MICROPROCESSOR HANDBOOK

Joseph D. Greenfield

JOHN WILEY & SONS
New York • Chichester • Brisbane • Toronto • Singapore

Library of Congress Cataloging in Publication Data:

Greenfield, Joseph D., 1930–
Microprocessor handbook.

(Wiley electrical and electronic technology handbook series)
Includes bibliographies and indexes.
1. Microprocessors. 2. Microcomputers.
I. Title. II. Series.
QA76.5.G688 1985 001.64 85-6443
ISBN 0-471-08791-2

Printed in the United States of America

10 9 8 7 6 5 4 3 2

PREFACE

This *Microprocessor Handbook* is intended to give engineers, scientists, and technicians an understanding of the features and capabilities of the most popular microprocessors currently available.

The Handbook is divided into four sections. Section I (chapters 1 through 3) is a general introduction to computers, computer arithmetic, and terminology, with an emphasis on microprocessor applications. Experienced and advanced readers may skip or skim this section.

Section II (chapters 4 through 9) consists of individual chapters on six 8-bit microprocessors (μPs). The older μPs, **8080**, **8085**, **6502**, and **6800**, and two later μPs, the **Z80** and **6809**, are presented. The study of 8-bit μPs is practical, because they are still the workhorses of the industry. Their study also forms a basis for understanding the 16-bit μPs.

Section III (chapters 10 through 12) concentrates on three of the most popular 16-bit μPs. The basic 16-bit μPs in the Intel, Zilog, and Motorola lines are presented.

Section IV (chapters 13 through 15) presents the peripheral μP ICs that work with the Intel, Zilog, and Motorola μPs. We describe the most important and widely used peripheral ICs in each family.

Most of the μPs and peripheral ICs described in this Handbook have been the subjects of entire books (see the references at the end of each chapter). Obviously, space constraints somewhat limit the presentation, but the devices are described in sufficient detail to give the reader a firm grasp of their capabilities. There is an emphasis on practical problems and their solution throughout so the reader can understand the use of a μP or peripheral after reading the section.

I would like to thank Hank Stewart, my editor at John Wiley, and Arthur Seidman, my series adviser, for their help and encouragement throughout the preparation of this Handbook. I would also like to thank the various authors for their cooperation. Above all, I must thank my wife, Gladys, who typed the manuscript and agonized with me during the years it was in preparation.

Joseph D. Greenfield

Rochester, New York
July 1984

CONTENTS

SECTION ONE INTRODUCTION TO MICROPROCESSORS 1

CHAPTER 1 Introduction to Microcomputers 3

Joseph D. Greenfield, Professor of Electrical Engineering Technology, Rochester Institute of Technology

1-1 INTRODUCTION 3
1-2 INTRODUCTION TO THE COMPUTER 4
1-3 THE MEMORY 5
1-3.1 Memory Concepts 5
1-3.2 Reading Memory 7
1-3.3 Writing Memory 7
1-4 SEMICONDUCTOR MEMORIES 8
1-4.1 Interfacing with a RAM Memory 8
1-4.2 Memory Timing 9
1-4.3 Dynamic RAMs 10
1-4.4 Read-Only Memories (ROMs) 10
1-4.5 Programmable Read-Only Memories (PROMs) 12
1-4.6 Erasable PROMs 12
1-5 THE ARITHMETIC-LOGIC UNIT (ALU) 12
1-5.1 The Condition Code Register 13
1-6 THE CONTROL SECTION 13
1-6.1 Control Unit FFs 14
1-7 EXECUTION OF A SIMPLE ROUTINE 14
1-7.1 Sample Problem 15
1-7.2 Hardware Execution of the Rountine 15
1-8 INTRODUCTION TO PROGRAMMING 17
1-8.1 Machine Language Programming 17
1-8.2 Assembly Language 18
1-8.3 Higher-Level Languages 18
1-9 FLOWCHARTS 18
1-9.1 Flowchart Symbols 19
1-9.2 Elementary Programming 20
1-10 BRANCH INSTRUCTIONS AND LOOPS 21

1-10.1 Branch Instructions 22
1-10.2 Decision Boxes and Conditional Branches 23
1-10.3 Event Detection 25
1-11 INPUT/OUTPUT 26
1-11.1 Port I/O 26
1-11.2 Memory-Mapped I/O 27
1-11.3 Command and Status Registers 27
1-12 INTERRUPTS 28
1-12.1 Vectored Interrupts 28
1-12.2 Maskable and Nonmaskable Interrupts 29
1-13 SUMMARY 30
1-14 REFERENCES 30

CHAPTER 2 **Computer Arithmetic and Shifting** **31**

Joseph D. Greenfield, Professor of Electrical Engineering Technology, Rochester Institute of Technology

2-1 INTRODUCTION 31
2-1.1 Bits, Bytes, and Words 33
2-1.2 Bytes and Nibbles 33
2-2 BINARY-TO-DECIMAL CONVERSION 34
2-3 DECIMAL-TO-BINARY CONVERSION 36
2-4 ADDITION AND SUBTRACTION OF BINARY NUMBERS 38
2-4.1 Addition of Binary Numbers 38
2-4.2 Subtraction of Binary Numbers 39
2-5 2s COMPLEMENT ARITHMETIC 40
2-5.1 2s Complement Numbers 41
2-5.2 The Range of 2s Complement Numbers 42
2-5.3 Adding 2s Complement Numbers 42
2-5.4 Subtraction of Binary Numbers 43
2-6 LOGICAL OPERATIONS 44
2-6.1 The Logical OR Operation 44
2-6.2 The Logical AND Operation 45
2-6.3 The EXCLUSIVE OR Operation 45
2-6.4 Complementation 45
2-7 HEXADECIMAL NOTATION 46
2-7.1 Conversion Between Hexadecimal and Binary Numbers 46
2-7.2 Conversion of Hex Numbers to Decimal Numbers 47
2-7.3 Hexadecimal Addition 48
2-7.4 Negating Hex Numbers 49

	2-7.5	Octal Notation	50
2-8	BRANCHING IN MICROPROCESSORS		50
	2-8.1	Calculating Offsets	51
	2-8.2	Long and Short Branches	52
2-9	SHIFT AND ROTATE INSTRUCTIONS		52
	2-9.1	Rotations	54
2-10	REFERENCES		55

CHAPTER 3 **Hardware and Software Considerations in a Microprocessor** **56**

Joseph D. Greenfield, Professor of Electrical Engineering Technology, Rochester Institute of Technology

3-1	MACHINE, ASSEMBLY, AND HIGHER-LEVEL LANGUAGES		56
	3-1.1	Machine Language	56
	3-1.2	Assembly Language Programming	58
	3-1.3	High-Level Languages	62
3-2	INSTRUCTION MODES		63
	3-2.1	Inherent or Implied Instructions	63
	3-2.2	Immediate Instructions	63
	3-2.3	Direct Instructions	64
	3-2.4	Indexed Instructions	64
	3-2.5	Indirect Addressing	65
	3-2.6	Relative Instructions	65
3-3	REGISTERS AND ACCUMULATORS		66
	3-3.1	The **8080/8085** Registers and Accumulator	66
	3-3.2	The **6800, 6809,** and **6502** Registers	66
3-4	SUBROUTINES AND STACKS		67
	3-4.1	Subroutines	67
	3-4.2	Stacks	68
	3-4.3	The Stack Pointer	69
	3-4.4	PUSHes and PULLs or POPs	69
	3-4.5	Stacks in Newer Microprocessors	70
3-5	INTERRUPTS		70
	3-5.1	Level- and Edge-Sensitive Interrupts	71
	3-5.2	Maskable Interrupts	71
	3-5.3	Nonmaskable Interrupts (NMI)	72
	3-5.4	Interrupts on the **8080** and **8085**	73
	3-5.5	Interrupts on the **6800**	73
3-6	MICROPROCESSOR BUSES		74
	3-6.1	The Data Bus	74
	3-6.2	The Address Bus	75
	3-6.3	The Control Bus	75

3-6.4 Multiplexed Buses 76
3-6.5 Direct Memory Access 76
3-7 REFERENCES 77

SECTION TWO EIGHT-BIT MICROPROCESSORS 79

CHAPTER 4 The Intel 8080 81

Walter Foley, Eastman Kodak Corp.

4-1 Architecture 81
4-1.1 Registers 81
4-1.2 The Accumulator 83
4-1.3 The Flags 83
4-1.4 Stack 84
4-2 ADDRESSING MODES 84
4-2.1 Implied Addressing 85
4-2.2 Register Addressing 85
4-2.3 Immediate Addressing 85
4-2.4 Direct Addressing 85
4-2.5 Register Indirect Addressing 86
4-3 INSTRUCTION FORMAT 86
4-4 INSTRUCTION SET 86
4-4.1 The Data Transfer Group 87
4-4.2 The Arithmetic Group 93
4-4.3 The Logical Group 104
4-4.4 The Branch Group 107
4-4.5 Stack, I/O, and Machine Control 110
4-5 THE CPU 112
4-5.1 Clock Generation 115
4-5.2 Machine Cycles and T States 115
4-5.3 Status Byte Decoding 121
4-5.4 Instruction Timing 123
4-5.5 System Control Devices 124
4-5.6 RESET Signal 125
4-6 MEMORY INTERFACE 126
4-7 REFERENCES 127

CHAPTER 5 The Intel 8085 142

Walter Foley, Eastman Kodak Corp.

5-1 ARCHITECTURE 142
5-1.1 The **8085** Oscillator Circuit 143
5-1.2 The Multiplexed Data Bus 143
5-1.3 Other **8085** Lines 146
5-2 INPUT AND OUTPUT PORTS 146

5-2.1 IN and OUT Timing 148
5-2.2 Execution of the OUT Instruction 148
5-2.3 Execution of the IN Instruction 149
5-2.4 SID and SOD 150
5-3 INTERRUPTS ON THE **8080** AND **8085** 150
5-3.1 The RESTART Instruction 150
5-3.2 New **8085** Interrupt Vectors 152
5-3.3 The CALL Instruction 153
5-4 INSTRUCTION SET 156
5-4.1 The Interrupt Mask Register 156
5-4.2 SIM 156
5-4.3 RIM 158
5-4.4 Other Instructions 159
5-5 THE CPU 161
5-5.1 Status Information Decoding 163
5-5.2 Demultiplexing Address and Data 163
5-5.3 Wait States 164
5-6 SPECIAL PERIPHERAL DEVICES 165
5-6.1 The **8255** 168
5-6.2 Strobed Input Mode 171
5-6.3 Strobed Output Mode 173
5-6.4 Mode 2 Operation 176
5-6.5 The Status Word 177
5-6.6 A Data Communications Controller Using the **8255** 178
5-7 REFERENCES 183

CHAPTER 6 **The Zilog Z80** **184**

Glenn A. Barlis, Mobil Chemical Co.

6-1 INTRODUCTION 184
6-2 ARCHITECTURE 185
6-3 ADDRESSING MODES 189
6-3.1 Immediate Addressing 189
6-3.2 Immediate Extended Addressing 199
6-3.3 Modified Page Zero Addressing 200
6-3.4 Register Addressing 200
6-3.5 Implied Addressing 200
6-3.6 Register Indirect Addressing 201
6-3.7 Stack Addressing 201
6-3.8 Extended Addressing 201
6-3.9 Relative Addressing 202
6-3.10 Indexed Addressing 203
6-3.11 Bit Addressing 203
6-4 INSTRUCTION SET 204
6-4.1 8-Bit Load Group 204
6-4.2 16-Bit Load Group 206

6-4.3 Exchange Group 207
6-4.4 Block Transfer Group 208
6-4.5 Block Search Group 210
6-4.6 8-Bit Arithmetic and Logic Group 212
6-4.7 General-Purpose AF Group 213
6-4.8 Miscellaneous CPU Control Group 213
6-4.9 16-Bit Arithmetic Group 214
6-4.10 ROTATE and SHIFT Group 216
6-4.11 Bit Manipulation Group 220
6-4.12 JUMP Group 221
6-4.13 CALL and RETURN Group 224
6-4.14 RESTART Group 224
6-4.15 Input Group 224
6-4.16 Output Group 227
6-5 CPU PIN OUT AND DESCRIPTION 227
6-6 I/O PROCESSING AND INTERRUPTS 229
6-6.1 WAIT and BUS Requests 230
6-6.2 Nonmaskable Interrupts 230
6-6.3 Maskable Interrupts 231
6-7 SAMPLE APPLICATION 233
6-7.1 **Z80** CPU 233
6-7.2 Clock Circuit 233
6-7.3 RESET Circuit 236
6-7.4 READ/WRITE Encoding 236
6-7.5 Memory 236
6-7.6 Memory Address Selection 236
6-7.7 I/O Port Address Decoding 236
6-7.8 Counter/Timer Circuit 237
6-7.9 Parallel Interface Controller 238
6-7.10 Serial I/O Circuit 238
6-7.11 Program Listing 239
6-8 REFERENCES 252

CHAPTER 7 The Motorola 6800 253

Joseph D. Greenfield, Professor of Electrical Engineering, Rochester Institute of Technology

7-1 INTRODUCTION 253
7-2 THE **6800** REGISTERS AND ACCUMULATORS 253
7-2.1 The 8-Bit Registers 253
7-2.2 The 16-Bit Registers 254
7-3 **6800** Addressing Modes 254
7-3.1 Immediate Addressing Instructions 257
7-3.2 Direct Instructions 257
7-3.3 Extended Instructions 258
7-3.4 Indexed Instructions 259

7-3.5 Implied Addressing 259
7-3.6 Relative Instructions 260

7-4 CONDITION CODES 260
7-4.1 The Z Bit 260
7-4.2 The C Bit 261
7-4.3 The N Bit 261
7-4.4 The V Bit 261
7-4.5 Manipulations of the Condition Code Register 263

7-5 BCD ADDITION AND THE H BIT 263
7-5.1 Adding BCD Numbers 263
7-5.2 The DAA Instruction 264

7-6 LOGIC INSTRUCTIONS 265
7-6.1 Setting and Clearing Specific Bits 265
7-6.2 Testing Bits 266
7-6.3 Compare Instructions 266
7-6.4 The TEST Instruction 267

7-7 OTHER **6800** INSTRUCTIONS 267
7-7.1 CLEAR, INCREMENT, and DECREMENT Instructions 267
7-7.2 SHIFT and ROTATE Instructions 267
7-7.3 Accumulator Transfer Instructions 268
7-7.4 COMPLEMENT and NEGATE Instructions 268

7-8 BRANCH AND JUMP INSTRUCTIONS 268
7-8.1 JUMP Instructions 268
7-8.2 Unconditional BRANCH Instructions 269
7-8.3 Out-of-Range BRANCHes 270
7-8.4 Conditional BRANCH Instructions 270
7-8.5 Other Conditional BRANCH Instructions 272

7-9 STACKS 274
7-9.1 The Stack Pointer 274
7-9.2 PUSH and PULL 275

7-10 SUBROUTINES 275
7-10.1 JUMPS to Subroutines 277
7-10.2 RETURN FROM SUBROUTINE 277
7-10.3 Nested Subroutines 278
7-10.4 Use of Registers During Subroutines 279

7-11 THE **6800** SIGNAL LINES 280
7-11.1 READ/WRITE (R/W) 280
7-11.2 Valid Memory Address (VMA) 280
7-11.3 Data Bus Enable (DBE) 282
7-11.4 Interrupt Request, Nonmaskable Interrupt, and RESET 282

7-11.5 Phase 1 (ϕ1) and Phase 2 (ϕ2) of the Clock 282
7-11.6 Halt and Run Modes 282
7-11.7 Bus Available (BA) 282
7-11.8 Tri-State Control (TSC) 282

7-12 CLOCK OPERATION 283
7-12.1 Instruction Bytes and Clock Cycles 283

7-13 INTRODUCTION TO INTERRUPTS 285
7-13.1 Vectored Interrupts 286
7-13.2 Reset (RST) 287
7-13.3 The IRQ Interrupt 287
7-13.4 Nested Interrupts 289
7-13.5 Return from Interrupt (RTI) 289
7-13.6 Nonmaskable Interrupt 289
7-13.7 The Software Interrupt (SWI) 290
7-13.8 The WAI Instruction 290

7-14 INPUT/OUTPUT 290
7-14.1 The PIA Registers 290
7-14.2 The PIA/**6800** Interface 291
7-14.3 The Interface Between the PIA and External Devices 292
7-14.4 Data Transfers Between the PIA and External Devices 292
7-14.5 The Direction Register 293
7-14.6 The Data Register 294
7-14.7 Initializing the PIA 294

7-15 HANDSHAKING WITH THE PIA 296
7-15.1 Control Lines CA1 and CB1 296
7-15.2 Control Lines CA2 and CB2 300
7-15.3 Use of CB2 as an Output in the Handshake Mode 300
7-15.4 Use of CB2 in the Pulse Mode 304
7-15.5 ON-OFF Control of CB2 305
7-15.6 Control of CA2 as an Output (Handshaking Mode) 305
7-15.7 Pulse Mode for CA2 307
7-15.8 ON-OFF Mode for CA2 307

7-16 REFERENCES 307

CHAPTER 8 THE MC6809 308

Tim Ahrens, Motorola

8-1 ARCHITECTURE OF THE **MC6809** 308
8-1.1 Accumulators 308
8-1.2 Index Registers 309
8-1.3 Stack Pointers (S, U) 309
8-1.4 Direct Page Register (DP) 309

8-1.5 Condition Code Register (CC) 310
8-1.6 Program Counter (PC) 312

8-2 MODES OF INSTRUCTION EXECUTION (ADDRESSING MODES) 312
8-2.1 Inherent 313
8-2.2 Immediate Addressing 313
8-2.3 Extended Addressing 313
8-2.4 Extended Indirect 313
8-2.5 Direct Addressing 314
8-2.6 Register Addressing 314

8-3 INDEXED ADDRESSING 314
8-3.1 Zero-Offset Indexed 317
8-3.2 Constant-Offset Indexed 317
8-3.3 Accumulator-Offset Indexed 318
8-3.4 Auto Increment/Decrement Indexed 318
8-3.5 Indexed Indirect 319
8-3.6 Relative Addressing 320
8-3.7 Program Counter Relative 320

8-4 **M6809** INSTRUCTION SET 320
8-4.1 PSHU/PSHS 321
8-4.2 PULU/PULS 321
8-4.3 TFR/EXG 322
8-4.4 LEAX/LEAY/LEAU/LEAS 322
8-4.5 MUL 324

8-5 LONG AND SHORT RELATIVE BRANCHES 324

8-6 SYNC 324

8-7 SOFTWARE INTERRUPTS 324

8-8 16-BIT OPERATION 325

8-9 PIN OUT AND SIGNAL DESCRIPTIONS 325
8-9.1 Power (Vss, Vcc) 325
8-9.2 XTAL, EXTAL* 329
8-9.3 E, Q* 329
8-9.4 Address Bus (A0–A15) 329
8-9.5 Data Bus (D0–D7) 329
8-9.6 READ/WRITE (R/W) 329
8-9.7 RESET 330
8-9.8 HALT 330
8-9.9 Bus Available, Bus Status (BA, BS) 330
8-9.10 INTERRUPT ACKNOWLEDGE 331
8-9.11 NONMASKABLE INTERRUPT (NMI) 331
8-9.12 FAST INTERRUPT REQUEST (FIRQ) 332
8-9.13 INTERRUPT REQUEST (IRQ) 332
8-9.14 MRDY* 332
8-9.15 DMA/BREQ* 332

8-10 PINS IMPLEMENTED ONLY ON THE **MC6809E** 333
8-10.1 Clock Inputs E, Q 333
8-10.2 BUSY 333
8-10.3 AVMA 334

8-10.4 LIC 334
8-10.5 TSC 335
8-11 MPU OPERATION 335
8-12 THE **MC6809** EVALUATION BOARD 335
8-13 CONVERSION CONSIDERATIONS 346
8-14 SUMMARY 346
8-15 REFERENCES 346

CHAPTER 9 The 6500 Family of Microprocessors 347

Marvin L. De Jong, Department of Mathematics–Physics. The School of the Ozarks

9-1 INTRODUCTION 347
9-2 A PROGRAMMER'S MODEL OF THE **6500** ARCHITECTURE 348
9-3 THE **6500** FAMILY INSTRUCTION SET 353
9-4 BRANCHES, JUMPS, AND SUBROUTINE CALLS 358
9-5 INTERRUPTS 360
9-6 ADDRESSING MODES 362
9-7 THE **6502** SIGNALS 364
9-8 **6502** SYSTEM TIMING 369
9-9 INPUT/OUTPUT 372
9-10 APPLICATIONS 376
9-11 REFERENCES 383

SECTION THREE SIXTEEN-BIT MICROPROCESSORS 385

CHAPTER 10 Intel 8086 and 8088 Microprocessors 387

Windsor Thomas, Professor of Electrical Engineering Technology, State University of New York

10-1 INTRODUCTION 387
10-2 **8086** ARCHITECTURE 387
10-3 **8086** REGISTERS 388
10-3.1 General Registers 388
10-3.2 Segment Registers 389
10-3.3 Instruction Pointer 390
10-3.4 Status Register 391
10-4 COMPARISON OF THE **8086** AND **8080/8085** ARCHITECTURE 392
10-5 THE STACK 393
10-6 SYSTEM RESET 393

10-7 ADDRESSING MODES 393
10-7.1 Register Addressing 394
10-7.2 Immediate Addressing 394
10-7.3 Effective Address Calculation 394
10-7.4 Direct Addressing 394
10-7.5 Register Indirect Addressing 394
10-7.6 Based Addressing 395
10-7.7 Indexed Addressing 395
10-7.8 Based Indexed Addressing 395
10-7.9 String Addressing 395
10-7.10 I/O Port Addressing 395

10-8 **8086** INSTRUCTION SET 395
10-8.1 Data Transfer Instruction 396
10-8.2 Arithmetic and Logical Instructions 397
10-8.3 String Instructions 397
10-8.4 Program Transfer Instruction 400
10-8.5 Processor Control Instructions 402

10-9 **8086/8088** PINS AND MODE SELECTION 403
10-9.1 **8086/8088** Pin Out 403
10-9.2 Mode Selection 408

10-10 INTERRUPT CAPABILITIES 408

10-11 COPROCESSORS 410
10-11.1 The **8089** Input/Output Processor 410
10-11.2 Functional Description 411
10-11.3 I/O Coprocessor Operation 416
10-11.4 Initialization 417
10-11.5 Numeric Data Processor 426

10-12 REFERENCES 441

CHAPTER 11 **The Z8000 16-Bit Microprocessors** **442**

Steve Sharp, American Microsystems, Inc.

11-1 INTRODUCTION 442

11-2 GENERAL ARCHITECTURE 443
11-2.1 General-Purpose Register Set 444
11-2.2 Instruction Set 447
11-2.3 Data Types 448
11-2.4 Addressing Modes 448
11-2.5 Memory Address Spaces 450
11-2.6 System/Normal Modes of Operation 451
11-2.7 Separate I/O Address Spaces 452
11-2.8 Interrupt Structure 452
11-2.9 Multiprocessing 453
11-2.10 Large Address Space for **Z8001** and **Z8003** 453
11-2.11 Segmented Address for **Z8001** and **Z8003** 453

11-3 THE **Z800** FAMILY OF CPUs 454
11-3.1 **Z8002** Nonsegmented CPU 454
11-3.2 **Z8001** Segmented CPU 454
11-3.3 **Z8003** Virtual Memory CPU 455
11-4 INSTRUCTION SET 455
11-4.1 Load and Exchange 455
11-4.2 Arithmetic 456
11-4.3 Logical 456
11-4.4 Program Control 457
11-4.5 Bit Manipulation 457
11-4.6 Rotate and Shift 457
11-4.7 Block Transfer and String Manipulation 458
11-4.8 Input/Output 459
11-4.9 CPU Control 459
11-4.10 Extended Instructions 460
11-5 HARDWARE INTERFACE 460
11-5.1 Multiplexed Bus (Z-Bus) 460
11-5.2 Address Strobe and Data Strobe 460
11-5.3 Input/Output Operation 461
11-5.4 Interrupts and Traps 462
11-5.5 Bus Request and Acknowledge 462
11-6 CPU SUPPORT DEVICES 462
11-6.1 **Z8010** MMU 463
11-6.2 **Z8016** DTC 463
11-6.3 **Z8070** APU 463
11-7 SOFTWARE INTERFACE 464
11-7.1 Context Switching 464
11-7.2 Interrupts 464
11-7.3 System Call Instruction 465
11-7.4 Segment Trap and Abort 465
11-8 REFERENCES 466

CHAPTER 12 **THE MOTOROLA 68000** **475**

Dennis Pfleger, Motorola Microsystem

12-1 PRIMARY FEATURES 475
12-2 THE SOFTWARE DESIGNER'S VIEW OF THE **MC68000** 478
12-2.1 Data Registers 479
12-2.2 Address Registers 479
12-2.3 Status Registers 479
12-3 ADDRESSING TYPES 480
12-3.1 Assemblers 495
12-4 SPECIAL INSTRUCTIONS 495
12-5 STACKS AND PROCEDURE CALLS 496

12-6 TRAPS AND ERROR RECOVERY 499
12-6.1 User and Supervisory States 499
12-7 INTERRUPTS AND I/O 501
12-7.1 Memory-Mapped I/O 501
12-7.2 Interlocks 501
12-8 DATA ORGANIZATION 501
12-9 THE HARDWARE DESIGNER'S VIEW OF THE **MC68000** 505
12-9.1 The Address Bus 505
12-9.2 The Data Bus 506
12-9.3 System Control 506
12-9.4 Systems Control 507
12-10 THE DATA SHEET AND USER'S GUIDE 508
12-10.1 Timing 508
12-10.2 The *Programmer's Reference Manual* 511
12-11 THE **MC68451** MEMORY MANAGEMENT UNIT 512
12-12 REFERENCES 513

SECTION FOUR PERIPHERAL ICs 515

CHAPTER 13 Intel Peripheral Circuits 517

Windsor Thomas, Professor of Electrical Engineering Technology, State University of New York

13-1 INTRODUCTION 517
13-2 **8251A** USART 517
13-2.1 Functional Description 517
13-2.2 Major Functional Blocks and Pins 519
13-2.3 Device Pins 520
13-2.4 General Operation 523
13-2.5 Asynchronous Mode 525
13-2.6 Synchronous Mode 526
13-2.7 Command Instructions 526
13-2.8 Status Register 528
13-2.9 Design Considerations 529
13-3 **8253** PROGRAMMABLE TIMER/COUNTER 530
13-3.1 Functional Description 530
13-3.2 Device Pins 530
13-3.3 Principles of Operation 533
13-3.4 Counter Initialization 533
13-3.5 Modes of Operation 535
13-3.6 Reading the Counter 538
13-4 **8275** PROGRAMMABLE CRT CONTROLLER 540
13-4.1 Functional Description 540
13-4.2 Device Pins 542
13-4.3 General Operation 544

13-4.4 Display Format 545
13-4.5 Device Initialization 547
13-5 THE **8279** PROGRAMMABLE KEYBOARD/DISPLAY INTERFACE 551
13-5.1 Functional Description 551
13-5.2 Device Pins 555
13-5.3 Device Operation 556
13-6 REFERENCES 558

CHAPTER 14 Motorola Peripherals 559

Joseph D. Greenfield, Professor of Electrical Engineering, Rochester Institute of Technology, and Tom Hardy, Motorola

14-1 THE **6840** PROGRAMMABLE TIMER MODULE 559
14-1.1 The Hardware Interface to the **6840** 560
14-1.2 General System Operation 561
14-1.3 Programming the Control Registers 563
14-1.4 Resets 564
14-1.5 Counter Initialization 564
14-1.6 16-Bit and Dual 8-Bit Modes 564
14-1.7 Single-Shot Mode 567
14-2 SERIAL DATA TRANSMISSION 568
14-2.1 Asynchronous Transmission 570
14-2.2 Synchronous Communications 571
14-3 THE ACIA 572
14-3.1 Parallel-to-Serial and Serial-to-Parallel Conversion 573
14-3.2 ACIA Registers 574
14-3.3 ACIA Signal Lines 575
14-3.4 The ACIA Control Register 575
14-3.5 ACIA POWER-ON RESET 580
14-3.6 The ACIA Status Register 580
14-3.7 Uses of the ACIA 583
14-4 HIGH-SPEED SERIAL COMMUNICATION WITH THE **MC6854** ADVANCED DATA LINK CONTROLLER 584
14-4.1 The Fields Within a Frame 585
14-4.2 Abort Conditions 587
14-4.3 FIFOs 587
14-4.4 Loop Transmission 589
14-4.5 **MC6854** ADLC Hardware 591
14-4.6 **MC6854** Used with DMA 592
14-4.7 Internal Registers in the **MC6854** 594

14-4.8 The **MC6852** Synchronous Serial Data Adapter (SSDA) 595

14-5 THE **MC6845** CRTC 595

14-5.1 The **MC6845** Signals 598

14-5.2 The **MC6845** Registers 601

14-5.3 Setting Up a CRTC System 604

14-5.4 An Example of a CRTC Design 606

14-6 REFERENCES 610

CHAPTER 15 Zilog Peripherals 611

Steve Sharp, American Microsystems, Inc.

15-1 OVERVIEW 611

15-2 HARDWARE INTERFACE 612

15-2.1 The Z-Bus Series of Peripherals 612

15-2.2 Signal Lines 612

15-2.3 Nonmultiplexed Bus Peripherals 614

15-3 INTERRUPT STRUCTURE 614

15-4 **Z8036** Z-CIO 617

15-5 **Z8030** Z-SCC 620

15-6 **Z8038** Z-FIO 624

15-7 FIFO BUFFER EXPANSION 626

15-8 **Z8065** Z-BEP 627

15-9 **Z8068** Z-DCP 628

15-10 **Z80** FAMILY PERIPHERALS 629

15-10.1 Interface 629

15-11 **Z80** PIO 630

15-12 **Z80** CTC 630

15-13 **Z80** SIO 630

15-14 REFERENCES 632

INDEX 633

INDEX OF INTEGRATED CIRCUITS 635

SECTION ONE

INTRODUCTION TO MICROPROCESSORS

CHAPTER 1

Introduction to Microcomputers

Joseph D. Greenfield
Professor of Electrical Engineering Technology
Rochester Institute of Technology
Rochester, New York

1-1 INTRODUCTION

The introduction of the digital computer in the early 1950s revolutionized methods of computing and manipulating data. The development of the microcomputer (one or more integrated circuit chips that provide all the functions of a computer) is revolutionizing the computer industry and many other industries as well. The microcomputer has reduced the cost of computing by an order of magnitude. The small size and small cost of a microcomputer has greatly increased the use of computers for calculations, command, and control. The use of microcomputers in automobiles, for example, represents a market for millions of them in this one application.

A *microcomputer* (μC) system is generally built around a *microprocessor* (μP). The μP chip contains within it most of the control and arithmetic functions of a computer. To become a complete μC, it is augmented by other integrated circuit (IC) chips, such as RAMs (random access memories), ROMs (read-only memories), and peripheral drivers. Common μC systems, such as Apples and TRS-80s, abound. Their low cost has made them available to many businesses and individuals who could not previously consider owning their own computer.

This handbook contains a chapter on each of the most popular and commonly used microprocessors. Each chapter has sufficient detail to allow the engineer to thoroughly understand the microprocessor being discussed. The book is intended to help the engineer who must select the best microprocessor for his or her particular application or who must understand the operation of a microprocessor in a piece of equipment his or her company is using.

The handbook is divided into four sections. Chapters 1 to 3 are an introduction to computers in general and microprocessors in particular. Readers who are experienced with microprocessors and are familiar with the basic software and hardware concepts may be able to skip all or most of this introductory material. Chapters 4 through 9 present six of the most popular 8-bit μPs in use today. Chapters 10 through 12 present three of the most popular 16-bit μPs that are currently available, and chapters 13 through 15 discuss the peripheral ICs manufactured by the leading companies in the field. These ICs work in conjunction with the μP and allow it to perform specific tasks, typically associated with input and output.

1-2 INTRODUCTION TO THE COMPUTER

A microcomputer system is a computer, and to fully understand it, one must understand how computers function.

A computer consists of four basic parts, as shown in Figure 1-1:

1 The memory

2 The arithmetic-logic unit (ALU)

3 The input/output system

4 The control unit

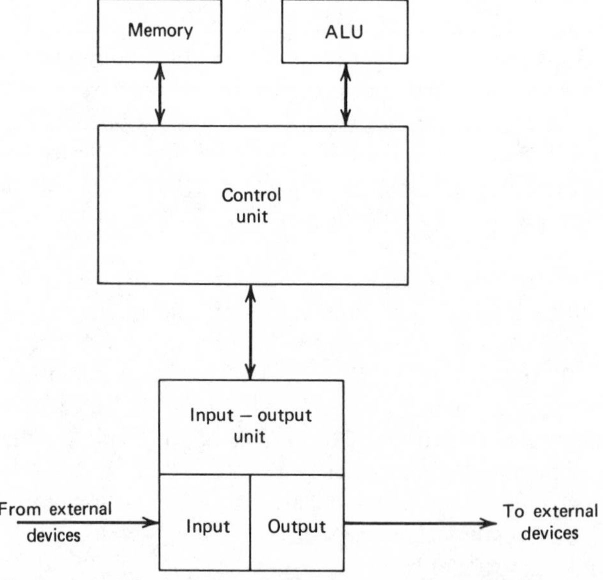

Figure 1-1 Block diagram of a basic computer. (From Greenfield and Wray, *Using Microprocessors and Microcomputers: The 6800 Family*, Wiley, 1981.)

The *memory* is an indispensable part of a computer. It contains the *data* used in a program as well as the *instructions* for executing the program. A *program* is a group of instructions telling the computer what to do with the data. An extremely simple program might instruct the computer to add two numbers in its data area; another program might command the computer to subtract the same numbers. Obviously, completely different results can be obtained from the same data by applying different programs.

The *arithmetic-logic unit* (ALU) is the part of the computer that performs those arithmetic or logic operations required by the routine or program, and generates the status bits (condition codes) that are the heart of the decision-making capabilities of any computer.

The *input/output system* controls communication between the computer and its external devices. The computer must receive data and status information from external devices such as sensors, analog-to-digital (A/D) converters, or disk or tape units. It must also produce outputs that depend on its program and the data it receives. If the computer is solving a problem, the output is usually a printout of the results. In this case it must issue commands to a printer to cause the results to be printed for the user to read. If the function of the computer is to control a physical process, however, its output will be electronic pulses that are translated into *commands* (open a valve, reduce the air flow, etc.) to regulate a process.

The *control unit* consists of a group of flip-flops (FFs) and registers that regulate the operation of the computer itself. The function of the control unit is to cause the proper sequence of events to occur during the execution of each computer instruction.

The microprocessor (μP) chip generally contains the ALU and control portions of the computer, while memory and input/output (I/O) are handled by auxiliary ICs. Some of the newer μPs, however, have incorporated some memory and I/O capability within the IC and manufacturers are calling them "single-chip computers."

1-3 THE MEMORY

Even the smallest minicomputer or microprocessor system requires a memory of several thousand bits to store its programs and data. Large-scale memories for computers are constructed of magnetic cores or integrated circuit flip-flops. A flip-flop (FF) is an electronic circuit that can be placed in one of two states (SET or RESET), and remains there until commanded to change states. Thus a single FF functions as a 1-bit memory. It remembers whether it was last set or reset.

Many FFs (presently up to 65,536) can be placed within a single IC. These ICs constitute one type of *semiconductor memory* (static) and are available from many manufacturers (see section 1-4).

1-3.1 Memory Concepts

The binary bits of a block of memory can be organized in various ways. It is usual for most computers to be arranged so that the bits are grouped into *words* of 8 or 16 bits each. The μPs discussed in chapters 4 through 9 use 8-bit words, while those discussed in chapters 10 through 12 use 16-bit words.

Modern computers are *word-oriented* in that they transfer 1 byte (or word) at a time by means of the data bus. This bus, the internal computer registers, and the ALU (arithmetic logic unit) are *parallel* devices that handle all the bits of a word *at the same time*. The memory can be thought of as a post office box arrangement with each location containing a word. The boxes are set up in an orderly sequence so that they can be addressed easily. Each instruction or data word is *written* into a specific location in memory (a word at a selected address) *when it must be preserved* for future use, and read at a later time *when the information is needed*. During the interval between writing and reading, other information may be stored or read at other locations.

Microprocessor instructions require 1, 2, or 3 bytes (or words) and typical routines include 5 to 50 instructions. Since IC memories are physically small and relatively inexpensive, they can include thousands of words and thereby provide very comprehensive computer programs.

A typical microcomputer memory size is 1K to 4K words. Unlike standard engineering terminology where K is an abbreviation for kilo, or 1000, K equals 2^{10} or 1024 when applied to memories. This value of K is used because normal memory design leads to sizes that are even powers of 2.

Each word in memory has *two parameters*: its *address*, which locates it within memory, and the *data*, which is stored at that location. The process of accessing the contents of the memory locations requires two registers: one associated with address and one with data. The memory address register (MAR) holds the *address of the word currently being accessed*, and the memory data register (MDR) holds the *data being written into or read out of the addressed memory location*. These registers can be considered part of the memory or of the control unit (see section 1-6).

A block diagram of a typical 1K word by 8-bit IC RAM memory is shown in Figure 1-2. The address information in the MAR selects one of the 1024 words in

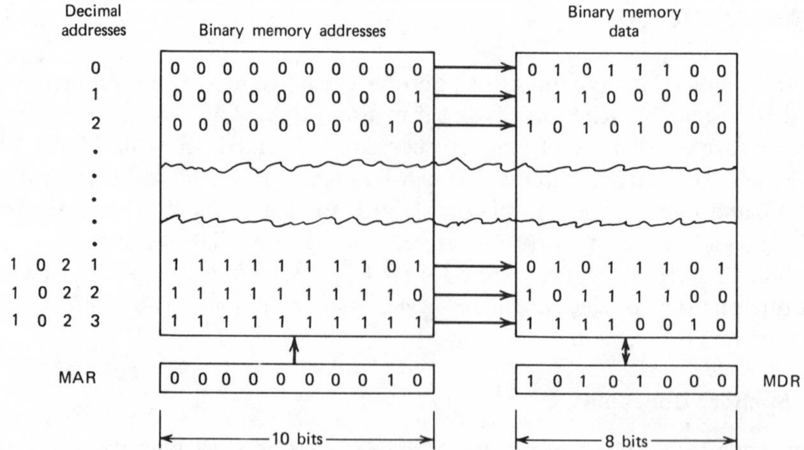

Figure 1-2 A typical 1024-word by 8-bit memory. (From Greenfield and Wray, *Using Microprocessors and Microcomputers: The 6800 Family*, Wiley, 1981.)

memory. While this is a very small memory by today's standards, it serves well for illustrative and tutorial purposes.

EXAMPLE 1-1 The 1K by 8-bit memory of Figure 1-2 is used as part of a μP system with a 16-bit address bus.

a How many bits are required to address all locations in this IC?

b How many address bits are used for the whole μP system?

c How many bits are required in the MDR?

d How many data bits are contained in this memory IC?

Solution

a A memory specification of 1K $\times$ 8 means 1024 (2^{10}) words of 8 bits each. The MAR must hold an address value between 0 to 1023 (1024 total locations) to select any word in this IC. Thus, 10 bits are needed to address the memory.

b The μP uses 16 address lines (or bits in the MAR). Since 10 are used to select the locations in this memory IC, the other 6 are available to select other ICs.

c Each memory location contains 8 bits. Consequently, the MDR must be 8 bits long to accommodate one data word.

d A 1K $\times$ 8 memory contains 2^{10} words times 2^3 (8) bits per word = 2^{13} or 8192 bits. For a microcomputer, this is a relatively small memory and several such ICs would typically be used.

In Figure 1-2 the MAR is shown to contain address 2 and the MDR register contains the value that is in that location.

1-3.2 Reading Memory

Memories operate in two basic modes: READ or WRITE. A memory is read when the information at a particular address is required by the system. To *read* a memory:

1 The location to be read is loaded into the MAR.

2 A READ command is given.

3 The data is transferred from the addressed word in memory to the MDR, where it is accessible to the system.

Normally, *the word being read must not be altered by the READ operation,* so the word in a particular location can be read many times. The process of reading a location without changing it is called *nondestructive readout.*

1-3.3 Writing Memory

A memory location is written when the data must be preserved for future use. In the process of writing, the previous information in the specified location is *destroyed* (overwritten). To *write* into a memory:

1 The address (the memory location where the data is to be written) is loaded into the MAR.

2 The data to be written is loaded into the MDR.

3 The WRITE command is then given (by means of the READ/WRITE line), which transfers the data from the MDR to the selected memory location.

1-4 SEMICONDUCTOR MEMORIES

Microcomputers use memories built of semiconductor ICs. These are packaged in a dual-in-line package (DIP) as is the μP and the rest of the components in the system.

Most μCs use at least some RAM memory. Literally speaking, the term RAM means *random access memory*, but it generally means a READ/WRITE memory, a memory that can both be *read* and *written into.*

Semiconductor RAMs are built primarily of MOS gates and store their information in FFs or capacitors within the IC. These two implementations are designated as *static* or *dynamic*. Static RAMs use FFs and are the simplest to understand and use, but require more circuitry on the chip for each cell (bit). Dynamic memories use capacitors to store their information and require constant clocking (pulsing) to refresh them. Because of the simpler geometry, however, they can contain significantly more memory in a given size. Both of these types are said to be *volatile*, since the circuits lose their information whenever power is turned OFF or inadvertently fails. To overcome this drawback, well-developed μP programs are written in ROMs (read-only memories) or PROMs (programmable ROMs) which are *nonvolatile*.

In most μPs, the memory consists of two parts with different memory addresses, a *ROM area* used to hold the *program*, *constant data*, and *tables*, and a *RAM area*, used to hold *variable data*. Generally, the data on which the program operates must be rewritten every time the system is started again (restarted), and the system must always be restarted (going through a startup procedure) after any power failure occurs. This is not a severe drawback because data is usually invalid after a power failure. Fortunately, the program, if it is contained in ROM, can be restarted immediately because a power failure does not affect a ROM.

Monitor programs that control the operation of μC systems and languages such as Basic are always stored in ROM so the systems can be turned off and restarted. The internal structure of the FFs and gates comprising a memory are not considered in this book. Instead, we concentrate on the input/output (I/O) characteristics that must be understood if one is to use a memory.

1-4.1 Interfacing with a RAM Memory

A semiconductor RAM normally has pins for the following inputs and outputs:

1 m output bits

2 m input bits

3 n address bits (for 2^n words)

4 READ/WRITE input

5 CHIP SELECT or ENABLE input

To read a location in a static semiconductor memory, the READ/WRITE line is set to the READ level. The memory chip is then *selected* or *enabled.* The memory contents at the addressed location are transferred to the output, and continue to be present until the address, READ/WRITE line or CHIP SELECT signals change. Reading is *nondestructive* (it does not change the information in the memory cells); the state of the internal memory cells at the selected address is simply brought to the outputs.

Writing into a memory requires that the address of the desired location be in the MAR and the data be in the MDR prior to the enabling of the memory. These registers (MAR and MDR) are connected to the memories by means of bus lines. When the READ/WRITE line is switched to write and the memory is enabled, the data on the bus lines is entered into the memory at the addressed location. One must be careful about changing the input data while in write mode. Any change of data is gated into the memory and overwrites the previous contents of the memory, which are lost.

The CHIP SELECT or ENABLE inputs are used to turn the memory ON or OFF and, more importantly, to disconnect it from the bus. This allows the μP designer to multiplex several memory or I/O devices onto a common bus.

EXAMPLE 1-2 The **MC6810** is the RAM usually used in **6800** μCs. It is a 1024-bit memory organized as 128 bytes (128 words by 8 bits). What input and output lines are required?

Solution This memory requires:

1 Seven address bits to select 1 of 128 words

2 Eight data input lines, one for each bit of the word

3 Eight data output lines, one for each bit of the word

4 One READ/WRITE line

5 CHIP SELECT or ENABLE

6 Power and ground

Actually the **6810** has 6 CHIP SELECT lines to make decoding easier, and the data input and output lines are on a common bidirectional data bus.

1-4.2 Memory Timing

For high-speed systems, memory timing is very important. A READ cycle is limited by the access time of a memory, and a WRITE cycle is limited by the cycle time.[1]

Access time is the time required for the memory to present valid data after the address and select signals are firm. *Cycle time* or WRITE time is the length of time the address and data must be held constant in order to write the memory.

[1] A more complete discussion of memory timing is given in Leucke, Mize, and Carr, *Semiconductor Memory Design and Application*, Sec. 9-3, McGraw-Hill, New York 1973.

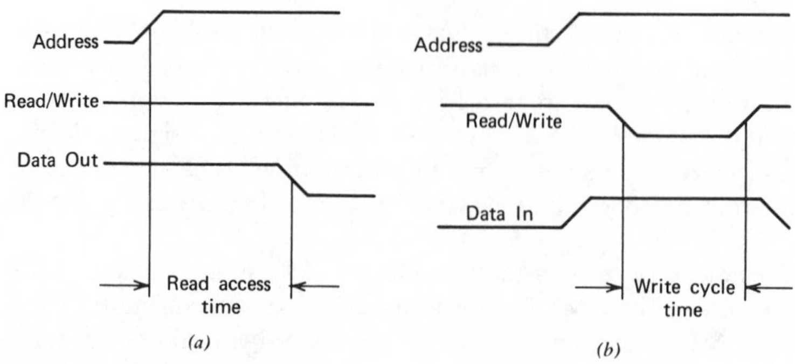

Figure 1-3 Memory timing. (*a*) READ cycle. (*b*) WRITE cycle. (From Greenfield and Wray, *Using Microprocessors and Microcomputers: The 6800 Family*, Wiley, 1981.)

Access time and cycle time are illustrated in Figure 1-3. Similar figures with specific times are supplied by the manufacturers of IC memories.

Figure 1-3*a* shows the normal situation where the memory is constantly in READ mode. The output data will change in response to an address change and the time for this response, the access time, is clearly visible.

Figure 1-3*b* shows the WRITE cycle. Note that the address and data are firm before the WRITE pulse occurs on the R/W line and do not change while the memory is in write mode. This is necessary to prevent spurious writes that could enter unwanted information into the memory.

If a memory has a long access or cycle time, the μP might have to be slowed down to accommodate the memory. For the **6800** or **6502** μPs, this means slowing down the basic clock driving the μP. Intel and Zilog μPs have an optional WAIT state that can be used to temporarily halt the μP until the memory has had sufficient time to respond to its command.

1-4.3 Dynamic RAMs

Dynamic RAMs are memories that store their information on capacitors, rather than on the FFs used in the static RAMs previously discussed. Dynamic RAMs are smaller and less expensive than static RAMs and are used in many μP systems, such as Apples and TRS-80s. The **4116** is a popular 16K by 1-bit dynamic RAM, but the **4164** (a 64K-bit dynamic RAM) and even larger dynamic RAMs are coming into current use.

The charges on the capacitors of a dynamic RAM tend to leak off and they must be refreshed periodically. They also use control signals such as $\overline{RAS}$ and $\overline{CAS}$. Unfortunately, space precludes a detailed discussion of dynamic RAMs here.[2]

1-4.4 Read-Only Memories (ROMs)

As its name implies, a *read-only memory* is read but not written into during the course of computer operation. Data is permanently written into a ROM when it is

[2] For a discussion of dynamic RAMs, see Greenfield, *Practical Digital Design Using ICs*, section 15-8 (see References).

manufactured. Usually μP users write their programs into ROM because it is permanent and nonvolatile. With its program in ROM, a μP can be restarted after a power failure with no need to reload or bootstrap its program.

The most popular manufacturing process involves generating a special mask from the user's program with which to make the chips. This is economically feasible only when a production run of a thousand or more ROMs are manufactured.

The operation of a ROM is identical to the read mode of a RAM; the user supplies an address and the ROM provides the data output of the word prewritten at that address. As with RAMs, ROMs are organized on an n-word by m-bit basis. Supplying the proper address results in an m-bit output. Access time for a ROM is the time between the setting of the address input and the appearance of the resulting data word on the output pins.

EXAMPLE 1-3 A memory has dimensions of 8K words by 8 bits. What input and output lines are required if the memory is:

a a RAM?

b a ROM?

Solution

a A RAM of this size requires:
  1 Eight data input bits
  2 Eight data output bits
  3 Thirteen address bits ($2^{13} = 8192$)
  4 A READ/WRITE line

b An 8K by 8 ROM requires:
  1 Eight data output bits
  2 Thirteen address bits

Since a ROM cannot be written into, the data input and READ/WRITE lines are not required.

Programs for μPs are generally developed using RAMs or PROMs (see section 1-4.6), because programs are changed many times during development and debugging. Once their programs are fully developed and not expected to change, users may order a custom built ROM from a manufacturer. They must supply the manufacturer of the ROM with the code they wish each word to contain. The manufacturer then builds a mask that is used to produce the ROM. Because of the custom programming involved, a mask costs about \$1000. Users should be sure of their inputs before they incur the masking charge, because the ROM is normally useless if a single bit is wrong. Once the mask is made, identical ROMs can be produced inexpensively.

1-4.5 Programmable Read-Only Memories (PROMs)

Programmable read-only memories are designed to be programmed by the users at their facility, instead of being programmed by the manufacturer. Most of these PROMs come with all outputs at 0. By following the programming procedure specified by the manufacturer, users can change bits at selected locations to a 1. Often this is done by driving high current through the IC that opens fusible links. Each open link provides a 1 instead of a 0 output. Thus users must open a link for a 1 in every location of their programs. Again, a mistake may cause the PROM to be useless. A 0 can always be changed to a 1, but a 1 cannot be changed back to a 0. If only a small quantity of identical ROMs is required, it is less expensive to use fusible link PROMs than a custom-masked ROM.

1-4.6 Erasable PROMs

Some PROMs can be *erased* and *reprogrammed* in the field if users have the proper equipment. The **2708**, manufactured by Intel, or the **MC68708**, made by Motorola, can be erased by exposing them to ultraviolet light. Because these are erasable and reprogrammable, they are very popular for developing programs for μPs, where programming mistakes are common and changes in the program occur frequently.

1-5 THE ARITHMETIC-LOGIC UNIT (ALU)

The ALU performs all the arithmetic and logical operations required by the computer. It accepts two operands as inputs (each operand contains as many bits as the basic word length of the computer) and performs the required arithmetic or logical operation upon them. ALUs are readily available as ICc (the **74181** is an ALU that provides for a variety of operations on two 4-bit operands), but μPs contain their ALUs within the μP chip.

Most ALUs perform the following arithmetic or logical operations:

1 Addition

2 Subtraction

3 Logical OR

4 Logical AND

5 EXCLUSIVE OR

6 Complementation

7 Shifting

Computers are capable of performing more sophisticated arithmetic operations such as multiplication, division, extracting square roots, and taking trigonometric functions; however, in most computers these operations are performed as *software subroutines*. A multiplication command, for example, is translated by the appropriate subroutine into a series of add and shift operations that can be performed by the ALU.

1-5.1 The Condition Code Register

All μPs have a condition code register associated with the ALU. The individual bits of the condition code register are called *flags* and indicate the status of the last operation of the μP. Flags are used by the μP to determine whether conditional jumps should be taken. They are also needed for arithmetic operations involving more than 1-byte operands.

The most common flags are

1 *The C flag.* Set when an arithmetic operation produces a carry.
2 *The Z flag.* Set to 1 when the last result is 0. Note that Z = 1 indicates the last result was 0, and Z = 0 indicates that the last result was not 0.
3 *The N (negative) or S (sign) flag.* This flag is set when the result of the last operation was negative, as indicated by a 1 in the MSB of the result.
4 *The V (overflow) flag.* This flag is set when the last operation produced a 2s complement overflow.
5 *The P (parity) flag.* Set to 1 when the parity of the result is even.
6 *The H (half-carry) flag.* Set to 1 when there is a carry from the lower to the upper half-byte in addition. This flag is used for decimal arithmetic.
7 *The I (interrupt) flag.* This flag determines whether interrupts will be accepted by the μP.

There are also some specialized flags, such as FIRQ, used by particular μPs. Detailed examples of the use of the arithmetic flags are presented in the chapters on the individual μPs.

1-6 THE CONTROL SECTION

The function of the *control section* is to regulate the operation of the computer. It decodes the instructions and causes the proper events to occur in the correct order.

The control section of a computer consists of a group of registers and FFs and the timing circuitry necessary to make them operate properly. In a rudimentary computer the following registers might be part of the control section.

1 *The MAR and MDR.*
2 *The program counter (PC).* This is a register that contains as many bits as the MAR. *It holds the memory address of the next instruction word to be executed.* It is usually *incremented* during the execution of an instruction so that it contains the address of the next instruction to be executed.
3 *The instruction register.* This register holds the instruction while it is in the process of being executed.
4 *The instruction decoder.* This decodes the instruction presently being executed. Its inputs come from the instruction register.

5 *The accumulator.* The accumulator is a register containing as many bits as the MDR. It contains the basic operand used in each instruction. In ALU operations where two operands are required, one of the operands is stored in the accumulator as a result of previous instructions. The other operand is generally read from memory. The two operands form the inputs to the ALU and the result is normally sent back to the accumulator.

1-6.1 Control Unit FFs

An FF is an electronic circuit that can function as a 1-bit memory. A FF can be set into the 1 or 0 state and remain there until another command causes it to change states. Large computer memories are made up of many thousands of integrated circuit FFs.

Individual FFs are used where small quantities of data (several bits) must be remembered and changed frequently.

The control unit usually contains several FFs. The flags or condition codes are FFs. Most μPs also have FETCH and EXECUTE FFs.

The FETCH and EXECUTE FFs determine the state of the computer. The instructions are contained in the computer's memory. *The computer starts by fetching the instruction.* This is the fetch portion of the computer's cycle. *It then executes, or performs, the instruction.* At this time, the computer is in execute mode. When it has finished executing the instruction, it returns to fetch mode and reads the next instruction from memory. Thus *the computer alternates between fetch and execute modes* and the FETCH and EXECUTE FFs determine its current mode of operation.

1-7 EXECUTION OF A SIMPLE ROUTINE

A μP starts to execute instructions by fetching the byte at the address contained in the PC. Most μPs use this first byte as an 8-bit Op code (short for operations code). The Op code tells the μP what to do (what instruction to execute). Since μPs have an 8-bit Op code, they can execute up to 256 different instructions.

In most cases the μP then executes a second fetch cycle[3] to get the address required by the instruction. It then has both the Op code and the address and can execute the instruction. When execution is complete the μP proceeds to execute the next instruction. Once started it continues to execute instructions until it is halted by a HALT instruction or an external signal. The **6800**, **6809**, and **6502** μPs have no HALT instruction as such. They can be halted by an instruction that branches to itself, but this instruction does not truly stop the computer; it reexecutes itself over and over again.

[3] The number of bytes and cycles required for each instruction depends upon the instruction itself and the mode of the instruction.

1-7.1 Sample Problem

As a simple example, let us consider what a μP must do to add two numbers. Before starting the μP, both the numbers to be added and the program must be written into memory. Suppose we are trying to add the numbers 2 and 3. We can arbitrarily set aside location 80 to hold the number 2 and location 81 to hold the number 3. Location 82 is also set aside to hold the result.

The program, or set of instructions, required to add the numbers might be this:

LOAD 80	First instruction
ADD 81	Second instruction
STORE 82	Third instruction

The first instruction loads or takes the contents of location 80 (2 in this example) and stores it into the accumulator. Note that it leaves the contents of 80 unchanged.

The second instruction reads the contents of 81 (3) and adds it to the accumulator, which contains a 2 because of the first instruction. The sum, 5, is then placed in the accumulator.

The third instruction causes the contents of the accumulator to be written to memory. Thus, 5 is written into location 82 and the program is complete.

1-7.2 Hardware Execution of the Routine

This section describes how the registers and ALU within the μP are coordinated and work together to execute the above program. The instructions must reside at specific locations in memory. Let us assume that location 10 is set aside for the start of the program. Thus, location 10 contains the LOAD, location 11 contains 80, location 12 contains the ADD instruction, and so on. The contents of the registers and memory are shown in Figure 1-4.

Before starting execution, the starting address of the program (10 in this example) must be written into the PC. Program execution then proceeds as follows.

1 The 10 is transferred from the PC to the MAR and the memory is read at location 10.

2 Since this is the first part of the FETCH cycle, the data read is placed in the instruction register and the instruction decoder determines that it is a LOAD instruction. Note that the μP cannot actually read the word "load" in location 10. It reads a byte of 1s and 0s that are decoded as a LOAD command.

3 The μP then increments the PC and MAR and reads the contents of 11 (80), which it places in the MAR.

4 The μP is now ready to execute the LOAD instruction. It does so by reading the contents of 80, which is already in the MAR, and placing it in the accumulator. The accumulator now contains the contents of 80 (the number 2).

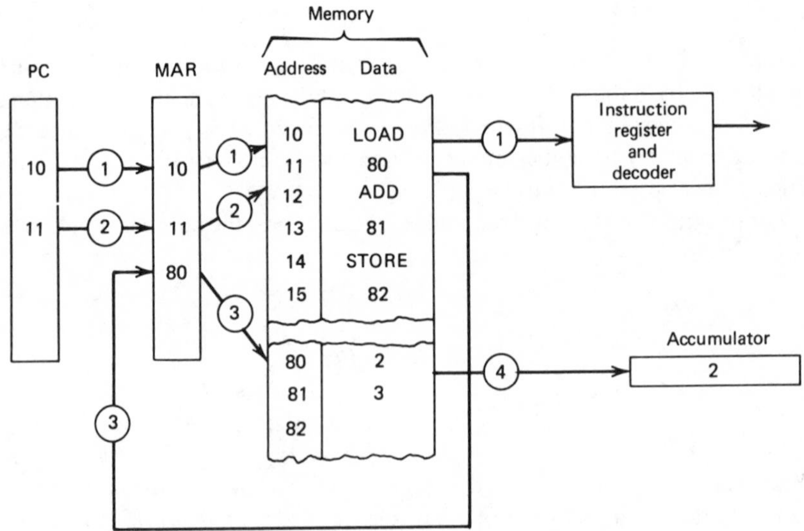

Figure 1-4 Execution of a LOAD instruction of a rudimentary μP. (From Greenfield and Wray, *Using Microprocessors and Microcomputers: The 6800 Family*, Wiley, 1981.)

5 The instruction execution is now finished and the fetch mode for the next instruction is entered. The PC is again incremented to 12 and placed in the MAR.

6 The code for ADD is fetched from location 12 and decoded.

7 The PC is again incremented and 81 is read from memory and placed in the MAR.

8 The execute portion of the ADD instruction is entered. The contents of 81 (3) are read and added to the contents of the accumulator. This uses the ALU within the μP. The results (5) are written to the accumulator and the ADD instruction is complete.

9 The PC is again incremented and transferred to the MAR. The Op code for the STORE instruction is fetched and decoded.

10 The address for the store instruction (82) is fetched from location 15 and placed in the MAR.

11 The store instruction is now executed by taking the contents of the accumulator (5) and writing them to memory at location 82.

The hardware execution of the LOAD instruction is shown in Figure 1-4, where the numbers in the circles indicate the step number. In step 1 the contents of the PC (10) are transferred to the MAR and the LOAD Op code is read from memory to the instruction register and decoded. The PC is then incremented (step 2), sent to the MAR and 80 is read. In step 3 the 80 is transferred to the MAR and the number 2 is read, which is sent to the accumulator in step 4. Thus, LOAD 80 placed the contents of location 80 in the accumulator.

Table 1-1 shows the contents of the registers at each step in the program. It correlates with the outline description of the program's progress.

Table 1-1 **Register changes as the example of section 1-7.2 progresses**

PC	*MAR*	*Memory data*	*Accumulator*	
10	10	LOAD	X	LOAD instruction
11	11	80	X	
11	80	2	2	
12	12	ADD	2	ADD instruction
13	13	81	2	
13	81	3	5	
14	14	STORE	5	STORE instruction
15	15	82	5	
15	82	5	5	

1-8 INTRODUCTION TO PROGRAMMING

The previous sections discussed the hardware of a computer, but computers are actually controlled by the *software* or programs written for them. This makes computers very versatile because their operation can be changed simply by changing the program.

A *program* is a group of instructions that cause the computer to perform a given task. Each instruction causes the computer to do something specific. As shown in the previous section, each microprocessor instruction consists of an Op code, a byte that tells the computer what to do, and usually some additional bytes that specify the address of an operand.

1-8.1 Machine Language Programming

Computers and microprocessors can only use numbers. The Op codes and addresses that they fetch from memory during program execution are simply numbers, which are the only things a memory can contain.

Programs written using the numbers the computers will actually use are called *machine language programs.* These programs can be *directly* entered into the computer. Programs written in higher-level languages must be translated into machine language before a computer can use them.

In any computer each Op code is designated by its own number. Most of the authors in this book use a modified form of machine language, as that is the most direct way of explaining the operation of microprocessors. Actually most instructions are expressed as both a *mnemonic* that describes the instruction and its machine language equivalent. The reader is liable to see code such as

```
LDA A 80        96    80
```

which means load the contents of 80 into the accumulator. The 96 80 is the machine language expression of this instruction; it is what would actually be written in memory. The 96 is the number for the Op code of the LOAD instruction whose mnemonic is LDA.

1-8.2 Assembly Language

Machine language is used by the engineer who must troubleshoot and debug hardware systems containing μPs. Machine language, however, makes programming slow and cumbersome and programmers prefer to write in *assembly language* or higher-level languages.

In assembly language programming, mnemonics are used for Op codes, addresses, and labels; instead of writing 96 80 an assembly language programmer might write

```
LDA    SAM
```

where SAM becomes the symbol for an address, 80 in this case. Assembly language programming is easier because the programmer does not have to remember the numeric values of Op codes and because it is easier to keep track of variables when calling them by symbolic names.

Assembly language programs cannot be directly entered into a μP. First an assembly language program must be converted into a machine language program. This is done by feeding the program in assembly language, called the *source program*, into a computer. The computer must also have another program in it called an *assembler*. The assembler operates on the source program and converts it into a *machine language or object program*, that contains all the numbers and can be loaded directly into the μP's memory.

Each individual μP has an assembler written specifically for it. After the engineer decides which μP to use, he should investigate the assemblers available for that μP.

1-8.3 Higher-Level Languages

Higher-level languages such as Basic, Fortran, and Pascal are the most efficient for a programmer. One high-level language statement can generate several machine language instructions. Now, however, a *compiler* program is necessary to translate the high-level language program to machine code. Many μPs do not have compilers for all languages.

There are some objections to using high-level languages with μPs. They are not good when bit manipulation is required, they cannot be used to generate precise time delays, and the execution of their code is generally slow. They are, however, the most convenient way to write programs. In general, programs written to get answers to problems are usually written in higher-level languages, whereas programs to control processes and devices, which must operate in "real time," use assembly language.

1-9 FLOWCHARTS

Flowcharts are used by programmers to show the progress of their programs graphically. They are a clear and concise method of presenting the programmer's approach to a problem. They are often used as a part of programming documenta-

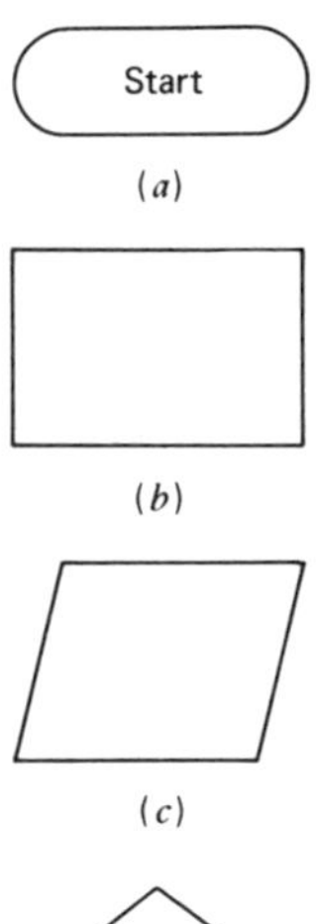

Figure 1-5 The most common standard flowchart symbols. (*a*) Beginning or termination block. (*b*) Processing or command block. (*c*) Input/output block. (*d*) Decision block. (From Greenfield and Wray, *Using Microprocessors and Microcomputers: The 6800 Family*, Wiley, 1981.)

tion, where the program must be explained to those unfamiliar with it. Since good documentation is essential for proper use of any computer, the rudiments of flowcharts are presented in this section.

1-9.1 Flowchart Symbols

The flowchart symbols used in this book are shown in Figure 1-5.

1 The *oval* symbol is either a *beginning* or *termination* box. It is used simply to denote the start or end of a program.
2 The *rectangular block* is the *processing or command block*. It states what must be done at that point in the program.
3 The *parallelogram* is an *input/output block*. Such commands as READ or WRITE, especially from an external device such as a disk or card reader, are flowcharted using these boxes.
4 The *diamond box* is a *decision box*. It usually contains a question within it. There are typically two output paths; one if the answer to the question is yes, and the other if the answer is no. Sometimes when a comparison between two numbers is made, there might be three exit paths corresponding to the greater than, less than, and equal, possibilities.

EXAMPLE 1-4 Draw a flowchart to add the numbers 1, 4, 7, and 10 together.

Solution The solution is shown in Figure 1-6. It consists simply of a start box, four command boxes, and a stop box. This is an example of straight-line programming since no

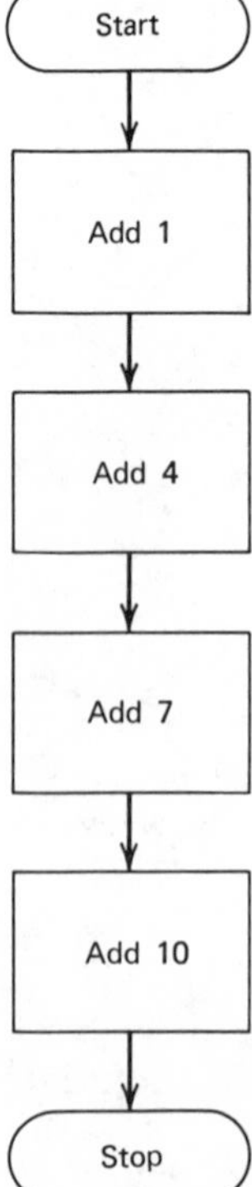

Figure 1-6 Flowchart for Example 1-4. (From Greenfield and Wray, *Using Microprocessors and Microcomputers*: *The 6800 Family*, Wiley, 1981.)

decisions were made. It was also assumed that the numbers 1, 4, 7, and 10 were available in the computer's memory and were not read from an external device.

1-9.2 Elementary Programming

To introduce the concepts of programming in this chapter, we use a rudimentary computer, such as that described in section 1-6. The instructions are really binary data words stored in various memory locations. Each instruction is assumed to consist of words that contain the Op code and the address of the data. The Op codes used in this section are ADD, SUBTRACT, MULTIPLY, DIVIDE, LOAD, and STORE.

For example, consider the problem of writing instructions for the flowchart of Figure 1-6. The first problem is to allocate memory areas for the instructions and the data. All these words must be in memory before the program can be started.

Most μP systems contain a keyboard and a monitor for data entry. The *monitor* is a program in ROM that controls the microcomputer system and allows the user to enter programs and data into memory directly from the keyboard. This method of data entry is slow, but must be used the first time a program is to be executed. Once entered, the program can be preserved on disk or tape and rapidly reentered when needed.

As in section 1-7, assume we are using a μP where the first byte of each instruction is the Op code and the next byte is the address of the data. Again we arbitrarily decide to start the program at location 10 and the data at 80. The program would then be as follows.

Location	*Instruction*
10	LOAD
11	80
12	ADD
13	81
14	ADD
15	82
16	ADD
17	83
18	STORE
19	84
1A	HALT

The operation of the LOAD, ADD, and STORE instructions is explained in section 1-7.

The data might then be this:

Location	*Contents*
80	1
81	4
82	7
83	10
84	Reserved for result

Once the data areas and all the required constants are written in memory, the code can be executed by starting at location 10. Note that the data could be changed and the same program executed any number of times.

1-10 BRANCH INSTRUCTIONS AND LOOPS

The program of the previous section is extremely simple; indeed, the user can compute the answer more quickly than he can write the program. Suppose, however, the program is expanded so that we are required to add the numbers 1, 4, 7, 10, . . . ,

10,000.[4] Conceptually, this could be done by expanding the program and flowchart of Section 1-9.2. However, the program and data areas would then require 3333 locations each and just writing them would become very tedious. Obviously, something else must be done.

1-10.1 Branch Instructions

Branch instructions provide the solution to the above problem. *A branch or jump instruction alters the normal sequence of program execution and is used to create loops that allow the same sequence of instructions to be executed many times.*

In the normal course of program execution the program counter (PC) is incremented during the execution of each instruction and contains the location of the next instruction to be fetched. A branch instruction might look like this:

```
BRANCH 500
```

where "branch" is the Op code and 500 is the branch address. It causes the branch address to be written into the PC. Thus the location of the next instruction to be executed is the branch address (500 in this case), rather than the sequential address.

There are two types of BRANCH instructions, unconditional and conditional.

The unconditional BRANCH always causes the program to jump to the branch address. It is written as BRA, which stands for "branch always."

The CONDITIONAL BRANCH causes the program to branch only if a specified condition is met. For this introductory chapter only two CONDITIONAL BRANCH instructions are used:

BPL—branch on positive (0 is considered as a positive number.)
BMI—branch on negative.

Therefore, should the computer encounter one of these instructions, it simply tests the negative bit of the condition code register. The state of this bit (which is established during the execution of the previous instructions) determines whether the branch should be taken.

EXAMPLE 1-5 A computer is to add the numbers 1, 4, 7, 10, ..., 10,000.[5] Draw a flowchart for the program.

Solution The flowchart is shown in Figure 1-7. We recognize that we must keep track of two quantities. One is the number to be added. This has been labeled N in the flowchart and progresses 1, 4, 7, 10.... The second quantity is the sum S, which progresses 1, $1 + 4$, $1 + 4 + 7$,... or 1, 5, 12.... The first box in the flowchart is an initialization box. It sets N to 1 and S to 0 at the beginning of the program. The next box ($S = N + S$) sets the new sum equal to the old sum plus the number to be added. The number to be added is then increased by 3. At

[4] Since the object of this section is to teach programming and not mathematics, we ignore the fact that this is an arithmetic progression whose sum is given by a simple formula.

[5] For the introductory problems of this section we have ignored the fact that decimal 10,000 cannot be contained within a single byte.

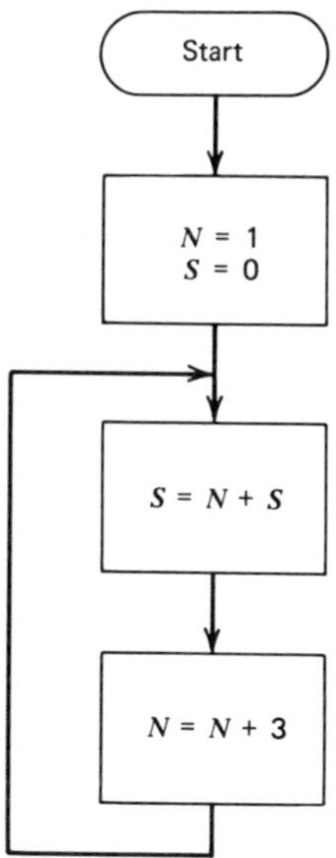

Figure 1-7 Flowchart for Example 1-5. (From Greenfield and Wray, *Using Microprocessors and Microcomputers: The 6800 Family*, Wiley, 1981.)

this point the flowchart loops around to repeat the sequence. This is accomplished by placing an unconditional branch instruction in the program. The quantities S and N will progress as specified.

1-10.2 Decision Boxes and Conditional Branches

The reader has probably already realized that there is a serious problem with Example 1-5; the loop never terminates. Actually, putting a program into an endless loop is one of the most common programming mistakes.

There are two common ways to determine when to end a loop: *loop counting* and *event detection.* Either method requires the use of decision boxes in the flowchart and corresponding conditional branch instructions in the program. Loop counting is considered first.

Loop counting is done by determining the number of times the loop should be traversed, counting the actual number of times through and comparing the two.

EXAMPLE 1-6 Improve the flowchart of Figure 1-7 so that it terminates properly.

Solution The program should terminate not when $N = 10{,}000$, but when 10,000 is added to the sum. For the flowchart of Figure 1-8, N is increased to 10,003 immediately after this occurs. At the end of the first loop $N = 4$, the second loop $N = 7$, and so on. It can be seen here that $N = 3L + 1$ where L is the number of times through the loop. If N is set to 10,003, $L = 3334$. The loop must be traversed 3334 times.

The correct flowchart is shown in Figure 1-8. The loop counter L has been added and set initially to -3334. It is incremented each time through the loop and tested to see if it is

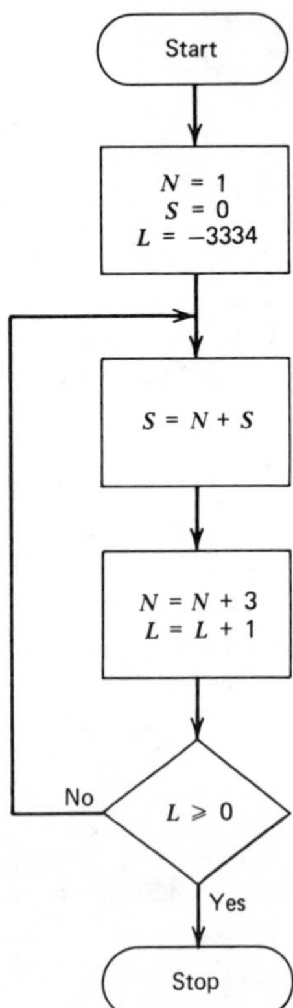

Figure 1-8 Flowchart for Example 1-6. (From Greenfield and Wray, *Using Microprocessors and Microcomputers: The 6800 Family*, Wiley, 1981.)

positive. After 3334 loops, it becomes 0. Then the yes path from the decision box is taken and the program halts.

EXAMPLE 1-7 Write the code for the flowchart of Figure 1-8.

Solution As in section 1-9.2, the program is started at location 10 and the data area at location 80. In the data area three variables, *N*, *S*, and *L* are needed. These should be initialized to 1, 0, and −3334, respectively, before the program starts. In addition, two constants, 1 and 3, are needed during the execution of the program. Before the program starts, the data area should look like this:

Location	*Term*	*Initial value*
80	*N*	1
81	*S*	0
82	*L*	−3334
83	Constant	3
84	Constant	1

The program can now be written directly from the flowchart.

Locations	*Instruction*	*Comments*
10,11	LOAD 81	
12,13	ADD 80	$S = N + S$
14,15	STORE 81	
16,17	LOAD 80	
18,19	ADD 83	$N = N + 3$
1A,1B	STORE 80	
1C,1D	LOAD 82	
1E,1F	ADD 84	$L = L + 1$
20,21	STORE 82	
22,23	BMI 10	
24,25	HALT	

Each instruction takes two bytes as it could in a μP. Two locations are therefore assigned to each instruction and the addresses are in hex.

Note that the instructions follow the flowchart. The decision box has been implemented by the BMI instruction. The program loops as long as L remains negative.

Check: as a check on the program, we can write the contents of N, S, and L at the end of each loop in the following table.

Times through the loop	N	S	L
1	4	1	−3333
2	7	5	−3332
3	10	12	−3331

The chart shows that each time around the loop:

$$\frac{N-1}{3} + |L| = 3334$$

Therefore, when $N = 10{,}003$, L indeed equals 0 and the loop terminates.

1-10.3 Event Detection

Event detection terminates a loop when an event occurs that should make the loop terminate. In Example 1-7, that event could be the fact that N is greater than 10,000. Using event detection, locations 1C through 21 could be replaced by:

```
1C,1D     LOAD N
1E,1F     SUBTRACT 105
20,21     Not needed (NOP)
22,23     BMI 10
```

where location 105 contains 10,001. This program branches back until $N =$ 10,003. In this problem, the use of event detection is conceptually simpler and saves one instruction.

1-11 INPUT/OUTPUT

To do anything useful, a microprocessor must communicate with external devices. This communication is called *input/output*. If the μP is being used as a computer, to solve problems, or do word processing, for example, it usually receives input from a keyboard on a teletype or CRT terminal. The output may also be to a CRT terminal, but if a permanent record of the result (hard copy) is needed, a printer must be added to the system. Conversely, if the μP is being used as a controller, to control the events occurring in some external process such as an automobile ignition system, the inputs come from sensors, transducers, and A/D converters. These tell the μP the status of the system. The μP then processes this information and sends commands to the system via relays or A/D converters to control the system and assure that it continues to operate optimally. In either case, *signals coming from an external device to the μP are input, and signals going from the μP to an external device are output.*

There are two types of I/O that μPs commonly use: port I/O, and memory-mapped I/O. Intel μPs (the **8080** and **8085**) and the Zilog **Z80** tend to use port I/O, whereas Motorola μPs and the **6502** use memory-mapped I/O exclusively. Both types of I/O are explained further in the following paragraphs.

1-11.1 Port I/O

The Intel **8080** and **8085** μPs execute their I/O instructions primarily by using input or output *ports*. A port designates the *source* of data on an I/O input or I/O READ instruction. Thus input devices like UARTs, card readers, or cassettes would have to be connected to an input port. For an output or I/O WRITE instruction, the port designates which external device (lineprinter, tape, etc.) is to *receive* information from the μP. The architecture of the **8080** and **8085** allows for 256 input and 256 output ports.

There are two special instructions for handling input and output: the IN instruction and the OUT instruction. An IN instruction causes data to be *read from the external device* into the accumulator, while an OUT instruction causes a byte from the accumulator to be *sent to an external device.*

Part of each IN or OUT instruction is a *port designation.* This tells the various input or output devices which port is being used for the data transfer. Suppose, for example, that several devices are connected to a μP to input data. Then the instruction

```
IN    34
```

commands only the device connected to port 34 to input data. All other input devices are deselected and must not attempt to put data on the lines. Thus each input device may be thought of as having an address that corresponds to its port number. It must not be active unless it detects an IN instruction and decodes its own port number on the address lines. IN and OUT instructions are covered more thoroughly in section 5-2.

1-11.2 Memory-Mapped I/O

While Intel uses primarily port I/O, Motorola uses *memory-mapped I/O* exclusively. In memory-mapped I/O *all peripheral interface ICs occupy locations in the address field.* The most commonly used Motorola peripheral is the **6821** Peripheral Interface Adapter (PIA). Of course, addresses used by PIAs or other I/O ICs cannot also be used by memory. This reduces the available memory space. Furthermore, each peripheral IC generally occupies only a few addresses (a PIA takes four addresses), so in a large system, considerable decoding may be needed to access a particular IC. The advantages of memory-mapped I/O are that the μP treats the I/O ICs just like memory; thus any instructions that access memory (LOADs, STOREs, SHIFTs[6], etc.) can also access the I/O ICs. No special instructions such as IN and OUT are needed and this simplifies programming.

Memory-mapped I/O is rapidly becoming the dominant form of I/O. Motorola peripheral ICs are all designed specifically for memory-mapped I/O, while the newer Intel ICs can work with either port or memory-mapped I/O.

1-11.3 Command and Status Registers

Most ICs that use memory-mapped I/O have several registers in them. Each register has its own memory address. The main registers are:

1 *The data register*. This holds the data being transferred from the I/O ICs to the μP on an I/O READ and from the μP on an I/O WRITE.

2 *The command register*. Most I/O ICs have several *modes* of operation, or ways they operate. The particular mode they use at any time is determined by the bits in a command register. The command register is written by the μP. Thus the μP can command the I/O IC to operate in a given mode, and the μP can change these commands as the program progresses. Often, however, the appropriate mode of operation is selected at the beginning of the program and does not change.

3 *The status register*. The status register of the I/O IC is written into by the external device. It contains information about the status of the external device such as: is the printer out of paper, does the tape drive need another character, and so on. The μP can read the status register to monitor the progress of data transfers and take appropriate action when required.

4 *Command-status register*. Sometimes the command and status registers are combined. The PIA is an example.

[6] The **6800** has instructions that allow the user to shift, increment, decrement, and perform other operations on a memory location. The **8080/8085** does not have this capability.

5 *The data direction register* (*DDR*). This register determines whether each line of the data register is input or output. Generally a 0 written into a bit in the DDR forces the corresponding bit in the data register to be an input and a 1 in the DDR forces the data register bit to be an output. The DDR is written to by the μP. This allows the μP to control the direction of data flow.

EXAMPLE 1-8 A DDR contains F0. What is the direction of data flow?

Solution Because the four LSBs of the DDR are 0, the corresponding four LSBs of the data register are inputs. The four MSBs of the data register are outputs. Thus this IC can take data in on its four LSBs and send data to the peripheral on its four MSBs. This situation will continue until the μP commands a change in the DDR.

In many ICs the command register is WRITE-ONLY (the μP cannot read it) and the status register is READ-ONLY (the μP cannot write it).

The Motorola **6821** Peripheral Interface Adapter (PIA) is a typical example of an I/O chip that uses these registers. The PIA has six internal registers and occupies four memory addresses. All of the PIA's registers can be both read and written to, which may be a help in debugging.[7]

1-12 INTERRUPTS

In many systems the peripherals must be able to request, or even demand, attention from the μP. These situations might occur when a peripheral needs data, or has data for the μP, or must inform the μP of a change of status in the external system.

It is often desirable, and sometimes necessary, to heed the peripheral's request as soon as it is made. In these cases, the peripheral makes its request by interrupting the μP. This is the fastest and most direct way to get the μP's attention.

An *interrupt* is a signal from a peripheral to a μP. It causes the μP to discontinue the program it is currently running and jump to a *service routine*, a program that takes the action required by the peripheral. When the μP finishes its service routine, it usually resumes executing the main program at the point it left off when it was interrupted.

1-12.1 Vectored Interrupts

In complex systems several devices might be capable of interrupting the μP, and each device has its own service routine in the μP's software. The μP must then determine which device interrupted it so it can execute the service routine for that device. One way of doing this is for the μP to *poll* or query each device until it finds

[7] The PIA's control registers do have 2 bits that are set by external events and cannot be written to. They are read-only to the μP.

the one that caused the interrupt. When very high speed is required this method is slow and inefficient.

Identification of the interrupting device is facilitated by using *vectored interrupts*. With vectored interrupts, the interrupting peripheral provides the μP with an indication of the device that caused the interrupt, and allows the μP to jump to the proper service routine quickly. The Intel **8080** and **8085** and the **Z80** have eight RESTART instructions (see section 4-4.4), which allow eight devices to interrupt using a particular RESTART. Each RESTART jumps or vectors the μP to a different service routine. The **8085** also allows interrupting devices to enter a CALL instruction that can jump the program to any predetermined location in memory. By using the CALL an unlimited number of devices can interrupt.

The Motorola **6800** always goes to the same routine upon interrupt and therefore must poll its peripherals. Motorola has, however, developed a priority interrupt controller (PIC) chip. Used in conjunction with the **6800**, it will vector the **6800** to one of several interrupt service routines. Other manufacturers have also developed similar ICs. Priority interrupt controllers not only facilitate interrupts but can be used to establish priorities among the peripheral devices so if several devices interrupt simultaneously, the one with the most urgent request is recognized.

1-12.2 Maskable and Nonmaskable Interrupts

A *nonmaskable interrupt* (NMI) will interrupt the μP as soon as it occurs. These interrupts have the highest priority and should be used with discretion. Nonmaskable interrupts are generally reserved for emergency situations, such as sensing that the μP or a peripheral is about to lose power. In most systems, only one event can cause a NMI so there is no need to determine which device caused the interrupt. NMIs vector most μPs to different locations than ordinary interrupts so the NMI service routine can be entered immediately.

Most interrupts are *maskable*; they will be ignored if the I bit in the condition code register is *set*. All μPs contain instructions to set and clear the I bit.

EXAMPLE 1-9 A programmer must be sure that the program segment between locations CO and DF is not interrupted. How can this be done?

Solution The programmer can set the I bit just before the program goes to CO. Of course the I bit must be cleared after finishing the code segment at DF or interrupts will be permanently disabled.

If a μP is to use interrupts it must clear the I bit at some point in the program. When a peripheral interrupts, the I bit is automatically set while the μP jumps to the service routine. This prevents a second peripheral from interrupting the service routine (sometimes called the interrupt of an interrupt). If a low priority device causes an interrupt it is sometimes necessary to allow a high priority device to interrupt. This can be done by placing an ENABLE INTERRUPT instruction in the low-priority device's service routine. Note that by allowing some devices routines to be interrupted but not others, we have effectively allocated priorities among the peripherals.

1-13 SUMMARY

This chapter served as an introduction to the concepts required for understanding μPs. The hardware (memories, ALUs, etc.) and software were introduced briefly. Other necessary concepts such as flags, input/output, and interrupts were also introduced. Further discussion of these concepts as they apply to specific μPs are included in the following chapters of this book.

1-14 REFERENCES

Joseph D. Greenfield and William C. Wray, *Using Microprocessors and Microcomputers: The 6800 Family*, Wiley, New York, 1981.

Lance A. Leventhal, *Introduction to Microprocessors: Software, Hardware, Programming*, Prentice-Hall, Englewood Cliffs, N.J., 1978.

Rodnay Zaks, *Microprocessors, from Chips to Systems*, 2nd Edition, Sybex, Inc., Berkeley, Calif., 1977.

CHAPTER 2

Computer Arithmetic and Shifting

Joseph D. Greenfield

Professor of Electrical Engineering Technology
Rochester Institute of Technology
Rochester, New York

2-1 INTRODUCTION

Almost all modern microprocessors use hexadecimal notation and 2s complement arithmetic. They are both derived from the binary number system, which is the basis of these systems. This chapter explains these number systems. Examples of applications to μPs are given in section 2-8.

The output of a digital electronic circuit is a single binary digit, commonly called a *bit*. A single bit has one of only two possible values, 0 or 1. In digital circuits, a certain range of voltages is defined as a logic 1 and another voltage range is defined as a logic 0. In transistor-transistor logic (TTL) circuits, for example, any voltage between 0 and 0.8 V is a logic 0, and any voltage between +2 and +5 is a logic 1. Digital circuits have a range of *undefined* or *forbidden* voltages that separate logic 1s from logic 0s. For TTL this range is from 0.8 to 2.0 V. If a circuit should produce a sustained output voltage in the undefined range, it is malfunctioning and should be investigated.

There are two advantages to restricting the output of an electronic circuit to one of two possible ranges. First, it is rarely necessary to make fine distinctions. Whether an output is 3.67 or 3.68 V is immaterial; both voltages correspond to a logic 1. Well-designed logic circuits produce voltages near the middle of the range defined for 1 or 0, so there is no difficulty in distinguishing between them. In addition, a digital circuit is very tolerant of any drift in the output caused by component aging or changes. A change in a component would almost have to be catastrophic to cause the output voltage to drift from a 1 to a 0 or an undefined value. The second advantage of digital circuits is that it is far easier to remember a 1 or a 0 than to remember an analog quantity like 3.67 V. Since computers are required to remember many bits, this is a very important consideration.

The output of a single digital circuit, a single bit, is enough to answer any question that has only two possible answers. For example, a typical job application might ask, "What is your sex?" The answer "male" could arbitrarily be assigned 1 and "female" 0, so a programmer needs to reserve only a single bit of space in the computer for this answer.

Another question on the job application might be, "What is the color of your hair?" If the possible answers are black, brown, blond, and red, a single bit cannot possibly describe them all; several bits are needed to describe all possible answers. We could assign one bit to each answer (e.g., brown = 0001, black = 0010, blond = 0100, red = 1000), but if there are many possible answers to the given question, many bits are required. The coding scheme presented above is not optimum; it requires more bits than are really necessary to answer the question.

It is most economical to use as few bits as possible to express the answer to a question, or a number, or a choice. So the crucial question arises:

"*What is the minimum number of bits required to distinguish between* n *different things?*"

Whether these n things are objects, possible answers, or n numbers is immaterial. To answer this question, we realize that each bit has two possible values. Therefore k bits can represent 2^k possible values. This gives rise to Theorem 1.

THEOREM 1 The minimum number of bits required to express n different things is k, where k is the smallest number such that $2^k \geqslant n$.

A few examples should make this clear.

EXAMPLE 2-1 What is the minimum number of bits required to answer the hair color question, and how could they be coded to give distinct answers?

Solution There are four possible answers to this question; therefore $2^k = 4$. Since 2 is the smallest number such that $2^2 \geqslant 4$, $k = 2$, and 2 bits are needed. One way of coding the answers is 00 = brown, 01 = black, 10 = blond, 11 = red.

EXAMPLE 2-2 How many bits are needed to express a single-decimal digit?

Solution There are 10 possible values for a single-decimal digit (0 through 9); therefore $2^k \geqslant 10$. Since $k = 4$ is the smallest *integer* such that $2^k \geqslant 10$, 4 bits are required.

EXAMPLE 2-3 A computer must store the names of a group of people. If we assume that no name is longer than 20 letters, how many bits must the computer reserve for each name?

Solution To express a name, only the 26 letters of the alphabet, plus a space and perhaps a period, are needed. This is a total of 28 characters. Since $2^k \geqslant 28$, $k = 5$ and 5 bits are required for each character. Because space must be reserved for 20 such characters, 100 bits are needed for each name.

2.1.1 Bits, Bytes, and Words

For use in computers, bits are grouped into *words*. The *word length* of a computer is the *number of bits involved in each memory data transfer*. While word lengths vary from computer to computer, each has a definite word length and its registers are generally built to accommodate words of that length.

Large computers generally use long words. The IBM **360/370** series, for example, uses 32-bit words. Minicomputers use intermediate word lengths; 16 bits is the most popular minicomputer word size.

Microprocessors use both 8- and 16-bit words. This book discusses six microprocessors that use 8-bit words and three that use 16-bit words. (Microprocessors using 32-bit words such as the National Semiconductor **32032** and the Motorola **68020** are starting to appear in the market, but they are too new to be discussed in this book.) In general, the smaller μPs are being used in control applications, while the 16-bit μPs are taking over some of the tasks previously reserved for minicomputers or mainframes. Microprocessors will not replace minis and mainframes, but they have caused an explosion in the general use of computers so that a large demand exists for all types of computers.

There are two advantages to using long word sizes:

1 Larger numbers can be accommodated within a single word.

2 Instruction words are larger and more flexible; they allow the instructions to contain more options.

The newer 16- and 32-bit μPs can now be used to solve complex mathematical problems, especially with coprocessors attached. Smaller μPs are most often used to control physical processes and can use shorter word lengths, which keeps the cost of the microprocessor and memory down, and allows the user to adjust the size of his system to fit the job requirements. Shorter word lengths complicate the programming, and the additional effort required to program μPs must be compensated for by the low cost of the hardware.

EXAMPLE 2-4 How many numbers can be represented by:

a a single IBM **360/370** word?

b an 8-bit microprocessor word?

Solution

a Since an IBM **360/370** word contains 32 bits, any one of $2^{32} = 4{,}294{,}967{,}296$ numbers may be represented in a single word.

b For the microprocessor word of 8 bits, $2^8 = 256$ numbers may be represented by a single word.

2-1.2 Bytes and Nibbles

A group of 8 bits is called a *byte*. This is a convenient size for storing a single *alphanumeric character* (a character from a teletype or typewriter that could be an alphabetic character, a number, a punctuation mark, or a control character). For the many μPs that have an 8-bit word size, the words byte and word are used interchangeably.

Groups of four bits are sometimes called a *nibble*. They also comprise a *hexadecimal digit* (see section 2-7). In addition, 32-bit computers use the terms *half word* and *double word*. Thus we have the following conversions:

$$\begin{aligned} 4 \text{ bits} &= 1 \text{ nibble} \\ 2 \text{ nibbles} &= 1 \text{ byte} \\ 2 \text{ bytes} &= 1 \text{ half word} = 16 \text{ bits} \\ 4 \text{ bytes} &= 1 \text{ word} = 32 \text{ bits} \\ 2 \text{ words} &= 1 \text{ mouthful (double word)} = 64 \text{ bits} \end{aligned}$$

2-2 BINARY-TO-DECIMAL CONVERSION

Because computer operation is based on the *binary* (base 2) number system and people use the *decimal* (base 10) number system, it is often necessary to convert numbers given in one system to their equivalents in the other system. To eliminate any possible confusion, a subscript is used to indicate which number system is employed. Thus, 101_{10} is the decimal number whose value is one hundred and one, while 101_2 is a binary number whose decimal value is five. Of course, any number containing a digit from 2 to 9 is a decimal number.

The value of a decimal number depends on the *magnitude* of the decimal digits expressing it and on their *position*. A decimal number is equal to the sum $D_0 \times 10^0 + D_1 \times 10^1 + D_2 \times 10^2 + \cdots$, where D_0 is the least significant digit, D_1 the next significant, and so on.

EXAMPLE 2-5 Express the decimal number 7903 as a sum to the base 10.

Solution Here D_0, the least significant digit is 3, $D_1 = 0, D_2 = 9$, and $D_3 = 7$. Therefore 7903 equals:

$$\begin{array}{lr} 3 \times 10^0 & 3 \\ + \ 0 \times 10^1 & 0 \\ + \ 9 \times 10^2 & 900 \\ + \ 7 \times 10^3 & 7000 \\ \hline & 7903 \end{array}$$

Similarly, a group of binary bits can represent a number in the binary system. The binary base is 2; therefore the digits can only be 0 or 1. However, a binary number is also equal to a sum, namely $B_0 \times 2^0 + B_1 \times 2^1 \cdots$, where B_0 is the least significant bit, B_1 the next significant bit, and so on. The powers of 2 are given in the *binary boat* of Table 2-1. In this table, n is the exponent and the corresponding positive and negative powers of 2 are listed to the left and right of n, respectively.

A binary number is a group of ones (1s) and zeros (0s). To find the equivalent decimal number, we simply add those powers of 2 that correspond to the 1s in the number and omit those powers of 2 that correspond to the 0s of the number.

EXAMPLE 2-6 Convert 100011011_2 to a decimal number.

Solution The first bit to the left of the decimal point corresponds to $n = 0$, and n increases by one (increments) for each position further to the left. The number 100011011 has 1s in

Table 2-1 **Positive and Negative Powers of 2**

2^n	n	2^{-n}
1	0	1.0
2	1	0.5
4	2	0.25
8	3	0.125
16	4	0.062 5
32	5	0.031 25
64	6	0.015 625
128	7	0.007 812 5
256	8	0.003 906 25
512	9	0.001 953 125
1 024	10	0.000 976 562 5
2 048	11	0.000 488 281 25
4 096	12	0.000 244 140 625
8 192	13	0.000 122 070 312 5
16 384	14	0.000 061 035 156 25
32 768	15	0.000 030 517 578 125
65 536	16	0.000 015 258 789 062 5
131 072	17	0.000 007 629 394 531 25
262 144	18	0.000 003 814 697 265 625
524 288	19	0.000 001 907 348 632 812 5
1 048 576	20	0.000 000 953 674 316 406 25
2 097 152	21	0.000 000 476 837 158 203 125
4 194 304	22	0.000 000 238 418 579 101 562 5
8 388 608	23	0.000 000 119 209 289 550 781 25
16 777 216	24	0.000 000 059 604 644 775 390 625
33 554 432	25	0.000 000 029 802 322 387 695 312 5
67 108 864	26	0.000 000 014 901 161 193 847 656 25
134 217 728	27	0.000 000 007 450 580 596 923 828 125
268 435 456	28	0.000 000 003 725 290 298 461 914 062 5
536 870 912	29	0.000 000 001 862 645 149 230 957 031 25
1 073 741 824	30	0.000 000 000 931 322 574 615 478 515 625
2 147 483 648	31	0.000 000 000 465 661 287 307 739 257 812 5
4 294 967 296	32	0.000 000 000 232 830 643 653 869 628 906 25
8 589 934 592	33	0.000 000 000 116 415 321 826 934 814 453 125
17 179 869 184	34	0.000 000 000 058 207 660 913 467 407 226 562 5
34 359 738 368	35	0.000 000 000 029 103 830 456 733 703 613 281 25
68 719 476 736	36	0.000 000 000 014 551 915 228 366 851 806 640 625
137 438 953 472	37	0.000 000 000 007 275 957 614 183 425 903 320 312 5
274 877 906 944	38	0.000 000 000 003 637 978 807 091 712 951 660 156 25
549 755 813 888	39	0.000 000 000 001 818 989 403 545 856 475 830 078 125
1 099 511 627 776	40	0.000 000 000 000 909 494 701 772 928 237 915 039 062 5
2 199 023 255 552	41	0.000 000 000 000 454 747 350 886 464 118 957 519 531 25
4 398 046 511 104	42	0.000 000 000 000 227 373 675 443 232 059 478 759 765 625
8 796 093 022 208	43	0.000 000 000 000 113 686 837 721 616 029 739 379 882 812 5
17 592 186 044 416	44	0.000 000 000 000 056 843 418 860 808 014 869 689 941 406 25
35 184 372 088 832	45	0.000 000 000 000 028 421 709 430 404 007 434 844 970 703 125
70 368 744 177 664	46	0.000 000 000 000 014 210 854 715 202 003 717 422 485 351 562 5
140 737 488 355 328	47	0.000 000 000 000 007 105 427 357 601 001 858 711 242 675 781 25
281 474 976 710 656	48	0.000 000 000 000 003 552 713 678 800 500 929 355 621 337 890 625
562 949 953 421 312	49	0.000 000 000 000 001 776 356 839 400 250 464 677 810 668 945 312 5
1 125 899 906 842 624	50	0.000 000 000 000 000 888 178 419 700 125 232 338 905 334 472 656 25
2 251 799 813 685 248	51	0.000 000 000 000 000 444 089 209 850 062 616 169 452 667 236 328 125
4 503 599 627 370 496	52	0.000 000 000 000 000 222 044 604 925 031 308 084 726 333 618 164 062 5
9 007 199 254 740 992	53	0.000 000 000 000 000 111 022 302 462 515 654 042 363 166 809 082 031 25
18 014 398 509 481 984	54	0.000 000 000 000 000 055 511 151 231 257 827 021 181 583 404 541 015 625
36 028 797 018 963 968	55	0.000 000 000 000 000 027 755 575 615 628 913 510 590 791 702 270 507 812 5
72 057 594 037 927 936	56	0.000 000 000 000 000 013 877 787 807 814 456 755 295 395 851 135 253 906 25
144 115 188 075 855 872	57	0.000 000 000 000 000 006 938 893 903 907 228 377 647 697 925 567 626 953 125
288 230 376 151 711 744	58	0.000 000 000 000 000 003 469 446 951 953 614 188 823 848 962 783 813 476 562 5
576 460 752 303 423 488	59	0.000 000 000 000 000 001 734 723 475 976 807 094 411 924 481 391 906 738 281 25
1 152 921 504 606 846 976	60	0.000 000 000 000 000 000 867 361 737 988 403 547 205 962 240 695 953 369 140 625
2 305 843 009 213 693 952	61	0.000 000 000 000 000 000 433 680 868 994 201 773 602 981 120 347 976 684 570 312 5
4 611 686 018 427 387 904	62	0.000 000 000 000 000 000 216 840 434 497 100 886 801 490 560 173 988 342 285 156 25
9 223 372 036 854 775 808	63	0.000 000 000 000 000 000 108 420 217 248 550 443 400 745 280 086 994 171 142 578 125
18 446 744 073 709 551 616	64	0.000 000 000 000 000 000 054 210 108 624 275 221 700 372 640 043 497 085 571 289 062 5
36 893 488 147 419 103 232	65	0.000 000 000 000 000 000 027 105 054 312 137 610 850 186 320 021 748 542 785 644 531 25
73 786 976 294 838 206 464	66	0.000 000 000 000 000 000 013 552 527 156 068 805 425 093 160 010 874 271 392 822 265 625
147 573 952 589 676 412 928	67	0.000 000 000 000 000 000 006 776 263 578 034 402 712 546 580 005 437 135 696 411 132 812 5
295 147 905 179 352 825 856	68	0.000 000 000 000 000 000 003 388 131 789 017 201 356 273 290 002 718 567 848 205 566 406 25
590 295 810 358 705 651 712	69	0.000 000 000 000 000 000 001 694 065 894 508 600 678 136 645 001 359 283 924 102 783 203 125
1 180 591 620 717 411 303 424	70	0.000 000 000 000 000 000 000 847 032 947 254 300 339 068 322 500 679 641 962 051 391 601 562 5
2 361 183 241 434 822 606 848	71	0.000 000 000 000 000 000 000 423 516 473 627 150 169 534 161 250 339 820 981 025 695 800 781 25
4 722 366 482 869 645 213 696	72	0.000 000 000 000 000 000 000 211 758 236 813 575 084 767 080 625 169 910 490 512 847 900 390 625

positions 0, 1, 3, 4, and 8. The conversion is made by obtaining those powers of 2 corresponding to these n values (using Appendix A, if necessary) and adding them:

n	2^n
0	1
1	2
3	8
4	16
8	256
	283

Therefore, $100011011_2 = \mathbf{283}_{10}$.

EXAMPLE 2-7 In the PDP-8 computer, each word consists of 12 bits, that is, $k = 12$. How many numbers can be represented by a single PDP-8 word?

Solution Since 12 bits are available, any one of 4096 (2^{12}) numbers can be expressed. These numbers range from a minimum of twelve 0s to a maximum of twelve 1s, which is the binary equivalent of 4095. Therefore, the 4096 different numbers that can be expressed by a single word are the decimal numbers 0 through 4095.

2-3 DECIMAL-TO-BINARY CONVERSION

It is often necessary to convert decimal numbers to binary. Humans, for example, supply and receive decimal numbers from computers that work in binary; consequently, computers are continually making binary-to-decimal and decimal-to-binary conversions.

To convert a decimal number to its equivalent binary number, the following *algorithm* (or procedure) may be used:

1 Obtain N. (The decimal number to be converted.)

2 Determine if N is odd or even.

3a If N is odd, write 1 and subtract 1 from N. Go to step 4.

3b If N is even, write 0.

4 Obtain a new value of N by dividing the N of step 3 by 2.

5a If $N > 1$, go back to step 1 and repeat the procedure.

5b If $N = 1$, write 1. The number written is the binary equivalent of the original decimal number. The number written first is the least significant bit, and the number written last is the most significant bit.

This procedure can also be implemented by following the flowchart of Figure 2-1. Computer programmers often use *flowcharts* to describe their programs graphically. For the rudimentary flowcharts drawn in this text, the square box is a command, which must be obeyed unconditionally. The diamond-shaped box is a decision box. Within the decision box is a question that must be answered yes or no. If the answer is yes, the *yes* path must be followed; otherwise the *no* path is followed.

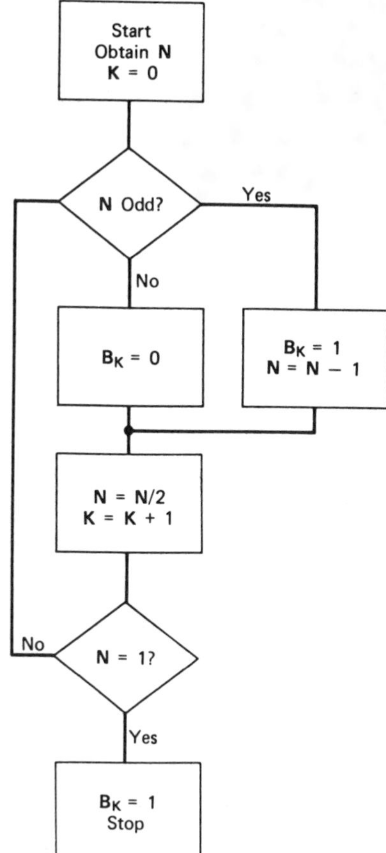

Figure 2-1 Flowchart for decimal-to-binary conversion of whole numbers. (From Greenfield and Wray, *Using Microprocessors and Microcomputers: The 6800 Family*, Wiley, 1981.)

The flowchart of Figure 2-1 starts with the given number N and since K equals 0, initially we are writing B_0, the least significant digit. Note that equations in a flowchart are programmer's equations, not algebraic equations. The "equation" $N = N - 1$ makes no sense mathematically. What it means here is that N is *replaced* by $N - 1$.

On the initial pass through the flowchart, B_0, the least significant bit, is written as 0 or 1, depending on whether N is even or odd. Next N is divided by 2 and K is incremented so that on the following pass, B_1, the second least significant bit (LSB) will be written. We continue looping through the flowchart and repeating the procedure until $N = 1$. Then the most significant bit (MSB) is written as a 1, and the process stops. The bits written are the binary equivalent of the decimal number.

EXAMPLE 2-8 Find the binary equivalent of the decimal number 217.

Solution The solution proceeds according to the algorithm or flowchart. When an odd number is encountered, a 1 is written as the binary digit and subtracted from the remaining number; when the remaining number is even, 0 is written as the binary digit. The number is then divided by 2. The process continues until the number is reduced to 1.

Remaining Number		**Binary Digit or Bit**
217	Odd—subtract 1	1
216	Divide by 2	
108	Even—divide by 2	0
54	Even—divide by 2	0
27	Odd—subtract 1	1
26	Divide by 2	
13	Odd—subtract 1	1
12	Divide by 2	
6	Even—divide by 2	0
3	Odd—subtract 1	1
2	Divide by 2	
1	Finish	1

Note that the *least significant bit* (LSB) was written first. Therefore $\mathbf{217_{10} = 11011001_2}$. To check this, convert back from binary to decimal.

$$11011001 = 128 + 64 + 16 + 8 + 1 = 217_{10}$$

2-4 ADDITION AND SUBTRACTION OF BINARY NUMBERS

The binary number system is a valid system, and mathematical operations such as addition, subtraction, multiplication, and division can be performed on binary numbers. In this section, the most commonly performed arithmetic operations, addition and subtraction, will be discussed. These are the arithmetic operations performed by a microprocessor or minicomputer. The reader should consult more specialized texts (section 2.10) for multiplication, division, squares, square roots, and other arithmetic operations.

2-4.1 Addition of Binary Numbers

The addition of binary numbers is similar to the addition of decimal numbers, except that $1 + 1 = 0$ with a carry out to the next significant place. A carry into a more significant position acts like an additional 1.

EXAMPLE 2-9 Add the binary numbers $A = 11101100$ and $B = 1100110$.

Solution

Column	9	8	7	6	5	4	3	2	1	**(Decimal Addition)**
A		1	1	1	0	1	1	0	0	(236)
B			1	1	0	0	1	1	0	(102)
	1	0	1	0	1	0	0	1	0	(338)

The above addition proceeded as follows:

1 Column 1 (least significant digit)	$0 + 0 = 0$
2 Column 2	$0 + 1 = 1$
3 Column 3	$1 + 1 = 0$ plus a carry output
4 Column 4	$0 + 1$ plus a carry input from column 3 sums to a 0 and produces a carry out to column 5.
5 Column 5	$0 + 0 = 0$, but the carry input from column 4 makes the sum 1.
6 Column 6	$1 + 1 = 0$ and a carry output to column 7.
7 Column 7	$1 + 1$ plus a carry input results in a sum of 1 and a carry output.
8 Column 8	B does not have an eighth bit; therefore a leading 0 can be assumed. Here $0 + 1$ plus a carry input yields a 0 sum plus a carry output.
9 Column 9	Neither A nor B has a ninth digit so leading 0s are written for both. In column 9 we have $0 + 0$ plus a carry in from column 8 that gives a sum of 1. Since there is no carry out of column 9, the addition is complete.

The sum of Example 2-9 can be checked by converting the numbers to their decimal equivalents. These numbers are shown in parentheses beside the sum.

2-4.2 Subtraction of Binary Numbers

The rules for the subtraction of binary numbers are:

1 $1 - 1 = 0$

2 $0 - 0 = 0$

3 $1 - 0 = 1$

4 $0 - 1 = 1$ with a *borrow out*

In order to borrow, change the next 1 in the minuend to a 0 and change all intervening 0s to 1s.

EXAMPLE 2-10 Subtract 101101001 from 100011010011.

Solution

Column	12	11	10	9	8	7	6	5	4	3	2	1	**(Decimal Subtraction)**
	1	0	0	0	1	1	0	1	0	0	1	1	(2259)
				1	0	1	1	0	1	0	0	1	− (361)
		1	1	1	0	1	1	0	1	0	1	0	(1898)

1 Column 1	$1 - 1 = 0$
2 Column 2	$1 - 0 = 1$
3 Column 3	$0 - 0 = 0$

4 Column 4 — $0 - 1 = 1$ The 1 in column 5 is changed to a 0 due to the borrow out generated in column 4.

5 Column 5 — This is now $0 - 0 = 0$

6 Column 6 — $0 - 1 = 1$ The 1 in column 7 is changed to a 0.

7 Column 7 — Due to the borrow from column 6, this now becomes $0 - 1$ or 1 with a borrow out that changes the 1 in column 8.

8 Column 8 — This becomes $0 - 0 = 0$

9 Column 9 — $0 - 1 = 1$ columns 10 and 11 are 0 so the borrow must be from column 12. Columns 10 and 11 contain intervening 0s so they change to 1s and column 12 changes to a 0.

10 Column 10 — This is now $1 - 0 = 1$

11 Column 11 — This is now $1 - 0 = 1$

12 Column 12 — $0 - 0 = 0$

The results were checked by converting the binary numbers to their decimal equivalents, which are shown in parentheses beside the numbers.

2-5 2s COMPLEMENT ARITHMETIC

When building hardware such as computers to accommodate binary numbers, two problems arise:

1 The number of bits in a hardware register is finite.

2 Negative integers must also be represented.

These problems do not arise in conventional pencil-and-paper arithmetic. If additional bits are needed, the number can always be extended to the left and negative numbers can always be represented by a minus sign.

Since a hardware register consists of a finite number of bits, the range of numbers that can be represented is finite. An n-bit register can contain one of 2^n numbers. If positive binary numbers are used, the 2^n numbers that can be represented are 0 through $2^n - 1$ (a string of n 1s represents the number $2^n - 1$).

The simplest approach to the problem of representing negative integers is to use the MSB to denote the *sign* of the number. Normally an *MSB of 0 indicates a positive number, and an MSB of 1 indicates a negative number*. The remaining bits denote the *magnitude* of the number. This is called *sign-magnitude* representation.

EXAMPLE 2-11 What range of positive and negative numbers can be represented in sign-magnitude notation by a 16-bit computer?

Solution Since the sixteenth bit is reserved for the sign, the largest number that can be represented is a string of fifteen 1s, which is $2^{15} - 1$, or 32,767.

Therefore 32,767 positive and 32,767 negative numbers can be represented. Zero, of course, can also be represented for a total range of 65,535 different numbers. There are two representations for 0; a positive 0 (all 0s) and a negative 0 (an MSB or sign bit of 1 followed by all 0s).

Some computers use sign-magnitude representation. The vast majority, however, use the *2s complement* method of representing numbers. It does not have the double representation of 0, and has other advantages that will soon become clear.

2-5.1 2s Complement Numbers

As in sign-magnitude representation, the *MSB of a 2s complement number denotes the sign* (0 means the number is positive, 1 means the number is negative), but *the MSB is also a part of the number.* In 2s complement notation, positive numbers are represented as simple binary numbers with the restriction that the MSB is 0. Negative numbers are somewhat different. To obtain the representation of a negative number, use the following algorithm:

1 Represent the number as a positive binary number.

2 Complement it (write 0s where there are 1s and 1s where there are 0s in the positive number).

3 Add 1.

4 Ignore any carries out of the MSB.

EXAMPLE 2-12 Given 8-bit words find the 2s complement representation of:

a 25

b −25

c −1

Solution

a The number +25 can be written as 11001. Since 8 bits are available, there is room for three leading 0s, making the MSB 0.

+25 = 00011001

b To find −25, complement +25 and add 1. (*Note*: The overbar notation means complementation or the inversion of all the bits.)

$$
\begin{aligned}
+25 &= 00011001 \\
\overline{(+25)} &= 11100110 \\
&\quad\;\; + \;\; 1 \\
\mathbf{-25} &= \mathbf{11100111}
\end{aligned}
$$

Note that the MSB is 1.

c To write −1, take the 2s complement of +1.

$$
\begin{aligned}
+1 &= 00000001 \\
\overline{(+1)} &= 11111110 \\
&\quad\;\; + \;\; 1 \\
\mathbf{-1} &= \mathbf{11111111}
\end{aligned}
$$

From this example, we see that a solid string of 1s represents the number −1 in 2s complement form.

To determine the magnitude of any unknown negative number, simply take its 2s complement as described above. The result is a positive number whose *magnitude equals that of the original number.*

EXAMPLE 2-13 What decimal number does 11110100 represent?

Solution Complementing the given number, we obtain:

$$\begin{array}{lr} & 00001011 \\ \text{Adding 1} & +\ 1 \\ \hline & 00001100 \end{array}$$

This is the equivalent of +12. Therefore, **11110100 = −12.**

2-5.2 The Range of 2s Complement Numbers

The *maximum positive* number that can be represented in 2s complement form is a single 0 followed by all 1s, or $2^{n-1} - 1$ for an n-bit number. The *most negative* number that can be represented has an MSB of 1 followed by all 0s, which equals -2^{n-1}. Therefore, an n-bit number can represent any one of $2^{n-1} - 1$ positive numbers, plus 2^{n-1} negative numbers, plus 0 which is 2^n total numbers. Every number has a *unique* representation.

Other features of 2s complement arithmetic are:

1 Even numbers (positive or negative) have an LSB of 0.

2 Numbers divisible by 4 have the two LSBs equal to 0 (see Example 2-13).

3 In general, numbers divisible by 2^n have n LSBs of 0.

EXAMPLE 2-14 What range of numbers can be represented by an 8-bit word (a byte) using 2s complement representation?

Solution The most positive is 01111111 = 127. The most negative number in eight bits is 10000000 = −128. Therefore, any number between +127 and −128 can be represented by an 8-bit number in 2s complement form. There are 256 numbers in this range, as expected. since $2^8 = 256$. Note also that the seven LSBs of −128 are 0, as required, since −128 is divisible by 2^7.

2-5.3 Adding 2s Complement Numbers

Consider the simple equation $C = A$ plus B. While it seems clear enough, we cannot immediately determine whether an addition or subtraction operation is required. If A and B are both positive, addition is required. But if one of the operands is negative and the other is positive, a subtraction operation must be performed.

The major advantage of 2s complement arithmetic is: *If an addition operation is to be performed, the numbers are added regardless of their signs. The answer is in 2s complement form with the correct sign.* Any carries out of the MSB are meaningless and should be ignored.

EXAMPLE 2-15 Express the numbers 19 and −11 as 8-bit, 2s complement numbers, and add them.

Solution The number +19 is simply 00010011. To find −11, take the 2s complement of 11.

$$11 = 00001011$$
$$(\overline{11}) = 11110100$$
$$-11 = 11110101$$

Now +19 plus (−11) equals:

	1111 111	**Carry**
	00010011	19
+	11110101	−11
	00001000	+ 8

Note that there is a carry out of the MSB that is ignored. The 8-bit answer is simply the number +8.

EXAMPLE 2-16 Add −11 and −19.

Solution First −19 must be expressed as a 2s complement number:

$$19 = 00010011$$
$$(\overline{19}) = 11101100$$
$$-19 = 11101101$$

Now the numbers can be added:

1	111111 1	**Carry**
(−19)	11101101	
+(−11)	11110101	
	11100010	Answer (−30)

Again, a carry out of the MSB has been ignored.

2-5.4 Subtraction of Binary Numbers

Subtraction of binary numbers in 2s complement form is also very simple and straightforward. The *2s complement of the subtrahend is taken and added to the minuend.* This is essentially subtraction by changing the sign and adding. As in addition, the signs of the operands and carries out of the MSB are ignored.

EXAMPLE 2-17 Subtract 30 from 53. Use 8-bit numbers.

Solution Note 30 is the subtrahend and 53 the minuend.

53 = 00110101 (minuend)
30 = 00011110 (subtrahend)

Taking the 2s complement of 30 and adding, we obtain:

$$\begin{aligned} (\overline{30}) &= 11100001 \\ -30 &= 11100010 \\ +53 &= \underline{00110101} \\ & \quad \mathbf{00010111} = 23 \end{aligned}$$

EXAMPLE 2-18 Subtract -30 from -19.

Solution Here

$$\begin{aligned} -19 &= 11101101 \quad \text{(See Example 2-16.)} \\ -30 &= 11100010 \quad \text{(subtrahend)} \end{aligned}$$

Note: -30 is the subtrahend. 2s complementing -30 gives $+30$ or 00011110.

$$\begin{aligned} -19 &\quad 11101101 \\ +30 &\quad \underline{00011110} \\ &\quad \mathbf{00001011} = +11 \end{aligned}$$

The carry out of the MSB is ignored and the answer $+11$ is correct.

2-6 LOGICAL OPERATIONS

Besides addition and subtraction, computers must be able to execute a variety of *logical* instructions. These logical operations are performed between words or bytes, on a bit-by-bit basis. There is no interaction (such as borrows or carries) between the bits.

2-6.1 The Logical OR Operation

If two words are ORed together, the result, or output word, has a 1 in each bit position where either or both of the input words had a 1. The logical OR of two operands, A and B, is expressed as $A + B$. Note that this is different from A *plus* B, which means the arithmetic *sum* of A and B.

EXAMPLE 2-19 Given two words, $A = 10111001$ and $B = 11011010$, find $A + B$.

Solution The words are lined up as follows:

Bit Position	**7**	**6**	**5**	**4**	**3**	**2**	**1**	**0**
A	1	0	1	1	1	0	0	1
B	1	1	0	1	1	0	1	0
$A + B$	**1**	**1**	**1**	**1**	**1**	**0**	**1**	**1**

For all bit positions except position 2, either word A or word B, or both, contain a 1. Therefore the logical OR ($A + B$) results in a 1 in all bit positions except position 2.

2-6.2 The Logical AND Operation

When two words are ANDed, the output word is a 1 only in those bit positions where both input words are 1. Since the operation is analogous to multiplication, $Y = AB$ means that Y is the logical AND of words A and B.

EXAMPLE 2-20 If the two words of Example 2-19 are ANDed, what is the output word?

Solution The words are ANDed bit-by-bit:

Bit Position	**7 6 5 4 3 2 1 0**
A	1 0 1 1 1 0 0 1
B	1 1 0 1 1 0 1 0
AB	**1 0 0 1 1 0 0 0**

A and B are both 1 only in bit positions 3, 4, and 7 as the answer shows.

2-6.3 The EXCLUSIVE OR Operation

Another logical operation that has many uses (parity checking is one example) is the *EXCLUSIVE OR* (XOR) operation. The symbol for the XOR operation is $\oplus$. If two words are XORed, the bits of the output word are a 1 if *either, but not both,* of the corresponding bits of the input words are 1.

EXAMPLE 2-21 Find the XOR of words A and B of Example 2-19.

Solution The words are XORed on a bit-by-bit basis.

Bit Position	**7 6 5 4 3 2 1 0**
A	1 0 1 1 1 0 0 1
B	1 1 0 1 1 0 1 0
$A \oplus B$	**0 1 1 0 0 0 1 1**

The output word is seen to be 1 wherever exactly one of the input words contains a 1.

2-6.4 Complementation

The *complement* of a word is obtained simply by *inverting each bit of the word.* Because complementation is often used in computer arithmetic, most microprocessors contain a complementation instruction.

EXAMPLE 2-22 Complement word A of Example 2-19.

Solution Complementation is obtained simply by changing each bit of the word.

A = 10111001
$\bar{A}$ (the complement of A) = 01000110

2-7 HEXADECIMAL NOTATION

Most μPs, including the **6800**, the **8080/85**, the **6502**, and the **Z80**, use 16 address lines and eight data lines. They therefore can use a memory of up to 64K bytes. To express the 16 bits needed for an address (or the 8 bits needed for a data byte) as 1s and 0s results in a long string of bits and is very tedious. In most literature and documentation today, the convention of using *hexadecimal notation* has been adopted.

The hexadecimal system is a *base 16* arithmetic system. Since such a system requires 16 different digits, the letters A through F are added to the ten decimal digits (0–9). The advantage of having 16 hexadecimal digits is that each digit can represent a unique combination of 4 bits, and that any combination of 4 bits can be represented by a single hex[1] digit. Table 2-2 gives both the decimal and binary value associated with each hexadecimal digit.

Table 2-2

Hexadecimal digit	*Decimal value*	*Binary value*
0	0	0000
1	1	0001
2	2	0010
3	3	0011
4	4	0100
5	5	0101
6	6	0110
7	7	0111
8	8	1000
9	9	1001
A	10	1010
B	11	1011
C	12	1100
D	13	1101
E	14	1110
F	15	1111

2-7.1 Conversions Between Hexadecimal and Binary Numbers

To convert a binary number to hexadecimal, start at the least significant bit (LSB) and divide the binary number into groups of 4 bits each. Then replace each 4-bit group with its equivalent hex digit obtained from Table 2-2.

[1] The word hex is often used as an abbreviation for hexadecimal.

EXAMPLE 2-23 Convert the binary number 110000010111111101 to hex.

Solution We start with the LSB and divide the number into 4-bit nibbles. Each nibble is then replaced with its corresponding hex digit as shown:

0011	0000	0101	1111	1101
3	0	5	F	D

When the most significant group has less than 4 bits, as in this example, leading 0s are added to complete the 4-bit nibble.

To convert a hex number to binary, simply replace each hex digit by its 4-bit binary equivalent.

EXAMPLE 2-24 Convert the hex number 1CB09 to binary.

Solution We simply expand the hex number:

1	C	B	0	9
0001	1100	1011	0000	1001

Thus the equivalent binary number is:

11100101100001001

It is not necessary to write the leading 0s.

2-7.2 Conversion of Hex Numbers to Decimal Numbers

The hex system is a base 16 system; therefore any hex number can be expressed as:

$$H_0 \times 1 + H_1 \times 16 + H_2 \times 16^2 + H_3 \times 16^3 \ldots$$

where H_0 is the least significant hex digit, H_1 the next, and so on. This is similar to the binary system of numbers discussed in section 2-2.

EXAMPLE 2-25 Convert 2FC to decimal.

Solution The least significant hex digit, H_0, is C or 12. The next digit (H_1) is F or 15. This must be multiplied by 16 giving 240. The next digit, H_2, is 2, which must be multiplied by 16^2, or 256. Hence, 2FC = 512 + 240 + 12 = 764.

An alternate solution is to convert 2FC to the binary number 1011111100 and then perform a binary to decimal conversion.

Decimal numbers can be converted to hex by repeatedly dividing them by 16. After each division, the remainder becomes one of the hex digits in the final answer.

EXAMPLE 2-26 Convert 9999 to hex.

Solution Start by dividing by 16 as shown in the following table. After each division, the quotient becomes the number starting the next line and the remainder is the hex digit with the least significant digit on the top line.

Number	*Quotient*	*Remainder*	*Hex digit*
9999	624	15	F
624	39	0	0
39	2	7	7
2	0	2	2

This example shows that $(9999)_{10} = (270F)_{16}$. The result can be checked by converting 270F to decimal, as shown in Example 4-3. By doing so we obtain:

$$(2 \times 4096) + (7 \times 256) + 0 + 15 = 9999$$
$$8192 \quad + \quad 1792 \quad + 0 + 15 = 9999$$

2-7.3 Hexadecimal Addition

When working with μPs, it is often necessary to add or subtract hex numbers. They can be added by referring to hexadecimal addition tables, but we suggest the following procedure.

1 Add the two hex digits (mentally substituting their decimal equivalent).

2 If the sum is 15 or less, it can be directly expressed in hex.

3 If the sum is greater than or equal to 16, subtract 16 and carry 1 to the next position.

The following examples should make this procedure clear.

EXAMPLE 2-27 Add D + E.

Solution D is the equivalent of decimal 13 and E is the equivalent of decimal 14. Together they sum to 27 = 16 + 11. The 11 is represented by B and there is a carry. Therefore, D + E = **1B**.

EXAMPLE 2-28 Add B2E6 and F77.

Solution The solution is shown below.

Column	**4**	**3**	**2**	**1**
Augend	B	2	E	6
Addend		F	7	7
Sum	**C**	**2**	**5**	**D**

Column 1 6 + 7 = 13 = D. The result is less than 16 so there is no carry.
Column 2 E + 7 = 14 + 7 = 21 = 5 + a carry because the result is greater than 16.
Column 3 F + 2 + 1 (the carry from column 2) = 15 + 2 + 1 = 18 = 2 + a carry.
Column 4 B + 1 (the carry from column 3) = C.

Like addition, *hex subtraction* is analogous to decimal subtraction. If the subtrahend digit is larger than the minuend digit, one is borrowed from the next most significant digit. If the next most significant digit is 0, a 1 is borrowed from the next digit and the intermediate digit is changed to an F.

EXAMPLE 2-29 Subtract 32F from C02.

Solution The subtraction proceeds as follows:

Column	**1**	**2**	**3**
Minuend	C	0	2
Subtrahend	3	2	F
Difference	**8**	**D**	**3**

Column 1 Subtracting F from 2 requires a borrow. Because a borrow is worth 16, it raises the minuend to 18. Column 1 is therefore 18 − F = 18 − 15 = 3.
Column 2 Because column 2 contains a 0, it cannot provide the borrow out for column 1. Consequently the borrow out must come from column 3, while the minuend of column 2 is changed to an F. Column 2 is therefore F − 2 = 15 − 2 = 13 = D.
Column 3 Column 3 can provide the borrow out needed for column 1. This reduces the C to a B and B − 3 = 8.

As in decimal addition, the results can be checked by adding the subtrahend and difference to get the minuend.

2-7.4 Negating Hex Numbers

The negative equivalent of a positive hex number can always be found by converting the hex number to binary and taking the 2s complement of the result (section 2-5). A shorter method exists, however.

1 Add to the least significant hex digit the hex digit that makes it sum to 16.
2 Add to all other digits the digits that make it sum to 15.
3 If the least significant digit is 0, write 0 as the least significant digit of the answer and start at the next digit.
4 The number written is the negative equivalent of the given hex number.

This procedure works because the sum of the original number and the new number is always 0.

EXAMPLE 2-30 Find the negative equivalent of the hex number 20C3.

Solution The least significant digit is 3. To make 16, D must be added to 3. The other digits are 2, 0, and C. To make 15 in each case, we add D, F, and 3, respectively. The negative equivalent of 20C3 is therefore **DF3D**. This example can be checked by adding the negative equivalent to the positive number. Since X plus −X always equals 0, the result should be 0.

```
  2 0 C3
+DF 3 D
--------
  0 0 0 0
```

The carry out of the most significant digit is ignored.

2-7.5 Octal Notation

Octal notation is an alternate form of concise notation used by many minicomputer manufacturers. It divides binary numbers into 3-bit groups and each group represents the particular digit (0 through 7) that corresponds to the value of the 3-bit group.

Octal notation is a base 8 system. The rules for conversions and addition and subtraction in octal are analogous to those for hexadecimal.

Octal is not as convenient as hex when expressing two bytes as a bit word. For example, compare these three ways to describe the same 16 bits of information:

Octal	2 6 5	3 0 6
Binary	1 0 1 1 0 1 0 1	1 1 0 0 0 1 1 0
Hexadecimal	B 5	C 6

When expressed as a 16-bit address, these same bits would be:

132706	in octal or
B5C6	in hex

It is obvious that the hex version is much easier to use when combining groups of 8-bit words because the hex notation is simply the linking of the two 8-bit notations, while octal requires conversion to different numbers to express the 16-bit value. Because hex is far more popular among μP users, it is used exclusively throughout this book.

2-8 BRANCHING IN MICROPROCESSORS

Many μPs use BRANCH instructions in addition to JUMP instructions to direct the program to a different address. Hexadecimal arithmetic is used in BRANCH instructions to calculate the location to be jumped to.

The difference between a BRANCH instruction and a JUMP instruction is that a JUMP instruction generally specifies an absolute address. The instruction

```
JUMP    500
```

for example, tells the μP to jump to location 500.

A BRANCH instruction is accompanied by an *offset*. The offset is a number that is added to the current value of the program counter to determine where the μP will go. Thus BRANCH *instructions are relative to the program counter*. A typical BRANCH instruction may jump the PC forward or backward a specific number of locations. Note that if an entire program is moved or relocated to a new set of memory locations, JUMP instructions must be changed but BRANCH instructions need not be changed.

EXAMPLE 2-31 A program resides in locations 0–1000 and contains within it a JUMP 500 instruction. This program is to be moved or relocated to locations 2000 and 3000. How must the JUMP instruction be changed?

Solution Note that location 500 is no longer within the program. Due to the move it has become location 2500. So an instruction like JUMP 500 must be changed to JUMP 2500 to be compatible with the new program.

BRANCH instructions, which say typically "move up 6 locations" or "go back 10 locations," are not affected by relocation, and thus have an advantage if the programmer is writing relocatable code.

2-8.1 Calculating Offsets

Branches were originally used in the **6800** and **6502** μPs, and are now used in the same way by many μPs. A BRANCH instruction for the **6800** or **6502** consists of the BRANCH Op code in 1 byte and an 8-bit offset in the following byte. If N is the location of the BRANCH instruction and T is the target address, the address the program will jump to, then formula (2-1) can be used to calculate the offset.

$$\text{Offset} = T - (N + 2) \tag{2-1}$$

Note that both forward and backward BRANCHes can be accommodated. Backward BRANCHes have negative offsets.

EXAMPLE 2-32 The Op code of the BRANCH instruction is in 011A. What should the offset (in 011B) be if the program must branch to 0150?

Solution From (2-1) we obtain:

$$\text{Offset} = 0150 - (011\text{A} + 2) = 34$$

Thus the BRANCH instruction would look like:

```
011A BRANCH Op code
011B 34            (offset)
```

EXAMPLE 2-33 The Op code of the BRANCH instruction is in 011A. What should the offset be if the program must branch to 00EA?

Solution From the formula:

$$\text{Offset} = 00EA - 011C = FFCE$$

For an 8-bit negative offset the FF is discarded and the program looks like this:

```
011A BRANCH Op code
011B CE            (offset)
```

Note that the offset is a negative number (CE) and the program branches backward from 11C to EA.

EXAMPLE 2-34

a If the instruction in 011A is BRA 39, where will the program branch to?

b Repeat if the instruction is BRA 93.

Solution

a Formula (2 – 1) can be transposed to read:

$$T = (N + 2) + \text{offset}$$

Because the Op code is in 011A, $N + 2 = 011C$. Therefore $T = 011C + 39 = 0155$.

b The procedure can be repeated but 93 is a negative offset. Negative 8-bit offset should be preceded by FF to convert them to 16-bit numbers.

$$T = 011C + FF93 = 00AF$$

In this case the program will branch backward to AF.

2-8.2 Long and Short Branches

An 8-bit offset is limited; the program can only branch forward 129 steps or backward 126 steps. This is usually sufficient for small programs but is a constraint as the programs become larger. In the **6800** or **6502**, BRANCHes to more remote locations must use JUMPs. The newer 8-bit μPs, like the **6809**, and all the 16-bit μPs, permit long BRANCHes by allowing the use of a 16-bit offset. This allows the programmer to branch to any location within a 64K-byte memory. For 16-bit μPs that can have more than 64K address, even this is not enough and Intel has introduced the concept of *far jumps* in the **8086**, which has a 20-bit address bus.

2-9 SHIFT AND ROTATE INSTRUCTIONS

Microprocessors can perform a variety of SHIFT and ROTATE instructions. Minicomputers and mainframes have a minor advantage over a μP because they can

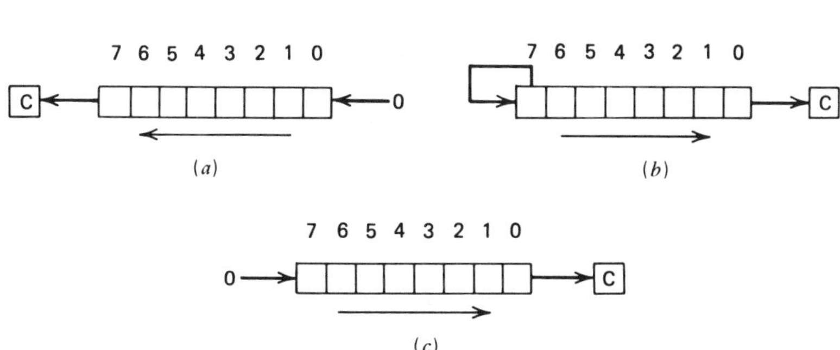

Figure 2-2 Shift instructions. (*a*) Arithmetic shift left (ASL). (*b*) Arithmetic shift right (ASR). (*c*) Logical shift right (LSR). (From Greenfield and Wray, *Using Microprocessors and Microcomputers: The 6800 Family*, Wiley, 1981.)

command a multiple shift in a single instruction. For example, it only takes one instruction in a mainframe to shift a register or accumulator 4 bits, whereas it would require four instructions in a μP. The ASL (ARITHMETIC SHIFT LEFT), ASR (ARITHMETIC SHIFT RIGHT), and LSR (LOGICAL SHIFT RIGHT) instructions are shown in Figure 2-2. Note that the carry FF that is part of the condition code register is used in the SHIFT operations.

In the ASL operation, the MSB is shifted out of the data word and into the carry FF. The LSB is filled with a 0.

The ASR operation shifts each bit to the right and moves the LSB into the carry FF. The MSB, however, is retained and also shifted into bit 6. If the bits in the register are considered a 2s complement number, this method of shifting *preserves the sign of the number*. The ASR is equivalent to dividing the number in the register by 2, regardless of the sign of the number.

The LSR operation simply shifts each bit one position to the right. The MSB becomes a 0 and the LSB goes into the carry FF.

EXAMPLE 2-35 An 8-bit word contains the bit pattern 10011010 (hexidecimal 9A).

a What is the contents of the word after two SHIFTs to the right (ASR, ASR)?

b What is its contents after three ARITHMETIC SHIFTs to the left (ASL, ASL, ASL)?

c What is its contents after two LOGIC SHIFTs to the right (LSR, LSR)?

Solution

a Here every bit is moved two places to the right, except bit 7. Since the rightmost bits are shifted through the carry register, bit 0 is lost and bit 1 becomes the carry bit. After execution of these two instructions, the word is:

11100110

Note that bits 7, 6, and 5 are 1s because bit 7 was originally 1.

b The bits are shifted three positions to the left and the two most significant bits are lost. Since bit 5 was 0, the carry is now 0. The least significant bit positions are filled with 0s; the word is now:

11010000

c After two LSRs the word becomes:

00100110

and the carry bit is a 1. Note that 0s are shifted into the MSBs in an LSR.

EXAMPLE 2-36

a If the number in an accumulator is 50, show that an ASR is equivalent to a division by 2.

b Repeat for −50.

Solution

a Since +50 = 00110010, an ASR causes the accumulator to become 00011001, or +25.

b Since −50 = 11001110, an ASR causes the accumulator to become 11100111, or −25. Again, division by 2 has occurred. This would not have been so if a 0 had been shifted into bit 7 instead of a 1.

2-9.1 Rotations

Two additional shifting instructions are ROL (ROTATE LEFT) and ROR (ROTATE RIGHT), shown in Figure 2-3. These are special forms of circular shifting where the bits coming off one end of the word are inserted into the carry FF, while the contents of the carry FF are transferred into the vacated bit position.

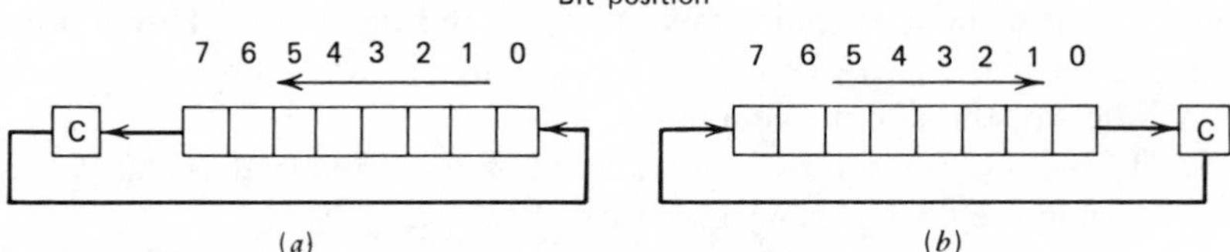

Figure 2-3 The **6800** ROTATE instructions. (*a*) ROTATE LEFT (ROL). (*b*) ROTATE RIGHT (ROR). (From Greenfield and Wray, *Using Microprocessors and Microcomputers: The 6800 Family*, Wiley, 1981.)

EXAMPLE 2-37 If a computer word is 11011100, what is it after the following commands?

a ROTATE RIGHT three times (ROR, ROR, ROR). Assume the carry FF is CLEAR.

b ROTATE LEFT twice (ROL, ROL). Assume the carry FF is SET.

Solution

a In response to three ROR instructions, the three LSBs are moved through the carry FF to the other end of the word. The word becomes

00011011

and the carry FF contains the 1 that was originally in bit 2.

b In rotating left twice, the carry now contains the original bit 6 (1) and the 1 that was bit 7 is now the LSB of the word. The result is

01110011

The 1 that was originally in the carry FF has been shifted through bit 0 and appears in bit 1 of the result.

There are many uses for ROTATE instructions. One application is to determine the *parity* of a byte. If the bits of the byte are successively shifted into the carry FF, the number of 1s in the byte can be counted and its parity can be determined.

2-10 REFERENCES

Joseph D. Greenfield and William C. Wray, *Using Microprocessors and Microcomputers: The 6800 Family*, Wiley, New York, 1981.

Louis Nashelsky, *Introduction to Digital Technology*, 3rd Edition, Wiley, New York, 1983.

Mohamed Rafiquzzaman, *Microcomputer Theory and Application*, Wiley, New York, 1982.

CHAPTER 3

Hardware and Software Considerations in a Microprocessor

Joseph D. Greenfield
Professor of Electrical Engineering Technology
Rochester Institute of Technology
Rochester, New York

This chapter presents an overview of microprocessors. The topics and concepts introduced are common to most, if not all, of the μPs discussed in the succeeding chapters. The topics are considered generally so that they apply to many μPs. To determine how each feature is used in a specific μP the reader should read the chapter on that μP.

3-1 MACHINE, ASSEMBLY, AND HIGHER-LEVEL LANGUAGES

Programs must be in *machine language* to be executed by the μP. They can be written directly in machine language or in a higher-level language (assembler or compiler), and then translated into machine language. Generally it is more efficient to write in higher-level languages and the modern trend is definitely in this direction.

3-1.1 Machine Language

Each Op code and each address in a computer is a specific pattern of 1s and 0s, and the code must be written into the computer in this form. This is machine language, the actual bit patterns that the machine can use and understand. The bit patterns are usually written in hexadecimal for brevity. For any instruction, the Op code is written first, followed by the address.

EXAMPLE 3-1 If the instruction at location 10 requires that the contents of location 0C40 be written into the accumulator, give the machine language code for:

a an Intel **8080/8085**

b a Motorola **6800**

Solution

a For an **8080** or **8085** the instruction is a LOAD DIRECT.

The code is:

Location	*Data*	
10	3A	Op code (LDA)
11	40	Low byte of address
12	0C	High byte of address

b For a Motorola **6800** the instruction is a LOAD EXTENDED and the code is:

Location	*Data*	
10	B6	Op code (LOAD EXTENDED)
11	0C	High byte of address
12	40	Low byte of address

Example 3-1 reveals at least three of the disadvantages of using machine language programming:[1]

1 The hex Op codes have to be looked up and used.

2 The addresses must be specified numerically instead of symbolically.

3 The user must remember where the high and low bytes of the address go. Example 3-1 shows that this depends on the μP being used.

Machine language or hand coding must be used where the program is typed in directly from a keyboard, as in some educational kits. A knowledge of machine language is also needed when debugging a hardware system (e.g., when it is necessary to determine if the μP is sending and receiving correct data, or if there is an open wire or bus). For general μP programming, however, machine language is an inefficient way to write programs.

[1] The technique of writing machine language instructions, as shown in Example 3-1, is sometimes called *hand coding.*

3-1.2 Assembly Language Programming

When using *assembly language*, the original program is written in *source code*, using symbols. Each line of source code is later translated to 1, 2, or 3 bytes of machine language code (there is a one-to-one correspondence between assembly and machine language), but it is much easier to write in assembly language because symbols are used. For example, the machine code B6 0C40 can simply be written as LDA A MAX. Here LDA A is the mnemonic for LOAD ACCUMULATOR A and the user does not have to remember that the corresponding Op code is B6. MAX becomes a *symbolic name* for the address so it is not necessary for the user to specify a memory location for the data.

Of course a statement like LDA A MAX has to be translated to its machine language equivalent before it can be used in a μP. This is done by using an *assembler, a computer program that translates source code into machine language* and prints both out in the form of a *paper listing*. The assembler and source code must both be entered into a computer. The assembler then operates on the source code to produce a machine language output. Usually assembly is done on a larger computer than a μP. An assembler program designed to work on one computer to produce machine language code for another computer or μP is called a *cross-assembler*.

Many computer companies have built special-purpose *microprocessor development systems*. Intel's is called the INTELLEC and Motorola's is called the EXORCISER. These development systems facilitate the use of μPs in many ways. One of their uses is to assemble a source code and produce an object or machine language program for the μP.

An example of a source program to convert BCD to binary numbers is given in Figure 3-1 and the resulting assembled program is given in Figure 3-2. Figures 3-1 and 3-2 used a **6800** assembler. It uses several prefixes to identify the various types of numbers that occur in a program. These prefixes are

1 A blank or no symbol indicates the number is a decimal number.

2 A $ immediately preceding a number indicates it is a *hex* number ($24, for example, is 24 in hex, or the equivalent of 36 in decimal).

3 A # sign indicates an *immediate* operand.

4 A @ sign indicates an *octal* value.

5 A % sign indicates a *binary* number (01011001, for example).

An examination of Figure 3-1 shows that the source program consists of three sections: comments, directives, and source code. Comment lines are preceded by an asterisk. In Figure 3-1 they tell what the program does, give the author and date written, and help clarify the program flow by such statements as "Add Algorithm Subroutine," which show where the subroutine begins.

The *directives* are *commands* given by the programmer to the assembler program to control it. Unlike source code instructions, which they resemble, directives do not result in machine language or Op codes. The directives used depend on the particular assembler being used and the assembler manual should be

```
 NAM BCDBIN
*PROGRAM TO CONVERT BCD NUMBERS TO BINARY
*WORD1 & WORD2 CONTAIN THE BCD WORDS
*SUM1 &SUM2 CONTAIN THE BINARY EQUIVALENT
*WRITTEN BY J. D. GREENFIELD 1/24/78
 OPT O OUTPUT OBJECT PGM
 OPT S OUTPUT SYMBOL TABLE
*
 ORG $20
WORD1 FCB 1 MSB BCD NUMBER
WORD2 FCB $69 LSB  PACKED BCD NUMBER
SUM1 FCB 0 BINARY RESULT
SUM2 FCB 0 2ND BINARY BYTE
 SPC 1
START1 LDS #$200 SET STACK
 LDX #LIST
 LDA A WORD2 GET LSB WORD TO BE CONVERTED
SHIFT2 ASR A SHIFT RIGHT
 BCC INCR
 BSR START2 GO TO ADD SUBROUTINE
INCR INX
 INX
 CPX #$120 LIST COMPLETED?
 BEQ HALT YES-GO INTO LOOP ON SELF
 CPX #$110 TEST FOR WORD1
 BNE SHIFT2 LOOP FOR NEXT BIT
 SPC 1
 LDA A WORD1 LOAD MSB BCD WORD
 BRA SHIFT2
 SPC 1
HALT BRA * LOOP BACK 2 BYTES
 SPC 1
* ADD ALGORITHM SUBROUTINE
 SPC 1
START2 PSH A
 LDA A 1,X LOAD LSB FROM LIST
 ADD A SUM2 ADD LSB OF SUM
 STA A SUM2 UPDATE SUM
 LDA A 0,X LOAD MSB FROM LIST
 ADC A SUM1 ADD MSB OF SUM
 STA A SUM1 UPDATE SUM
 PUL A
 RTS RETURN TO MAIN PROGRAM
 SPC 2
 ORG $100
LIST FDB 1
 FDB 2
 FDB 4
 FDB 8
 FDB 10
 FDB 20
 FDB 40
 FDB 80
 FDB 100
 FDB 200
 FDB 400
 FDB 800
 FDB 1000
 FDB 2000
 FDB 4000
 FDB 8000
 SPC 1
 END
```

Figure 3-1 A source program for a **6800**. (From Greenfield and Wray, *Using Microprocessors and Microcomputers*: *The 6800 Family*, Wiley, 1981.)

```
                        NAM    BCDBIN
                  *PROGRAM TO CONVERT BCD NUMBERS TO BINARY
                  *WORD1 & WORD2 CONTAIN THE BCD WORDS
                  *SUM1 &SUM2 CONTAIN THE BINARY EQUIVALENT
                  *WRITTEN BY J. D. GREENFIELD 1/24/78
                        OPT    O        OUTPUT OBJECT PGM
                        OPT    S        OUTPUT SYMBOL TABLE
                  *
0020                    ORG    $20
0020 01           WORD1 FCB    1        MSB BCD NUMBER
0021 69           WORD2 FCB    $69      LSB  PACKED BCD NUMBER
0022 00           SUM1  FCB    0        BINARY RESULT
0023 00           SUM2  FCB    0        2ND BINARY BYTE

0024 8E 0200     START1 LDS    #$200    SET STACK
0027 CE 0100            LDX    #LIST
002A 96 21              LDA A  WORD2    GET LSB WORD TO BE CONVERTED
002C 47          SHIFT2 ASR A           SHIFT RIGHT
002D 24 02              BCC    INCR
002F 8D 12              BSR    START2   GO TO ADD SUBROUTINE
0031 08          INCR   INX
0032 08                 INX
0033 8C 0120            CPX    #$120    LIST COMPLETED?
0036 27 09              BEQ    HALT     YES-GO INTO LOOP ON SELF
0038 8C 0110            CPX    #$110    TEST FOR WORD1
003B 26 EF              BNE    SHIFT2   LOOP FOR NEXT BIT

003D 96 20              LDA A  WORD1    LOAD MSB BCD WORD
003F 20 EB              BRA    SHIFT2

0041 20 FE       HALT   BRA    *        LOOP BACK 2 BYTES

                 * ADD ALGORITHM SUBROUTINE

0043 36          START2 PSH A
0044 A6 01              LDA A  1,X      LOAD LSB FROM LIST
0046 9B 23              ADD A  SUM2     ADD LSB OF SUM
0048 97 23              STA A  SUM2     UPDATE SUM
004A A6 00              LDA A  0,X      LOAD MSB FROM LIST
004C 99 22              ADC A  SUM1     ADD MSB OF SUM
004E 97 22              STA A  SUM1     UPDATE SUM
0050 32                 PUL A
0051 39                 RTS             RETURN TO MAIN PROGRAM


0100                    ORG    $100
0100 0001        LIST   FDB    1
0102 0002               FDB    2
0104 0004               FDB    4
0106 0008               FDB    8
0108 000A               FDB    10
010A 0014               FDB    20
010C 0028               FDB    40
010E 0050               FDB    80
0110 0064               FDB    100
0112 00C8               FDB    200
0114 0190               FDB    400
0116 0320               FDB    800
0118 03E8               FDB    1000
011A 07D0               FDB    2000
011C 0FA0               FDB    4000
011E 1F40               FDB    8000

     0000               END
WORD1  0020 WORD2  0021 SUM1   0022 SUM2   0023 START1 0024
SHIFT2 002C INCR   0031 HALT   0041 START2 0043 LIST   0100

TOTAL ERRORS 00000
```

Figure 3-2 Assembly listing for the source program of Figure 3-1. (From Greenfield and Wray, *Using Microprocessors and Microcomputers: The 6800 Family*, Wiley, 1981.)

consulted for a precise explanation. The directives used in this example are:

NAM—the name of the program.
OPT—Options. Generally the options specify the format of the output, such as whether a listing including the object program and symbol table is required.
ORG—Origin. The starting address of program sections and of lists.
SPC—Line. This directive places spaces (skips lines) in the output listing for clarity.
FCB—Form constant byte. This directive defines the initial value of a byte and gives it a symbolic name. For example, the line SUM1 FCB 0 sets aside a location called SUM1 and initializes its value to 0. The value in SUM1 changes as the program progresses.
FDB—Form double byte. Like FCB, except that a double byte or 16-bit word is used.

EXAMPLE 3-2 The term FDB 20 appears in the list. What does it mean and what is the result?

Solution FDB 20 means that a 16-bit word whose value is $(20)_{10}$ must be placed in the list. In the final listing (see Figure 3-2), it appears as $(0014)_{16}$.

Other directives that are often used (but not in this program) include:

FCC—Form constant character. Sets aside a location for an ASCII character.
RMB—Reserve memory block. Sets aside a word or group of words and reserves memory space for them. This directive is sometimes used to define the stack area (see section 3-4).
EQU—Equates. Defines or sets the value of a label. A *label* is a mnemonic for an address. For example, the expression CRA EQU $8005 sets the label CRA equal to $(8005)_{16}$. This label might be used if CRA is the address of the control register for the A side of a PIA (see section 7-14) located at $8005.

Each line of the source program consists of four parts: label, instruction mnemonic or directive, operand, and comments. If the first column of a line starts with an asterisk it is a comment; if it starts with a letter it is a label. Many lines do not have labels. These lines must all start with at least one space.

In Figure 3-1, some typical labels are SUM1 and SUM2, the memory addresses of the locations holding the binary sum and START1, where the program starts.

In assembly language programming *the destination of all branches must have a label.* A label is put in the operand field of each instruction so the program knows where to branch to.

The second field in the source code is a three-letter field that is either a directive to the assembler or a mnemonic for an Op code for the μP. The next field is the operand or address, often a symbol or label, and the fourth field is reserved for the programmer's comments.

EXAMPLE 3-3 At various points in the source code listing of Figure 3-1 the following statements occur:

a `* PROGRAM TO CONVERT BCD NUMBER TO BINARY`

b `INCR INX`

c (space) `BNE SHIFT2 LOOP FOR NEXT BIT`

Describe each of these statements.

Solution

a The line starts with an asterisk. Consequently the entire line is a comment and there is no formatting.

b The line starts with a label (INCR). The next field is INX, a mnemonic Op code for the instruction INCREMENT THE X REGISTER. The address field and comment field have been omitted; no address is needed for this instruction.

c The line starts with a space. This means the label field is blank and there is no label attached to this particular line. The second field is BNE, the mnemonic Op code for BRANCH IF NOT EQUAL TO ZERO. The third field, SHIFT2, is the object of the branch. Note that SHIFT2 must be a label on another line of the program, so the program knows where to branch to. The rest of the line, LOOP FOR NEXT BIT, is the comment the programmer attached to that line.

The assembly listing for the program is shown in Figure 3-2. It consists of seven columns: line numbers, address, hex Op code, and the four columns of the source program lined up in a more orderly manner. The program can now be written into the μP's memory using the addresses and Op codes developed by the assembler. Some assemblers and development systems allow the user to transfer the machine language program directly into the μP's memory and execution can start immediately.

3-1.3 High-Level Languages

High-level languages such as Basic, Fortran, Pascal, and C have been used for most programs written for mainframes and minicomputers and are coming to be used more and more in microprocessors. Each line of a high-level language is called a *statement*. A high-level language statement generates several lines of machine language code. For example, the statement $A = B + C + D$ might generate assembly code such as:

```
LOAD B
ADD C
ADD D
STORE A
```

Such statements must be put through a compiler, a program that translates high-level languages into machine language.

Present theories of programmer efficiency state that a programmer can write about ten lines of debugged code per day, and it does not matter whether this code is in assembly language or high-level language. Since each high-level language statement is equivalent to several assembly or machine language statements, it is more efficient to write in high-level languages.

High-level languages do have some drawbacks. They are not as well-suited to changing individual bits in memory, and sometimes they are inefficient in the sense that they do not generate optimum code; they use more machine language instructions than necessary and they do not execute as quickly as well-written assembly language programs.

In most cases these drawbacks are outweighed by the advantages. Often small programs will be written in assembly language, but large programs, even for μPs, tend to be written in high-level languages.

3-2 INSTRUCTION MODES

Instructions can often be executed in one of several *modes*. (A mode is a way of executing an instruction.) The various modes of executing instructions are described in this section.

3-2.1 Inherent or Implied Instructions

Inherent or implied instructions are those instructions that require only an Op code fetch. All the information required for the instruction is already within the CPU and no additional operands from memory or from the program are needed. Since no memory references are needed, implied instructions only require 1 byte for their Op code. Examples of implied instructions are CLEAR, INCREMENT and DECREMENT, COMPLEMENT, SHIFT and ROTATE registers and accumulators.

In the **8080/8085/Z80** family an instruction such as ADD C, for example, is implied since the addend and augend are within the μP in the A and C registers.

3-2.2 Immediate Instructions

Immediate instructions generally consist of 1 byte of Op code and 1 or 2 bytes of data that are the operand. Thus, in immediate instructions, the operand is written directly into the program. The pound sign (#) is the assembler symbol for an immediate instruction. Figure 3-3 is an example of an immediate instruction.

Immediate instructions are followed by 1 or 2 bytes of *data* depending on whether an 8- or 16-bit register is being used. In **8085** code, for example, MVI A takes 1 additional byte because an 8-bit accumulator is being loaded, but LXI H requires two additional bytes because the H and L registers are both being loaded. Similarly, the LDX instruction of a **6800** requires 2 additional bytes because a 16-bit register (X) is being loaded.

Location		Example of Code	Instruction and Effect
10	OP Code	8B	ADD A #$33
11	Immediate value	33	Adds $(33)_{16}$ to A.

Figure 3-3 An immediate instruction. (From Greenfield and Wray, *Using Microprocessors and Microcomputers: The 6800 Family*, Wiley, 1981.)

3-2.3 Direct Instructions

In *direct* instruction the bytes following the Op code specify the memory address of the operand. Examples of the direct mode for the **8080/8085/Z80** and for the **6800** have been given in Example 3-1 (see section 3-1.1). In a direct instruction for a Motorola μP only the low byte is specified. The high byte is implied (00 for the **6800** or the direct page register for the **6809**). An *extended instruction* is a form of a direct instruction that has 2 *bytes* of address following it so it can access the entire 64K memory space. Extended instructions are used by Motorola μPs and are equivalent to direct instructions used in the **8080/8085/Z80**. They are followed by a 2-byte address.

3-2.4 Indexed Instructions

Many μPs contain an index register that allows them to do *indexed instructions.* An indexed instruction usually contains an *offset* as part of the instruction. The instruction address is the contents of the *index register added to the offset.* Those μPs that have index registers must have both indexed instructions and instructions that can be used to *change* the value in the index register. Generally indexed instructions do not change the index register, they just use the index register to calculate the address. Examples of instructions that change the index register are LOAD INDEX REGISTER, INCREMENT INDEX REGISTER, and so on.

EXAMPLE 3-4 What does the following program accomplish?

```
LDX #$0123
ADD A $A0,X
```

Solution The first instruction is an immediate LOAD of the index register. It causes the number 0123 to be loaded into X. The second instruction is an INDEXED ADD. In executing this instruction the μP adds the second byte (A0) to the contents of X (0123) to get the data address. Thus the contents of memory location 01C3 are added to the A accumulator.

The number and size of index registers varies from μP to μP:

The **8080** and **8085** do not have index registers.
The **6800** has one 16-bit index register and uses an 8-bit offset.
The **6502** has two 8-bit index registers.
The **6809** has two 16-bit index registers, and the offset can be 5, 8, or 16 bits long.

The user must consult the specifications for a particular μP for information about its index registers.

3-2.5 Indirect Addressing

Indirect addressing means that the location specified in the instruction is not the address of the data, but rather that *the location contains the address of the data.* The assembler symbol for indirect addressing is the business at (@) sign.

EXAMPLE 3-5 If location 500 contains 20 and location 20 contains 30, what is loaded into the accumulator in response to each of the following instructions?

a `LDA A #$500`

b `LDA A $500`

c `LDA 2 @$500`

Solution

a The # symbol indicates this is an immediate instruction. Therefore $(500)_{16}$ is loaded into the accumulator.

b This is a direct instruction. The contents of 500 (20) are loaded into the accumulator.

c The @ symbol indicates this is an indirect instruction. Therefore 500 contains the address of the data, or 20 is the address where the data is stored. Since location 20 contains the number 30, this number is loaded into the accumulator.

Most indirect addressing in μPs is done via registers. Many of the **8080/8085/Z80** instructions are indirect on the H and L registers. For example, the instruction MOV M, C stores the contents of the C register in memory. The memory address for this instruction is contained in the H and L registers.

The **6809** allows indirect addressing in the X, Y, U, and S registers. When those registers are accessed indirectly they can also be automatically incremented or decremented by one or two at each access. This is a nice feature because the registers are often used as pointers to memory and the program would otherwise need a specific instruction to increment or decrement them.

The **6502** has indirect addressing for its JUMP instruction. It also has two other modes of its own, indexed indirect and indirect indexed. For further information, see Chapter 9.

3-2.6 Relative Instructions

Relative instructions are *relative to the program counter.* The instruction usually contains an *offset* that is *added* to the *program counter* to give the operand address. Relative addressing has the advantage of being *relocatable*; if the entire program is moved there is no need to change the operands in a BRANCH or JUMP instruction because they remain at the same place relative to the PC.

Relative addressing is most often used with BRANCH or JUMP instructions. Motorola makes a distinction between the words BRANCH and JUMP. A JUMP is to an *absolute address.* A BRANCH is always a JUMP *relative* to the program counter. In the **6800** the length of this BRANCH is constrained by the 1-byte offset, but the **6809** has the ability to provide a 16-bit offset and can be branched to any address in the 64K memory space, making many programs completely relocatable.

3-3 REGISTERS AND ACCUMULATORS

Registers and accumulators generally exist within the μP instead of in memory or another peripheral. They contain data that is used either in arithmetic calculations or in the calculation of the effective memory address. An accumulator is a register that must be part of any arithmetic operation, and it retains the results. For example, a register or accumulator can be loaded from memory, but an ADD instruction must have one of its operands in an accumulator. It is good programming practice to keep as much frequently used data as possible in registers, because instructions that reference registers instead of memory execute faster.

The registers and accumulators are part of the internal structure of a μP and vary from μP to μP. This section is intended to be a brief introduction. The registers and accumulators for any particular μP are covered in more detail, with examples, in the chapter on that μP.

3-3.1 The 8080/8085 Registers and Accumulator

The **8080** and **8085** have one accumulator (A) and six general-purpose 8-bit registers (B, C, D, E, H, and L). An instruction such as ADD A,C adds the accumulator and the contents of register C. It is an inherent or implied instruction since both operands are in the μP and the Op code fetch is the only memory reference required. This instruction executes in four clock cycles.

The instruction ADD A,M adds the contents of a memory location to the accumulator. Two memory references are needed (the Op code fetch and a memory read to obtain the data) and this instruction takes seven clock cycles. An instruction such as ADD C,M does not exist because the accumulator must be involved in all arithmetic operations.

The H and L registers function primarily as a pointer to a memory location. The instruction ADD A,M, for example, uses the contents of H and L as the memory address. This scheme allows most memory reference instructions to be only 1 type byte long since the address is in H and L.

3-3.2 The 6800, 6809, and 6502 Registers

The **6800** has two 8-bit accumulators, A and B, and one 16-bit index register. Each instruction must specify which accumulator it references. LDA A and LDA B are different instructions to LOAD the A and B accumulators, respectively.

The **6800** has a single 16-bit index register, while the **6502** has two 8-bit index registers. For indexed instructions, the **6800** index register is added to an 8-bit offset to compute the effective address, while a 16-bit offset is added to the 8-bit index register of the **6502**.

The **6809** is perhaps the most sophisticated 8-bit μP. It has two accumulators, but they can be concatenated to form a 16-bit accumulator (D) and the **6809** has the ability to perform 16-bit arithmetic. It also has four 16-bit registers, U, S, X, and Y. U and S function as stack pointers and X and Y form two 16-bit index registers. All the registers can be used as index registers with 5-, 8-, or 16-bit offsets, auto-incrementing and auto-decrementing, and other features.

Most 16-bit μPs have several registers that can be used as either accumulators or index registers. They also have a wide variety of addressing modes, and operate similarly to modern minicomputers.

3-4 SUBROUTINES AND STACKS

All microprocessors make use of subroutines and stacks. Indeed, with modern structured programming, some programs consist primarily of JUMPs to subroutines.

3-4.1 Subroutines A *subroutine* is usually a small program meant to do a specific task. The main program can call, jump, or branch to the subroutine when the task must be done. Often the same task is executed several times at several points in the main program.

EXAMPLE 3-6 At point A in a program to control a machine, the program must delay for 1 ms. At point B in the same program it must delay for 3 ms. What is the easiest way to write this program?

Solution Perhaps the easiest way is to write a subroutine for a 1-ms delay. When the main program reaches point A it calls the subroutine. When the program reaches point B it can call the same subroutine three times and the code might look like:

```
CALL (subroutine address)
CALL (subroutine address)
CALL (subroutine address)
CONTINUE
  :
```

The main feature of a subroutine that distinguishes it from a JUMP is that the subroutine can be called from several places in the main program. *When the subroutine is finished, it must always return to the instruction following the CALL.*

Figure 3-4 illustrates the use of the same subroutine by two different parts of the main program. The subroutine located at 200 can be entered from either location

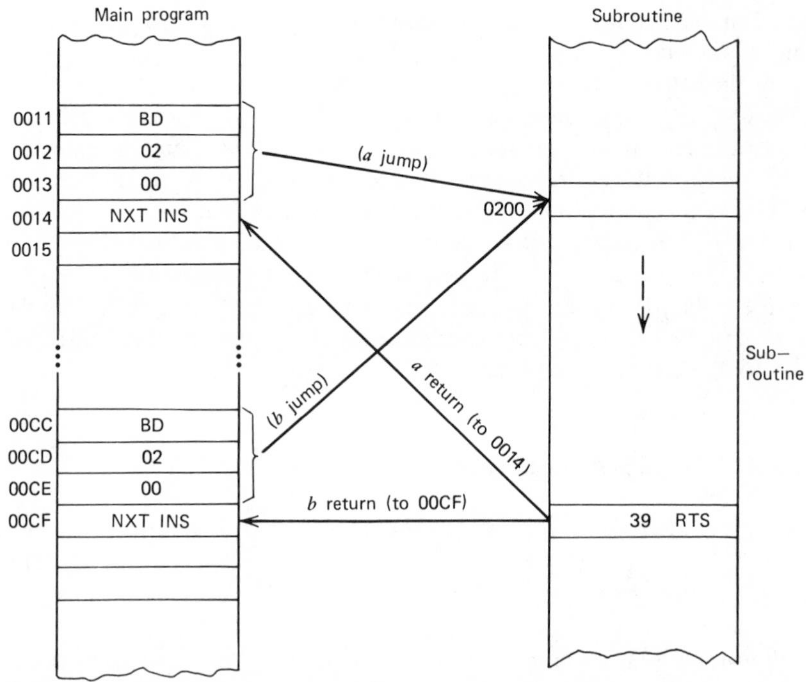

Figure 3-4 Use of a subroutine. (From Greenfield and Wray, *Using Microprocessors and Microcomputers*: *The 6800 Family*, Wiley, 1981.)

0011 or 00CC by placing a JUMP TO SUBROUTINE (AD, BD, or 8D, depending on the mode) in these addresses. The PC actions, as a result of the subroutine jump at 0011, are identified by Figure 3-4*a*, and *b* identifies jumps from 00CC.

After the subroutine is complete, the program resumes from the instruction following the location where it called the subroutine. Because the subroutine must return to one of several locations, depending on which one caused it to be entered, the original contents of the PC must be preserved so the subroutine knows where to return.

3-4.2 Stacks

The *stack* is an area of RAM (READ/WRITE memory) reserved for the temporary storage of important information or data that is changed frequently. Subroutines must return to the point in the main program they were called from. During the CALL instruction, the current program counter contents are written to the stack. This allows the μP to remember where each subroutine was called from. Subroutines end with a RETURN instruction that causes the return address to be written from the stack to the PC so the main program can resume at the proper point. If the register contents of a main program must be preserved but that register is used in a subroutine, the register contents are generally saved on the stack (see section 3-4.4).

3-4.3 The Stack Pointer

The *stack pointer* is an address register that points to the stack. When something is to be written to the stack in the **6800**, it is written at the stack pointer. The stack pointer is automatically decremented by the μP so the next byte written to the stack will be written into the next lower location and will not overwrite previously written data. The **8080/8085/Z80** decrements the stack pointer first and then write to memory. The reader must check the specifications for each particular μP to determine if the stack pointer is pre- or postdecremented.

The stack pointer is incremented when something is read from the stack. Incrementing the stack pointer implies that the information read has been used and is no longer available. Because the stack pointer has been incremented, the data in that location will be overwritten by the next write to the stack. The information actually remains in memory until it is overwritten.

3-4.4 PUSHes and PULLs or POPs

A PUSH instruction writes the accumulator contents to the stack and decrements the stack pointer. A PULL (Motorola) or POP (Intel) does the reverse; it reads from the stack, at the stack pointer, into an accumulator and increments the stack pointer. Again the user should check the μP specifications to see if the stack pointer is incremented before or after the PULL or POP.

A **6800** or **6502** PUSH writes a single byte to the stack and decrements the stack pointer once. A CALL or JUMP TO SUBROUTINE must write the return address (a 16-bit word) to the stack and therefore decrements the stack pointer twice.

The **8080/8085** use only 16-bit PUSHes and POPs. They combine registers into pairs as follows:

`PSH B`	Pushes the B and L registers
`PSH D`	Pushes the D and E registers
`PSH H`	Pushes the H and L registers
`PSH PSW`	Push the accumulator and the flags

The program status word (PSW) is a combination of the accumulator and the flags (see chapter 4). Each **8080/8085** PUSH decrements the SP twice and its corresponding POP increments the SP twice.

EXAMPLE 3-7 An **8080/8085** subroutine must use the accumulator and register C, but it must return to the main program with the original values of those registers. How can this be done?

Solution This can be done by pushing the registers that must be saved at the start of the subroutine, and then popping them in reverse order at the end of the subroutine. The subroutine program should look like this:

```
PUSH   PSW
PUSH   B
  :
Main body of subroutine
  :
POP B
POP PSW
RETURN
```

The stack is shown in Figure 3-5. The CALL routine and beginning of the subroutine

Address	*Data*	
SP-7		
SP-6	Flags	← Final contents of SP
SP-5	A	
SP-4	C	
SP-3	B	
SP-2	PCL	
SP-1	PCH	
SP		← Original contents of SP
⋮		

Figure 3-5 Contents of the stack for Example 3-7. (From Greenfield and Wray, *Using Microprocessors and Microcomputers*: *The 6800 Family*, Wiley, 1981.)

decremented the SP six times (twice for the CALL to stack the return address, twice to store B and C, and twice to store the PSW, A, and the flags). The exit routine (PUSH B, PUSH PSW, RETURN) will increment the SP six times so that it ends up where it was before the subroutine was started.

3-4.5 Stacks in Newer Microprocessors

Stacks have proven so useful that many newer μPs use more than one stack. The **6809** is typical; it has an S (hardware) stack and a U (user) stack. The hardware stack automatically stores the return address on subroutine calls and interrupts. Pushes and pulls can be made to either stack, however, giving the user more flexibility. Most 16-bit μPs have more than one register that can be used as a stack pointer.

3-5 INTERRUPTS

One of the most important features of a μP is its ability to control and act on feedback from peripheral devices, such as line printers or machinery controllers. It must be able to sense the operation of the system under its control and respond quickly with corrective commands when necessary.

When conditions that require fast response arise, the system is wired so as to send a signal called an *interrupt* to the μP. An interrupt causes the μP to *stop* execution of its main program and jump to a special program, an *interrupt service routine*, that responds to the needs of the external device. The main program resumes when the interrupt service routine is finished.

3-5.1 Level- and Edge-Sensitive Interrupts

All μPs have one or more pins that are activated by external devices when they need to interrupt. Most of these inputs are *level sensitive*; the interrupt signal persists as long as the level is active. Some μPs and peripherals use *edge-sensitive* interrupts. In these systems the interrupt takes effect when a *transition* occurs on a line, and the level of the signal by itself does not cause an interrupt.

For level-sensitive interrupts, the occurrence of an interrupt disables further interrupts, so the service routine will not be further interrupted. Usually interrupts are enabled when the service routine finishes and the main program resumes. Therefore the interrupt service routine must take some action to *terminate* the source of interrupt and return the interrupt input to its inactive state, so the same level does not generate a second interrupt. This is not required in edge-sensitive systems because a second interrupt can only be generated by another transition.

3-5.2 Maskable Interrupts

An interrupt is *maskable* if it can be *enabled or disabled by a command.* If the interrupt is masked off or disabled, the μP will not respond to any interrupt requests.

EXAMPLE 3-8 In a program there is a segment of code that must not be interrupted. How can this be arranged?

Solution The mask can be set at the start of the segment, so no further interrupts will be recognized. The mask must then be cleared at the end of the segment or the interrupting devices will never be able to interrupt again.

In the **6800** series of μPs the mask bit is part of the condition code or flag register. The **8080** and **8085** use ENABLE INTERRUPT (EI) and DISABLE INTERRUPT (DI) instructions to mask or enable interrupts. The **8085** also has several RESTART interrupts that can be enabled or disabled using the SET INTERRUPT MASK (SIM) instruction.

Interrupts are disabled in one of three ways:

1 The mask bit is set by the program.

2 The μP is restarted.

3 An interrupt occurs.

It is generally wise to have the μP restarted with *interrupts disabled.* The program can then do its initialization and set up the interrupt routines before allowing any interrupts. It is also wise to have the interrupt masked when an interrupt occurs. This prevents level-sensitive interrupts from interrupting the interrupt routine. Most μPs automatically disable interrupts in both of these cases.

3-5.3 Nonmaskable Interrupts (NMI)

An NMI, called a TRAP in the **8085** and an $\overline{\text{NMI}}$ in the **6800**, *cannot* be masked off by the program. Consequently, an interrupt occurs every time the NMI pin on the μP is activated and NMIs must be activated by an edge-triggered signal.

NMIs function as very high-priority interrupts. Because they cannot be masked off they must be used very carefully. They are usually reserved for events like a power failure in the μP or in a peripheral, which could be catastrophic if the μP did not recognize them and take immediate action.

EXAMPLE 3-9 Assume a system like Figure 3-6 is being used as a part of a financial terminal where transactions involving customer bank accounts are being handled, and the information must be preserved in the event of a power failure. Describe the interrupt service routines required.

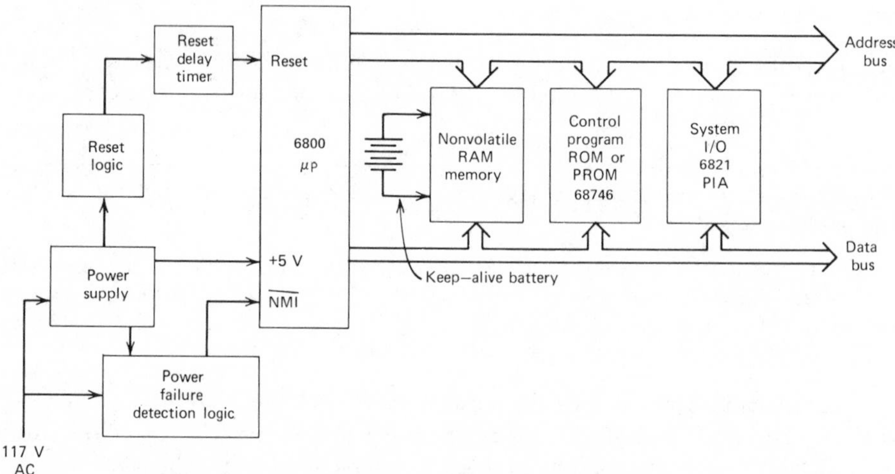

Figure 3-6 A **6800** system for automatic recovery from a power failure. (From Greenfield and Wray, *Using Microprocessors and Microcomputers*: *The 6800 Family*, Wiley, 1981.)

Solution Since it is necessary in this type of system to save all calculations and status, a nonvolatile RAM is needed with a *powerfail* detector, as shown in Figure 3-6.

The function of the battery is to act as an auxiliary source of energy for the RAM so the RAM will not lose information when the main power fails.

When a power failure occurs, the NMI line is pulled down by the powerfail logic, the main program is interrupted at the end of the current instruction, and the registers are stored in the stack. (The power supply will take many milliseconds before the voltage is too low to operate the system, and this routine only takes microseconds.) The vector for the powerfail routine is fetched and the processor starts its execution. This routine's main function is to save, in nonvolatile memory, all relevant information such as the contents of PIA and ACIA registers. The stack should also be in nonvolatile memory. The program should then use a PIA (see section 7-14) to pull down the HALT line and wait until the power fails.

Figure 3-6 also includes the circuitry necessary to resume operation when the power comes on again. The box labeled "reset logic" must decide when the voltage is normal and it then initiates a RESET pulse. The RESET routine fetched by the RESET vector must not only reconfigure the PIAs and the ACIAs, for example, but must reload all interim products or data into the appropriate registers (the RTI restores the μP registers). The program then resumes from the address restored to the PC register without loss of any vital data.

3-5.4 Interrupts on the 8080 and 8085

On the **8080** and **8085** an interrupt is initiated when the interrupting device places a HIGH on the INTR line. The μP responds by placing a LOW pulse on its $\overline{\text{INTA}}$ (INTERRUPT ACKNOWLEDGE) line. While this pulse is LOW the μP must receive the Op code of the next instruction it will execute on its AD0–AD7 lines. The interrupting device is responsible for placing the Op code on the AD0–AD7 lines.

The function of the instruction whose Op code is read in during $\overline{\text{INTA}}$ is to jump the program to the start of the interrupt service routine. It must also place the contents of the program counter (PC) on the μP's stack so the main program can be resumed after the interrupt routine is finished. For the **8080**, there is only one instruction that performs these functions and should be placed on the AD0–AD7 lines. This is a RESTART. The **8085** can accept either a RESTART or a CALL.

RESTARTs and CALLs are discussed further in chapters 4 and 5 on the **8080** and **8085**.

3-5.5 Interrupts on the 6800

The **6800** uses four different types of interrupts: RESET (RST), NONMASKABLE (NMI), SOFTWARE (SWI), and HARDWARE INTERRUPT REQUEST (IRQ). Unique interrupt servicing routines must be written by the system designer for each type of interrupt used, and they can be located anywhere in memory. When an interrupt occurs the processor reads the starting address for the interrupt service routine from a pair of memory locations. The two locations addressed must contain the address of the required interrupt service routine. The locations where the starting addresses are stored for the four interrupt types are:

1 RESET (RST)	FFFE—FFFF
2 NONMASKABLE INTERRUPT (NMI)	FFFC—FFFD
3 SOFTWARE INTERRUPT (SWI)	FFFA—FFFB
4 INTERRUPT REQUEST (IRQ)	FFT8—FFF9

The normal interrupt on the **6800** is an IRQ.

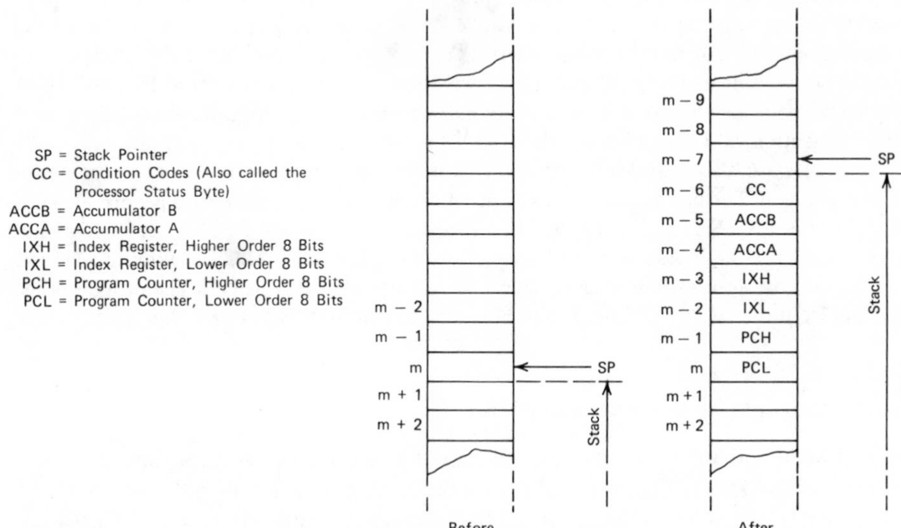

Figure 3-7 Saving the status of the μP in the stack. (From Greenfield and Wray, *Using Microprocessors and Microcomputers: The 6800 Family*, Wiley, 1981.)

When an interrupt is initiated, *the instruction in progress is completed before the μP begins its interrupt sequence.* The first step in this sequence is to save the program status by storing the PC, X, A, B, and CC registers on the stack in the order shown in Figure 3-7. These seven bytes are written into memory starting at the location in the stack pointer (SP) register, which is decremented on each write. When completed, the SP is pointing to the next empty memory location. The condition of the stack before and after accepting an interrupt is shown in Figure 3-8. The μP next sets the interrupt mask bit (I), which allows the service program to run without being interrupted. After setting the interrupt mask, the μP fetches the address of the interrupt service routine from the IRQ vector location by placing FFF8 and FFF9 on the address bus, and inserts it into the PC. The μP then fetches the first instruction of the service routine from the location now designated by the PC.

Most μPs handle their interrupts similarly to one of the two methods described in the preceding paragraphs. To understand the interrupt system on any particular μP, the reader should consult the chapter in this book on that μP or other sources.

3-6 MICROPROCESSOR BUSES

A μP communicates with the other ICs (memories and I/O chips) in the microcomputer system via a group of signal and control lines that are collectively called a *bus.* Microprocessor buses can generally be divided into three parts: the data bus, the address bus, and the control lines.

3-6.1 The Data Bus

The data bus is a *bidirectional* bus used for the transfer of data between the μP and the other ICs in the system in *either* direction. During a READ cycle, data goes from the selected peripheral device to the μP; the μP receives information at this time.

During a WRITE cycle the μP is the source of the information. It drives the data bus and the peripherals must receive the information.

In general, there are as many lines on the data bus as there are bits in the μP. Thus the 8-bit μPs have 8 bidirectional lines (generally labeled D0–D7) and the 16-bit μPs have 16 data lines. Some μPs, however, like the Intel **8088**, are 16-bit μPs with an 8-bit interface. They only have 8 data lines.

3-6.2 The Address Bus

The address lines are controlled and driven by the μP. They are often also divided into two groups. The high-order bits are used to select a memory or peripheral IC, while the low-order bits on the address lines are used to select a location in that IC.

EXAMPLE 3-10 A microcomputer system has a 16-bit address bus and uses 1K RAMs. How many address lines are needed to select the word on a RAM, and how many are available to select a particular RAM?

Solution A 1K RAM IC has 2^{10} bits on it and therefore needs 10 bits (addresses A0–A9) to select it. This leaves the upper 6 address bits available to select a particular RAM or other I/O chip. Generally the selection of a particular IC is made by decoding the upper addresses for that IC's address and properly setting the CHIP SELECT lines on the IC only when that address occurs.

The 8-bit μPs have a standard 16-bit address bus, which limits their address range to 64K bytes. The 16-bit μPs generally have a larger address bus that gives them the ability to address from one to several megabytes of memory.

3-6.3 The Control Bus

The control bus is a set of signals that are neither address nor data, but *control* the flow of information between the μP and its peripherals. Most control bus lines are driven by the μP so that it is generally the master of the bus and the other devices are the slaves.

The most important line of the control bus is the READ/WRITE line, which determines whether data is flowing to or from the μP. In most μPs the READ/WRITE line is HIGH for READ and LOW for WRITE, and most memories or other peripheral ICs react accordingly; they can be written into when their chip select ($\overline{\text{CS}}$) and $\overline{\text{WRITE}}$ inputs and LOW, and they can be read when their $\overline{\text{CS}}$ input is LOW but their $\overline{\text{WRITE}}$ input is HIGH. The Intel **8085**, and some other μPs, have both a $\overline{\text{RD}}$ and a $\overline{\text{WR}}$ output. They only read when $\overline{\text{RD}}$ goes LOW and write when

$\overline{WR}$ goes LOW. Many peripheral ICs manufactured by Intel respond directly to $\overline{RD}$ and $\overline{WR}$.

Another control line found on most μP buses is the $\overline{RESET}$ line. This line is driven LOW when the μP is first turned on and it is used to start the program. In Intel μPs the $\overline{RESET}$ line forces the PC to address 0, which either starts the user's program or contains a JUMP to the starting address. In Motorola μPs a $\overline{RESET}$ places the contents of FFFE and FFFF in the PC. Thus locations FFFE and FFFF must contain the starting address of the user's program.

The **8080/8085/Z80** series of μPs also have a READY input. If this input is HIGH the μP enters a WAIT state and delays execution of instructions until the line goes HIGH. In case the μP is faster than the memroy, the READY input is used to cause the μP to wait for the memory. It goes LOW at the start of each memory cycle, causing the μP to go into the WAIT state for one or two clock cycles to allow the memory time to present its data. Motorola μPs generally have a slower clock and do not use a READY signal.

Another set of signals on the **8080/8085/Z80** control bus are the status lines; they tell the user what kind of a cycle is about to be executed. They can be used to distinguish between a coming memory cycle and an I/O READ (IN) or I/O WRITE (OUT) cycle. This is important because the address bus contains memory addresses during memory READ or WRITE cycles, but contains a port address during I/O cycles. The **8085** simplifies matters by using an IO/$\overline{M}$ signal on its control bus that only goes HIGH during an I/O cycle.

3-6.4 Multiplexed Buses

Some μPs, in particular the **8085**, use a time multiplexed bus, where different signals appear on the same lines at different times. The **8085** multiplexes its data bus with the 8 low-order bits of the address bus; these lines are called AD0–AD7 because they contain both address and data. At the start of a memory cycle the AD lines contain the lower 8 bits of the address. Another signal on the control bus, ALE (ADDRESS LATCH ENABLE), goes HIGH at this time to indicate that there are addresses on the multiplexed bus. Later in the memory cycle, when data is available, ALE goes LOW and the data replaces the addresses on the AD lines. The **8085** multiplexed bus is discussed more thoroughly in chapter 5 on the **8085**.

The advantage of a multiplexed bus is that more information can be transmitted over fewer wires. They do, however, present latching and timing problems. With an **8085**, if the addresses must remain firm throughout the memory cycle, they must be latched into a group of external flip-flops. Usually the flip-flops are clocked with ALE.

3-6.5 Direct Memory Access

In DIRECT MEMORY ACCESS (DMA) the μP relinquishes control of the memory to an external device for a short time. DMA is used when an external device has many bytes of data to write into or read from the memory. It is the fastest way to transfer data and has the least effect on the μP. One use of DMA is with a CRT controller that constantly reads the screen image from the μP's memory (see chapter 13).

To effect a DMA, the following events must occur:

1 The external device or peripheral IC must indicate that it requires a DMA.
2 The μP must relinquish control of the address and data buses and the READ/WRITE line, generally by placing them in high impedance mode. The μP must also inform the peripheral that it has control of the bus.
3 The peripheral uses the bus to read or write memory. It may transfer many bytes during a single access depending on the system.
4 The peripheral returns control of the buses to the μP.

The lines to control DMA form part of the control bus. The **8080/8085/Z80** μPs use the HOLD and HLDA signals for DMA. A device requests a DMA by asserting the HOLD input to the μP. The μP then finishes its present instruction, 3-states the address and data buses and READ/WRITE (high impedance), and asserts HLDA (HOLD ACKNOWLEDGE). The requesting peripheral can now take control of the buses for its data transfer. It retains control of the bus as long as it asserts HOLD.

The **6800** uses such control signals as TSC (three-state control), DBE (data bus enable), and BA (bus available) for DMA accesses. DMA on other μPs are also similar. The user should consult the manufacturer's specification for the DMA procedure on any particular μP.

3-7 REFERENCES

Joseph D. Greenfield and William C. Wray, *Using Microprocessors and Microcomputers: The 6800 Family*, Wiley, New York, 1981.

Lance A. Leventhal, *Introduction to Microprocessors: Software, Hardware, Programming*, Prentice-Hall, Englewood Cliffs, N.J., 1978.

SECTION TWO

EIGHT-BIT MICROPROCESSORS

CHAPTER 4

The Intel 8080

Walter Foley
Eastman Kodak Corp.
Rochester, New York

The **8080** microprocessor was the first of the second generation 8-bit μPs. It had numerous advantages over the first generation 8-bit μPs, such as the **8008**. Some of the features of the **8080** are as follows:

1 64K-byte memory addressing
2 256 I/O port addresses
3 Three general-purpose 16-bit registers
4 Three special-purpose 16-bit registers
5 Eight vectored interrupts
6 An instruction set of 78 instructions

4-1 ARCHITECTURE

The entire architecture of the **8080** is shown in Figure 4-1. It shows the registers, the accumulator, instruction decoder, ALU, and the rest of the logic necessary to allow the **8080** to function as a microprocessor.

4-1.1 Registers

The **8080** contains six 16-bit static registers, shown on the right side of Figure 4-1. There are three 16-bit general-purpose register pairs, B,C, D,E, H,L, which can also be used as six 8-bit registers. There is also a 16-bit stack pointer register that is used to reference the memory locations where program counter, register contents, and condition flags are stored during interrupt handling and subroutine calls. The fifth 16-bit register is the program counter (PC) that contains the memory address of the

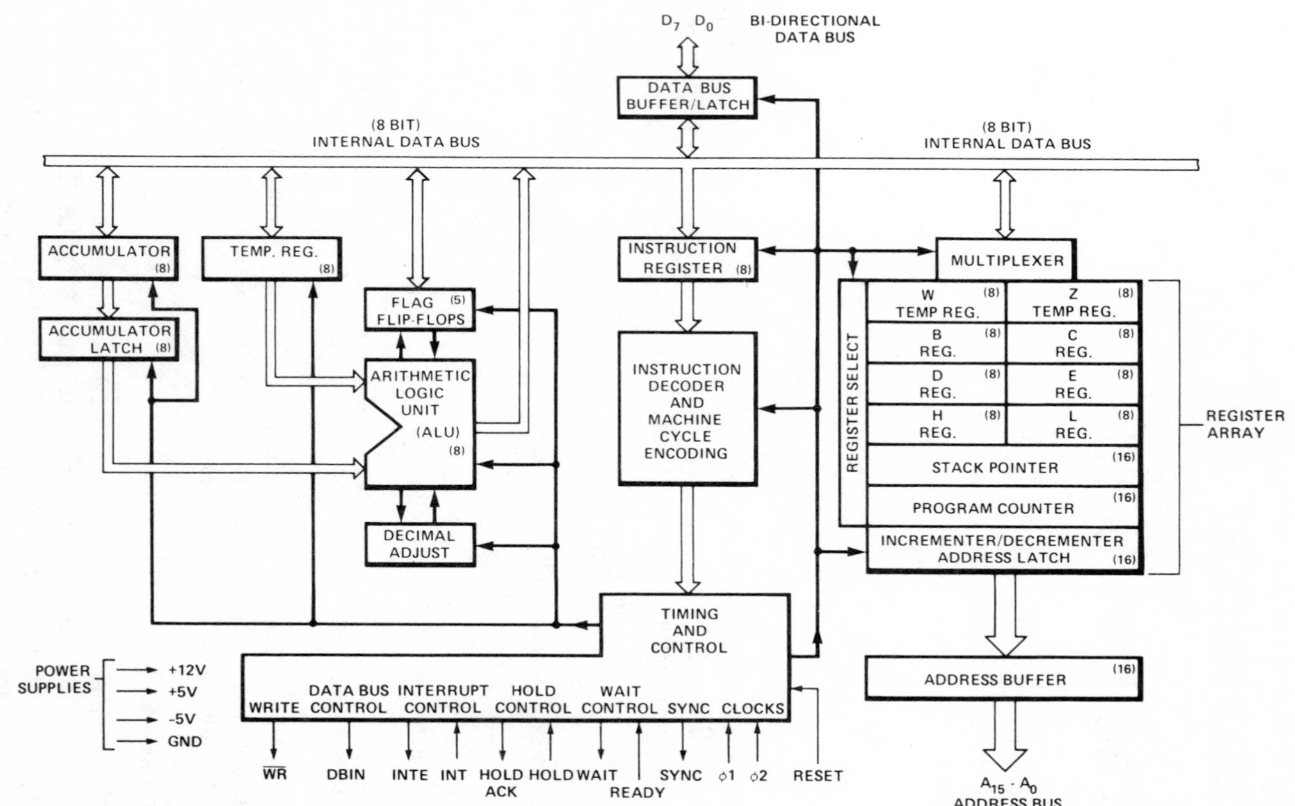

Figure 4-1 **8080** CPU functional block diagram. (Reprinted by permission of Intel Corp., copyright 1975.)

instruction currently being executed. The sixth 16-bit register pair is called W,Z. This register pair is used internally by the **8080** and is not program addressable.

The three 16-bit general-purpose register pairs are very useful, both as 16-bit registers and as 8-bit registers. As 16-bit registers, they can be used to perform double-precision arithmetic, hold the addresses of data memory locations, such as look up tables, and calculate offset addresses for modifying program execution. As 8-bit registers, they can be used for intermediate data storage and holding operands. This eliminates the need to go to memory for this type of data, which improves processing speed.

4-1.2 The Accumulator

There is a single 8-bit *accumulator* in the **8080**, called the *A register*. Single-precision arithmetic, logic, and rotate instructions are executed in the A register. Data going to or coming from I/O in an isolated I/O system is handled by the A register. Whenever the A register is moved to or from the stack, it is used as half of a 16-bit word, called the *processor status word* (PSW). The other half of the PSW word contains the condition flags.

4-1.3 The Flags

There are five *condition flags* that are associated with the execution of instructions in the **8080**. These flags are:

1 *Zero.* If the result of an operation has the value 0, the flag is set to a 1, otherwise it is reset to a 0.

2 *Sign.* If the most significant bit of the result of the operation is a 1, the flag is set to a 1, otherwise it is reset to a 0.

3 *Parity.* If the bits of the result of an operation have even parity, the flag is set to a 1, otherwise it is reset to a 0.

4 *Carry.* If the last arithmetic operation resulted in a carry or a borrow out of the high-order bit, the flag is set to a 1, otherwise it is reset to a 0.

5 *Auxiliary carry.* If an addition causes a carry out of bit 3 and into bit 4 of the resulting value, the flag is set to a 1, otherwise it is reset to a 0.

The first four condition flags can be tested by JUMP or CALL instructions in a program and normal sequential program flow can be altered by their values. The fifth condition flag, auxiliary carry, is used only when doing decimal arithmetic and is not directly testable by instructions. To test the AUX CARRY flag, the PSW (processor status word) must be pushed onto the stack. Then the byte containing the flags can be popped back off the stack into one of the general-purpose registers to test for the AUX CARRY bit.

The 16-bit word that is the combination of the flags (8 bits) and the accumulator is called the processor status word (PSW). The location of the FLAG WORD and A accumulator in the PSW is shown in Figure 4-2.

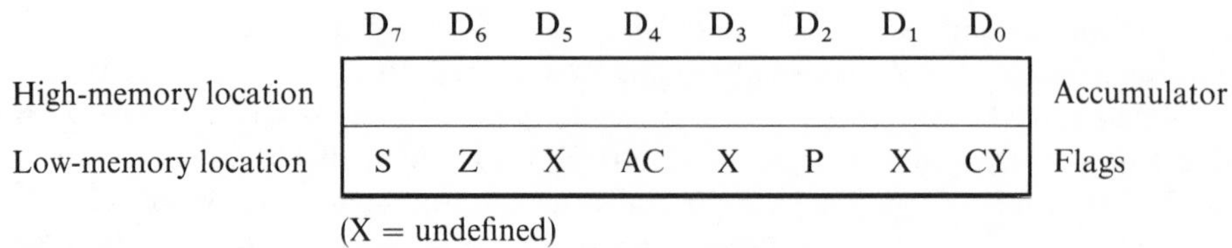

Figure 4-*2* The processor status word (PSW) as it appears in memory.

4-1.4 Stack

The *stack* in an **8080** system is a section of READ/WRITE data memory that is used by the processor for housekeeping purposes, and is also used by the programmer for temporary data storage. The processor uses the stack to store the address it will return to after it has handled either an *interrupt* or a *subroutine call.* The processor responds to an interrupt, for example, as follows:

1 It completes execution of the current instruction.

2 It increments the program counter to point to the next instruction.

3 It decrements the stack pointer.

4 It pushes the high-order byte of the program counter onto the stack.

5 It decrements the stack pointer.

6 It pushes the low-order byte of program counter onto the stack.

7 It jumps to the interrupt service routine and responds to the interrupt. When the processor has finished servicing the interrupt, it returns to the main program, at the point it was interrupted, by popping a byte off the stack to restore it to the low byte of the program counter.

8 It increments the stack pointer.

9 It pops a byte off the stack to restore the high-order byte of the program counter.

10 It increments the stack pointer.

11 It then resumes execution of the program that was interrupted.

In the **8080** only the PC is automatically stacked in response to an interrupt or CALL. The programmer can push the register and flag values onto the stack when entering either an interrupt routine or a subroutine. This is necessary if the routine being entered uses some of the **8080**'s registers and flags and will overwrite them. Pushing them onto the stack at the start of a subroutine and popping them off at the end preserves them, despite their use by the subroutine. The programmer must remember to pop the registers and flags before leaving the routine; otherwise the processor will use the last 2 register bytes pushed on the stack as the return address and resume execution at the wrong location.

4-2 ADDRESSING MODES

There are five modes of addressing the hardware registers and/or memory in the **8080**. These modes are: implied addressing, register addressing, immediate addressing, direct addressing, and register indirect addressing. The addressing mode used by an instruction is implicit for that instruction. Listed below are explanations and examples of the different modes.

4-2.1 Implied Addressing

Implied addressing instructions require only one memory reference, an Op code fetch. All the information necessary to execute these instructions is already within the μP. An example of an implied instruction is the complement carry flag (CMC) instruction; since this instruction deals only with the carry flag, the addressing is implied. Another example would be the complement accumulator (CMA) instruction, since this instruction deals only with the accumulator.

4-2.2 Register Addressing

This type of addressing is used by a large set of instructions and is really a form of implied addressing because only one memory reference is required. In this mode the use of the accumulator as a second operand is implied, and the programmer must specify one of the other registers—A through E, H, or L—as the first operand, as well as the operation code. For example, the instruction ANA B is read as "logically AND the contents of the B register with the contents of the accumulator and store the results in the accumulator." Most of the register addressing instructions deal with 8-bit values. However, a few instructions of this type deal with 16-bit register pairs. For example, the XCHG instruction swaps the contents of the H and L register pair with the contents of the D and E register pair.

4-2.3 Immediate Addressing

Instructions that use *immediate addressing* have data assembled as a part of the instruction. As an example, the instruction ADI 23H is read to mean "add immediately the value 23 (hex) to the accumulator." When this instruction is assembled, it will use two bytes in memory. The first byte will be the code for the ADI instruction, the second byte will be the hex value 23. When the instruction is executed, the processor fetches the first byte, determines that it requires a second byte, fetches the second byte into an internal register, and then performs the operation requested by the first byte using the second byte as data.

4-2.4 Direct Addressing

This type of addressing is used by instructions that require a 16-bit address as part of the instruction. For example, the JUMP instructions include a 16-bit address that indicates where the processor should jump to. This type of instruction occupies three bytes in memory. The first byte contains the instruction code, the second byte contains the LS byte (least significant byte) of the 16-bit address, and the third byte contains the MS byte (most significant byte) of the 16-bit address. The processor fetches the first byte, the Op code, determines that it requires 2 more bytes to complete the address, and then fetches these 2 bytes into an internal register. It then replaces the current contents of the program counter with the value of these 2 bytes, and continues execution starting at the new address.

4-2.5 Register Indirect Addressing

This type of addressing uses a register pair to reference a location in memory. For example, the MOV M,A instruction moves the value in the accumulator to the memory location whose address is the 16-bit value stored in the H and L register pair. The H register contains the MS byte of the memory address and the L register contains the LS byte of the memory address.

Some instructions, such as the CALL instruction, use a combination of addressing modes. The CALL instructions combine direct addressing and register indirect addressing. The direct address is the address of the subroutine being called and the register indirect address is the stack pointer that contains the address where the contents of the program counter will be stored while the subroutine is being executed.

4-3 INSTRUCTION FORMAT

The **8080** instruction set consists of instructions of 1, 2- or 3-byte length. The format of the instructions in program memory depends upon the operation to be performed. The generalized instruction formats are shown in Figure 4-3. The instructions that operate on the 8-bit registers use a 3-bit pattern imbedded in the instruction to specify the source (SSS) and/or destination (DDD) register to be used. The instructions that operate on the 16-bit register pairs use a 2-bit pattern (RP) imbedded in the instruction to specify the register pair to be used. Figure 4-4 lists the bit patterns for the registers and register pairs.

4-4 INSTRUCTION SET

The **8080** instruction set can be separated into five main groups:

1 *Data transfer group.* These instructions handle the movement of data to and from the registers and memory.

2 *Arithmetic group.* These instructions direct all computational operations on data present in the accumulator.

3 *Logical group.* These instructions perform all logic operations on data present in the accumulator.

4 *Branch group.* These instructions control the sequence of program execution.

5 *Stack, I/O, and machine control.* These instructions control machine operation and the movement of data:

   a On and off the stack

   b To and from external devices

	Instruction Format Byte one	Byte two	Byte three
Single byte	[Op code]	—	—
Two byte	[Op code]	[Data or ADDR]	—
Three byte	[Op code]	[Low-order ADDR]	[High-order ADDR]

Figure 4-3 The **8080** instruction formats.

Register	*Code [SSS or DDD]*
Acc	111
B	000
C	001
D	010
E	011
H	100
L	101

Register pair	*Code [RP]*
B (B,C)	00
D (D,E)	01
H (H,L)	10
SP (STACK POINTER)	11

Figure 4-4 Bit patterns for the **8080** registers and register pairs.

Table 4-1, which begins on page 127, is a complete listing of the **8080** instruction set. It shows the mnemonic for each instruction, the format of each instruction, and explains its actions and its effect on the condition codes. It also shows the number of cycles and states taken by each instruction (see section 4-5.2). The last page is a one-page summary of the **8080** instructions. The instructions are explained further in the following sections, with examples.

4-4.1 The Data Transfer Group

These instructions transfer data from register to register, memory to register, or register to memory. Instructions exist to transfer data between any pair of registers, or between a register and memory. All MOVE instructions have 01 as the two MSBs of the Op code.

The condition flags are *not* affected by any instruction in this group.

Note: Throughout this chapter the suffix H will be used to indicate hexadecimal values.

`MOV R1,R2` (Move from register to register)

Definition: Move the contents of register 2 to register 1.
No. of memory locations required: 1
Op code: 0 1 D D D S S S
Addressing mode: Register
Execution time: 5 clock cycles

EXAMPLE

`MOV A,C` (with the C register contents being 44H)

D D D (A REG) = 1 1 1 S S S (C REG) = 0 0 1
Op code = 0 1 1 1 1 0 0 1 = 79H

After execution the A register will contain the value 44H, and the C register will not have been changed, and will also contain 44H.

`MVI R, DATA` (Move immediate to register)

Definition: Move the contents of byte 2 of the instruction into the register R.
No. of memory locations required: 2
Op code: 0 0 D D D 1 1 0 (Memory location N)
Data: X X X X X X X X (Memory location N + 1)
Addressing mode: Immediate
Execution time: 7 clock cycles

EXAMPLE

`MOV H,34H`

D D D (H Register) = 1 0 0
Op code = 0 0 1 0 0 1 1 0 = 26H
Data = 0 0 1 1 0 1 0 0 = 34H

After execution the H register will contain the value 34H.

`MOV R,M` (Move to register from memory)

Definition: Move the contents of the memory location M, whose address is given by registers H (MSB) and L (LSB) into the register R.

No. of memory locations required: 1
Op code: 0 1 D D D 1 1 0
Addressing mode: Register indirect
Execution time: 7 clock cycles

EXAMPLE

`MOV B,M` (The H register contains the value 01H)
(The L register contains the value A5H)
(Address of memory location M = 01A5H)
(The memory location 01A5H contains the value 88H)

D D D (B register) = 0 0 0
Op code = 0 1 0 0 0 1 1 0 = 46H
After execution the B register will contain the value 88H.

`MOV M,R` (Move to memory from register)

Definition: Move the contents of register R into the memory location M whose address is contained in the H (MSB) and L (LSB) registers.
No. of memory locations required: 1
Op code: 0 1 1 1 0 S S S
Addressing mode: Register indirect
Execution time: 7 clock cycles

EXAMPLE

`MOV M,L` (The H register contains the value 23H)
(The L register contains the value 10H)
(Address of memory location M = 2310H)

S S S (L register) = 1 0 1
Op code = 0 1 1 1 0 1 0 1 = 75H
After execution the memory location 2310H will contain the value 10H.

`MVI M, DATA` (Move immediate to memory)

Definition: Move the contents of byte 2 of the instruction into the memory location M whose address is contained in the H (MSB) and L (LSB) registers.
No. of memory locations required: 2
Op code: 0 0 1 1 0 1 1 0 = 36H (Program memory location N)
Data: X X X X X X X X (Program memory location N + 1)
Addressing mode: Immediate and register indirect
Execution time: 10 clock cycles

EXAMPLE

`MVI M,(DE)`$_{16}$ (The H register contains the value 30H)
(The L register contains the value 00H)
(The address of memory location M = 3000H)

Op code = 0 0 1 1 0 1 1 0 = 36H
Data = 1 1 0 1 1 1 1 0 = DEH
After execution the memory location 3000H will contain the value DEH.

LOAD and STORE instructions transfer information to or from registers. They are very similar to MOVE instructions.

`LXI RP,DATA` (Load immediate to register pair)

Definition: Move the contents of byte 2 of the instruction into the low-order (LS byte) register of the register pair RP, and then move the contents of byte 3 of the instruction into the high-order (MS byte) register of the register pair RP.
No. of memory locations required: 3
Op code: 0 0 R P 0 0 0 1 (Program memory location N)
Data (LSB): X X X X X X X X (Program memory location N + 1)
Data (MSB): Y Y Y Y Y Y Y Y (Program memory location N + 2)
Addressing mode: Immediate
Execution time: 10 clock cycles

EXAMPLE

`LXI D,1475H`

RP (DE register pair) = 0 1
Op code = 0 0 0 1 0 0 0 1 = 11H
Data (LSB) = 0 1 1 1 0 1 0 1 = 75H
Data (MSB) = 0 0 0 1 0 1 0 1 = 14H
After execution the D register will contain the value 14H and the E register will contain the value 75H.

`LDA ADDR` (Load accumulator direct)

Definition: Move the contents of memory location M, whose high-order address is contained in byte 3 of the instruction and whose low-order address is contained in byte 2 of the instruction into the accumulator.
No. of memory locations required: 3
Op code: 0 0 1 1 1 0 1 0 = 3AH (Program memory location N)
ADDR (LSB): X X X X X X X X (Program memory location N + 1)
ADDR (MSB): Y Y Y Y Y Y Y Y (Program memory location N + 2)
Execution time: 13 clock cycles

EXAMPLE

`LDA C003H` (The address of memory location M: C003H (Memory location M contains the value 9AH)

Op code = 0 0 1 1 1 0 1 0 = 3AH
ADDR (LSB) = 0 0 0 0 0 0 1 1 = 03H
ADDR (MSB) = 1 1 0 0 0 0 0 0 = C0H

After execution the accumulator will contain the value 9AH.

`STA ADDR` (Store accumulator direct)

Definition: Move the contents of the accumulator to the memory location M, whose high-order address is contained in byte 3 of the instruction and whose low-order address is contained in byte 2 of the instruction.
No. of memory locations required: 3

Op code:	0 0 1 1 0 0 1 0 = 32H	(Program memory location N)
ADDR (LSB):	X X X X X X X X	(Program memory location N + 1)
ADDR (MSB):	Y Y Y Y Y Y Y Y	(Program memory location N + 2)

Addressing mode: Direct
Execution time: 13 clock cycles

`LHLD ADDR` (Load H and L direct)

Definition: First move the contents of memory location M, whose high-order address is contained in byte 3 of the instruction and whose low-order address is contained in byte 2 of the instruction into register L. Next move the contents of memory location M + 1 into register H.
No. of memory locations required: 3

Op code:	0 0 1 0 1 0 1 0 = 2AH	(Program memory location N)
ADDR (LSB):	X X X X X X X X	(Program memory location N + 1)
ADDR (MSB):	Y Y Y Y Y Y Y Y	(Program memory location N + 2)

Addressing mode: Direct
Execution time: 16 clock cycles

EXAMPLE

`LHLD C6A7` (The address of memory location M = C6A7H)
(The contents of memory location C6A7 = 00H)
(The address of memory location M + 1 = C6A8H)
(The contents of memory location C6A8 = 27H)

Op code = 0 0 1 0 1 0 1 0 = 2AH
ADDR (LSB) = 1 0 1 0 0 1 1 1 = A7H
ADDR (MSB) = 1 1 0 0 0 1 1 0 = C6H

After execution the H register will contain the value 27H and the L register will contain the value 00H.

`SHLD ADDR` (Store H and L direct)

Definition: First move the contents of register L into the memory location M, whose high-order address is contained in byte 3 of the instruction and whose low-order address is contained in byte 2 of the instruction. Next move the contents of register H into the memory location M + 1.
No. of memory locations required: 3

Op code:	0 0 1 0 0 0 1 0 = ZZH	(Program memory location N)
ADDR (LSB):	X X X X X X X X	(Program memory location N + 1)
ADDR (MSB):	Y Y Y Y Y Y Y Y	(Program memory location N + 2)

Addressing mode: Direct
Execution time: 16 clock cycles

`LDAX RP` (Load accumulator indirect)

Definition: Move the contents of memory location M, whose address is contained in the register pair RP, into the accumulator. (Note: only the register BC or DE may be specified for RP.)
No. of memory locations: 1
Op code: 0 0 R P 1 0 1 0
Addressing mode: Register indirect
Execution time: 7 clock cycles

EXAMPLE

`LDAX B` (The B register contains the value 78H)
(The C register contains the value 12H)
(The address of memory location M = 7812H)
(The memory location 7812H contains the value B6H)

RP (BC register pair) = 00
Op code = 0 0 0 0 1 0 1 0 = 0AH
After execution the accumulator will contain the value B6H.

`STAX RP` (Store accumulator indirect)

Definition: Move the contents of the accumulator into the memory location M, whose address is contained in the register pair RP. (Note: only register pairs BC or DE may be specified for RP.)
No. of memory locations required: 1
Op code: 0 0 R P 0 0 1 0
Addressing mode: Register indirect
Execution time: 7 clock cycles

`XCHG` (Exchange H and L with D and E)

Definition: The contents of the H register are exchanged with the contents of the D

register and then the contents of the L register are exchanged with the contents of the E register.
No. of memory locations required: 1
Op code: 1 1 1 0 1 0 1 1 = CBH
Addressing mode: Register
Execution time: 4 clock cycles

EXAMPLE

XCHG (The H register contains the value 23H)
(The L register contains the value 67H)
(The D register contains the value 9AH)
(The E register contains the value F4H)

Op code = 1 1 1 0 1 0 1 1 = EBH

After execution the H register will contain the value 9AH, the L register will contain the value F4H, the D register will contain the value 23H, and the E register will contain the value 67H.

4-4.2 The Arithmetic Group

The arithmetic group includes ADD, SUBTRACT, ROTATE, and other instructions. Note: Flags affected for each instruction are indicated. All subtraction operations use 2s complement arithmetic and set the carry flag to indicate a borrow or clear it to indicate no borrow.

ADD R (Add register)

Definition: The contents of register R is added to the contents of the accumulator. The result is placed in the accumulator.
No. of memory locations required: 1
Op code: 1 0 0 0 0 S S S
Flags affected: Z, S, P, CY, AC
Addressing mode: Register
Execution time: 4 clock cycles

EXAMPLE

ADD C

S S S (C Register) = 0 0 1
Op code = 1 0 0 0 0 0 0 1 = 81H
ACC = 1 0 0 0 1 0 0 1 = 89H
C REG = 1 1 0 0 0 0 1 1 = C3H
After execution:
ACC = 0 1 0 0 1 1 0 0 = 4CH
The carry flag will be set; all other flags are reset.

`ADD M` (Add memory)

Definition: The contents of the memory location M, whose address is contained in the H and L registers, is added to the contents of the accumulator. The result is placed in the accumulator.
No. of memory locations required: 1
Op code: 1 0 0 0 0 1 1 0
Flags affected: Z, S, P, CY, AC
Addressing mode: Register indirect
Execution time: 7 clock cycles

`ADI DATA` (Add immediate)

Definition: The contents of the accumulator are added to the contents of byte 2 of the instruction. The result is placed in the accumulator.
No. of memory locations required: 2
Op code: 1 1 0 0 0 1 1 0
Flags affected: Z, S, P, CY, AC
Addressing mode: Immediate
Execution time: 7 clock cycles

EXAMPLE

`ADI 44H`

Op code = 1 1 0 0 0 1 1 0 = C6H (Program memory location N)
Data = 0 1 0 0 0 1 0 0 = 44H (Program memory location N + 1)
ACC = 0 0 0 1 0 0 0 1 = 11H
After execution:
ACC = 0 1 0 1 0 1 0 1 = 55H
The parity flag will be set; all other flags will be reset.

`ADC R` (Add register with carry)

Definition: The contents of the register R and the carry flag are added to the contents of the accumulator. The result is placed in the accumulator.
No. of memory locations required: 1
Op code: 1 0 0 0 1 S S S
Flags affected: Z, S, P, CY, AC
Addressing mode: Register
Execution time: 4 clock cycles

EXAMPLE

`ADC E`

S S S (E register) = 0 1 1
Op code = 1 0 0 0 1 0 1 1 = 8BH
ACC = 0 0 0 1 1 1 0 0 = 1CH

E reg = 0 0 1 1 0 0 0 0 = 30H
Carry = 1 = 01H
After execution:
ACC = 0 1 0 0 1 1 0 1 = 4DH
The parity flag will be set; all other flags will be reset.

ADC M (Add memory with carry)

Definition: The contents of the memory location M, whose address is contained in the H and L registers, and the carry flag are added to the accumulator. The result is placed in the accumulator.
No. of memory locations required: 1
Op code: 1 0 0 0 1 1 1 0 = 8EH
Flags affected: Z, S, P, CY, AC
Addressing mode: Register indirect
Execution time: 7 clock cycles

ACI DATA (Add immediate with carry)

Definition: The contents of the accumulator are added to the contents of byte 2 of the instruction and the carry flag. The result is placed in the accumulator.
No. of memory locations required: 2
Op code: 1 1 0 0 1 1 1 0
Flags affected: Z, S, P, CY, AC
Addressing mode: Immediate
Execution time: 7 clock cycles

SUB R (Subtract register)

Definition: Subtract the contents of register R from the contents of the accumulator. The result is placed in the accumulator.
No. of memory locations required: 1
Op code: 1 0 0 1 0 S S S
Flags affected: Z, S, P, CY, AC
Addressing mode: Register
Execution time: 4 clock cycles

EXAMPLE

SUB D

S S S (D register) = 0 1 0
Op code = 1 0 0 1 0 0 1 0 = 92H
ACC = 1 0 0 0 0 1 1 1 = 87H
D reg = 1 0 1 0 1 0 1 1 = ABH
After execution:
ACC = 1 1 0 1 1 1 0 0 = DCH
The sign and carry flags will be set; all other flags are reset.

`SUB M` (Subtract memory)

Definition: The contents of memory location M, whose address is contained in the H and L register, are subtracted from the accumulator. The result is placed in the accumulator.
No. of memory locations required: 1
Op code: 1 0 0 1 0 1 1 0 = 96H
Flags affected: Z, S, P, CY, AC
Addressing mode: Register indirect
Execution time: 7 clock cycles

`SUI DATA` (Subtract immediate)

Definition: The contents of byte 2 of the instruction are subtracted from the accumulator.
No. of memory locations required: 2
Op code: 1 1 0 1 0 1 1 0 = D6H
Flags affected: Z, S, P, CY, AC
Addressing mode: Immediate
Execution time: 7 clock cycles

`SBB R` (Subtract register with borrow)

Definition: The contents of register R and the carry flag are subtracted from the contents of the accumulator. The result is placed in the accumulator.
No. of memory locations required: 1
Op code: 1 0 0 1 1 S S S
Flags affected: Z, S, P, CY, AC
Addressing mode: Register
Execution time: 4 clock cycles

EXAMPLE

`SBB B`

S S S (B REG) = 0 0 0
Op code = 1 0 0 1 1 0 0 0 = 98H
ACC = 0 0 0 1 0 0 0 1 = 11H
B REG = 0 0 0 0 0 1 0 1 = 05H
Carry = 1 = 01H
After execution:
ACC = 0 0 0 0 1 0 1 1 = OBH
All flags are reset.

`SBB M` (Subtract memory with borrow)

Definition: The contents of memory location M, whose address is contained in the H and L registers, and the carry flag are subtracted from the accumulator. The result is placed in the accumulator.
No. of memory locations required: 1
Op code: 1 0 0 1 1 1 1 0 = 9EH

Flags affected: Z, S, P, CY, AC
Addressing mode: Register indirect
Execution time: 7 clock cycles

`SBI DATA` (Subtract immediate with borrow)

Definition: The contents of byte 2 of the instruction and the carry flag are subtracted from the accumulator.
No. of memory locations required: 2
Op code: 1 1 0 1 1 1 1 0 = DEH
Flags affected: Z, S, P, CY, AC
Addressing mode: Immediate
Execution time: 7 clock cycles

EXAMPLE

```
SBI 00H
```

Op code = 1 1 0 1 1 1 1 0 = DEH
Data = 0 0 0 0 0 0 0 0 = 00H
ACC = 0 1 0 1 0 0 0 1 = 51H
Carry = 1 = 01H
After execution:
ACC = 0 1 0 1 0 0 0 0 = 50H
The parity flag will be set; all others are reset.

(Double register add)

Definition: The 16-bit value of register pair RP is added to the contents of the HL register pair. The result is stored in HL.
No. of memory locations required: 2
Op code: 0 0 R P 1 0 0 1
Flags affected: CY
Addressing mode: Register
Execution time: 10 clock cycles

EXAMPLE The DAD instruction provides a means of saving the contents of the stack pointer, by adding it to H and L.

```
LXI H 00H        ;Clear H&L to zeros
DAD SP           ;Add the 16-bit stack pointer to H&L
SHLD 3E00        ;Store stack pointer in memory location 3E00H
```

The stack pointer contents are now in HL and in 3E00H and 3E01H. The DAD H instruction will add the contents of the H&L register pair to itself except when a carry out of the H register occurs, effectively doubling the value in H and L.

Rotate Instructions There are four ROTATE instructions in the **8080**. These are shown in Figure 4-5.

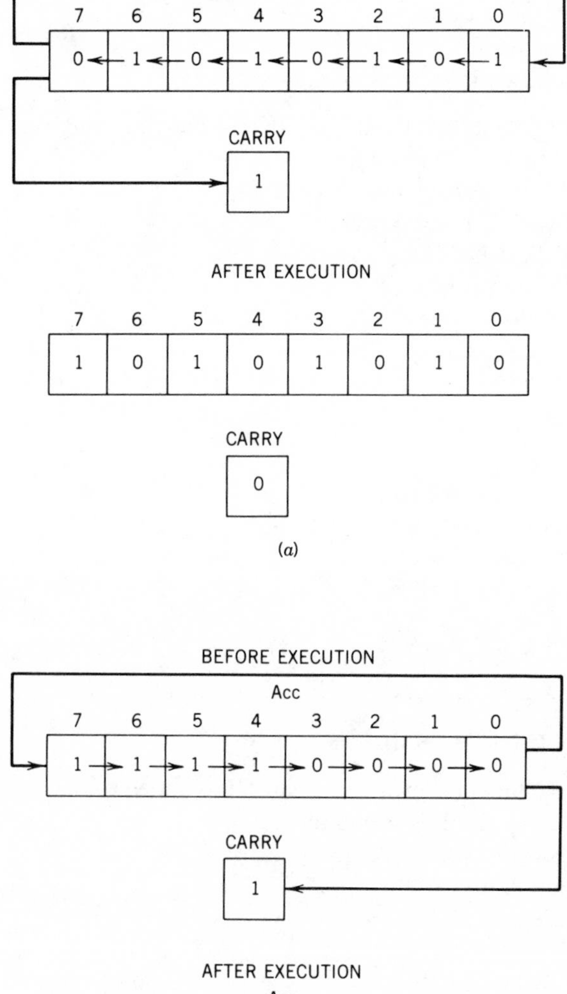

Figure 4-5 Diagrams for the **8080** ROTATE instructions. (*a*) RLC instruction. (*b*) RRC instruction. (*c*) RAL instruction. (*d*) RAR instruction.

BEFORE EXECUTION

Acc

7 6 5 4 3 2 1 0

0 1 1 1 0 0 0 0

CARRY

1

AFTER EXECUTION

Acc

7 6 5 4 3 2 1 0

1 1 1 0 0 0 0 1

0

(*c*)

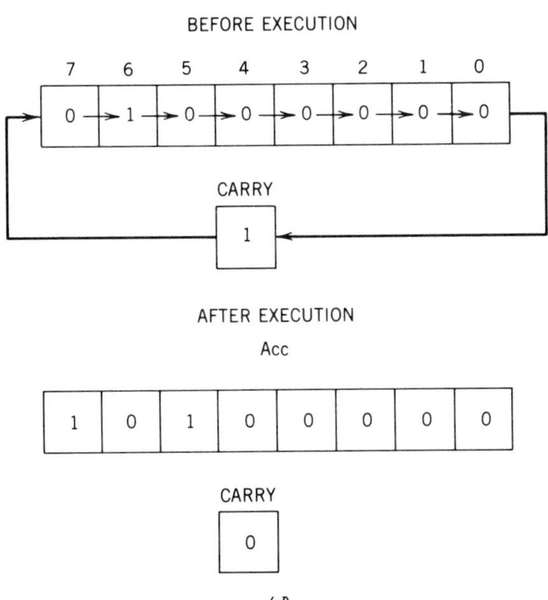

(*d*)

Figure 4-5 (Continued)

RLC (ROTATE ACCUMULATOR LEFT)

Definition: This instruction rotates the contents of the accumulator 1-bit position to the left with the MSB transferring to the LSB position in the accumulator. The carry flag is also set equal to the MSB.
No. of memory locations: 1
Op code: 0 0 0 0 0 1 1 1 = 07H
Flags affected: CY
Execution time: 4 clock cycles

EXAMPLE

RLC

ACC = 0 1 0 1 0 1 0 1 = 55H
CY = 1
After execution:
ACC = 1 0 1 0 1 0 1 0 = AAH
CY = 0

RRC (ROTATE ACCUMULATOR RIGHT)

Definition: Operation is identical to the RLC instruction, except rotation is to the right and the LSB replaces the CY flag.
Op code: 0 0 0 0 1 1 1 = 0FH
Flags affected: CY
Execution time: 4 clock cycles

RAL (ROTATE LEFT THROUGH CARRY)

Definition: The contents of the ACC and the CY flag are rotated 1-bit position to the left. The CY flag is treated as part of the ACC. The CY contents are transferred to the LSB of the ACC and the MSB of the ACC is transferred to the CY flag.
Op code: 0 0 0 1 0 1 1 1 = 17H
Flags affected: CY
Execution time: 4 clock cycles

RAR (ROTATE RIGHT THROUGH CARRY)

Definition: The operation is identical to the RAL instruction, except rotation is to the right.
Op code: 0 0 0 1 1 1 1 1 = 1FH
Flags affected: CY
Execution time: 4 clock cycles

A complete set of increment and decrement instructions are available on the **8080**.

`INR R` (INCREMENT REGISTER)

Definition: INR adds one to the contents of the specified register.
Op code: 0 0 D D D 1 0 0
Flags affected: All except CY
Addressing mode: Register
Execution time: 5 clock cycles

EXAMPLE

```
INR B
```

Op code = 0 0 0 0 0 1 0 0 = 04H

If the B register contained the value 3FH then after the execution of the INR B instruction the B register would contain the value 40H.

`INR M` (INCREMENT MEMORY)

Definition: Add one to the contents of the memory location specified by the contents of the H and L register pair.
No. of memory locations required: 1
Op code: 0 0 1 1 0 1 0 0 = 34H
Flags affected: All except CY
Addressing mode: Register indirect
Execution time: 10 clock cycles

EXAMPLE

```
INR M
```

If the register pair H and L contain the value 3E10H then after execution of the INR M instruction, the value contained in memory location 3E10H will be incremented by one.

`INX RP` (Increment register pair)

Definition: Add one to the contents of the 16-bit register pair specified.
No. of memory locations required: 1
Op code: 0 0 R P 0 0 1 1
Flags affected: None
Addressing mode: Register
Execution time: 5 clock cycles

EXAMPLE

`INX B`

Op code = 0 0 0 0 0 0 1 1 = 03H

If the B&C register pair contains the value 1FFFH then after execution of the INX B instruction the register pair will contain the value 2000H.

Note: No flags are changed by the INX or DEX instructions. This is a drawback if a program requires a register pair to be counted down to 0.

`DCR R` (Decrement register)

Definition: Subtract 1 from the value of the specified register.
No. of memory locations required: 1
Op code: 0 0 D D D 1 0 1
Flags affected: All except carry
Addressing mode: Register
Execution time: 5 clock cycles

`DCR M` (Decrement memory)

Definition: The contents of the memory location, whose address is specified by the value of the H and L register pair, will have 1 subtracted from it.
No. of memory locations required: 1
Op code: 0 0 1 1 0 1 0 1 = 35H
Flags affected: All except carry
Addressing mode: Register indirect
Execution time: 10 clock cycles

`DCX RP` (Decrement register pair)

Definition: Decrement the 16-bit value of the register pair specified by 1.
No. of memory locations required: 1
Op code: 0 0 R P 1 0 1 1
Flags affected: None
Addressing mode: Register
Execution time: 5 clock cycles

`CMA` (Complement accumulator)

Definition: Produces the 1s complement of the accumulator.
No. of memory locations required: 1
Op code: 0 0 1 0 1 1 1 1 = 2FH
Flags affected: None
Execution time: 4 clock cycles

EXAMPLE

`CMA`

ACC = 1 1 0 0 0 1 1 1 = 0C7H
After execution:
ACC = 0 0 1 1 1 0 0 0 = 38H

`STC` (Set carry)

Definition: Sets the carry flag to 1.
No. of memory locations required: 1
Op code: 0 0 1 1 0 1 1 1 = 37H
Flags affected: CY
Execution time: 4 clock cycles

`CMC` (Complement carry)

Definition: If the carry flag equals 0 it will be set to a 1. If the carry flag equals 1 it will be set to a 0.
No. of memory locations required: 1
Op code: 0 0 1 1 1 1 1 1 = 3FH
Flags affected: CY
Execution time: 4 clock cycles

`DAA` (Decimal adjust accumulator)

Definition: Adjust the 8-bit value of the accumulator to form two 4-bit BCD digits.
No. of memory locations required: 1
Op code: 0 0 1 0 0 1 1 1 = 27H
Flags affected: All
Addressing mode: Register
Execution time: 4 clock cycles

The DAA operates as follows:

1 If (a) the lower 4 bits of the ACC have a value > 9, or (b) the AC flag is set then 6 is added to the ACC.

2 If (a) the upper 4 bits of the ACC have a value > 9, or (b) the CY flag is set then 6 is added to the upper 4 bits of the ACC.

Note: The B section above may set the carry flag. If this is important to the program, the carry flag should be tested before executing another instruction that could change the carry flag's value.

EXAMPLE 4-1 How does the **8080** behave if 48 and 59 are added, followed by a DAA?

Solution First binary addition is performed:

48 + 59 = A1H

This addition sets the AC flag, but clears the CY flag. In accordance with items 1 and 2, the DAA adds 6 to both nibbles of the results.

$$\begin{array}{r} \text{A1} \\ +66 \\ \hline 07 \end{array}$$

The addition also sets the CY flag. The results can be interpreted as 107, the correct BCD answer.

4-4.3 The Logical Group

This group contains the logic instructions (AND, OR, XOR) available on the **8080**.

Note: All flags are affected by operations contained in this group. Examples are not given for the instructions in this group since their operations are simple logic.

`ANA R` (AND register)

Definition: AND the contents of the specified register with the contents of the accumulator. The result is placed in the accumulator.
No. of memory locations required: 1
Op code: 1 0 1 0 0 S S S
Addressing mode: Register
Addressing time: 4 clock cycles

`ANA M` (AND memory)

Definition: AND the contents of the memory location, whose address is contained in the H and L RP, with the contents of the accumulator. The result is placed in the accumulator.
No. of memory locations required: 1
Op code: 1 0 1 0 0 1 1 0 = A6H
Addressing mode: Register indirect
Execution time: 7 clock cycles

`ANI DATA` (AND immediate)

Definition: AND the contents of the second byte of the instruction with the accumulator. The result is placed in the accumulator.
No. of memory locations required: 2
Op code: 1 1 1 0 0 1 1 0 = E6H
Addressing mode: Immediate
Execution time: 7 clock cycles

`XRA R` (EXCLUSIVE OR register)

Definition: EXCLUSIVE OR the contents of the specified register with the accumulator. The result is placed in the accumulator.

No. of memory locations required: 1
Op code: 1 0 1 0 1 S S S
Addressing mode: Register
Executive time: 4 clock cycles

`XRA M` (EXCLUSIVE OR memory)

Definition: EXCLUSIVE OR the contents of the memory location, whose address is contained in the H and L RP, with the accumulator. The result is placed in the accumulator.
No. of memory locations required: 1
Op code: 1 0 1 0 1 1 1 0 = AEH
Addressing mode: Register indirect
Execution time: 7 clock cycles

`XRI DATA` (EXCLUSIVE OR immediate)

Definition: EXCLUSIVE OR the second byte of the instruction with the accumulator. The result is placed in the accumulator.
No. of memory locations required: 2
Op code: 1 1 1 0 1 1 1 0 = EEH
Addressing mode: Immediate
Execution time: 7 clock cycles

`ORA R` (OR register)

Definition: OR the contents of the register specified with the contents of the accumulator. The result is placed in the accumulator.
No. of memory locations required: 1
Op code: 1 0 1 1 0 S S S
Addressing mode: Register
Execution time: 4 clock cycles

`ORA M` (OR memory)

Definition: OR the contents of the memory location, whose address is contained by the H and L RP, with the accumulator. The result is placed in the accumulator.
No. of memory locations required: 1
Op code: 1 0 1 1 0 1 1 0 = B6H
Addressing mode: Register indirect
Execution time: 7 clock cycles

`ORI DATA` (OR immediate)

Definition: OR the second byte of the instruction with the accumulator. The result is placed in the accumulator.

No. of memory locations required: 2
Op code: 1 1 1 1 0 1 1 0 = F6H
Addressing mode: Immediate
Execution time: 7 clock cycles

COMPARE instructions are used to compare two registers or a register and a value. The flags are set according to the result. The values in the registers are never changed by a COMPARE instruction.

`CMP R` (COMPARE register)

Definition: Compare the contents of the specified register with the contents of the accumulator. The result is indicated by the flag settings. Below is a list of the flags and the conditions that set them:

Flag	Condition
Zero	Set if accumulator = R, otherwise reset
Carry	Set if accumulator > R, reset if accumulator < R

The meaning of the carry flag is reversed when the two values being compared have different signs or one of the values is complemented. *The values being compared are not changed.*
No. of memory locations required: 1
Op code: 1 0 1 1 1 S S S
Addressing mode: Register
Execution time: 4 clock cycles

`CMP M` (COMPARE memory)

Definition: Compare the contents of the memory location, whose address is contained in the H and L RP, with the accumulator. The results are indicated in the flags as shown in the CMP R instruction. The values being compared are not changed.
No. of memory locations required: 1
Op code: 1 0 1 1 1 1 1 0 = BEH
Addressing mode: Register indirect
Execution time: 7 clock cycles

`CPI DATA` (COMPARE immediate)

Definition: Compare the second byte of the instruction with the accumulator. The results are indicated in the flags as shown in the CMP R instruction. The values being compared are not changed.
No. of memory locations required: 2
Op code: 1 1 1 1 1 1 1 0 = FEH
Addressing mode: Immediate
Execution time: 7 clock cycles

4-4.4 The Branch Group

This group of instructions includes JUMPs, CALLs (jumps to subroutines), RETURNs, and RESTARTs.

Note: None of the instructions in this group affect the flags. Where an address is specified as part of the instruction the LS byte of the address is located in the second byte of the instruction and the MS byte of the address in the third byte.

JMP ADDR (JUMP)

Definition: The address contained in the next two bytes of the instruction is placed in the program counter. Execution resumes at this new address.
No. of memory locations required: 3
Op code: 1 1 0 0 0 0 1 1 = C3H
LSB ADDR
MSB ADDR
Addressing mode: Immediate
Execution time: 10 clock cycles

J(FLAG) ADDR (JUMP CONDITIONAL)

Definition: The address contained in the next two bytes of the instruction is placed in the program counter if the condition specified is true, otherwise execution continues at the next sequential address. There are eight instructions in this set dealing with the two possible settings of the zero, carry, parity, and sign flags. Below is a table of these instructions:

Instruction	*Op code*	*Condition*	*Hex*
JNZ	1 1 0 0 0 0 1 0	JUMP NOT ZERO (Z = 0)	C2
JZ	1 1 0 0 1 0 1 0	JUMP ZERO (Z = 1)	CA
JNC	1 1 0 1 0 0 1 0	JUMP NO CARRY (CY = 0)	D2
JC	1 1 0 1 1 0 1 0	JUMP CARRY (CY = 1)	DA
JPO	1 1 1 0 0 0 1 0	JUMP PARITY ODD (P = 0)	E2
JPE	1 1 1 0 1 0 1 0	JUMP PARITY EVEN (P = 1)	EA
JP	1 1 1 1 0 0 1 0	JUMP POSITIVE (S = 0)	F2
JM	1 1 1 1 1 0 1 0	JUMP MINUS (S = 1)	FA

No. of memory locations required: 3 (Op code + 2 address bytes)
Addressing mode: Immediate
Execution time: 10 clock cycles

PCHL (Move H and L to program counter)

Definition: The contents of the H and L RP are moved into the program counter and execution resumes at that address.

No. of memory locations required: 1
Op code: 1 1 1 0 1 0 0 1 = E9H
Addressing mode: Register
Execution time: 5 clock cycles

`CALL ADDR` (Call subroutine immediate)

Definition: The address of the next sequential instruction is pushed onto the stack and then the **8085** jumps to the address specified in the next two bytes of the CALL instruction.
No. of memory locations required: 3
Op code: 1 1 0 0 1 1 0 1 = CDH
L S B A D D R
M S B A D D R
Addressing mode: Immediate/register indirect
Execution time: 17 clock cycles

`C(FLAG) ADDR` (Call subroutine conditional)

Definition: If the condition specified in the instruction is true, the address of the next sequential instruction is pushed onto the stack and then the address specified in the next two bytes of the CALL instruction is placed in the PC. The conditions are the same eight as in the JUMP conditional instructions. Below is a table of these instructions:

Instruction	*Op code*	*Hex*
CNZ	1 1 0 0 0 1 0 0	C4
CZ	1 1 0 0 1 1 0 0	CC
CNC	1 1 0 1 0 1 0 0	D4
CC	1 1 0 1 1 1 0 0	DC
CPO	1 1 1 0 0 1 0 0	E4
CPE	1 1 1 0 1 1 0 0	EC
CP	1 1 1 1 0 1 0 0	F4
CM	1 1 1 1 1 1 0 0	FC

No. of memory locations required: 3 (Op code + 2 byte ADDR)
Addressing mode: Immediate/register indirect
Execution time: 11 clock cycles (if condition specified is false)
17 clock cycles (if condition specified is true)

`RET` (Return immediate)

Definition: Two bytes are popped off the stack and moved into the program counter. Execution resumes at the new address. This instruction is used to return to the instruction located after a CALL instruction when the execution

of the subroutine is complete. It is also used to return to the correct address after handling an interrupt request.
No. of memory locations required: 1
Op code: 1 1 0 0 1 0 0 1 = C9H
Addressing mode: Register indirect
Execution time: 10 clock cycles

R(FLAG) (Return conditional)

Definition: If the condition specified is true, execute a return instruction; otherwise continue execution at the next sequential address. The conditions are the same eight as in the JMP conditional instructions. Below is a table of the return conditional instructions:

Instruction	*Op code*	*Hex*
RNZ	1 1 0 0 0 0 0 0	C0
RZ	1 1 0 0 1 0 0 0	C8
RNC	1 1 0 1 0 0 0 0	D0
RC	1 1 0 1 1 0 0 0	D8
RPO	1 1 1 0 0 0 0 0	E0
RPE	1 1 1 0 1 0 0 0	E8
RP	1 1 1 1 0 0 0 0	F0
RM	1 1 1 1 1 0 0 0	F8

No. of memory locations required: 1
Addressing mode: Register indirect
Execution time: 5 clock cycles (if condition specified is false)
11 clock cycles (if condition specified is true)

RST # (Restart)

Definition: RESTART is a special purpose CALL instruction that pushes a return address on the stack and then jumps to one of eight predetermined addresses. The address it jumps to is specified by bits 3, 4, and 5 of the instruction. The table below lists the instructions and the predetermined address for each.

Instruction	*Op code*	*Jump address*
RST 0	1 1 0 0 0 1 1 1	0000H
RST 1	1 1 0 0 1 1 1 1	0008H
RST 2	1 1 0 1 0 1 1 1	0010H
RST 3	1 1 0 1 1 1 1 1	0018H
RST 4	1 1 1 0 0 1 1 1	0020H
RST 5	1 1 1 0 1 1 1 1	0028H
RST 6	1 1 1 1 0 1 1 1	0030H
RST 7	1 1 1 1 1 1 1 1	0038H

EXAMPLE 4-2 What effect does a RESTART 3 have on the **8080**?

Solution A RESTART pushes the present value of the PC onto the stack (decrementing the SP twice) and places 0018H into the PC so the program's execution resumes at this address.

The RESTART instruction is used to vector an interrupt to its proper subroutine (see Section 4-5.2).

4-4.5 Stack, I/O, and Machine Control

These are the instructions that affect the stack, the stack pointer, input/output, and several miscellaneous instructions.

PUSH RP (Push register pair)

Definition: Decrement the stack pointer register, place the high-order byte of the register pair specified into the memory location, whose value is contained in the stack pointer register, decrement the stack pointer register again, and place the low-order byte of the specified register pair into the memory location that the stack pointer is now pointing to. If the two RP bits are both ones the processor status word (PSW, the accumulator plus the flags) is pushed onto the stack.
No. of memory locations required: 1
Op code: 1 1 R P 0 1 0 1
Flags affected: None
Addressing mode: Register indirect
Execution time: 11 clock cycles

POP RP (Pop register pair)

Definition: The opposite of the PUSH instruction. The low-order byte is removed from the stack, placed in the register specified, the stack pointer is incremented, the high-order byte is removed from the stack and placed in the register specified. The stack pointer is incremented again. If the RP bits are 11 the PSW is popped into the accumulator and the flags.
No. of memory locations required: 1
Op code: 1 1 R P 0 0 0 1
Flags affected: None
Addressing mode: Register indirect
Execution time: 10 clock cycles

XTHL (Exchange H and L with top of stack)

Definition: The top 2 bytes from the stack are exchanged with the contents of the H and L register pair.
No. of memory locations required: 1
Op code: 1 1 1 0 0 0 1 1 = E3H

Flags affected: None
Addressing mode: Register indirect
Execution time: 18 clock cycles

`SPHL` (Move H and L to stack pointer)

Definition: The contents of the H and L register pair are loaded into the stack pointer.
No. of memory locations required: 1
Op code: 1 1 1 1 1 0 0 1 = F9H
Flags affected: None
Addressing mode: Register
Execution time: 5 clock cycles

`OUT PORT` (Output to port)

Definition: The contents of the accumulator are output to the port whose address is contained in the second byte of the instruction (see Example 4-4).
No. of memory locations required: 2
Op code: 1 1 0 1 0 0 1 1 = D3H
P O R T A D D R
Flags affected: None
Addressing mode: Direct
Execution time: 10 clock cycles

`IN PORT` (Input from port)

Definition: The value read from the port, whose address is contained in the second byte of the instruction, and is placed into the accumulator (see Example 4-4).
No. of memory locations required: 2
Op code: 1 1 0 1 1 0 1 1 = 0DB H
P O R T A D D R
Flags affected: None
Addressing mode: Direct
Execution time: 10 clock cycles

`DI` (Disable interrupts)

Definition: The **8080** contains an internal flip-flop that is used to enable and disable the external interrupt system. The execution of the DI instruction turns off this flip-flop and while the flip-flop is off, the CPU will not respond to any external interrupts.
No. of memory locations required: 1
Op code: 1 1 1 1 0 0 1 1 = F3H
Flags affected: None
Addressing mode: Immediate
Execution time: 4 clock cycles

EI (Enable interrupts)

Definition: This instruction allows external interrupts to be recognized by enabling the internal interrupt FF. This instruction is used after a power on reset has occurred, after the processing of a previous interrupt request, or after the DI instruction has been executed.
No. of memory locations required: 1
Op code: 1 1 1 1 1 0 1 1 = FBH
Flags affected: None
Addressing mode: Immediate
Execution time: 4 clock cycles

NOP (No operation)

Definition: This instruction performs no operation. It is useful as a filler in a timing loop.
No. of memory locations required: 1
Op code: 0 0 0 0 0 0 0 0 = 00H
Flags affected: None
Execution time: 4 clock cycles

HLT (Halt)

Definition: After execution of this instruction the processor will halt. The program counter contains the address of the next sequential instruction. If interrupts are enabled, then an external interrupt will restart the processor. If interrupts are disabled, then only a RESET signal will restart the processor.
No. of memory locations required: 1
Op code: 0 1 1 1 0 1 1 0 = 76H
Flags affected: None
Addressing mode: Immediate
Execution time: 7 clock cycles

4-5 THE CPU

The **8080** CPU, as shown in Figure 4-6, is contained in a 40 pin, dual-in-line, plastic or ceramic package. A listing of the pins by number with a brief description of their function follows. (I means "in," O means "out," and B means "bidirectional.")

Pin no.	*Name*	*Direction*	*Function*
1	A10	O	Bit 10 of the address bus
2	GND	I	Power supply and signal-ground reference
3, 4, 5, 6	DATA	B	Bits 4, 5, 6, 7 of the bidirectional data/status bus
7, 8, 9, 10	DATA	B	Bits 3, 2, 1, 0 of the bidirectional data/status bus

Pin no.	Name	Direction	Function
11	V_{BB}	I	−5 V DC + −5% (substrate bias)
12	RESET	I	Active HIGH, when active program counter is cleared to 0000H, where execution will start after reset. The interrupt enable and the hold acknowledge internal FFs are reset. The reset signal must be active at least 3 clock cycles.
13	HOLD	I	Active HIGH, signals the CPU to enter the HOLD state. The CPU does this by tri-stating the address and data bus. This allows another device to access the system memory for DMA purposes.
14	INT	I	Interrupt, active HIGH, signals the CPU that an interrupt is being requested. The interrupt enable (INTE) FF must be set by an EI instruction and/or the CPU must not be in the hold state for it to recognize the interrupt.
15	ϕ2	I	ϕ2 of the CPU (**8080**) clock. Non-TTL compatible signal. Its voltage swing must be from 0.6 to 11 V with rise and fall times less than 50 ns.
16	INTE	0	Interrupt enable, active HIGH, indicates the internal INTE FF is set
17	DBIN	0	Data bus in, active HIGH, indicates the CPU data bus is in the input mode
18	WR	0	Write, active LOW, indicates stable data from the CPU is on the data bus
19	SYNC	0	Active HIGH, indicates the start of a machine cycle
20	V_{CC}	I	+5 V DC + −5%, power
21	HLDA	0	Hold acknowledge, active HIGH, indicates the buses will go tri-state after the rising edge of the next ϕ2 clock cycle.
22	ϕ1	I	ϕ1 of the CPU clock. Same signal levels as ϕ2.
23	READY	I	Active HIGH, indicates that external devices can accept or receive data. If ready is LOW when the CPU sends out an address, the CPU will enter wait states until ready goes HIGH. Ready is used to synchronize the CPU with slow memory or I/O and it also can be used to single step the CPU.
24	WAIT	0	Active HIGH, indicates the CPU is in a wait state.
25, 26, 27	ADDR	0	Bit 0, 1, 2 of the address bus
28	VDD	I	+12 V DC + −15%, power
29–35	ADDR	0	Bits 3–9 of the address bus
36	A15	0	Bit 15 (MSB) of the address bus
37, 38, 39	ADDR	0	Bits 12, 13, 14 of the address bus
40	A11	0	Bit 11 of the address bus

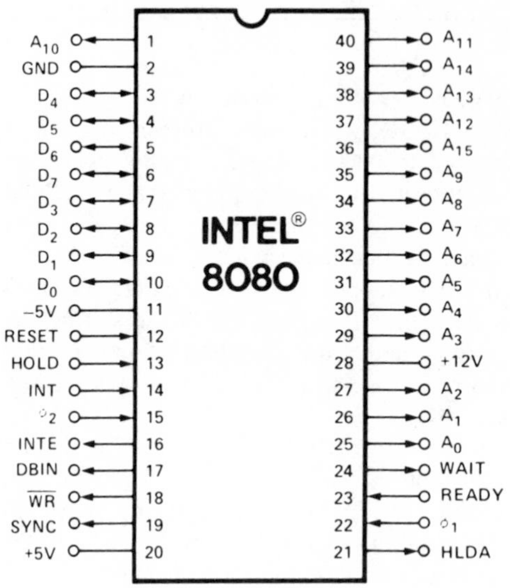

Figure 4-6 **8080** CPU pin connection. (Courtesy of Intel Corporation.)

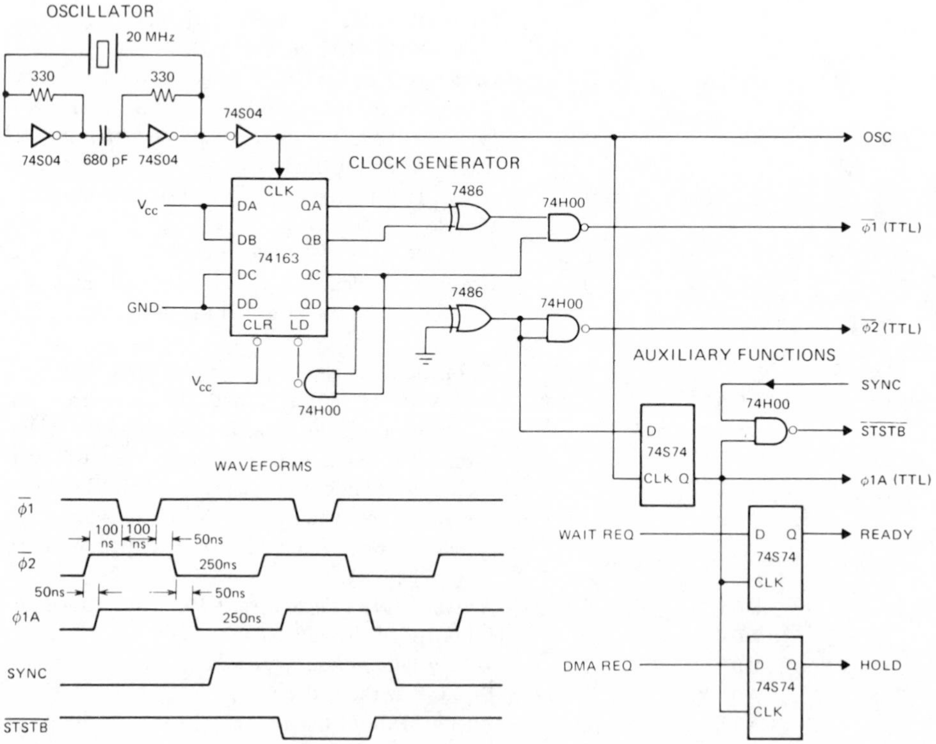

Figure 4-7 A timing generator for the **8080**. (Reprinted by permission of Intel Corp., copyright 1975.)

4-5.1 Clock Generation

The two-phase clock signals that the **8080** runs on have several special requirements. The time from rising edge of $\phi 1$ to rising edge of the next $\phi 1$ can be a maximum of 2 μs or a clock frequency of 500 kHz, minimum. This is because the **8080** is a dynamic device and its internal registers will lose their values if the clock is too slow or it stops. The voltage levels of the clock are not TTL compatible. The clock signals must swing from a low level of 0.6 V to a high level of 11 V. A simple two-phase clock generator circuit is shown in Figure 4-7. This circuit also generates a status strobe ($\overline{\text{STSTB}}$) for system use and synchronizes the READY and HOLD signals for the CPU. The waveforms generated by this circuit are also shown in Figure 4-7. The problem with this circuit is that it produces only TTL level outputs.

Figure 4-8 shows a possible circuit for a high-level clock driver for the 8080. It uses the $\phi 1$ and $\phi 2$ signals generated in Figure 4-7 as inputs. The **MH0026** is a dual MOS clock driver that produces the output voltages required by the **8080**. The output rise and fall times are less than the required 50 ns and the low level of the clock output is close to ground. The low-value resistors in series with the clock signals are used to reduce overshoot.

4-5.2 Machine Cycles and T States

The *execution time* of an instruction is defined as the time required to fetch and execute that instruction. During the fetch phase of an instruction, the Op code for the instruction is read from memory and placed in the CPU's instruction register and the number of bytes required by that instruction (1, 2, or 3) is determined. During the execution phase of an instruction, the instruction register is decoded and the specific CPU functions required are performed by that instruction.

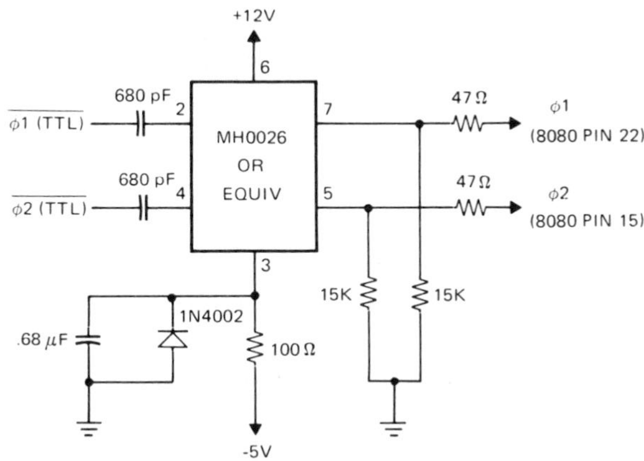

Figure 4-8 A high-level clock driver for the **8080**.
(Reprinted by permission of Intel Corp., copyright 1975.)

TYPE OF MACHINE CYCLE

DATA BUS BIT	STATUS INFORMATION	INSTRUCTION FETCH ①	MEMORY READ ②	MEMORY WRITE ③	STACK READ ④	STACK WRITE ⑤	INPUT READ ⑥	OUTPUT WRITE ⑦	INTERRUPT ACKNOWLEDGE ⑧	HALT ACKNOWLEDGE ⑨	INTERRUPT ACKNOWLEDGE WHILE HALT ⑩
D_0	INTA	0	0	0	0	0	0	0	1	0	1
D_1	$\overline{WO}$	1	1	0	1	0	1	0	1	1	1
D_2	STACK	0	0	0	1	1	0	0	0	0	0
D_3	HLTA	0	0	0	0	0	0	0	0	1	1
D_4	OUT	0	0	0	0	0	0	1	0	0	0
D_5	M_1	1	0	0	0	0	0	0	1	0	1
D_6	INP	0	0	0	0	0	1	0	0	0	0
D_7	MEMR	1	1	0	1	0	0	0	0	1	0

Ⓝ STATUS WORD

Figure 4-9 Machine cycles. (Reprinted by permission of Intel Corp., copyright 1975.)

Each instruction consists of a number of *machine cycles*. A machine cycle is defined as a CPU access of memory or I/O. There can be from one to five machine cycles required for a given instruction, depending upon the functions to be performed. For example, the ROTATE ACCUMULATOR LEFT instruction requires one machine cycle, while the LOAD H AND L DIRECT instruction requires five machine cycles. At the start of a machine cycle, the CPU places a *status word* onto the data bus. Figure 4-9 shows the ten possible machine cycles and their respective status words. The method of reading and decoding the status word is discussed later in this chapter.

Each machine cycle is divided into transition states (T states). There can normally be from three to five T states in a machine cycle. For example, a MEMORY READ machine cycle requires three T states, while an INSTRUCTION FETCH machine cycle requires four, and sometimes, five T states. A T state is defined as a complete CPU clock cycle (from rising edge of $\phi 1$ to the next rising edge of $\phi 1$). There are six possible T states that can make up a machine cycle. These are shown in Figure 4-10. The exception to the maximum of five T states in a machine cycle occurs when WAIT states are inserted during an instruction.

WAIT states occur when the READY input to the **8080** is pulled LOW. The **8080** will then enter a wait mode and do nothing until the READY input goes HIGH again.

Figure 4-11 shows a basic machine cycle consisting of three necessary T states and optional states, T4 and T5, that depend on the instruction. The figure also shows that a LOW on the READY line causes one WAIT state (T_W). It also shows the action of the bus signals during the cycle. Note that the cycle shown is a WRITE cycle because $\overline{WR}$ goes LOW during T3. Ordinary READ or WRITE cycles take

STATE	ASSOCIATED ACTIVITIES
T_1	A memory address or I/O device number is placed on the Address Bus ($A_{15\text{-}0}$); status information is placed on Data Bus ($D_{7\text{-}0}$).
T_2	The CPU samples the READY and HOLD inputs and checks for halt instruction.
TW (optional)	Processor enters wait state if READY is low or if HALT instruction has been executed.
T3	An instruction byte (FETCH machine cycle), data byte (MEMORY READ, STACK READ) or interrupt instruction (INTERRUPT machine cycle) is input to the CPU from the Data Bus; or a data byte (MEMORY WRITE, STACK WRITE or OUTPUT machine cycle) is output onto the data bus.
T4 T5 (optional)	States T_4 and T_5 are available if the execution of a particular instruction requires them; if not, the CPU may skip one or both of them. T_4 and T_5 are only used for internal processor operations.

Figure 4-10 T states. (Reprinted by permission of Intel Corp., copyright 1975.)

three T states (plus any WAIT states). Instruction FETCH cycles require four or more T states: three for the μP to fetch the instruction and at least one more to decide what to do.

Figure 4-12 shows the timing for an input instruction cycle (an IN instruction or any instruction that requires a memory READ) that consists of three machine cycles with no WAIT states. The action of each signal on the bus is shown.

Figure 4-13 shows the timing for an output instruction (a WRITE or OUT instruction such as MVI M). The illustrated instruction also takes three machine cycles and ten T states.

EXAMPLE 4-3 How many machine cycles and T states does the instruction MOV M,A have? What kind of cycles are they?

Solution Table 4-1 shows this instruction takes two machine cycles and seven T states. The first machine cycle is an INSTRUCTION FETCH and the second is a memory WRITE to write the contents of the accumulator into memory.

READ or WRITE cycles require three T states so the instruction fetch requires four T states. This is the minimum number of T states for an INSTRUCTION FETCH.

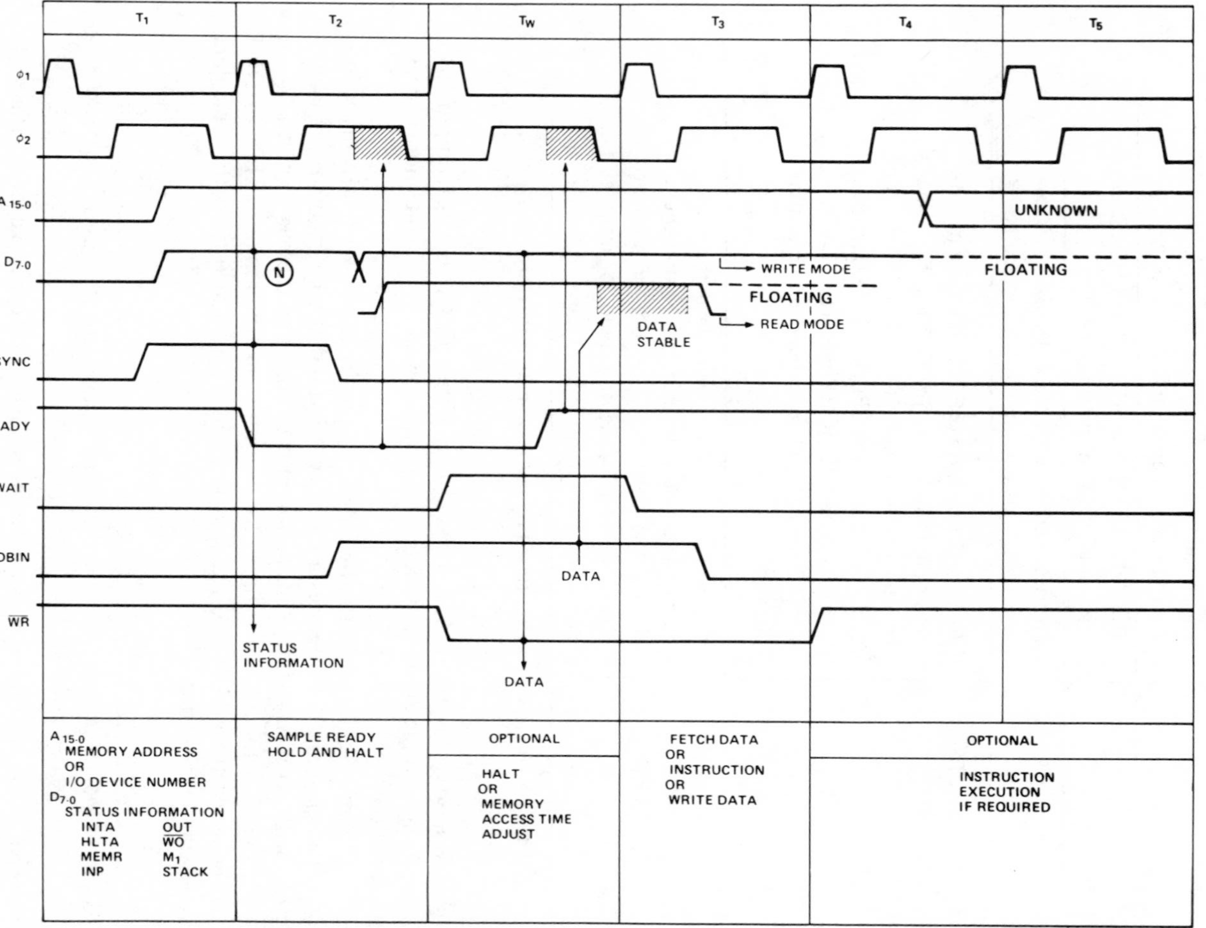

Figure 4-11 Basic **8080** instruction cycle. (Reprinted by permission of Intel Corp., copyright 1975.)

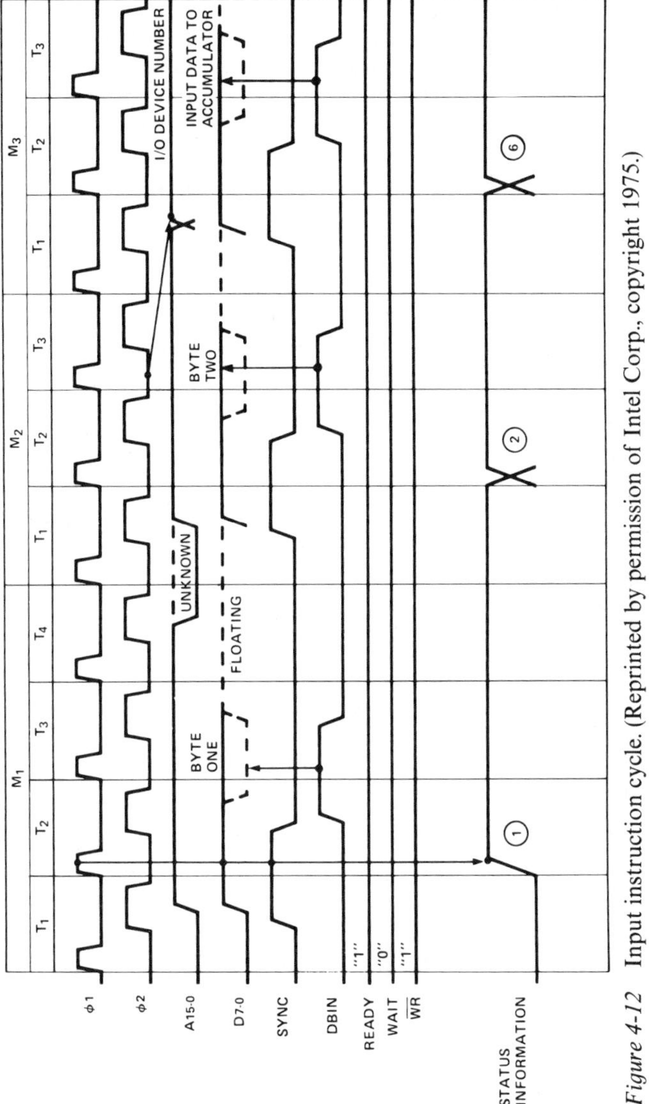

Figure 4-12 Input instruction cycle. (Reprinted by permission of Intel Corp., copyright 1975.)

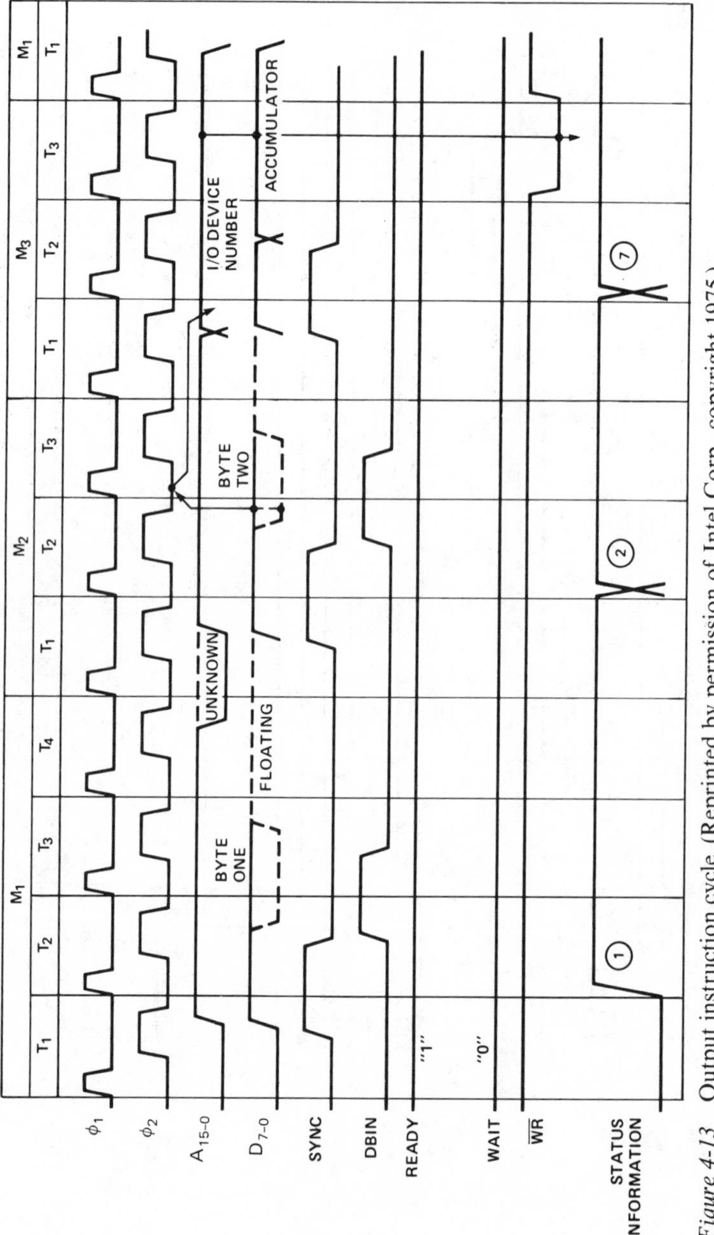

Figure 4-13 Output instruction cycle. (Reprinted by permission of Intel Corp., copyright 1975.)

4-5.3 Status Byte Decoding

At the start of each machine cycle the **8080** puts out status information on the data bus lines (see Figures 4-10 and 4-12) that indicates the operation to be performed during that cycle. The circuit in Figure 4-14 shows a simple method of status decoding to obtain the required system signals. The STSTB signal produced by the clock circuit is used to enable a **8212** octal latch. When STSTB is LOW, the CPU status is on the data bus. The latch is transparent. When STSTB goes HIGH, the status byte is latched. The outputs of the status latch are as follows:

Bit no.	*Name*	*Function*
0	INTA	INTERRUPT ACKNOWLEDGE, active HIGH is used to gate a restart vector onto the data bus when DBIN is active.
1	$\overline{\text{WO}}$	WRITE or OUTPUT, active LOW indicates the current machine cycle will be a WRITE memory or output function. When HIGH the cycle will be a READ memory or input operation.
2	STACK	Indicates the address bus contains the stack pointer value.
3	HLTA	HALT ACKNOWLEDGE, active HIGH indicates response to the HALT instruction.
4	OUT	Active HIGH indicates the address bus contains the address of an output device and the data to be output will be on the data bus when the WR signal goes LOW.
5	M1	Active HIGH indicates the CPU is fetching the first byte of an instruction (Op code fetch).
6	INP	Active HIGH indicates the address bus contains the address of an input device and the data to be input should be on the bus when DBIN goes active.
7	MEMR	Active HIGH indicates the data bus will be used to read memory.

The NAND gates shown in Figure 4-14 on the output of the **8212** are used to decode the five major signals needed for system interface. Those signals are as follows:

$\overline{\text{INTA}}$	INTERRUPT ACKNOWLEDGE
$\overline{\text{I/O RD}}$	INPUT PORT READ
$\overline{\text{MEM RD}}$	MEMORY READ
$\overline{\text{I/O WR}}$	OUTPUT PORT WRITE
$\overline{\text{MEM WR}}$	MEMORY WRITE

All the signals above are active LOW.

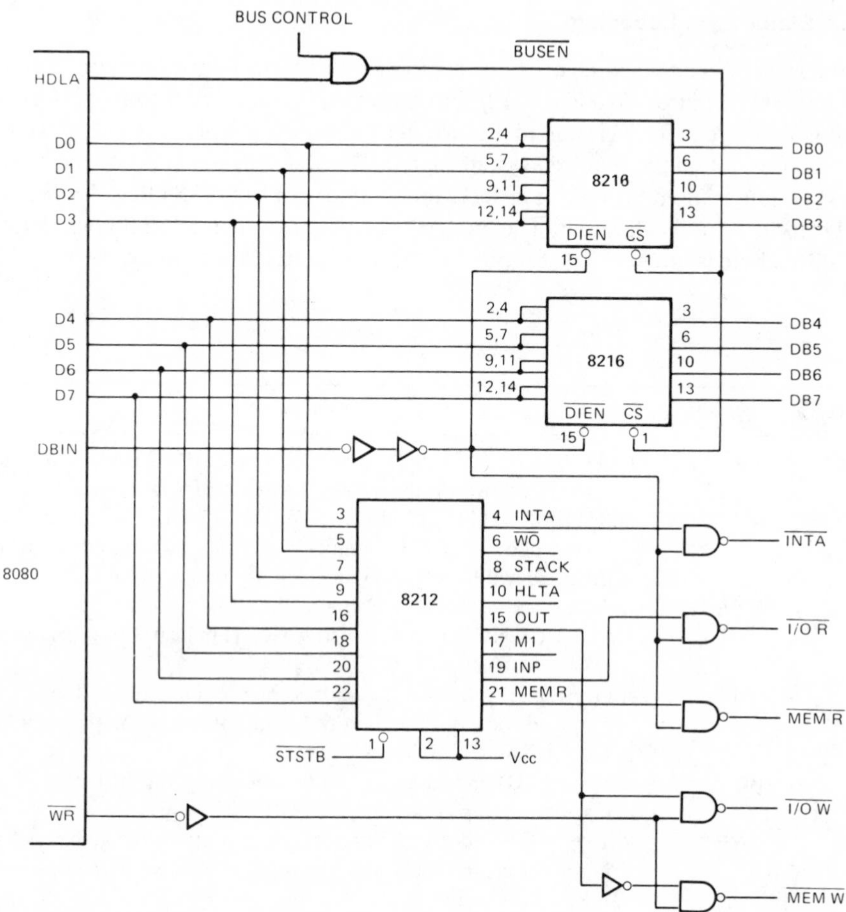

Figure 4-14 **8080** system control. Courtesy of Intel, Inc.

EXAMPLE 4-4 What happens when an IN 35 instruction is executed?

Solution During the third machine cycle of the IN instruction, the number 35 is placed on the address bus (both on address lines 0–7, and on address lines 8–15), and the $\overline{\text{I/O RD}}$ signal goes LOW. This commands I/O device #35 to send a byte to the **8080**, where it is placed in the accumulator. OUT instructions operate similarly, except that the contents of the accumulator are sent to the addressed port and then to the specified I/O device.

The $\overline{\text{BUSEN}}$ signal, shown in Figure 4-14, is used when direct memory access (DMA) is required. When $\overline{\text{BUSEN}}$ is LOW, the data bus and control signals are enabled to the rest of the system. If $\overline{\text{BUSEN}}$ goes HIGH, the data bus and control signals will go tri-state to the rest of the system, thereby allowing an external device to access the memory. The $\overline{\text{BUSEN}}$ signal must be gated by the HLDA signal from the CPU, which indicates the CPU is responding to a HOLD request. If the address bus is buffered, then the buffer devices must also go tri-state. The device that buffers the data lines from the CPU to the rest of the system should not be a standard TTL device. The **8080** data lines require an input high-level voltage of 3.3 V minimum. Most TTL devices have specifications that allow the output high-level voltage to be 2.4 to 2.8 V maximum. A solution to this problem is to use a part Intel specifically designed for this requirement, the **8216**. The **8216** is a 4-bit bidirectional bus driver that has output drive of 50 mA and on the CPU side has an output high level of 3.65 V minimum. Figure 4-14 illustrates the interface of two **8216**s to the CPU.

4-5.4 Instruction Timing

The execution time of a given instruction is determined by several factors. These factors are:

1 *8080 clock frequency.* The frequency at which the **8080** μP is clocked determines the length of time required for each state of an instruction cycle.

2 *Number of clock cycle states required.* This number is determined by the number of memory READ or WRITE cycles needed to fetch or store all the information required by the instruction. The number of clock cycles required for each instruction is specified by Intel. They are listed as the execution time for each instruction in Section 4-4.

3 *Number of WAIT states inserted by hardware.* The use of either slow memory or slow I/O devices may require the insertion of WAIT state(s) into the instruction cycle. The execution time will increase one clock cycle for each WAIT state inserted.

4 *The result of a conditional branch instruction.* The execution of a conditional branch instruction will have two values, depending upon whether a branch must be taken or not. The time difference is caused by the extra memory READ cycles that are needed to fetch the branch address if it is required. The extra memory READ cycles and WRITE cycles to the stack area, when they are needed by the conditional CALL and RET instructions, will also increase execution time.

5 *The execution of a HALT instruction will stop the processor.* The processor will remain halted until either a RESET or an interrupt occurs.

EXAMPLE 4-5 An **8080** system is running at a clock frequency of 2 MHz.

CPU clock cycle state time = 500 ns
Memory access time = 450 ns
I/O device access time = 450 ns
Number of WAIT states required = 0 (for both memory and I/O)

Find the instruction time for an IN 00 instruction.

Solution Table 4-1 (page 129) shows that the IN instruction takes three cycles and ten T states (see Figure 4-13 for its sequence of execution). The execution time would be as follows:

4 T states to fetch and decode the IN Op Code (M1)
+3 T states to read the 00 port address (M2)
+3 T states to input data from the port into the A register (M3)
=10 clock cycle states × 500 ns = 5-μs execution time

EXAMPLE 4-6 Repeat Example 4-5 when the system uses slow memory.

Clock cycle state time = 500 ns
Memory access time = 650 ns
I/O device access time = 450 ns
Number of WAIT states required = 1 (for memory operations)
= 0 (for I/O operations)

Note: If the system is designed correctly, WAIT states will be inserted only for the operations that require them. Here they will be inserted in the INSTRUCTION FETCH and READ cycles (M1 and M2) of the IN instruction. The third cycle (M3) is an input cycle that does not require a memory reference.

Solution For the same IN 00 instruction used previously, the execution time is now:

5 T states to fetch and decode the IN Op code (M1)
+4 T states to read the 00 port address (M2)
+3 T states to input data from the port into the A register (M3)
=12 clock cycle states × 500 ns = 6-μs execution time

The number of cycles an instruction requires is important if delay loops are used in the program. The time of a delay loop is then the product of the number of cycles in the loop and the number of times the loop is traversed.

4-5.5 System Control Devices

The **8224** and **8228** are integrated circuits that combine many of the functions that previously required many more ICs to accomplish. The **8224** accepts a crystal input and generates the high-level two-phase clock required by the **8080**. With the addition of a resistor and capacitor, it also provides power on reset. The **8224** also generates the synchronized $\overline{\text{STSTB}}$ and READY signals required by the CPU and the rest of the system. The interface of the **8224** to an **8080** is shown in Figure 4-15.

The **8228** is also shown in Figure 4-15. It combines the functions of status byte decoding and bidirectional data bus driver in one package. It uses the $\overline{\text{STSTB}}$ signal generated by the clock generator for status byte synchronization. It also allows for the use of multiple byte instructions (e.g., CALL) for INTERRUPT ACKNOWLEDGE. The **8228** can sink 10 mA or source −1 mA onto the data bus and timing specifications for the device are given for load capacitances of 100 pF. If the system being designed only requires one interrupt, then the interrupt ACK (INTA) pin of the **8228** should be tied to +12 V through a 1000-Ω resistor. This causes the **8228** to place a RST 7 instruction on the data lines to the processor when it requests an INTERRUPT ACKNOWLEDGE.

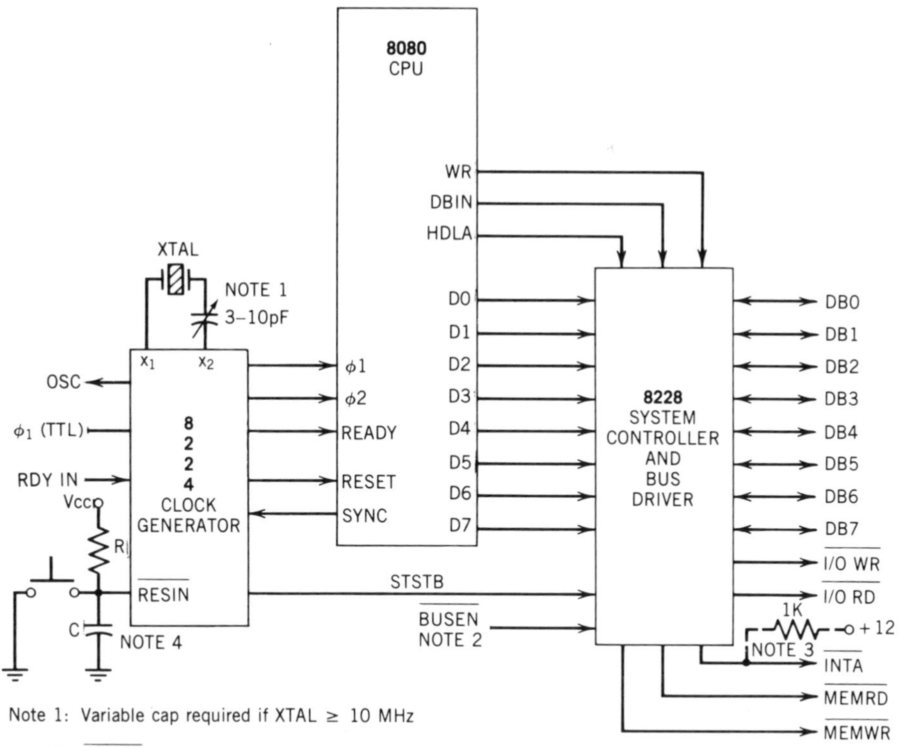

Note 1: Variable cap required if XTAL ≥ 10 MHz

Note 2: $\overline{\text{BUSEN}}$ signal required for DMA.
If DMA is not used tie $\overline{\text{BUSEN}}$ to GND

Note 3: Tying $\overline{\text{INTA}}$ to + 12 V through a 1K resistor forces a RST 7 code into the **8080** for every $\overline{\text{INTA}}$. Use for a system that only needs one interrupt.

Note 4: R and C values must cause reset to **8080** to be at least 3 clock cycles long.

Figure 4-15 Using the **8224** and **8228** to clock the **8080** and develop its signals.

4-5.6 RESET Signal

The generation of a reliable RESET signal to the **8080** is very important. The R-C system, shown in Figure 4-15 for use with an **8224**, is good enough for most cases. When using linear power supplies, however, a momentary loss of line voltage can cause the logic power to sag below the minimum operating voltage specifications for parts of the system, but still not trip the RESET circuit. In most cases, a momentary sag in logic voltage will cause the RAM memory to become scrambled, which destroys any program or stack information stored in the RAM. The circuit shown in Figure 4-16 is an example of a method for detecting these momentary power sags and forcing a RESET. The U1 circuits are comparators that compare the power supply voltage to the proper voltage and generate a $\overline{\text{RESET}}$ signal when a problem

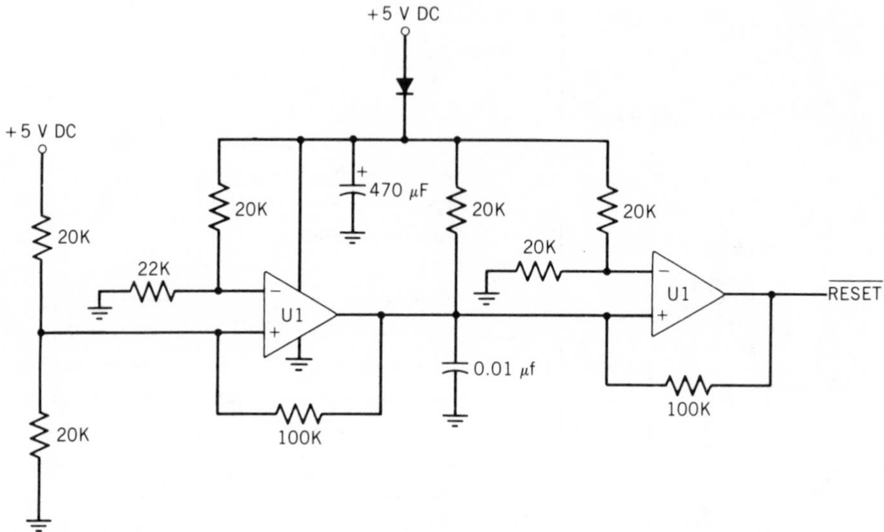

Figure 4-16 A circuit for detecting an under-voltage condition for resetting the **8080**.

occurs. These should be low power comparators, such as the LM393, because they must operate off the stored energy in the capacitor when power goes down.

The use of switching power supplies will help alleviate the power problem, since most of them hold the DC voltage level for some time period after line voltage is removed. This feature should allow the system to continue operating despite momentary losses of power.

Another feature of some switching power supplies is an output signal that indicates that the AC line power has been removed and the logic voltage will fail shortly. This signal can be used, through an interrupt, to inform the CPU of an imminent power loss so that the CPU can perform certain tasks, such as turning off motors, before the power actually fails. The output signal can also be used to force a RESET to occur.

4-6 MEMORY INTERFACE

Any TTL compatible memory devices can be interfaced to an **8080**. The memory access time and the CPU clock frequency will determine if, and how many, WAIT states are needed. Address decoding must be provided to select which memory device of several the CPU is accessing at any given time. Care must be taken when designing the address decoding so that only one device, be it memory or I/O, is able to place or accept data from the bus. Obviously, if memory such as the **2102** (a 1024 × 1-bit memory) is used, then eight devices would be selected simultaneously with each device being connected to a different line of the data bus.

The normal memory configuration of a system consists of a mixture of PROM (programmable read-only memory) and RAM (random access memory). The PROM memory is nonvolatile, so that when system power is turned off the memory does not lose the values programmed into it. RAM memory, on the other hand, will generally forget the values placed in it when power is removed. The amount of memory each provides to the total system depends upon system requirements. A computer system that is designed to do only one task, such as a car engine controller, needs only enough RAM for stack and temporary buffers. The majority of its memory will be contained in PROM because it is required to be available immediately upon the application of power. Another type of computer system, such as a word processor, will require large amounts of RAM memory to hold the text information that will have to be manipulated by the system. The word processor will still require some amount of PROM, though. The PROM is required to provide the computer with enough intelligence to enable it to get its main operating program or text information from some form of mass media and to then load it into the RAM.

A block diagram of two **2114** (1024-word × 4-bit) RAMs and two **2716** (2048-word × 8-bit) PROMs connected to an **8080** bus is shown in Figure 4-17 (page 128). The address decoding needed to select each memory is also given in the figure.

4-7 REFERENCES

Intel Corp., *Intel 8080 Microcomputer Systems User's Manual*, Santa Clara, Calif., 1975.

Intel Corp., *The 8080/8085 Microprocessor Book*, Wiley-Interscience, New York, 1980.

Kenneth L. Short, *Microprocessors and Programmed Logic*, Prentice-Hall, Englewood Cliffs, N.J., 1981.

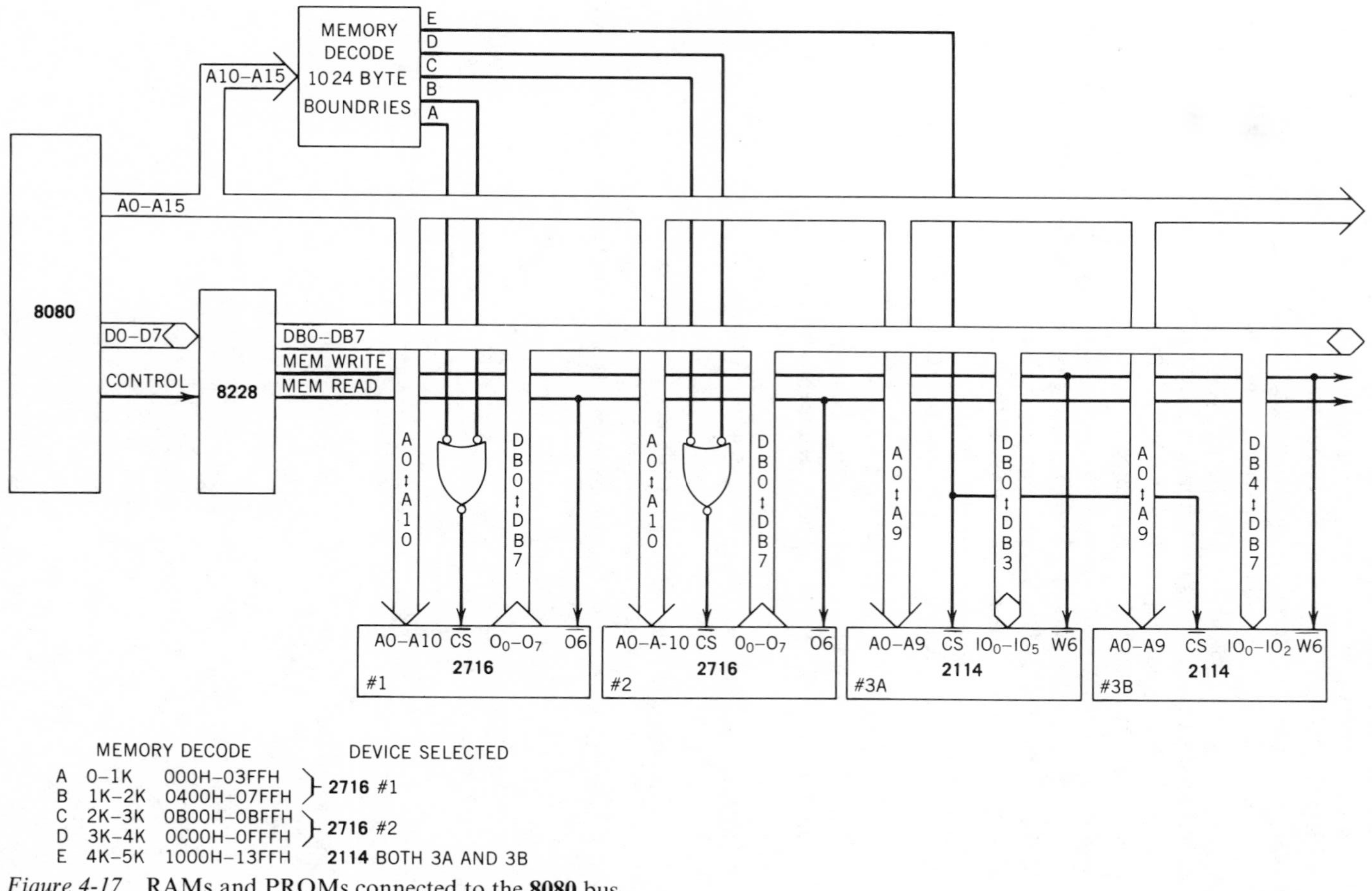

Figure 4-17 RAMs and PROMs connected to the **8080** bus.

Table 4-1 **8080 instruction set**

Data Transfer Group:

This group of instructions transfers data to and from registers and memory. **Condition flags are not affected** by any instruction in this group.

MOV r1, r2 (Move Register)

(r1) ← (r2)

The content of register r2 is moved to register r1.

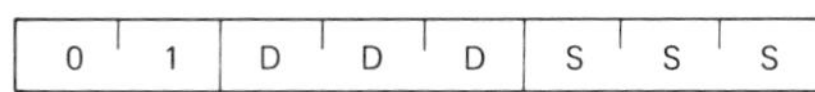

Cycles: 1
States: 5
Addressing: register
Flags: none

MOV r, M (Move from memory)

(r) ← ((H) (L))

The content of the memory location, whose address is in registers H and L, is moved to register r.

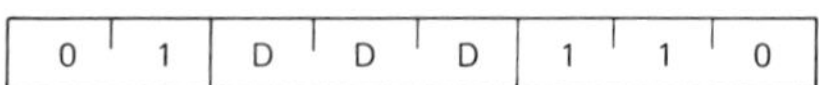

Cycles: 2
States: 7
Addressing: reg. indirect
Flags: none

MOV M, r (Move to memory)

((H) (L)) ← (r)

The content of register r is moved to the memory location whose address is in registers H and L.

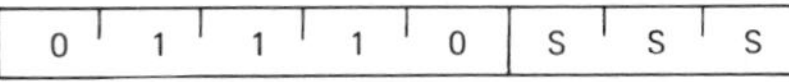

Cycles: 2
States: 7
Addressing: reg. indirect
Flags: none

MVI r, data (Move Immediate)

(r) ← (byte 2)

The content of byte 2 of the instruction is moved to register r.

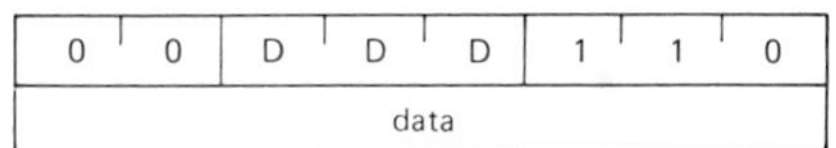

Cycles: 2
States: 7
Addressing: immediate
Flags: none

MVI M, data (Move to memory immediate)

((H) (L)) ← (byte 2)

The content of byte 2 of the instruction is moved to the memory location whose address is in registers H and L.

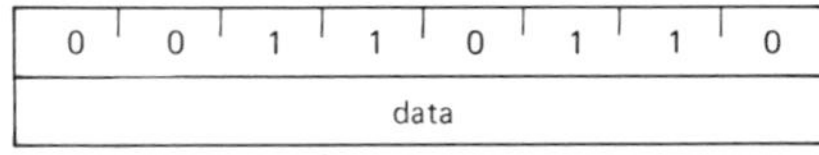

Cycles: 3
States: 10
Addressing: immed./reg. indirect
Flags: none

LXI rp, data 16 (Load register pair immediate)

(rh) ← (byte 3),

(rl) ← (byte 2)

Byte 3 of the instruction is moved into the high-order register (rh) of the register pair rp. Byte 2 of the instruction is moved into the low-order register (rl) of the register pair rp.

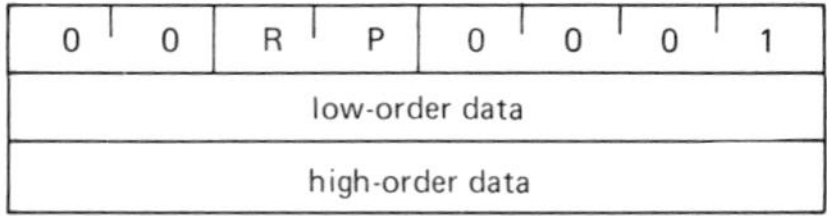

Cycles: 3
States: 10
Addressing: immediate
Flags: none

Table 4-1 (Continued)

LDA addr (Load Accumulator direct)

(A) ← ((byte 3)(byte 2))

The content of the memory location, whose address is specified in byte 2 and byte 3 of the instruction, is moved to register A.

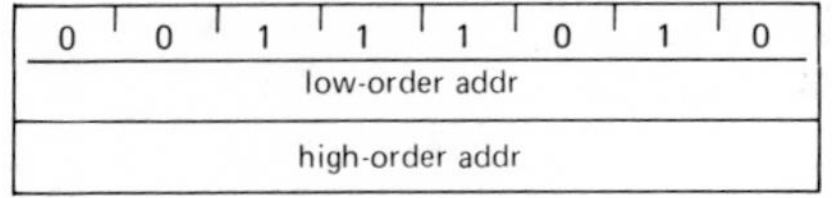

Cycles: 4
States: 13
Addressing: direct
Flags: none

STA addr (Store Accumulator direct)

((byte 3)(byte 2)) ← (A)

The content of the accumulator is moved to the memory location whose address is specified in byte 2 and byte 3 of the instruction.

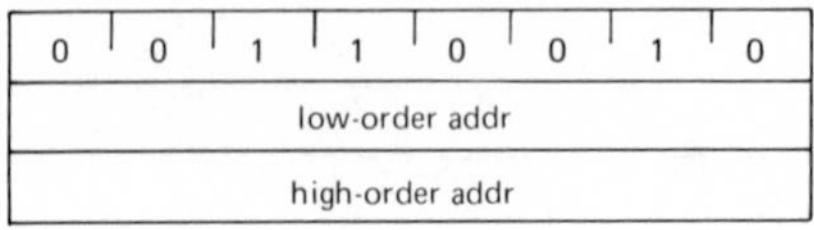

Cycles: 4
States: 13
Addressing: direct
Flags: none

LHLD addr (Load H and L direct)

(L) ← ((byte 3)(byte 2))

(H) ← ((byte 3)(byte 2) + 1)

The content of the memory location, whose address is specified in byte 2 and byte 3 of the instruction, is moved to register L. The content of the memory location at the succeeding address is moved to register H.

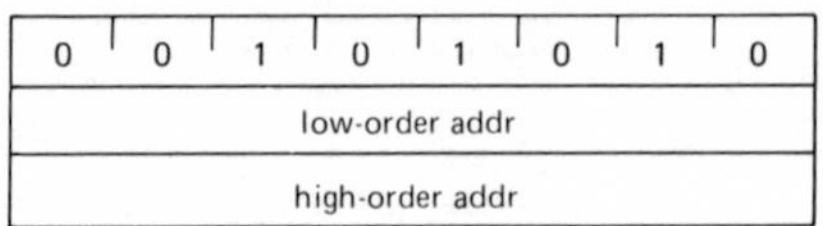

Cycles: 5
States: 16
Addressing: direct
Flags: none

SHLD addr (Store H and L direct)

((byte 3)(byte 2)) ← (L)

((byte 3)(byte 2) + 1) ← (H)

The content of register L is moved to the memory location whose address is specified in byte 2 and byte 3. The content of register H is moved to the succeeding memory location.

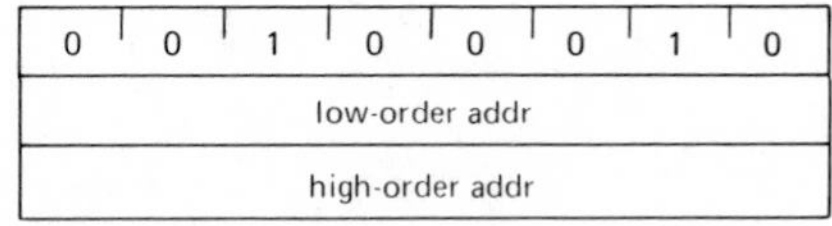

Cycles: 5
States: 16
Addressing: direct
Flags: none

LDAX rp (Load accumulator indirect)

(A) ← ((rp))

The content of the memory location, whose address is in the register pair rp, is moved to register A. Note: only register pairs rp=B (registers B and C) or rp=D (registers D and E) may be specified.

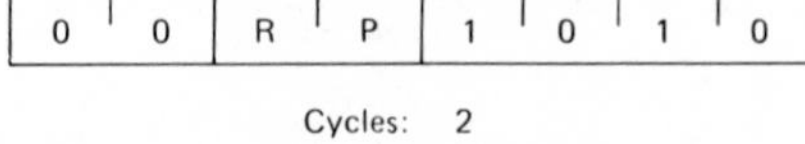

Cycles: 2
States: 7
Addressing: reg. indirect
Flags: none

STAX rp (Store accumulator indirect)

((rp)) ← (A)

The content of register A is moved to the memory location whose address is in the register pair rp. Note: only register pairs rp=B (registers B and C) or rp=D (registers D and E) may be specified.

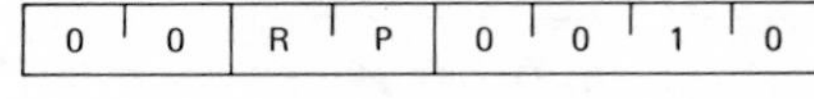

Cycles: 2
States: 7
Addressing: reg. indirect
Flags: none

XCHG (Exchange H and L with D and E)

(H) ↔ (D)

(L) ↔ (E)

The contents of registers H and L are exchanged with the contents of registers D and E.

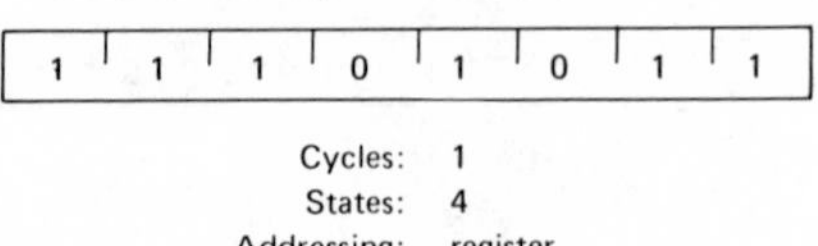

Cycles: 1
States: 4
Addressing: register
Flags: none

Table 4-1 (Continued)

Arithmetic Group:

This group of instructions performs arithmetic operations on data in registers and memory.

Unless indicated otherwise, all instructions in this group affect the Zero, Sign, Parity, Carry, and Auxiliary Carry flags according to the standard rules.

All subtraction operations are performed via two's complement arithmetic and set the carry flag to one to indicate a borrow and clear it to indicate no borrow.

ADD r (Add Register)

(A) ← (A) + (r)

The content of register r is added to the content of the accumulator. The result is placed in the accumulator.

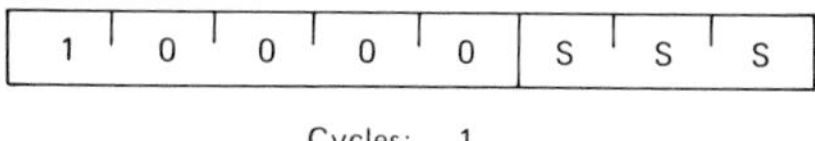

1	0	0	0	0	S	S	S

Cycles: 1
States: 4
Addressing: register
Flags: Z,S,P,CY,AC

ADD M (Add memory)

(A) ← (A) + ((H) (L))

The content of the memory location whose address is contained in the H and L registers is added to the content of the accumulator. The result is placed in the accumulator.

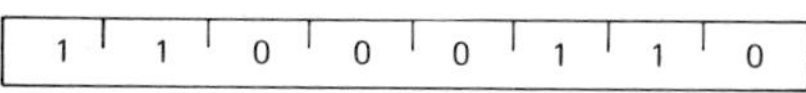

1	1	0	0	0	1	1	0

Cycles: 2
States: 7
Addressing: reg. indirect
Flags: Z,S,P,CY,AC

ADI data (Add immediate)

(A) ← (A) + (byte 2)

The content of the second byte of the instruction is added to the content of the accumulator. The result is placed in the accumulator.

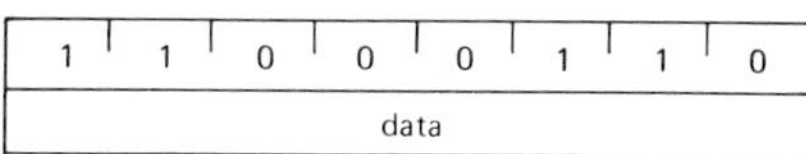

1	1	0	0	0	1	1	0
data							

Cycles: 2
States: 7
Addressing: immediate
Flags: Z,S,P,CY,AC

ADC r (Add Register with carry)

(A) ← (A) + (r) + (CY)

The content of register r and the content of the carry bit are added to the content of the accumulator. The result is placed in the accumulator.

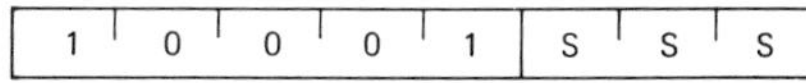

1	0	0	0	1	S	S	S

Cycles: 1
States: 4
Addressing: register
Flags: Z,S,P,CY,AC

ADC M (Add memory with carry)

(A) ← (A) + ((H) (L)) + (CY)

The content of the memory location whose address is contained in the H and L registers and the content of the CY flag are added to the accumulator. The result is placed in the accumulator.

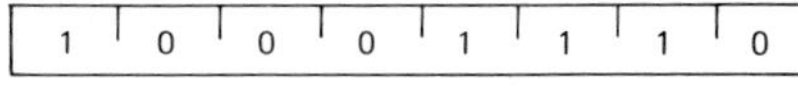

1	0	0	0	1	1	1	0

Cycles: 2
States: 7
Addressing: reg. indirect
Flags: Z,S,P,CY,AC

ACI data (Add immediate with carry)

(A) ← (A) + (byte 2) + (CY)

The content of the second byte of the instruction and the content of the CY flag are added to the contents of the accumulator. The result is placed in the accumulator.

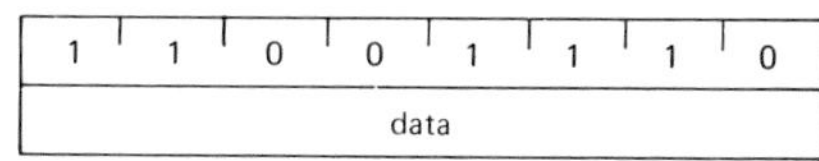

1	1	0	0	1	1	1	0
data							

Cycles: 2
States: 7
Addressing: immediate
Flags: Z,S,P,CY,AC

SUB r (Subtract Register)

(A) ← (A) − (r)

The content of register r is subtracted from the content of the accumulator. The result is placed in the accumulator.

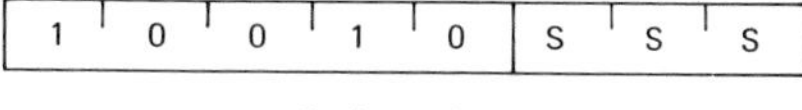

1	0	0	1	0	S	S	S

Cycles: 1
States: 4
Addressing: register
Flags: Z,S,P,CY,AC

Table 4-1 **(*Continued*)**

SUB M (Subtract memory)

(A) ← (A) – ((H) (L))

The content of the memory location whose address is contained in the H and L registers is subtracted from the content of the accumulator. The result is placed in the accumulator.

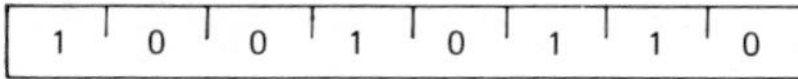

Cycles: 2
States: 7
Addressing: reg. indirect
Flags: Z,S,P,CY,AC

SUI data (Subtract immediate)

(A) ← (A) – (byte 2)

The content of the second byte of the instruction is subtracted from the content of the accumulator. The result is placed in the accumulator.

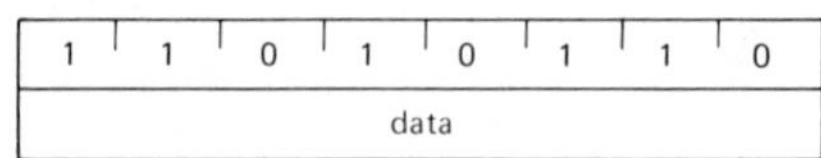

Cycles: 2
States: 7
Addressing: immediate
Flags: Z,S,P,CY,AC

SBB r (Subtract Register with borrow)

(A) ← (A) – (r) – (CY)

The content of register r and the content of the CY flag are both subtracted from the accumulator. The result is placed in the accumulator.

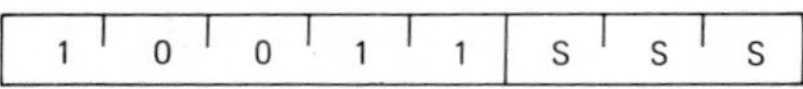

Cycles: 1
States: 4
Addressing: register
Flags: Z,S,P,CY,AC

SBB M (Subtract memory with borrow)

(A) ← (A) – ((H) (L)) – (CY)

The content of the memory location whose address is contained in the H and L registers and the content of the CY flag are both subtracted from the accumulator. The result is placed in the accumulator.

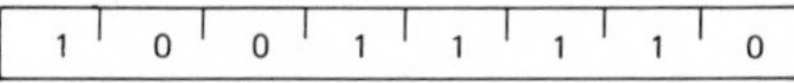

Cycles: 2
States: 7
Addressing: reg. indirect
Flags: Z,S,P,CY,AC

SBI data (Subtract immediate with borrow)

(A) ← (A) – (byte 2) – (CY)

The contents of the second byte of the instruction and the contents of the CY flag are both subtracted from the accumulator. The result is placed in the accumulator.

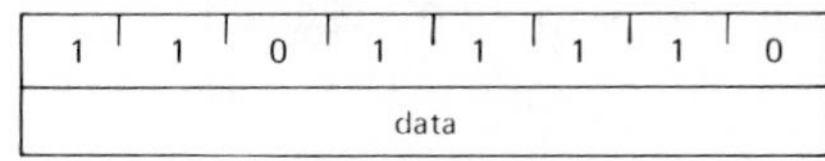

Cycles: 2
States: 7
Addressing: immediate
Flags: Z,S,P,CY,AC

INR r (Increment Register)

(r) ← (r) + 1

The content of register r is incremented by one. Note: All condition flags **except CY** are affected.

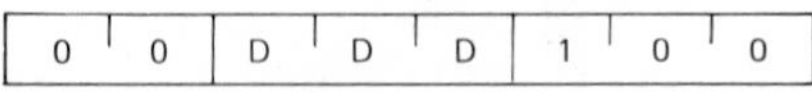

Cycles: 1
States: 5
Addressing: register
Flags: Z,S,P,AC

INR M (Increment memory)

((H) (L)) ← ((H) (L)) + 1

The content of the memory location whose address is contained in the H and L registers is incremented by one. Note: All condition flags **except CY** are affected.

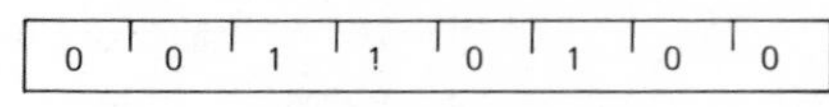

Cycles: 3
States: 10
Addressing: reg. indirect
Flags: Z,S,P,AC

DCR r (Decrement Register)

(r) ← (r) – 1

The content of register r is decremented by one. Note: All condition flags **except CY** are affected.

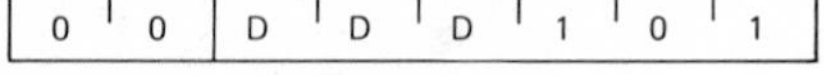

Cycles: 1
States: 5
Addressing: register
Flags: Z,S,P,AC

Table 4-1 (Continued)

DCR M (Decrement memory)

((H) (L)) ← ((H) (L)) – 1

The content of the memory location whose address is contained in the H and L registers is decremented by one. Note: All condition flags **except CY** are affected.

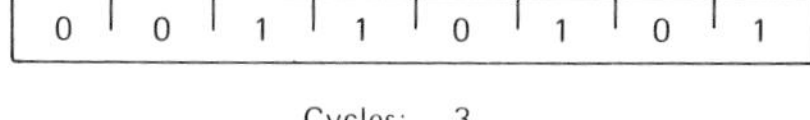

0 0 1 1 0 1 0 1

Cycles: 3
States: 10
Addressing: reg. indirect
Flags: Z,S,P,AC

INX rp (Increment register pair)

(rh) (rl) ← (rh) (rl) + 1

The content of the register pair rp is incremented by one. Note: **No condition flags are affected.**

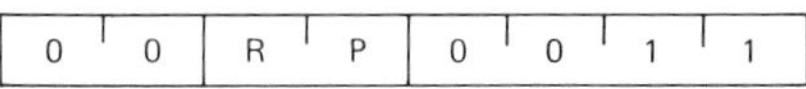

0 0 R P 0 0 1 1

Cycles: 1
States: 5
Addressing: register
Flags: none

DCX rp (Decrement register pair)

(rh) (rl) ← (rh) (rl) – 1

The content of the register pair rp is decremented by one. Note: **No condition flags are affected.**

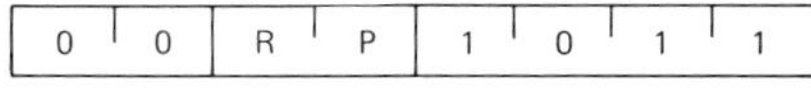

0 0 R P 1 0 1 1

Cycles: 1
States: 5
Addressing: register
Flags: none

DAD rp (Add register pair to H and L)

(H) (L) ← (H) (L) + (rh) (rl)

The content of the register pair rp is added to the content of the register pair H and L. The result is placed in the register pair H and L. Note: **Only the CY flag is affected.** It is set if there is a carry out of the double precision add; otherwise it is reset.

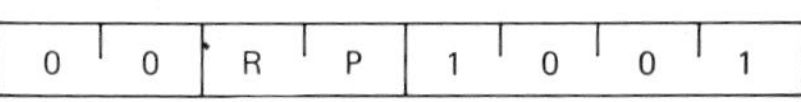

0 0 R P 1 0 0 1

Cycles: 3
States: 10
Addressing: register
Flags: CY

DAA (Decimal Adjust Accumulator)

The eight-bit number in the accumulator is adjusted to form two four-bit Binary-Coded-Decimal digits by the following process:

1. If the value of the least significant 4 bits of the accumulator is greater than 9 **or** if the AC flag is set, 6 is added to the accumulator.
2. If the value of the most significant 4 bits of the accumulator is now greater than 9, **or** if the CY flag is set, 6 is added to the most significant 4 bits of the accumulator.

NOTE: All flags are affected.

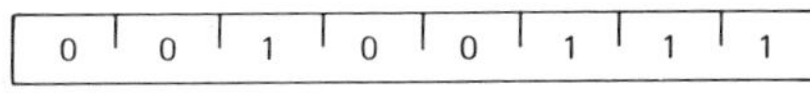

0 0 1 0 0 1 1 1

Cycles: 1
States: 4
Flags: Z,S,P,CY,AC

Logical Group:

This group of instructions performs logical (Boolean) operations on data in registers and memory and on condition flags.

Unless indicated otherwise, all instructions in this group affect the Zero, Sign, Parity, Auxiliary Carry, and Carry flags according to the standard rules.

ANA r (AND Register)

(A) ← (A) ∧ (r)

The content of register r is logically anded with the content of the accumulator. The result is placed in the accumulator. **The CY and AC flags are cleared.**

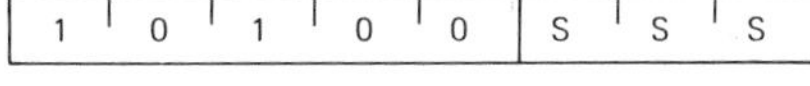

1 0 1 0 0 S S S

Cycles: 1
States: 4
Addressing: register
Flags: Z,S,P,CY,AC

ANA M (AND memory)

(A) ← (A) ∧ ((H) (L))

The contents of the memory location whose address is contained in the H and L registers is logically anded with the content of the accumulator. The result is placed in the accumulator. **The CY and AC flags are cleared.**

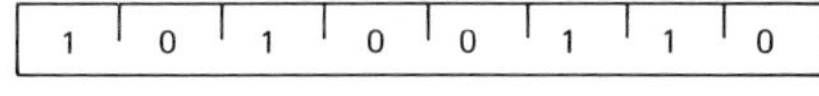

1 0 1 0 0 1 1 0

Cycles: 2
States: 7
Addressing: reg. indirect
Flags: Z,S,P,CY,AC

Table 4-1 (Continued)

ANI data (AND immediate)

$(A) \leftarrow (A) \wedge (\text{byte } 2)$

The content of the second byte of the instruction is logically anded with the contents of the accumulator. The result is placed in the accumulator. **The CY and AC flags are cleared.**

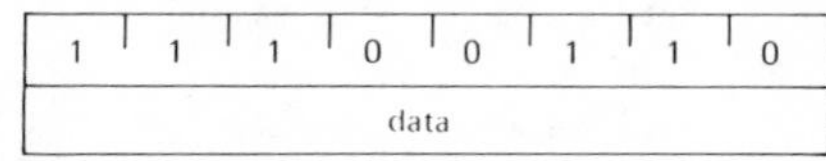

Cycles: 2
States: 7
Addressing: immediate
Flags: Z,S,P,CY,AC

XRA r (Exclusive OR Register)

$(A) \leftarrow (A) \forall (r)$

The content of register r is exclusive-or'd with the content of the accumulator. The result is placed in the accumulator. **The CY and AC flags are cleared.**

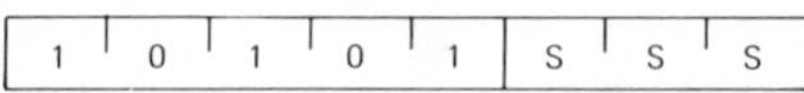

Cycles: 1
States: 4
Addressing: register
Flags: Z,S,P,CY,AC

XRA M (Exclusive OR Memory)

$(A) \leftarrow (A) \forall ((H)\ (L))$

The content of the memory location whose address is contained in the H and L registers is exclusive-OR'd with the content of the accumulator. The result is placed in the accumulator. **The CY and AC flags are cleared.**

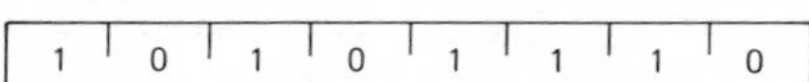

Cycles: 2
States: 7
Addressing: reg. indirect
Flags: Z,S,P,CY,AC

XRI data (Exclusive OR immediate)

$(A) \leftarrow (A) \forall (\text{byte } 2)$

The content of the second byte of the instruction is exclusive-OR'd with the content of the accumulator. The result is placed in the accumulator. **The CY and AC flags are cleared.**

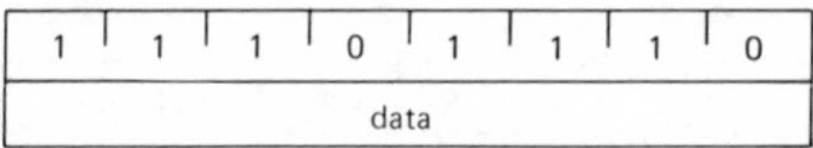

Cycles: 2
States: 7
Addressing: immediate
Flags: Z,S,P,CY,AC

ORA r (OR Register)

$(A) \leftarrow (A) \vee (r)$

The content of register r is inclusive-OR'd with the content of the accumulator. The result is placed in the accumulator. **The CY and AC flags are cleared.**

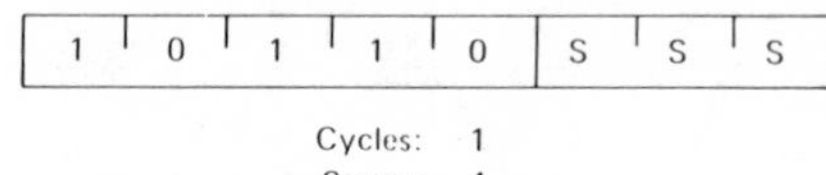

Cycles: 1
States: 4
Addressing: register
Flags: Z,S,P,CY,AC

ORA M (OR memory)

$(A) \leftarrow (A) \vee ((H)\ (L))$

The content of the memory location whose address is contained in the H and L registers is inclusive-OR'd with the content of the accumulator. The result is placed in the accumulator. **The CY and AC flags are cleared.**

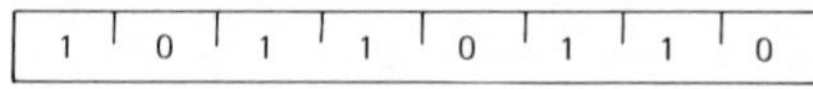

Cycles: 2
States: 7
Addressing: reg. indirect
Flags: Z,S,P,CY,AC

ORI data (OR Immediate)

$(A) \leftarrow (A) \vee (\text{byte } 2)$

The content of the second byte of the instruction is inclusive-OR'd with the content of the accumulator. The result is placed in the accumulator. **The CY and AC flags are cleared.**

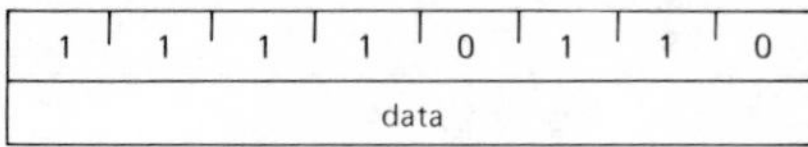

Cycles: 2
States: 7
Addressing: immediate
Flags: Z,S,P,CY,AC

CMP r (Compare Register)

$(A) - (r)$

The content of register r is subtracted from the accumulator. The accumulator remains unchanged. The condition flags are set as a result of the subtraction. **The Z flag is set to 1 if $(A) = (r)$. The CY flag is set to 1 if $(A) < (r)$.**

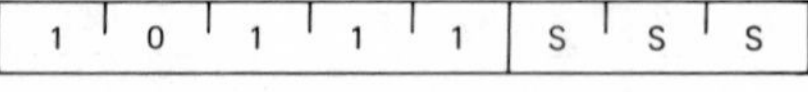

Cycles: 1
States: 4
Addressing: register
Flags: Z,S,P,CY,AC

Table 4-1 (Continued)

CMP M (Compare memory)

(A) – ((H) (L))

The content of the memory location whose address is contained in the H and L registers is subtracted from the accumulator. The accumulator remains unchanged. The condition flags are set as a result of the subtraction. The Z flag is set to 1 if (A) = ((H) (L)). The CY flag is set to 1 if (A) < ((H) (L)).

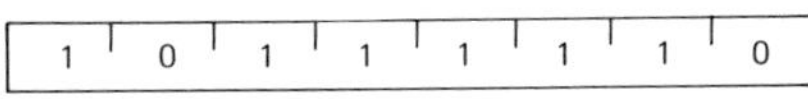

Cycles: 2
States: 7
Addressing: reg. indirect
Flags: Z,S,P,CY,AC

CPI data (Compare immediate)

(A) – (byte 2)

The content of the second byte of the instruction is subtracted from the accumulator. The condition flags are set by the result of the subtraction. The Z flag is set to 1 if (A) = (byte 2). The CY flag is set to 1 if (A) < (byte 2).

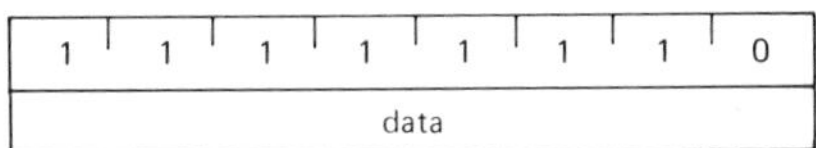

Cycles: 2
States: 7
Addressing: immediate
Flags: Z,S,P,CY,AC

RLC (Rotate left)

$(A_{n+1}) \leftarrow (A_n)$; $(A_0) \leftarrow (A_7)$

$(CY) \leftarrow (A_7)$

The content of the accumulator is rotated left one position. The low order bit and the CY flag are both set to the value shifted out of the high order bit position. **Only the CY flag is affected.**

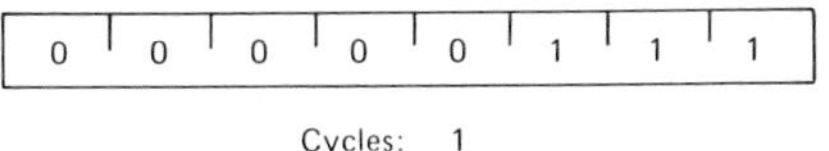

Cycles: 1
States: 1
Flags: CY

RRC (Rotate right)

$(A_n) \leftarrow (A_{n-1})$; $(A_7) \leftarrow (A_0)$

$(CY) \leftarrow (A_0)$

The content of the accumulator is rotated right one position. The high order bit and the CY flag are both set to the value shifted out of the low order bit position. **Only the CY flag is affected.**

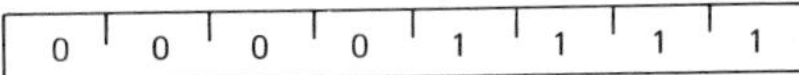

Cycles: 1
States: 4
Flags: CY

RAL (Rotate left through carry)

$(A_{n+1}) \leftarrow (A_n)$; $(CY) \leftarrow (A_7)$

$(A_0) \leftarrow (CY)$

The content of the accumulator is rotated left one position through the CY flag. The low order bit is set equal to the CY flag and the CY flag is set to the value shifted out of the high order bit. **Only the CY flag is affected.**

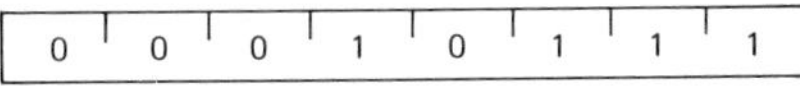

Cycles: 1
States: 4
Flags: CY

RAR (Rotate right through carry)

$(A_n) \leftarrow (A_{n+1})$; $(CY) \leftarrow (A_0)$

$(A_7) \leftarrow (CY)$

The content of the accumulator is rotated right one position through the CY flag. The high order bit is set to the CY flag and the CY flag is set to the value shifted out of the low order bit. **Only the CY flag is affected.**

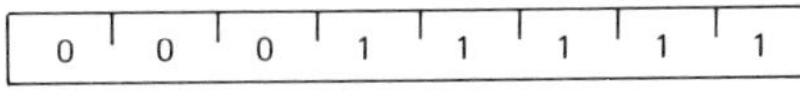

Cycles: 1
States: 4
Flags: CY

CMA (Complement accumulator)

$(A) \leftarrow (\overline{A})$

The contents of the accumulator are complemented (zero bits become 1, one bits become 0). **No flags are affected.**

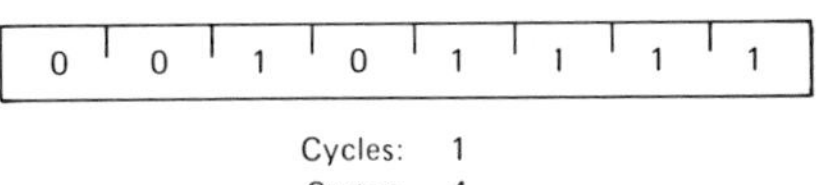

Cycles: 1
States: 4
Flags: none

Table 4-1 (Continued)

CMC (Complement carry)

The CY flag is complemented. **No other flags are affected.**

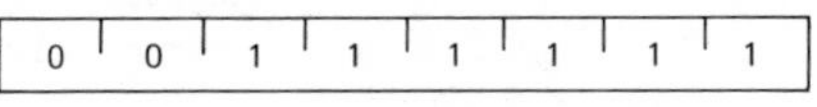

Cycles: 1
States: 4
Flags: CY

STC (Set carry)

(CY) ← 1

The CY flag is set to 1. **No other flags are affected.**

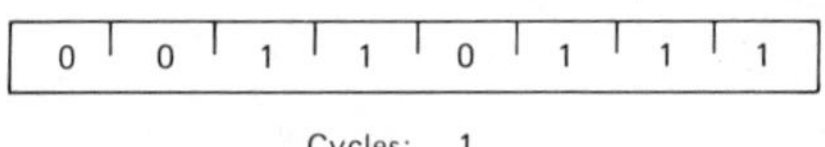

Cycles: 1
States: 4
Flags: CY

Branch Group:

This group of instructions alter normal sequential program flow.

Condition flags are not affected by any instruction in this group.

The two types of branch instructions are unconditional and conditional. Unconditional transfers simply perform the specified operation on register PC (the program counter). Conditional transfers examine the status of one of the four processor flags to determine if the specified branch is to be executed. The conditions that may be specified are as follows:

CONDITION		CCC
NZ	– not zero (Z = 0)	000
Z	– zero (Z = 1)	001
NC	– no carry (CY = 0)	010
C	– carry (CY = 1)	011
PO	– parity odd (P = 0)	100
PE	– parity even (P = 1)	101
P	– plus (S = 0)	110
M	– minus (S = 1)	111

JMP addr (Jump)

(PC) ← (byte 3) (byte 2)

Control is transferred to the instruction whose address is specified in byte 3 and byte 2 of the current instruction.

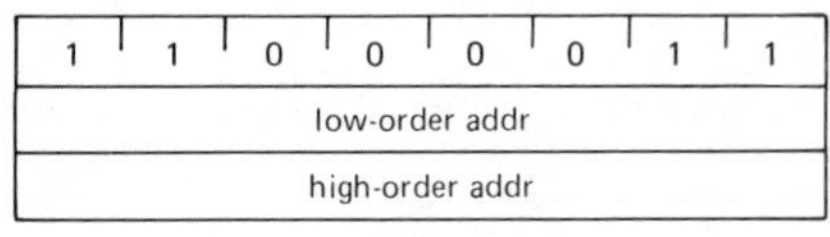

Cycles: 3
States: 10
Addressing: immediate
Flags: none

Jcondition addr (Conditional jump)

If (CCC),

(PC) ← (byte 3) (byte 2)

If the specified condition is true, control is transferred to the instruction whose address is specified in byte 3 and byte 2 of the current instruction; otherwise, control continues sequentially.

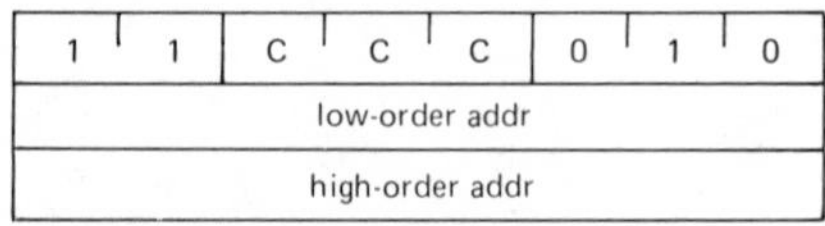

Cycles: 3
States: 10
Addressing: immediate
Flags: none

CALL addr (Call)

((SP) – 1) ← (PCH)
((SP) – 2) ← (PCL)
(SP) ← (SP) – 2
(PC) ← (byte 3) (byte 2)

The high-order eight bits of the next instruction address are moved to the memory location whose address is one less than the content of register SP. The low-order eight bits of the next instruction address are moved to the memory location whose address is two less than the content of register SP. The content of register SP is decremented by 2. Control is transferred to the instruction whose address is specified in byte 3 and byte 2 of the current instruction.

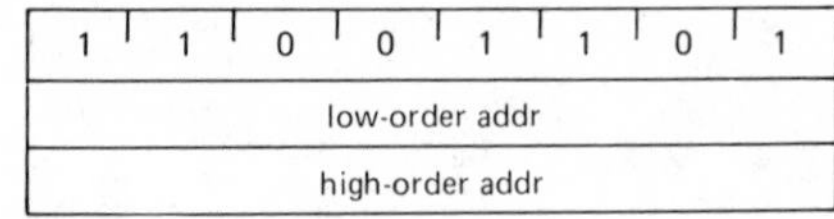

Cycles: 5
States: 17
Addressing: immediate/reg. indirect
Flags: none

Table 4-1 (Continued)

Ccondition addr (Condition call)

If (CCC),
((SP) − 1) ← (PCH)
((SP) − 2) ← (PCL)
(SP) ← (SP) − 2
(PC) ← (byte 3) (byte 2)

If the specified condition is true, the actions specified in the CALL instruction (see above) are performed; otherwise, control continues sequentially.

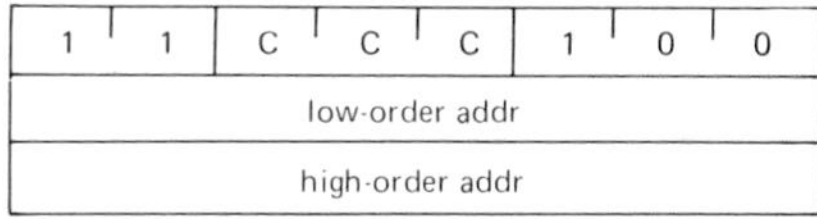

Cycles: 3/5
States: 11/17
Addressing: immediate/reg. indirect
Flags: none

RET (Return)

(PCL) ← ((SP));
(PCH) ← ((SP) + 1);
(SP) ← (SP) + 2;

The content of the memory location whose address is specified in register SP is moved to the low-order eight bits of register PC. The content of the memory location whose address is one more than the content of register SP is moved to the high-order eight bits of register PC. The content of register SP is incremented by 2.

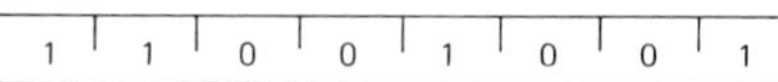

Cycles: 3
States: 10
Addressing: reg. indirect
Flags: none

Rcondition (Conditional return)

If (CCC),
(PCL) ← ((SP))
(PCH) ← ((SP) + 1)
(SP) ← (SP) + 2

If the specified condition is true, the actions specified in the RET instruction (see above) are performed; otherwise, control continues sequentially.

1	1	C	C	C	0	0	0

Cycles: 1/3
States: 5/11
Addressing: reg. indirect
Flags: none

RST n (Restart)

((SP) − 1) ← (PCH)
((SP) − 2) ← (PCL)
(SP) ← (SP) − 2
(PC) ← 8 * (NNN)

The high-order eight bits of the next instruction address are moved to the memory location whose address is one less than the content of register SP. The low-order eight bits of the next instruction address are moved to the memory location whose address is two less than the content of register SP. The content of register SP is decremented by two. Control is transferred to the instruction whose address is eight times the content of NNN.

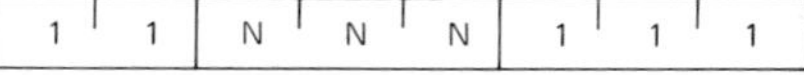

Cycles: 3
States: 11
Addressing: reg. indirect
Flags: none

15	14	13	12	11	10	9	8	7	6	5	4	3	2	1	0
0	0	0	0	0	0	0	0	0	0	N	N	N	0	0	0

Program Counter After Restart

PCHL (Jump H and L indirect – move H and L to PC)

(PCH) ← (H)
(PCL) ← (L)

The content of register H is moved to the high-order eight bits of register PC. The content of register L is moved to the low-order eight bits of register PC.

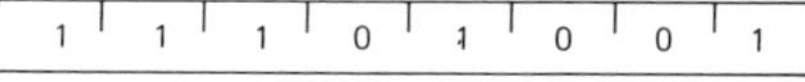

Cycles: 1
States: 5
Addressing: register
Flags: none

Table 4-1 (Continued)

Stack, I/O, and Machine Control Group:

This group of instructions performs I/O, manipulates the Stack, and alters internal control flags.

Unless otherwise specified, **condition flags are not affected by any instructions in this group.**

FLAG WORD

D_7	D_6	D_5	D_4	D_3	D_2	D_1	D_0
S	Z	0	AC	0	P	1	CY

PUSH rp (Push)

((SP) − 1) ← (rh)
((SP) − 2) ← (rl)
(SP) ← (SP) − 2

The content of the high-order register of register pair rp is moved to the memory location whose address is one less than the content of register SP. The content of the low-order register of register pair rp is moved to the memory location whose address is two less than the content of register SP. The content of register SP is decremented by 2. **Note: Register pair rp = SP may not be specified.**

1	1	R	P	0	1	0	1

Cycles: 3
States: 11
Addressing: reg. indirect
Flags: none

PUSH PSW (Push processor status word)

((SP) − 1) ← (A)
$((SP) - 2)_0$ ← (CY) , $((SP) - 2)_1$ ← 1
$((SP) - 2)_2$ ← (P) , $((SP) - 2)_3$ ← 0
$((SP) - 2)_4$ ← (AC) , $((SP) - 2)_5$ ← 0
$((SP) - 2)_6$ ← (Z) , $((SP) - 2)_7$ ← (S)
(SP) ← (SP) − 2

The content of register A is moved to the memory location whose address is one less than register SP. The contents of the condition flags are assembled into a processor status word and the word is moved to the memory location whose address is two less than the content of register SP. The content of register SP is decremented by two.

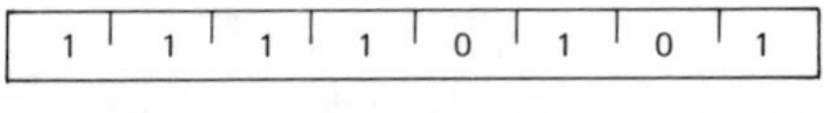

1	1	1	1	0	1	0	1

Cycles: 3
States: 11
Addressing: reg. indirect
Flags: none

POP rp (Pop)

(rl) ← ((SP))
(rh) ← ((SP) + 1)
(SP) ← (SP) + 2

The content of the memory location, whose address is specified by the content of register SP, is moved to the low-order register of register pair rp. The content of the memory location, whose address is one more than the content of register SP, is moved to the high-order register of register pair rp. The content of register SP is incremented by 2. **Note: Register pair rp = SP may not be specified.**

1	1	R	P	0	0	0	1

Cycles: 3
States: 10
Addressing: reg. indirect
Flags: none

POP PSW (Pop processor status word)

(CY) ← $((SP))_0$
(P) ← $((SP))_2$
(AC) ← $((SP))_4$
(Z) ← $((SP))_6$
(S) ← $((SP))_7$
(A) ← ((SP) + 1)
(SP) ← (SP) + 2

The content of the memory location whose address is specified by the content of register SP is used to restore the condition flags. The content of the memory location whose address is one more than the content of register SP is moved to register A. The content of register SP is incremented by 2.

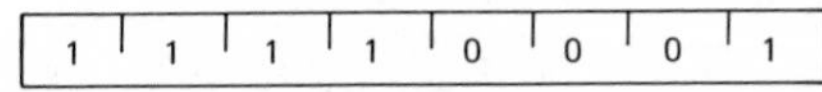

1	1	1	1	0	0	0	1

Cycles: 3
States: 10
Addressing: reg. indirect
Flags: Z,S,P,CY,AC

Table 4-1 (Continued)

XTHL (Exchange stack top with H and L)

(L) ↔ ((SP))

(H) ↔ ((SP) + 1)

The content of the L register is exchanged with the content of the memory location whose address is specified by the content of register SP. The content of the H register is exchanged with the content of the memory location whose address is one more than the content of register SP.

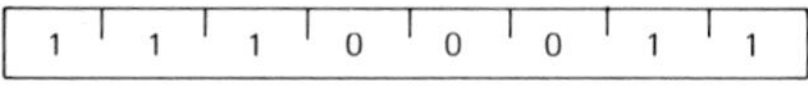

1	1	1	0	0	0	1	1

Cycles: 5
States: 18
Addressing: reg. indirect
Flags: none

SPHL (Move HL to SP)

(SP) ← (H) (L)

The contents of registers H and L (16 bits) are moved to register SP.

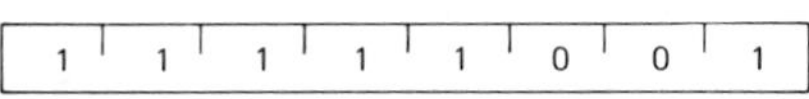

1	1	1	1	1	0	0	1

Cycles: 1
States: 5
Addressing: register
Flags: none

IN port (Input)

(A) ← (data)

The data placed on the eight bit bi-directional data bus by the specified port is moved to register A.

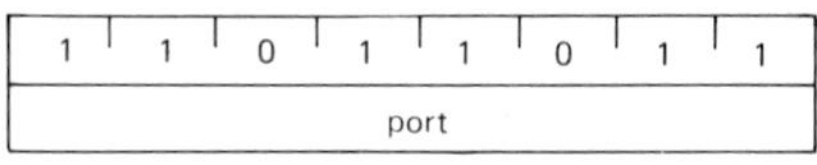

1	1	0	1	1	0	1	1
port							

Cycles: 3
States: 10
Addressing: direct
Flags: none

OUT port (Output)

(data) ← (A)

The content of register A is placed on the eight bit bi-directional data bus for transmission to the specified port.

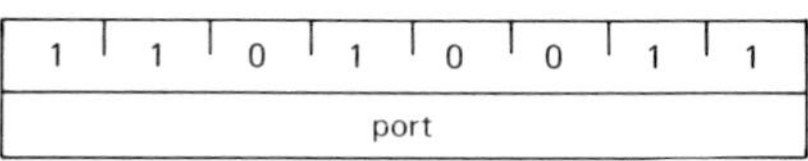

1	1	0	1	0	0	1	1
port							

Cycles: 3
States: 10
Addressing: direct
Flags: none

EI (Enable interrupts)

The interrupt system is enabled **following the execution of the next instruction.**

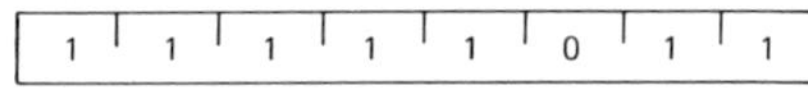

1	1	1	1	1	0	1	1

Cycles: 1
States: 4
Flags: none

DI (Disable interrupts)

The interrupt system is disabled **immediately following the execution of the DI instruction.**

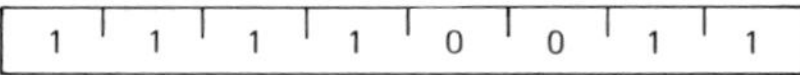

1	1	1	1	0	0	1	1

Cycles: 1
States: 4
Flags: none

HLT (Halt)

The processor is stopped. The registers and flags are unaffected.

0	1	1	1	0	1	1	0

Cycles: 1
States: 7
Flags: none

NOP (No op)

No operation is performed. The registers and flags are unaffected.

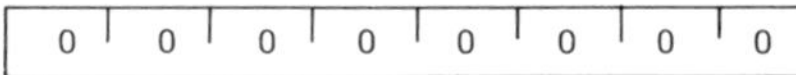

0	0	0	0	0	0	0	0

Cycles: 1
States: 4
Flags: none

Table 4-1 (Continued)

INSTRUCTION SET

Summary of Processor Instructions

Mnemonic	Description	Instruction Code[1] D_7	D_6	D_5	D_4	D_3	D_2	D_1	D_0	Clock[2] Cycles
MOV r1, r2	Move register to register	0	1	D	D	D	S	S	S	5
MOV M, r	Move register to memory	0	1	1	1	0	S	S	S	7
MOV r, M	Move memory to register	0	1	D	D	D	1	1	0	7
HLT	Halt	0	1	1	1	0	1	1	0	7
MVI r	Move immediate register	0	0	D	D	D	1	1	0	7
MVI M	Move immediate memory	0	0	1	1	0	1	1	0	10
INR r	Increment register	0	0	D	D	D	1	0	0	5
DCR r	Decrement register	0	0	D	D	D	1	0	1	5
INR M	Increment memory	0	0	1	1	0	1	0	0	10
DCR M	Decrement memory	0	0	1	1	0	1	0	1	10
ADD r	Add register to A	1	0	0	0	0	S	S	S	4
ADC r	Add register to A with carry	1	0	0	0	1	S	S	S	4
SUB r	Subtract register from A	1	0	0	1	0	S	S	S	4
SBB r	Subtract register from A with borrow	1	0	0	1	1	S	S	S	4
ANA r	And register with A	1	0	1	0	0	S	S	S	4
XRA r	Exclusive Or register with A	1	0	1	0	1	S	S	S	4
ORA r	Or register with A	1	0	1	1	0	S	S	S	4
CMP r	Compare register with A	1	0	1	1	1	S	S	S	4
ADD M	Add memory to A	1	0	0	0	0	1	1	0	7
ADC M	Add memory to A with carry	1	0	0	0	1	1	1	0	7
SUB M	Subtract memory from A	1	0	0	1	0	1	1	0	7
SBB M	Subtract memory from A with borrow	1	0	0	1	1	1	1	0	7
ANA M	And memory with A	1	0	1	0	0	1	1	0	7
XRA M	Exclusive Or memory with A	1	0	1	0	1	1	1	0	7
ORA M	Or memory with A	1	0	1	1	0	1	1	0	7
CMP M	Compare memory with A	1	0	1	1	1	1	1	0	7
ADI	Add immediate to A	1	1	0	0	0	1	1	0	7
ACI	Add immediate to A with carry	1	1	0	0	1	1	1	0	7
SUI	Subtract immediate from A	1	1	0	1	0	1	1	0	7
SBI	Subtract immediate from A with borrow	1	1	0	1	1	1	1	0	7
ANI	And immediate with A	1	1	1	0	0	1	1	0	7
XRI	Exclusive Or immediate with A	1	1	1	0	1	1	1	0	7
ORI	Or immediate with A	1	1	1	1	0	1	1	0	7
CPI	Compare immediate with A	1	1	1	1	1	1	1	0	7
RLC	Rotate A left	0	0	0	0	0	1	1	1	4
RRC	Rotate A right	0	0	0	0	1	1	1	1	4
RAL	Rotate A left through carry	0	0	0	1	0	1	1	1	4
RAR	Rotate A right through carry	0	0	0	1	1	1	1	1	4
JMP	Jump unconditional	1	1	0	0	0	0	1	1	10
JC	Jump on carry	1	1	0	1	1	0	1	0	10
JNC	Jump on no carry	1	1	0	1	0	0	1	0	10
JZ	Jump on zero	1	1	0	0	1	0	1	0	10
JNZ	Jump on no zero	1	1	0	0	0	0	1	0	10
JP	Jump on positive	1	1	1	1	0	0	1	0	10
JM	Jump on minus	1	1	1	1	1	0	1	0	10
JPE	Jump on parity even	1	1	1	0	1	0	1	0	10
JPO	Jump on parity odd	1	1	1	0	0	0	1	0	10
CALL	Call unconditional	1	1	0	0	1	1	0	1	17
CC	Call on carry	1	1	0	1	1	1	0	0	11/17
CNC	Call on no carry	1	1	0	1	0	1	0	0	11/17
CZ	Call on zero	1	1	0	0	1	1	0	0	11/17
CNZ	Call on no zero	1	1	0	0	0	1	0	0	11/17
CP	Call on positive	1	1	1	1	0	1	0	0	11/17
CM	Call on minus	1	1	1	1	1	1	0	0	11/17
CPE	Call on parity even	1	1	1	0	1	1	0	0	11/17
CPO	Call on parity odd	1	1	1	0	0	1	0	0	11/17
RET	Return	1	1	0	0	1	0	0	1	10
RC	Return on carry	1	1	0	1	1	0	0	0	5/11
RNC	Return on no carry	1	1	0	1	0	0	0	0	5/11
RZ	Return on zero	1	1	0	0	1	0	0	0	5/11
RNZ	Return on no zero	1	1	0	0	0	0	0	0	5/11
RP	Return on positive	1	1	1	1	0	0	0	0	5/11
RM	Return on minus	1	1	1	1	1	0	0	0	5/11
RPE	Return on parity even	1	1	1	0	1	0	0	0	5/11
RPO	Return on parity odd	1	1	1	0	0	0	0	0	5/11
RST	Restart	1	1	A	A	A	1	1	1	11
IN	Input	1	1	0	1	1	0	1	1	10
OUT	Output	1	1	0	1	0	0	1	1	10
LXI B	Load immediate register Pair B & C	0	0	0	0	0	0	0	1	10
LXI D	Load immediate register Pair D & E	0	0	0	1	0	0	0	1	10
LXI H	Load immediate register Pair H & L	0	0	1	0	0	0	0	1	10
LXI SP	Load immediate stack pointer	0	0	1	1	0	0	0	1	10
PUSH B	Push register Pair B & C on stack	1	1	0	0	0	1	0	1	11
PUSH D	Push register Pair D & E on stack	1	1	0	1	0	1	0	1	11
PUSH H	Push register Pair H & L on stack	1	1	1	0	0	1	0	1	11
PUSH PSW	Push A and Flags on stack	1	1	1	1	0	1	0	1	11
POP B	Pop register pair B & C off stack	1	1	0	0	0	0	0	1	10
POP D	Pop register pair D & E off stack	1	1	0	1	0	0	0	1	10
POP H	Pop register pair H & L off stack	1	1	1	0	0	0	0	1	10
POP PSW	Pop A and Flags off stack	1	1	1	1	0	0	0	1	10
STA	Store A direct	0	0	1	1	0	0	1	0	13
LDA	Load A direct	0	0	1	1	1	0	1	0	13
XCHG	Exchange D & E, H & L Registers	1	1	1	0	1	0	1	1	4
XTHL	Exchange top of stack, H & L	1	1	1	0	0	0	1	1	18
SPHL	H & L to stack pointer	1	1	1	1	1	0	0	1	5
PCHL	H & L to program counter	1	1	1	0	1	0	0	1	5
DAD B	Add B & C to H & L	0	0	0	0	1	0	0	1	10
DAD D	Add D & E to H & L	0	0	0	1	1	0	0	1	10
DAD H	Add H & L to H & L	0	0	1	0	1	0	0	1	10
DAD SP	Add stack pointer to H & L	0	0	1	1	1	0	0	1	10
STAX B	Store A indirect	0	0	0	0	0	0	1	0	7
STAX D	Store A indirect	0	0	0	1	0	0	1	0	7
LDAX B	Load A indirect	0	0	0	0	1	0	1	0	7
LDAX D	Load A indirect	0	0	0	1	1	0	1	0	7
INX B	Increment B & C registers	0	0	0	0	0	0	1	1	5
INX D	Increment D & E registers	0	0	0	1	0	0	1	1	5
INX H	Increment H & L registers	0	0	1	0	0	0	1	1	5
INX SP	Increment stack pointer	0	0	1	1	0	0	1	1	5
DCX B	Decrement B & C	0	0	0	0	1	0	1	1	5
DCX D	Decrement D & E	0	0	0	1	1	0	1	1	5
DCX H	Decrement H & L	0	0	1	0	1	0	1	1	5
DCX SP	Decrement stack pointer	0	0	1	1	1	0	1	1	5
CMA	Complement A	0	0	1	0	1	1	1	1	4
STC	Set carry	0	0	1	1	0	1	1	1	4
CMC	Complement carry	0	0	1	1	1	1	1	1	4
DAA	Decimal adjust A	0	0	1	0	0	1	1	1	4
SHLD	Store H & L direct	0	0	1	0	0	0	1	0	16
LHLD	Load H & L direct	0	0	1	0	1	0	1	0	16
EI	Enable Interrupts	1	1	1	1	1	0	1	1	4
DI	Disable interrupt	1	1	1	1	0	0	1	1	4
NOP	No-operation	0	0	0	0	0	0	0	0	4

NOTES: 1. DDD or SSS – 000 B – 001 C – 010 D – 011 E – 100 H – 101 L – 110 Memory – 111 A.
2. Two possible cycle times, (5/11) indicate instruction cycles dependent on condition flags.

Table 4-1 (Continued)

INSTRUCTION SET

Summary of Processor Instructions

Mnemonic	Description	Instruction Code[1] D_7	D_6	D_5	D_4	D_3	D_2	D_1	D_0	Clock[2] Cycles
MOV $_{r1, r2}$	Move register to register	0	1	D	D	D	S	S	S	5
MOV M, r	Move register to memory	0	1	1	1	0	S	S	S	7
MOV r, M	Move memory to register	0	1	D	D	D	1	1	0	7
HLT	Halt	0	1	1	1	0	1	1	0	7
MVI r	Move immediate register	0	0	D	D	D	1	1	0	7
MVI M	Move immediate memory	0	0	1	1	0	1	1	0	10
INR r	Increment register	0	0	D	D	D	1	0	0	5
DCR r	Decrement register	0	0	D	D	D	1	0	1	5
INR M	Increment memory	0	0	1	1	0	1	0	0	10
DCR M	Decrement memory	0	0	1	1	0	1	0	1	10
ADD r	Add register to A	1	0	0	0	0	S	S	S	4
ADC r	Add register to A with carry	1	0	0	0	1	S	S	S	4
SUB r	Subtract register from A	1	0	0	1	0	S	S	S	4
SBB r	Subtract register from A with borrow	1	0	0	1	1	S	S	S	4
ANA r	And register with A	1	0	1	0	0	S	S	S	4
XRA r	Exclusive Or register with A	1	0	1	0	1	S	S	S	4
ORA r	Or register with A	1	0	1	1	0	S	S	S	4
CMP r	Compare register with A	1	0	1	1	1	S	S	S	4
ADD M	Add memory to A	1	0	0	0	0	1	1	0	7
ADC M	Add memory to A with carry	1	0	0	0	1	1	1	0	7
SUB M	Subtract memory from A	1	0	0	1	0	1	1	0	7
SBB M	Subtract memory from A with borrow	1	0	0	1	1	1	1	0	7
ANA M	And memory with A	1	0	1	0	0	1	1	0	7
XRA M	Exclusive Or memory with A	1	0	1	0	1	1	1	0	7
ORA M	Or memory with A	1	0	1	1	0	1	1	0	7
CMP M	Compare memory with A	1	0	1	1	1	1	1	0	7
ADI	Add immediate to A	1	1	0	0	0	1	1	0	7
ACI	Add immediate to A with carry	1	1	0	0	1	1	1	0	7
SUI	Subtract immediate from A	1	1	0	1	0	1	1	0	7
SBI	Subtract immediate from A with borrow	1	1	0	1	1	1	1	0	7
ANI	And immediate with A	1	1	1	0	0	1	1	0	7
XRI	Exclusive Or immediate with A	1	1	1	0	1	1	1	0	7
ORI	Or immediate with A	1	1	1	1	0	1	1	0	7
CPI	Compare immediate with A	1	1	1	1	1	1	1	0	7
RLC	Rotate A left	0	0	0	0	0	1	1	1	4
RRC	Rotate A right	0	0	0	0	1	1	1	1	4
RAL	Rotate A left through carry	0	0	0	1	0	1	1	1	4
RAR	Rotate A right through carry	0	0	0	1	1	1	1	1	4
JMP	Jump unconditional	1	1	0	0	0	0	1	1	10
JC	Jump on carry	1	1	0	1	1	0	1	0	10
JNC	Jump on no carry	1	1	0	1	0	0	1	0	10
JZ	Jump on zero	1	1	0	0	1	0	1	0	10
JNZ	Jump on no zero	1	1	0	0	0	0	1	0	10
JP	Jump on positive	1	1	1	1	0	0	1	0	10
JM	Jump on minus	1	1	1	1	1	0	1	0	10
JPE	Jump on parity even	1	1	1	0	1	0	1	0	10
JPO	Jump on parity odd	1	1	1	0	0	0	1	0	10
CALL	Call unconditional	1	1	0	0	1	1	0	1	17
CC	Call on carry	1	1	0	1	1	1	0	0	11/17
CNC	Call on no carry	1	1	0	1	0	1	0	0	11/17
CZ	Call on zero	1	1	0	0	1	1	0	0	11/17
CNZ	Call on no zero	1	1	0	0	0	1	0	0	11/17
CP	Call on positive	1	1	1	1	0	1	0	0	11/17
CM	Call on minus	1	1	1	1	1	1	0	0	11/17
CPE	Call on parity even	1	1	1	0	1	1	0	0	11/17
CPO	Call on parity odd	1	1	1	0	0	1	0	0	11/17
RET	Return	1	1	0	0	1	0	0	1	10
RC	Return on carry	1	1	0	1	1	0	0	0	5/11
RNC	Return on no carry	1	1	0	1	0	0	0	0	5/11
RZ	Return on zero	1	1	0	0	1	0	0	0	5/11
RNZ	Return on no zero	1	1	0	0	0	0	0	0	5/11
RP	Return on positive	1	1	1	1	0	0	0	0	5/11
RM	Return on minus	1	1	1	1	1	0	0	0	5/11
RPE	Return on parity even	1	1	1	0	1	0	0	0	5/11
RPO	Return on parity odd	1	1	1	0	0	0	0	0	5/11
RST	Restart	1	1	A	A	A	1	1	1	11
IN	Input	1	1	0	1	1	0	1	1	10
OUT	Output	1	1	0	1	0	0	1	1	10
LXI B	Load immediate register Pair B & C	0	0	0	0	0	0	0	1	10
LXI D	Load immediate register Pair D & E	0	0	0	1	0	0	0	1	10
LXI H	Load immediate register Pair H & L	0	0	1	0	0	0	0	1	10
LXI SP	Load immediate stack pointer	0	0	1	1	0	0	0	1	10
PUSH B	Push register Pair B & C on stack	1	1	0	0	0	1	0	1	11
PUSH D	Push register Pair D & E on stack	1	1	0	1	0	1	0	1	11
PUSH H	Push register Pair H & L on stack	1	1	1	0	0	1	0	1	11
PUSH PSW	Push A and Flags on stack	1	1	1	1	0	1	0	1	11
POP B	Pop register pair B & C off stack	1	1	0	0	0	0	0	1	10
POP D	Pop register pair D & E off stack	1	1	0	1	0	0	0	1	10
POP H	Pop register pair H & L off stack	1	1	1	0	0	0	0	1	10
POP PSW	Pop A and Flags off stack	1	1	1	1	0	0	0	1	10
STA	Store A direct	0	0	1	1	0	0	1	0	13
LDA	Load A direct	0	0	1	1	1	0	1	0	13
XCHG	Exchange D & E, H & L Registers	1	1	1	0	1	0	1	1	4
XTHL	Exchange top of stack, H & L	1	1	1	0	0	0	1	1	18
SPHL	H & L to stack pointer	1	1	1	1	1	0	0	1	5
PCHL	H & L to program counter	1	1	1	0	1	0	0	1	5
DAD B	Add B & C to H & L	0	0	0	0	1	0	0	1	10
DAD D	Add D & E to H & L	0	0	0	1	1	0	0	1	10
DAD H	Add H & L to H & L	0	0	1	0	1	0	0	1	10
DAD SP	Add stack pointer to H & L	0	0	1	1	1	0	0	1	10
STAX B	Store A indirect	0	0	0	0	0	0	1	0	7
STAX D	Store A indirect	0	0	0	1	0	0	1	0	7
LDAX B	Load A indirect	0	0	0	0	1	0	1	0	7
LDAX D	Load A indirect	0	0	0	1	1	0	1	0	7
INX B	Increment B & C registers	0	0	0	0	0	0	1	1	5
INX D	Increment D & E registers	0	0	0	1	0	0	1	1	5
INX H	Increment H & L registers	0	0	1	0	0	0	1	1	5
INX SP	Increment stack pointer	0	0	1	1	0	0	1	1	5
DCX B	Decrement B & C	0	0	0	0	1	0	1	1	5
DCX D	Decrement D & E	0	0	0	1	1	0	1	1	5
DCX H	Decrement H & L	0	0	1	0	1	0	1	1	5
DCX SP	Decrement stack pointer	0	0	1	1	1	0	1	1	5
CMA	Complement A	0	0	1	0	1	1	1	1	4
STC	Set carry	0	0	1	1	0	1	1	1	4
CMC	Complement carry	0	0	1	1	1	1	1	1	4
DAA	Decimal adjust A	0	0	1	0	0	1	1	1	4
SHLD	Store H & L direct	0	0	1	0	0	0	1	0	16
LHLD	Load H & L direct	0	0	1	0	1	0	1	0	16
EI	Enable Interrupts	1	1	1	1	1	0	1	1	4
DI	Disable interrupt	1	1	1	1	0	0	1	1	4
NOP	No-operation	0	0	0	0	0	0	0	0	4

NOTES: 1. DDD or SSS – 000 B – 001 C – 010 D – 011 E – 100 H – 101 L – 110 Memory – 111 A.

2. Two possible cycle times, (5/11) indicate instruction cycles dependent on condition flags.

CHAPTER 5

The Intel 8085

Walter Foley
Eastman Kodak Corp.
Rochester, New York

The Intel **8085** is an improved, second-generation, 8-bit microprocessor. It was developed to simplify system design, reduce system parts count, and increase processing speed. At this time the **8085** is still Intel's most advanced 8-bit μP and is completely software compatible with the **8080**. The **8085** includes all the functions of the **8080** and has a number of additional functions. A list of the functions that are included within the **8085** follows:

1 Internal clock generator
2 Clock output
3 Synchronized ready
4 Reset in (Schmitt triggered)
5 Reset out pin
6 Bus control signals (RD, WR, and IO/M)
7 Encoded status information
8 Multiplexed address and data
9 Four vectored hardware interrupts
10 Serial input/output lines

The **8085** also requires only a single 5-V power supply, as compared to three power supplies for the **8080**.

5-1 ARCHITECTURE

The **8085** contains all the instructions of the **8080** and adds two more (the RIM and SIM instructions, see section 5-2.1). The **8085** differs largely from its predecessor in the manner in which it interfaces with the other devices which make up a system.

5-1.1 The 8085 Oscillator Circuit

The **8085** has a built-in crystal oscillator circuit that requires only the connection of a parallel resonant crystal for operation. The connection of the crystal is shown in Figure 5-1. The **8085** divides the crystal frequency by two to derive its basic cycle time. For example, the specifications for the **8085A** state that the minimum clock cycle time is 320 ns. This corresponds to a frequency of 3.125 MHz, which means that a 6.25-MHz crystal would be connected to the **8085** for operation at this speed. The **8085** is also a dynamic part, as is the **8080**. Therefore a maximum cycle time for correct operation is specified. This clock cycle time is 2 μs, which converts to a frequency of 500 kHz. This means that the slowest crystal that can be used with an **8085** is 1 MHz.

There is a problem that can be encountered with the **8085** crystal system. The internal clock oscillator can sometimes start operating at the third harmonic of the crystals being used. This has been observed mostly at crystal frequencies above 5 MHZ. The best way of solving this problem is to add capacitance to the crystal. There have been many different recommendations concerning the addition of capacitors to the crystal connections of the **8085**. The experience of many years of use of the **8085** and the large numbers of devices encountered have shown that the best method of construction is to connect two 10–20 pF caps from ground to both leads of the crystal and to keep all interconnections in this area short.

5-1.2 The Multiplexed Data Bus

A major area of difference between the **8080** and **8085** is the address and data bus structure. In order to get more functions in the device and still keep the same IC package size, some of the IC pins have to do double duty.

In the **8085** the 8 data bits and the 8 LSBs of the address are multiplexed onto the same lines. During the *first T state* of each machine cycle the bus contains the *memory address* and during the *later T states* the bus contains the *memory data*, which may be bidirectional. The **8085** bus also contains an ALE (address latch enable) signal, which goes HIGH when the bus contains addresses rather than data.

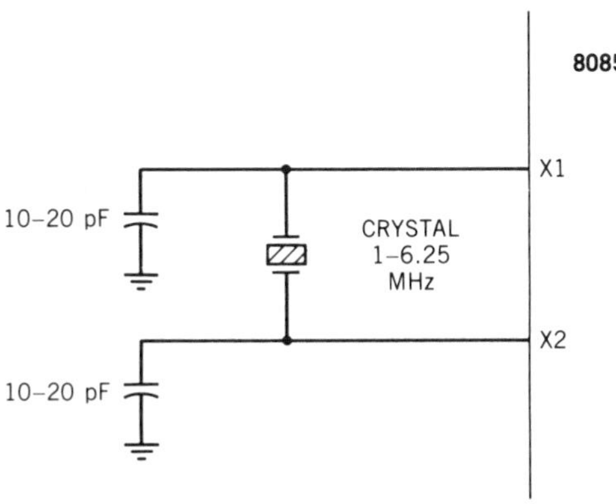

Figure 5-1 Connecting a crystal to the **8085**. (From the *MCS-85 User's Manual*, September 1978. Reprinted by permission of Intel, Inc.)

The **8085** bus also contains the following lines:

$\overline{RD}$. A READ line that goes LOW when the μP is reading (from memory or a peripheral device).

$\overline{WR}$. A WRITE line that goes LOW when the **8085** is writing to memory or a peripheral.

$IO/\overline{M}$. This line distinguishes between a memory request ($IO/\overline{M} = 0$) and an IO Port Request ($IO/\overline{M} = 1$). See section 5-2 for further details.

S_1, S_0. These two lines can be decoded to determine what type of memory cycle (I/O READ, MEMORY WRITE, OP CODE FETCH, etc.) is taking place. This was important for the **8080** μP, but for the **8085** the information is rarely required. The SDK-85 kit, for example, does not use these lines, although they are made available to the user on an external connector.

READY. The READY line is an input to the **8085**. During T2 of each machine cycle the status of the READY line is determined. If it is LOW the **8085** enters the WAIT state, and suspends operation until READY goes HIGH. This line is used to synchronize the **8085** with slow memories. If the memory's response is too slow for the **8085**, the READY line can be held LOW until the memory had had sufficient time to READ or WRITE the byte.

The **8085** bus operation is shown in Figure 5-2. Two READ cycles are shown: the first with no WAIT states (READY always HIGH) and the second with one WAIT state. Note that the addresses appear on AD0–AD7 (the multiplexed portion of the address/data bus) at T1 and the data appears on the same lines at the end of T2.

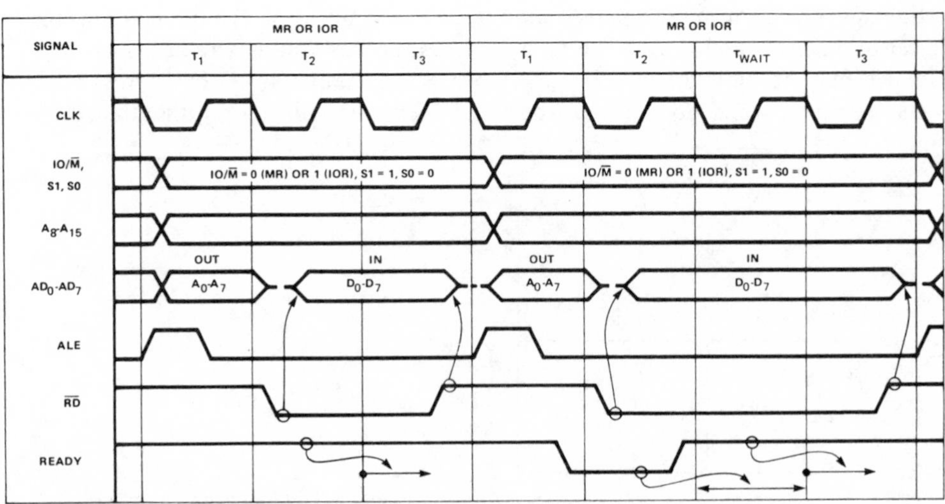

Figure 5-2 Memory READ (or I/O READ) machine cycles. (Reprinted by permission of Intel Corporation, copyright 1978.)

EXAMPLE 5-1 If a slow memory is being used with the **8085**, how can the READY line be connected so that it goes LOW on each memory cycle?

Solution One way is to use ALE, which occurs at the beginning of each cycle, to trigger a one-shot. The output of the one-shot can be tied to READY and the time adjusted until the memory and μP speeds are compatible.

EXAMPLE 5-2 Design a circuit to connect an **8085** to a 1K-byte memory using **2114**s.

Solution For a 1K-byte memory, two **2114**s (which are 1K words by four bits) are required. The circuit is shown in Figure 5-3. The multiplexed ADO–AD7 lines are connected to the data inputs of the **2114**s and to the inputs of **7475** 4-bit latches. The **7475**s are clocked by ALE and supply the eight LSBs of the address. The two MSBs of the address lines are tied directly to A8 and A9 coming from the **8085** because these lines are not multiplexed.

The **2114**s are selected when either $\overline{RD}$ or $\overline{WR}$ go LOW. Note that the **2114**s cannot always be selected because if they were, they would drive data onto the bus at the same time the **8085** was putting addresses on the bus.

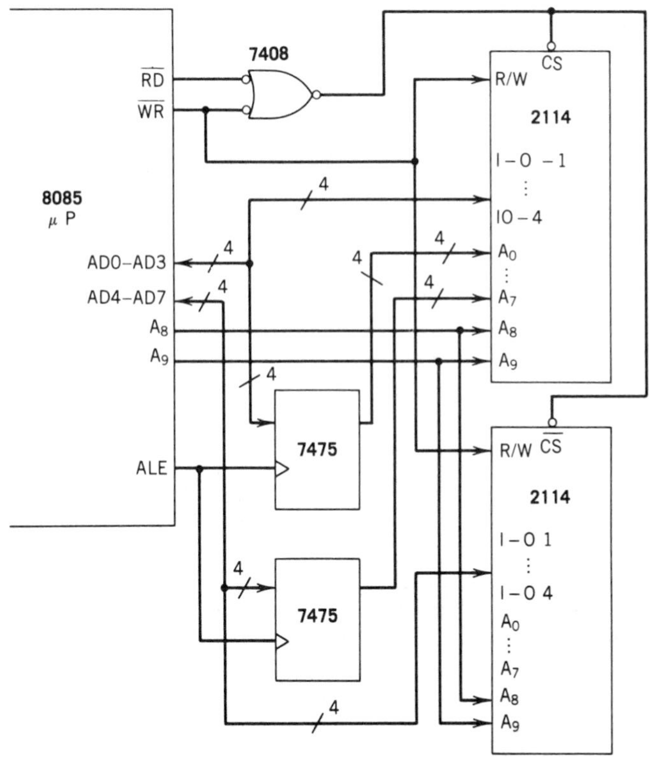

Figure 5-3 Connecting a **2114** memory to an **8085** μP. (From J. D. Greenfield, *Practical Digital Design Using ICs*, 2nd Edition, Wiley, 1983.)

When the CPU cycles the READ signal, if there is no device driving the address/data bus, then the CPU reads the lower eight bits of the address as the data. This can occur if a memory device fails, or if the CPU tries to read a memory location where there is no memory. Assume, for example, that an **8085** is placed in a system with no memory or I/O and the μP has power applied and a reset pulse applied. Then the **8085** should do the following:

Address	*Data*	*Instruction*
0000	00	NOP
0001	01	LXI B
0002	02	STAX B
0003	03	INX B
0004	04	INR B
0005	05	DCR B

and so on until address 0076 is reached. The address (76) will be read as the instruction for a HALT which will stop the processor.

5-1.3 Other 8085 lines

The other major differences between the **8085** and the **8080** are the addition of the RESET OUT, CLOCK OUT, IO/MEMORY, READ, and WRITE lines. The RESET OUT line is an active HIGH signal that can be used to reset all other system components synchronously with the resetting of the **8085**. It is generated by the application of a LOW level to the RESET IN line. The RESET IN line is claimed to have Schmitt action, but the same reservations that were mentioned when referring to the **8224** reset in the chapter on the **8080** still apply. The CLOCK OUT line provides a square wave running at half the crystal frequency. This signal is used to clock or synchronize other system components or to derive other clock frequencies for other purposes, such as baud rates. The IO/MEMORY line is used in conjunction with the address bus for device decoding. The signal is HIGH only during the third cycle of IN and OUT instructions; the signal is LOW for all other instructions. The READ and WRITE lines are just what they seem. READ pulses low during any instruction that gets data from memory or I/O, and WRITE pulses low any time that an instruction sends data to memory or I/O. The timing of these signals is shown in Figures 5-2 and 5-4.

One major internal difference between the **8080** and the **8085** is the addition of the *interrupt mask register*. The layout of this register, along with an explanation of the SIM and RIM instructions, is discussed in section 5-4.

5-2 INPUT AND OUTPUT PORTS

The **8080** and **8085** execute their I/O instructions primarily by using input or output *ports*. A port designates the *source* of data on an I/O input or I/O READ

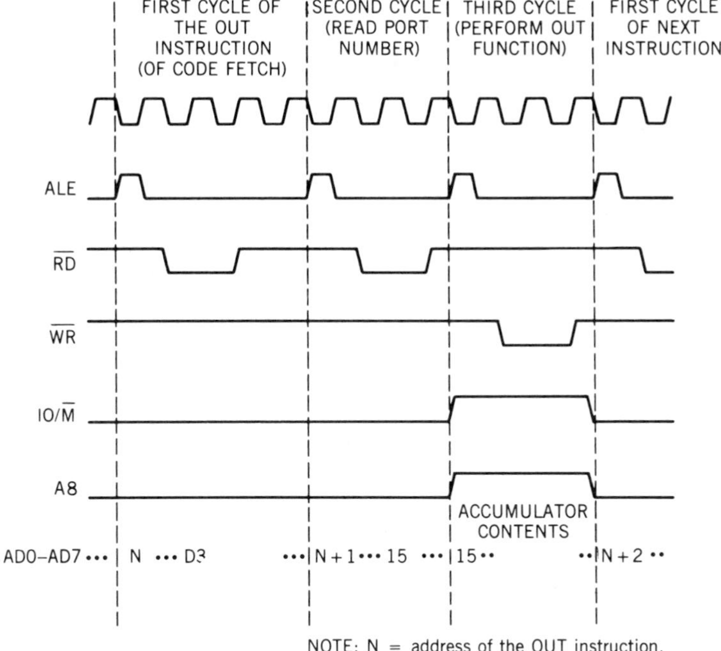

Figure 5-4 Timing for an OUT instruction. (From J. D. Greenfield, *Practical Digital Design Using ICs*, 2nd Edition, Wiley, 1983.)

instruction. Thus input devices like UARTs, card readers, or cassettes would have to be connected to an input port. For an output or I/O WRITE instruction, the port designates which external device (lineprinter, tape, etc.) is to *receive* information from the μP. The architecture of the **8080** and **8085** allows for 256 input and 256 output ports.

There are two special instructions for handling input and output: the IN instruction and the OUT instruction. An IN instruction causes data to be *read from the external device* into the accumulator, while an OUT instruction causes a byte from the accumulator to be *sent to an external device.* Both use two bytes and three machine cycles. The first byte is the Op code (DB for an IN, D3 for an OUT). The second byte is the port address (1 of 256 ports may be selected). During the first machine cycle, the μP reads the IN or OUT Op code, during the second machine cycle it reads the port address.

Data transfer occurs during the third machine cycle. *The 8-bit port address from the second byte of the instruction is placed on the 16 address lines twice.* It occupies *both* bits 0–7 and bits 8–15 of the address bus. An IN instruction also causes $\overline{RD}$ to go LOW, and a byte is read from the external device to the accumulator. Thus an IN instruction is sometimes called an I/O READ (IOR). An OUT instruction causes $\overline{WR}$ to go LOW and a byte is written from the accumulator. This is also called an I/O WRITE (IOW).

Both IN and OUT instructions must inform all components connected to the μP that an I/O cycle is occurring instead of a memory cycle. In the **8080** it is necessary to decode the S1 and S2 lines to determine this. The **8085** simplifies I/O by using the IO/$\overline{\text{M}}$ line. IN and OUT are the *only* two **8085** instructions that cause IO/$\overline{\text{M}}$ to go HIGH.

5-2.1 IN and OUT Timing

The timing for an OUT instruction for the **8085** is shown in Figure 5-4. IN and OUT instructions take three machine cycles consisting of 10 clock cycles, or T states. Figure 15-4 shows the relationship of the clock, ALE, $\overline{\text{RD}}$, $\overline{\text{WR}}$, A8, and the lower 8 bits of the multiplexed address/data bus for an OUT 15 instruction. The instruction proceeds as follows:

1 The first machine cycle is an Op code fetch. This requires four clock cycles. During the first clock cycle, the instruction address (N) is on the address-data bus and ALE goes HIGH. During the second and third cycles, $\overline{\text{RD}}$ goes LOW while the Op code (D3 for an OUT instruction) is placed on the bus. The fourth clock cycle gives the **8085** time to decode the instruction and prepare for the following cycles.

2 The second cycle of the OUT instruction is a memory read of the second byte. The memory address is (N + 1), the location of the second byte, and the data read from memory is the port address (15 in this example).

3 The data transfer takes place during the third machine cycle. During this cycle IO/$\overline{\text{M}}$ is HIGH. The port address is placed on the address/data bus, but is quickly replaced by the accumulator data. At this time the $\overline{\text{WR}}$ line goes LOW. Address bits 8–15 will also contain the port address (15), but they will remain there throughout the entire cycle as the behavior of A8 shows.

The timing for an IN instruction is identical except that an additional pulse occurs on the $\overline{\text{RD}}$ line instead of on the $\overline{\text{WR}}$ line. All timing can be checked on an oscilloscope by using the simple program:

```
2010 OUT 15    (or IN)
2012 JMP 2012
```

5-2.2 Execution of the OUT Instruction

The OUT instruction (I/O WRITE) can be executed by tying the address/data bus to the inputs of the various peripherals and then strobing the data in with a pulse that gates IO/$\overline{\text{M}}$ and the $\overline{\text{WR}}$ line.

EXAMPLE 5-3 An **8085** system has 16 output devices. Design the circuitry so the **8085** can send data to any of these devices.

Solution The output devices can be set up so they use ports 0–15. In this way only the four LSBs of the address lines need to be used. The circuit is shown in Figure 5-5. It operates as follows.

a The AD0–AD7 lines go to all devices. These lines are shown going through a **74LS241**, eight input, noninverting, buffer/line driver. If the data input to all devices is CMOS, the **74LS241** might be omitted, but it has two advantages: it alleviates *fanout* or *loading*

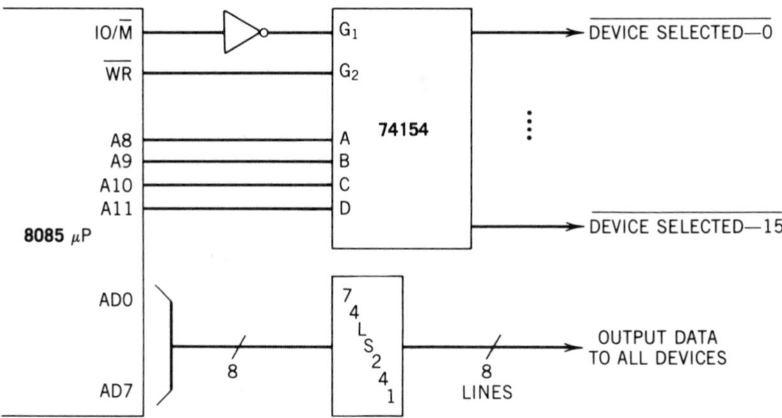

Figure 5-5 Sending data from an **8085** to 16 peripherals. (From J. D. Greenfield, *Practical Digital Design Using ICs*, 2nd Edition, Wiley, 1983.)

problems, and it *isolates* the μP from the external devices. Isolation is important. Otherwise, a miswire or other catastrophe on an external device could disable the μP. The buffer is enabled by IO/$\overline{M}$ so that it transmits data only during OUT or IN instructions.

b The 4-bit port address is sent to a **74154** decoder. Addresses A8 through A11 are used (instead of ADO–AD3) because the higher address lines are not multiplexed and this eliminates the need for an address latch.

c The decoder is enabled by the inverse of IO/$\overline{M}$ and by $\overline{WR}$. Thus it will only function during the write portion of an OUT instruction. When enabled the decoder provides a LOW input to the DEVICE-SELECTED line of the addressed peripheral. The peripheral must use this signal to *strobe* in the data. Note that the AD lines contain data at this time, not addresses, because DEVICE-SELECTED is synchronized with the $\overline{WR}$ signal.

d More than 16 (up to 256) peripherals may be accommodated by enlarging the decoder and adding more drive capability if necessary.

5-2.3 Execution of the IN Instruction

The IN instruction (I/O READ) brings data in from the peripherals and enters them into the accumulator. The IN instruction can be executed by a circuit similar to Figure 5-5. The major differences are:

1 The $\overline{RD}$ line would enable the decoder instead of $\overline{WR}$.

2 The peripherals must all put their data on the AD lines of the μP. If this data is present at the wrong time (when the μP is executing other instruction, for example), it will cause a conflict and cripple the μP. Therefore, all peripherals that are inputs must be tied to the address/data bus via tri-state gates that are only enabled during the third machine cycle of an IN instruction. Fortunately, the DEVICE-SELECTED outputs from the decoder only go LOW at this time, so DEVICE-SELECTED provides an ideal signal for enabling the tri-state drivers going from the peripherals to the μP.

5-2.4 SID and SOD

The **8085** has additional I/O capability because of its serial in data (SID) and serial out data (SOD) lines. These lines can be used to move data to and from the processor in a serial format under software control. The instructions used to control these lines are the SIM and RIM instructions (see section 5-4). Data can be sent out a bit at a time via the SOD line by using the SIM instruction. Data can also be received a bit at a time through the SID line by using the RIM instruction. Very fast baud rates cannot be achieved using this method because the data speed is determined by the processor instruction cycle time and other system factors. However, baud rates of around 1200 BPS are achievable. A nice feature of using the SID and SOD lines is that the **8085** can monitor the SID line after a reset and if a known character, such as a carriage return, is sent over the SID line, the **8085** can determine the baud rate being used, and then reply via the SOD line at the correct speed. This is useful because several different types of terminals, such as CRTs or TTYs, can be used with the processor, without having to determine, and then set, baud rate controls.

5-3 INTERRUPTS ON THE 8080 AND 8085

An interrupt is a high priority request for service made by a peripheral. An interrupt causes the μP to *jump* out of the program it is currently running and go to a *service routine* for the peripheral. When it finishes the service routine it returns to its main program.

On the **8080** and **8085** an interrupt is initiated when the interrupting device places a HIGH on the INTR line. The μP responds by placing a LOW pulse on its $\overline{\text{INTA}}$ (interrupt acknowledge) line. While this pulse is LOW the μP must receive the Op code of the next instruction it will execute on its AD0–AD7 lines. The interrupting device is responsible for placing the Op code on the AD0–AD7 lines.

The function of the instruction whose Op code is read in during $\overline{\text{INTA}}$ is to jump the program to the start of the interrupt service routine. It must also place the contents of the program counter (PC) on the μP's stack so the main program can be resumed after the interrupt routine is finished. For the **8080**, there is only one instruction that performs these functions and should be placed on the AD0–AD7 lines. This is a RESTART. The **8085** can accept either a RESTART or a CALL.

5-3.1 The RESTART Instruction

The RESTART instruction looks like this:

11NNN111

During execution it first writes the PC onto the stack to preserve it, and then places NNN000 into the program counter, so the first instruction of the service routine is executed there. There are eight RESTARTS (RESTART-0 through RESTART-7), where the number of the RESTART is the binary value of NNN.

EXAMPLE 5-4 What does the Op code of a RESTART-5 look like? Where does the service routine start?

Solution A RESTART-5 looks like

$$11\underbrace{101}_{5}111$$

The service routine will start at 0000 0000 00$\underbrace{10\ 1}_{5}$000 or $(0028)_{16}$.

EXAMPLE 5-5 Design a circuit to connect a RESTART to the AD0–AD7 lines.

Solution Since the RESTART Op code should only be placed on the AD lines when $\overline{\text{INTA}}$ is LOW, it must come in through tri-state gates that are enabled by $\overline{\text{INTA}}$. The circuit is

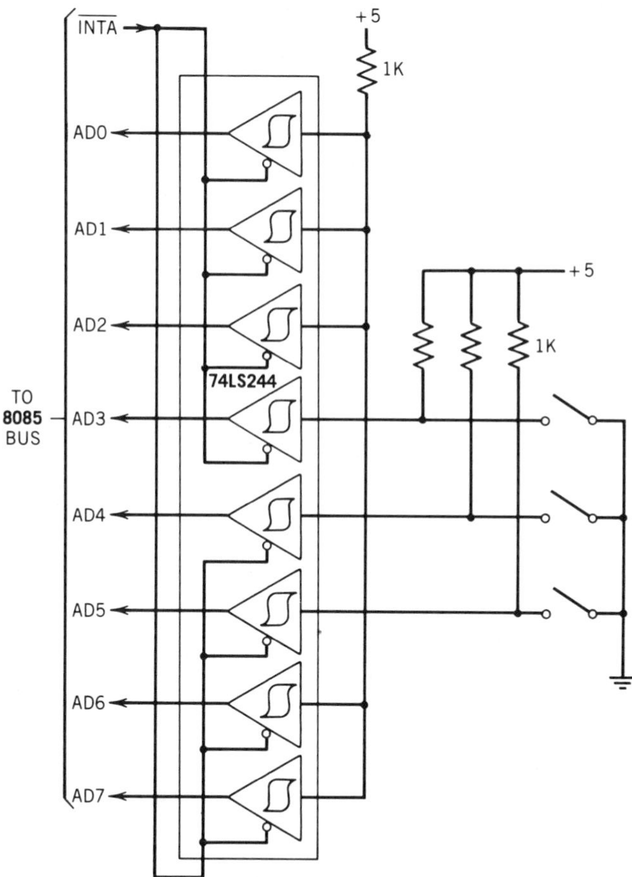

Figure 5-6 Connecting a RESTART to an **8085**. (From J. D. Greenfield, *Practical Digital Design Using ICs*, 2nd Edition, Wiley, 1983.)

shown in Figure 5-6. It can use either two **74125**s or a **74LS244**. The **74LS244** is shown. The switches can be set to give any desired RESTART (0–7). Of course peripherals that generate RESTARTs will probably use gates rather than switches to drive the AD lines during $\overline{\text{INTA}}$.

The possibility of eight different RESTART addresses allows the service routines for the various interrupting devices to start at (or vector to) eight different addresses. This is called *vectored interrupts* by Intel since each interrupting device can use a different RESTART that vectors the μP to that device's service routine. There are only eight locations between the RESTART vectors, however, so programs cannot really be written there. Most RESTART addresses contain a JUMP to the actual start of the service routine.

The **8080** and **8085** also contain a $\overline{\text{RESET IN}}$ pin. A LOW on this input causes the μP to go to location 0. Location 0 is thus reserved for the start of the main program. Turning power on also causes a $\overline{\text{RESET}}$. Note that both a $\overline{\text{RESET}}$ and a RESTART-0 vector the μP to location 0.

5-3.2 New 8085 Interrupt Vectors

Four vectored interrupt lines have been added to the **8085**. Three of these four interrupts are maskable through software instructions, and one of them is an edge-triggered interrupt. These four interrupts operate by forcing RESTARTs to certain locations in memory. These four lines and their RESTART addresses are given in Table 5-1.

Table 5-1 **RESTART addresses for the 8085**

Name	*RESTART address*
TRAP	$(24)_{16}$
RST 5.5	$(2C)_{16}$
RST 6.5	$(34)_{16}$
RST 7.5	$(3C)_{16}$

EXAMPLE 5-6 In the event of a power failure, the **8085** must TRAP to location 2000 to start a service routine. How does it get there?

Solution The power failure indicator is connected to the TRAP input. Locations 24, 25, and 26 must contain the code:

```
24  C3 )
25  00 }  JUMP $2000
26  20 )
```

Thus the TRAP will vector the μP to location 24 and it will then jump to 2000.

The priority of interrupts is given in Table 5-1. TRAP is the highest and RST 5.5 the lowest. TRAP is a *nonmaskable edge-triggered* interrupt that is not affected by the state of any interrupt mask. TRAP is therefore most generally used to signal problems, such as imminent power failure, to the processor. RST 7.5 is a rising edge-sensitive interrupt. An external device need only provide a pulse to set an internal flip-flop that generates the interrupt. RST 6.5 and RST 5.5 are level-sensitive interrupts whose timing is the same as the interrupt line of the **8080**. The two instructions, SIM and RIM, are used to control the masking and unmasking of the RST 7.5, RST 7.5, and RST 5.5 interrupts. The use of these instructions will be covered later in this chapter. In addition to the above four interrupts, the **8085** also has a line called interrupt request (INTR) whose function is the same as the INT line of the **8080**.

5-3.3 The CALL Instruction

The **8085** will also accept an unconditional CALL instruction. The CALL instruction can be considered as a jump to subroutine. It places the address of the next instruction (the contents of the PC) on the stack and jumps to the address specified by the 2 bytes following the Op code. For example, a CALL instruction to location **2050**, that is in **2010**, looks like the following:

Address	*Data*	*Function*
2010	CD	Op code for an unconditional CALL
2011	50	LS byte of destination address
2012	20	MS byte of destination address

This instruction causes the program to jump to the subroutine at **2050**, and it places the address of the next instruction, **2013**, on the stack so the program can resume after the subroutine finishes and RETURNs.

The advantage of using a CALL in response to an interrupt is that the **8085** can be vectored to a service routine *anywhere* in memory. Of course, it requires more hardware to do this. The interrupting peripheral must place the CALL Op code (CD) on the AD0–AD7 lines in response to INTA. It will then receive two more INTAs, and it must place the address on the bus.

The timing for a CALL response to an interrupt is shown in Figure 5-7. It requires five machine cycles. During the first three cycles INTA goes LOW and the **8085** receives the CALL Op code and the 2 bytes of the address (B2 and B3). During cycles 4 and 5 $\overline{WR}$ goes LOW and the PC is written to the stack. Figure 5-2 also shows the Op code fetch for the next instruction. Note that addresses A8–A15 contain B3 throughout the machine cycle, and AD0–AD7 contain B2 during ALE.

EXAMPLE 5-7 A peripheral is to interrupt and place a CALL **2050** on the AD0–AD7 lines when the **8085** responds. Design the circuitry.

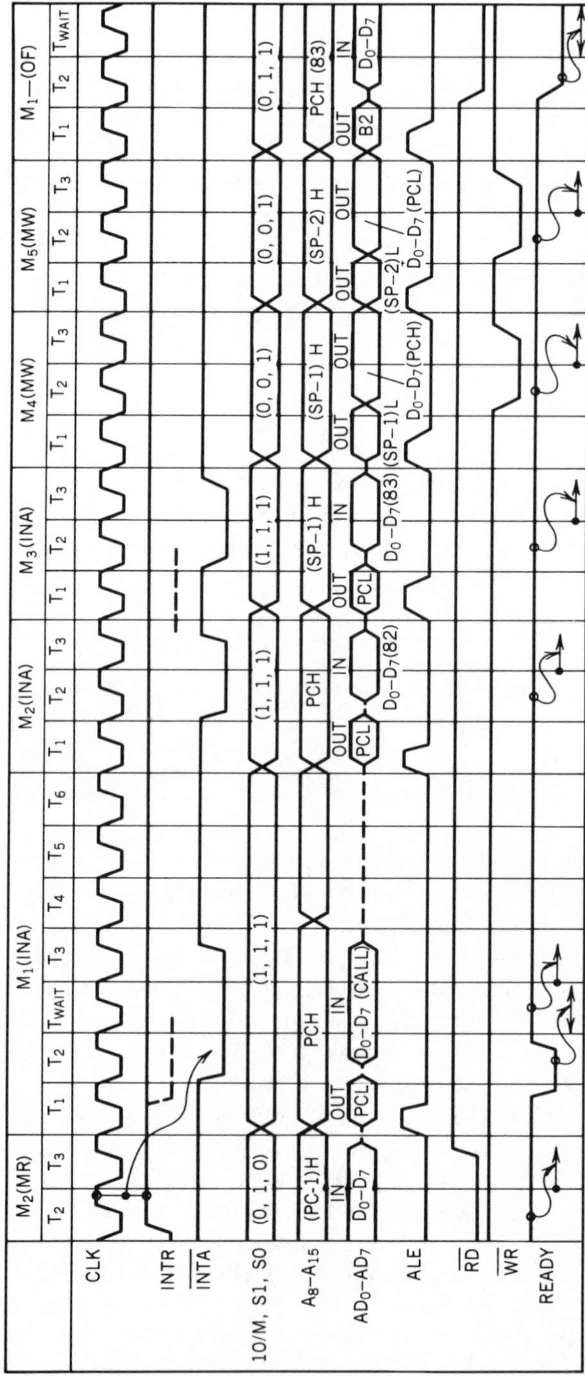

Figure 5-7 INTERRUPT ACKNOWLEDGE machine cycles with CALL instructions in response to INTR. (Reprinted by permission of Intel Corporation, copyright 1978.)

Solution The circuit is shown in Figure 5-8. It was designed as follows:

a The outputs to the AD0–AD7 lines must only be active when INTA is LOW. This suggests a **74LS244** (or two **74125**s) enabled by $\overline{\text{INTA}}$.

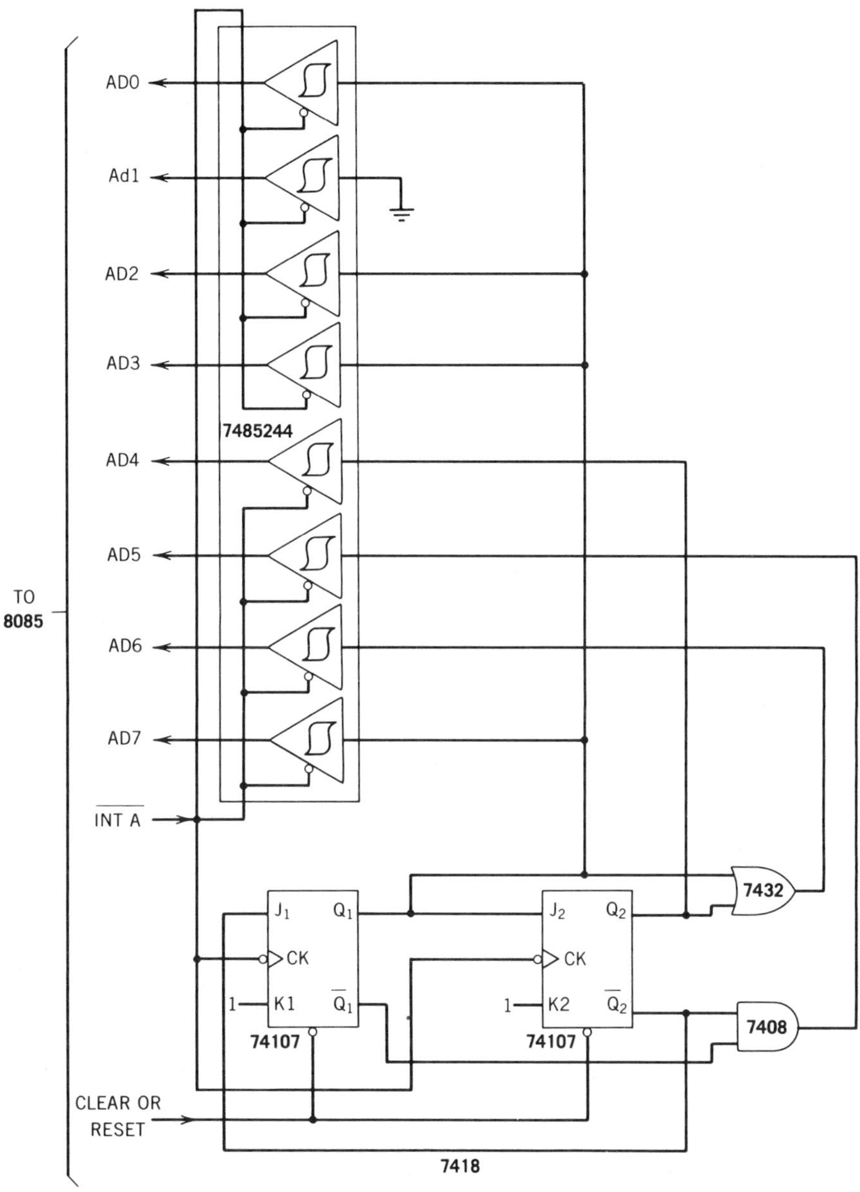

Figure 5-8 A circuit to generate a CALL 2050 in response to an interrupt for an **8085**. (From J. D. Greenfield, *Practical Digital Design Using ICs*, 2nd Edition, Wiley, 1983.)

b Three different outputs are required in response to an interrupt. This suggests a 3s counter triggered by $\overline{\text{INTA}}$. Assuming the 3s counter is cleared prior to the start, the leading edge of the first INTA will set it to a count of 1, so for each interrupt it counts 1, 2, 0.

c The bits to be placed on the line are shown in Table 5-2.

d By examining the table we see that bits 0, 2, 3, and 7 should only be 1s during the first pulse, when Q_1 is 1. Therefore, Q_1 is connected to the inputs of these gates.

e Bit 1 is always 0. Therefore, the input to that gate is grounded.

f By looking at the logic required for the other bits we can complete the circuit as shown in Table 5-2.

Table 5-2 **Bit configuration for a CALL 2050**

$\overline{\text{INTA}}$	Q_1	Q_2	AD									
			7	6	5	4	3	2	1	0		
1	1	0	1	1	0	0	1	1	0	1	CD	CALL
2	0	1	0	1	0	1	0	0	0	0	50	50
3	0	0	0	0	1	0	0	0	0	0	20	20

5-4 INSTRUCTION SET

The **8085** uses all of the instructions that were presented in the previous chapter on the **8080**. The differences between the **8080** and the **8085** are that the **8085** has two additional instructions and that the **8085** uses different numbers of clock cycles to execute certain instructions.

5-4.1 The Interrupt Mask Register

The **8085** has an *interrupt mask register*, which is not available on the **8080** (see Figures 5-9 and 5-10). It is used to *mask* (disable) or *enable* the various interrupts. It can also be used to check the state of the serial input data line (SID) or set the state of the serial output data line (SOD). The interrupt mask register is controlled by the SIM and RIM instructions.

5-4.2 SIM

The SIM (set interrupt mask) instruction is used to transfer the contents of the accumulator into the interrupt mask register. This transfer performs several functions. It loads the mask for RST5.5, RST6.5, and RST7.5. It also resets the edge-sensitive input for RST7.5 and it can output to the SOD line. Figure 5-9 shows what functions the bit locations of the accumulator perform when a SIM instruction is executed.

A SIM instruction has the following characteristics:

No. of memory locations required: 1
Op code: 0 0 1 1 0 0 0 0 = 30H
Addressing: Register
Execution time: 4 clock cycles

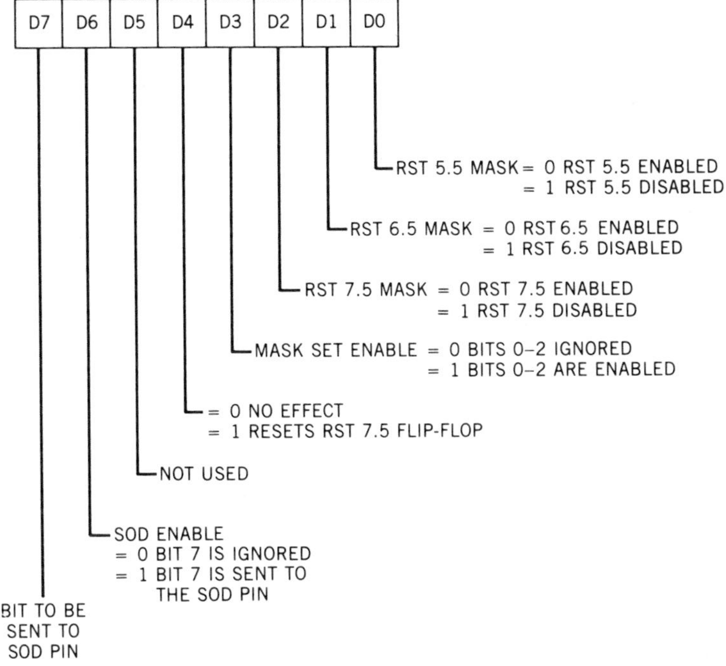

Figure 5-9 Definition of accumulator bits when executing a SIM instruction.

EXAMPLE 5-8 If the accumulator contained the value 0CC (hex) when the SIM instruction is executed, what is the effect on the interrupt mask register?

Solution The SIM instruction causes the following:

a A HIGH is output on the **8085** SOD pin, because bit 6 is a 1, enabling SOD, and bit 7 is a 1, setting SOD to a 1.

b RST7.5 is masked off (bit 2 = 1). Bringing the RST7.5 pin HIGH will not cause an interrupt.

c RST5.5 and RST6.5 are masked on (bit 3 is a 1, enabling the bits to be SET, and bits 0 and 1 are 0s, enabling RESTARTs 5.5 and 6.5); bringing either pin HIGH will cause an interrupt.

If the accumulator contains the value 87 hex when the SIM instruction is executed, there is no effect. This is because both the SOD enable bit is low and the mask set enable bit is low.

Even when RST7.5 is disabled, its request flip-flop is still active. This means that if a pulse occurs on the RST7.5 line when it is disabled, the flip-flop will latch this pulse and a RST7.5 interrupt will be generated as soon as RST7.5 is reenabled. To keep this from occurring, the accumulator should first be loaded with the value 10 hex and then a SIM instruction executed. Doing this will have no effect on the interrupt mask or the SOD line, but it will reset the RST7.5 flip-flop to the off state. After this, RST7.5 can be enabled without unwanted interrupts being generated.

5-4.3 RIM

The RIM (read interrupt mask) instruction transfers the contents of the interrupt mask register into the accumulator. The resulting bit pattern in the accumulator indicates the value of the SID line, the setting of the interrupt mask, the setting of the interrupt enable flag, and if any interrupts are pending. Figure 5-10 indicates what the values of the bits in the accumulator mean after a RIM instruction is executed.

A RIM instruction has the following characteristics:

No. of memory locations required: 1
Op code: 0 0 1 0 0 0 0 0 = 20H
Addressing mode: Register
Execution time: 4 clock cycles

EXAMPLE 5-9 If after execution of the RIM instruction the accumulator contained the value 0AF hex, what would this indicate?

Solution The status of the interrupt mask register is as follows:

a The **8085** SID pin is high (bit 7 = 1).

b The RST6.5 pin is high (interrupt pending, bit 5 = 1).

c The **8085** interrupt system is enabled (bit 3 = 1).

d RST7.5, RST6.5, and RST5.5 are disabled (bits 2, 1, and 0 = 1).

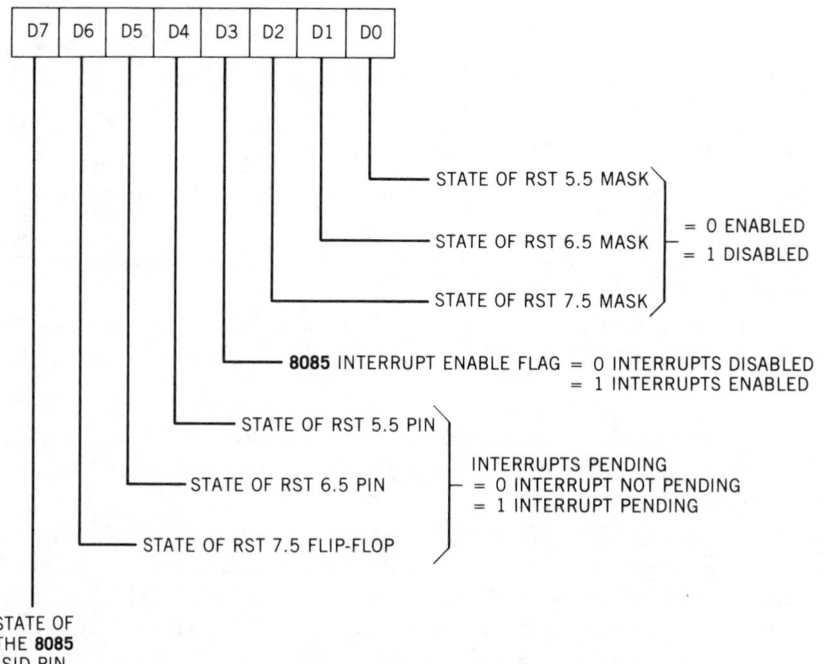

Figure 5-10 Definition of accumulator bits after executing a RIM instruction.

If the RIM instruction is executed immediately following a trap interrupt, the interrupt enable flag (bit 3) will indicate the status that was present before the trap occurred. (The TRAP sets the flag and disables interrupts.) Executing this RIM instruction causes the flag to change to the correct state and the execution of subsequent RIM instructions will indicate the correct flag status.

5-4.4 Other Instructions

There are 10 unused Op codes in the **8085** instruction set that nothing is said about. It has been determined that in some, but not all, **8085**s these Op codes are usable instructions. What is known about these Op codes is given below.

Note: These codes may not work in all **8085**s. If their use in a program is contemplated, it would be a good idea to verify that at least two available devices can use these instructions so that a spare **8085** is on hand in case of failure. Intel does not warrant that these instructions work.

New Condition Codes

V — Bit 1 of the PSW
This indicates a 2s complement overflow

X 5 — Bit 5 of the PSW
This indicates underflow from the DCX instruction or overflow from the INX instruction.

DSUB (Double subtraction)
The contents of the register pair BC are subtracted from the contents of the register pair HL. The result is placed in the HL register pair.

Op code: 0 0 0 0 1 0 0 0 = 08H
Addressing: Register
Execution time: 10 clock cycles
Flags affect: All

ARHL (Arithmetic shift of H and L to the right)
The contents of the register pair HL are shifted one bit to the right. The MSB is duplicated and the LSB is shifted into the carry flag.

Op code: 0 0 0 1 0 0 0 0 = 10H
Addressing: Register
Execution time: 7 clock cycles
Flags affected: Carry

RDEL (Rotate DE left through carry)
The contents of the DE register pair are rotated left 1-bit position through the carry flag. The LSB is set equal to the carry flag and then the carry flag is set equal to the MSB.

Op code: 0 0 0 1 1 0 0 0 = 18H
Addressing: Register
Execution time: 10 clock cycles
Flags affected: Carry, V

LDHI (Load DE with HL plus immediate byte)
The contents of the byte immediately following the instruction is added to the contents of the HL register pair and the result is placed into the DE register pair.

Op code: 0 0 1 0 1 0 0 0 = 28H
Addressing: Immediate register
Execution time: 10 clock cycles
Flags affected: None

LDSI (Load DE with SP plus immediate byte)
As above, except SP register pair instead of HL register pair.

Op code: 0 0 1 1 1 0 0 0 = 38H
All other parameters as above.

RSTV (Restart on overflow)
If V is set when this instruction is executed, then the program counter is pushed onto the stack and the address 0040H is loaded into the program counter. If the V flag is not set, then the instruction is ignored.

Op code: 1 1 0 0 1 0 1 1 = CBH
Addressing: Register indirect
Execution time: 6 or 12 clock cycles
Flags affected: None

SHLX (Store HL indirect through DE)
The contents of the L register are moved to the memory location whose address is contained in the DE register pair. The contents of the H register are moved to the succeeding memory location.

Op code: 1 1 0 1 1 0 0 1 = D9H
Addressing: Register indirect
Execution time: 10 clock cycles
Flags affected: None

JNX5 (Jump on not X5)
If the X5 flag is reset, then the address specified by the next 2 program bytes becomes the new execution address. If the X5 flag is set, the instruction is ignored.

Op code: 1 1 0 1 1 1 0 1 = DDH
Addressing: Immediate
Execution time: 7 or 10 clock cycles
Flags affected: None

LHLX (Load HL indirect through DE)
The contents of the memory location whose address is contained in the DE register pair are moved to register L. The contents of the succeeding memory location are moved to the H register.

Op code: 1 1 1 0 1 1 0 1 = EDH
Addressing: Register indirect
Execution time: 10 clock cycles
Flags affected: None

JX5 (Jump on X5)
If the X5 flag is set, then program control is transferred to the memory location whose address is contained in the next 2 bytes of the instruction. If the flag is not set, then the instruction is ignored.

Op code: 1 1 1 1 1 1 0 1 = FDH
Addressing: Immediate
Execution time: 7 or 10 clock cycles
Flags affected: None

5-5 THE CPU

The **8085** CPU, as shown in Figure 5-11, is a 40-pin DIP of 0.6-in. width. Below is a listing of the pins with a brief description of their function.

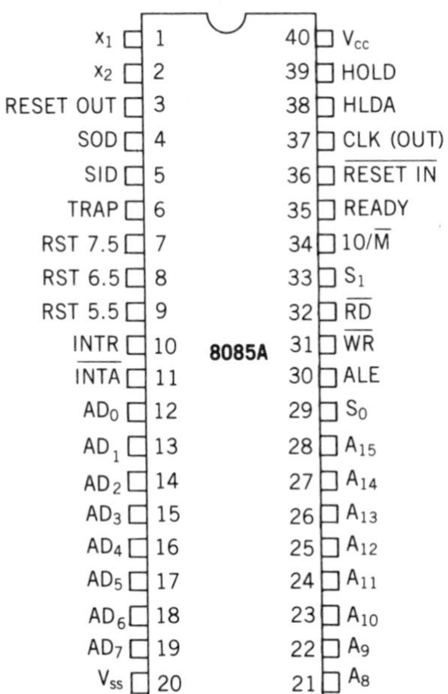

Figure 5-11 **8085A** pin out diagram. (From the *MCS-85 User's Manual*, September 1978. Reprinted by permission of Intel, Inc.)

Pin no.	*Name*	*Dir*	*Function*
1,2	X1, X2	I	The two pins for connection of a crystal
3	RESET OUT	O	An active HIGH signal that indicates a reset has been applied to the **8085**
4	SOD	O	Serial output data (see section 5-2.4)
5	SID	I	Serial input data (see section 5-2.4)
6	TRAP	I	Nonmaskable interrupt
7	RST 7.5	I	Rising edge sensitive, maskable, vectored interrupt (see section 5-3)
8	RST 6.5	I	High-level sensitive, maskable, vectored interrupt (see section 5-3)
9	RST 5.5	I	High-level sensitive, maskable, vectored interrupt (see section 5-3)
10	INTR	I	INTERRUPT REQUEST, same function as INT on 8080
11	$\overline{\text{INTA}}$	I	INTERRUPT ACKNOWLEDGE, indicates a response to the interrupt request
12–19	AD0–AD7	B	Address/data lines bits 0–7
20	Vss	I	Power and signal ground
21–28	A8–A15	O	Address lines bits 8–15
29	S0	O	Status bit 0, encoded bus cycle status
30	ALE	O	Address latch enable (see section 5-3)
31	$\overline{\text{WR}}$	O	WRITE, active LOW, signals a bus WRITE cycle is in progress
32	$\overline{\text{RD}}$	O	READ, active LOW, signals a bus READ cycle is in progress
33	S1	O	Status bit 1, encoded bus cycle status
34	IO/M	O	Input/output memory (see section 5-2)
35	READY	I	Active HIGH, when high signals to the **8085** that no WAIT states are required. If it is low during the second rising clock edge of an instruction cycle, WAIT states will be inserted until the next rising edge when ready is high.
36	RESET IN	I	Active LOW (see section 5-1.3)
37	CLK (OUT)	O	Clock OUT (see section 5-1.3)
38	HLDA	O	HOLD ACKNOWLEDGE, active HIGH, indicates the **8085** will respond to a HOLD request and tri-state the buses, RD, WR, and IO/M lines during the next clock cycle.
39	HOLD	I	Active HIGH, indicates to the CPU that another device wishes to gain control of the buses and control lines
40	VCC	I	+5-V power supply

5-5.1 Status Information Decoding

The S0 and S1 lines indicate the type of cycle the CPU is executing at any given time. Knowing how to read these signals can sometimes help when debugging a system. For example, if a CPU suddenly stops running, reading the states of S0 and S1 can indicate why the CPU stopped. Below is a table of the decoded status information from S0 and S1:

S0	*S1*	*State*
0	0	HALT
0	1	READ
1	0	WRITE
1	1	FETCH

The ALE line can be used as a status strobe; the falling edge is used to latch the status.

5-5.2 Demultiplexing Address and Data

There are many ways to demultiplex the address and data lines. Two of the most common methods are shown in Figures 5-12 and 5-13. The method shown in Figure 5-12 uses a **7465374** rising edge-triggered latch to hold the lower 8 bits of address. To do this requires the use of an inverter between the ALE line and the clock line of the latch. This method does not latch the address until the falling edge of ALE, and thus allows for maximum stability of the address lines. On the other hand, the method used in Figure 5-13 uses a high enable, transparent latch. The

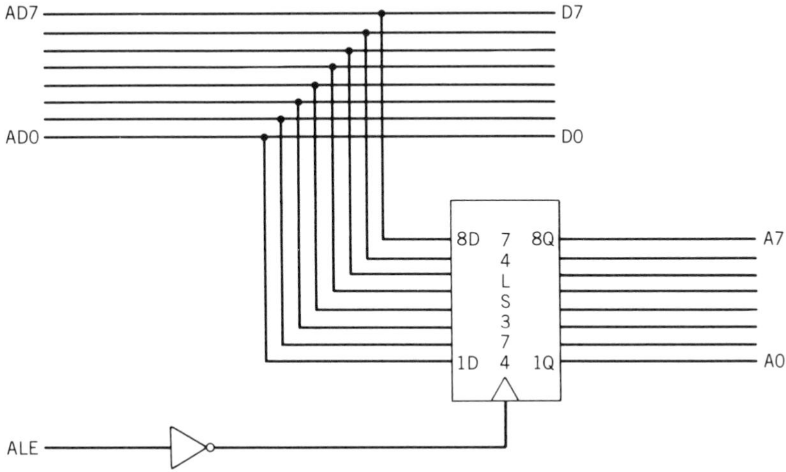

Figure 5-12 Latching ALE with an edge-triggered latch.

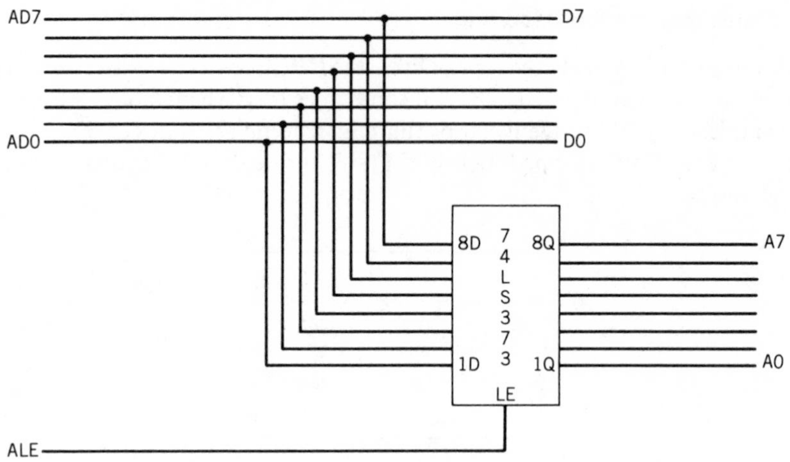

Figure 5-13 Latching ALE with a transparent latch.

advantage to this method is that the address signals pass through the latch while ALE is high and appear on the bus sooner than the signals from the edge-triggered latch would. This slight time advantage can be useful in systems where access speed of the memory or I/O is tight, and faster parts are not available or desirable.

5-5.3 WAIT States

The insertion of WAIT states into the CPU cycles is sometimes necessary. The circuit in Figure 5-14 can be used to insert one WAIT state into every **8085** machine cycle. However, this is not always acceptable. The alternate circuit shown in Figure 5-15 will insert one WAIT state into a machine cycle whenever a given device chip select is active. This has the advantage of allowing the CPU to run at full speed, except when it is actually required to slow down.

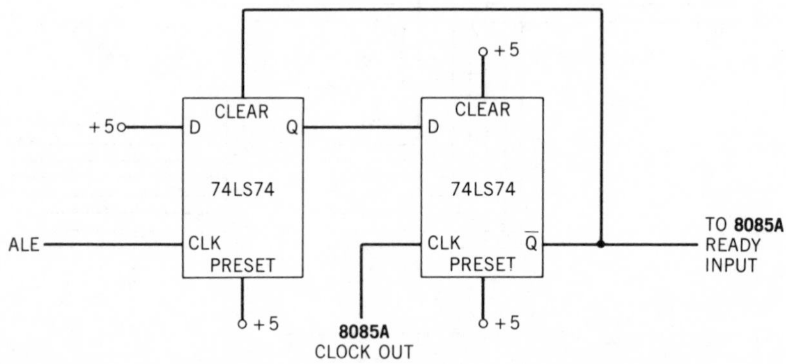

Figure 5-14 Inserting a WAIT state in every **8085** machine cycle.

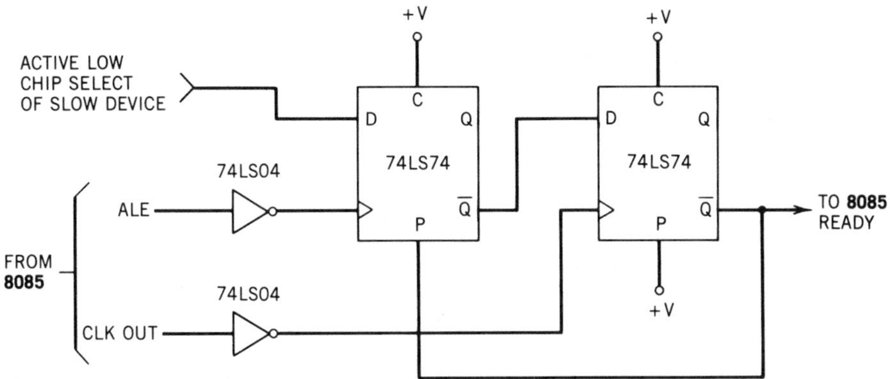

Figure 5-15 Selective WAIT state insertion.

5-6 SPECIAL PERIPHERAL DEVICES

There are several special memory and I/O devices that are designed for use with the **8085**. These devices are special in that they contain a built-in address latch for the lower 8 bits of address and have a pin that connects directly to the **8085** ALE line for use of this function. The devices that are in this category are as follows:

1 8755/8355 A combination memory (EPROM in the **8755**, ROM in the **8355**) and I/O device (two 8-bit bidirectional ports).

2 8155/8156 A combination memory (256 8-bit bytes of RAM), I/O (two 8-bit and one 6-bit bidirectional ports), and timer/counter (or 14-bit programmable timer with separate input and output lines). The difference between the **8155** and **8156** is the active state of their chip select lines. The **8155** chip select is active LOW, while the **8156** has an active HIGH chip select.

3 8185 An 8K (1K × 8 bits) RAM memory device.

The above devices are very useful in designing and building a very powerful microcomputer system with a minimum number of components. Figure 5-16 illustrates a four-chip **8085** system with the following specifications:

1 2048 bytes of EPROM
2 1280 bytes of RAM
3 38 input/output lines
4 14-bit timer
5 4 vectored interrupts
6 Serial I/O port

The preceding specifications are more than adequate for a small, control-oriented computer for applications such as heating control, alarm system, intelligent

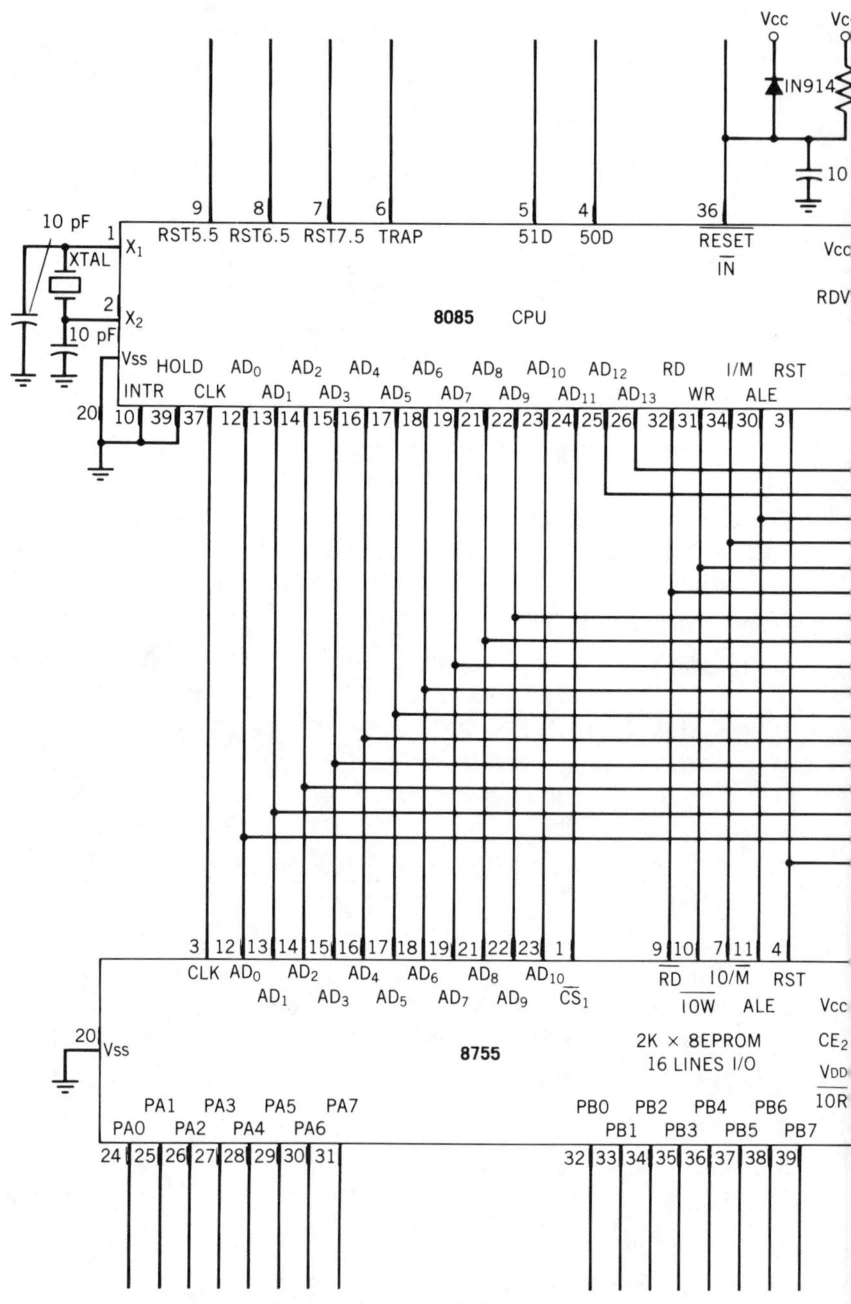

Figure 5-16 An **8085** four-chip system.

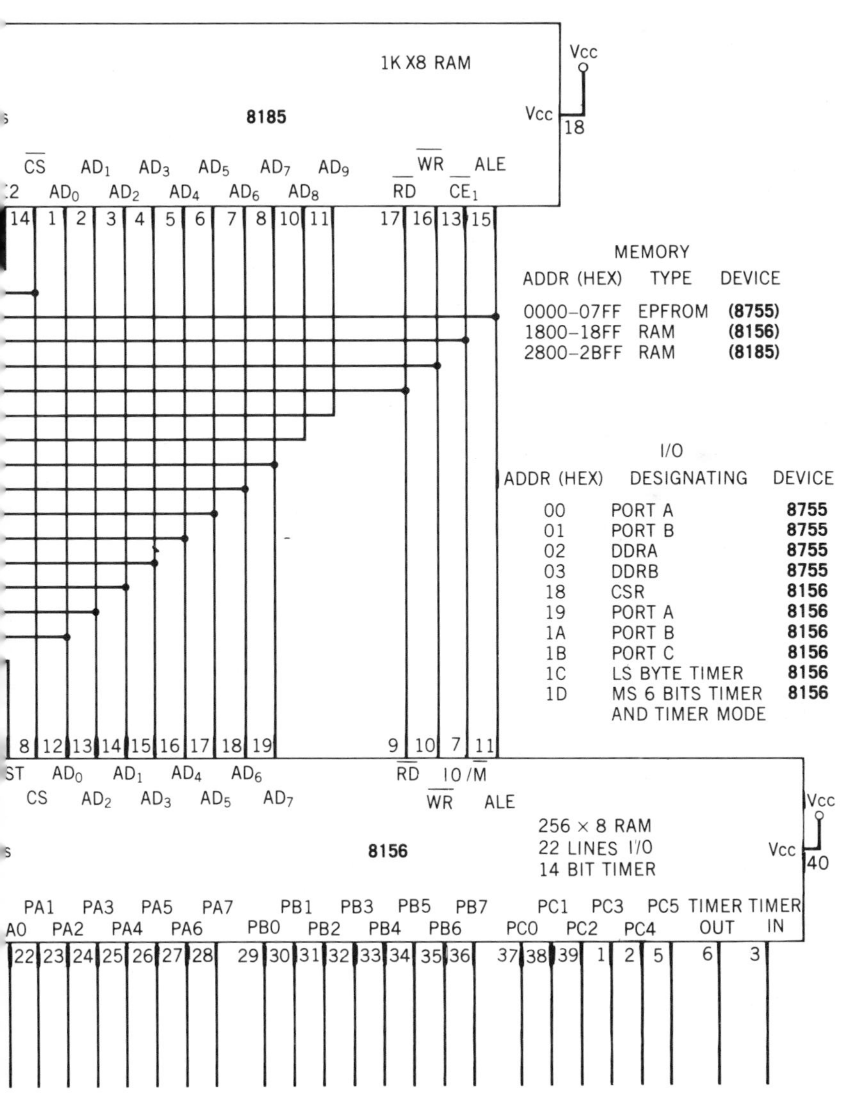

1K X8 RAM
8185
Vcc
Vcc
18
CS AD1 AD3 AD5 AD7 AD9 WR ALE
AD0 AD2 AD4 AD6 AD8 RD CE1
MEMORY
ADDR (HEX) TYPE DEVICE
0000–07FF EPFROM (8755)
1800–18FF RAM (8156)
2800–2BFF RAM (8185)
I/O
ADDR (HEX) DESIGNATING DEVICE
00 PORT A 8755
01 PORT B 8755
02 DDRA 8755
03 DDRB 8755
18 CSR 8156
19 PORT A 8156
1A PORT B 8156
1B PORT C 8156
1C LS BYTE TIMER 8156
1D MS 6 BITS TIMER AND TIMER MODE 8156
AD0 AD1 AD4 AD6 RD IO/M
CS AD2 AD3 AD5 AD7 WR ALE
256 × 8 RAM
22 LINES I/O
14 BIT TIMER
8156
Vcc
Vcc
40
PA1 PA3 PA5 PA7 PB1 PB3 PB5 PB7 PC1 PC3 PC5 TIMER OUT TIMER IN
PA2 PA4 PA6 PB0 PB2 PB4 PB6 PC0 PC2 PC4

controllers for computer peripherals, or other process-related operations. The memory and I/O addresses for the RAMs, EPROMs, timer, and I/O ports are also given in Figure 5-16.

5-6.1 The 8255

The **8255** is a programmable peripheral interface (PPI) device for use in **8080/8085** computer systems. The **8255** is contained in a 40 pin package, whose pin out is shown in Figure 5-17. It consists of three 8-bit bidirectional I/O ports that can be configured to meet many different system I/O needs. The device occupies four address locations in a system address map; three of these locations are used to address the I/O ports, referred to as ports A, B, and C. Port A contains one 8-bit output latch/buffer and one 8-bit input buffer. Port B is the same as port A. Port C is also the same as ports A and B. However, it can also be split into two separate 4-bit ports by the control register. Each 4-bit port can input or output data or be used in conjunction with ports A or B as control/status lines.

The fourth **8085** location is used to address the control register that determines the mode of operation of the device. The I/O ports of the **8255** are divided into two groups. Group A consists of port A and the upper 4 bits (C4–C7) of port C. Group B consists of port B and the lower 4 bits (CO–C3) of port C. Each group has a control block that accepts *control words* from the data bus and then sends commands to its respective ports. These control words consist of mode commands and bit SET/RESET commands that are written into the control register by the system CPU. The mode commands are used to set up the ports as inputs or outputs. The bit SET/RESET function allows individual setting and resetting of the bits of port C when it is an output port. The control register can only be written into. Under *no* circumstances can the control register be *read*.

Table 5-3 shows the addressing scheme of the **8255**. It shows the addresses required to read or write data to the data ports (A, B, and C). It also shows the address of the control register ($A1 = A0 = \overline{RD} = 1$ and $\overline{CS} = \overline{WR} = 0$). The table also shows that attempting to read the register results in an "illegal condition."

There are three basic modes of operation of the **8255** that can be selected by the control words. These modes are:

1 mode 0—basic input/output

2 mode 1—strobed input/output

3 mode 2—bidirectional bus

After the RESET pin goes HIGH all ports are set to mode 0 as inputs, which means that all 24 lines are in a high impedance state and can be used as normal input lines after the RESET pin is brought back LOW. The mode definition format of the control word is shown in Figure 5-18.

The mode operating conditions follow.

Mode 0 This mode provides simple input/output operations for the three ports. After the mode is set, data is simply read from or written to the ports. The mode 0

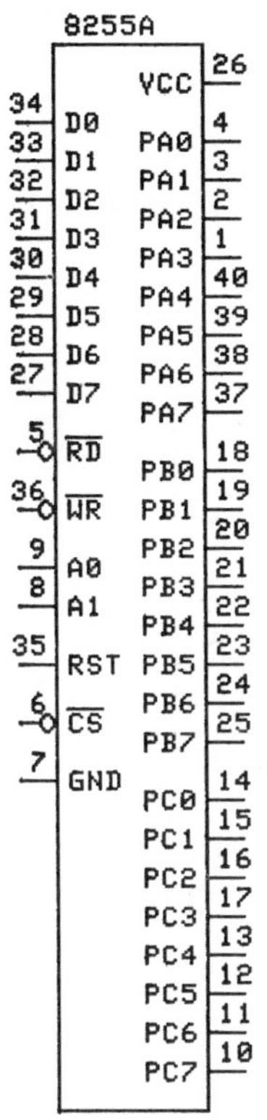

Figure 5-17 The pin out of the **8255A** (fractional arrangement).

Table 5-3 **8255A basic operation**

A_1	A_0	$\overline{RD}$	$\overline{WR}$	$\overline{CS}$	*Input operation* (*read*)
0	0	0	1	0	PORT A ⇒ DATA BUS
0	1	0	1	0	PORT B ⇒ DATA BUS
1	0	0	1	0	PORT C ⇒ DATA BUS
					Output operation (*write*)
0	0	1	0	0	DATA BUS ⇒ PORT A
0	1	1	0	0	DATA BUS ⇒ PORT B
1	0	1	0	0	DATA BUS ⇒ PORT C
1	1	1	0	0	DATA BUS ⇒ CONTROL
					Disable function
X	X	X	X	1	DATA BUS ⇒ 3-STATE
1	1	0	1	0	ILLEGAL CONDITION
X	X	1	1	0	DATA BUS ⇒ 3-STATE

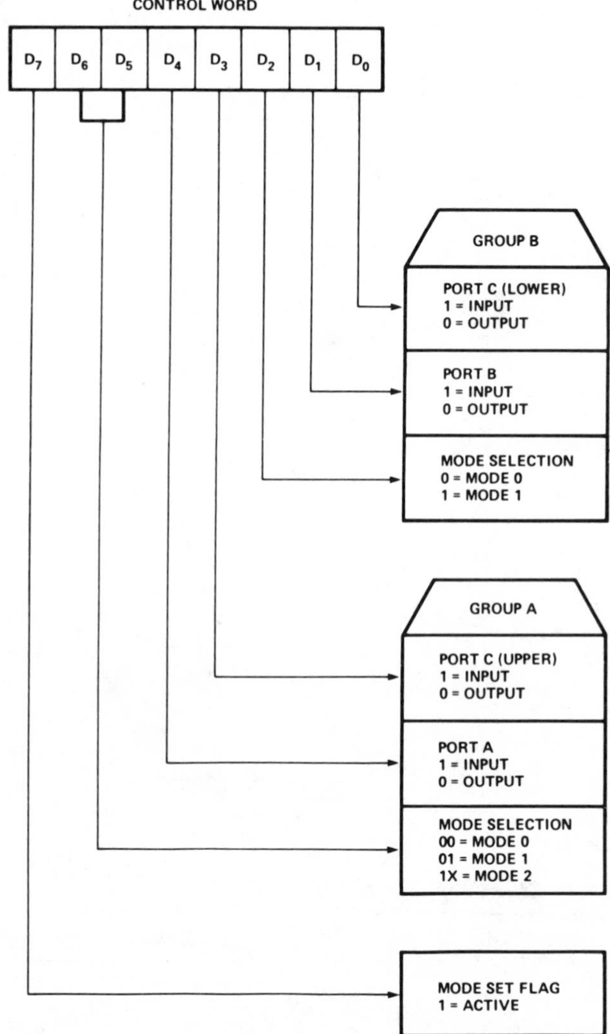

Figure 5-18 Mode definition format. (Reprinted by permission of Intel Corp.)

functional conditions are as follows:

1 Any port can be input or output.

2 Two 8-bit ports and two 4-bit ports.

3 Outputs are latched.

4 Inputs are not latched.

5 16 different input/output configurations are possible.

6 Writing to the made register resets any bits that are outputs.

Mode 1 In this mode data can be transferred to and from the **8255** with the use of strobe or handshaking lines. Some of the bits of port C are used for the strobe lines in this mode. The mode 1 functional conditions are as follows:

1 Group A or group B can be set independently.
2 Each group contains an 8-bit data port and a 4-bit control/data port.
3 The 8-bit ports can be used as either input or output. Both inputs and outputs are latched.
4 The 4-bit port is used for control and status of the 8-bit data port.

Mode 2 This mode allows a bidirectional 8-bit I/O bus to be created. Control and status lines are provided to handle the flow of data on the I/O bus. The mode 2 functional conditions are as follows:

1 Used by group A only.
2 An 8-bit bidirectional I/O port (port A) and a 5-bit control port (port C) are created.
3 Both inputs and outputs are latched.
4 The 5 bits of port C are used for control and status of port A.

5-6.2 Strobed Input Mode

Figure 5-19 illustrates an **8255** set up with port A as mode 1 input and with port B also as mode 1 input. The mode word to set up this condition is also given in the same figure.

The basic timing for the strobed input mode is shown in Figure 5-20. The device or peripheral that is inputting the data places the data byte in the PA or PB

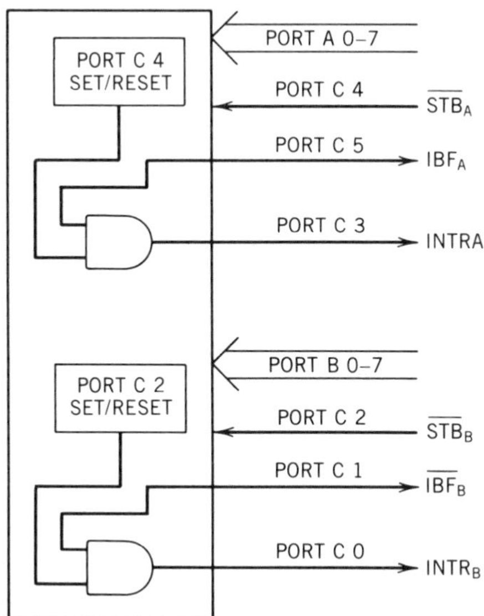

Figure 5-19 Mode 1 input.

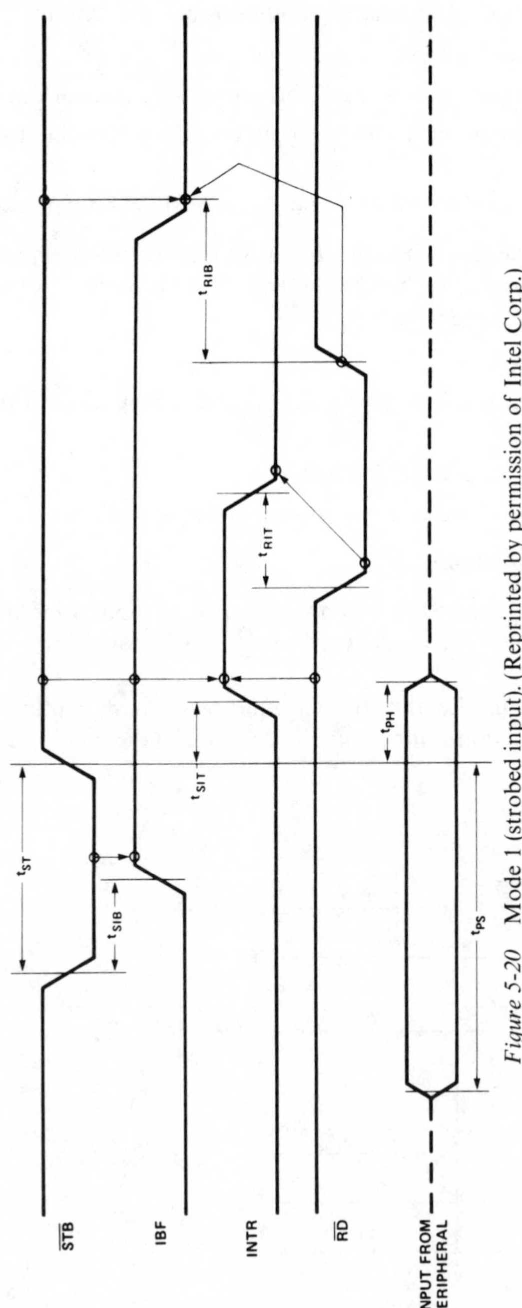

Figure 5-20 Mode 1 (strobed input). (Reprinted by permission of Intel Corp.)

lines and then provides a strobe to indicate to the **8255** that data is available. The **8255** reacts by raising IBF (input buffer full). The **8085** can determine that IBF = 1 by reading register C and looking at bit 1 (for the B side) and bit 5 (for the A side). A read of the A or B data register takes in the data and resets the corresponding IBF, which indicates to the peripheral that it can send more data.

The trailing edge of the strobe pulse also causes INTR to go HIGH. This can be used to interrupt the **8085** if interrupt programming is required. INTR is also reset by a READ of the corresponding (A or B) data register.

The functions of the port C lines as determined by the mode are as described below.

Port C Bit 4 — $\overline{\text{STBA}}$ Input strobe for port A
When STBA is pulsed LOW the data presented to the port A lines is latched into port A.

Port C Bit 5 — IBFA Input buffer full port A
This line goes HIGH after data is strobed into port A by the STBA signal. The line returns LOW after a CPU read of port A. This signal is used to identify when data can be written into port A by an external device.

Port C Bit 3 — INTRA Interrupt request port A
This signal will go HIGH after the IBFA line goes HIGH if its internal INTERRUPT ENABLE is set. The INTERRUPT ENABLE is controlled by the bit SET/RESET of port C bit 4. When this signal is set, INTRA will follow IBFA. If the bit is reset, then INTRA will always be LOW. INTRA can therefore be used as a maskable interrupt to the CPU to indicate a data transfer into port A.

Port C Bit 2 — $\overline{\text{STBB}}$ Input strobe for port B
Port B version of $\overline{\text{STBA}}$

Port C Bit 1 — IBFB Input buffer full port B
Port B version of IBFA

Port C Bit 0 — INTRB Interrupt request port B
Port B version of INTRA, except that the INTERRUPT ENABLE bit is port C bit 2.

Port C bits 6 and 7 are not used as control or status lines and therefore they can be used as either input or ouput. Bit 3 of the control word determines whether these lines are input or output.

5-6.3 Strobed Output Mode

Figure 5-21 illustrates an **8255** set up with both ports A and B as mode 1 output. The mode word to set up this condition is also given in the same figure.

The basic output timing is shown in Figure 5-22. In output mode a WRITE from the **8085** into port A or B causes the corresponding $\overline{\text{OBF}}$ (Output Buffer Full) line to go LOW, indicating that data is available. When the peripheral has read the

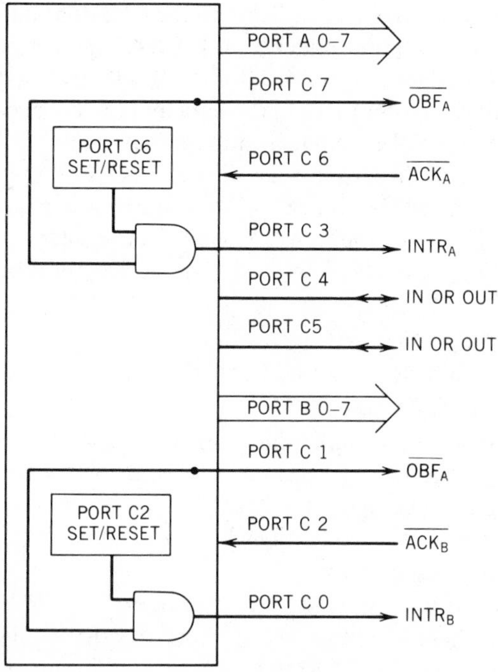

Figure 5-21 Mode 1 output.

data, it responds with a LOW going $\overline{\text{ACK}}$ pulse. The trailing edge of ACK causes $\overline{\text{OBF}}$ to go HIGH. This can be read by the **8085** reading the C port, and indicates that the output buffer is empty and the next data byte can be written to the **8255**. The trailing edge of $\overline{\text{ACK}}$ also causes an INTR to go HIGH so that interrupt programming may be used. INTR goes LOW on a WRITE to the A or B data register.

The functions of the port C lines as determined by the mode are described below.

Port C Bit 7 — $\overline{\text{OBFA}}$ Output buffer full port A
When data is written into port A by the CPU, this signal goes LOW to indicate that data is available at port A.

Port C Bit 6 — $\overline{\text{ACKA}}$ Acknowledge port A
When this signal goes LOW it indicates that an external device has accepted the data that was written out port A. This signal going LOW, then back HIGH, will reset the $\overline{\text{OBFA}}$ signal back HIGH.

Port C Bit 5 — INTRA Interrupt request port A
This signal is similar to INTRB. It is set HIGH when $\overline{\text{ACKA}}$ goes HIGH after a data transfer and if its INTERRUPT ENABLE port C bit 6 has been set. This signal can be used as a CPU interrupt to indicate that data written into port A has been accepted by an external device. This means that the CPU can now load the next output word into port A.

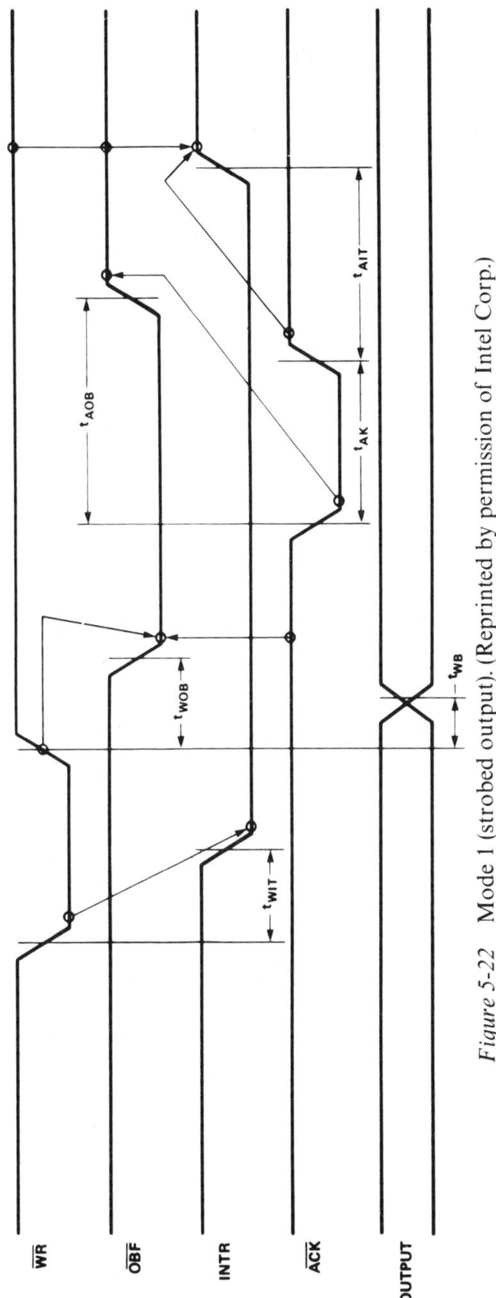

Figure 5-22 Mode 1 (strobed output). (Reprinted by permission of Intel Corp.)

Port C Bit 1 — OBFB — Output buffer full port B
Port B version of $\overline{OBFA}$

Port C Bit 2 — $\overline{ACKB}$ — Acknowledge port B
Port B version of ACKA

Port C Bit 0 — INTRB — Interrupt request port B
Port B version of INTRA, except that its ENABLE bit is port C bit 2.

Port C bits 4 and 5 are not used as control or status lines and therefore they can be used as either input or output. Their direction is determined by bit 3 of the control word (see Figure 5-21).

5-6.4 Mode 2 Operation

Figure 5-23 illustrates an **8255** set up with port A in mode 2. Port B is not shown, as mode 2 has no effect on it. The mode word used to set up a mode 2 condition is also given in the same figure. The functions of port C, as determined by mode 2, are shown below.

Port C Bit 7 — $\overline{OBFA}$ — Output buffer full port A
This signal is identical in function to the mode 1 OBFA signal.

Port C Bit 6 — $\overline{ACKA}$ — Acknowledge port A
This signal is similar in function to the mode 1 ACKA signal. The difference between their functions is that in mode 2 the output of port A is normally in a tri-state condition, so the ACKA signal enables the output buffers of port A, in addition to indicating that the external device has accepted the port A data.

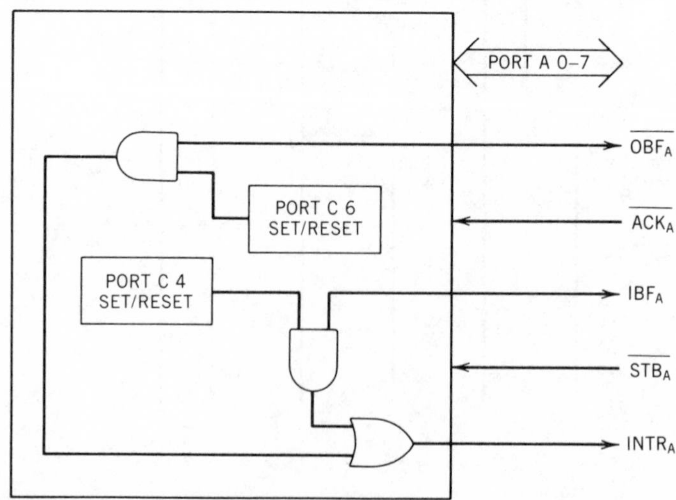

Figure 5-23 Mode 2 operation.

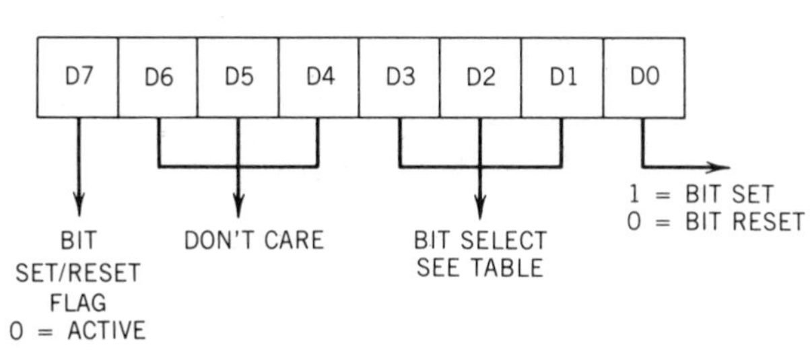

BIT SELECTED	D1	D2	D3
0	0	0	0
1	1	0	0
2	0	1	0
3	1	1	0
4	0	0	1
5	1	0	1
6	0	1	1
7	1	1	1

Figure 5-24 Control word for bit SET/RESET.

Port C Bit 4 $\overline{\text{STBA}}$ Input strobe for port A
This signal is identical in function to the mode 1 STBA signal.

Port C Bit 5 IBFA Input buffer full port A
This signal is identical in function to the mode 1 IBFA signal.

Port C Bit 3 INTRA Interrupt request port A
When port C bit 6 is set, this signal indicates that data written into port A by the CPU has been accepted by the external device. When port C bit 4 is set, this signal indicates that data has been written into port A by an external device. By proper control of port C bits 4 and 6 an interrupt driven, bidirectional, 8-bit data bus between the CPU and a peripheral device, or even another CPU, can be established.

The remaining bits of port C and all of port B can be used as either mode 1 or mode 2.

When using mode 1 or mode 2, there are special considerations in trying to read or write to the unused port C bits. Figure 5-24 shows how to use the control word to set and reset bits in port C. If the unused bits are programmed as outputs, then bits 7 through 4 (the upper bits) must be accessed individually using the bit SET/RESET function. Bits 3 through 0 (the lower bits) can be accessed either by using the bit SET/RESET function or by writing into port C.

5-6.5 The Status Word

In mode 1 or mode 2 operation, a read of port C becomes a status word input to the CPU. The bits in the status word and their definition are shown in Figure 5-25. A read of the status word allows the CPU to monitor the states of the interrupt

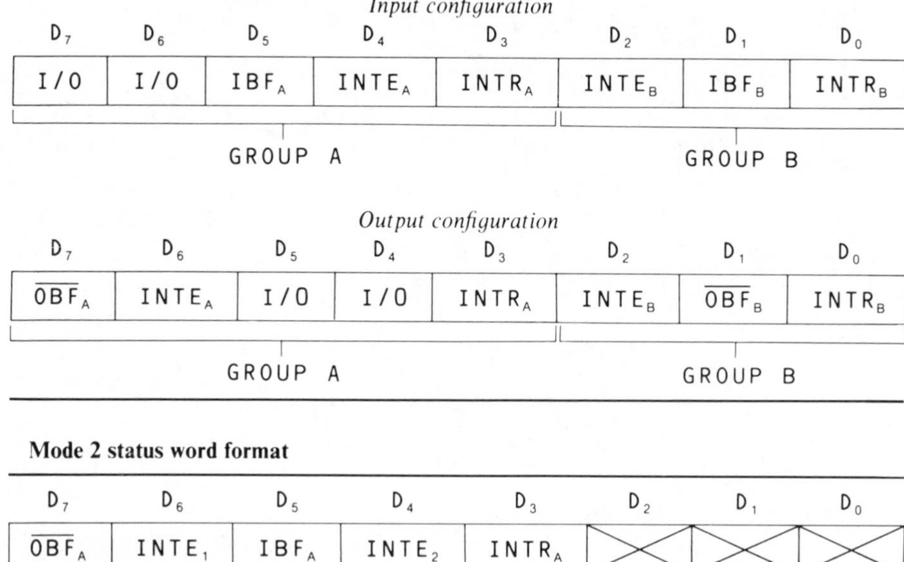

Mode 2 status word format

D_7	D_6	D_5	D_4	D_3	D_2	D_1	D_0
$\overline{OBF}_A$	$INTE_1$	IBF_A	$INTE_2$	$INTR_A$	X	X	X
GROUP A					GROUP B		

(Defined by mode 0 or mode 1 selection)

Figure 5-25 **8255** modes 1 and 2 status word definition.

and buffer full lines and the bits of port C that are used as I/O, and to react appropriately.

5-6.6 A Data Communications Controller Using the 8255

The program of Table 5-4 demonstrates a peripheral communications link using an **8255**. The program uses port A, in mode 1, as the output port, and it uses port B, in mode 1, as the input port. Bit 6 of port C is used as an attention signal that indicates to the peripheral device that a message will be sent. Bit 7 of port C is unused and bits 0–5 are handshake lines. In this program, the **8255** is assumed to reside at addresses 00H through 03H.[1] In practice, however, the **8255** could be located anywhere in the I/O map by changing lines 6 through 9 of the example program to the correct addresses. The program also assumes that there are at least 222 bytes of memory located at 800H, and that there is 512 bytes of RAM memory starting at location 1000H. The 222 bytes are used to hold the actual program, and the 512 bytes are used as message buffers.

This program will transmit and then receive messages, from 1 to 255 bytes long, to and from a peripheral device. The message format is 1 byte indicating the

[1] Notice on line 6 that port A equals 00H, etc.

Table 5-4 **A program for a communications link using the 8255 programmable peripheral interface**

```
                         ASM80 :F5:8255EX.1 MOD85 SYMBOLS XREF LIST


ISIS-II 8080/8085 MACRO ASSEMBLER, V4.0          MODULE   PAGE    1


 LOC  OBJ          SOURCE STATEMENT

                   ;        8255A MODE 1 COMMUNICATIONS EXAMPLE
                   ;
                   ;        8255A SETUP PROCEDURE
                   ;
0800               ORG      800H            ;SET THE STARTING ADRESS OF PROCEDURE EQUAL TO 800HEX
0000               PORTA    EQU     00H     ;EQUATE THE LABEL PORTA WITH THE ADDRESS 00H
0001               PORTB    EQU     01H     ;EQUATE THE LABEL PORTB WITH THE ADDRESS 01H
0002               PORTC    EQU     02H     ;EQUATE THE LABEL PORTC WITH THE ADDRESS 02H
0003               CWR      EQU     03H     ;EQUATE THE LABEL CWR (CONTROL WORD REGISTER) WITH 03H
1000               OBUF     EQU     1000H   ;EQUATE THE LABEL OUTBUF WITH THE VALUE 1000H
1100               IBUF     EQU     1100H   ;EQUATE THE LABEL INBUF WITH THE VALUE 1100H
                   ;
0800 3EA6                   MVI     A,0A6H  ;LOAD THE A REGISTER WITH THE MODE CONTROL WORD
0802 D303                   OUT     CWR     ;OUTPUT THE MODE CONTROL WORD TO THE CONTROL WORD REG
0804 210010                 LXI     H,OBUF  ;LOAD THE HL REG PAIR WITH THE OUTPUT DATA POINTER
0807 46                     MOV     B,M     ;LOAD THE B REG WITH THE NUM OF BYTES TO BE SENT
0808 23                     INX     H       ;INCREMENT THE MESSAGE POINTER TO THE FIRST BYTE
                   ;
                   ;        THE 8255 IS NOW SET UP WITH PORT A AS A MODE 1 OUTPUT PORT, PORT B AS A
                   ;        MODE 1 INPUT PORT, AND PORT C BITS 6 AND 7 AS OUTPUT.
                   ;
                   ;        THIS PROCEDURE NOTIFIES THE THE EXTERNAL DEVICE THAT DATA IS READY
                   ;        TO BE SENT AND CLEARS PORT B IF IT IS FULL.
                   ;
0809 3E0D                   MVI     A,0DH   ;LOAD A REG WITH THE CODE TO SET PORT C BIT 6
080B D303                   OUT     CWR     ;OUTPUT THE CODE TO THE CWR
080D 00                     NOP             ;WASTE SOME TIME
080E 00                     NOP
080F 3E0C                   MVI     A,0CH   ;LOAD A REG WITH THE CODE TO RESET PORT C BIT 6
0811 D303                   OUT     CWR     ;OUTPUT THE CODE TO THE CWR
0813 DB02                   IN      PORTC   ;READ THE STATUS WORD
0815 E602                   ANI     02H     ;MASK OFF ALL BITS EXCEPT IBFB
0817 CA1C08                 JZ      OUTLNG  ;IF THE IBFB BIT IS CLEAR THEN JUMP TO OUTLNG PROCEDURE
                   ;
                   ;        IF THE IBFB BIT IS SET THEN CLEAR IT
                   ;
081A DB01                   IN      PORTB   ;READ THE BYTE CONTAINED IN THE PORT B REG
                   ;
                   ;        THIS PROCEDURE OUTPUTS THE MESSAGE LENGTH TO THE EXTERNAL DEVICE
                   ;
081C 78            OUTLNG:  MOV     A,B     ;LOAD A WITH THE BYTE COUNT
081D D300                   OUT     PORTA   ;WRITE THE DATA TO PORT A
081F DB02          LOOPB1:  IN      PORTC   ;READ THE STATUS WORD
0821 E680                   ANI     80H     ;MASK OFF ALL BITS EXCEPT OBFA NOT
0823 CA1F08                 JZ      LOOPB1  ;IF OBFA NOT IS LOW THEN GO BACK AND READ IT AGAIN
0826 DB02          LOOPB2:  IN      PORTC   ;READ THE STATUS WORD
0828 E602                   ANI     02H     ;MASK OFF ALL BITS EXCEPT IBFB
082A CA2608                 JZ      LOOPB2  ;IF IBFB IS LOW THEN GO BACK AND READ IT AGAIN
082D DB01                   IN      PORTB   ;READ THE ECHOED DATA
082F B8                     CMP     B       ;COMPARE IT WITH THE DATA WRITTEN
0830 CA3908                 JZ      NEXT1   ;IF THEY ARE EQUAL JUMP TO THE MESSAGE OUTPUT PROCEDURE
```

Table 5-4 **(*Continued*)**

```
LOC  OBJ        SOURCE STATEMENT

0833 CDAD08            CALL   ERR1    ;IF THEY ARE NOT EQUAL CALL THE OUTPUT ERROR PROCEDURE
0836 C31C08            JMP    OUTLNG
                ;
                ;
                ;      THIS PROCEDURE OUTPUTS A BYTE OF DATA, WAITS FOR IT TO BE ECHOED
                ;      BACK, AND TESTS THAT THE ECHOED DATA IS CORRECT
                ;
0839 7E         NEXT1: MOV    A,M     ;LOAD THE A REG WITH THE FIRST BYTE OF DATA
083A D300              OUT    PORTA   ;WRITE THE DATA TO PORT A
083C 4F                MOV    C,A     ;SAVE THE DATA IN REG C
083D DB02       LOOP1: IN     PORTC   ;READ THE STATUS WORD
083F E680              ANI    80H     ;MASK OFF ALL BITS EXCEPT OBFA NOT
0841 CA3D08            JZ     LOOP1   ;IF OBFA NOT IS LOW THEN GO BACK AND READ IT AGAIN
0844 DB02       LOOP2: IN     PORTC   ;READ THE STATUS WORD
0846 E602              ANI    02H     ;MASK OFF ALL BITS EXCEPT IBFB
0848 CA4408            JZ     LOOP2   ;IF IBFB IS LOW THEN GO BACK AND READ IT AGAIN
084B DB01              IN     PORTB   ;READ THE INPUT DATA FROM PORT B
084D B9                CMP    C       ;COMPARE THE DATA READ WITH THE DATA WRITTEN
084E CA5708            JZ     OK1     ;IF EQUAL THEN JUMP TO THE OK1 PROCEDURE
0851 CDAD08            CALL   ERR1    ;IF NOT EQUAL THEN CALL THE OUTPUT ERROR PROCEDURE
0854 C33908            JMP    NEXT1   ;RETRANSMIT THE BYTE THE HAD THE ERROR
0857 05         OK1:   DCR    B       ;DECREMENT THE MESSAGE LENGTH COUNTER
0858 23                INX    H       ;INCREMENT THE MESSAGE POINTER ADDRESS
0859 C23908            JNZ    NEXT1   ;IF MESSAGE NOT COMPLETE THEN OUTPUT THE NEXT BYTE
085C 210011            LXI    H,IBUF  ;IF THE MESSAGE IS COMPLETE THEN LOAD HL WITH THE
                                      ;INPUT MESSAGE BUFFER POINTER AND THEN READ THE INPUT
                                      ;MESSAGE
                ;
                ;      THIS PROCEDURE INPUTS THE MESSAGE LENGTH FROM THE EXTERNAL DEVICE
                ;
085F DB02       INLNG: IN     PORTC   ;READ THE STATUS WORD
0861 E602              ANI    02H     ;MASK OFF ALL BITS EXCEPT IBFB
0863 CA5F08            JZ     INLNG   ;IF IBFB IS LOW THEN READ IT AGAIN
0866 DB01              IN     PORTB   ;READ THE MESSAGE LENGTH
0868 47         ECLNG: MOV    B,A     ;SAVE THE LENGTH IN REG B
0869 D300              OUT    PORTA   ;ECHO THE DATA BACK
086B DB02       LOOPB3: IN    PORTC   ;READ THE STATUS WORD
086D E680              ANI    80H     ;MASK OFF ALL BITS EXCEPT OBFA NOT
086F CA6B08            JZ     LOOPB3  ;IF OBFA NOT IS LOW THEN READ IT AGAIN
0872 DB02       LOOPB4: IN    PORTC   ;READ THE STATUS WORD
0874 E602              ANI    02H     ;MASK OFF ALL BITS EXCEPT IBFB
0876 CA7208            JZ     LOOPB4  ;IF IBFB IS LOW THEN READ IT AGAIN
0879 DB01              IN     PORTB   ;READ THE DATA
087B FEFF              CPI    0FFH    ;CHECK FOR ERROR INDICATOR BYTE
087D C28608            JNZ    OK2     ;IF NO ERROR THEN CONTINUE
0880 CDC708            CALL   ERR2    ;IF ERROR THEN CALL THE RECEPTION ERROR PROCEDURE
0883 C36808            JMP    ECLNG   ;GO BACK AND ECHO THE LENGTH AGAIN
0886 70         OK2:   MOV    M,B     ;SAVE THE LENGTH IN THE MESSAGE BUFFER
0887 23                INX    H       ;INCREMENT THE MESSAGE BUFFER POINTER
                ;
                ;      THIS PROCEDURE LOOKS FOR INPUT DATA THEN ECHOS IT
                ;
0888 4F         NEXT2: MOV    C,A     ;IF NO ERROR LOAD THE DATA INTO REG C
0889 D300              OUT    PORTA   ;ECHO THE DATA BACK
088B DB02       LOOP4: IN     PORTC   ;READ THE STATUS WORD
088D E680              ANI    80H     ;MASK OFF ALL BITS EXCEPT OBFA NOT
088F CA8B08            JZ     LOOP4   ;WAIT UNTIL ECHO IS READ
0892 DB02       LOOP5: IN     PORTC   ;READ THE STATUS WORD
```

Table 5-4 (Continued)

```
LOC  OBJ             SOURCE STATEMENT

0894 E602                   ANI   02H     ;MASK OFF ALL BITS EXCEPT IBFB
0896 CA9208                 JZ    LOOP5   ;IF IBFB IS LOW THEN READ IT AGAIN
0899 DB01                   IN    PORTB   ;READ THE DATA
089B FEFF                   CPI   0FFH    ;TEST FOR ERROR INDICATOR BYTE
089D C2A608                 JNZ   OK3     ;IF NO ERROR THEN SAVE THE BYTE
08A0 CDC708                 CALL  ERR2    ;IF ERROR THEN CALL THE RECEPTION ERROR PROCEDURE
08A3 C38808                 JMP   NEXT2   ;ECHO THE DATA BYTE AGAIN
08A6 71              OK3:   MOV   M,C     ;IF NO ERROR THEN LOAD THE DATA INTO THE MESSAGE BUF
08A7 23                     INX   H       ;INCREMENT THE MESSAGE POINTER
08A8 05                     DCR   B       ;DECREMENT THE BYTE COUNT
08A9 C28808                 JNZ   NEXT2   ;IF MESSAGE NOT COMPLETE THEN CONTINUE READING DATA
08AC C9                     RET           ;IF MESSAGE COMPLETE THEN RETURN TO CALLING ROUTINE
                     ;
                     ;
                     ;      THIS PROCEDURE HANDLES DATA TRANSMISSION ERRORS
                     ;
08AD 3EFF            ERR1:  MVI   A,0FFH  ;LOAD A WITH THE ERROR INDICATOR BYTE
08AF D300                   OUT   PORTA   ;WRITE THE BYTE TO PORT A
08B1 4F                     MOV   C,A     ;SAVE THE DATA IN REG C
08B2 DB02            LOOPE1: IN   PORTC   ;READ THE STATUS WORD
08B4 E680                   ANI   80H     ;MASK OFF ALL BITS EXCEPT OBFA NOT
08B6 CAB208                 JZ    LOOPE1  ;IF OBFA NOT IS LOW THEN GO BACK AND READ IT AGAIN
08B9 DB02            LOOPE2: IN   PORTC   ;READ THE STATUS WORD
08BB E602                   ANI   02H     ;MASK OFF ALL BITS EXCEPT IBFB
08BD CAB908                 JZ    LOOPE2  ;IF IBFB IS LOW THEN GO BACK AND READ IT AGAIN
08C0 DB01                   IN    PORTB   ;READS THE ECHOED DATA
08C2 B9                     CMP   C       ;COMPARE READ DATA WITH SAVED DATA
08C3 C4DF08                 CNZ   FAIL    ;IF DATA NOT EQUAL CALL THE FAILURE ROUTINE
08C6 C9                     RET           ;IF DATA EQUAL THEN RETURN TO CALL POINT
                     ;
                     ;      THIS PROCEDURE HANDLES DATA RECEPTION ERRORS
                     ;
08C7 D300            ERR2:  OUT   PORTA   ;ECHO BACK THE ERROR INDICATOR BYTE
08C9 DB02            LOOPE3: IN   PORTC   ;READ THE STATUS WORD
08CB E680                   ANI   80H     ;MASK OFF ALL BITS EXCEPT OBFA NOT
08CD CAC908                 JZ    LOOPE3  ;IF OBFA NOT IS LOW THEN READ IT AGAIN
08D0 DB02            LOOPE4: IN   PORTC   ;READ THE STATUS WORD
08D2 E602                   ANI   02H     ;MASK OFF ALL BITS EXCEPT IBFB
08D4 CAD008                 JZ    LOOPE4  ;IF IBFB IS LOW THEN READ IT AGAIN
08D7 DB01                   IN    PORTB   ;READ PORT B
08D9 FEFF                   CPI   0FFH    ;TEST FOR ANOTHER ECHO ERROR
08DB CCDF08                 CZ    FAIL    ;IF IT IS ANOTHER ECHO ERROR CALL THE FAIL PROCEDURE
08DE C9                     RET           ;IF NOT AN ERROR THEN RETURN TO CALL POINT
                     ;
                     ;      THIS IS THE COMMUNICATION FAILURE ROUTINE
                     ;
08DF 76              FAIL:  HLT           ;THE HALT INSRUCTION SHOWN HERE IS A DUMMY. THIS
                                          ;ROUTINE WOULD NORMALLY INDICATE A SYSTEM COMMUNICATION
                                          ;ERROR. THE FIRST TWO BYTES ON THE STACK WOULD BE
                                          ;THE RETURN ADDRESS OF THE ERROR PROCEDURE THAT CALLED
                                          ;FAIL AND THE NEXT TWO BYTES ON THE STACK WOULD BE
                                          ;THE RETURN ADDRESS OF THE PROCEDURE THAT CALLED THE
                                          ;ERROR PROCEDURE. THESE CAN BE USED TO DETERMINE WHAT
                                          ;TYPE OF ERROR OCURRED.
                            END
```

Table 5-4 (Continued)

```
LOC  OBJ          LINE         SOURCE STATEMENT
PUBLIC SYMBOLS

EXTERNAL SYMBOLS

USER SYMBOLS
CWR    A 0003   ECLNG  A 0868   ERR1   A 08AD   ERR2   A 08C7   FAIL   A 08DF   IBUF   A 1100   INLNG  A 085F
LOOP1  A 083D   LOOP2  A 0844   LOOP4  A 088B   LOOP5  A 0892   LOOPB1 A 081F   LOOPB2 A 0826   LOOPB3 A 086B
LOOPB4 A 0872   LOOPE1 A 08B2   LOOPE2 A 08B9   LOOPE3 A 08C9   LOOPE4 A 08D0   NEXT1  A 0839   NEXT2  A 0888
OBUF   A 1000   OK1    A 0857   OK2    A 0886   OK3    A 08A6   OUTLNG A 081C   PORTA  A 0000   PORTB  A 0001
PORTC  A 0002

ASSEMBLY COMPLETE,   NO ERRORS

ISIS-II ASSEMBLER SYMBOL CROSS REFERENCE, V2.1                    PAGE   1

CWR       9#    14     26     30
ECLNG    86#    98
ERR1     52     71    126#
ERR2     97    115    142#
FAIL    137    151    156#
IBUF     11#    76
INLNG    82#    84
LOOP1    62#    64
LOOP2    65#    67
LOOP4   106#   108
LOOP5   109#   111
LOOPB1   43#    45
LOOPB2   46#    48
LOOPB3   88#    90
LOOPB4   91#    93
LOOPE1  129#   131
LOOPE2  132#   134
LOOPE3  143#   145
LOOPE4  146#   148
NEXT1    51     59#    72     75
NEXT2   104#   116    120
OBUF     10#    15
OK1      70     73#
OK2      96     99#
OK3     114    117#
OUTLNG   33     41#    53
PORTA     6#    42     60     87    105    127    142
PORTB     7#    37     49     68     85     94    112    135    149
PORTC     8#    31     43     46     62     65     82     88     91    106    109    129    132    143    146

CROSS REFERENCE COMPLETE
```

message length, followed by the rest of the message. Before calling this program, location 1000H should be loaded with the length of the message to be sent. Locations 1001H through 10FFH should be loaded with the message to be sent, using as many sequential locations as required. When the program returns to where it was called from, location 1100H will contain the length of the message received. The message itself will be located between 1101H and 11FFH in memory, using as many locations as required.

The program verifies the integrity of each byte transmitted and received by means of *data echoing*. After a byte is sent out, it should be echoed back immediately by the receiving device. The byte received is then compared to the byte that was transmitted and, if they are equal, the next byte of the message is sent. However, if the bytes are not equal, the value 0FFH is sent to the peripheral device indicating a *bad echo*. The program then looks for the echoing of the 0FFH value and if it is received correctly, then the byte that was echoed incorrectly is retransmitted. If the error indicator byte (0FFH) is not echoed correctly, then the program calls another program named FAIL. The FAIL program should indicate to an operator that the communications link is not functioning. The procedure for verifying received data is similar. In this case, this program does the echoing of the data and checks to see if an error indicator byte has been received.

The format of the program listing is as follows:

Column 1	Location	Hex value of address where the first byte of the instruction on the program line is to be placed in memory.
Column 2	Object	Hex value(s) of the instruction. There is 1 byte for a single-byte instruction, 2 bytes for a 2-byte instruction, and so on.
Column 3	Line	Program line number.
Column 4	Label	Labels are used to identify constants that are used frequently in the program. They are also used to identify specific points in a program that are referenced by instructions such as the JUMP or CALL instructions.
Column 5	Op code	The mnemonic code that is used to represent an instruction.
Column 6	Operand	The register, data, port, and so on, that the instruction operates upon.
Column 7	Comments	A semicolon, followed by text used to explain the program. Semicolons can also be placed in column 4 to insert blank lines, or to add headers at the start of program sections.

5-7 REFERENCES

Kenneth L. Short, *Microprocessors and Programmed Logic*, Prentice-Hall, Englewood Cliffs, N.J., 1981.

Mohamed Rafiquzzaman, *Microcomputer Theory and Application*, Wiley, New York, 1982.

Lance A. Leventhal, *Introduction to Microprocessors: Software, Hardware, Programming*, Prentice-Hall, Englewood Cliffs, N.J., 1978.

Intel Corp., *MCS-85 User's Manual*, Santa Clara, Calif., 1978.

CHAPTER 6

The Zilog Z80

Glenn A. Barlis
Mobil Chemical Co.
Macedon, New York

6-1 INTRODUCTION

The **Z80**[1] is one of the most popular of the 8-bit microprocessors. It has achieved this position in large part because it is an enhancement of the ubiquitous **8080A**. The **Z80** is not pin compatible with the **8080A** but it does include all of the **8080A** instructions as a subset of its own. Because of this instruction compatibility, the **Z80** user is able to capitalize on the vast amount of available **8080A** software while gaining more power because of the additional instructions, registers, and addressing modes the **Z80** offers.

The **Z80** uses a form of NMOS technology which requires only a single +5-V power supply instead of the three voltages required by the **8080A**. Other features of the **Z80** include a single clock signal, dynamic memory refresh logic, and two types of interrupts. This chapter concentrates on the aspects of the **Z80** that are enhancements to the **8080A** and only touch briefly on those items that the two have in common. The reader is referred to Chapter 4 on the **8080A** for details on items not covered in depth here.

Intel has produced its own enhancement of the **8080A** called the **8085**. Like the **Z80**, it is not pin compatible with the **8080A** but uses the **8080A** instruction set, with only two additional instructions. The two instructions RIM and SIM are not included in the **Z80**. Except for these two instructions, all future references to the **8080A** instruction set also apply to the **8085**.

A comment on the notation used in this chapter is in order. Zilog chose not to use Intel's (copyrighted) assembler mnemonics for the **Z80** instruction set. This can

[1] **Z80** is a trademark of Zilog, Inc., with whom the publisher is not associated.

be a nuisance when comparing **Z80** and **8080A** assembly code, but the **Z80** mnemonics will be used in this chapter. Table 6-1 provides a comparison of the Zilog and Intel mnemonics for the instructions that the **Z-80** and **8080A** have in common.

6-2 ARCHITECTURE

Figure 6-1 shows the register set of the **Z80**. Note that all of the **8080A** registers are included. The program counter (PC), stack pointer (SP), A, B, C, D, E, H, and L registers and the F flag register are identical to those in the **8080A**. The operation of these registers, with the exception of the flags as described later, is also identical to their use in the **8080A**.

The **Z80** has an additional register set, labeled A′, F′, B′, C′, D′, E′, H′, and L′, which duplicates the unprimed registers of the same name. Only one of the register sets can be *active* at any one time. The alternative set can be reached by means of one of the two exchange commands EX AF, AF′ and EXX) in the **Z80** instruction set. The alternative register set has been added as a means of providing a fast way to switch registers during single-level interrupt operations such as high-speed serial I/O. The use of the exchange commands is much faster than pushing registers on the stack as a way of saving their values during an interrupt. Since there is only one

Main accumulator	A	s	z	—	h	—	p/v	n	c	Main flag register
	B	C								Main general-purpose registers
	D	E								
	H	L								
Alternate accumulator	A′	s′	z′	—	h′	—	p/v′	n′	c′	Alternate flag register
	B′	C′								Alternate general-purpose registers
	D′	E′								
	H′	L′								
Interrupt vector	I	R								Refresh register
	IX									Index register
	IY									Index register
	SP									Stack pointer
	PC									Program counter

Figure 6-1 **Z80** CPU registers.

Table 6-1 **8080–Z80 mnemonic comparison**

8080	Z80	8080	Z80	8080	Z80
ACI N	ADC A,N	IN	IN A,(N)	POP H	POP HL
ADC M	ADC A,(HL)	INR M	INC (HL)	POP PSW	POP AF
ADC R	ADC A,R	INR R	INR R	PUSH B	PUSH BC
ADD M	ADD A,(HL)	INX B	INC BC	PUSH D	PUSH DE
ADD R	ADD A,R	INX D	INC DE	PUSH H	PUSH HL
ADI N	ADD A,N	INX H	INC HL	PUSH PSW	PUSH AF
ANA M	AND A,(HL)	INX SP	INC SP	RAL	RLA
ANA R	AND A,R	JC NN	JP C,NN	RAR	RRA
ANI N	AND A,N	JM NN	JP M,NN	RC	RET C
CALL NN	CALL NN	JMP NN	JP NN	RET	RET
CC NN	CALL C,NN	JNC NN	JP NC,NN	RLC	RLCA
CM NN	CALL M,NN	JNZ NN	JP NZ,NN	RM	RET M
CMA	CPL	JP NN	JP P,NN	RNC	RET NC
CMC	CCF	JPE NN	JP PE,NN	RNZ	RET NZ
CMP M	CP (HL)	JPO NN	JP PO,NN	RP	RET P
CMP R	CP A,R	JZ NN	JP Z,NN	RPE	RET PE
CNC NN	CALL NC,NN	LDA	LD A,(NN)	RPO	RET PO
CNZ NN	CALL NZ,NN	LDAX B	LD A,(BC)	RRC	RRCA

CP NN	CALL P,NN	LDAX D	LD A,(DE)	RST	RST
CPE NN	CALL PE,NN	LHLD	LD HL,(NN)	RZ	RET Z
CPI	CP A,N	LXI B	LD BC,NN	SBB M	SBC A,(HL)
CPO NN	CALL PO,NN	LXI D	LD DE,NN	SBB R	SBC A,R
CZ NN	CALL Z,NN	LXI H	LD HL,NN	SBI	SBC A,N
DAA	DAA	LXI SP	LD SP,NN	SHLD	LD (NN),HL
DAD B	ADD HL,BC	MVI M	LD (HL),N	SPHL	LD SP,HL
DAD D	ADD HL,DE	MVI R	LD (HL),R	STA	LD (NN),A
DAD H	ADD HL,HL	MOV M,R	LD (HL),R	STAX B	LD (BC),A
DAD SP	ADD HL,SP	MOV R,M	LD R,(HL)	STAX D	LD (DE),A
DCR M	DEC (HL)	MOV R,R1	LD R,R1	STC	SCF
DCR R	DEC R	NOP	NOP	SUB M	SUB A,(HL)
DCX B	DEC BC	ORA M	OR A,(HL)	SUB R	SUB A,R
DCX D	DEC DE	ORA R	OR A,R	SUI	SUB A,N
DCX H	DEC HL	ORI	OR A,N	XCHG	EX DE,HL
DCX SP	DEC SP	OUT	OUT (N),A	XRA M	XOR A,(HL)
DI	DI	PCHL	JP (HL)	XRA R	XOR A,R
EI	EI	POP B	POP BC	XRI	XOR A,N
HLT	HALT	POP D	POP DE	XTHL	EX (SP),HL

duplicate register set, this technique only works with a single level of interrupt. Multiple interrupt levels require the use of the stack.

The **Z80** has two 16-bit *index registers*, labeled IX and IY in Figure 6-1, which are not found in the **8080A**. The index registers allow the user to access tables of data by using as an address the sum of the contents of the index register and an 8-bit value included in the instruction. The operation of these registers will be detailed in section 6-3.

The 8-bit *interrupt vector register* is used during the **Z80** mode 2 interrupt cycle. As will be explained in section 6-5, this register is used to form an address to a table of interrupt vectors. This register has no equivalent in the **8080A**.

Dynamic memory chips must have each location read every few milliseconds in order to maintain the data stored in them. The **Z80** includes a *memory refresh register* to automatically provide this function. While the CPU is decoding and executing the instruction fetched during an Op code cycle, it places a refresh address on the address bus and pulls the RFSH line low. The CPU places the I and R register contents on the address bus, but only the low 7 bits are used as the refresh address. These signals can be used with a small amount of logic to cause a read of all system dynamic memory chips. The low 7 bits of the refresh register are incremented after each instruction fetch so that all memory locations are refreshed in the required time.

EXAMPLE 6-1 How large a dynamic RAM can the **Z80** refresh? How long does it normally take?

Solution Dynamic RAMs are usually "square." That is, their number of rows and columns are equal, and all cells in the same row are refreshed at the same time. Since the **Z80** provides 7 bits for the refresh address, it can address 128 rows. Typically, each row has 128 cells (or columns) so the **Z80** can refresh a 16K RAM. The average **Z80** instruction may take 8 T states and the clock runs at 2 MHz. Therefore, a new refresh address is presented every 4 μs, and it requires 512 μs to refresh an entire 16K memory.

The two flag registers, F and F′, are not registers that can be manipulated by the user in the same manner as the general-purpose registers. There are only three operations that can be done on these registers as a whole—PUSH to stack, POP from stack, and EXchange one with the other. Since the **Z80** stack operations always involve 16 bits, all of these operations are done in conjunction with the respective A register. Their purpose is to save the status flag conditions for future use while other operations which may change them are being performed. CPU operations only alter the individual bits of the active flag register.

Each of the flag registers has 6 bits, which are set or reset by certain CPU operations. Four of the bits (P/V, Z, C, and S) may be tested for condition by the JUMP, CALL, and RETURN instructions. The other two flags (H and N) are used for BCD arithmetic.

The *sign flag* (s) represents the state of bit 7 (MSB) of the accumulator after arithmetic or logical operations. The **Z80** does binary arithmetic using 2s complement numbers so bit 7 represents the sign of the number. The sign flag bit is also affected by certain I/O and 16-bit arithmetic operations.

The zero *flag* (z) bit is set to 1 if the result of an operation leaves a zero in the accumulator. It is also affected by certain I/O and 16-bit arithmetic operations.

The *parity/overflow flag* (p/v) is a dual purpose flag which indicates the *parity* of the result of logical operations and *overflow* of 2s complement arithmetic operations. Since parity and overflow are mutually exclusive conditions for any given operation, the use of one flag with two meanings is not a problem. The parity flag operation is identical to that in the **8080A**. The flag is set to 1 if the result of a logical operation is a byte with even parity. If the byte has odd parity, the flag is reset to 0.

The overflow status has no counterpart in the **8080A**. This flag is set to 1 if the result of a signed binary arithmetic operation is in error (overflow has occurred). This flag is needed for signed binary arithmetic since the carry flag does not reflect the true result of such an operation. Unless a program written for the **8080A** uses the parity flag in an unorthodox manner, this flag difference will cause no difficulty when the program is run on a **Z80**.

The *carry flag* (c) holds the result of any carry from the highest bit of the accumulator during arithmetic operations. The flag is set to 1 if a carry results during an addition or a borrow during a subtraction. ROTATE instructions also affect this flag bit. The **Z80** instruction set includes commands for setting and complementing this bit.

The *half-carry flag* (h) is one of the two nontestable flags in the **Z80**. It represents any carry or borrow resulting from BCD operations on the least significant 4 bits of the operands. The decimal adjust accumulator (DAA) instruction uses this bit to correct the result of BCD add and subtracts.

The *subtract flag* (n) is the other nontestable flag. It is used by the DAA instruction to determine if the value to be adjusted is the result of an addition or a subtraction. This is necessary because the algorithm for making the correction differs for the two operations. The **8080A** does not have this flag, since it performs the DAA operation internally in a different manner.

The exact nature in which the flag bits are affected by **Z80** operations can be found in Tables 6-2 through 6-13, which summarize the **Z80** instruction set.

6-3 ADDRESSING MODES

The most significant improvement of the **Z80** over the **8080A**, from the programmer's viewpoint, is the addition of several useful addressing modes and the extension of existing **8080A** modes to more instruction types. The standard **8080A** addressing modes will be discussed first with comments on the new instructions that use them.

6-3.1 Immediate Addressing

In the immediate addressing mode, the operand is the byte in memory following the Op code, for example,

Mnemonic	`LD A,0BH`
Hex	`3E 0B`

Note: Text resumes after Table 6-13 on page 199.

Table 6-2 **Summary of flag operation and symbolic notation**

Summary of Flag Operation

Instruction	D_7 S	Z		H		P/V	N	D_0 C	Comments
ADD A, s; ADC A, s	↕	↕	X	↕	X	V	0	↕	8-bit add or add with carry.
SUB s; SBC A, s; CP s; NEG	↕	↕	X	↕	X	V	1	↕	8-bit subtract, subtract with carry, compare and negate accumulator
AND s	↕	↕	X	1	X	P	0	0	Logical operations.
OR s, XOR s	↕	↕	X	0	X	P	0	0	Logical operations.
INC s	↕	↕	X	↕	X	V	0	•	8-bit increment.
DEC s	↕	↕	X	↕	X	V	1	•	8-bit decrement.
ADD DD, ss	•	•	X	X	X	•	0	↕	16-bit add.
ADC HL, ss	↕	↕	X	X	X	V	0	↕	16-bit add with carry.
SBC HL, ss	↕	↕	X	X	X	V	1	↕	16-bit subtract with carry.
RLA, RLCA, RRA; RRCA	•	•	X	0	X	•	0	↕	Rotate accumulator.
RL m; RLC m; RR m; RRC m; SLA m; SRA m; SRL m	↕	↕	X	0	X	P	0	↕	Rotate and shift locations.
RLD; RRD	↕	↕	X	0	X	P	0	•	Rotate digit left and right.
DAA	↕	↕	X	↕	X	P	•	↕	Decimal adjust accumulator.
CPL	•	•	X	1	X	•	1	•	Complement accumulator.
SCF	•	•	X	0	X	•	0	1	Set carry.
CCF	•	•	X	X	X	•	0	↕	Complement carry.
IN r (C)	↕	↕	X	0	X	P	0	•	Input register indirect.
INI, IND, OUTI; OUTD	X	↕	X	X	X	X	1	•	Block input and output. Z = 0 if B ≠ 0 otherwise Z = 0.
INIR; INDR; OTIR; OTDR	X	1	X	X	X	X	1	•	Block input and output. Z = 0 if B ≠ 0 otherwise Z = 0.
LDI; LDD	X	X	X	0	X	↕	0	•	Block transfer instructions. P/V = 1 if BC ≠ 0, otherwise P/V = 0.
LDIR; LDDR	X	X	X	0	X	0	0	•	Block transfer instructions. P/V = 1 if BC ≠ 0, otherwise P/V = 0.
CPI; CPIR, CPD; CPDR	X	↕	X	X	X	↕	1	•	Block search instructions. Z = 1 if A = (HL), otherwise Z = 0. P/V = 1 if BC ≠ 0, otherwise P/V = 0.
LD A, I, LD A, R	↕	↕	X	0	X	IFF	0	•	The content of the interrupt enable flip-flop (IFF) is copied into the P/V flag.
BIT b, s	X	↕	X	1	X	X	0	•	The state of bit b of location s is copied into the Z flag.

Symbolic Notation

Symbol	Operation
S	Sign flag. S = 1 if the MSB of the result is 1.
Z	Zero flag. Z = 1 if the result of the operation is 0.
P/V	Parity or overflow flag. Parity (P) and overflow (V) share the same flag. Logical operations affect this flag with the parity of the result while arithmetic operations affect this flag with the overflow of the result. If P/V holds parity, P/V = 1 if the result of the operation is even, P/V = 0 if result is odd. If P/V holds overflow, P/V = 1 if the result of the operation produced an overflow.
H	Half-carry flag. H = 1 if the add or subtract operation produced a carry into or borrow from bit 4 of the accumulator.
N	Add/Subtract flag. N = 1 if the previous operation was a subtract.
H & N	H and N flags are used in conjunction with the decimal adjust instruction (DAA) to properly correct the result into packed BCD format following addition or subtraction using operands with packed BCD format.
C	Carry/Link flag. C = 1 if the operation produced a carry from the MSB of the operand or result.

Symbol	Operation
↕	The flag is affected according to the result of the operation.
•	The flag is unchanged by the operation.
0	The flag is reset by the operation.
1	The flag is set by the operation.
X	The flag is a "don't care."
V	P/V flag affected according to the overflow result of the operation.
P	P/V flag affected according to the parity result of the operation.
r	Any one of the CPU registers A, B, C, D, E, H, L.
s	Any 8-bit location for all the addressing modes allowed for the particular instruction.
ss	Any 16-bit location for all the addressing modes allowed for that instruction.
ii	Any one of the two index registers IX or IY.
R	Refresh counter.
n	8-bit value in range < 0, 255 >.
nn	16-bit value in range < 0, 65535 >.

Table 6-3 8-bit load group

8-Bit Load Group

Mnemonic	Symbolic Operation	S	Z		H		P/V	N	C	Opcode 76 543 210	Hex	No. of Bytes	No. of M Cycles	No. of T States	Comments
LD r, r'	r ← r'	•	•	X	•	X	•	•	•	01 r r'		1	1	4	r, r' Reg.
LD r, n	r ← n	•	•	X	•	X	•	•	•	00 r 110		2	2	7	000 B
										← n →					001 C
LD r, (HL)	r ← (HL)	•	•	X	•	X	•	•	•	01 r 110		1	2	7	010 D
LD r, (IX + d)	r ← (IX + d)	•	•	X	•	X	•	•	•	11 011 101	DD	3	5	19	011 E
										01 r 101					100 H
										← d →					101 L
LD r, (IY + d)	r ← (IY + d)	•	•	X	•	X	•	•	•	11 111 101	FD	3	5	19	111 A
										01 r 110					
										← d →					
LD (HL), r	(HL) ← r	•	•	X	•	X	•	•	•	01 110 r		1	2	7	
LD (IX + d), r	(IX + d) ← r	•	•	X	•	X	•	•	•	11 011 101	DD	3	5	19	
										01 110 r					
										← d →					
LD (IY + d), r	(IY + d) ← r	•	•	X	•	X	•	•	•	11 111 101	FD	3	5	19	
										01 110 r					
										← d →					
LD (HL), n	(HL) ← n	•	•	X	•	X	•	•	•	00 110 110	36	2	3	10	
										← n →					
LD ('X + d), n	(IX + d) ← n	•	•	X	•	X	•	•	•	11 011 101	DD	4	5	19	
										00 110 110	36				
										← d →					
										← n →					
LD (IY + d), n	(IY + d) ← n	•	•	X	•	X	•	•	•	11 111 101	FD	4	5	19	
										00 110 110	36				
										← d →					
										← n →					
LD A, (BC)	A ← (BC)	•	•	X	•	X	•	•	•	00 001 010	0A	1	2	7	
LD A, (DE)	A ← (DE)	•	•	X	•	X	•	•	•	00 011 010	1A	1	2	7	
LD A, (nn)	A ← (nn)	•	•	X	•	X	•	•	•	00 111 010	3A	3	4	13	
										← n →					
										← n →					
LD (BC), A	(BC) ← A	•	•	X	•	X	•	•	•	00 000 010	02	1	2	7	
LD (DE), A	(DE) ← A	•	•	X	•	X	•	•	•	00 010 010	12	1	2	7	
LD (nn), A	(nn) ← A	•	•	X	•	X	•	•	•	00 110 010	32	3	4	13	
										← n →					
										← n →					
LD A, I	A ← I	↕	↕	X	0	X	IFF	0	•	11 101 101	ED	2	2	9	
										01 010 111	57				
LD A, R	A ← R	↕	↕	X	0	X	IFF	0	•	11 101 101	ED	2	2	9	
										01 011 111	5F				
LD I, A	I ← A	•	•	X	•	X	•	•	•	11 101 101	ED	2	2	9	
										01 000 111	47				
LD R, A	R ← A	•	•	X	•	X	•	•	•	11 101 101	ED	2	2	9	
										01 001 111	4F				

NOTES: r, r' means any of the registers A, B, C, D, E, H, L.
IFF the content of the interrupt enable flip-flop, (IFF) is copied into the P/V flag.
For an explanation of flag notation and symbols for mnemonic tables, see Symbolic Notation section following tables.

Table 6-4 16-bit load group

Mnemonic	Symbolic Operation	S	Z		H		P/V	N	C	76 543 210	Hex	No. of Bytes	No. of M Cycles	No. of T States	Comments
LD dd, nn	dd ← nn	•	•	X	•	X	•	•	•	00 dd0 001 ← n → ← n →		3	3	10	dd Pair 00 BC 01 DE 10 HL 11 SP
LD IX, nn	IX ← nn	•	•	X	•	X	•	•	•	11 011 101 00 100 001 ← n → ← n →	DD 21	4	4	14	
LD IY, nn	IY ← nn	•	•	X	•	X	•	•	•	11 111 101 00 100 001 ← n → ← n →	FD 21	4	4	14	
LD HL, (nn)	H ← (nn + 1) L ← (nn)	•	•	X	•	X	•	•	•	00 101 010 ← n → ← n →	2A	3	5	16	
LD dd, (nn)	dd_H ← (nn + 1) dd_L ← (nn)	•	•	X	•	X	•	•	•	11 101 101 01 dd1 011 ← n → ← n →	ED	4	6	20	
LD IX, (nn)	IX_H ← (nn + 1) IX_L ← (nn)	•	•	X	•	X	•	•	•	11 011 101 00 101 010 ← n → ← n →	DD 2A	4	6	20	
LD IY, (nn)	IY_H ← (nn + 1) IY_L ← (nn)	•	•	X	•	X	•	•	•	11 111 101 00 101 010 ← n → ← n →	FD 2A	4	6	20	
LD (nn), HL	(nn + 1) ← H (nn) ← L	•	•	X	•	X	•	•	•	00 100 010 ← n → ← n →	22	3	5	16	
LD (nn), dd	(nn + 1) ← dd_H (nn) ← dd_L	•	•	X	•	X	•	•	•	11 101 101 01 dd0 011 ← n → ← n →	ED	4	6	20	
LD (nn), IX	(nn + 1) ← IX_H (nn) ← IX_L	•	•	X	•	X	•	•	•	11 011 101 00 100 010 ← n → ← n →	DD 22	4	6	20	
LD (nn), IY	(nn + 1) ← IY_H (nn) ← IY_L	•	•	X	•	X	•	•	•	11 111 101 00 100 010 ← n → ← n →	FD 22	4	6	20	
LD SP, HL	SP ← HL	•	•	X	•	X	•	•	•	11 111 001	F9	1	1	6	
LD SP, IX	SP ← IX	•	•	X	•	X	•	•	•	11 011 101 11 111 001	DD F9	2	2	10	
LD SP, IY	SP ← IY	•	•	X	•	X	•	•	•	11 111 101 11 111 001	FD F9	2	2	10	
PUSH qq	(SP − 2) ← qq_L (SP − 1) ← qq_H SP → SP − 2	•	•	X	•	X	•	•	•	11 qq0 101		1	3	11	qq Pair 00 BC 01 DE 10 HL 11 AF
PUSH IX	(SP − 2) ← IX_L (SP − 1) ← IX_H SP → SP − 2	•	•	X	•	X	•	•	•	11 011 101 11 100 101	DD E5	2	4	15	
PUSH IY	(SP − 2) ← IY_L (SP − 1) ← IY_H SP → SP − 2	•	•	X	•	X	•	•	•	11 111 101 11 100 101	FD E5	2	4	15	
POP qq	qq_H ← (SP + 1) qq_L ← (SP) SP → SP + 2	•	•	X	•	X	•	•	•	11 qq0 001		1	3	10	
POP IX	IX_H ← (SP + 1) IX_L ← (SP) SP → SP + 2	•	•	X	•	X	•	•	•	11 011 101 11 100 001	DD E1	2	4	14	
POP IY	IY_H ← (SP + 1) IY_L ← (SP) SP → SP + 2	•	•	X	•	X	•	•	•	11 111 101 11 100 001	FD E1	2	4	14	

NOTES: dd is any of the register pairs BC, DE, HL, SP.
qq is any of the register pairs AF, BC, DE, HL.
$(PAIR)_H$, $(PAIR)_L$ refer to high order and low order eight bits of the register pair respectively,
e.g., BC_L = C, AF_H = A.

Table 6-5 Exchange group and block transfer and search group

Mnemonic	Symbolic Operation	S	Z		H		P/V	N	C	Opcode 76 543 210	Hex	No. of Bytes	No. of M Cycles	No. of T States	Comments
EX DE, HL	DE ↔ HL	•	•	X	•	X	•	•	•	11 101 011	EB	1	1	4	
EX AF, AF′	AF ↔ AF′	•	•	X	•	X	•	•	•	00 001 000	08	1	1	4	
EXX	BC ↔ BC′ DE ↔ DE′ HL ↔ HL′	•	•	X	•	X	•	•	•	11 011 001	D9	1	1	4	Register bank and auxiliary register bank exchange
EX (SP), HL	H ↔ (SP+1) L ↔ (SP)	•	•	X	•	X	•	•	•	11 100 011	E3	1	5	19	
EX (SP), IX	IX_H ↔ (SP+1) IX_L ↔ (SP)	•	•	X	•	X	•	•	•	11 011 101 11 100 011	DD E3	2	6	23	
EX (SP), IY	IY_H ↔ (SP+1) IY_L ↔ (SP)	•	•	X	•	X	•	•	•	11 111 101 11 100 011	FD E3	2	6	23	
LDI	(DE) ← (HL) DE ← DE+1 HL ← HL+1 BC ← BC−1	•	•	X	0	X	① ↕	0	•	11 101 101 10 100 000	ED A0	2	4	16	Load (HL) into (DE), increment the pointers and decrement the byte counter (BC)
LDIR	(DE) ← (HL) DE ← DE+1 HL ← HL+1 BC ← BC−1 Repeat until BC = 0	•	•	X	0	X	① 0	0	•	11 101 101 10 110 000	ED B0	2 2	5 4	21 16	If BC ≠ 0 If BC = 0
LDD	(DE) ← (HL) DE ← DE−1 HL ← HL−1 BC ← BC−1	•	•	X	0	X	① ↕	0	•	11 101 101 10 101 000	ED A8	2	4	16	
LDDR	(DE) ← (HL) DE ← DE−1 HL ← HL−1 BC ← BC−1 Repeat until BC = 0	•	•	X	0	X	② 0	0	•	11 101 101 10 111 000	ED B8	2 2	5 4	21 16	If BC ≠ 0 If BC = 0
CPI	A − (HL) HL ← HL+1 BC ← BC−1	↕	③ ↕	X	↕	X	① ↕	1	•	11 101 101 10 100 001	ED A1	2	4	16	
CPIR	A − (HL) HL ← HL+1 BC ← BC−1 Repeat until A = (HL) or BC = 0	↕	③ ↕	X	↕	X	① ↕	1	•	11 101 101 10 110 001	ED B1	2 2	5 4	21 16	If BC ≠ 0 and A ≠ (HL) If BC = 0 or A = (HL)
CPD	A − (HL) HL ← HL−1 BC ← BC−1	↕	③ ↕	X	↕	X	① ↕	1	•	11 101 101 10 101 001	ED A9	2	4	16	
CPDR	A − (HL) HL ← HL−1 BC ← BC−1 Repeat until A = (HL) or BC = 0	↕	③ ↕	X	↕	X	① ↕	1	•	11 101 101 10 111 001	ED B9	2 2	5 4	21 16	If BC ≠ 0 and A ≠ (HL) If BC = 0 or A = (HL)

NOTES: ① P/V flag is 0 if the result of BC − 1 = 0, otherwise P/V = 1.
② P/V flag is 0 at completion of instruction only.
③ Z flag is 1 if A = (HL), otherwise Z = 0.

Table 6-6 8-bit arithmetic and logical group

Mnemonic	Operation									Opcode					Comments
ADD A, r	A ← A + r	↕	↕	X	↕	X	V	0	↕	10 [000] r		1	1	4	r Reg.
ADD A, n	A ← A + n	↕	↕	X	↕	X	V	0	↕	11 [000] 110		2	2	7	000 B
										← n →					001 C
															010 D
ADD A, (HL)	A ← A + (HL)	↕	↕	X	↕	X	V	0	↕	10 [000] 110		1	2	7	011 E
ADD A, (IX+d)	A ← A + (IX+d)	↕	↕	X	↕	X	V	0	↕	11 011 101	DD	3	5	19	100 H
										10 [000] 110					101 L
										← d →					111 A
ADD A, (IY+d)	A ← A + (IY+d)	↕	↕	X	↕	X	V	0	↕	11 111 101	FD	3	5	19	
										10 [000] 110					
										← d →					
ADC A, s	A ← A+s+CY	↕	↕	X	↕	X	V	0	↕	[001]					s is any of r, n,
SUB s	A ← A − s	↕	↕	X	↕	X	V	1	↕	[010]					(HL), (IX + d),
SBC A, s	A ← A − s − CY	↕	↕	X	↕	X	V	1	↕	[011]					(IY + d) as shown for ADD instruction.
AND s	A ← A ∧ s	↕	↕	X	1	X	P	0	0	[100]					The indicated bits
OR s	A ← A ∨ s	↕	↕	X	0	X	P	0	0	[110]					replace the [000] in
XOR s	A ← A ⊕ s	↕	↕	X	0	X	P	0	0	[101]					the ADD set above.
CP s	A − s	↕	↕	X	↕	X	V	1	↕	[111]					
INC r	r ← r + 1	↕	↕	X	↕	X	V	0	•	00 r [100]		1	1	4	
INC (HL)	(HL) ← (HL) + 1	↕	↕	X		X	V	0	•	00 110 [100]		1	3	11	
INC (IX + d)	(IX + d) ←	↕	↕	X	↕	X	V	0	•	11 011 101	DD	3	6	23	
	(IX + d) + 1									00 110 [100]					
										← d →					
INC (IY + d)	(IY + d) ←	↕	↕	X	↕	X	V	0	•	11 111 101	FD	3	6	23	
	(IY + d) + 1									00 110 [100]					
										← d →					
DEC m	m ← m − 1	↕	↕	X	↕	X	V	1	•	[101]					m is any of r, (HL), (IX + d), (IY + d) as shown for INC. DEC same format and states as INC. Replace [100] with [101] in opcode.

Table 6-7 General-purpose arithmetic and CPU control groups

Mnemonic	Symbolic Operation	Flags S	Z		H		P/V	N	C	Opcode 76 543 210 Hex	No. of Bytes	No. of M Cycles	No. of T States	Comments
DAA	Converts acc. content into packed BCD following add or subtract with packed BCD operands.	↕	↕	X	↕	X	P	•	↕	00 100 111 27	1	1	4	Decimal adjust accumulator.
CPL	A ← $\bar{A}$	•	•	X	1	X	•	1	•	00 101 111 2F	1	1	4	Complement accumulator (one's complement).
NEG	A ← 0 − A	↕	↕	X	↕	X	V	1	↕	11 101 101 ED 01 000 100 44	2	2	8	Negate acc. (two's complement).
CCF	CY ← $\overline{CY}$	•	•	X	X	X	•	0	↕	00 111 111 3F	1	1	4	Complement carry flag.
SCF	CY ← 1	•	•	X	0	X	•	0	1	00 110 111 37	1	1	4	Set carry flag.
NOP	No operation	•	•	X	•	X	•	•	•	00 000 000 00	1	1	4	
HALT	CPU halted	•	•	X	•	X	•	•	•	01 110 110 76	1	1	4	
DI ★	IFF ← 0	•	•	X	•	X	•	•	•	11 110 011 F3	1	1	4	
EI ★	IFF ← 1	•	•	X	•	X	•	•	•	11 111 011 FB	1	1	4	
IM 0	Set interrupt mode 0	•	•	X	•	X	•	•	•	11 101 101 ED 01 000 110 46	2	2	8	
IM 1	Set interrupt mode 1	•	•	X	•	X	•	•	•	11 101 101 ED 01 010 110 56	2	2	8	
IM 2	Set interrupt mode 2	•	•	X	•	X	•	•	•	11 101 101 ED 01 011 110 5E	2	2	8	

NOTES: IFF indicates the interrupt enable flip-flop.
CY indicates the carry flip-flop.
★ indicates interrupts are not sampled at the end of EI or DI.

Table 6-8 16-bit arithmetic group

Mnemonic	Symbolic Operation	S	Z		H		P/V	N	C	Opcode	Bytes	M Cycles	T States	Comments
ADD HL, ss	HL ← HL + ss	•	•	X	X	X	•	0	↕	00 ss1 001	1	3	11	ss Reg. 00 BC 01 DE 10 HL 11 SP
ADC HL, ss	HL ← HL + ss + CY	↕	↕	X	X	X	V	0	↕	11 101 101 ED 01 ss1 010	2	4	15	
SBC HL, ss	HL ← HL − ss − CY	↕	↕	X	X	X	V	1	↕	11 101 101 ED 01 ss0 010	2	4	15	
ADD IX, pp	IX ← IX + pp	•	•	X	X	X	•	0	↕	11 011 101 DD 01 pp1 001	2	4	15	pp Reg. 00 BC 01 DE 10 IX 11 SP
ADD IY, rr	IY ← IY + rr	•	•	X	X	X	•	0	↕	11 111 101 FD 00 rr1 001	2	4	15	rr Reg. 00 BC 01 DE 10 IY 11 SP
INC ss	ss ← ss + 1	•	•	X	•	X	•	•	•	00 ss0 011	1	1	6	
INC IX	IX ← IX + 1	•	•	X	•	X	•	•	•	11 011 101 DD 00 100 011 23	2	2	10	
INC IY	IY ← IY + 1	•	•	X	•	X	•	•	•	11 111 101 FD 00 100 011 23	2	2	10	
DEC ss	ss ← ss − 1	•	•	X	•	X	•	•	•	00 ss1 011	1	1	6	
DEC IX	IX ← IX − 1	•	•	X	•	X	•	•	•	11 011 101 DD 00 101 011 2B	2	2	10	
DEC IY	IY ← IY − 1	•	•	X	•	X	•	•	•	11 111 101 FD 00 101 011 2B	2	2	10	

NOTES: ss is any of the register pairs BC, DE, HL, SP.
pp is any of the register pairs BC, DE, IX, SP.
rr is any of the register pairs BC, DE, IY, SP.

Table 6-9 ROTATE and SHIFT group

Mnemonic	Symbolic Operation	S	Z		H		P/V	N	C	Opcode 76 543 210	Hex	No. of Bytes	No. of M Cycles	No. of T States	Comments
RLCA	CY ← 7 ← 0 (A)	•	•	X	0	X	•	0	↕	00 000 111	07	1	1	4	Rotate left circular accumulator.
RLA	CY ← 7 ← 0 (A)	•	•	X	0	X	•	0	↕	00 010 111	17	1	1	4	Rotate left accumulator.
RRCA	7 → 0 → CY (A)	•	•	X	0	X	•	0	↕	00 001 111	0F	1	1	4	Rotate right circular accumulator.
RRA	7 → 0 → CY (A)	•	•	X	0	X	•	0	↕	00 011 111	1F	1	1	4	Rotate right accumulator.
RLC r		↕	↕	X	0	X	P	0	↕	11 001 011 00 [000] r	CB	2	2	8	Rotate left circular register r.
RLC (HL)		↕	↕	X	0	X	P	0	↕	11 001 011 00 [000] 110	CB	2	4	15	r Reg. 000 B 001 C
RLC (IX + d)	CY ← 7 ← 0 r,(HL),(IX + d),(IY + d)	↕	↕	X	0	X	P	0	↕	11 011 101 11 001 011 ← d → 00 [000] 110	DD CB	4	6	23	010 D 011 E 100 H 101 L 111 A
RLC (IY + d)		↕	↕	X	0	X	P	0	↕	11 111 101 11 001 011 ← d → 00 [000] 110	FD CB	4	6	23	
RL m	CY ← 7 ← 0 m ≡ r,(HL),(IX + d),(IY + d)	↕	↕	X	0	X	P	0	↕	[010]					Instruction format and states are as shown for RLC's To form new opcode replace [000] or RLC's with shown code.
RRC m	7 → 0 → CY m ≡ r,(HL),(IX + d),(IY + d)	↕	↕	X	0	X	P	0	↕	[001]					
RR m	7 → 0 → CY m ≡ r,(HL),(IX + d),(IY + d)	↕	↕	X	0	X	P	0	↕	[011]					
SLA m	CY ← 7 ← 0 ← 0 m ≡ r,(HL),(IX + d),(IY + d)	↕	↕	X	0	X	P	0	↕	[100]					
SRA m	7 → 0 → CY m ≡ r,(HL),(IX + d),(IY + d)	↕	↕	X	0	X	P	0	↕	[101]					
SRL m	0 → 7 → 0 → CY m ≡ r,(HL),(IX + d),(IY + d)	↕	↕	X	0	X	P	0	↕	[111]					
RLD	7-4 3-0 (A) 7-4 3-0 (HL)	↕	↕	X	0	X	P	0	•	11 101 101 01 101 111	ED 6F	2	5	18	Rotate digit left and right between the accumulator and location (HL).
RRD	7-4 3-0 (A) 7-4 3-0 (HL)	↕	↕	X	0	X	P	0	•	11 101 101 01 100 111	ED 67	2	5	18	The content of the upper half of the accumulator is unaffected

Table 6-10 Bit SET, RESET, and test group

BIT b, r	$Z \leftarrow \overline{r_b}$	X	↕	X	1	X	X	0	•	11 001 011 CB 01 b r	2	2	8	r Reg. 000 B 001 C 010 D 011 E 100 H 101 L 111 A
BIT b, (HL)	$Z \leftarrow \overline{(HL)}_b$	X	↕	X	1	X	X	0	•	11 001 011 CB 01 b 110	2	3	12	
BIT b, $(IX + d)_b$	$Z \leftarrow \overline{(IX + d)}_b$	X	↕	X	1	X	X	0	•	11 011 101 DD 11 001 011 CB ← d → 01 b 110	4	5	20	
BIT b, $(IY + d)_b$	$Z \leftarrow \overline{(IY + d)}_b$	X	↕	X	1	X	X	0	•	11 111 101 FD 11 001 011 CB ← d → 01 b 110	4	5	20	b Bit Tested 000 0 001 1 010 2 011 3 100 4 101 5 110 6 111 7
SET b, r	$r_b \leftarrow 1$	•	•	X	•	X	•	•	•	11 001 011 CB [11] b r	2	2	8	
SET b, (HL)	$(HL)_b \leftarrow 1$	•	•	X	•	X	•	•	•	11 001 011 CB [11] b 110	2	4	15	
SET b, (IX + d)	$(IX + d)_b \leftarrow 1$	•	•	X	•	X	•	•	•	11 011 101 DD 11 001 011 CB ← d → [11] b 110	4	6	23	
SET b, (IY + d)	$(IY + d)_b \leftarrow 1$	•	•	X	•	X	•	•	•	11 111 101 FD 11 001 011 CB ← d → [11] b 110	4	6	23	
RES b, m	$m_b \leftarrow 0$ m ≡ r, (HL), (IX + d), (IY + d)	•	•	X	•	X	•	•	•	[10]				To form new opcode replace [11] of SET b, s with [10]. Flags and time states for SET instruction.

NOTES: The notation m_b indicates bit b (0 to 7) or location m.

Table 6-11 JUMP group table

Mnemonic	Symbolic Operation	Flags S	Z		H		P/V	N	C	Opcode 76 543 210 Hex	No. of Bytes	No. of M Cycles	No. of T States	Comments
JP nn	PC ← nn	•	•	X	•	X	•	•	•	11 000 011 C3 ← n → ← n →	3	3	10	
JP cc, nn	If condition cc is true PC ← nn, otherwise continue	•	•	X	•	X	•	•	•	11 cc 010 ← n → ← n →	3	3	10	cc Condition 000 NZ non-zero 001 Z zero 010 NC non-carry 011 C carry 100 PO parity odd 101 PE parity even 110 P sign positive 111 M sign negative
JR e	PC ← PC + e	•	•	X	•	X	•	•	•	00 011 000 18 ← e − 2 →	2	3	12	
JR C, e	If C = 0, continue	•	•	X	•	X	•	•	•	00 111 000 38 ← e − 2 →	2	2	7	If condition not met.
	If C = 1, PC ← PC + e										2	3	12	If condition is met.
JR NC, e	If C = 1, continue	•	•	X	•	X	•	•	•	00 110 000 30 ← e − 2 →	2	2	7	If condition not met.
	If C = 0, PC ← PC + e										2	3	12	If condition is met.
JP Z, e	If Z = 0 continue	•	•	X	•	X	•	•	•	00 101 000 28 ← e − 2 →	2	2	7	If condition not met.
	If Z = 1, PC ← PC + e										2	3	12	If condition is met.
JR NZ, e	If Z = 1, continue	•	•	X	•	X	•	•	•	00 100 000 20 ← e − 2 →	2	2	7	If condition not met.
	If Z = 0, PC ← PC + e										2	3	12	If condition is met.
JP (HL)	PC ← HL	•	•	X	•	X	•	•	•	11 101 001 E9	1	1	4	
JP (IX)	PC ← IX	•	•	X	•	X	•	•	•	11 011 101 DD 11 101 001 E9	2	2	8	
JP (IY)	PC ← IY	•	•	X	•	X	•	•	•	11 111 101 FD 11 101 001 E9	2	2	8	
DJNZ, e	B ← B − 1 If B = 0, continue	•	•	X	•	X	•	•	•	00 010 000 10 ← e − 2 →	2	2	8	If B = 0.
	If B ≠ 0, PC ← PC + e										2	3	13	If B ≠ 0.

NOTES: e represents the extension in the relative addressing mode.
e is a signed two's complement number in the range < −126, 129 >.
e − 2 in the opcode provides an effective address of pc + e as PC is incremented by 2 prior to the addition of e.

Table 6-12 CALL and RETURN group

Mnemonic	Symbolic Operation	S	Z		H		P/V	N	C	Opcode	No. of Bytes	No. of M Cycles	No. of T States	Comments
CALL nn	(SP − 1) ← PC_H (SP − 2) ← PC_L PC ← nn	•	•	X	•	X	•	•	•	11 001 101 CD ← n → ← n →	3	5	17	
CALL cc, nn	If condition cc is false continue, otherwise same as CALL nn	•	•	X	•	X	•	•	•	11 cc 100 ← n → ← n →	3	3	10	If cc is false.
											3	5	17	If cc is true.
RET	PC_L ← (SP) PC_H ← (SP + 1)	•	•	X	•	X	•	•	•	11 001 001 C9	1	3	10	
RET cc	If condition cc is false continue, otherwise same as RET	•	•	X	•	X	•	•	•	11 cc 000	1	1	5	If cc is false.
											1	3	11	If cc is true. cc Condition 000 NZ non-zero 001 Z zero 010 NC non-carry 011 C carry 100 PO parity odd 101 PE parity even 110 P sign positive 111 M sign negative
RETI	Return from interrupt	•	•	X	•	X	•	•	•	11 101 101 ED 01 001 101 4D	2	4	14	
RETN[1]	Return from non-maskable interrupt	•	•	X	•	X	•	•	•	11 101 101 ED 01 000 101 45	2	4	14	
RST p	(SP − 1) ← PC_H (SP − 2) ← PC_L PC_H ← 0 PC_L ← p	•	•	X	•	X	•	•	•	11 t 111	1	3	11	t p 000 00H 001 08H 010 10H 011 18H 100 20H 101 28H 110 30H 111 38H

NOTE: [1]RETN loads $IFF_2 \rightarrow IFF_1$

Table 6-13 **Input/output group table**

Mnemonic	Symbolic Operation	S	Z		H		P/V	N	C	Opcode 76 543 210 Hex	No. of Bytes	No. of M Cycles	No. of T States	Comments
IN A, (n)	A ← (n)	•	•	X	•	X	•	•	•	11 011 011 DB ← n →	2	3	11	n to A_0 ~ A_7 Acc. to A_8 ~ A_{15}
IN r, (C)	r ← (C) if r = 110 only the flags will be affected	↕	↕	X	↕	X	P	0	•	11 101 101 ED 01 r 000	2	3	12	C to A_0 ~ A_7 B to A_8 ~ A_{15}
INI	(HL) ← (C) B ← B − 1 HL ← HL + 1	X	① ↕	X	X	X	X	1	X	11 101 101 ED 10 100 010 A2	2	4	16	C to A_0 ~ A_7 B to A_8 ~ A_{15}
INIR	(HL) ← (C) B ← B − 1 HL ← HL + 1 Repeat until B = 0	X	② 1	X	X	X	X	1	X	11 101 101 ED 10 110 010 B2	2 2	5 (If B≠0) 4 (If B = 0)	21 16	C to A_0 ~ A_7 B to A_8 ~ A_{15}
IND	(HL) ← (C) B ← B − 1 HL ← HL − 1	X	① ↕	X	X	X	X	1	X	11 101 101 ED 10 101 010 AA	2	4	16	C to A_0 ~ A_7 B to A_8 ~ A_{15}
INDR	(HL) ← (C) B ← B − 1 HL ← HL − 1 Repeat until B = 0	X	② 1	X	X	X	X	1	X	11 101 101 ED 10 111 010 BA	2 2	5 (If B≠0) 4 (If B = 0)	21 16	C to A_0 ~ A_7 B to A_8 ~ A_{15}
OUT (n), A	(n) ← A	•	•	X	•	X	•	•	•	11 010 011 D3 ← n →	2	3	11	n to A_0 ~ A_7 Acc. to A_8 ~ A_{15}
OUT (C), r	(C) ← r	•	•	X	•	X	•	•	•	11 101 101 ED 01 r 001	2	3	12	C to A_0 ~ A_7 B to A_8 ~ A_{15}
OUTI	(C) ← (HL) B ← B − 1 HL ← HL + 1	X	① ↕	X	X	X	X	1	X	11 101 101 ED 10 100 011 A3	2	4	16	C to A_0 ~ A_7 B to A_8 ~ A_{15}
OTIR	(C) ← (HL) B ← B − 1 HL ← HL + 1 Repeat until B = 0	X	② 1	X	X	X	X	1	X	11 101 101 ED 10 110 011 B3	2 2	5 (If B≠0) 4 (If B = 0)	21 16	C to A_0 ~ A_7 B to A_8 ~ A_{15}
OUTD	(C) ← (HL) B ← B − 1 HL ← HL − 1	X	① ↕	X	X	X	X	1	X	11 101 101 ED 10 101 011 AB	2	4	16	C to A_0 ~ A_7 B to A_8 ~ A_{15}
OTDR	(C) ← (HL) B ← B − 1 HL ← HL − 1 Repeat until B = 0	X	① 1	X	X	X	X	1	X	11 101 101 ED 10 111 011	2 2	5 (If B≠0) 4 (If B = 0)	21 16	C to A_0 ~ A_7 B to A_8 ~ A_{15}

NOTE: ① If the result of B − 1 is zero the Z flag is set, otherwise it is reset.
② Z flag is set upon instruction completion only.

This example places the value 0B hex into the accumulator. The H following the value in the mnemonic indicates that it is a hex value.

The **Z80** has no new instructions using simple immediate addressing.

6-3.2 Immediate Extended Addressing

The word "extended" in the title means that the CPU is dealing with 2 bytes of data, for example,

Mnemonic	`LD BC,1CD0H`
Hex	`01 D0 1C`

This instruction loads 1CD0 hex into the BC register pair. Notice that the low byte of the 16-bit word comes first in memory.

Many of the *new* **Z80** instructions require a *2-byte Op code* as the next example illustrates. Because the **Z80** has two additional 16-bit registers, it is natural that additional immediate extended mode instructions have been added to handle the IX and IY registers, for example,

Mnemonic	`LD IX,1CD0H`
Hex	`DD 21 D0 1C`

The Op code in this example requires 2 bytes, DD 21 and loads 1CD0 into IX.

6-3.3 Modified Page Zero Addressing

Page zero is defined as the first 256 bytes of address space (0000H to 00FFH). The CALL to page zero or **8080A** RESTART instructions are the only instructions using this addressing form. The eight RESTART instructions all set the program counter to an address of a location in page zero, for example,

Mnemonic	`RST 20H`
Hex	`E7`

This instruction results in a CALL to location 0020H.

6-3.4 Register Addressing

This addressing mode uses a bit pattern within the Op code to specify the register to be used as a source or destination for the operation, for example,

Mnemonic	`LD A,B`
Hex	`78`
Binary	`01111000`

The instruction shown loads A with the contents of B. Bits 0, 1, and 2 (000) specify the source as B, while bits 3, 4, and 5 (111) specify the A register as the destination. Many instructions have been added to the **Z80** instruction set that use the register addressing mode. These instructions are of two types—ROTATEs and SHIFTs, and bit manipulation, for example,

Mnemonic	`RLC B`
Hex	`CB 00`

The instruction shown rotates the contents of the B register left in a circular fashion. Bits 0, 1, and 2 (000) in the second byte specify that the B register is the object of the operation.

6-3.5 Implied Addressing

Implied addressing does not require an explicit address for the operand. The nature of the Op code itself implies the only possible address, for example,

Mnemonic	`DAA`
Hex	`27`

This instruction is the decimal adjust accumulator command. Obviously, the only possible address for the operand is the accumulator, so no further information is required.

The new **Z80** instructions using this addressing mode are those that set the interrupt mode register, exchange registers, and negate (2s complement) the accumulator.

6-3.6 Register Indirect Addressing

The 16-bit CPU register specified by the Op code contains the address of the operand in this form of addressing, for example,

Mnemonic	`LD A,(HL)`
Hex	`7E`

This instruction loads the accumulator with the byte from the memory location whose address is found in the HL register.

Register indirect addressing using the HL register is the fundamental memory addressing mode of the **8080A**. It is not surprising, therefore, that the **Z80** instruction set includes a number of new instructions using this addressing mode. These instruction types are: block transfer; block search; ROTATE and SHIFT; bit manipulation; and block I/O. The HL register is the indirect address source in all of these instructions except for some of the I/O instructions in which the C register is the source of the 8-bit I/O port address.

6-3.7 Stack Addressing

This mode is a special form of register indirect addressing in which the address is held in the stack pointer register. When a PUSH instruction is executed, the contents of the stack pointer is decremented (auto predecrement) and then used as the address. (Since the **Z80** always saves a 16-bit register pair on the stack, the operation actually takes place twice, once for each byte.) This action is known as *auto predecrement* of the register contents, for example,

Mnemonic	`PUSH AF`
Hex	`F1`

This command causes the stack pointer contents to be decremented, and then used as the address at which the contents of A are stored. The stack pointer is decremented again, and the contents of F stored at the address pointed to by the stack pointer.

During a POP instruction, the contents of the stack pointer is used as the address of a register indirect load from memory and the contents of the stack pointer is then incremented (auto postincrement). The **Z80** has new instructions for pushing and popping the IX and IY registers.

6-3.8 Extended Addressing

In this addressing mode, the 2 bytes following the Op code are the address of the operand, for example,

Mnemonic	`LD BC,01FEH`
Hex	`ED 4B FE 01`

In the example, the C register is loaded with the contents of memory location 01FE hex and the B register is loaded from 01FF hex.

The **8080A** has only two instructions using this addressing mode—load the accumulator and load the HL register pair. The **Z80** has instructions to load the BC, DE, SP, IX, and IY registers using extended addressing.

This concludes the discussion of the **8080A** addressing modes used in the **Z80**. The following addressing modes are the powerful enhancements found in the **Z80**.

6-3.9 Relative Addressing

The JUMP instructions of the **8080A** use the 2 bytes following the Op code as the address to which control is to be transferred. Since loops in programs often require a jump to a location close to the point at which the decision to jump is made, the concept of *relative addressing* has been added to the **Z80**. In this addressing method, a byte following the Op code is added in 2s complement fashion to the program counter. This provides a JUMP range of +127 to −128 from the program counter contents at the time the addition is made. The **Z80** has a number of JUMP instructions that use the relative addressing mode. Besides saving a byte per JUMP instruction, this addressing mode helps in writing relocatable code.[2]

EXAMPLE 6-2 If the instruction in location 00C3H is a JR 0EH (HEX 18 0E), to what address does the program jump?

Solution After reading the second byte of the instruction, the program counter will have the value 00C5H. The offset value must be added to this:

```
00C5H + 0EH = 00D3H
```

EXAMPLE 6-3 Show the JUMP instruction that must be placed at 02CFH to transfer control to location 02ABH. How is the offset calculated?

Solution Try the unconditional relative JUMP instruction. The Op code value is 18H placed at 02CFH. The offset value is placed at 02D0H. The offset is calculated in the following manner: The program counter value will be 02D1H after reading the offset byte. Subtract this value from the destination.

```
02ABH - 02D1H = 0DAH
```

Since the JUMP is backward, the result is a negative (BIT 7 set) number. We can use the relative JUMP since the offset only requires 1 byte.

Unfortunately, the **Z80** does not have relative addressing using a full 16-bit offset value. This means that the total address space cannot be reached with a relative JUMP and true relocatable code cannot be written. One other aspect of the relative address JUMPs should be noted. While the instructions use 1 less byte than the standard JUMP, the execution time (due to the need to calculate the jump address) can be longer for the relative JUMP.

[2] Relative branching is also discussed in section 2-8.

6-3.10 Indexed Addressing

Indexed addressing, naturally enough, makes use of the index registers that have been provided in the **Z80**. Instructions using index addressing have a byte following the Op code that is added to the contents of the index register. The result is used as the address of the operand for the instruction. The contents of the index register is unaltered by this operation. This addressing mode can be very useful for accessing data that is located in a tabular form in memory.

EXAMPLE 6-4 Assume that there is a table of 8-bit data starting at location 2000H in memory, and assume that the IX register has been loaded with the value 2000H. What instruction will load the third byte of the table into the accumulator?

Solution The correct instruction is the indexed 8-bit load instruction. The offset value (the value added to the contents of IX) will be 2 to access the third byte in the table. An offset of 0 will access byte 1, offset of 1 will access byte 2, and so on.

Hex code	`DD 7E 02`
Mnemonic	`LD A,(IX + 2)`

The **Z80** instructions which use this form of addressing are: 8-bit register load; 8-bit arithmetic and logical; ROTATEs and SHIFTs; and bit manipulation.

By letting the offset value be 0, this addressing mode is equivalent in operation to register indirect addressing. This particular instruction mode can be used to advantage where the contents of the HL register will be used in 16-bit arithmetic operations. The IX or IY register can be used as the register indirect source in this case, leaving the HL register free for the arithmetic operations.

6-3.11 Bit Addressing

This is the final addressing mode to be discussed. The **Z80** instruction set has a large number of instructions for setting, resetting, and testing an individual bit in a byte. Bit-wise instructions can be very useful in I/O and control type operations. The only way these types of operations can be done in the **8080A** is by means of a logical operation involving the A register contents. The **Z80** bit instructions operate directly on the byte involved. This is especially helpful in the case of a bit test since status flags are set but no changes are made to any of the registers, for example,

Mnemonic	`BIT 2,B`
Hex	`CB 50`

This instruction tests the value of bit 2 in register B and sets the zero flag according to the result of the test (1 if the bit is zero, 0 if it is not).

As can be seen from the example, the bit addressing mode is always used with another one of the addressing modes specifying the byte to be operated upon. In the example, register addressing was used. Register indirect and indexed addressing may also be used to specify the byte. The bit addressing mode saves time and program space for bit-wise operations.

6-4 INSTRUCTION SET

In this section, the instruction set of the **Z80** will be described. **8080A** compatible instructions will not be discussed in great detail, since these are covered in the chapter on the **8080A**. The assembler mnemonics used are those defined by Zilog and have the following general format:

$$\langle \text{Op code} \rangle \qquad \langle \text{Destination} \rangle \qquad \langle \text{Source} \rangle$$

where

Op code defines the operation to be done.
Destination (if required) is where the result is to be placed.
Source (if required) identifies the operand to be used by the instruction.

Some instructions may have the destination implied and thus only the source operand needs to be explicitly written. Instructions using implied addressing for both source and destination require only the Op code.

Before the instructions are described, there are a few characteristics of the **Z80** instruction set that should be understood. The **8080A** uses almost all of the single-byte Op codes available. In order to provide a large number of additional instructions, the designers of the **Z80** had to use *2-byte Op codes* for many instructions. Since the CPU can only fetch 1 byte at a time, this means that these instructions take more memory and execution time than they ideally should. The decision to adopt the **8080A** instruction set as a subset of the **Z80** is thus seen as a mixed blessing. It provides a large base of ready software for the **Z80** but results in a less than ideal set of Op codes in terms of length versus frequency of use. This is the sort of decision which computer designers must always face and hindsight (i.e., success of the **Z80**) shows that Zilog made the correct choice. The user, however, must evaluate byte count and timing in determining the best instruction sequence, since the **Z80** often offers more than one way of obtaining a desired result.

6-4.1 8-Bit Load Group

The **8080A** instruction set is very complete in terms of 8-bit load instructions. The accumulator or any of the general registers may be used as a source and/or destination using the immediate, register, and register indirect (HL) modes of addressing. The accumulator may also be the source or destination, using the register indirect (BC) or (DE) and extended addressing modes. The instructions Zilog has added to this group include indexed addressing and implied loads involving the accumulator and special I and R registers. There are 28 indexed 8-bit load instructions in the **Z80**. Half of these instructions use the accumulator or one of the general registers as the destination and either the IX or IY register as the indexed source.

EXAMPLE 6-5 The IX register has the base address of a table of character bytes. Show the code to load the seventh byte of this table into the accumulator.

Solution

Code	Mnemonic
DD 7E 06	LD A, (IX + 6)
Op code (DD 7E)	

The offset number 6 is used since the IX register is pointing to the first byte in the table. This first byte in the table is addressed as (IX + 0). Note that this instruction is an example of a 2-byte Op code. Indexed instructions do not exist in the **8080A** instruction set.

The other half of the indexed instructions use the accumulator or one of the general registers as the source and either the IX or IY register as the indexed destination.

EXAMPLE 6-6 The IY register is used as a pointer to an output buffer area. Load the contents of the E register into the current buffer location.

Solution

Code	Mnemonic
FD 73 00	LD (IY + 0), E

This is an example of how indexed addressing can be used as a simple register indirect mode. This can be a very useful way of freeing the more powerful HL register pair from addressing tables and buffer areas. The extra bytes and time involved in using the index register may not be a real penalty in many cases since the HL register, having been used in other operations, usually will have to be loaded with the indirect address. The less used index register will often already have the indirect address from a previous iteration of the code.

The I and R registers are usually accessed only during the initialization portion of a program where their values are set. The contents of these registers can also be read at any time. All of these 8-bit load operations use implied addressing in which the accumulator is the implied source or destination.

EXAMPLE 6-7 The starting address of the interrupt vector table is to be located at F000 hex in memory. The I register must be loaded with the most significant byte of this address.

Solution

Code	Mnemonic
3E	LD A,0F0H
ED 47	LD I, A

Loading the accumulator with either the I or R register also results in the P/V flag being set to the status of IFF2, the maskable interrupt status flag. This use of this flag will be explained in the section on interrupts.

EXAMPLE 6-8 Load the accumulator with the contents of the refresh register.

Solution

Code	Mnemonic
ED 4F	LD A, R

This instruction can be used as the source of a seed for a random number generator since the R register is being incremented with each instruction fetch.

6-4.2 16-Bit Load Group

This set of instructions is more limited since the **Z80** is basically an 8-bit machine. The 16-bit loads are primarily intended for address manipulation. This group also includes the stack addressing PUSH and POP instructions.

The **8080A** has instructions for immediate extended loading of the BC, DE, HL, and SP registers, loading the HL register pair using extended addressing, and loading the SP register with the contents of HL. Stack addressing is used to load the register pairs to and from the stack (PUSH and POP, respectively). The **Z80** has added similar instructions involving the index registers and has included instructions to cover all 16-bit registers with extended addressing.

EXAMPLE 6-9 A system servicing multiple users will maintain a stack for each user. The stack pointer of tasks not in use will be stored in a specific area of memory. Show the instruction sequence to transfer the stack address from task 1 to task 2. The stack pointer for task 1 is stored at 100H and the stack pointer for task 2 is stored at 102H.

Solution

Code	Mnemonic
ED 73 00 01	LD (0100H), SP
ED 7B 02 01	LD SP, (0102H)

EXAMPLE 6-10 A process control algorithm is designed to access a table using indexed addressing. There is a table for each loop controlled by the microprocessor. The table for control loop 1 is located at address 2300H. Show how the IY register is loaded with this table address before the algorithm subroutine is called.

Solution

Code	Mnemonic
FD 21 00 23	LD IY, 2300H

EXAMPLE 6-11 Transfer the contents of the IX register to the DE register.

Solution Since there are no instructions for doing the 16-bit register transfer directly, it must be done through the stack.

Code	Mnemonic
DD E5	PUSH IX
D1	POP DE

Observe the hex code for these two instructions. The POP DE instruction was part of the original **8080A** instruction set and only requires a single byte. PUSH IX is a new **Z80** instruction and requires 2 bytes and more execution time.

6-4.3 Exchange Group

The **8080A** instructions provide for only two types of register exchange. The EX DE, HL instruction is very useful in arithmetic routines. The EX (SP), HL instruction can be used to pass parameters to subroutines. The **Z80** instruction set has four additional commands in the exchange group. All exchange instructions involve 16-bit register pairs.

Two of the **Z80** instructions are used to swap the current register contents with the alternate set. Since the routine using these instructions may not use all registers (typically it is an interrupt routine), the exchange of register sets was defined as two instructions to add flexibility.

The EX AF, AF′ instruction swaps the active accumulator and flag register contents with the alternate set. After the exchange, the CPU flags reflect the new register contents and conditional instructions will be executed accordingly. Care must be taken not to use flag dependent operations based on actions that take place before the exchange since the flags no longer represent that state.

The EXX instruction swaps the BC, DE, and HL active registers with their alternates and combined with the above instruction provides a complete exchange of all general registers in the **Z80** that have alternates.

Two instructions are also available for exchanging the contents of the stack top with the index registers. These instructions are similar to the EX (SP), HL instruction of the **8080A**.

EX (SP), IX exchanges the top 2 bytes of the stack with the IX register. EX (SP), IY does the similar operation with the IY register. In both of the instructions the actual stack pointer value never changes and the CPU flags are unaffected.

EXAMPLE 6-12 The content of the top of the stack and the IX and SP registers are shown before an EX (SP), IX instruction. What will be the state of these locations after this instruction is executed?

Contents	*Register*	*Address*	*Contents*
2B3E H	IX	F012 H	FF H
F011 H	SP	F011 H	00 H

Solution

FF00 H	IX	F012 H	2B H
F011 H	SP	F011 H	3E H

6-4.4 Block Transfer Group

The need to transfer a block of data from one memory location to another is frequently encountered. One example of such use might be to transfer initial variable values from ROM to RAM on system startup. The designers of the **Z80** felt that this requirement was so common and so easily implemented in the CPU that they included instructions for moving data among the expanded instructions. There are four such instructions and all use register indirect addressing with the following format: The HL register points to the *source data*; the DE register points to *destination location*; and the BC register acts as a *counter* for the number of bytes transferred.

The LDI instruction moves the byte pointed to by HL to the location pointed to by DE. The HL and DE registers are both then incremented by 1. The contents of BC is decremented by 1 and the P/V flag is cleared if the contents of BC becomes 0 (it is set otherwise). This instruction would typically be used within a loop in which the data being transferred is to be checked for a specified value. The BC counter can be ignored or used as a loop terminator to limit the number of bytes transferred.

EXAMPLE 6-13 An 80-byte input buffer is located at 0100H. Write a program to move the contents of this buffer to location 1000H until either a 00H is encountered or the buffer contents are exhausted.

Solution First the CPU registers are loaded with the appropriate contents, then the move routine is used (Note: This example is shown in the output format of a typical **Z80** assembler. This format will be used to illustrate the more complex examples in this chapter.)

Memory address (hex)	*Code*	*Label*	*Instruction (mnemonic)*	*Comments*
0000	210001		LD HL,0100H	;Source address.
0003	110010		LD DE,1000H	;Destination address.
0006	018000		LD BC,0080H	;Max. # bytes to move.
0009	3E00		LD A,00H	;Test byte.
000B	EDA0	MOVBUF:	LDI	;This instruction does ;the actual move.
000D	E21400		JP PO, NEXT	;Exit loop if this is ;the last byte.
0010	BE		CP (HL)	;Is next value a 00H?
0011	C20B00		JP NZ,MOVBUF	;If not, go move another ;byte.
			⋮	
0014		NEXT:	⋮	

The four instruction MOVBUF loop could be written as a general-purpose subroutine. If this were done, the two conditional JUMP instructions would be rewritten as conditional returns. The CPU registers would all be set to the desired values before the subroutine call. The use of the BC counter as a terminator, as illustrated in this example, is highly recommended. Otherwise, the LDI instruction could be executed indefinitely if the match byte is never encountered.

The LDIR instruction is similar to the LDI instruction except that the transfer is automatically repeated until the BC register is decremented to 0. The instruction works by the following means: the contents of the location pointed to by HL is transferred to the location pointed to by DE; HL and DE are both incremented by 1; the contents of BC is decremented by 1; a conditional test is then done on BC, and if the contents of BC is not 0, the program counter is decremented by 2 so that it points back to the instruction for another execution; finally, the interrupt flags are checked and any pending interrupts acknowledged before the next instruction is executed. If BC is set to 0 before execution of this instruction, 65,536 bytes will be moved.

EXAMPLE 6-14 Unconditionally, move 200H bytes of memory from the location starting at 0200H to memory starting at 0100H.

Memory address (hex)	*Code*	*Label*	*Instruction (mnemonic)*	*Comments*
	210002		LD HL,0200H	;Source.
	110001		LD DE,0100H	;Destination.
	010002		LD BC,0200H	;# of bytes to move.
	EDB0		LDIR	;Move it.

This instruction does an overlapping downward move of memory. The original memory locations from 0100H through 01FFH will be overwritten with the data in locations 0200H through 02FFH. There is no problem with the move, however, since it is started from the bottom of the block to be moved and the locations overwritten have already been moved by the time they are lost.

The previous instructions fail to accomplish the desired results if the programmer is trying to move a block of memory up to an area which overlaps the block to be moved, since the last part of the block will be overwritten with the first part of the block before it has a change to be moved. There are also times in which it would be desirable to do a conditional block transfer in descending order. To provide for these cases, the **Z80** instruction set has the LDD and LDDR commands.

LDD and LDDR work in the same manner as LDI and LDIR, respectively, except that HL and DE are decremented after the byte transfer instead of being incremented. This operation results in the block being moved starting with the highest memory locations first so that a block can be moved up into an overlapping area without the overwrite problem.

EXAMPLE 6-15 Unconditionally move 200H bytes starting at location 0100H to memory starting at 0200H.

Solution The LDIR instruction would not work in this case, since the values from 0200H to 2FFH will be overwritten before they are moved. Instead, we must move in descending order.

Memory address (hex)	*Code*	*Label*	*Instruction (mnemonic)*	*Comments*
	21FF02		LD HL,02FFH	;Starting from the top.
	11FF03		LD DE,03FFH	;With the destination ;also.
	01002		LD BC,0200H	;200 bytes.
	EDB8		LDDR	;Move it.

6-4.5 Block Search Group

Another programming requirement, which the designers of the **Z80** decided to incorporate as a set of instructions, is the search for a specific bit pattern. There are four search commands similar in form to the block move functions. Only byte searches can be done directly with these instructions, but multibyte searches can be easily implemented using additional commands. All of the instructions compare the contents of the location pointed to by the HL register to the contents of the accumulator. The BC register serves as a counter.

The CPI instruction works in the following way: Compare (HL) to A and set the S, Z, and H flags according to the results of the comparison; increment HL; decrement BC and clear P/V if the result is 0 (set P/V otherwise). The two flags of interest at the end of this instruction are Z and P/V.

If the Z flag is a 1, then there was a match between A and (HL). The P/V flag is used, as in the block transfer group, to signify that the counter has reached 0. As with the LDI instructions, the use of BC as a terminator is highly recommended.

EXAMPLE 6-16 Show the code required to search memory from 0100H through 0200H for the value 0DH.

Solution The byte counter will be set to 0101H to cover the range 0100H to 0200H inclusively.

Memory address (hex)	*Code*	*Label*	*Instruction (mnemonic)*	*Comments*
0000	010101		LD BC,0101H	;Byte count.
0003	210001		LD HL,0100H	;Starting address.
0006	3E0D		LD A,0DH	;Value to be found.

Memory address (hex)	*Code*	*Label*	*Instruction (mnemonic)*	*Comments*
0008	EDA1	SRCH:	CPI	
000A	E21000		JP PO,DONE	;Exit if last byte.
000D	C20800		JP NZ,SRCH	;Try again if no match.
0010		DONE:	⋮	

The code at the label "DONE" can check the Z flag to see if a successful match was found. The location of the successful match is HL-1 since the CPI instruction is incremented after the comparison.

The CPI instruction has a secondary usage which is just as useful as its primary compare function. The result of the compare can simply be ignored and the instruction used as a way to step through a block of memory. HL serves as the memory location pointer, while BC is the byte count.

EXAMPLE 6-17 Set memory locations 0100 through 01FFH to the value 0E5H.

Solution

Memory address (hex)	*Code*	*Label*	*Instruction (mnemonic)*	*Comments*
0000	010001		LD BC,0100H	;The count.
0003	210001		LD HL,0100H	;The starting location.
0006	36E5	LOOP:	LD (HL),0E5H	;Set the value.
0008	EDA1		CPI	;Adjust registers.
000A	EA0600		JP PE,LOOP	;Loop until count = zero.

In this example, the CPI instruction is only used as an easy way to increment the location pointer and decrement the counter. The result of the compare is ignored (the contents of the accumulator is not even specified). The jump on parity even command is used since the loop must be continued until the counter reaches zero and the P/V flag is cleared (parity odd). This use of the CPI command is especially handy for multibyte arithmetic and logical operations.

The CPIR command provides automatic repetition of the CPI function. The flag operation of this instruction is identical to CPI. The command will be repeated until (a) a match is found and the Z flag is set, or (b) the BC count goes to zero and the P/V flag is cleared. As with the LDIR and LDDR instructions, the interrupt flags are checked and interrupts serviced at the end of each execution of the instruction. The CPIR instruction automatically performs the operations of flag checking and jumping shown in the previous search example.

EXAMPLE 6-18 Write the search routine to find 0DH using the CPIR command.

Solution

Memory address (hex)	*Code*	*Label*	*Instruction (mnemonic)*	*Comments*
0000	010101		LD BC,0101H	;Count
0003	210001		LD HL,0100H	;Starting address
0006	3E0D		LD A,0DH	;Object byte
0008	EDB1		CPIR	;Search for it

The CPIR instruction is the instruction to use for a simple-byte search while the CPI instruction should be used when additional operations are required within the search loop.

The CPD and CPDR instructions are identical to the CPI and CPIR instructions, respectively, except that the HL register is decremented after the comparison. These instructions, therefore, search memory in descending order. All comments on the CPI and CPIR commands pertain to the CPD and CPDR with the above-mentioned exception.

6-4.6 8-Bit Arithmetic and Logic Group

The **8080A** has a very complete set of instructions for doing arithmetic and logic on 8-bit values. These commands are ADD; ADD WITH CARRY; SUBTRACT; SUBTRACT WITH CARRY (BORROW); AND; EXCLUSIVE OR; INCLUSIVE OR; COMPARE; INCREMENT; and DECREMENT. The accumulator is always an implied operand and the destination of these commands, with the exception of the increment and decrement commands.

The **Z80** expands this group of instructions by permitting the use of indexed addressing for a command operand.

EXAMPLE 6-19 A previous example showed how the IY register could be loaded with the base address of a table of values used by a process control algorithm. Show how the fourth entry in that table can be subtracted from the fifth element and the result placed in the sixth location. Finally, increment the seventh element.

Solution (IY was previously loaded with 2300H, the table base address.)

Memory address (hex)	*Code*	*Label*	*Instruction (mnemonic)*	*Comments*
0000	FD7E04		LD A,(IY + 4)	;This is the 5th element ;of the table (IY + 0 is ;the 1st).
0003	FD9603		SUB A,(IY + 3)	;Subtract 4th element.
0006	FD7705		LD (IY + 5), A	;Store the result.
0009	FD3406		INC (IY + 6)	;Increment 7th element.

All of the 8-bit arithmetic and logic commands can be used with indexed addressing with either the IX or IY register.

6-4.7 General-Purpose AF Group

This set of instructions uses implied addressing on the accumulator or flag register. The **8080A** instructions in this group are DECIMAL ADJUST ACCUMULATOR, COMPLEMENT ACCUMULATOR (1s complement), COMPLEMENT CARRY FLAG, and SET CARRY FLAG.

The only **Z80** addition to this group is NEGATE ACCUMULATOR (NEG). This command makes the contents of the accumulator into its 2s complement. This instruction is equivalent to the following code sequence:

Code	*Mnemonic*	*Comments*
2F	CPL	Complement accumulator.
C601	ADD A,1	Add 1 to create the 2s complement.

Using the NEG command instead of the above sequence saves 1 byte of memory and 36 percent in execution time, and results in the same flag status.

6-4.8 Miscellaneous CPU Control Group

The **8080A** miscellaneous commands are NOP, HALT, DISABLE INTERRUPT, and ENABLE INTERRUPT. The **Z80** has three maskable interrupt modes compared to the **8080A**'s one mode. Three commands have been added to this group to allow the user to set the interrupt mechanism to the desired mode. The three instructions are:

```
IM 0    ;Set interrupt mode 0 (the default 8080A mode).
IM 1    ;A restart to location 0038H.
IM 2    ;Indirect call using the I register and 8 bits supplied by the interrupting
         device.
```

A detailed description of the operation of these commands is given in the section on interrupts.

6-4.9 16-Bit Arithmetic Group

A limited number of instructions are provided in the **8080A** for doing 16-bit arithmetic. The instructions were originally included primarily to allow for address calculations and use the HL register pair as the 16-bit "accumulator" since it is also the main data pointer. These instructions are ADD, INCREMENT, and DECREMENT.

The **8080A** 16-bit add instruction allows the BC, DE, HL, or SP register to be added to the contents of HL with the result in HL. The only status flag set is the carry flag to indicate overflow. These instructions are fine for adding an offset to a base address, but they make multiple precision arithmetic cumbersome and time consuming. The designers of the **Z80**, realizing that programmers do indeed want to perform multiprecision arithmetic, provided additional instructions to make these operations easier to do.

The add with carry and set flag (ADC) instruction of the **Z80** overcomes the two main objections to the simple 16-bit add instruction: the failure to set the zero and sign flags and the inability to easily include the carry flag in the addition. With this instruction, the carry from a previous instruction can be included in the add. The following segments of code illustrate the advantage of this instruction. The

EXAMPLE 6-20 Using only **8080A** instructions we have the following:

Memory address (hex)	*Code*	*Label*	*Instruction (mnemonic)*	*Comments*
		ACC	EQU 100H	;Location of ACC
0000	A7		AND A	;Clear carry flag
0001	19		ADD HL, DE	;Add the low 16 bits
0002	220001		LD (ACC), HL	;Store the low result
0005	E1		POP HL	;Get the high 16 bits of ;one number
0006	D20A00		JP NC, SKIP	;Check if a carry was ;provided
0009	23		INC HL	;If so, include it
000A	D1	SKIP:	POP DE	;Get the high 16 bits of ;the second number
000B	19		ADD HL, DE	;Add the high 16 bits
000C	220201		LD (ACC + 2), HL	;Store the high result

program adds 2 32-bit numbers and puts the result into 4 consecutive bytes in memory labeled "ACC." The low-order 16-bits of each number are in DE and HL, while the higher-order 16 bits of each number have been pushed onto the stack.

EXAMPLE 6-21 The same program segment, taking advantage of the **Z80** ADC instruction is as follows:

Memory address (hex)	*Code*	*Label*	*Instruction (mnemonic)*	*Comments*
		ACC	EQU 100H	
0000	A7		AND A	;Clear carry flag
0001	19		ADD HL, DE	;Add low 16 bits
0002	220001		LD (ACC), HL	;Add store in memory
0005	E1		POP HL	;Get the high 16 bits
0006	D1		POP DE	;For each number
0007	ED5A		ADC HL, DE	;Add them with any carry
0009	220201		LD (ACC + 2), HL	;And store the high 16 ;bit result

The subtract with carry and set flags (SBC) instruction of the **Z80** can offer even better efficiency since the **8080A** has no form of 16-bit subtract. Multibyte subtractions on the **8080A** must be done a byte at a time or by doing a 2s complement on a 16-bit number and then using the 16-bit add. Contrast the code required to subtract the contents of DE from the contents of HL with the result in HL.

EXAMPLE 6-22 Using only **8080A** instructions we have the following:

Memory address (hex)	*Code*	*Instruction (mnemonic)*	*Comments*
0000	7D	LD A,L	;Subtract the low
0001	93	SUB A,E	;byte
0002	6F	LD L,A	;Put result in L
0003	7C	LD A,H	;Subtract the high byte
0004	9A	SBC A,D	;With any borrow
0005	67	LD H,A	;Put result in H

EXAMPLE 6-23 Using the **Z80** 16-bit SBC instruction we have the following:

Memory address (hex)	*Code*	*Instruction (mnemonic)*	*Comments*
0001	A7	AND A	;Clear carry
0002	ED52	SBC HL, DE	;Do the 16 bit subtract

The **Z80** also includes instructions for 16-bit ADD, INC, and DEC using the IX or IY register as the destination and source of one operand. These instructions operate identically to the **8080A** instructions and are provided to allow easy calculation of the index register address values. Only the carry flag is affected by these operations. Note that the HL register cannot be used as a source in the ADD instructions and that the two index registers cannot be added directly together.

6-4.10 ROTATE and SHIFT Group

The **Z80** has a wealth of SHIFT and ROTATE instructions in contrast to the four instructions provided by the **8080A**. The contents of any of the 8-bit CPU registers, memory addressed indirectly by HL, or the memory addressed by IX or IY using indexed indirect, may be shifted or rotated in seven different ways. The **Z80** instructions also set the sign and zero flags which the **8080A** instructions fail to do. In addition, memory addressed indirectly by HL can be rotated left or right 4 bits at a time with the low 4 bits of the accumulator. These instructions permit rapid execution of packed binary coded decimal (BCD) arithmetic.

The ROTATE LEFT CIRCULAR (RLC) instruction moves each bit of the addressed register or memory location one position to the left. The most significant bit is moved to the least significant bit position. The carry flag is set to the value of the most significant bit before the rotation is done. This operation is shown in Figure 6-2.

The **8080A** can only perform this operation on the A register while the **Z80** can use any of the indicated registers or memory locations. An interesting result of the way the **Z80** circuitry was designed is that two different Op code sequences may be used to rotate the accumulator. The difference between the two is that the **8080A** code (07) does not affect the S and Z flags while the **Z80** code (CB 07) does. Unless

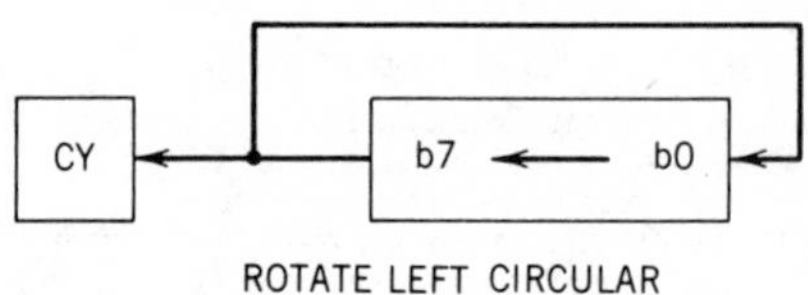

Figure 6-2 ROTATE LEFT CIRCULAR.

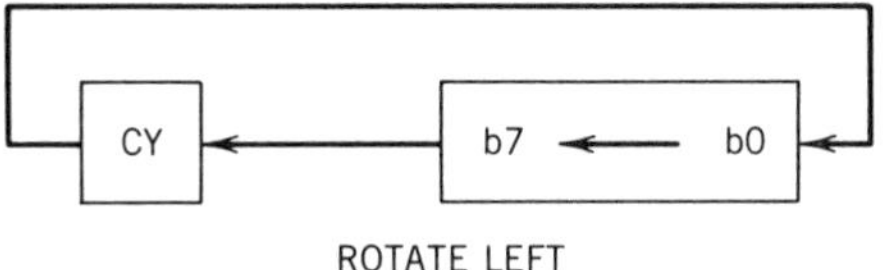

Figure 6-3 ROTATE LEFT.

the flags are to be tested, the **8080A** code is preferred since it is shorter and faster. These comments also apply to the RLA, RRCA, and RRA instructions.

The ROTATE LEFT instruction moves all bits to the left and includes the carry in the move. The contents of the most significant bit is put into the carry while the original contents of the carry is placed into the least significant bit position. This operation is shown in Figure 6-3.

The ROTATE RIGHT CIRCULAR and the ROTATE RIGHT instructions are similar to the above except that the direction is changed. These operations are shown in Figures 6-4 and 6-5. Note that in these instructions, the carry gets set to the value of the least significant bit.

There are times when it is desirable to do a simple shift rather than a rotation of bits. The **Z80** provides three types of shifting instructions: SHIFT LEFT ARITHMETIC; SHIFT RIGHT ARITHMETIC; and SHIFT RIGHT LOGICAL. The names correspond to the types of operation in which the shifting action is usually used.

The SHIFT LEFT ARITHMETIC operation is shown in Figure 6-6. Notice that the carry flag receives the contents of the most significant bit (the original contents of the carry is lost), all bits are shifted left, and that the least significant bit receives a 0. This operation is equivalent to multiplying the register contents by 2. The S, Z, and P/V flags are affected by this operation, with P/V indicating the parity of the shifted byte.

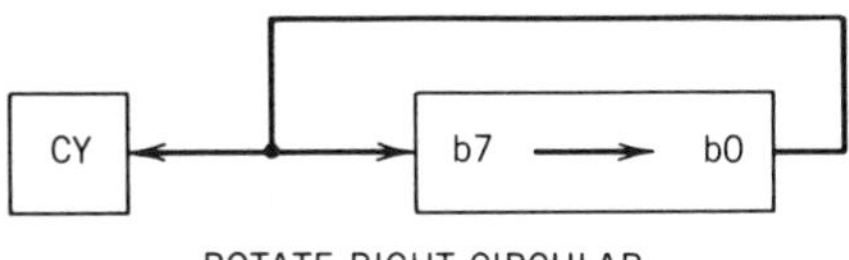

Figure 6-4 ROTATE RIGHT CIRCULAR.

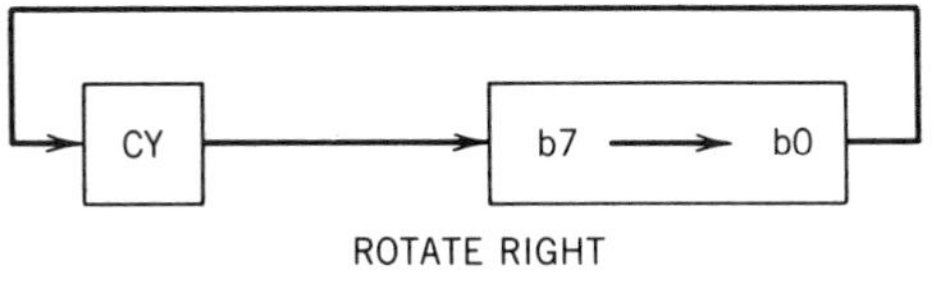

Figure 6-5 ROTATE RIGHT.

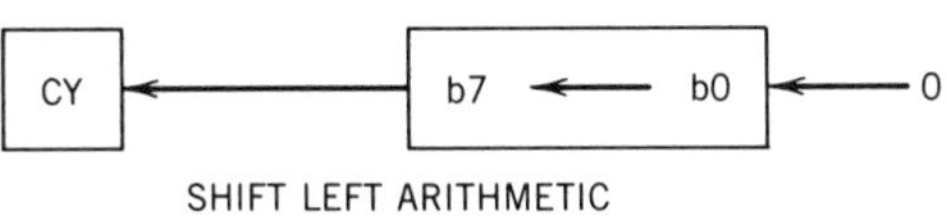

Figure 6-6 SHIFT LEFT ARITHMETIC.

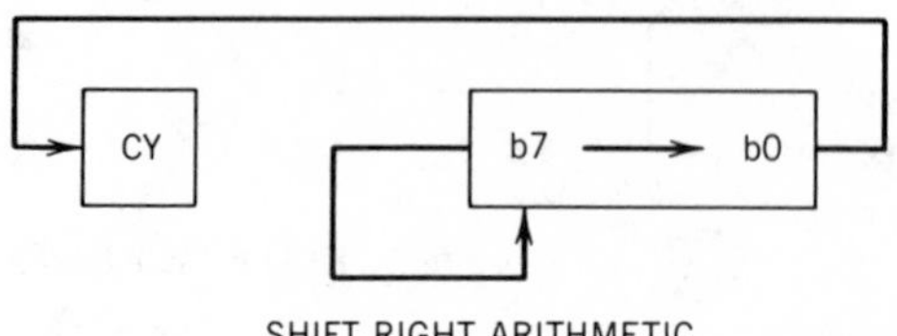

Figure 6-7 SHIFT RIGHT ARITHMETIC.

The SHIFT RIGHT ARITHMETIC operation is shown in Figure 6-7. In this operation, the carry flag receives the contents of the least significant bit, all bits are shifted right, and the contents of bit 7 remains the same. This operation is equivalent to dividing the register contents by 2. The sign of the number is maintained by keeping its contents the same. The flags are affected in the same manner as the SHIFT LEFT ARITHMETIC instruction.

The SHIFT ARITHMETIC commands may be combined with the ROTATE instructions to perform multibyte arithmetic shifts as shown in the following example:

EXAMPLE 6-24 Divide the triple-precision number, starting at location 0100H, by 2.

Solution

Memory address (hex)	*Code*	*Label*	*Instruction (mnemonic)*	*Comments*
0000	0201		LD HL, 0102H	;Point to the most ;significant byte
0003	CB 2E		SRA (HL)	;Shift right maintaining ;sign
0005	2B		DEC HL	;Point to next byte
0006	CB 1E		RR (HL)	;Shift in the carry bit
0008	2B		DEC HL	;Complete for the least
0009	CB 1E		RR (HL)	;Significant byte

The SHIFT RIGHT LOGICAL instruction is shown in Figure 6-8. In this case, the bits are shifted right with the least significant byte shifting into the carry.

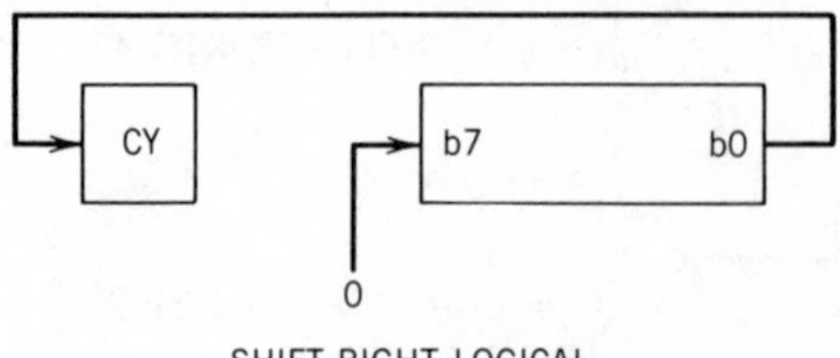

Figure 6-8 SHIFT RIGHT LOGICAL.

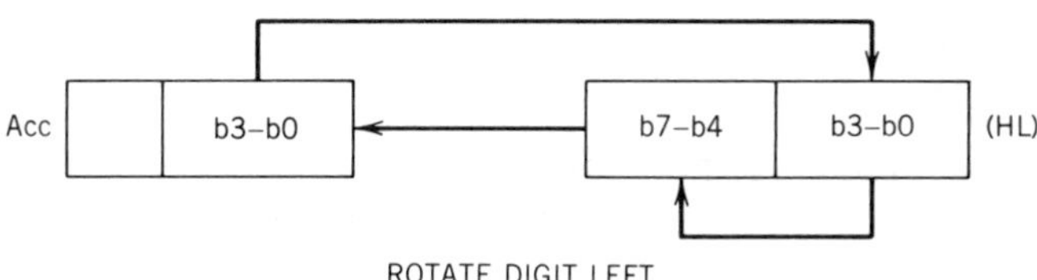

Figure 6-9 ROTATE DIGIT LEFT.

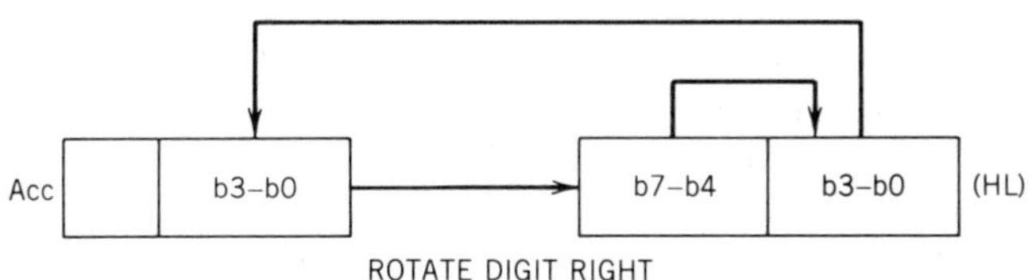

Figure 6-10 ROTATE DIGIT RIGHT.

The most significant bit is cleared to 0. The flags are affected in the same manner as the other SHIFT operations.

The ROTATE LEFT DIGIT (RLD) and ROTATE RIGHT DIGIT (RRD) instructions are unique to the **Z80**. Instead of rotating by 1 bit, these two instructions rotate by 4 bits to implement a BCD digit rotate. As Figures 6-9 and 6-10 show, the rotates are done between the accumulator and a memory location indirectly addressed by HL. The S and Z flags conditions represent the memory location status after the rotate. The P/V flag will be set to the parity of the memory contents.

EXAMPLE 6-25 Create a subroutine to SHIFT LEFT ARITHMETIC a 14-digit BCD number. The least significant digit memory location will be passed to the subroutine in the HL register. This routine will be used as part of a BCD multiply and divide routines.

Solution

```
            LD B, 7         ;Set up count
            XOR A           ;Clear accumulator

SHIFT       RLD             ;Rotate left digit
            INC HL          ;Point to next byte
            DJNZ SHIFT      ;Continue rotating until done
            RET
```

Example 6-25 uses the DJNZ instruction, which, as explained later, is a combination decrement of B and relative jump if the result is not zero.

6-4.11 Bit Manipulation Group

The manipulation of individual bits is frequently necessary in signal processing and control applications. Surprisingly, few microprocessors offer instructions to manipulate bits directly; most bit manipulation must be done through a combination of load and logical operations.

The **Z80** provides three types of bit manipulation commands which efficiently operate on individual bits. There are a total of 240 distinct Op codes to cover all possible addressing modes and bit positions. The addressing modes used are: register; register indirect using HL; and indexed with either IX or IY. Fortunately, we need only discuss the three instruction types—BIT SET, BIT CLEAR, and BIT TEST—since all of the instructions are only variations of one of these three. These instructions can only operate on a single bit.

The BIT TEST instruction uses the Z flag to indicate the status of the indicated bit. If the bit being tested is a 1, then the Z flag will be cleared. Conversely, if the bit is a 0, the Z flag will be set. By this action, the Z flag is in the appropriate state for conditional jump and call instructions.

EXAMPLE 6-26 Test the sixth bit in the accumulator and jump to CALC, at 0100H, if the bit is zero.

Solution

Code	**Mnemonic**
CB6F	BIT 5, A
CA 0001	JP Z, CALC

Since the bits are numbered 0 (least significant) through 7 (most significant), the sixth bit of the accumulator is labeled as 5 for the mnemonic. This point is confusing to beginning assembly language programmers and is a common source of error.

The BIT SET instruction is used to SET the addressed bit to a binary 1. No flags are affected by this instruction.

EXAMPLE 6-27 SET the fifth bit of the byte pointed to by HL without disturbing the contents of any of the CPU registers. Show the solution two ways:

a using the **Z80** instruction set;

b using only **8080A** instructions.

Solution

a Using the **Z80** instruction set:

Code	**Mnemonic**
CB E6	SET 4, (HL)

b Using only **8080A** instructions:

Code	Mnemonic
F5	PUSH AF
7E	LD A, (HL)
F6 10	OR A, 00010000B
77	LD (HL), A
F1	POP AF

The PUSH and POP instructions are necessary to preserve the accumulator and flag contents.

Notice the use of the binary form for the logical mask byte in the OR instruction. The binary form should be used for logical operation mnemonics since the bits affected are more obvious than if the octal, decimal, or hexadecimal formats are used.

The BIT RES instruction type resets the addressed bit to a zero. As with the set instruction type, no flags are affected by this instruction.

EXAMPLE 6-28 Reset the fourth bit in the seventh byte of TABLE, starting at 1000H.

Solution

Code	Mnemonic
FD 21 0010	LD IY, TABLE
FD CB 06 9E	RES 3, (IY + 6)

To appreciate the power of these instructions, the reader should program the last example using only the **8080A** instruction set. Write the code so that no CPU registers or flags are disturbed.

6-4.12 JUMP Group

All of the instructions described so far provide for simple linear flow of the program. The JUMP instructions have been shown in some of the examples as a means of redirecting the flow of the program to another part of memory, usually based on some condition indicated by one of the flag bits.

The **8080A** instruction set has nine 3-byte JUMP instructions using the immediate extended addressing mode and a single-byte JUMP register indirect instruction (PCHL) using the HL register. Eight of the immediate extended JUMPs are conditional on the status of one of the flag bits: CARRY, NON-CARRY, ZERO, NON-ZERO, PARITY EVEN, PARITY ODD, SIGN NEGATIVE (1), SIGN POSITIVE (0). The register indirect JUMP and simple JUMP commands are unconditional.

A large number of JUMPs used in a program cause the program counter to be changed to a location quite close to its current position. This occurs when the JUMP is back to a previous location as in a loop or when a JUMP is made around a piece of code that is only to be executed on certain conditions. The **8080A** instructions for conditional JUMPs require 3 bytes of code because the absolute address is provided. For these short JUMPs the **Z80** provides five types of relative JUMPs, which require only 2 bytes. The details of this addressing mode were described earlier.

The relative JUMPs in the **Z80** instruction set are UNCONDITIONAL, CARRY, NON-CARRY, ZERO, and NON-ZERO. Relative JUMPs based on the sign and parity flags are not provided. An interesting effect of the way the relative JUMP instruction is implemented is that the amount of time the instruction takes is dependent on whether the condition is met or not. If the condition is not met, the program just falls through to the next instruction and the execution time is less than it would be for the standard JUMP. On the other hand, if the condition is met, the JUMP address must be calculated by adding the offset to the program counter. The time required to do the addition results in a longer execution time than the standard JUMP. This timing difference is usually not important except for programs involving real-time applications, but the programmer should always keep it in mind. Relative JUMPs are usually used whenever possible because of the byte savings.

EXAMPLE 6-29 A terminal output routine often sends out a line feed whenever a carriage return is printed since many terminals do not provide an automatic line feed. Show the portion of the code to perform this action. The output port is at 01.

Solution

Memory address (hex)	*Code*	*Label*	*Instruction (mnemonic)*	*Comments*
0110	D3 01		OUT A, PORT	;A has character to ;to be printed
0112	FE OD		CP A, ODH	;Is it a CR(0DH)?
0114	20 04		JR NZ, SKIP	;Skip if not,
0116	3E OA		LD A, OAH	;Else send out
0118	D3 01		OUT A, PORT	;a line feed (0AH)
011A	⋮	SKIP	⋮	

Assembler programs automatically calculate the relative offset based on the JUMP address and give an error if it is outside the single-byte offset range.

The JUMP can be backward as well as forward, as shown in the next example:

EXAMPLE 6-30 An output routine expands the tab character (09H) into eight single spaces. Many terminals do not recognize the tab command. Show that portion of the code that expands tabs.

Solution

Memory address (hex)	*Code*	*Label*	*Instruction (mnemonic)*	*Comments*
				;Character in A
00F0	FE 09		CP A, 09H	;Is it a tab
00F2	20 09		JR NX, NOTAB	;Skip expansion if not
00F4	06 08		LD B, 08	;Else load count
00F6	3E 20		LD A, 20H	;Output spaces
00F8	D3 01	TAB:	OUT A, PORT	;
00FA	05		DEC B	;
00FB	20 FB		JR NZ, TAB	;Until count is zero
00FD	⋮	NOTAB:	⋮	

The relative JUMP address requires an offset of −5, which is 0FBH.

The type of loop shown in the last example is so common that the **Z80** instruction set has a special relative JUMP that combines the DECREMENT and JUMP function. The DJNZ instruction decrements the B register and does a relative JUMP if the result is not zero. One byte (and a small amount of time per iteration) can be saved by using the DJNZ instruction as shown below:

Memory address	*Code*	*Label*	*Operation (mnemonic)*	*Comments*
⋮	⋮		⋮	⋮
00F8	D3 01	TAB:	OUT A, PORT	;Output spaces
00FA	10 FC		DJNZ TAB	;Until count is zero
00FC	⋮	NOTAB:	⋮	⋮

The register indirect JUMP is useful for transferring control to a calculated address or an address from a table. Since the IX and IY registers can be used as accumulators for 16-bit addition, they can also be used for register indirect JUMPs.

EXAMPLE 6-31 A JUMP table is a useful device for transferring control based on a table index value. As an example, the index could be a value returned from a terminal input routine. The table consists of 2 byte addresses. Show the code to JUMP to the appropriate table routine using the IX register. The index is in the A register and the table starts at 0500H.

Solution

Memory address (hex)	*Code*	*Label*	*Op code (mnemonic)*	*Comments*
0100	21 00 05		LD HL, TABLE	;Point to table
0103	DD 21 00 00		LD IX, 0	;Clear IX
0107	87		ADD A	;Double index value to
0108	5F		LD E, A	;Get into word table
0109	16 00		LD D, 0	;Put index into DE
010B	19		ADD HL, DE	;& add offset to table
010C	5E		LD E, (HL)	;Get address from
010D	23		INC HL	;Table into DE,
010E	56		LD D, (HL)	
010F	DD 19		ADD IX, DE	;Add to IX
0111	DD E9		JP (IX)	;JUMP to routine

6-4.13 CALL and RETURN Group

The **8080A** has a very complete set of CALL and RETURN instructions. Conditional CALLs and RETURNs can be made on the same basis as conditional JUMPs. There are only two additional **Z80** instructions in this group.

The return from interrupt (RETI) and return from nonmaskable interrupt (RETN) are special instructions used in conjunction with **Z80** peripheral chips. They act like the standard RETURN instruction as far as the program is concerned, but also cause **Z80** peripheral chips to be conditioned for priority interrupts. This action will be explained in detail in the section on interrupts.

6-4.14 RESTART Group

The eight RESTART instructions of the **8080A** are used identically in the **Z80**. These instructions act as single-byte call instructions to special location in page zero of memory. See the chapter on the **8080A** for details on these commands.

6-4.15 Input Group

Like the **8080A**, the **Z80** provides instructions for input and output using special I/O addressing techniques that provide for 256 input and 256 output locations. The

8080A has only one input command using immediate addressing. The **Z80** instruction set includes significant improvements in this area.

One of the problems with immediate mode I/O addressing is that the I/O address cannot be dynamically changed if the program is in read-only memory. This can be a significant limitation in microprocessor systems. Designers of **8080A** ROM-based systems must resort to awkward program "fixes" to get around this limitation. The **Z80** has a set of *register indirect* I/O instructions in which the C register contains the I/O address number. The 8-bit data byte can be input into the accumulator or any of the general registers. An added feature of these instructions is that the S, Z, and P/V flags reflect the status of the data input (the P/V flag shows the parity).

EXAMPLE 6-32 Show a subroutine, located at 1000H, which will cause a program to wait until a specific bit pattern is available on a given port. The port number is passed in register C, and the bit pattern is passed in register B.

Solution

Memory address (hex)	*Code*	*Label*	*Instruction (mnemonic)*	*Comments*
1000	ED78	WAIT	IN A, C	;Get input byte
1002	B8		CP B	;Is it desired pattern?
1003	C8		RET Z	;Return if so
1004	18FA		JR WAIT	;Else, keep trying

The conditional return is used in this example to illustrate its use. Note that this is a general subroutine not specifying any particular input port and could be placed in ROM if desired.

The **Z80** also has a series of block I/O instructions similar in nature to the block search and move instructions. The block input instructions use the HL register as a memory pointer for the destination of the input byte. The B register is used as a byte counter.

The INI instruction inputs a byte from the port addressed by C into the memory location pointed to by HL, increments HL, and decrements B. The Z flag is set if the contents of B goes to zero.

The INIR instruction is similar except that it repeats the input sequence until B becomes zero. Notice the similarity to the other block type instructions.

The IND and INDR instructions operate the same as the INI and INIR instructions, respectively, except that HL is decremented after each input instruction. This allows memory to be loaded in descending order.

The INI and IND instructions are the more generally useful of the set, since they permit additional instructions to be inserted between repetitions of the input command. The use of the REPEAT type instructions requires that the CPU and external device be syncronized in some manner. This can be done by the external device pulling the **Z80** WAIT line LOW until data is ready, and monitoring the address lines to determine that the I/O device has been read. This approach requires additional hardware and the added performance is seldom worth the effort. Direct memory access (DMA) techniques should probably be used for truly high-speed I/O requirements.

EXAMPLE 6-33 A controller requires a periodic scan of input ports. The scan will be done on an interrupt basis and the contents of each port are to be placed in a table for further processing. The number of ports to be scanned will be found in location 0110H (noports). The first port number is found at location 0111H (inports). The input data table starts at 6000H (intabl). The scan interrupt vectors to location 0500H. Show the scan interrupt routine.

Solution

Memory address (hex)	*Code*	*Label*	*Op code*	*Comments*
0500	21 10 01	SCANIN	LD HL, NOPORTS	;Point to setup ;data
0503	46		LD B, (HL)	;Get number of ;ports
0504	23		INC HL	
0505	4E		LD C, (HL)	;Point to first ;port Inports
0506	21 00 60		LD HL, INTABL	;Point to input ;table
0509	0D		DEC C	;Set up for loop
050A	0C	INLOOP	INC C	;Point to next ;port
050B	ED AZ		INI	;Get data to ;table
050D	20 FB		JR NZ, INLOOP	;If not last port ;Do it again
050F	ED 4D		RETI	;Return from ;interrupt ;When done

Note the use of RETI to return from this interrupt routine. The increment of the C register was placed before the INI instruction instead of after it, so that the flags would not be affected for the conditional JUMP instruction. This required a preceding decrement for the first time through the loop. The decrement C instruction could be eliminated if inports contained the address of the first port minus 1.

6-4.16 Output Group

The **Z80** output instructions are grouped the same as the input instructions and simply reverse the direction of data flow. As with the input instruction, the **8080A** single-output instruction uses immediate mode addressing which limits its use with ROM-based code.

The **Z80** register indirect output commands use the C register to point to the desired output port. The source of the byte to be output can be the accumulator or any 8-bit general register. Unlike the input instruction, the register indirect output command does not affect the flags.

The block output commands OUTI and OUTD use HL to point to the table of bytes to be output while B maintains the byte count. Again, C contains the port address and the table address is either incremented or decremented after each byte output, depending on the instruction used.

The repeated block output instructions (OTIR and OTDR) repeat the OUTI and OUTD instructions until the byte count in B is decremented to zero.

EXAMPLE 6-34 The repeated block output instruction is useful for configuring **Z80** family I/O devices such as the PIO. Show a program which will send 5 configuration bytes to the PIO control register at port address 10H. The table of bytes is located at 1000H.

Solution

Memory address (hex)	*Code*	*Label*	*Op Code*	*Comments*
100	0605	CONFIG:	LD B, 5	;No. of bytes
102	0E10		LD C, 10H	;Port address
104	21 00 10		LD HL, 1000H	;Table of bytes
107	ED B3		OTIR	;Send it

6-5 CPU PINOUT AND DESCRIPTION

This section describes the function of each of the 40 pins on the **Z80** package. Figure 6-11 illustrates the pin designations.

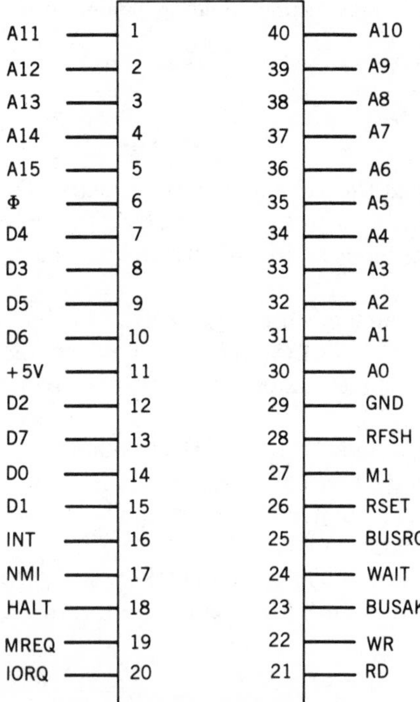

Figure 6-11 **Z80** CPU pin out.

Pin name	*Description*
A0–A7	16-bit address bus. Outputs are tri-state, active HIGH. The lower 8 bits (A0–A7) are also used for I/O addressing. The lower 7 bits (A0–A6) provide a refresh address when pin 28 (RFSH) is LOW.
D0–D7	8-bit data bus. Bidirectional, tri-state active HIGH.
$\overline{\text{M1}}$	Machine cycle one output indication. An active LOW on this pin indicates that the current machine cycle is the Op code fetch cycle of an instruction. M1 is generated for each byte of a 2-byte Op code. M1 is also active LOW with IORQ to indicate an interrupt acknowledge cycle.
$\overline{\text{MREQ}}$	Memory request signal. This is a tri-state, active LOW output which indicates that the address bus holds a valid memory address. Used with all memory READ and WRITE operations.
$\overline{\text{IORQ}}$	Input/output request indicator. Tri-state, active LOW output used to indicate that A0–A7 holds a valid address for I/O operations. IORQ concurrent with M1 during an interrupt acknowledge cycle indicates that an interrupt vector can be placed on the data bus.
$\overline{\text{RD}}$	Memory read tri-state active LOW output. Used by memory or I/O device to gate data onto the data bus.
$\overline{\text{WR}}$	Memory write tri-state active LOW output. Used to indicate to memory or an I/O device that the data bus contains valid data to be stored.

Pin name	Description
$\overline{\text{RFSH}}$	Refresh signal. An active LOW output used with MREQ to indicate to dynamic memories that A0–A6 has a refresh address.
$\overline{\text{HALT}}$	Halt state indicator. This is an active LOW output which indicates that the CPU has executed a software HALT instruction and is executing NOPs. Operation will resume with receipt of an interrupt or RESET.
$\overline{\text{WAIT}}$	Wait active LOW input signal to the CPU. Provided by a memory or I/O device to request that the CPU insert WAIT states in its machine cycle. Used to synchronize slow memory or I/O to the CPU.
$\overline{\text{INT}}$	This is the maskable interrupt line. Active LOW input. See the following section on interrupts for a detailed description.
$\overline{\text{NMI}}$	Nonmaskable interrupt input. This is a negative edge-triggered input used to force the CPU to restart at location 0066H.
$\overline{\text{RESET}}$	Reset is an active LOW input that forces the program counter to 0000H and initializes the CPU in the following manner: (a) Disable interrupt enable flip flop. (b) Set I and R registers to 00H. (c) Set interrupt mode 0. During reset time the address and data lines are placed in the high impedance state and all control outputs are placed in the inactive state.
$\overline{\text{BUSRQ}}$	Bus request input, active LOW. Used by external devices for direct memory access. Upon receipt, the CPU places tri-state lines in the high impedance state when the current machine cycle is terminated.
$\overline{\text{BUSAK}}$	This is an active LOW output provided by the CPU to indicate that it has placed all tri-state lines in the high impedance state in response to BUSRQ. The external device has control of these lines until it takes BUSRQ HIGH.
$\overline{\Phi}$	Single-phase TTL level clock input line. The clock must be generated by external circuitry.

6-6 I/O PROCESSING AND INTERRUPTS

The operation of the **Z80** I/O instructions was explained in section 6-4. This section will consist of some general comments on I/O processing and a discussion of **Z80** interrupts which are often closely related to I/O functions.

While the **Z80** provides special instructions for I/O operations, memory-mapped I/O such as that used in the **68XX** and **65XX** series processors is perfectly feasible. The use of memory-mapped I/O can frequently be useful since this technique treats an I/O port the same as any memory location. This means that a larger number of operations (e.g., logical operations) can be done directly on the port contents. These advantages are purchased at the cost of the memory dedicated to the I/O ports and (usually) more complex address decoding circuits for the I/O ports. In small systems, where the memory allocation is not a problem, the decoding can usually be simplified and memory-mapped I/O techniques deserve design consideration.

The use of register indirect I/O via the C register is a powerful addition to the **Z80** instruction set. As was pointed out earlier, it allows I/O code to be placed in

ROM and provides means for the block I/O instructions. It also means that general I/O subroutines can be written to which the port number is simply passed in the C register. Operations of this type cannot be written on the **8080A** without the use of self-modifying code.

Caution should be used with the repetitive block I/O functions. These commands operate at full CPU speed and, unless the external I/O device can accept or provide data at this rate, incorrect operation will result. Since the external device usually runs asynchronous to the **Z80**, the device must synchronize repetitive block I/O operations through the **Z80** $\overline{\text{WAIT}}$ line. Unless the external device is very close in speed to the CPU, the nonrepetitive block I/O operation with status checking is preferred.

6-6.1 WAIT and BUS Requests

External devices or events can alter the normal operation of the CPU by a variety of methods. The $\overline{\text{WAIT}}$ signal will introduce $\overline{\text{WAIT}}$ cycles into the current machine cycle until the $\overline{\text{WAIT}}$ line goes high. The purpose of this line is to synchronize slow memory devices to the CPU. Since the $\overline{\text{WAIT}}$ line prevents completion of the machine cycle, bus request and interrupt signals will not be acknowledged until the $\overline{\text{WAIT}}$ line goes HIGH. This is the prime reason for not using the $\overline{\text{WAIT}}$ line to synchronize slow I/O devices.

External events are accorded the following priority:

1 Bus request ($\overline{\text{BUSRQ}}$)

2 Nonmaskable interrupt ($\overline{\text{NMI}}$)

3 Maskable interrupt ($\overline{\text{INT}}$)

The lines associated with these signals are sampled on the rising edge of the last clock period of a machine cycle. Bus requests are acknowledged on any machine cycle, but interrupts are only acknowledged at the end of instructions. If the signal is active, the CPU alters its normal operation and executes the actions associated with the lines in the priority listed. If $\overline{\text{BUSRQ}}$ is active, the CPU will set its address, data, and tri-state control lines to the high impedance state and take the $\overline{\text{BUSAK}}$ line low. This is the direct memory access (DMA) mode with which external devices can gain direct access to the system for fast data transfers. The CPU will stay in this state as long as the $\overline{\text{BUSRQ}}$ line is active.

6-6.2 Nonmaskable Interrupts

After the bus request has been serviced, the interrupts can be acted upon. Two internal flip-flops (IFF1 and IFF2) are provided to indicate the status of the interrupt sequence. A nonmaskable interrupt will reset IFF1, the flip-flop that enables maskable interrupts. This prevents a maskable interrupt from interrupting the $\overline{\text{NMI}}$ routine. The status of IFF1 just prior to the $\overline{\text{NMI}}$ is placed in IFF2 so that the CPU can return to the correct status at the end of the $\overline{\text{NMI}}$ routine.

The nonmaskable interrupt works in the following manner:

1 Push the current program counter to stack.
2 Store IFF1 status in IFF2.
3 Reset IFF1, preventing further interrupts.
4 Jump to location 0066H, executing the code found there until a RETN instruction is encountered.
5 The RETN instruction causes the IFF1 status to be restored.
6 The address on top of the stack is placed in the program counter.

The RETN instruction should always be used to return from the $\overline{\text{NMI}}$ interrupt, since it is the only return instruction that restores the IFF1 status.

6-6.3 Maskable Interrupts

The **Z80** has three modes of maskable interrupt operation. Which of the three will operate when the $\overline{\text{INT}}$ goes low is determined by the IMx commands. The power up default mode is mode 0, identical to the **8080A** interrupt mode. In this mode, IFF1 and IFF2 are both reset when $\overline{\text{INT}}$ goes low. The $\overline{\text{IORQ}}$ and $\overline{\text{M1}}$ lines are activated to request a command. This is usually a RESTART instruction placed on the data bus by the interrupting device. This instruction is then executed. As you will recall, the RESTART instructions are 1-byte CALLs to a location in page zero of memory. The restart interrupt routine usually ends with an EI (enable interrupts) and RET command. The EI sets IFF1 flip flop so that further interrupts can be processed.

Two things should be noticed about this interrupt mode. First, the CPU will execute any instruction supplied on the data bus, not just RST instructions. If a multibyte instruction is given, the CPU continues to read these bytes with the program counter stationary. The interrupting device must supply the full instruction. This means that vectored interrupt operations to any place in memory are possible with mode 0 as long as the interrupting device can supply a 3-byte CALL instruction. Second, the EI instruction can be given at any time in the interrupt routine to allow multiple, nested interrupts.

Interrupt mode 1 is a very simple interrupt, which operates in a manner similar to $\overline{\text{NMI}}$. If the $\overline{\text{INT}}$ signal is received with the mode set to 1 by the IM1 instruction, interrupts are disabled, the program counter is pushed to the stack, and control jumps to 0038H. As with mode 0, interrupts can be enabled at any time to allow for nested interrupts. Control is returned to the interrupted code by the standard RET instruction.

The most complex and powerful of the **Z80** interrupts is mode 2. This mode takes advantage of the special circuitry included in the **Z80** family peripheral chips to provide a priority vectored interrupt system. This mode uses a table of interrupt vector addresses which can be placed anywhere in memory. The following actions occur when an $\overline{\text{INT}}$ is received in mode 2:

1 Interrupts are disabled.

2 An 8-bit interrupt vector is read from the data bus. This vector is supplied from the interrupting device as with mode 0.

3 The program counter is pushed to the stack.

4 The vector table address is formed with the high byte being the contents of the I register and the low byte being the unique vector just supplied by the interrupting device.

5 The 2 bytes read at the vector table address are then placed in the program counter and control is passed to the interrupt routine at this address.

Interrupts may be reenabled at any time to allow for nested interrupts. Control is returned to the interrupted code by means of the RETI instruction. This is a special form of the RETURN instruction that resets the priority interrupt circuitry in the peripheral device.

The **Z80** family of peripheral devices are based on a daisy-chain interrupt design that requires a minimum amount of external hardware. Each peripheral chip has 3 signal lines used to implement the interrupt system.

1 interrupt enable input (IEI)

2 interrupt enable output (IEO)

3 interrupt request ($\overline{\text{INT}}$)

The interrupt request lines on each device may be wire ORed to the CPU INT line to provide the interrupt signal. Priority is established by wiring the IEO line of one device to the IEI line of the next. The first device in the chain, and the device with the highest priority, has its IEI line tied permanently HIGH. A device makes an interrupt request by pulling its INT and IEO lines LOW. The INT line informs the CPU of the interrupt request. The IEO line going LOW prevents devices lower in the chain from making an interrupt request since an interrupt can only be generated if the IEI line on the device is HIGH. A low IEI line on a device is reflected as a low IEO line on the same device, thus propagating the interrupt disable to all lower devices in the chain. The physical daisy chain of the devices provides the priority structure to the system.

The CPU acknowledges the interrupt by a special $\overline{\text{M1}}$ cycle in which $\overline{\text{IORQ}}$ is taken LOW. An active M1 line prevents further interrupts during the cycle, to ensure that the highest of the interrupting devices receives the $\overline{\text{IORQ}}$ signal. When the interrupting devices see an active $\overline{\text{M1}}$ and $\overline{\text{IORQ}}$ it places the 8-bit vector previously programmed into it onto the data bus. This vector is used to form the vector table address, as described earlier. After this action, the peripheral device takes its $\overline{\text{INT}}$ line HIGH and monitors the data bus for an RETI instruction. The RETI (ED 4D) is interpreted by the device as completion of the interrupt sequence and the peripheral takes its IEO line HIGH to restore the chain to its normal state. The IEI line must be HIGH for the RETI instruction to be recognized. This requirement is the means by which multiple priority interrupts is implemented. If the interrupt routine enables interrupts with the EI instruction, a higher-priority device may in turn interrupt the current interrupt routine. That device will, as part of the interrupt sequence, take its

IEO line LOW, prohibiting the first interrupting device from recognizing the RETI instruction of the higher priority interrupt routine. This technique ensures that interrupts are properly nested and acknowledged.

The number of peripheral devices that may be chained with no external circuitry in the manner described above is limited because of the propagation time down the chain of the IEI-IEO and $\overline{\text{IORQ}}$ signals. The manufacturer's literature provides schemes by which $\overline{\text{WAIT}}$ states may be introduced to allow for the propagation time in long daisy chains.

The use of the peripheral devices is best shown by a real example. This is done in the next section, which describes a practical application of the **Z80** and two of its most popular peripheral devices.

6-7 SAMPLE APPLICATION

To illustrate the application of the **Z80** and its peripheral devices, this section describes a small single board computer. This circuit could form the heart of a remote data acquisition unit or a dedicated machine controller. The sample application illustrates the following:

1 **Z80** CPU and typical clock circuit

2 byte-wide read-only memory (ROM and RAM)

3 **Z80** PIO (parallel I/O interface device)

4 **Z80** CTC (counter/timer circuit)

5 **8251** serial I/O device

The **8251** (see Chapter 13) is used for serial communication instead of the **Z80** SIO (serial I/O device) to show how **8080A** or other non-**Z80** peripheral devices may be interfaced to the **Z80** using the CTC as a priority interrupt generator.

The complete circuit of the computer is shown in Figure 6-12. Each of the major sections in the figure will now be detailed.

6-7.1 Z80 CPU

The **Z80** is configured for a minimal system with no bus buffers because of the small number of chips that it must drive. The $\overline{\text{WAIT}}$, $\overline{\text{NMI}}$, and $\overline{\text{BUSRQ}}$ lines are pulled HIGH since they are not needed in this simple application. Likewise, $\overline{\text{BUSAK}}$, $\overline{\text{RFSH}}$, and $\overline{\text{HALT}}$ outputs do not lead anywhere since they too are not needed. The memory and I/O peripherals do not require WAIT states and DMA and nonmaskable interrupts will not be implemented. The **Z80** peripherals are connected to the $\overline{\text{INT}}$ line and will use the mode 2 interrupt capability.

6-7.2 Clock Circuit

The clock circuitry is a simple crystal oscillator using two gates of a **7400** TTL two-input NAND gate. The oscillator runs at 4 MHz and is divided by half of a **74LS74**

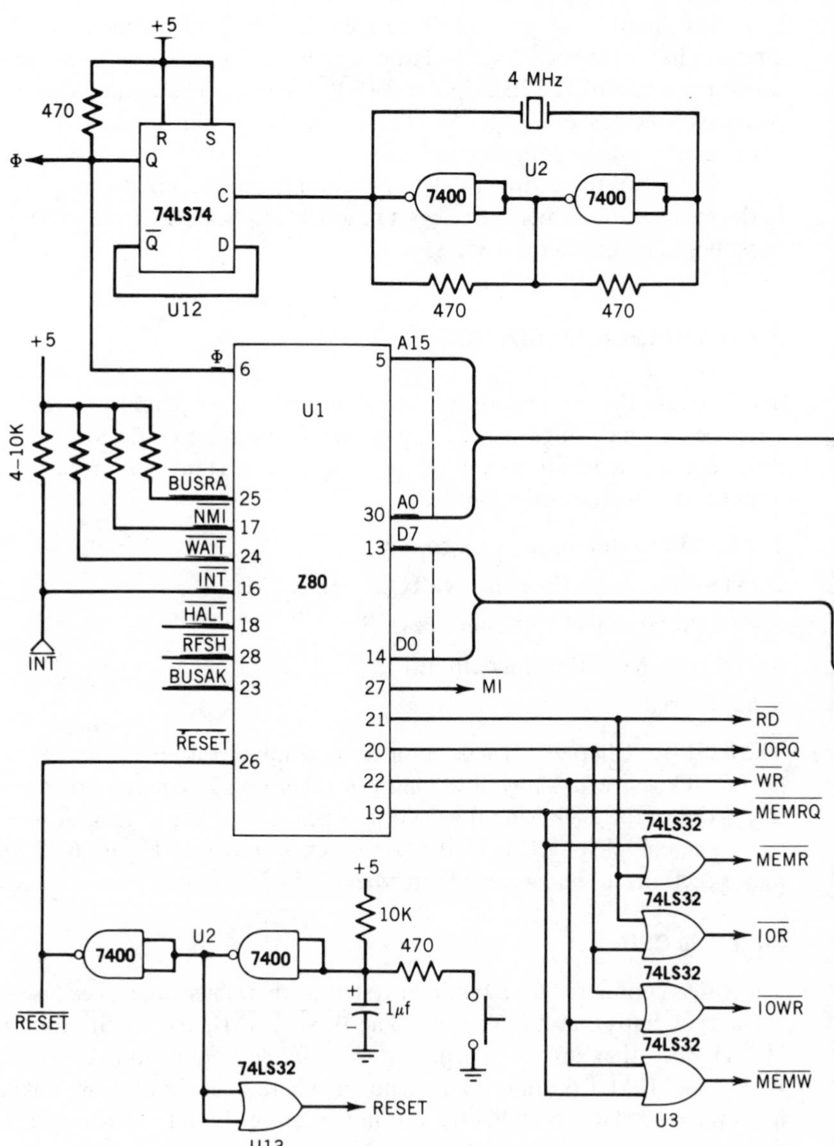

Figure 6-12 A **Z80** connected to several peripheral drivers.

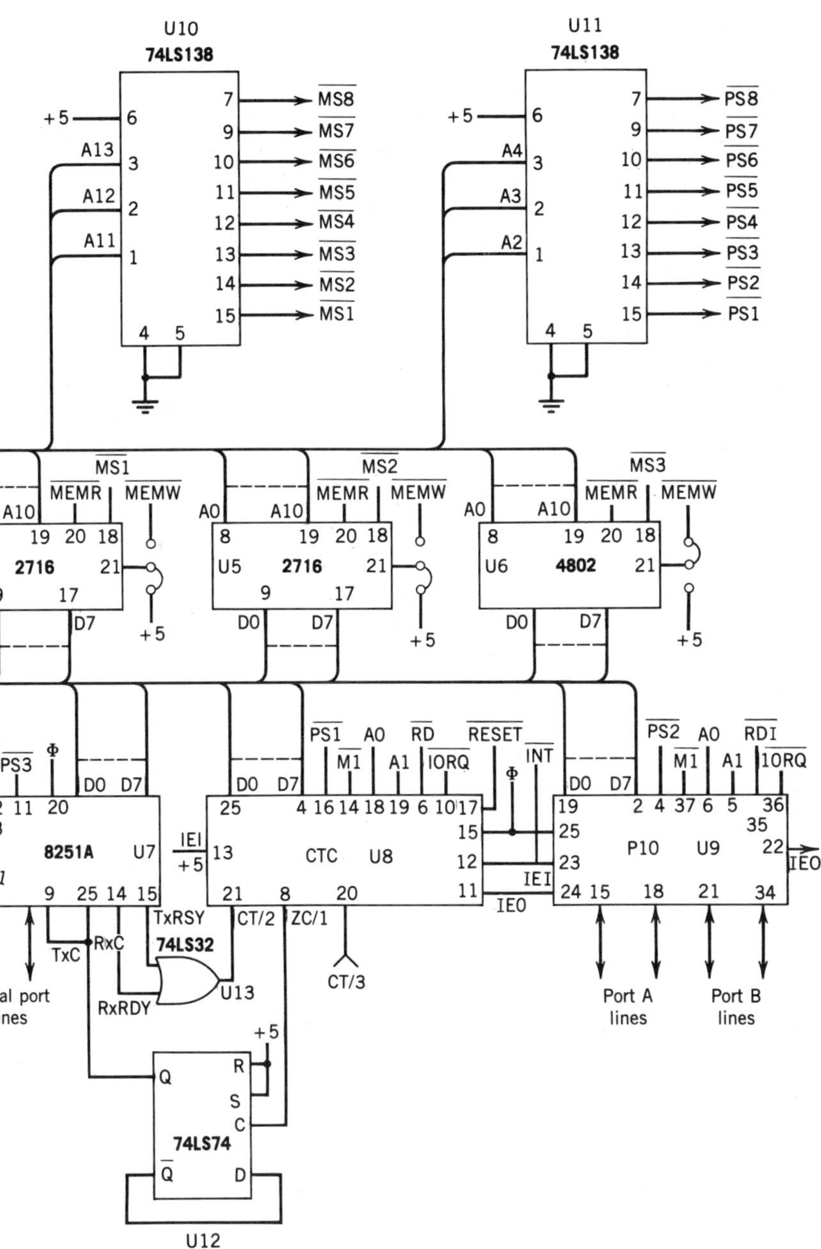
U10
74LS138
+5
A13
A12
A11
MS8
MS7
MS6
MS5
MS4
MS3
MS2
MS1
U11
74LS138
A4
A3
A2
PS8
PS7
PS6
PS5
PS4
PS3
PS2
PS1
MS1
MEMR
MEMW
A10
2716
D7
A0
MS2
U5
2716
D0
MS3
U6
4802
PS3
Φ
8251A
U7
D0 D7
IEI
PS1
A0
RD
RESET
INT
M1
A1
IORQ
CTC
U8
IEO
CT/2
ZC/1
CT/3
PS2
RDI
P10
U9
Port A lines
Port B lines
TxC
RxC
TxRSY
74LS32
U13
RxRDY
ial port lines
74LS74
U12

flip-flop to provide a symmetrical 2 MHz clock (Φ) to the **Z80**, CTC, and **8251** devices.

6-7.3 RESET Circuit

The other two gates of the **7400** are wired to provide a $\overline{\text{RESET}}$ signal for the **Z80** and peripheral devices. Whenever PB1 is pushed, C1 is discharged and the RESET line is pulled LOW. This line remains LOW until PB1 is released and C1 charges to a voltage that allows the gates to change state. The R-C network debounces the pushbutton and provides a RESET signal of adequate duration to all devices in the system. An OR gate supplies a noninverted RESET signal.

6-7.4 READ/WRITE Encoding

The **Z80** control lines must be encoded to produce standard memory and I/O READ/WRITE signals for the memory and **8251** chips. The **Z80** peripherals accept the CPU control signals directly. The encoding is done with a **74LS32** quad two-input OR gate to produce distinct memory READ ($\overline{\text{MEMR}}$), memory WRITE ($\overline{\text{MEMW}}$), I/O READ ($\overline{\text{I/OR}}$), and I/O WRITE ($\overline{\text{IOW}}$) signals.

6-7.5 Memory

Memory capability is supplied in the form of three sockets that can accept byte-wide RAM/ROM/EPROM. The address decoding shown is for 2K byte devices of the **4802** RAM/**2316** ROM/**2716** EPROM type. A total of 6K of memory is available. A jumper on pin 21 for each socket allows the user to select $\overline{\text{MEMW}}$ for the **4802** or +5 V for the **2316** and **2716** devices. The sockets are addressed as follows:

Device	**Address Range**
U4	0000H–07FFH
U5	0800H–0FFFH
U6	1000H–17FFH

6-7.6 Memory Address Selection

The 11 low address lines (A0–A11) drive the address inputs of the memory chips directly. Chip select decoding is done with a **74LS138** 1-of-8 decoder. Address lines A11–A13 are used as inputs to the decoder. The three address lines are decoded into eight memory chip select signals $\overline{\text{MS1}}$ through $\overline{\text{MS8}}$. Each signal can enable a distinct 2K-byte memory chip. Only $\overline{\text{MS1}}$–$\overline{\text{MS3}}$ are required for the sockets provided. The other signals are available for memory expansion.

6-7.7 I/O Port Address Decoding

A second **74LS138** is used to provide eight I/O port select lines PS1 through PS8. Each I/O device is allotted four port addresses, so address lines A2–A4 are used as inputs to the decoder. A1 and A2 are input directly to the peripheral device. The port address range for each line is as follows:

I/O Select Line	Port Address Range
PS1	00H–03H
PS2	04H–07H
PS3	08H–0BH
PS4	0CH–0FH
PS5	10H–13H
PS6	14H–17H
PS7	18H–1BH
PS8	1CH–1FH

6-7.8 Counter/Timer Circuit

The CTC device is addressed as four consecutive ports at 00H–03H by using PS1 as the chip enable line. The **Z80** $\overline{\text{RD}}$ and $\overline{\text{IORQ}}$ signals are used directly by the CTC instead of the $\overline{\text{IOR}}$ and $\overline{\text{IOW}}$ encoded signals. $\overline{\text{RESET}}$ and Φ are also used by the chip. $\overline{\text{M1}}$ is required for the interrupt cycle as detailed in section 6-5. The IEI line of the CTC is tied to +5 V making it the highest-priority device in the daisy chain. IEO from the CTC is tied to IEI of the PIO, making the PIO the next device in the chain.

The CTC contains four counter/timers. They can be allocated in the following way:

Counter/timer 0	System real-time clock
Counter/timer 1	**8251** Baud rate clock
Counter/timer 2	**8251** Interrupt detector
Counter/timer 3	User assigned

The port addresses for the CTC are

Port	Read	Write
00H	Ctr 0	Ctr 0/Control register 0
01H	Ctr 1	Ctr 1/Control register 1
02H	Ctr 2	Ctr 2/Control register 2
03H	Ctr 3	Ctr 3/Control register 3

Counter/timer 0 is programmed as a timer that interrupts the processor on a regular basis (e.g., every 20 ms). This interrupt provides a fixed sampling time for I/O devices such as an A/D converter, which might be accessed through the PIO. This timer is the highest-priority device in the interrupt chain.

Counter/timer 1 is programmed as a pulse generator running at twice the desired baud rate clock for the **8251**. The output pulse lasts for only one cycle of the system clock O. The output of the CTC is divided by the U 10 flip-flop to create a

50-percent duty cycle clock for the **8251** UART T × C and R × C imputs. C/T 1 is not programmed to provide an interrupt.

Counter/timer 2 is programmed as a counter with preset value of 1. The rising edge of the signal at its input will cause the counter to decrement to 0 and cause a system interrupt. The routine to which this interrupt vectors will be the UART handler since it is either a transmit ready (T × RDY) or receive ready (R × RDY) which provides the signal to the counter input.

6-7.9 Parallel Interface Controller

The PIO provides two programmable 8-bit ports with interrupt driven "handshake." The ports may be programmed in various configurations, depending on the user's needs. The PIO is addressed as ports 04H–07H with the following assignments:

Port	Read	Write
04H	Port A data	Port A data
05H	Port B data	Port B data
06H	—	Port A control buffer
07H	—	Port B control buffer

6-7.10 Serial I/O Circuit

The **8251** is a device from the **8080A** family of peripherals, which is used as an asynchronous UART in this application. The CTC provides the T × C and R × C clock signals which determine the operating baud rate. The CTC also acts as the priority interrupt generator for the **8251**, which does not have the daisy chain capability. The **8251** is addressed as four ports with the following assignments:

Port	Read	Write
08H	Receive data	Transmit data
09H	Status	Control
0AH	Receive data	Transmit data
0BH	Status	Control

The **8251** only requires two data ports but the decoding logic allocates four port addresses to it. This results in the UART ports being available at two addresses. In this application there is no reason to add the additional circuitry required to address the UART at only two ports. The OR gate is used to combine the T × RDY and R × RDY signals into a single interrupt line to the **Z80** through the CTC. The interrupt routine will read the UART status byte to determine if the interrupt was caused by a receive or transmit request (or both). The outputs of the **8251** are TTL compatible. Additional circuitry not shown would be required to connect this device to a standard serial line such as RS-232C or TTY current loop.

6.7-11 Program Listing

The program that follows shows typical initialization procedures and an interrupt vector table for the **Z80**. No application program is provided. The listings are well commented and should be self-explanatory. The reader should consult the appropriate device application manual to clarify any portions of the code that are not understood.

```
CROMEMCO Z80 Macro Assembler version 03.08
*** Z80SAMP! ***


                ;;;;;;;;;;;;;;;;;;;;;;;;;;;;;;;;;;;;;;;;;;
                ;
                ;
                ;       SAMPLE PROGRAM
                ;          by Glenn A. Barlis
                ;
                ;;;;;;;;;;;;;;;;;;;;;;;;;;;;;;;;;;;;;;;;;;
                ;
                ;
                ;       This program illustrates Z80
                ;       assembly code and the use of
                ;       the Z80 PIO and CTC chips.
                ;
                ;;;;;;;;;;;;;;;;;;;;;;;;;;;;;;;;;;;;;;;;;;
                ;
                ;
                ;
                ;
                ;       SYSTEM EQUATES
                ;
      (1000)    RAMBOT: EQU     1000H           ;BOTTOM OF RAM
      (17FF)    RAMTOP: EQU     17FFH           ;TOP OF RAM
      (0800)    RAMSIZE:EQU     RAMTOP-RAMBOT+1 ;NUMBER OF BYTES OF RAM
      (1800)    STACK:  EQU     RAMTOP+1        ;INITIAL SP VALUE
      (0000)    COLD:   EQU     0               ;COLD START LOCATION
                ;

                ;;;;;;;;;;;;;;;;;;;;;;;;;;;;;;;;;;;;;;;;;;;;;;;;;
                ;;
                ;       RAM DEFINITIONS
                ;
                ;       We will define some RAM memory locations needed
                ;       by the routines which follow.
                ;
                ;
      (1000)            ORG     RAMBOT          ;ORIGIN ASSEMBLER PROGRAM COUNTER
                                                ;TO RAM BOTTOM
                ;
                ;       6 BYTES ARE NEEDED FOR A CLOCK
                ;
1000  (0006)    CLKRAM: DS      6               ;THE DEFINE STORAGE (DS) PSEUDO OP
                                                ;RESERVES RAM SPACE
                ;
                ;       NEXT WE NEED A PRINTER BUFFER
```

```
CROMEMCO Z80 Macro Assembler version 03.08
*** Z80SAMPL ***

                ;
1006  (0001)    PBUFCNT:DS      1               ;HOLDS COUNT OF CHARACTERS IN PRINTER
                                                ;BUFFER
1007  (0001)    PBUFBOT:DS      1               ;HOLDS LOW BYTE OF CURRENT BUFFER
                                                ;BOTTOM ADDRESS
1008  (0001)    PBUFTOP:DS      1               ;HOLDS LOW BYTE OF CURRENT BUFFER
                                                ;TOP ADDRESS
1009  (0050)    PBUFF:  DS      80              ;RESERVE SPACE FOR BUFFER
      (1059)    PBTOP:  DL      $               ;TOP OF PRINT BUFFER
      (0009)    PBUFINIT:       EQU     LOW[ PBUFF ]
                                                ;INITIAL VALUE OF BUFFER
                                                ;NOTE BUFFER MUST BE ON ONE PAGE
                ;
                ;       DEFINE THE SERIAL I/O XMIT AND RECEIVE BUFFERS
                ;
1059  (0001)    CMDBYTE:DS      1               ;HOLDS CURRENT UART COMMAND BYTE
105A  (0001)    RBUFCNT:DS      1               ;HOLDS RECEIVE BUFFER CHAR COUNT
105B  (0001)    RBUFBOT:DS      1               ;LOW BYTE OF CURRENT BOTTOM OF
                                                ;RECEIVE BUFFER ADDRESS
105C  (0001)    RBUFTOP:DS      1               ;LOW BYTE OF CURRENT TOP OF
                                                ;RECEIVE BUFFER ADDRESS
105D  (0040)    RBUFF:  DS      64              ;RESERVE SPACE FOR RECEIVE BUFFER
      (109D)    RBTOP:  DL      $               ;TOP OF RECEIVE BUFFER
      (005D)    RBUFINIT:       EQU     LOW[ RBUFF ]
                                                ;INITIAL VALUE OF BUFFER ADDRESS
                                                ;BUFFER MUST BE ON ONE PAGE
                ;
109D  (0001)    XBUFCNT:DS      1               ;XMIT BUFFER CHAR COUNT
109E  (0001)    XBUFBOT:DS      1               ;LOW BYTE OF CURRENT BOTTOM
                                                ;OF XMIT BUFFER ADDRESS
109F  (0001)    XBUFTOP:DS      1               ;LOW BYTE OF CURRENT TOP OF
                                                ;XMIT BUFFER ADDRESS
10A0  (0040)    XBUFF:  DS      64              ;RESERVE SPACE FOR XMIT BUFFER
      (10E0)    XBTOP:  DL      $               ;TOP OF XMIT BUFFER
      (00A0)    XBUFINIT:       EQU     LOW[ XBUFF ]
                                                ;INITIAL VALUE OF RECEIVE BUFFER ADDRESS
                                                ;BUFFER MUST BE ON ONE PAGE
                ;

                ;;;;;;;;;;;;;;;;;;;;;;;;;;;;;;;;;;;;;;;;
                ;
                ;
                ;
                ;       COLD START
                ;
                ;       The Z80 will start at location 0000H on power
                ;       up or when the reset line is toggled. Interrupts
                ;       will be disabled at this time and the CTC and
                ;       PIO will also be initialized to their default
                ;       states.
                ;
      (0000)            ORG     COLD            ;ORIGIN TO COLD START LOCATION
                ;
                COLDSTRT:
```

```
0000 310018            LD      SP,STACK        ;INITIALIZE SP
0003 C38000    R       JP      INIT            ;GO DO THE INITIALIZATION
                 ;
                 ;
                 ;       Locations 0 thru 38H are reached by the RST commands.
                 ;       These will be left to the user for use as 1 byte
                 ;       calls for frequently used subroutines. Location 66H
                 ;       is the NMI vector location. 3 bytes will be left here
                 ;       for a jump to an NMI handler. The program will be re-
                 ;       origined at 69H to continue.
                 ;
     (0069)            ORG     69H
                 ;
                 ;       Mode 2 interrupts will be used so a vector table
                 ;       must be set up. We will also establish at this
                 ;       point a set of tables used to initialize the
                 ;       PIO and CTC.
                 ;

                 ;;;;;;;;;;;;;;;;;;;;;;;;;;;;;;;;;;;;;;;;;;;;;;;;;;;;
                 ;
                 ;       INTERRUPT VECTOR TABLE
                 ;
     (0069)      IVECTBL:DL      $               ;LABLE IS DEFINED AT THE
                                                 ;CURRENT PROGRAM LOCATION
0069 E100        RTCINT: DW      RTCHNDLR        ;ADDRESS OF REAL TIME CLOCK
                                                 ;HANDLER
006B 3B01        SIOINT: DW      SIOHNDLR        ;ADDRESS OF SERIAL I/O
                                                 ;HANDLER
006D EE00        APIOINT:DW      APHNDLR         ;ADDRESS OF PIO PORT A
                                                 ;HANDLER
006F 1801        BPIOINT:DW      BPHNDLR         ;ADDRESS OF PIO PORT B
                                                 ;HANDLER

                 ;;;;;;;;;;;;;;;;;;;;;;;;;;;;;;;;;;;;;;;;;;
                 ;
                 ;       PIO INITIALIZATION TABLE
                 ;
0071 6D          APCTBL: DB      LOW[ APIOINT ]  ;PIO GETS LOW BYTE OF TABLE
                                                 ;LOCATION WHICH HOLDS PORT A
                                                 ;HANDLER
0072 CF                  DB      11001111B       ;OPERATING MODE = 3 (CONTROL)
0073 F0                  DB      11110000B       ;HIGH 4 BITS INPUT, LOW 4 BITS
                                                 ;OUTPUT
0074 B7                  DB      10110111B       ;INTERRUPT ENABLED,INPUTS OR'ED,
                                                 ;HIGH LEVEL ACTIVE,MASK FOLLOWS
0075 C0                  DB      11000000B       ;ONLY TOP 2 BITS WILL CAUSE
                                                 ;INTERRUPT
                 ;
0076 6F          BPCTBL: DB      LOW[ BPIOINT ]  ;LOW BYTE OF TABLE LOCATION WHICH
                                                 ;HOLDS PORT B HANDLER
0077 0F                  DB      00001111B       ;OPERATING MODE = 1 (OUTPUT)
                 ;
                 ;
                 ;;;;;;;;;;;;;;;;;;;;;;;;;;;;;;;;;;;;;;;;;;;;;
                 ;
                 ;       CTC INITIALIZATION TABLE
```

```
CROMEMCO Z80 Macro Assembler version 03.08
*** Z80SAMPL ***

                    ;
0078  69            CTC0TBL:DB      LOW[ RTCINT ]   ;LOW BYTE OF TABLE LOCATION HOLDING
                                                    ;REAL TIME CLOCK HANDLER
0079  B7                    DB      10110111B       ;INTERRUPTS, TIMER MODE,
                                                    ;PRESCALER = 256
007A  7E                    DB      126             ;COUNT REQUIRED FOR 16 MSEC INTERRUPTS
                    ;
007B  17            CTC1TBL:DB      00010111B       ;NO INTERRUPTS, TIMER MODE,
                                                    ;PRESCALER = 16
007C  0D                    DB      13              ;PRESET FOR 9600 HZ OUTPUT
                    ;
007D  6B            CTC2TBL:DB      LOW[ SIOINT ]   ;LOW BYTE OF TABLE LOCATION HOLDING
                                                    ;SERIAL I/O HANDLER
007E  D7                    DB      11010111B       ;INTERRUPTS, COUNTER MODE,
                                                    ;COUNT ON RISING EDGE
007F  01                    DB      1               ;COUNT OF 1 READY FOR INTERRUPT
                                                    ;FROM 8251A
                    ;

                    ;;;;;;;;;;;;;;;;;;;;;;;;;;;;;;;;;;;;;;;;;;;;;;;;;;;
                    ;
                    ;       The first step in the initialization will be to clear
                    ;       RAM memory.
                    ;
0080  AF            INIT:   XOR     A,A             ;SET A REG TO 0
0081  210010                LD      HL,RAMBOT       ;POINT TO RAM BOTTOM
0084  010008                LD      BC,RAMSIZE      ;BC GETS COUNT
0087  110110                LD      DE,RAMBOT+1     ;DE GETS NEXT TO BOTTOM
008A  77                    LD      (HL),A          ;ZERO FIRST BYTE OF RAM
008B  EDB0                  LDIR                    ;ZERO THE REST

                    ;
                    ;
                    ;       The I register in the Z80 must be set with the
                    ;       high byte of the interrupt vector table
                    ;
008D  3E00                  LD      A,HIGH[ IVECTBL ]       ;PUT HIGH BYTE IN A
008F  ED47                  LD      I,A                     ;SO IT CAN BE TRANSFERRED TO I
                    ;
                    ;
                    ;       Initialize the PIO by using the OTIR command to move
                    ;       the values from the table to the PIO.
                    ;
      (0004)        ADATA:  EQU     04H             ;PORT A DATA I/O ADDRESS
      (0005)        BDATA:  EQU     ADATA+1         ;PORT B DATA I/O ADDRESS
      (0006)        ACONT:  EQU     ADATA+2         ;PORT A CONTROL ADDRESS
      (0007)        BCONT:  EQU     ADATA+3         ;PORT B CONTROL ADDRESS
                    ;
                    ;       SET UP PORT A
                    ;
0091  0E06                  LD      C,ACONT         ;USE REG INDIRECT PORT ADDRESSING
0093  217100                LD      HL,APCTBL       ;POINT TO TABLE OF PROGRAM BYTES
0096  0605                  LD      B,5             ;THERE ARE 5 BYTES FOR PORT A
0098  EDB3                  OTIR                    ;MOVE THEM
```

```
                ;
                ;       SET UP PORT B
                ;
009A  0C                INC     C               ;POINT TO BCONT
009B  0602              LD      B,2             ;2 BYTES TO MOVE. HL IS ALREADY
                                                ;POINTING TO START BECAUSE OF OTIR
                                                ;OPERATION
009D  EDB3              OTIR                    ;SO MOVE THEM
                ;
                ;       SET UP CTC CHANNELS 0,1,AND 2
                ;
      (0000)    CTR0:   EQU     0               ;COUNTER 0 PORT ADDRESS
      (0001)    CTR1:   EQU     CTR0+1          ;COUNTER 1 PORT ADDRESS
      (0002)    CTR2:   EQU     CTR0+2          ;COUNTER 2 PORT ADDRESS
      (0003)    CTR3:   EQU     CTR0+3          ;COUNTER 3 PORT ADDRESS
                ;
                ;
009F  0E00              LD      C,CTR0          ; POINT TO COUNTER 0
00A1  0603              LD      B,3             ;3 BYTES TO MOVE. HL ALREADY SET
                                                ;UP FROM ABOVE
00A3  EDB3              OTIR                    ;INIT CTR 0
                ;

00A5  0C                INC     C               ;COUNTER 1
00A6  0602              LD      B,2
00A8  EDB3              OTIR
                ;
00AA  0C                INC     C               ;COUNTER 2
00AB  0602              LD      B,2
00AD  EDB3              OTIR
                ;
                ;       INITIALIZE THE 8251A UART
                ;
      (004E)    UARTMODE:       EQU     01001110B
                                                ;16x BAUD RATE, ASYNCH, 8 BITS/CHAR
                                                ;ONE STOP BIT,PARITY DISABLED
      (0036)    UARTCMD:        EQU     00110110B
                                                ;ENABLE RxRDY, DISABLE XMIT,RESET ERROR
                                                ;FLAGS, RTS AND DTR LOW
      (0037)    XMITCMD:        EQU     00110111B
                                                ;SAME AS UARTCMD EXCEPT XMIT ENABLED
                                                ;
      (0009)    UARTDP: EQU     09H             ;UART DATA PORT ADDRESS
      (000A)    UARTCP: EQU     UARTDP+1        ;UART CONTROL/STATUS PORT ADDRESS
                ;
                ;
00AF  3E4E              LD      A,UARTMODE      ;SET 8251A MODE
00B1  D30A              OUT     (UARTCP),A
00B3  3E36              LD      A,UARTCMD       ;SET CONTROL COMMAND RECV ONLY
00B5  D30A              OUT     (UARTCP),A
00B7  DB09              IN      A,(UARTDP)      ;CLEAR OUT ANY GARBAGE IN THE
00B9  DB09              IN      A,(UARTDP)      ;INPUT BUFFER OF THE UART

                ;
                ;;;;;;;;;;;;;;;;;;;;;;;;;;;;;;;;;;;;;;;;;;;;;
                ;
                ;       That initializes the hardware of the computer
```

```
CROMEMCO Z80 Macro Assembler version 03.08
*** Z80SAMPL ***

                ;       The buffers used by the interrupt routines must
                ;       be initialized.
                ;
00BB  3E36              LD      A,UARTCMD       ;UART INITIAL COMMAND TO
00BD  325910            LD      (CMDBYTE),A     ;HOLDER
00C0  3E09              LD      A,PBUFINIT      ;START OF PRINT BUFFER
00C2  320710            LD      (PBUFBOT),A     ;INTO ADDRESS HOLDERS
00C5  320810            LD      (PBUFTOP),A
00C8  3E5D              LD      A,LOW[ RBUFF ]  ;START OF RCV BUFFER
00CA  325B10            LD      (RBUFBOT),A     ;INTO ADDRESS HOLDRES
00CD  325C10            LD      (RBUFTOP),A
00D0  3EA0              LD      A,LOW[ XBUFF ]  ;START OF XMIT BUFFER
00D2  329E10            LD      (XBUFBOT),A     ;INTO ADDRESS HOLDERS
00D5  329F10            LD      (XBUFTOP),A
                ;
                ;       At this time a call will be provided to a user
                ;       initialization routine. This can be used for
                ;       any application specific init operations.
                ;
00D8  CDFB01            CALL    USERINIT
                ;
                ;       With all of the initialization done, the interrupt mode
                ;       can be set, interrupts enabled, and we can proceed to the
                ;       application program.
                ;
00DB  ED5E              IM      2               ;INTERRUPT MODE 2
00DD  FB                EI                      ;ENABLE INTERRUPTS
00DE  C3FD01            JP      USRPROG         ;GOTO THE USER PROGRAM
                ;

                ;
                ;
                ;;;;;;;;;;;;;;;;;;;;;;;;;;;;;;;;;;;;;;;;;;;;;
                ;
                ;       SYSTEM SUBROUTINES
                ;
                ;       The following subroutines are the system
                ;       interrupt handlers.
                ;
                ;;;;;;;;;;;;;;;;;;;;;;;;;;;;;;;;;;;;;;;;;;;;;
                ;
                ;
                ;       REAL TIME CLOCK HANDLER
                ;
                ;       Note the use of the RETI instruction as required
                ;       to reset the PIO and CTC priority interrupt
                ;       structure for mode 2 interrupts
                ;
                RTCHNDLR:
00E1  08                EX      AF,AF'          ;SAVE ALL OF THE MAIN REGISTERS
00E2  D9                EXX
00E3  CD9B01            CALL    CLOCK           ;UPDATE THE CLOCK
00E6  CDFF01            CALL    USRSVC          ;PROVIDE FOR A USER REAL TIME
                                                ;INTERRUPT SERVICE ROUTINE
00E9  08                EX      AF,AF'          ;RESTORE THE MAIN REGISTERS
```

```
00EA  D9                     EXX
00EB  FB                     EI                      ;ENABLE INTERRUPTS
00EC  ED4D                   RETI                    ;AND RETURN FROM THE INTERRUPT
                   ;

                   ;
                   ;;;;;;;;;;;;;;;;;;;;;;;;;;;;;;;;;;;;;;;;
                   ;
                   ;         PIO PORT A HANDLER
                   ;
                   ;         Port A of the PIO is set up in MODE 3 which is
                   ;         the bit control mode. Because of the way the port
                   ;         was initialized, this routine is entered if either
                   ;         bit 6 or bit 7 on port A goes high.
                   ;         A somewhat trivial process control situation will
                   ;         be used as an example of this feature. Port A output
                   ;         bit 0 will be used to control an electric heater.
                   ;         The temperature must be maintained within 2 degrees
                   ;         of setpoint. A thermostat monitors the temperature and
                   ;         causes bit 6 to o high if the temperature drops 2 degrees
                   ;         below setpoint. The computer should turn on the heater if
                   ;         this happens. Bit 7 will go high if the temperature
                   ;         goes 2 degrees over the setpoint. The computer should
                   ;         then shut off the heater. If both bits are high, the
                   ;         thermostat is malfunctioning and the heat should be
                   ;         shut off and an alarm set on bit 1 of Port A.
                   ;         This example illustrates the use of the Z80 bit
                   ;         manipulation commands.
                   ;
                   ;
                   ;         EQUATES
      (00C0)       APMASK: EQU     11000000B       ;BIT MASK TO TEST FOR THERMOSTAT
      (0002)       TALARM: EQU     00000010B       ;ALARM OUTPUT BYTE
      (0001)       HEATON: EQU     00000001B       ;HEAT ON OUTPUT BYTE
      (0000)       HEATOFF:EQU     00000000B       ;HEAT OFF OUTPUT BYTE
                   ;

                   ;
                   APHNDLR:
00EE  CDE301               CALL    SAVAL           ;SAVE THE REGS (NOTE: EXCHANGE COMMANDS
                                                   ; COULD ALSO BE USED)
00F1  DB04                 IN      A,(ADATA)       ;GET PORT A DATA
00F3  47                   LD      B,A             ;SAVE FOR LATER
00F4  E6C0                 AND     A,APMASK        ;MASK OFF INPUT
00F6  FEC0                 CP      A,APMASK        ;BOTH BITS SET?
00F8  280A                 JR      Z,TBAD          ;GO HANDLE MALFUNCTION
                   ;
00FA  CB78                 BIT     7,B             ;SHUT OFF?
00FC  280C                 JR      Z,ONTEST        ;NO, SEE IF ON
                   ;
00FE  3E00                 LD      A,HEATOFF       ;SHUT IT OFF
0100  D304                 OUT     (ADATA),A
0102  180E                 JR      AEXIT           ;AND LEAVE
                   ;
                   ;
0104  3E02         TBAD:   LD      A,TALARM        ;BAD THERMOSTAT
0106  D304                 OUT     (ADATA),A       ;SHUT OFF AND ALARM
0108  1808                 JR      AEXIT
```

```
CROMEMCO Z80 Macro Assembler version 03.08
*** Z80SAMPL ***

                    ;
                    ;
                    ONTEST:
010A  CB70                  BIT     6,B             ;TURN IT ON?
010C  2804                  JR      Z,AEXIT         ;IF NOT JUST EXIT
010E  3E01                  LD      A,HEATON
0110  D304                  OUT     (ADATA),A       ;TURN ON HEATER
                    ;
0112  CDEE01        AEXIT:  CALL    RESAL           ;RESTORE THE REGS
0115  FB                    EI                      ;AND RETURN
0116  ED4D                  RETI                    ;FROM INTERRUPT
                    ;

                    ;
                    ;;;;;;;;;;;;;;;;;;;;;;;;;;;;;;;;;;;;;;;;;;;;;;;;;;;;;;
                    ;
                    ;       PIO PORT B HANDLER
                    ;
                    ;       Port B is set up in MODE 0, the output mode.
                    ;       Each time the Z80 writes to this port the
                    ;       B RDY line on the PIO goes high. This is used to
                    ;       inform an external device that data is available
                    ;       at the port. The external device then reads the
                    ;       data and acknowledges by pulsing the B STB line.
                    ;       The low going acknowledge strobe clears the B RDY
                    ;       line and causes an interrupt.
                    ;       The example which follows assumes that a printer
                    ;       working with the handshake protocol described above
                    ;       is connected to Port B. BPHNDLR sends characters from
                    ;       a print buffer PBUFF. The buffer is assumed to be filled
                    ;       by some user routine which also initiates the printer
                    ;       action. This simple routine assumes a buffer which does
                    ;       not cross a page address boundary. A more realistic design
                    ;       would utilize a circular queue which involves a more
                    ;       complex buffer arrangement than shown here.
                    ;
                    ;
                    BPHNDLR:
0118  CDE301                CALL    SAVAL           ;SAVE THE REGS
011B  210610                LD      HL,PBUFCNT      ;GET CHAR CNT
011E  AF                    XOR     A,A             ;SET A TO ZERO
011F  BE                    CP      A,(HL)          ;IS COUNT ZERO?
0120  200A                  JR      NZ,BOUT
                    ;
0122  3E09                  LD      A,PBUFINIT      ;QUIT IF EMPTY BY
0124  320710                LD      (PBUFBOT),A     ;INITIALIZING
0127  320810                LD      (PBUFTOP),A     ;THE BUFFER
012A  1809                  JR      BEXIT
                    ;
                    ;
012C  23            BOUT:   INC     HL              ;POINT TO BOTTOM ADDR HOLDER
012D  5E                    LD      E,(HL)          ;GET IT
012E  54                    LD      D,H             ;SAME PAGE,REMEMBER
012F  1A                    LD      A,(DE)          ;GET CHARACTER TO OUTPUT
```

```
0130  D305         OUT    (BDATA),A      ;DO IT
0132  34           INC    (HL)           ;UPDATE BUFFER POINTER
0133  2B           DEC    HL             ;POINT TO COUNT
0134  35           DEC    (HL)           ;AND DECREMENT IT
             ;
0135  CDEE01 BEXIT: CALL  RESAL          ;RESTORE REGS
0138  FB           EI                    ;AND RETURN
0139  ED4D         RETI                  ;FROM INTERRUPT
             ;

             ;
             ;
             ;;;;;;;;;;;;;;;;;;;;;;;;;;;;;;;;;;;;;
             ;
             ;
             ;      SERIAL I/O HANDLER
             ;
             ;      This routine is entered whenever Counter 2 of the
             ;      CTC counts out to zero. The counter input is received
             ;      from either RxRDY or TxRDY of the 8251A UART.
             ;      These signals are generated whenever the UART buffers
             ;      are needed to be serviced. TxRDY can be disabled by
             ;      setting bit 0 of the 8251A command byte to 0. Since the
             ;      CTC channel 2 is preset to 1, the first input
             ;      decrements the down counter register contents
             ;      from 1 to 0 and causes an interrupt. The counter
             ;      is automatically reloaded to a 1 for the next input.
             ;      This technique alows the CTC to be used as
             ;      a programmable priority vector interrupt generator.
             ;      The following code is for a simple serial interrupt
             ;      handler. Like the printer routine, it uses a buffer
             ;      scheme which would need refinement for  a really practical
             ;      system. How the transmit and receive buffers are handled
             ;      by the application program and how it and the interrupt
             ;      routine interact are ignored here even though they are
             ;      critical to a working system. The objective here
             ;      is to show the workings of the CTC and some more Z80
             ;      programming techniques.
             ;      The 8251A is initialized with a command byte (UARTCMD) which
             ;      disables the xmit mode. The user routine which fills the
             ;      xmit RAM buffer can start transmission by writing a new
             ;      control command (XMITCMD) to the 8251A to enable xmit.
             ;      When the interrupt handler empties the xmit RAM buffer it
             ;      disables the UART xmit. The receive function is always active.
             ;

             ;;;;;;;;;;;;;;;;;;;;;;;;;;;;;;;;;;;;;;;;;;
             ;
             SIOHNDLR:
013B  CDE301       CALL   SAVAL          ;SAVE THE REGS
             ;
013E  DB0A         IN     A,(UARTCP)     ;GET THE UART STAUS BYTE
0140  CB4F         BIT    1,A            ;CHARACTER RECEIVED?
0142  281A         JR     Z,TRANS        ;NO, GO CHECK XMIT
             ;
0144  0601         LD     B,1            ;USED FOR CHARACTER COUNT
0146  DB09         IN     A,(UARTDP)     ;GET THE CHARACTER
```

```
CROMEMCO Z80 Macro Assembler version 03.08
*** Z80SAMPL ***

0148  F5                     PUSH   AF               ;SAVE IT
0149  215C10                 LD     HL,RBUFTOP       ;GET TOP OF BUFFER ADDRESS
014C  5E                     LD     E,(HL)           ;INTO DE
014D  54                     LD     D,H
014E  7B                     LD     A,E              ;CHECK IF AT END OF BUFFER
014F  FE9D                   CP     A,LOW[ RBTOP ]
0151  3802                   JR     C,ADDCHAR        ;IF SO,
                    ;
0153  1D                     DEC    E                ;PUT CHARACTER IN LAST POSITION
0154  05                     DEC    B                ;OVERWRITING WHAT IS THERE
                                                     ;CHAR CNT WILL NOT CHANGE
                    ;
                    ADDCHAR:
0155  F1                     POP    AF               ;GET THE CHAR
0156  12                     LD     (DE),A           ;PUT IN BUFFER
0157  1C                     INC    E
0158  73                     LD     (HL),E           ;UPDATE BUFFER POINTER
0159  2B                     DEC    HL
015A  2B                     DEC    HL               ;POINT TO COUNT
015B  7E                     LD     A,(HL)
015C  80                     ADD    A,B              ;ADJUST IT
015D  77                     LD     (HL),A
                    ;
015E  3A5910        TRANS:   LD     A,(CMDBYTE)      ;SEE IF IN XMIT MODE
0161  CB47                   BIT    0,A
0163  2830                   JR     Z,SIOEXIT        ;QUIT IF NOT
                    ;
0165  DB0A          TRANS1:  IN     A,(UARTCP)       ;UART STATUS
0167  F5                     PUSH   AF               ;SAVE IT
0168  CB47                   BIT    0,A              ;READY FOR CHARACTER?
016A  2829                   JR     Z,SIOEXIT        ;QUIT IF NOT
016C  219D10                 LD     HL,XBUFCNT       ;POINT TO CHAR COUNT
016F  7E                     LD     A,(HL)
0170  B7                     OR     A,A              ;COUNT ZERO?
0171  2016                   JR     NZ,OUTCHAR       ;OUTPUT IF NOT
                    ;
0173  F1                     POP    AF               ;STATUS
0174  CB57                   BIT    2,A              ;TxE EMPTY?
0176  281D                   JR     Z,SIOEXIT        ;QUIT IF NOT
                    ;

                    ;
0178  3E36                   LD     A,UARTCMD        ;SHUT XMIT OFF
017A  D30A                   OUT    (UARTCP),A
017C  325910                 LD     (CMDBYTE),A      ;AND UPDATE COMMAND STATUS
017F  3EA0                   LD     A,LOW[ XBUFF ]   ;INITIALIZE THE BUFFER
0181  329E10                 LD     (XBUFBOT),A
0184  329F10                 LD     (XBUFTOP),A
0187  180C                   JR     SIOEXIT          ;AND QUIT
                    ;
                    ;
                    OUTCHAR:
0189  23                     INC    HL               ;BUFFER BOTTOM ADDRESS
018A  5E                     LD     E,(HL)
```

```
018B  54                LD      D,H             ;IN DE
018C  1A                LD      A,(DE)          ;GET CHARACTER
018D  D309              OUT     (UARTDP),A      ;SEND IT
018F  1C                INC     E               ;UPDATE BUFFER ADDRESS
0190  73                LD      (HL),E
0191  2B                DEC     HL              ;UPDATE COUNT
0192  35                DEC     (HL)
0193  18D0              JR      TRANS1          ;CHECK IF UART READY FOR DATA
                                                ;THIS IS NECASSARY FOR FIRST
                                                ;CHAR SENT WHEN UART FIRST ENABLED
                                                ;FOR XMIT SINCE IT IS DOUBLE BUFFERED.
                  ;
                  ;
                  SIOEXIT:
0195  CDEE01            CALL    RESAL           ;RESTORE REGS
0198  FB                EI                      ;AND RETURN
0199  ED4D              RETI                    ;FROM INTERRUPT
                  ;

                  ;
                  ;
                  ;;;;;;;;;;;;;;;;;;;;;;;;;;;;;;;;;;;;;;;;
                  ;
                  ;       CLOCK
                  ;
                  ;       This is a subroutine which maintains a time
                  ;       of day clock in the first 6 bytes of RAM.
                  ;       The memory locations are defined as:
                  ;
                  ;       RAMBOT: FRACTION OF SECONDS
                  ;          +1 : SECONDS
                  ;          +2 : MINUTES
                  ;          +3 : HOURS
                  ;          +4 : DAYS (1-99)
                  ;          +5 : DAYS (100-365)
                  ;
                  ;
                  ;       The clock is a 24 hour, 365 day clock with no provision
                  ;       for leap years. Because of the 4MHz crystal, this clock
                  ;       will run slightly fast. This can be corrected by trimming
                  ;       the crystal or incorporating a software correction factor
                  ;       if desired. The clock is kept in decimal instead of binary
                  ;       form for simple display conversion and to illustrate the
                  ;       DAA instruction.

                  ;
019B  F5          CLOCK: PUSH   AF
019C  E5                PUSH    HL              ;SAVE REGS
019D  210010            LD      HL,RAMBOT       ;POINT TO FRACTION OF SECONDS
01A0  7E                LD      A,(HL)          ;GET CONTENTS
01A1  3C                INC     A               ;INCREMENT IT
01A2  27                DAA                     ;DECIMAL ADJUST
01A3  FE62              CP      62H             ;62 CLOCK TICS/SEC (NOTE DECIMAL FORM
                                                ;REQUIRES REPRESENTATION BY A HEX
                                                ;NUMBER)
01A5  2031              JR      NZ,CLKEND       ;EXIT IF NOT AN EVEN SECOND
01A7  CDDC01            CALL    INCCLK          ;INCREMENT THE NEXT CLOCK LOCATION
```

```
CROMEMCO Z80 Macro Assembler version 03.08
*** Z80SAMPL ***

01AA  FE60              CP      60H             ;END OF MINUTE?
01AC  202A              JR      NZ,CLKEND       ;END IF NOT
01AE  CDDC01            CALL    INCCLK          ;INCREMENT MINUTES
01B1  FE60              CP      60H             ;END OF AN HOUR
01B3  2023              JR      NZ,CLKEND
01B5  CDDC01            CALL    INCCLK          ;INCREMENT HOURS
01B8  FE24              CP      24H             ;END OF A DAY?
01BA  201C              JR      NZ,CLKEND
01BC  CDDC01            CALL    INCCLK          ;INCREMENT DAYS
01BF  FE41              CP      65              ;CHECKING FOR END OF YEAR
01C1  200D              JR      NZ,NEXTD        ;NOT
01C3  77                LD      (HL),A          ;UPDATE DAYS
01C4  23                INC     HL
01C5  7E                LD      A,(HL)          ;MIGHT BE END OF YEAR
01C6  FE03              CP      03H             ;IS IT?
01C8  200E              JR      NZ,CLKEND       ;IF SO,
01CA  AF                XOR     A,A             ;RESET THE DAYS
01CB  77                LD      (HL),A
01CC  3C                INC     A               ;TO DAY 1
01CD  2B                DEC     HL
01CE  1808              JR      CLKEND
                  ;
01D0  FE00        NEXTD: CP     0               ;END OF A HUNDREDTH DAY?
01D2  2004              JR      NZ,CLKEND       ;IF SO,
01D4  77                LD      (HL),A          ;UPDATE BOTH DAYS
01D5  23                INC     HL              ;LOCATIONS
01D6  7E                LD      A,(HL)
01D7  3C                INC     A
                  ;
01D8  77          CLKEND: LD    (HL),A          ;UPDATE THE LOCATION
01D9  E1                POP     HL
01DA  F1                POP     AF              ;RESTORE THE REGS
01DB  C9                RET                     ;AND RETURN
                  ;
                  ;
01DC  3600        INCCLK: LD    (HL),0          ;ZERO CURRENT LOCATION
01DE  23                INC     HL              ;AND INCREMENT THE NEXT
01DF  7E                LD      A,(HL)
01E0  3C                INC     A
01E1  27                DAA                     ;AND DECIMAL ADJUST
01E2  C9                RET
                  ;

                  ;
                  ;     SAVAL
                  ;
                  ;     This is a subroutine to save the main registers on the
                  ;     stack. It is written as a subroutine so that it can
                  ;     also be used in application programs.
                  ;     Note the use of the EX (SP),IY instruction to get the
                  ;     calling address to the top of the stack for the
                  ;     return.
                  ;
                  ;
```

```
01E3  FDE3       SAVAL:  EX      (SP),IY         ;RETURN ADDRESS IN IY, IY CONTENTS
                                                 ;TO TOP OF STACK
01E5  DDE5               PUSH    IX
01E7  E5                 PUSH    HL              ;THEN REST OF REGS TO STACK
01E8  D5                 PUSH    DE
01E9  C5                 PUSH    BC
01EA  F5                 PUSH    AF
01EB  FDE5               PUSH    IY              ;NOW RETURN ADDRESS ON STACK
01ED  C9                 RET                     ;FOR THE RETURN
                 ;
                 ;
                 ;       RESAL
                 ;
                 ;       This subroutine is the complement of SAVAL used to
                 ;       restore the processor status at the end of a routine which
                 ;       uses SAVAL.
                 ;
                 ;
01EE  FDE3       RESAL:  EX      (SP),IY         ;RETURN ADDRESS TO IY
01F0  33                 INC     SP              ;STEP OVER THE IY CONTENTS
01F1  33                 INC     SP
01F2  F1                 POP     AF              ;AND RESTORE REGS
01F3  C1                 POP     BC
01F4  D1                 POP     DE
01F5  E1                 POP     HL
01F6  DDE1               POP     IX
01F8  FDE3               EX      (SP),IY         ;RESTORE IY AND PUT RETURN
                                                 ;ADDRESS BACK ON STACK
01FA  C9                 RET                     ;FOR RETURN
                 ;
                 ;
                 ;

                 ;
                 ;;;;;;;;;;;;;;;;;;;;;;;;;;;;;;;;;;;;;;;;;;
                 ;
                 ;
                 ;       THE USER APPLICATION PROGRAM
                 ;       CAN START HERE.
                 ;
                 ;       IT MUST INCLUDE THE 3 FOLLOWING
                 ;       ROUTINES SHOWN AS DUMMIES HERE.
                 ;
                 USERINIT:
01FB  00                 NOP             ;NULL INITIALIZATION ROUTINE
01FC  C9                 RET
                 ;
                 USRPROG:
01FD  00                 NOP             :NULL MAIN APPLICATION
01FE  C9                 RET
                 :
                 USRSVC:
01FF  00                 NOP             :NULL USER INTERRUPT SERVICE
0200  C9                 RET

Errors          0
Range Count     1
```

6-8 REFERENCES

Elizabeth A. Nichols, Joseph C. Nichols, and Peter R. Rony, *Z-80 Microprocessor Programming and Interfacing, Book 1*, Howard W. Sams, Indianapolis, Ind., 1979.

Joseph Carr, *Z-80 User's Manual*, Reston, Reston, Va., 1980.

A. J. Khambata, *Introduction to the Z80 Microcomputer*, Wiley, New York, 1980.

Lance Levanthal, *Assembly Language Programming: Z80*, Osborne–McGraw-Hill, New York, 1979.

Rodnay Zaks, *Programming the Z80*, 3rd Edition, Sybex, Berkeley, Calif., 1982.

Zilog, Inc., *Z80-CPU Z80A-CPU Technical Manual*, Cupertino, Calif.

Zilog, Inc., *Z80-PIO Technical Manual*, Cupertino, Calif.

Zilog, Inc., *Z80-CTC Z80A-CTC Technical Manual*, Cupertino, Calif.

Zilog, Inc., *The Z80 Family Program Interrupt Structure Application Note*, Cupertino, Calif.

CHAPTER 7

The Motorola 6800

Joseph D. Greenfield
Professor of Electrical Engineering
Rochester Institute of Technology
Rochester, New York

7-1 INTRODUCTION

The **6800** μP, Motorola's first, was introduced in 1974. It has been succeeded by more powerful 8-bit μPs such as the **6805** and **6809** (see Chapter 8), and the 16-bit **68000** (see Chapter 12). But millions of **6800**s are still being used in existing designs. The newer 8-bit μPs, and to some extent the **68000**, are extensions of the **6800** instruction set and architecture. A thorough understanding of the **6800** is therefore necessary before the reader can attempt to master the newer, more sophisticated μPs.

7-2 THE 6800 REGISTERS AND ACCUMULATORS

Internally the **6800** has three 8-bit registers and three 16-bit registers, as shown in Figure 7-1.

7-2.1 The 8-Bit Registers

There are two 8-bit accumulators in the **6800**, labeled A and B. These are almost identical in operation. Any arithmetic operation must involve one of them. The accumulator to be used is generally specified by the Op code. For example, an Op code of 8B specifies an ADD IMMEDIATE to the A accumulator, and an Op code of CB specifies an ADD IMMEDIATE to B.

The 8-bit condition code register contains the condition codes or flags. It is described in section 7-4.

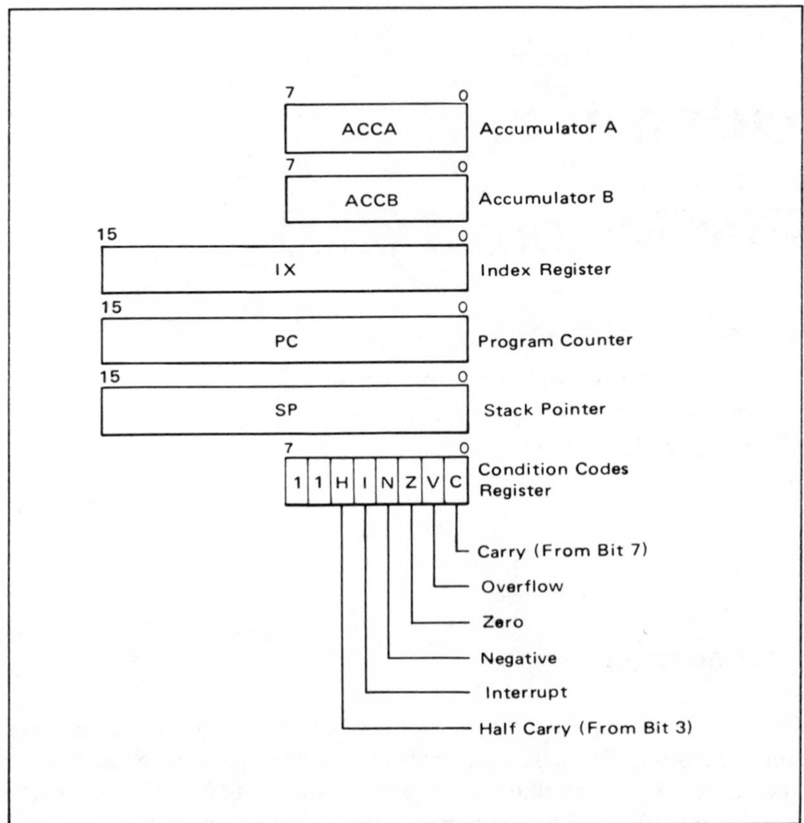

Figure 7-1 Programming model of the microprocessing unit. (From Greenfield and Wray, *Using Microprocessors and Microcomputers: The 6800 Family*, Wiley, 1981.)

7-2.2 The 16-Bit Registers

There are three 16-bit registers in the **6800**.

The program counter is the typical 16-bit PC found in 8-bit μPs. It contains the address of the next instruction to be executed.

The stack pointer and stack are used with PUSH and PULL instructions, JUMPs TO SUBROUTINES, and interrupts. They are discussed in section 7-9.

The index register is used when indexed instructions are executed (see section 7-3.4).

7-3 6800 ADDRESSING MODES

The complete **6800** instruction set is given in Tables 7-1 through 7-4. The instruction set is divided into four parts for clarity. The parts are:

Table 7-1	Accumulator and memory instructions
Table 7-2	Index register and stack manipulation instructions
Table 7-3	JUMP and BRANCH instructions
Table 7-4	Instructions for manipulating the condition code register and notes on the table.

Table 7-1 6800 accumulator and memory instructions

ADDRESSING MODES — BOOLEAN/ARITHMETIC OPERATION — COND. CODE REG.

		IMMED			DIRECT			INDEX			EXTND			IMPLIED			BOOLEAN/ARITHMETIC OPERATION (All register labels refer to contents)	5	4	3	2	1	0
OPERATIONS	MNEMONIC	OP	~	=	OP	~	=	OP	~	=	OP	~	=	OP	~	=		H	I	N	Z	V	C
Add	ADDA	8B	2	2	9B	3	2	AB	5	2	BB	4	3				A + M · A	↕	●	↕	↕	↕	↕
	ADDB	CB	2	2	DB	3	2	EB	5	2	FB	4	3				B + M · B	↕	●	↕	↕	↕	↕
Add Acmltrs	ABA													1B	2	1	A + B · A	↕	●	↕	↕	↕	↕
Add with Carry	ADCA	89	2	2	99	3	2	A9	5	2	B9	4	3				A + M + C · A	↕	●	↕	↕	↕	↕
	ADCB	C9	2	2	D9	3	2	E9	5	2	F9	4	3				B + M + C · B	↕	●	↕	↕	↕	↕
And	ANDA	84	2	2	94	3	2	A4	5	2	B4	4	3				A · M · A	●	●	↕	↕	R	●
	ANDB	C4	2	2	D4	3	2	E4	5	2	F4	4	3				B · M · B	●	●	↕	↕	R	●
Bit Test	BITA	85	2	2	95	3	2	A5	5	2	B5	4	3				A · M	●	●	↕	↕	R	●
	BITB	C5	2	2	D5	3	2	E5	5	2	F5	4	3				B · M	●	●	↕	↕	R	●
Clear	CLR							6F	7	2	7F	6	3				00 · M	●	●	R	S	R	R
	CLRA													4F	2	1	00 · A	●	●	R	S	R	R
	CLRB													5F	2	1	00 · B	●	●	R	S	R	R
Compare	CMPA	81	2	2	91	3	2	A1	5	2	B1	4	3				A M	●	●	↕	↕	↕	↕
	CMPB	C1	2	2	D1	3	2	E1	5	2	F1	4	3				B M	●	●	↕	↕	↕	↕
Compare Acmltrs	CBA													11	2	1	A B	●	●	↕	↕	↕	↕
Complement, 1's	COM							63	7	2	73	6	3				$\bar{M}$ · M	●	●	↕	↕	R	S
	COMA													43	2	1	$\bar{A}$ · A	●	●	↕	↕	R	S
	COMB													53	2	1	$\bar{B}$ · B	●	●	↕	↕	R	S
Complement, 2's	NEG							60	7	2	70	6	3				00 M · M	●	●	↕	↕	①	②
(Negate)	NEGA													40	2	1	00 – A · A	●	●	↕	↕	①	②
	NEGB													50	2	1	00 B · B	●	●	↕	↕	①	②
Decimal Adjust, A	DAA													19	2	1	Converts Binary Add. of BCD Characters into BCD Format	●	●	↕	↕	↕	③
Decrement	DEC							6A	7	2	7A	6	3				M – 1 · M	●	●	↕	↕	4	●
	DECA													4A	2	1	A 1 · A	●	●	↕	↕	4	●
	DECB													5A	2	1	B – 1 · B	●	●	↕	↕	4	●
Exclusive OR	EORA	88	2	2	98	3	2	A8	5	2	B8	4	3				A⊕M · A	●	●	↕	↕	R	●
	EORB	C8	2	2	D8	3	2	E8	5	2	F8	4	3				B⊕M · B	●	●	↕	↕	R	●
Increment	INC							6C	7	2	7C	6	3				M + 1 · M	●	●	↕	↕	⑤	●
	INCA													4C	2	1	A + 1 · A	●	●	↕	↕	⑤	●
	INCB													5C	2	1	B + 1 · B	●	●	↕	↕	⑤	●
Load Acmltr	LDAA	86	2	2	96	3	2	A6	5	2	B6	4	3				M · A	●	●	↕	↕	R	●
	LDAB	C6	2	2	D6	3	2	E6	5	2	F6	4	3				M · B	●	●	↕	↕	R	●
Or, Inclusive	ORAA	8A	2	2	9A	3	2	AA	5	2	BA	4	3				A + M · A	●	●	↕	↕	R	●
	ORAB	CA	2	2	DA	3	2	EA	5	2	FA	4	3				B + M · B	●	●	↕	↕	R	●
Push Data	PSHA													36	4	1	A · M_{SP}, SP 1 · SP	●	●	●	●	●	●
	PSHB													37	4	1	B · M_{SP}, SP 1 · SP	●	●	●	●	●	●
Pull Data	PULA													32	4	1	SP + 1 · SP, M_{SP} · A	●	●	●	●	●	●
	PULB													33	4	1	SP + 1 · SP, M_{SP} · B	●	●	●	●	●	●
Rotate Left	ROL							69	7	2	79	6	3				M	●	●	↕	↕	⑥	↕
	ROLA													49	2	1	A	●	●	↕	↕	⑥	↕
	ROLB													59	2	1	B C b7 ← b0	●	●	↕	↕	⑥	↕
Rotate Right	ROR							66	7	2	76	6	3				M	●	●	↕	↕	⑥	↕
	RORA													46	2	1	A	●	●	↕	↕	⑥	↕
	RORB													56	2	1	B C b7 → b0	●	●	↕	↕	⑥	↕
Shift Left, Arithmetic	ASL							68	7	2	78	6	3				M	●	●	↕	↕	⑥	↕
	ASLA													48	2	1	A ← 0	●	●	↕	↕	⑥	↕
	ASLB													58	2	1	B C b7 b0	●	●	↕	↕	⑥	↕
Shift Right, Arithmetic	ASR							67	7	2	77	6	3				M	●	●	↕	↕	⑥	↕
	ASRA													47	2	1	A	●	●	↕	↕	⑥	↕
	ASRB													57	2	1	B b7 b0 C	●	●	↕	↕	⑥	↕
Shift Right, Logic	LSR							64	7	2	74	6	3				M	●	●	R	↕	⑥	↕
	LSRA													44	2	1	A 0 →	●	●	R	↕	⑥	↕
	LSRB													54	2	1	B b7 b0 C	●	●	R	↕	⑥	↕
Store Acmltr	STAA				97	4	2	A7	6	2	B7	5	3				A · M	●	●	↕	↕	R	●
	STAB				D7	4	2	E7	6	2	F7	5	3				B · M	●	●	↕	↕	R	●
Subtract	SUBA	80	2	2	90	3	2	A0	5	2	B0	4	3				A M · A	●	●	↕	↕	↕	↕
	SUBB	C0	2	2	D0	3	2	E0	5	2	F0	4	3				B M · B	●	●	↕	↕	↕	↕
Subtract Acmltrs.	SBA													10	2	1	A B · A	●	●	↕	↕	↕	↕
Subtr. with Carry	SBCA	82	2	2	92	3	2	A2	5	2	B2	4	3				A M C · A	●	●	↕	↕	↕	↕
	SBCB	C2	2	2	D2	3	2	E2	5	2	F2	4	3				B M C · B	●	●	↕	↕	↕	↕
Transfer Acmltrs	TAB													16	2	1	A · B	●	●	↕	↕	R	●
	TBA													17	2	1	B · A	●	●	↕	↕	R	●
Test, Zero or Minus	TST							6D	7	2	7D	6	3				M 00	●	●	↕	↕	R	R
	TSTA													4D	2	1	A 00	●	●	↕	↕	R	R
	TSTB													5D	2	1	B 00	●	●	↕	↕	R	R
																		H	I	N	Z	V	C

LEGEND:

- OP Operation Code (Hexadecimal).
- ~ Number of MPU Cycles.
- = Number of Program Bytes.
- + Arithmetic Plus;
- Arithmetic Minus.
- · Boolean AND.
- M_{SP} Contents of memory location pointed to be Stack Pointer.
- + Boolean Inclusive OR.
- ⊙ Boolean Exclusive OR.
- $\bar{M}$ Complement of M.
- · Transfer Into.
- 0 Bit = Zero.
- 00 Byte = Zero.

Note: Accumulator addressing mode instructions are included in the column for IMPLIED addressing

CONDITION CODE SYMBOLS:

- H Half carry from bit 3.
- I Interrupt mask
- N Negative (sign bit)
- Z Zero (byte)
- V Overflow, 2's complement
- C Carry from bit 7
- R Reset Always
- S Set Always
- ↕ Test and set if true, cleared otherwise
- ● Not Affected

Table 7-2 **6800 index register and stack manipulation instructions**

Index Register and Stack Manipulation

		IMMED			DIRECT			INDEX			EXTND			IMPLIED				COND. CODE REG 5	4	3	2	1	0
POINTER OPERATIONS	MNEMONIC	OP	~	#	OP	~	#	OP	~	#	OP	~	#	OP	~	#	BOOLEAN/ARITHMETIC OPERATION	H	I	N	Z	V	C
Compare Index Reg	CPX	8C	3	3	9C	4	2	AC	6	2	BC	5	3				$X_H - M, X_L - (M + 1)$	•	•	(7)	↕	(8)	•
Decrement Index Reg	DEX													09	4	1	$X - 1 \to X$	•	•	•	↕	•	•
Decrement Stack Pntr	DES													34	4	1	$SP - 1 \to SP$	•	•	•	•	•	•
Increment Index Reg	INX													08	4	1	$X + 1 \to X$	•	•	•	↕	•	•
Increment Stack Pntr	INS													31	4	1	$SP + 1 \to SP$	•	•	•	•	•	•
Load Index Reg	LDX	CE	3	3	DE	4	2	EE	6	2	FE	5	3				$M \to X_H, (M + 1) \to X_L$	•	•	(9)	↕	R	•
Load Stack Pntr	LDS	8E	3	3	9E	4	2	AE	6	2	BE	5	3				$M \to SP_H, (M + 1) \to SP_L$	•	•	(9)	↕	R	•
Store Index Reg	STX				DF	5	2	EF	7	2	FF	6	3				$X_H \to M, X_L \to (M + 1)$	•	•	(9)	↕	R	•
Store Stack Pntr	STS				9F	5	2	AF	7	2	BF	6	3				$SP_H \to M, SP_L \to (M + 1)$	•	•	(9)	↕	R	•
Indx Reg → Stack Pntr	TXS													35	4	1	$X - 1 \to SP$	•	•	•	•	•	•
Stack Pntr → Indx Reg	TSX													30	4	1	$SP + 1 \to X$	•	•	•	•	•	•

Table 7-3 **6800 JUMP and BRANCH instructions**

		RELATIVE			INDEX			EXTND			IMPLIED				COND. CODE REG. 5	4	3	2	1	0
OPERATIONS	MNEMONIC	OP	~	#	OP	~	#	OP	~	#	OP	~	#	BRANCH TEST	H	I	N	Z	V	C
Branch Always	BRA	20	4	2										None	•	•	•	•	•	•
Branch If Carry Clear	BCC	24	4	2										C = 0	•	•	•	•	•	•
Branch If Carry Set	BCS	25	4	2										C = 1	•	•	•	•	•	•
Branch If = Zero	BEQ	27	4	2										Z = 1	•	•	•	•	•	•
Branch If ≥ Zero	BGE	2C	4	2										N ⊕ V = 0	•	•	•	•	•	•
Branch If > Zero	BGT	2E	4	2										Z + (N ⊕ V) = 0	•	•	•	•	•	•
Branch If Higher	BHI	22	4	2										C + Z = 0	•	•	•	•	•	•
Branch If ≤ Zero	BLE	2F	4	2										Z + (N ⊕ V) = 1	•	•	•	•	•	•
Branch If Lower Or Same	BLS	23	4	2										C + Z = 1	•	•	•	•	•	•
Branch If < Zero	BLT	2D	4	2										N ⊕ V = 1	•	•	•	•	•	•
Branch If Minus	BMI	2B	4	2										N = 1	•	•	•	•	•	•
Branch If Not Equal Zero	BNE	26	4	2										Z = 0	•	•	•	•	•	•
Branch If Overflow Clear	BVC	28	4	2										V = 0	•	•	•	•	•	•
Branch If Overflow Set	BVS	29	4	2										V = 1	•	•	•	•	•	•
Branch If Plus	BPL	2A	4	2										N = 0	•	•	•	•	•	•
Branch To Subroutine	BSR	8D	8	2										See Special Operations	•	•	•	•	•	•
Jump	JMP				6E	4	2	7E	3	3				See Special Operations	•	•	•	•	•	•
Jump To Subroutine	JSR				AD	8	2	BD	9	3				See Special Operations	•	•	•	•	•	•
No Operation	NOP										01	2	1	Advances Prog. Cntr. Only	•	•	•	•	•	•
Return From Interrupt	RTI										3B	10	1		(10)					
Return From Subroutine	RTS										39	5	1	See Special Operations	•	•	•	•	•	•
Software Interrupt	SWI										3F	12	1	See Special Operations	•	•	•	•	•	•
Wait for Interrupt*	WAI										3E	9	1	See Special Operations	•	(11)	•	•	•	•

*WAI puts Address Bus, R/W, and Data Bus in the three state mode while VMA is held low.

Table 7-4 **Instructions for manipulating the 6800 condition code register and notes on the table**

		IMPLIED				COND. CODE REG. 5	4	3	2	1	0
OPERATIONS	MNEMONIC	OP	~	#	BOOLEAN OPERATION	H	I	N	Z	V	C
Clear Carry	CLC	0C	2	1	0 → C	•	•	•	•	•	R
Clear Interrupt Mask	CLI	0E	2	1	0 → I	•	R	•	•	•	•
Clear Overflow	CLV	0A	2	1	0 → V	•	•	•	•	R	•
Set Carry	SEC	0D	2	1	1 → C	•	•	•	•	•	S
Set Interrupt Mask	SEI	0F	2	1	1 → I	•	S	•	•	•	•
Set Overflow	SEV	0B	2	1	1 → V	•	•	•	•	S	•
Acmltr A → CCR	TAP	06	2	1	A → CCR	(12)					
CCR → Acmltr A	TPA	07	2	1	CCR → A	•	•	•	•	•	•

CONDITION CODE REGISTER NOTES: (Bit set if test is true and cleared otherwise)

1	(Bit V)	Test: Result = 10000000?
2	(Bit C)	Test: Result = 00000000?
3	(Bit C)	Test: Decimal value of most significant BCD Character greater than nine? (Not cleared if previously set.)
4	(Bit V)	Test: Operand = 10000000 prior to execution?
5	(Bit V)	Test: Operand = 01111111 prior to execution?
6	(Bit V)	Test: Set equal to result of N⊕C after shift has occurred.
7	(Bit N)	Test: Sign bit of most significant (MS) byte = 1?
8	(Bit V)	Test: 2's complement overflow from subtraction of MS bytes?
9	(Bit N)	Test: Result less than zero? (Bit 15 = 1)
10	(All)	Load Condition Code Register from Stack. (See Special Operations)
11	(Bit I)	Set when interrupt occurs. If previously set, a Non-Maskable Interrupt is required to exit the wait state.
12	(All)	Set according to the contents of Accumulator A.

The instructions in each of the tables are discussed in section 7-4.

Tables 7-1 through 7-4 show that each instruction can be executed in one of several addressing *modes*. The modes are immediate, direct, indexed, extended, implied, and relative. Of course, not all instructions can be executed in all modes. The relative mode, for example, applies only to the BRANCH and JUMP instructions of Table 7-3 and is not included in the other tables.

7-3.1 Immediate Addressing Instructions

Those immediate instructions that affect an 8-bit register (an accumulator or the CCR) require 2 bytes. Immediate instructions that affect 16-bit registers such as the index register or stack pointer require 3 bytes. The first byte is the Op code and the second byte (or second and third byte) contains the operand (the information to be used). If, for example, the accumulator contains the number 2C and the following instruction occurs in a program,

```
ADD A #$23
```

the # indicates that the hex value, $23, is to be added to the A accumulator. The immediate mode of the instruction is indicated by the # sign. After the instruction is executed, A contains 4F (23 + 2C).

7-3.2 Direct Instructions

Immediate instructions are used if the variable or operand is known to the programmer when the program is being written. For example, if the programmer knows the program must add 5 to the accumulator, it is more efficient to add it immediately than to store 5 in memory and do a direct or extended ADD. Often the value to be added may change during program execution. In this case the value is stored in memory, and direct or extended instructions are required.

Like immediate instructions, direct instructions require 2 bytes. The second byte contains the address of the operand used in the instruction. Since the direct instruction is a two-byte instruction, only 8 address bits are available. The μP must provide a 16-bit address, so for this instruction, the 8 MSBs of the address are effectively set to 0. The memory locations that can be addressed by a direct instruction are therefore restricted to 0000 to 00FF. It is often wise to place variable data in these memory locations because this data is usually referenced frequently throughout the program. The programmer can then make maximum use of direct instructions and reduce memory requirements by up to 25%.

EXAMPLE 7-1 What happens when the instruction

```
LDA A $55
```

is encountered in a program? Assume that location 55 contains CA.

Solution This is a direct instruction. The second byte of this 2-byte instruction specifies the address (0055). The LDA A $55 instruction causes the μP to read location 0055 and load its contents into A. At the end of the instruction, the A accumulator contains CA.

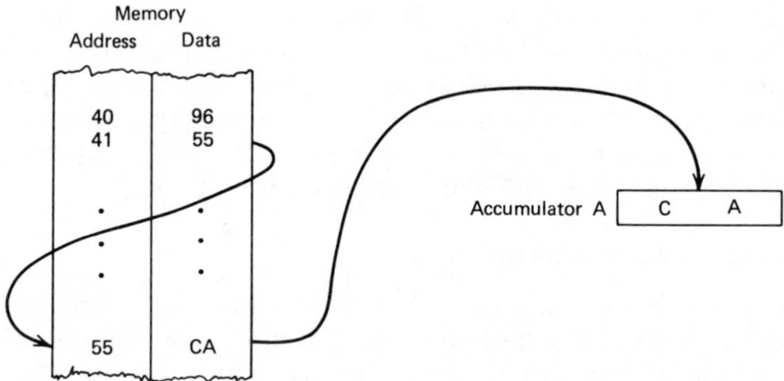

Figure 7-2 Action of a LOAD DIRECT instruction. (From Greenfield and Wray, *Using Microprocessors and Microcomputers: The 6800 Family*, Wiley, 1981.)

The action of this instruction is shown in Figure 7-2. The Op code for the LOAD A DIRECT (96) is in memory location 40 and the operand (55) is in 41. Because this is a direct instruction, the operand is an address (0055) and the contents of that address (CA) are loaded into accumulator A.

EXAMPLE 7-2 If location 55 contains CA and the B accumulator contains 13, what does B contain after execution of the following instructions?

a `ADD B #$55`

b `ADD B $55`

Solution

a The # indicates the immediate mode. This, ADD B #$55 causes 55 to be added to 13 and the result is 55 + 13 = **68**.

b Since the address of $55 is less than $100, this a direct mode instruction. It causes the contents of 55 to be added to B and the result stored in the B register. Since location 55 contains CA, the result stored is CA + 13 = **DD**.

7-3.3 Extended Instructions

Extended instructions are 3-byte instructions. The Op code is followed by 2 bytes that specify the address of the operand used by the instruction. The second byte contains the 8 high-order bits of the address. Because 16 address bits are available, any one of the 65,536 memory locations in the **6800** μC can be selected. Thus, extended instructions have the advantage of being able to select *any* memory locations, but direct instructions only require 2 bytes in the program instead of 3. Direct instructions also require one less cycle for execution so they are somewhat faster than the corresponding extended instructions.

EXAMPLE 7-3 What occurs when the instruction

```
STA A $13C
```

appears in a program?

Solution Since this operand is a hex address greater than $FF, this is an extended mode instruction. The instruction causes the contents of the A accumulator to be stored or written into location 013C.

7-3.4 Indexed Instructions

As its name implies, an indexed instruction makes use of the index register (X)[1] in the **6800** μP. For any indexed instruction, the address referred to is the sum of the number (called the OFFSET) in the second byte of the instruction, plus the contents of X. At this point a distinction should be made. There are *indexed instructions* and there are instructions that *affect* or *change* the index register. Indexed instructions typically do *not* change the index register, but use it to calculate the effective address.

Table 7-2 is a list of instructions that affect the index register and stack pointer. Notice the **6800** provides instructions to LOAD, STORE, INCREMENT, and DECREMENT X, as well as the stack pointer (SP).

EXAMPLE 7-4 What does the following program accomplish?

```
LDX #$0123
ADD A $A0,X
```

Solution The first instruction is an immediate LOAD of the index register. It causes the number 0123 to be loaded into X. The second instruction is an INDEXED ADD. In executing this instruction, the μP adds the second byte (A0) to the contents of X (0123) to get the data address. Thus, the contents of memory location 01C3 are added to the A accumulator.

Index registers are useful when it is necessary to *relocate* a program. For example, if a program that originally occupied locations 0000 to 00CF must be moved or relocated to locations 0400 to 04CF, all addresses used in the original program must be changed. In particular, direct instructions cannot be used because the program no longer occupies lower memory. If X is loaded with the base address of the program (400 in this example), then all direct instructions can be changed to indexed instructions and the program will function as before.

7-3.5 Implied Addressing

Implied instructions are used when *all* the information required for the instruction is already within the CPU and *no external operands* from memory or from the program (in the case of immediate instructions) are needed. Since no memory

[1] Most manufacturers refer to the index register as the X register or simply X.

references are needed, implied instructions only require one byte for their Op code. Examples of implied instructions are CLEAR, INCREMENT, and DECREMENT the accumulators, and SHIFT, ROTATE, ADD, or SUBTRACT accumulators.

EXAMPLE 7-5 What does the following instruction do?

SBA

Solution This is a 1-byte instruction. SBA is the mnemonic for SUBTRACT ACCUMULATORS. Table 7-1 shows that the operation is (A) − (B) → (A). Thus the number in the B accumulator is subtracted from the A accumulator and the results are stored in A. At the end of the instruction, A contains the result (difference), while B contains the original subtrahend and its value is unchanged.

7-3.6 Relative Instructions

BRANCH instructions are relative instructions. They depend on the condition codes described in section 7-4. Relative instructions are described in section 7-8.

7-4 CONDITION CODES

The condition code register is shown at the bottom of Figure 7-1. The **6800** uses six condition codes (sometimes called flags), labeled H, I, N, Z, V, and C. As shown in Figure 7-1, the 1s in the two MSBs of the CCR are merely to fill it out to 8 bits.

The function of most of the condition codes is to *retain information* about the *results of the last arithmetic or memory operation.* The effect of an instruction on each condition code is shown in the six rightmost columns of Tables 7-1 through 7-4. Two symbols dominate this part of the table; the dot (·) means that the instruction does not affect the condition codes, and the ↕ symbol indicates that the condition code is SET or CLEARED as a result of the instruction execution.

The I condition code is set or cleared to enable the μP to be interrupted. Its action is discussed in section 7-13.3. None of the accumulator and memory instructions affects the I bit, but CLI and SEI will clear or set it.

7-4.1 The Z Bit

The Z (for zero) bit in the condition code register is set whenever an instruction results in a 0 being entered into the destination register or memory location.

One function of the COMPARE instruction is simply to set the Z bit. COMPARE instructions internally subtract an operand from an accumulator, but do not change the contents of either. They simply change the bits of the CCR. A μP can determine if two operands are equal by comparing them. If the Z bit is SET after execution of the COMPARE instruction, it indicates the two operands are indeed equal. This information is often used by BRANCH instructions (see section 7-8).

7-4.2 The C Bit

The C or carry bit in the condition code register is mainly set in one of four ways:

1 It is set during ADD instructions when the result of the addition produces a carry output.

2 For subtraction and comparison instructions, it is set when the *absolute value* of the subtrahend is larger than the absolute value of the minuend. Generally this implies a *borrow*.

3 It is changed when executing SHIFT and ROTATE instructions. For these instructions the bit shifted out of the accumulator becomes the carry bit and is not lost.

4 It is SET when an SEC (set carry) instruction is executed.

Some other instructions, such as CLEAR and TEST, affect the carry bit. The careful programmer should consult the notes attached to Table 7-4 when there is any doubt about how an instruction affects the carry bit.

Two instructions, ADD WITH CARRY and SUBTRACT WITH CARRY, use the carry bit as part of the instruction. This simplifies the addition or subtraction of numbers that are longer than 8 bits. If, for example, the least significant bytes are added and produce a carry output, an ADC (add with carry) instruction is used to add the more significant bytes and also adds 1 if the sum of the least significant bytes produced a carry output.

7-4.3 The N Bit

The N (negative) bit, sometimes called the sign bit, of the CCR is set whenever the results of an operation are negative. The N bit is set whenever the MSB of the result is a 1 (an MSB of 1 indicates a negative number in 2s complement arithmetic). The Boolean equation for the N bit is $N = R_7$. Note that all accumulator and memory instructions, except PSH and PUL, affect the N bit.

7-4.4 The V Bit

The *V* or *overflow* bit is set when an arithmetic operation results in a 2s complement overflow or underflow. *Overflow* occurs when the result of an arithmetic operation produces a number larger than the register can accommodate (i.e., the sign bit is affected). *Underflow* occurs when the result produces a number more negative than the register can accommodate (less than 128). This also affects the *sign* bit.

The limitations on the numbers that can be handled by an *n*-bit register are $2^{n-1} - 1$ positive numbers, and 2^{n-1} negative numbers. A single 8-bit byte is thus restricted to numbers between $+127$ and -128.

There are two criteria for overflow and underflow in the **6800**.

1 For *addition* instructions the basic Boolean equation for overflow is

$$V = \bar{A}_7 \bar{B}_7 R_7 + A_7 B_7 \bar{R}_7 \tag{7-1}$$

where it is assumed that the operation is A plus $B \rightarrow R$ and A_7 is the MSB of A (the augend), B_7 is the MSB of B (the addend), and R_7 is the MSB of the result. The plus sign in the equation indicates the logical OR.

If the first term of the equation is 1, it indicates that two positive numbers have been added (because A_7 and B_7 are both 0) and the result is negative (because $R_7 = 1$). This possibility has been illustrated in the preceding paragraph.

The second term indicates that two negative numbers have been added and have produced a positive result.

EXAMPLE 7-6 Show how the hex numbers 80 and CO are added.

Solution 80 + CO = 40 plus a carry. Note that 80 and CO are both negative numbers, but their sum (as contained in a single byte) is positive. This corresponds to the second term of equation (7-1). Fortunately, this addition sets the V bit to warn the user that overflow (in this case underflow) has occurred.

---

2 For subtraction operations, the Boolean equation is

$$V = A_7\bar{B}_7\bar{R}_7 + \bar{A}_7B_7R_7 \tag{7-2}$$

The assumption here is that $A - B = R$. The first term indicates that a positive number has been subtracted from a negative number and has produced a positive result. The second term indicates that a negative number has been subtracted from a positive number and has produced a negative result. In either case, the overflow bit is set to positive to warn the user.

EXAMPLE 7-7 If the numbers 23C4 and FDAB are added, what flags are set after the:

a LS bytes are added?

b MS bytes are added?

Solution

a First the μP adds the LS bytes, C4 and AB, to obtain 6F. This addition sets the C and V bits. The V bit is set because two negative numbers were added and the result, 6F, is positive. This positive result also clears the N bit.

b The next part of the program adds the MS bytes, 23 and FD, and the 1 in the C bit. The result is 21. The C bit is SET, but both N and V are CLEAR. Because numbers of unlike sign were added, overflow is impossible and V is CLEAR.

The significance of the overflow bit depends on the program. In Example 7-7, the V bit was set after the first addition but, because this was an intermediate step, the V bit could be ignored. After the final addition the V bit was CLEAR, indicating that the result was correct.

7-4.5 Manipulations of the Condition Code Register

Table 7-4 shows those instructions that affect the CCR.

1 Specific instructions exist to SET or CLEAR the C, V, and I bits.

2 The CCR can be transferred to the A accumulator by a TPA instruction. This would be done if the program had to preserve the present contents of the CCR for future use. The CCR could be transferred to A and then saved in RAM by a STORE A or PUSH A instruction.

3 The contents of accumulator A can be transferred to the CCR by a TAP instruction. This would be done when the contents of the CCR are being restored from memory.

EXAMPLE 7-8 At a point in a program the H, I, and C bit of the CCR should be SET and the N, V, and Z bits should be CLEAR. Write a sequence of instructions to set the bits accordingly.

Solution According to Figure 7-1, the CCR should look like this:

11110001

It can be forced into this configuration by the following instructions.

Op code	*Mnemonic*	*Comment*
86 F1	LDA A #$F1	Load desired contents of CCR into A
06	TAP	Transfer A to CCR

7-5 BCD ADDITION AND THE H BIT

Although programmers and readers of this book can use hex fluently, most people prefer to communicate with their computers using ordinary *decimal numbers*. Normal input devices, such as teletypes or hand calculator keyboards, have only keys for the numbers 0 through 9, and their outputs, whether presented as a type-out by a teletype or on a seven-segment display by a hand calculator, must be in decimal form.

In applications that deal with money, such as cash registers, it is preferable to keep the numbers in decimal form, rather than converting them to binary or hex. The use of the H bit of the CCR and the DAA (decimal adjust accumulator) instruction makes decimal arithmetic possible.

7-5.1 Adding BCD Numbers

Since each **6800** memory location contains 8 bits and each BCD decade requires 4 bits, it is natural to store two BCD digits in a single memory location. This is sometimes called *packing*, or *packed BCD*, and is a function of the input/output routine.

Addition and subtraction of BCD numbers is possible, but since all addition and subtraction instructions in the **6800** assume *binary* numbers, the *binary results must be manipulated to convert them to BCD*. This is done by using the H bit and the DAA instruction.

Table 7-1 shows that the H bit is changed only by addition instructions. *It is SET when the addition produces a carry out of bit position 3 and into bit position 4.* For BCD numbers the *H* bit is SET whenever the sum of the two digits, plus carry, is equal to or greater than $(16)_{10}$. Because this carry occurs midway through the byte, the *H* bit is sometimes called the *half-carry* bit.

EXAMPLE 7-9 The A and B accumulators contain the decimal numbers 48 and 79, respectively. They are added by an ADD accumulator (ABA) instruction. What is the result and what are the conditions of the C and H bits after the addition?

Solution The **6800** adds 48 and 79 as though they were hex digits, placing the sum, C1, in the A accumulator. At the end of the addition the H bit is SET (because the sum of 8 and 9 produces a carry), but the carry bit is CLEAR because the sum of the two most significant digits is less than 16.

7-5.2 The DAA Instruction

The result of Example 7-9 (48 + 79 = C1) is unsatisfactory if decimal arithmetic is being used. Addition instructions must be followed by a *decimal adjust accumulator* (DAA) instruction to convert the hex result to the correct BCD result.

Table 7-5 **Action of the DAA instruction**

State of C bit before DAA (Col. 1)	*Upper half-byte (bits 4–7) (Col. 2)*	*Initial half-carry H bit (Col. 3)*	*Lower half-byte (bits 0–3) (Col. 4)*	*Number added by DAA (Col. 5)*	*State of C-bit after DAA (Col. 6)*
0	0–9	0	0–9	00	0
0	0–8	0	A–F	06	0
0	0–9	1	0–3	06	0
0	A–F	0	0–9	60	1
0	9–F	0	A–F	66	1
0	A–F	1	0–3	66	1
1	0–2	0	0–9	60	1
1	0–2	0	A–F	66	1
1	0–3	1	0–3	66	1

The DAA instruction modifies an answer as shown in Table 7-5. It examines four parts of the result:

1 the lower half-byte

2 the upper half-byte

3 the H bit

4 the C bit

It then adds 00, 06, 60, or 66 to the answer. This transforms the result to BCD.

EXAMPLE 7-10 What happens if a DAA instruction follows the result of Example 7-9?

Solution In Example 7-9, the sum was C1. The DAA notes:

1 The lower half-byte is 0–3.

2 The H bit is SET.

3 The upper half-byte is A–F.

4 The C bit is CLEAR.

These conditions occur on line 6 of Table 7-5. The table shows that the DAA adds 66 to the result and sets the C bit. After the DAA, A contains C1 + 66 = 27 and the carry bit is set, which indicates a carry (a weight of 100 in decimal arithmetic). Therefore the BCD sum is 127, which is correct.

7-6 LOGIC INSTRUCTIONS

The **6800** contains AND, OR, and EXCLUSIVE OR instructions. They allow the programmer to perform Boolean algebra manipulations on a variable, and to set or clear specific bits in a byte. They can also be used to test specific bits in a byte, but other logic instructions such as BIT, TEST, or COMPARE may be more useful for these tests.

Since logic operations are performed on a *bit-by-bit* basis, the C bit has no effect. It is unchanged by all logic operations. The V bit is cleared by logic operations. The N and Z bits are set in accordance with the result.

7-6.1 Setting and Clearing Specific Bits

AND and OR instructions can be used to set or clear a specific bit or bits in an accumulator or memory location. This is very useful in those systems where each bit has a specific meaning, rather than being part of a number. In the control and status registers of the PIA or ACIA, for example, each bit has a distinct meaning.

EXAMPLE 7-11 Bit 3 of A must be set, while all other bits remain unchanged. How can this be done?

Solution If A is ORed with 08, which contains 1 in bit position 3, bit 3 of the result will be set and all other bits will remain as they were. The instruction ORA A #08 accomplishes this.

EXAMPLE 7-12 Bits 3, 5, and 6 of A are to be cleared while all other bits remain unchanged. How can this be done?

Solution If A is ANDed with 97, which contains 0s in positions 3, 5, and 6, then these bits of the result are 0 and the rest are unchanged. The instruction 84 97 (AND A 97) accomplishes this.

7-6.2 Testing Bits

In addition to being able to set or clear specific bits in a register, it is also possible to *test* specific bits to determine if they are 1 or 0. In the peripheral interface adapter (PIA), for example, a 1 in the MSB of the control register indicates some external even has occurred. The μP can test this bit and react appropriately. Typically the results of the test sets the Z or N bit. The program then executes a conditional branch (see section 7-8) and takes one of two different paths depending on the results of the test.

Accumulator bits can be tested by the AND and OR instructions, but this modifies the contents of the accumulator. If the accumulator is to remain unchanged, the BIT TEST instruction is used. This ANDs memory (or an immediate operand) with the accumulator without changing either.

EXAMPLE 7-13 Determine if bit 5 of accumulator B is a 1 or 0 without changing B.

Solution The instruction BIT B #$20 (C5 20) is a BIT TEST immediate. It ANDs the contents of B with 20. Since 20 only contains a 1 in the bit 5 position, the result is 00 if bit 5 of B is 0 and 20 if bit 5 of B is 1. The Z bit is cleared or set accordingly and retains the result of this test.

7-6.3 Compare Instructions

A COMPARE instruction essentially subtracts a memory or immediate operand from an accumulator, leaving the *contents of both memory and accumulator unchanged.* The actual results of the subtraction are discarded; the only function of the COMPARE is to set the condition code bits.

There are two types of COMPARE instructions: those that involve accumulators and those that use the index register. Effectively, the two numbers that are being compared are subtracted, but neither value is changed. The subtraction serves to set or clear the condition codes. In the case of the CPX instruction, only the Z bit is significant, but for the COMPARE accumulator (CMP A or B) instruction, the carry, negative, zero, and overflow bits are affected and allow us to determine which of the operands is greater.

The COMPARE INDEX REGISTER instructions compare the contents of the index register with a 16-bit operand. They are often used to terminate loops. These instructions set the Z bit properly, but the N and V bits are often set *incorrectly* and the reader is warned *not* to use N or V after a COMPARE INDEX REGISTER instruction.

EXAMPLE 7-14 Determine if the contents of location CB are equal to the number F2.

Solution One program that does this is:

```
C6  F2      LDA  B  #$F2     (LOAD B IMMEDIATE)
D1  CB      CMP  B  $CB      (COMPARE B DIRECT)
```

The first instruction loads F2 into B. The second instruction compares the contents of B (F2) with the contents of CB. The Z bit is set if they are equal, since the result of the subtraction is 0.

7-6.4 The TEST Instruction

The TEST (TST) instruction subtracts 0 from an operand and therefore does not alter the operand. Its effect, like that of COMPAREs or BIT TESTs, is to set the N and Z bits. It differs in that it always clears the overflow and carry bits. It is used to set the condition codes in accordance with the contents of an accumulator or memory location.

EXAMPLE 7-15 Determine if the contents of location F0 are positive, zero, or negative.

Solution This problem is solved by using the TEST instruction. Since F0 is below FF it is generally addressed in direct mode, but this mode is not available with the test instruction (see Table 7-1). We can, however, use extended addressing. The instruction

```
TST $F0       7D 00F0
```

sets the N and Z bits and allows us to determine the sign of the number in F0.

7-7 OTHER 6800 INSTRUCTIONS

The remaining **6800** instructions listed in Table 7-1 are well described by their name and mnemonics.

7-7.1 CLEAR, INCREMENT, and DECREMENT Instructions

These allow the user to alter the contents of an accumulator or memory location as specified. Those instructions referring to memory locations can be executed in extended or indexed modes only. They are simple to write, but require six or seven cycles for execution because the contents of a memory location must be brought to the CPU, modified, and rewritten to memory.

7-7.2 SHIFT and ROTATE Instructions

SHIFTs and ROTATEs have already been discussed in section 2-9. The drawings in Table 7-1 show diagrammatically how they work. Note that they all use the carry bit, either for input, output, or both. ROTATEs are 9-bit ROTATEs that combine the 8-bit accumulator and the carry bit.

7-7.3 Accumulator Transfer Instructions

The TAB and TBA instructions allow the transfer of data from A to B and B to A, respectively. These instructions help the user make use of both accumulators, which simplifies the programming of the **6800**.

7-7.4 COMPLEMENT and NEGATE Instructions

The COMPLEMENT instructions invert all bits of a memory location. They are useful as logic instructions and in programs requiring complementation, such as a BCD subtraction program.

The NEGATE instructions take the 2s complement of a number and therefore negate it. The NEGATE instruction works by subtracting the operand from 00. Since the absolute value of the operand is always greater than the minuend, except when the operand itself is 00, the NEGATE instruction sets the carry flag for all cases, except when the operand is 00.

7-8 BRANCH AND JUMP INSTRUCTIONS

Table 7-3 shows the BRANCH and JUMP instructions available in the **6800** μP. They complete the **6800** instruction set and allow programs requiring decisions, branches, and subroutines to be written.

7-8.1 JUMP Instructions

One of the simplest instructions in Table 7-3 is the JUMP instruction. It loads the PC with a new value and thereby transfers or JUMPs the program to a new location.

The JUMP instruction can be specified in one of two modes, indexed or extended, as shown in Figure 7-3. The JUMP INDEXED (JMP 0,X) is a 2-byte instruction; its function is shown in Figure 7-3*a*. The second byte or offset is added to the index register and the sum is loaded into the PC.

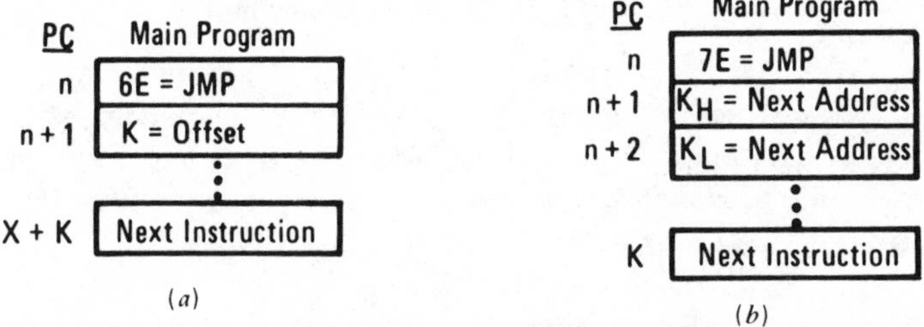

Figure 7-3 JUMP instruction in the **6800** μP. (*a*) Indexed. (*b*) Extended. (From Greenfield and Wray, *Using Microprocessors and Microcomputers: The 6800 Family*, Wiley, 1981.)

EXAMPLE 7-16 What does the following program accomplish?

```
LDX #$5234      CE 5234
JMP $2D,X       6E 2D
```

Solution The first instruction, LDX #$5234 is an immediate load and loads 5234 into the index register (X). The second instruction is an indexed JUMP. It adds the second byte, 2D, to the contents of X and loads the sum, 5261, into the PC. Thus the next Op code to be executed is in location 5261.

Extended JUMPs are 3-byte instructions, where the last 2 bytes are a 16-bit address. Their action is shown in Figure 7-3*b*. Since a 16-bit address is available, they allow the program to JUMP to any location in memory. They are very easily understood because they require no calculations.

7-8.2 Unconditional BRANCH Instructions

BRANCH instructions are 2-byte *relative address* instructions. The second byte contains a *displacement*. Normally, when a BRANCH instruction is executed, the contents of the PC are incremented twice to point to the address of the next instruction. When the BRANCH is taken, the PC is altered by the displacement, and the next Op code is found at *the address that equals the address of the BRANCH instruction plus two, plus the displacement*. The displacement is treated as an 8-bit *signed* number that is added to the PC. Displacements with MSBs of 1 are negative numbers, which cause the program to BRANCH *backward*. Since the maximum positive number that can be represented by an 8-bit signed byte is 127_{10} and the most negative number is -128, the program can BRANCH to any location between PC + 129 and PC − 126, where PC is the address of the first byte of the BRANCH instruction.

The *unconditional* BRANCH, BRA, causes the program to BRANCH whenever it is encountered. It is equivalent to a JUMP instruction, but since it is only a 2-byte instruction, it is used when the location being JUMPED to is within the range of +129 or −126 bytes relative to the current PC address.

The formula for calculating the target address of BRANCH instructions was given in Chapter 2 as

$$\text{Target} = \text{BRANCH address} + 2 + \text{offset}$$

and two examples were presented there (see section 2-8). Example 7-17 is another example of the use of a BRANCH.

EXAMPLE 7-17 The instruction 20 FE (BRA *) is often used to halt the program. Explain how it works.

Solution The displacement in this instruction is FE = −2. The instruction causes the program to BRANCH to PC + 2 − 2 = PC, or back to its own location where it executes the instruction again. Thus, BRA * causes the program to continuously BRANCH back to its own location and execute itself again, effectively halting the μP.

7-8.3 Out-of-Range BRANCHes

If a program is to branch to a location further than +126 or −129 bytes away from the BRANCH instruction, a JUMP instruction must be used. Conditional BRANCHes can still be taken by branching around the JUMP instruction, as Example 7-18 shows.

EXAMPLE 7-18 Assume the instruction in location 20 is COMPARE A IMMEDIATE TO CB (CMP A #$CB). If the contents of A is CB, the program is to go to location 5000; otherwise it is to continue. Write this section of the program.

Solution This problem can be solved by placing a JUMP to 5000 if the results of the comparison are 0, but now we must branch around the JUMP if the results are not 0. The portion of the program can look like this:

Add	Mnemonic	Codes
20	CMP A #$CB	81 CB
22	BNE $27	26 03
24	JMP 5000	7E 5000
27	Continue	

If the results are not 0, the conditional BRANCH (BNE) causes the program to skip the JUMP instruction.

7-8.4 Conditional BRANCH Instructions

A *conditional BRANCH instruction branches only* when a particular condition code or combination of condition codes are SET or CLEAR. Therefore the *results of instructions preceding the BRANCH determine whether or not the BRANCH is taken.* Conditional BRANCHes allow the user to write programs that make *decisions* and give the μP its ability to compute.

There are 14 conditional BRANCHes in the **6800** instruction set. Eight of them simply test the C, Z, N, and V bits and branch accordingly. They are listed below.

Instruction	*Mnemonic*	*Op code*	*Condition*
Branch if carry SET	BCS	25	C=1
Branch if carry CLEAR	BCC	24	C=0
Branch if zero	BEQ	27	Z=1
Branch if not zero	BNE	26	Z=0
Branch if minus	BMI	2B	N=1
Branch if plus	BPL	2A	N=0
Branch if overflow SET	BVS	29	V=1
Branch if overflow CLEAR	BVC	28	V=0

EXAMPLE 7-19 Assuming that all the bytes between 0100 and 01FF contain positive numbers, write a program to add them.

Solution Because there are no negative numbers in this problem, the N and V bits can be ignored. For example, 01100100 + 01100100 = 11001000, which can be interpreted as +200 or −56. Here it is interpreted as the straight binary result, +200, because all numbers are positive. We must, however, make provision for overflow out of the byte. This is indicated by the C bit, not the V bit, because bit 7 is used for magnitude, not sign. Note that the above sum sets V, but not C, and there is no overflow if the byte is treated as an 8-bit binary number.

Using the foregoing approach, the least significant part of the result can be placed in A, and B can be incremented each time a carry out appears. The addresses are most conveniently incremented by using the index register (X). X can also be used to determine when to end the program.

Before writing the program, the flowchart of Figure 7-4 was prepared. The program of Table 7-6 was then written and proceeds as follows.

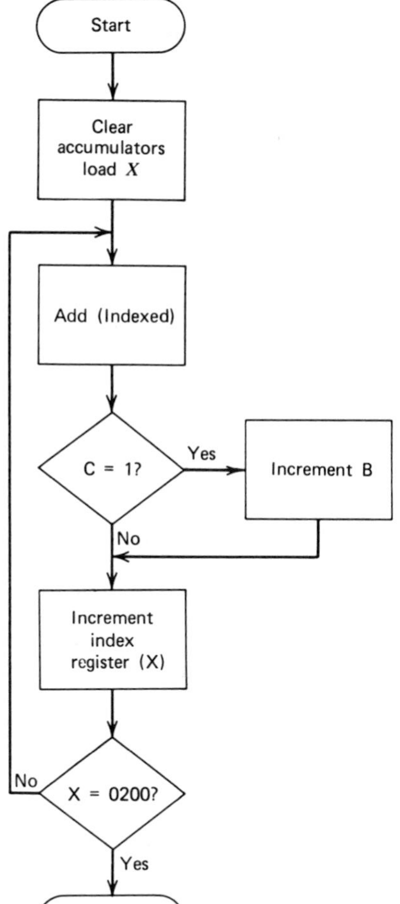

Figure 7-4 Flowchart for Example 7-19. (From Greenfield and Wray, *Using Microprocessors and Microcomputers: The 6800 Family*, Wiley, 1981.)

1 The first three instructions are initializations; they clear the accumulators and load the first address into X.

2 The contents of the first location are then added to A.

3 The carry flag is checked. If C = 1, the BRANCH is taken and B is incremented. If C = 0, the BCS instruction allows the PC to proceed to 29.

4 The index register is incremented and checked. If it equals 200, the program is complete and halts. If not, the program loops back and adds the contents of the next location to A.

Note that the program contains two conditional BRANCHes and two unconditional BRANCHes, one of which is the halt (20 FE).

Table 7-6 **Program for Example 7-19**

Location	*Code*	*Mnemonics*	*Comments*
20	4F	CLR A	Clear A
21	5F	CLR B	Clear B
22	CE 0100	LDX #$100	Load X with $100
25	AB 00	ADD A 0,X	Add number in 1st location to A
27	25 08	BCS $31	Branch if carry set to increment B
29	08	INX	Increment X
2A	8C 0200	CPX #$200	Reached end yet?
2D	26 F6	BNE $25	No, loop back to $25
2F	20 FE	BRA $2F	Halt program
31	5C	INC B	Increment B
32	20 F5	BRA $29	Branch back to $29

7-8.5 Other Conditional BRANCH Instructions

The six additional BRANCH instructions listed below depend on the result of the last ALU operations.

1 **Branch if greater than or equal to zero (BGE).** We have already seen that it is possible to add two positive numbers and get a negative result if overflow occurs (section 7-4.4). The BGE instruction takes the BRANCH if the result of the last operation was positive or 0, *even if the N bit is 1*. It is often used after subtraction or compare instructions and branches only if the minuend is greater than or equal to the subtrahend. The logic equation is $N \oplus V = 0$.

2 **Branch if greater than zero (BGT).** This instruction is very much like BGE. It branches only if the result of the last operation was positive and not equal to 0. The logic equation is $Z + N \oplus V = 0$.

3 **Branch if higher (BHI).** This instruction is meant to be executed after a compare or subtract instruction (CBA, CMP, SBA, or SUB). It branches if the minuend, considered as an unsigned binary number, is greater than the subtrahend. The logic equation is $C + Z = 0$, so the instruction will not branch if C is 1 (indicating

the results of the subtraction is negative; see section 7-4.2) or if Z is 1, indicating that the minuend and subtrahend are equal and the results of the subtraction are 0.

4 **Branch if less than or equal to zero (BLE).** This instruction branches if the result of the last operation is less than or equal to 0. It allows for the possibility that $N = 0$ due to overflow.

5 **Branch if less than zero (BLT).** Similar to the BLE, but no BRANCH is taken if the last result is 0.

6 **Branch if lower or the same (BLS).** This instruction complements the BHI. It is also meant to be executed after a compare or subtract instruction and causes a BRANCH if the subtrahend is greater than or equal to the minuend. Since the logic equation is $C + Z = 1$, the BRANCH is taken if the result of the subtraction is negative ($C = 1$) or 0 ($Z = 1$).

Note that the BHI and BLS instructions compare on the basis of *absolute magnitude*, while the BGE, BGT, BLE, and BLT use *signed numbers*.

EXAMPLE 7-20 Assume the A accumulator contains 60 and B contains 90.

a Which number is higher?
b With which of the following programs will it branch?

1 CBA	2 CBA	3 CBA
BHI	BGT	BPL

Solution

a Considered as unsigned numbers B > A, but if signed numbers are being used, the 60 is positive and 90 is negative, therefore A > B.

b CBA is the mnemonic for COMPARE accumulators. The result of the compare is $60 - 90 = \text{D0}$, with the C, N, and V bits all SET. The contents of the A and B accumulators remain 60 and 90, however, because they are not affected by a COMPARE instruction.

Program 1 will not branch because 90 is higher (in absolute value) than 60, and the subtraction SETs the C bit so that $C + Z \neq 0$.

Program 2 will branch because the BGT considers signed numbers and A > B. Note that the logic equation $Z + N \oplus V = 0$ is satisfied because $Z = 0$ and both N and $V = 1$.

Program 3 will not branch because the result SETs the N bit and the **6800** considers the result as negative.

The results of this program show that the BHI instruction should be used when comparing *absolute* numbers but, when comparing 2s complement signed numbers, the BGE or BGT instructions are correct.

EXAMPLE 7-21 If the following program is executed, what numbers must be in the B accumulator for the program to branch?

```
LDAA #$FD
CBA
BHI
```

Solution The first instruction loads FD into A and the second instruction compares the accumulators. Unless B contains FF, FE, or FD, the minuend is higher than the subtrahend and the program will branch.

7-9 STACKS

As with the other μPs, the **6800** uses a stack for *the temporary storage of important information or data that is changed frequently*. Subroutines and interrupts make use of the stack. Since it must be written to as well as read, the stack must be in RAM.

7-9.1 The Stack Pointer

The system designer must determine the area of memory allocated to the stack during initialization. The *stack pointer* (SP) is a register within the μP that contains the *address of the next location available for the stack*. Since SP decrements automatically when data or return addresses are stored, it must be initially set to the highest address in the stack area. This location is often called the *top of the stack*, and is pointed to when nothing is stored in the stack. The following instructions pertain to the stack pointer:

Mnemonic	**Description**
DES	Decrement stack pointer.
INS	Increment stack pointer.
LDS	Load stack pointer. (This instruction can be executed in the immediate, direct, indexed or extended modes.)
STS	Store stack pointer. (This instruction can be executed in the direct, indexed, or extended modes.)
TXS	Transfer the contents of the index register (minus 1) to the stack pointer register.
TSX	Transfer the contents of the stack pointer register (plus 1) to the index register (see Table 7-2).

EXAMPLE 7-22 The stack is to occupy locations \$0200 to \$02FF. What instructions are required at the beginning of the program to initialize the SP?

Solution The SP points to the highest vacant location in the stack. At the beginning of the program the entire stack is empty so the SP must point to 02FF. The single instruction

```
LDS #$2FF   (8E 02FF)
```

is a LOAD IMMEDIATE that loads 02FF into the SP. This instruction initializes the stack so that it starts at 02FF. Whenever the stack is used the SP is decremented. The stack must not be allowed to become so large that it invades memory area set aside for programs or data, or it will overwrite them. One common programming mistake is to do something that causes the stack pointer to decrement and to fail to increment it later. This can cause the stack to overflow and destroy the program.

7-9.2 PUSH and PULL

Two memory instructions that were not previously discussed because they involve the SP are PUSH and PULL.[2] These are implied instructions that refer to the A or B accumulators.

A PUSH takes the contents of the accumulator and *writes* it in the stack at the SP location. It then *decrements* the SP because the original stack location is no longer vacant; it contains the *pushed byte*.

EXAMPLE 7-23 If A contains CB, what do the following instructions accomplish?

```
LDS #$2FF
PSH A
```

Solution The first instruction loads 02FF into the SP, as in Example 7-22. The second instruction pushes A onto the stack. After execution, location 02FF contains CB and the SP contains 02FE, which points to the highest vacant location in the stack.

A PULL instruction first *increments* the SP, then *transfers* the contents of the stack at the new value of the SP to the accumulator. Note that once the contents of a stack location has been pulled, it is considered vacant although the byte is still there. It will be overwritten by the next PUSH or other usage of the stack.

EXAMPLE 7-24 If the SP contains \$200, location \$200 contains \$CB, and \$201 contains \$CC, what happens in response to a PULL B instruction?

Solution The SP is incremented to 201 and the stack is read. At the end of the instruction, B contains CC and the SP contains 201. Now 200 and 201 are both considered to be vacant.

Note that the stack acts as a last-in-first-out (LIFO) register. *A PULL retrieves the information that was last pushed onto the stack.*

7-10 SUBROUTINES

A *subroutine* is a small program that is generally used more than once by the main program. Multiplications, 16-bit adds, and square roots are typical subroutines.

Figure 7-5 illustrates the use of the same subroutine by two different parts of the main program. The subroutine located at 200 can be entered from either location 0011 or 00CC by placing a JUMP TO SUBROUTINE (AD, BD, or 8D, depending on the mode) in these addresses. The PC action, as a result of the subroutine JUMP at 0011, are identified by the *a* in Figure 7-5 and *b* identifies JUMPS from 00CC.

After the subroutine is complete, the program resumes from the instruction following the location where it called the subroutine. Because the subroutine must return to one of *several* locations, depending on which one caused it to be entered,

[2] The word POP is often used instead of PULL by other computer manufacturers.

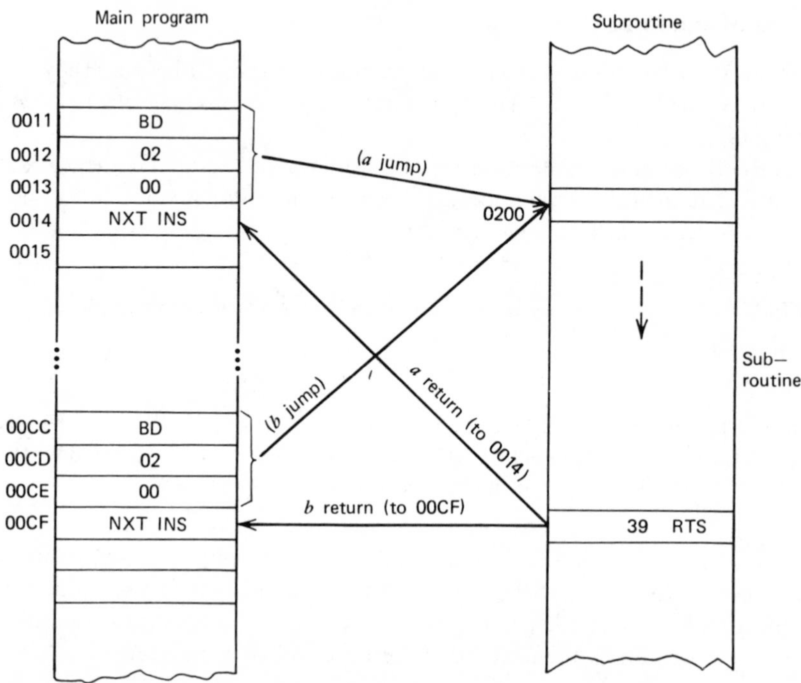

Figure 7-5 Use of a subroutine. (From Greenfield and Wray, *Using Microprocessors and Microcomputers: The 6800 Family*, Wiley, 1981.)

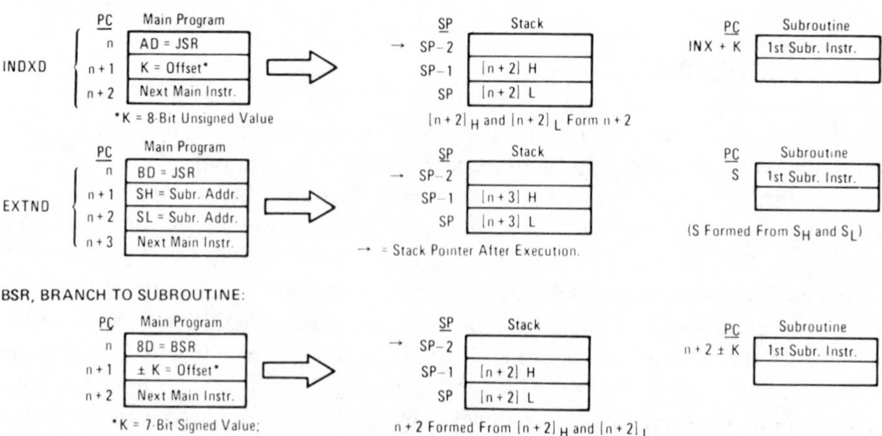

Figure 7-6 JUMPs and BRANCHes to subroutines in the **6800** μP. (From Greenfield and Wray, *Using Microprocessors and Microcomputers: The 6800 Family*, Wiley, 1981.)

the *original contents of the PC must be preserved* so the subroutine knows where to return.

7-10.1 JUMPs to Subroutines

The JUMP TO SUBROUTINE (JSR) instruction stores the address of the next main instruction by *writing it to the stack* before it takes the JUMP. The JSR can be executed in the indexed or extended mode. There is a BRANCH TO SUBROUTINE (BSR) that can be used if the starting address of the subroutine is within +129 to −126 locations of the program counter. The advantage of the BSR is that it requires 1 less byte in the main program.

The action of the subroutine instructions are illustrated in Figure 7-6. In each case they store the address of the next main instruction on the stack before taking the JUMP.

EXAMPLE 7-25 If the SP and X registers both contain 0200, what happens when the instruction.

```
JSR $20,X
```

in location 30 is executed?

Solution This is the indexed mode of the instruction JSR. Since the Op code for the JSR (AD) occupies location 30 and 20 (the offset) occupies location 31, the address of the next instruction, 0032, is written to the stack. Location 0200 then contains 32 and location 01FF contains 00. The SP has been decremented twice and contains 01FE. The program then jumps to 0220 (the sum of the contents of X and the offset), which is the starting location of the subroutine.

7-10.2 RETURN FROM SUBROUTINE

The JSR instructions preserve the contents of the PC on the stack, but a RETURN FROM SUBROUTINE (RTS) instruction is required to properly return. The RTS is the last instruction executed in a subroutine. Its action is shown in Figure 7-7. It places the contents of the stack in the PC and causes the SP to be incremented twice. Because these bytes contain the address of the next main instruction in the program (put there by the JSR or BSR that initiated the subroutine), the program resumes at the place where it left off before it entered the subroutine.

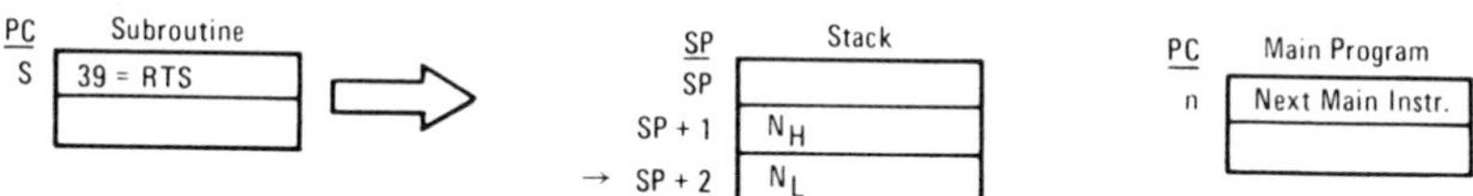

Figure 7-7 Action of the RETURN FROM SUBROUTINE (RTS) instruction. (From Greenfield and Wray, *Using Microprocessors and Microcomputers: The 6800 Family*, Wiley, 1981.)

Note: Pushing a value onto the stack during the subroutine and failing to pull it back off before executing the RTS instruction cause the processor to return to the wrong address, usually with catastrophic results.

7-10.3 Nested Subroutines

In some sophisticated programs the main program may call a subroutine, which then calls on a second subroutine. The second subroutine is called a *nested subroutine* because it is used by and returns to the first subroutine.

The situation is shown graphically in Figure 7-8. The main program does a JSR (JUMP TO SUBROUTINE) extended at address 40. This puts 0043 on the stack. The first subroutine does a JSR at 01C3, placing 01C6 on the stack and jumping to the second subroutine. When the second subroutine is complete, an RTS returns it to 01C6 and increments the SP twice. Now the first subroutine picks up where it left off. When the first subroutine finishes, it ends with an RTS that causes a return to the main program. By making use of the stack as shown, there can be any number of nested subroutines, limited only by the stack size.

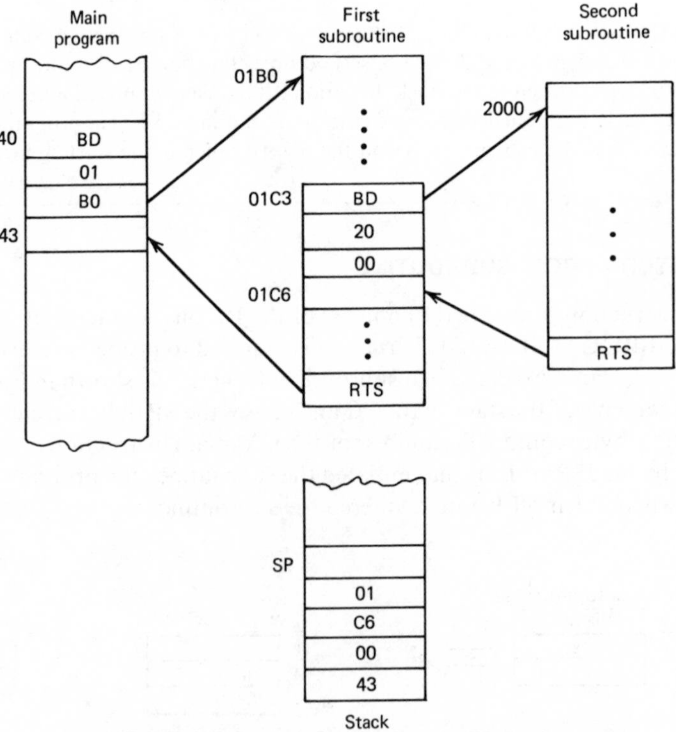

Figure 7-8 Nested subroutines. (From Greenfield and Wray, *Using Microprocessors and Microcomputers: The 6800 Family*, Wiley, 1981.)

7-10.4 Use of Registers During Subroutines

During the execution of a subroutine, the subroutine will use the accumulators; it may use X and it changes the contents of the CCR. When the main program is reentered, however, the contents of these registers must often be as they were before the JUMP to the subroutine.

The most commonly used method of preserving register contents during a subroutine is to write the subroutine so that it pushes those registers it must *preserve* onto the stack at the beginning of the subroutine and then pulls them at the end of the subroutine, thus *restoring their contents* before returning to the main program.

EXAMPLE 7-26 A subroutine uses the A and B accumulators and the CCR. How can the main program contents of these registers be preserved?

Solution To preserve the contents of these registers for the main program, the first four instructions of the subroutine should be:

Op Code	Mnemonic
36	PSH A
37	PSH B
07	TPA
36	PSH A

This puts the contents of A, B, and the CCR on the stack as shown in Figure 7-9.

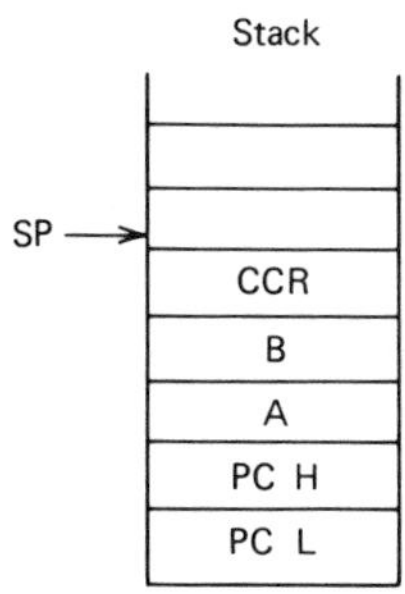

Figure 7-9 Contents of the stack after entering the subroutine of Example 7-26 and executing the first four instructions. (From Greenfield and Wray, *Using Microprocessors and Microcomputers: The 6800 Family*, Wiley, 1981.)

To restore these registers before returning to the main program, the instructions at the beginning must be executed in *reverse* order. The last five instructions of the subroutine must be:

Op Code	Mnemonic
32	PUL A
06	TAP
33	PUL B
32	PUL A
39	RTS

Note that the A register had to be preserved. Because it is also used by the TPA and TAP instructions, the contents of A are overwritten and will be lost unless it is first pushed onto the stack.

7-11 THE 6800 SIGNAL LINES

The pin out for the **6800** is shown in Figure 7-10. An even better drawing which shows the I/O lines and the internal registers of the **6800** is given in Figure 7-11. These figures show that the **6800** has the normal complement of eight data lines, 16 address lines, and a group of control lines. The function of each control line is described in the following paragraphs.

7-11.1 READ/WRITE (R/W)

This output line is used to signal all external devices that the μP is in a READ state (R/W = HIGH), or a WRITE state (R/W = LOW). The normal standby state of this line is HIGH. When tri-state control (TSC) (see section 7-11.8) goes HIGH, the R/W line enters the high impedance mode, otherwise it is driven HIGH or LOW by the **6800**.

7-11.2 Valid Memory Address (VMA)

The VMA output line (when in the HIGH state) tells all devices external to the μP that there is a valid address on the address bus. During the execution of certain instructions, the address bus may assume a random address because of internal calculations. VMA goes LOW to avoid enabling any device under those conditions. Note also that VMA is held LOW during HALT, TSC, or during the execution of a WAIT (WAI) instruction. VMA is not a 3-state line (it is always driven by the **6800**),

PIN ASSIGNMENT

Signal	Pin	Pin	Signal
V_{SS}	1	40	$\overline{RESET}$
$\overline{HALT}$	2	39	TSC
$\phi 1$	3	38	N.C.
$\overline{IRQ}$	4	37	$\phi 2$
VMA	5	36	DBE
$\overline{NMI}$	6	35	N.C.
BA	7	34	R/$\overline{W}$
V_{CC}	8	33	D0
A0	9	32	D1
A1	10	31	D2
A2	11	30	D3
A3	12	29	D4
A4	13	28	D5
A5	14	27	D6
A6	15	26	D7
A7	16	25	A15
A8	17	24	A14
A9	18	23	A13
A10	19	22	A12
A11	20	21	V_{SS}

Figure 7-10 The **6800** μP pin out. (From the Motorola 6800 Data Sheets. Reprinted courtesy of Motorola, Inc.)

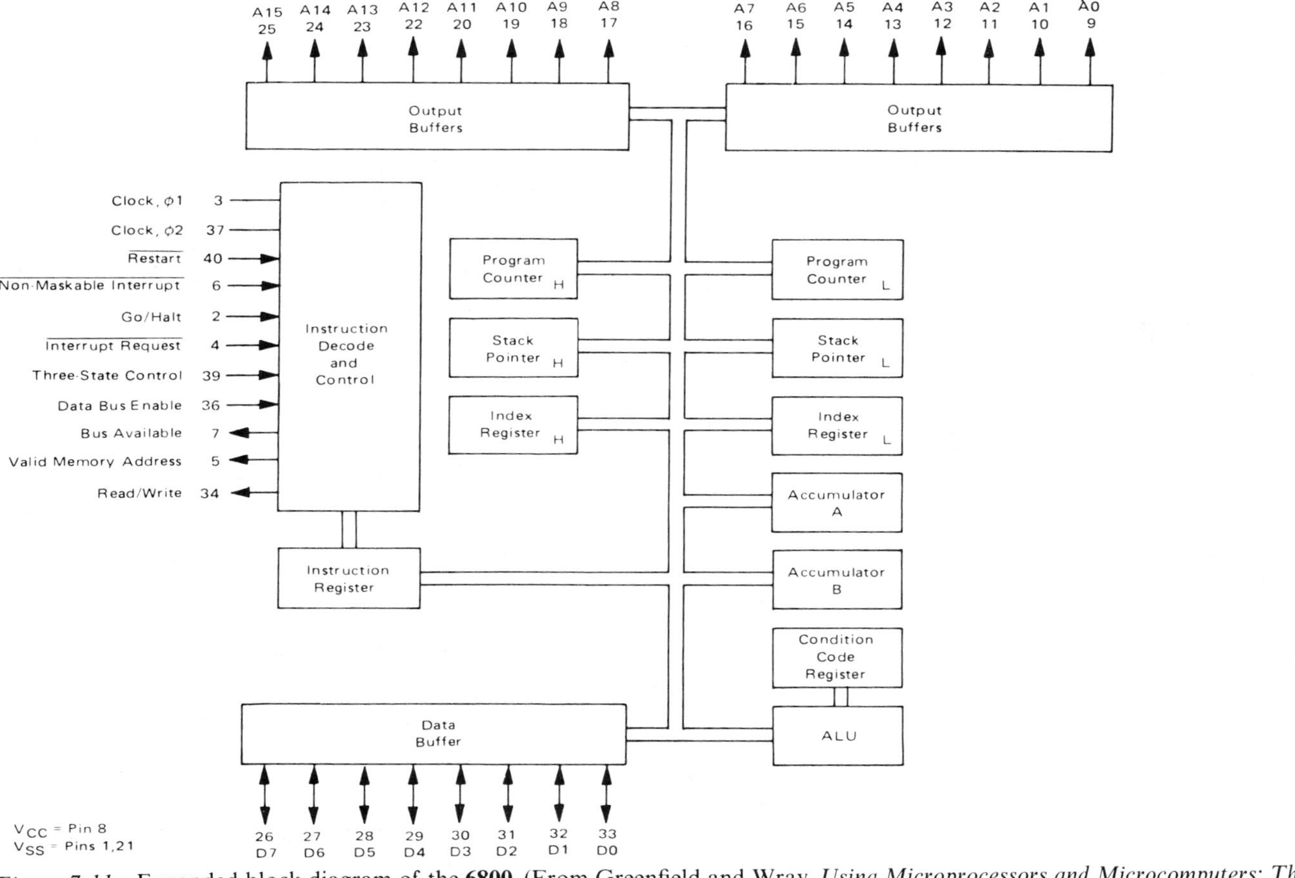

Figure 7-11 Expanded block diagram of the **6800**. (From Greenfield and Wray, *Using Microprocessors and Microcomputers: The 6800 Family*, Wiley, 1981.)

and therefore direct memory access (DMA) cannot be performed unless VMA is externally opened (or gated).

7-11.3 Data Bus Enable (DBE)

The DBE signal enables the data bus drivers of the μP when in the HIGH state. This input is normally connected to the phase 2 (ϕ2) clock but is sometimes delayed to assure proper operation with some memory devices. When HIGH, it permits data to be placed on the bus during a WRITE cycle. During a μP READ cycle, the data bus drivers within the μP are disabled internally. If an external signal holds DBE LOW, the μP data bus drivers are forced into their high impedance state. This allows other devices to control the I/O bus (as in DMA).

7-11.4 Interrupt Request, Nonmaskable Interrupt, and RESET

An active signal on the IRQ, NMI, or RESET lines initiates an interrupt sequence. The action of these lines is discussed in section 7-13 where interrupts are considered in detail.

7-11.5 Phase 1 (ϕ1) and Phase 2 (ϕ2) of the Clock

These two pins are used to accommodate a two-phase, nonoverlapping clock. This clock runs at a frequency up to 1 MHz for the **M6800B** and up to 2 MHz for the depletion mode versions of the **6800 (MC68B00)**.

7-11.6 Halt and Run Modes

When the HALT input to the **6800** is HIGH, the μP is in the run mode and is continually executing instructions. When the HALT line goes LOW, the μP halts after completing its present instruction. At that time the μP is in the halt mode. Bus available (BA) goes HIGH, VMA (section 7-11.2) becomes a 0, and all tri-state lines enter their high impedance state. Note that the μP does not enter the halt mode as soon as HALT goes LOW, but does so only when the μP has finished execution of its current instruction.

7-11.7 Bus Available (BA)

The bus available (BA) signal is a normally LOW signal generated by the μP. In the HIGH state it indicates that the μP has stopped and that the address bus is available to an external device for DMA. This occurs if the μP is in the halt mode or in a WAIT state as the result of the WAI instruction.

7-11.8 Tri-State Control (TSC)

TSC is an externally generated signal that effectively causes the μP to disconnect itself from the address and control buses. This allows an external device to assume control of the system for DMA. When TSC is HIGH, it causes the address lines and the READ/WRITE line to go to the high impedance state. The VMA and BA signals are forced LOW. The data bus is not affected by TSC and has its own enable (DBE).

The μP is a dynamic IC that must be periodically refreshed by its own clocks. Because TSC stops the clocking of the internal logic of the μP, it should not be HIGH longer that three clock pulses, or the dynamic registers in the μP may lose some of their internal data (up to 19 cycles at 2 MHz for the new **68B00**).

7-12 CLOCK OPERATION

The **6800** utilizes a *two-phase clock* to control its operation. The waveforms and timing of the clock are critical for the proper operation of the μP and the other components of the family. The timing requirements are shown in the waveforms and table of Figure 7-12. The clocks must be nonoverlapping and conform to the timing table (Figure 7-12b).

The clock synchronizes the internal operations of the μP, as well as all external devices on the bus. The program counter, for example, is advanced on the falling edge of $\phi 1$ and data is latched into the μP on the falling edge of $\phi 2$. All operations necessary for the execution of each instruction are synchronized with the clock.

Certain components and functions of the system affect the clock requirements. If dynamic memories are used, slow memories are involved, or direct memory access (DMA) is required, the clock may have to be stopped momentarily (that is, stretched). If the memory is slow, for example, $\phi 2$ has to be long enough to allow the memory to complete its READ or WRITE operation. Since a memory that is too slow to operate with a 1-MHz clock (such as an Intel **1702A** EPROM) may only be addressed periodically, there is no need to slow the clock for the entire system, provided that a "memory ready" feature can be included in the clock.

The **MC6875** shown in Figure 7-13 is a 16-pin IC that includes all the features necessary to control the timing of a **6800** system. It includes an internal oscillator whose frequency can be determined by an external crystal or RC network connected to pins X1 and X2. (An inexpensive 3.59-MHz crystal made for color TVs can be used.) Alternatively, an external timing signal can be connected to the Ext. In. pin. The oscillator frequency is divided by four and shaped to provide $\phi 1$ and $\phi 2$, the two-phase nonoverlapping clock required by the **6800** μP. If the system contains slow memories, the clock can be stretched with $\phi 2$ high by holding memory ready low until the data is transferred. The **6875** also contains a Schmitt trigger input that controls $\overline{\text{RESET}}$. A capacitor to ground (power ON RESET) and/or a RESET switch may be used. DMA or dynamic memory refresh can also be accommodated.

7-12.1 Instruction Bytes and Clock Cycles

In the **6800** instruction set (Tables 7-1 through 7-4), the number of bytes and clock cycles are listed for each instruction. The number of bytes for each instruction determines the size of the memory, and the number of cycles determines the time required to execute the program. LDA A $1234 (which is the extended addressing mode), for example, requires 3 bytes, 1 to specify the operation (Op) code and 2 to

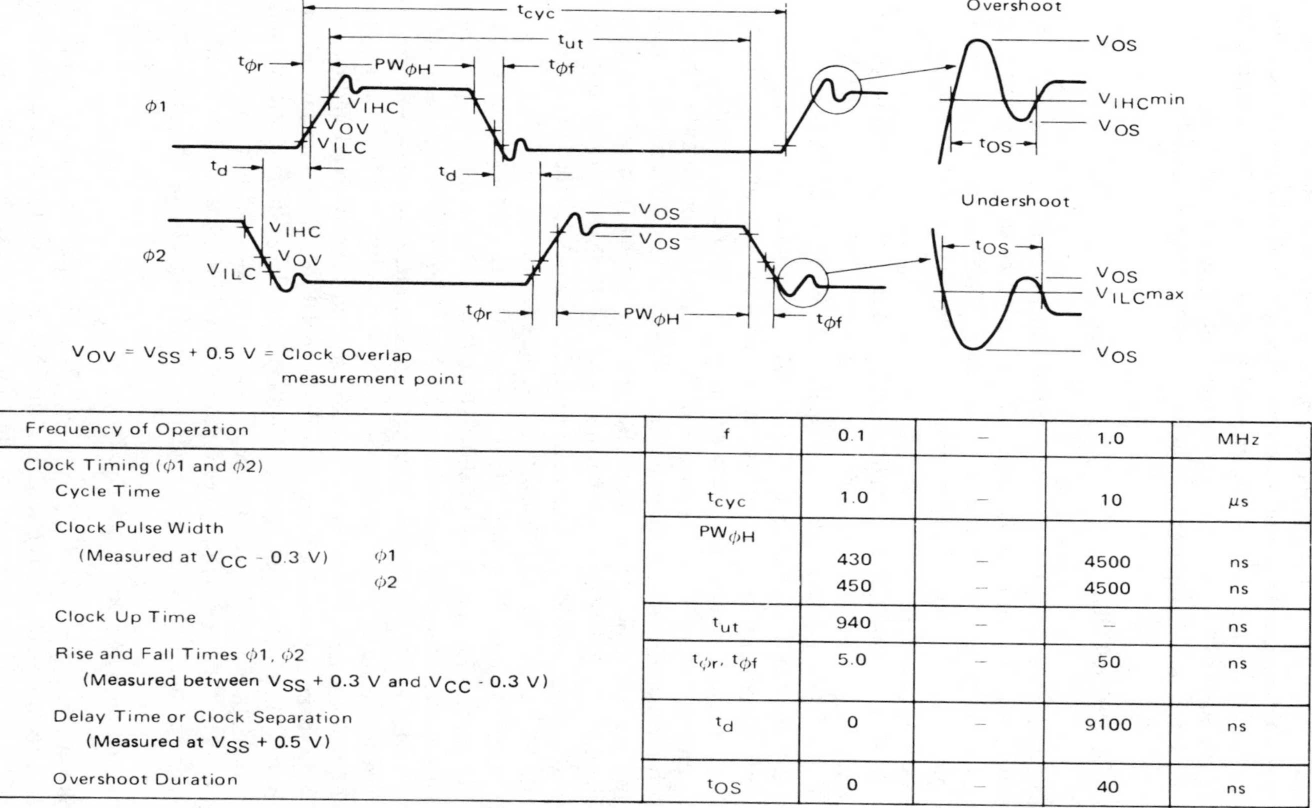

Frequency of Operation	f	0.1	–	1.0	MHz
Clock Timing ($\phi 1$ and $\phi 2$)					
Cycle Time	t_{cyc}	1.0	–	10	μs
Clock Pulse Width	$PW_{\phi H}$				
(Measured at $V_{CC} - 0.3$ V) $\phi 1$		430	–	4500	ns
$\phi 2$		450	–	4500	ns
Clock Up Time	t_{ut}	940	–	–	ns
Rise and Fall Times $\phi 1$, $\phi 2$ (Measured between $V_{SS} + 0.3$ V and $V_{CC} - 0.3$ V)	$t_{\phi r}$, $t_{\phi f}$	5.0	–	50	ns
Delay Time or Clock Separation (Measured at $V_{SS} + 0.5$ V)	t_d	0	–	9100	ns
Overshoot Duration	t_{OS}	0	–	40	ns

(b)

Figure 7-12 **6800** clock timing. Microprocessor $\phi 1$ and $\phi 2$ clocks. (*a*) Waveforms. (*b*) Timing table. (From Greenfield and Wray, *Using Microprocessors and Microcomputers: The 6800 Family*, Wiley, 1981.)

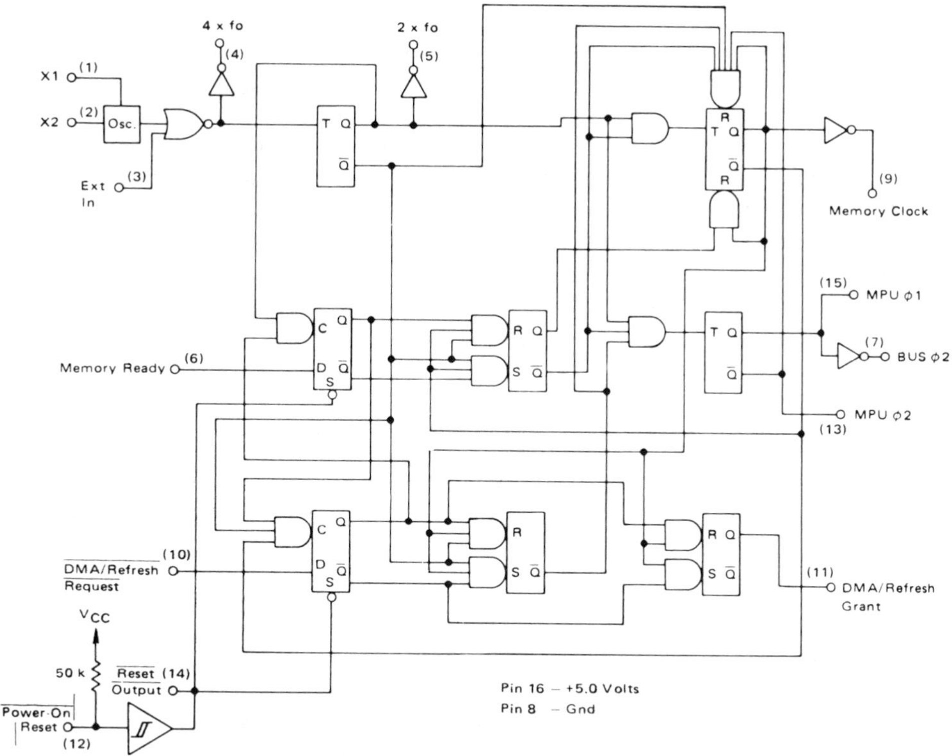

Figure 7-13 **6875** block diagram. (From Greenfield and Wray, *Using Microprocessors and Microcomputers: The 6800 Family*, Wiley, 1981.)

specify the address, but requires 4 cycles to execute. Often an instruction requires the processor to perform internal operations in addition to the fetch cycles. Consequently, for any instruction the number of cycles is generally larger than the number of bytes.

EXAMPLE 7-27 How long does it take to execute a LDAA 0,X (indexed) instruction if a 1-MHz oscillator is used as the system clock?

Solution From Table 7-1, we find that a LDAA 0,X instruction requires 2 bytes and 5 cycles. The 2 bytes are the Op code and the offset address. The μP must add the offset to the contents of its index register. This accounts for the large number of clock cycles required for this instruction. Since the instruction takes 5 cycles, it takes 5 μs to execute at a clock rate of 1 MHz.

7-13 INTRODUCTION TO INTERRUPTS

One of the most important features of a μP is its ability to control and act on feedback from peripheral devices such as line printers or machinery controllers. It must be able to sense the operation of the system under its control and respond quickly with corrective commands when necessary.

When conditions that require fast response arise, the system is wired so as to send a signal called an *interrupt* to the μP. *An interrupt causes the μP to stop execution of its main program and jump to a special program, an interrupt service routine, that responds to the needs of the external device.* The main program resumes when the interrupt service routine is finished.

Although a computer can perform many useful tasks without using or responding to an interrupt, the ability to do so is a necessary function for many system designs. The **6800** includes a powerful interrupt structure. Important aspects of this are the stack concept, the use of vectored interrupts, and the interrupt priority scheme provided by the μP logic.

As described in Section 7-9 the *stack* is an area in memory pointed to by the stack pointer (SP) register. The stack has three basic uses.

1 to save return addresses during the execution of subroutines;

2 to move or save data;

3 to save register contents during an interrupt.

Use of the stack during interrupts is discussed in this section.

7-13.1 Vectored Interrupts

The **6800** uses four different types of interrupts: *reset* (RST), *non-maskable* (NMI), *software* (SWI), and *hardware interrupt request* (IRQ). Unique interrupt servicing routines must be written by the system designer for each type of interrupt used, and they can be located anywhere in memory. Access to the routines is provided by the μP that outputs a pair of addresses for the appropriate interrupt. The two locations addressed must contain the address of the required interrupt service routine. The eight addresses put out by the μP for the four interrupt types are:

1 reset (RST)	FFFE–FFFF
2 non-maskable interrupt (NMI)	FFFC–FFFD
3 software interrupt (SWI)	FFFA–FFFB
4 interrupt request (IRQ)	FFF8–FFF9

These are shown in the memory map of Figure 7-14.

It should be noted that the actual ROM (or PROM) accessed may appear to be at some lower address as long as it also responds to the addresses shown above. When one of the four types of interrupts occurs, the μP logic fetches the contents of the appropriate 2 bytes and loads them into the program counter. This causes the program to jump to the proper interrupt routine. The fetched addresses are commonly called *vectors* or *vector addresses* since they *point to* the software routine used to service the interrupt.

Three of the interrupts (RST, NMI, and IRQ) are activated by signals on the pins of the μP, and the fourth (SWI) is initiated by an instruction. Each of these

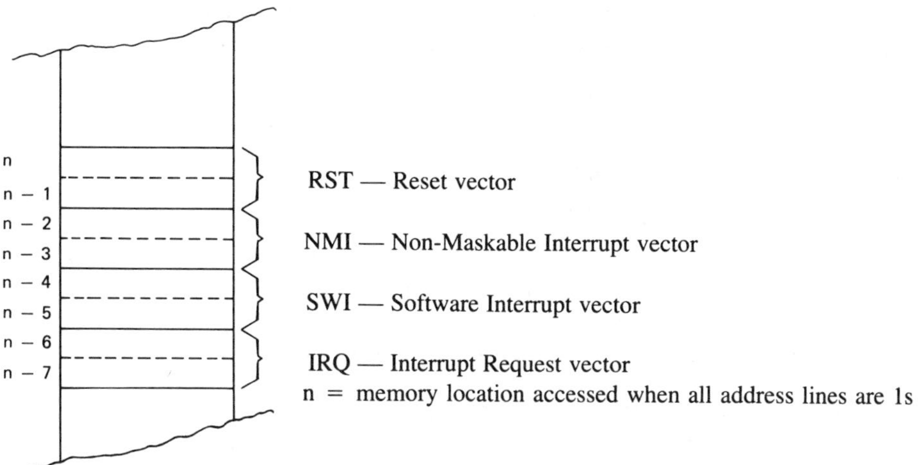

Figure 7-14 Memory map showing RESTART and INTERRUPT vector locations. (From Greenfield and Wray, *Using Microprocessors and Microcomputers: The 6800 Family*, Wiley, 1981.)

interrupts have similar but different sequences of operation and each will be described.

7-13.2 RESET (RST)

A RESET is used to start the program. A LOW pulse on the RESET pin of the μP causes the logic in the μP to be reset and also causes the starting location of the program to be fetched from the *reset vector* locations by the FFFE and FFFF that are put on the address bus by the μP and transferred to the PC.

EXAMPLE 7-28 The program starts at location 123 (hex). What must be done to assure a proper start?

Solution Before a program can be started automatically, the $\overline{\text{RESET}}$ vector must be in place. In this case a 01 must be stored in a location that is accessed when FFFE is on the address bus and a 23 must be in the following location.

When a RESTART is caused (perhaps by a RESTART timer or by a pushbutton switch), the **6800** fetches the vector in two steps by addressing FFFE and then FFFF. When each byte appears on the data bus (01, followed by 23), they are loaded into the program counter and the program starts in the proper place.

7-13.3 The IRQ Interrupt

The IRQ interrupt is typically used when peripheral devices must communicate with the μP. It is activated by a LOW signal on the $\overline{\text{IRQ}}$ pin (pin 4) of the μP. Even though this line is pulled LOW, the $\overline{IRQ}$ interrupt does not occur if the I bit of the condition code (CC) register is set. This is known as *masking the interrupt*. The I bit is set in one of three ways.

1 by the hardware logic of the μP as a part of the restart procedure;

2 whenever the μP is interrupted;

3 by an SEI (set interrupt mask) instruction.

Once set, the I bit can be cleared only by a CLI (clear interrupt mask) instruction. Therefore, if a program is to allow interrupts, it must have a CLI instruction near its beginning.

When an interrupt is initiated, *the instruction in progress is completed before the μP begins its interrupt sequence*. The first step in this sequence is to save the program status by storing the PC, X, A, B, and CC registers on the stack in the order shown in Figure 7-15. These 7 bytes are written into memory starting at the location in the stack pointer (SP) register, which is decremented on each WRITE. When completed, the SP is pointing to the next empty memory location. The condition of the stack before and after accepting an interrupt is shown in Figure 7-15. The μP next sets the interrupt mask bit (I), which allows the service program to run without being interrupted. After setting the interrupt mask, the μP fetches the address of the interrupt service routine from the IRQ vector location by placing FFF8 and FFF9 on the address bus, and inserts it into the PC. The μP then fetches the first instruction of the service routine from the location now designated by the PC.

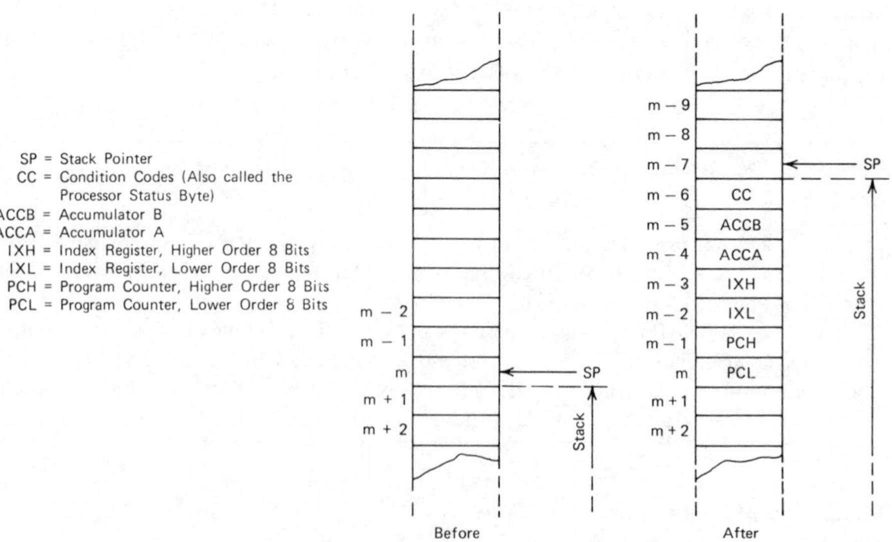

Figure 7-15 Saving the status of the μP in the stack. (From Greenfield and Wray, *Using Microprocessors and Microcomputers: The 6800 Family*, Wiley, 1981.)

7-13.4 Nested Interrupts

Normally an interrupt service routine proceeds until it is complete without being interrupted itself, because the I flag is set. If it is desirable to recognize another IRQ interrupt (or higher priority, for example), before the servicing of the first one is completed, the interrupt mask can be cleared by a CLI instruction at the beginning of the current service routine. This allows "an interrupt of an interrupt," or *nested interrupts*. It is handled in the **6800** by storing another sequence of registers on the stack. Because of the automatic decrementing of the stack pointer by each interrupt, and subsequent incrementing by the RTI instruction when an interrupt is completed, they are serviced in the proper order. Interrupts can be nested to any depth, limited only by the amount of memory available for the stack.

7-13.5 Return from Interrupt (RTI)

The interrupt service routine must end with an RTI (return from interrupt) instruction. The action of the RTI is shown in Figure 7-16. It reloads all the μP registers with the values they had before the interrupt and, in the process, moves the stack pointer to SP + 7, where it was before the interrupt. The RTI essentially consists of seven steps that write the contents of the stack into the μP registers and an additional one that allows the program to resume at the address restored to the PC (which is the same place it was before the interrupt occurred). Note that the RTI restores the CC register as it was previously, and interrupts will or will not be allowed as determined by the I bit.

7-13.6 Nonmaskable Interrupt

A nonmaskable interrupt (NMI) is initiated by placing a LOW level on the NMI pin (pin 6) of the **6800**. When an NMI occurs, the program counter is loaded with the vector accessed by FFFC and FFFD. This causes the μP to jump to the start of the NMI service routine.

As its name implies, the NMI is not affected by the I bit of the CCR and an interrupt occurs whenever the NMI pin is pulled LOW. Consequently, NMI

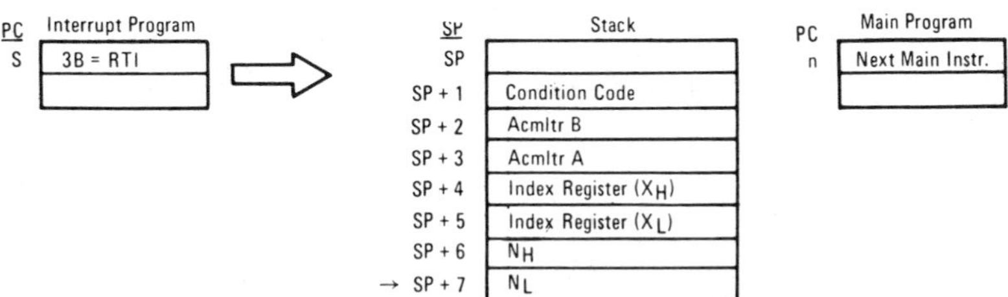

Figure 7-16 Operation of the RETURN FROM INTERRUPT (RTI) instruction. (From Greenfield and Wray, *Using Microprocessors and Microcomputers: The 6800 Family*, Wiley, 1981.)

functions as a *very high priority interrupt*. It is usually reserved for events like a power failure in the μP, or in a peripheral, which could be catastrophic if the μP did not recognize them and take immediate action.

7-13.7 The Software Interrupt (SWI)

An interrupt activated by an instruction is available in the **6800** and serves several interesting purposes. One use is as an aid in debugging systems, but it can be used for error indications or other uses. The SWI instruction, when encountered in a program, causes the registers to be put away on the stack and a vector to be fetched, just as for other interrupts. The vector for SWI is located at the address that responds to FFFA and FFFB. Monitor programs such as found in the MEK-6800-D2 kit use an SWI to store the register contents on the stack where they can be read out to the user.

7-13.8 The WAI Instruction

The **6800** μP also incorporates a wait-for-interrupt (WAI) instruction. When the WAI instruction occurs in a program, it causes the **6800** to stack all the registers and go into a quiescent state until an interrupt occurs. The WAI speeds up interrupt servicing because the registers are stacked before the interrupt occurs and the service routine can be entered directly.

7-14 INPUT/OUTPUT

Motorola uses only memory-mapped I/O (input/output). They have designed a series of ICs to control I/O. All I/O chips appear as a set of *memory locations* on the **6800** bus. The most common of these is the Motorola Peripheral Interface Adapter (PIA), the **MC6820** or **MC6821**. The **6821** is the newer and preferred part. The difference between the two parts is minimal and not essential for this discussion.

The PIA is a 40-pin LSI IC designed to control *parallel* data transfers between the **6800** system and external devices. PIAs are used to transfer data or commands when the equipment to be controlled is nearby, and the many lines are easily accommodated.

A block diagram of the **6820** (or **6821**) PIA that is used for parallel data transfer in **6800** systems is shown in Figure 7-17. It shows the registers within the PIA, the interface to the **6800** data, address, and control buses on the left, and the interface connections to external devices on the right.

7-14.1 The PIA Registers

Figure 7-17 shows that the PIA is a dual I/O port unit (a port is defined as an 8-bit parallel interface) with two similar sides labeled A and B. Each side contains three registers.

1 **The control/status register.** This controls the operation of its side of the PIA.

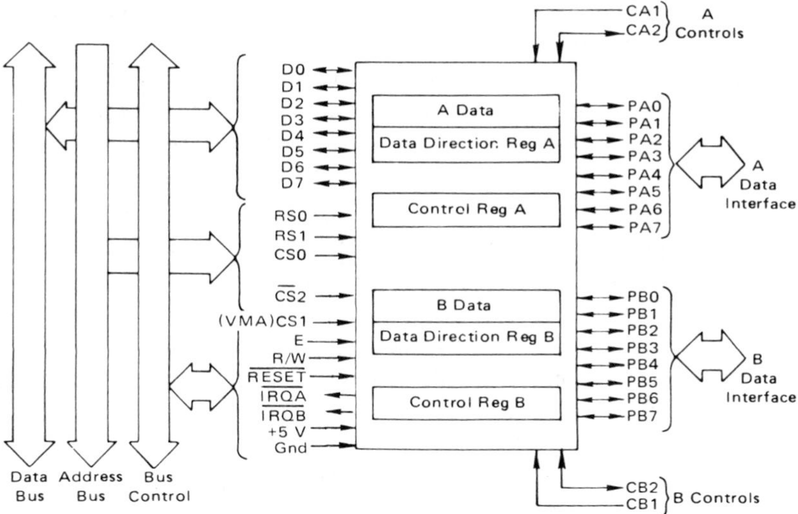

Figure 7-17 **6820** PIA bus interface. (From Greenfield and Wray, *Using Microprocessors and Microcomputers*: *The 6800 Family*, Wiley, 1981.)

2 **The direction register.** This register determines the direction of data flow (input or output) on each I/O line.

3 **The data register.** This holds the I/O data going between the external system and the PIA.

7-14.2 The PIA/6800 Interface

The PIA registers are treated as a *set of memory locations* by the **6800** system. It reads and writes these registers as it would any memory location. The user must assign these PIA addresses as he would other memory addresses.

The lines connecting the PIA to the **6800** I/O bus are shown on the left side of Figure 7-17. This interface consists of:

1 **Inputs D0–D7.** The 8-bit bidirectional data bus.

2 **Inputs RS0, RS1 and CS0, CS1, and $\overline{\text{CS2}}$.** These lines are normally connected to the **6800** address bus. RS0 and RS1 are usually connected to A0 and A1, and determine, along with a bit in the control register, which of the six registers within the PIA, is selected. The chip select lines CS0, CS1, and CS2 are used to select the particular PIA.

3 **Enable (E).** The enable (E) pin of the **6820** PIA must be clocked continuously, because it is a dynamic part. The E pin is generally connected to a signal that is derived from the $\phi 2$ clock. The **6821** is a static part that allows pin E to be used as another chip select.

4 **PIA READ/WRITE.** This signal is generated by the μP to control the direction of

data transfers on the data bus. A LOW state on the PIA READ/WRITE line allows data to be written into the PIA's registers. Data is transferred from the μP to the PIA on the E signal if the device has been selected. A HIGH on the READ/WRITE line sets up the PIA for a transfer of data to the μP via the bus. The PIA output buffers are enabled when the proper address and the E pulse are present.

5 **$\overline{\text{RESET}}$.** This active low reset line is used to reset all register bits in the PIA to a logical 0 (LOW). This pin of the PIA is normally connected to the RESET line of the μC system, and is usually activated by a momentary switch or automatic restart circuit during POWER ON.

6 **IRQA and IRQB.** These are the PIA interrupt lines. They are designed for wire OR operation and are generally tied together and wired to the interrupt input on the **6800**. A LOW signal on either of these lines causes the **6800** to be interrupted.

7-14.3 The Interface Between the PIA and External Devices

The connections between the PIA and external devices are shown on the right side of Figure 7-17. There are two groups of eight bidirectional data lines (PA0–PA7, and PB0–PB7) and two control lines (CA1, and CA2, or CB1, and CB2) for each side. The control lines are used to regulate communication between the PIA and the external devices.

7-14.4 Data Transfers Between the PIA and External Devices

Before any data transfers can take place via the PIA, its control registers and data direction registers have to be set up to determine the mode of operation and the direction of the data transfer (in or out of the PIA). This is known as *initialization.* Once initialized, these registers generally remain unchanged, although one of the PIA's outstanding capabilities is its programmable nature and ability to change system function during the operation of a program. This permits many unique features to be implemented in special programs with a minimum of external hardware, and also permits the same PIA to be used in many applications.

Figure 7-17 shows that there are six registers within the PIA. Each PIA occupies four memory locations. Generally the 14 high-order address bits are used to select a particular PIA and the two lowest address lines (A0, A1) are used to select a particular register on the PIA.

The reader may have noticed that there are six registers, but only four addresses can be specified with A0 and A1. The addressing scheme is shown in Table 7-7. Note that on both the A and B sides the control registers have a unique address, but the data and direction registers have the same address.

The control/status register contains 6 bits that control the operation of the PIA and 2 bits that show its status (see section 7-15.1). At present we will focus only on bit 2 of the control register. This is a *steering* bit. If a memory read or write request is made at the data/direction register address (where RS1, RS0, connected to A0, A1, are 00 for the A side and 10 for the B side), bit 2 of the control register

Table 7-7 **PIA addressing**

(*a*) *Internal addressing*				
RS1	*RS0*	*CRA2*	*CRB2*	*Registers*
0	0	1	X	Data register A
0	0	0	X	Direction register A
0	1	X	X	Control/status register A
1	0	X	1	Data register B
1	0	X	0	Direction register B
1	1	X	X	Control register B

(*b*) *Memory location*	
Address	*Registers*
XXX11	B control/status (1 register)
XXX10	B data/direction (2 registers)
XXX01	A control/status (1 register)
XXX00	A data/direction (2 registers)

determines whether the data or direction register will be accessed. If bit 2 of the control register is a 1, the data register is addressed; otherwise the direction register is addressed.

EXAMPLE 7-29 A PIA's register is addressed at location 803E.

a What addresses select this PIA?

b Which register is being addressed?

Solution

a The top 14 address bits (1000 0000 0011 11) select the PIA. Any address in the range 803C to 803F selects this PIA.

b Because the two lowest address lines are 10, the B data or B direction register is being addressed. To determine which one is actually addressed, we must know what CRB-2 is. This could be found by reading CRB-2 at 803F.

7-14.5 The Direction Register

The direction register determines the direction of each bit of data being transferred on the PIA's bidirectional data lines. The direction register is 8 bits long, so there is a one-to-one correspondence between the bits of the direction register and the PA0–PA7 or PB0–PB7 lines. A 1 in any bit of the direction register causes the corresponding PA or PB line to act as an output, whereas a 0 causes it to become an input. Typically direction registers contain 00 or FF so that an entire byte is transferred in or out, but some bits of either side of a PIA can act as inputs and some as outputs, as shown in Example 7-31.

7-14.6 The Data Register

The data register contains the data being transferred in or out of the PIA. The data and direction registers have the same address, but whether a word to that address reaches the data register or the direction register depends on bit 2 of the control register.

7-14.7 Initializing the PIA

The PIA is initialized by a system RESET. When the RESET line of the PIA is taken LOW, it clears (or 0s) all registers. This sets up the PA0–PA7, PB0–PB7, CA2, and CB2 lines as inputs and disables all interrupts. Since bit 2 is also 0, the direction registers are set to be accessed. The RESET line is normally connected to the μP RESET, and therefore a RESTART program routine is automatically accessed whenever RESET is activated. The desired PIA configuration is selected during the execution of this RESTART program routine.

If the PIA needs to be reconfigured without using the RESET line, it can be done in the following sequence.

1 Clear the control/status register (including bit 2).

2 Rewrite the direction register.

3 Rewrite the control word with bit 2 SET to select the data register.

4 Write or read data.

EXAMPLE 7-30 Write a program to send the contents of locations 40 and 41 to a peripheral device. Assume the control register is at address 8009, and the direction register and data register are both at address 8008.

Note that because bit 1 of the address is 0, the A side of the PIA is being used.

Solution The steps of the solution are listed below. The coding has been omitted to save space.

1 Accumulator A is cleared and stored in 8009. This clears all the bits of the control registers; in particular, it clears bit 2.

2 Accumulator A is loaded (immediate) with FF and stored in 8008. Because bit 2 of the control/status register is now a 0, when FF is written to address 8008, it enters the direction register and causes all the data lines to act as outputs.

3 An 04 is now loaded (LDA A immediate) into the accumulator and stored in 8009. This changes bit 2 of the control register to a 1, which latches the direction register and allows the data register to be accessed.

4 The contents of location 40 are loaded into the accumulator and stored at 8008. Because bit 2 of the control/status register is now a 1, these bits go to the data register and are output on the I/O lines.

5 After the first word has been read by the peripheral, and sensed by reading the status bits (usually signaled by one of the control lines, as described later), the contents of location 41 are loaded in A and stored at 8008. This places that data on the I/O lines.

Note that once the control and direction registers have been set up, data can be sent out repeatedly without reintializing those registers.

EXAMPLE 7-31 Write a program to read the state of four switches and send the data out to a hexadecimal display.

Solution One solution is shown in the circuit of Figure 7-18 where the four switches are connected to lines PA0 through PA3, and the display inputs are connected to peripheral lines PA4 to PA7. The program for the solution proceeds.

1 During initialization, F0 is written into the direction register. This configures the four LSBs as inputs and the four MSBs as outputs.
2 The control register is then rewritten to make bit 2 a 1. The instruction LOAD A (from) 8008 reads the switch contents into the four LSBs of the accumulator.
3 Four LEFT SHIFT instructions shift the switch settings into the MSBs of the accumulator.
4 Now a STORE A at 8008 places the switch settings on the output lines (PA4–PA7) where they can drive the display.

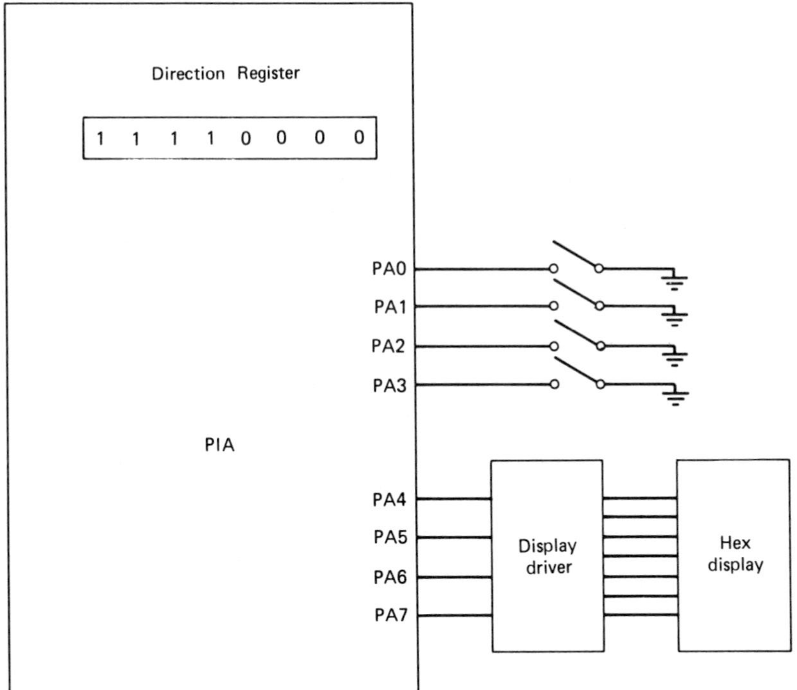

Figure 7-18 The PIA and its connections for Example 9-3. (From Greenfield and Wray, *Using Microprocessors and Microcomputers: The 6800 Family*, Wiley, 1981.)

7-15 HANDSHAKING WITH THE PIA

When an external device has information for the μC, it must send the PIA a signal (often called DATA READY). When the byte is read by the PIA, it typically acknowledges receipt of the information by sending an ACK (for acknowledge) signal to the device. A similar situation exists when the PIA is transmitting information to the device. The protocol and signals that control the exchange of information is called *handshaking*.

Previously we concentrated on the data lines and ignored the CA1 and CA2 (or CB1 and CB2) lines, which control the interchange of information. The operating mode of these control lines is determined by the bits in the A and B control/status registers. The control lines, in turn, affect the contents of bits 6 and 7 of the control/status registers as will be explained.

The configuration of the control/status register is shown in Table 7-8. The upper register (CRA) is for the A side of the PIA, and the lower one (CRB) is an identical register used to control the B side. The function of bit 2 (direction register access) has already been described. Status bits 6 and 7 are set by the transitions of the CA1 and CA2 (CB1–CB2) lines. The rest of the bits in the control/status register are used to select the functions of the control lines. Bits 6 and 7 cannot be changed by writing to them from the μP bus but are reset indirectly by a READ data or WRITE data operation, as explained later.

7-15.1 Control Lines CA1 and CB1

Control lines CA1 and CB1 are input only lines that function identically. As shown in Table 7-8, they are controlled by bits 0 and 1 of the control/status register, and their action can be determined from Table 7-9. Table 7-9 shows the following.

1 If CRA1 (CRB1) is a 0, status bit 7 of the control/status register is set HIGH whenever there is a negative *transition* (↓) on the CA1 (CB1) line. These lines are typically connected to an external device that causes a transition whenever it requires attention. If CRA1 (CRB1) is a 1, a positive *transition* (↑) on CA1 (CB1) sets status bit 7 of the corresponding control/status register.

2 If CRA0 of the control/status register is a 0, the interrupt line IRQA is disabled

Table 7-8 **PIA control word format**

	7	6	5	4	3	2	1	0
CRA	IRQA1	IRQA2	CA2 Control			DDRA Access	CA1 Control	

	7	6	5	4	3	2	1	0
CRB	IRQB1	IRQB2	CB2 Control			DDRB Access	CB1 Control	

***Table** 7-9* **Control of interrupt inputs CA1 and CB1**

CRA-1 (CRB-1)	*CRA-0 (CRB-0)*	*Interrupt input CA1 (CB1)*	*Interrupt flag CRA-7 (CRB-7)*	*MPU interrupt request $\overline{IRQA}$ ($\overline{IRQB}$)*
0	0	↓ Active	Set HIGH on ↓ of CA1 (CB1)	Disabled — $\overline{IRQ}$ remains HIGH
0	1	↓ Active	Set HIGH on ↓ of CA1 (CB1)	Goes LOW when the interrupt flag bit CRA-7 (CRB-7) goes HIGH
1	0	↑ Active	Set HIGH on ↑ of CA1 (CB1)	Disabled — $\overline{IRQ}$ remains HIGH
1	1	↑ Active	Set HIGH on ↑ of CA1 (CB1)	Goes LOW when the interrupt flag bit CRA-7 (CRB-7) goes HIGH

Notes: 1 ↑ indicates positive transition (LOW to HIGH).
2 ↓ indicates negative transition (HIGH to LOW).
3 The interrupt flag bit CRA-7 is cleared by an MPU read of the A data register, and CRB-7 is cleared by an MPU read of the B data register.
4 If CRA-0 (CRB-0) is LOW when an interrupt occurs (interrupt disabled) and is later brought HIGH, $\overline{IRQA}$ ($\overline{IRQB}$) occurs after CRA-0 (CRB-0) is written to a 1.

and IRQA remains HIGH, even when status bit 7 goes HIGH as a result of the CA1 line transitions. If CRA0 is a 1, the IRQA line goes LOW when bit 7 goes HIGH and interrupts the μP, provided that IRQA is connected to the μP IRQ line, and the interrupt is not masked in the μP.

EXAMPLE 7-32 What happens if 06 is written into control/status register A?

Solution A control word of 06 results in the conditions specified on line 3 of Table 7-9. Bit 7 is set by a positive transition of the CA1 line. IRQA is disabled. The Direction Register is unaffected because bit 2 is also set. If 06 is written to the Control/Status Register and read back before a positive transition on CA1 occurs, the μP reads it back as 06, but if a transition occurs between the writing and reading, the μP reads it back as an 86, because CRA7 is now set.

As stated in note 3 to Table 7-9, once bit 7 of the control register is set, it can only be *cleared* by *reading the corresponding data register*. Some readers have difficulty with the idea that to clear a bit in one register, *another* register at a *different address* must be read, but when the bit in the control register is set, it indicates that data from the peripheral is available. Reading the data register brings the data from the peripheral into the μP and resets bit 7, so the peripheral can set it again when it has another byte to transmit.

Often in a program the μP constantly monitors the PIA for input (similar to an INPUT statement in Basic). This is called *polling* and effectively halts the μP until an input byte is received.

EXAMPLE 7-33 Write a program to monitor constantly the CA1 line and to take action when a transition occurs. Assume the control/status register's address is 8009 (hex).

Solution First the control/status register must be initialized to select the proper transition (↓ or ↑) and disable interrupts. Then the program can proceed as shown in Table 7-10.

Table 7-10 **Program for Example 7-33**

Address	*Data*	*Mnemonic*	*Comment*
1000	B6 8009	LDA A $8009	Get status.
1003	2A FB	BPL *-3	If plus, branch back to 1000 and repeat.
1005	B6 8008	LDA A $8008	Get data.
Etc.	.. ..	... .	

The instruction at location 1000 loads the contents of the status register into the A accumulator and it is tested by the following instruction (at 1003), to see if bit 7 (the interrupt flag bit) is set. If not, the contents are positive and the instruction branches back to 1000 and fetches the status again. It continues to loop in this fashion until bit 7 goes HIGH. Since the resulting byte is then negative, the program falls through to the following instruction. The PIAs data register at 8008 is then read to reset CRA7 and get the data.

Note that this is a very tight loop; that is, the computer did nothing but monitor the PIA. If the PIA's interrupt line for the A side (IRQA), is connected to the μPs IRQ and the interrupt is enabled by a proper control word, the μP can be running a main program and doing useful work while waiting for this interrupt.

EXAMPLE 7-34 A PIA is located at 8004–8007. A debounced switch is connected to CA1 and the outputs PA0–PA6 drive a seven-segment display, as shown in Figure 7-19. Write a program to increment the number in the seven-segment display every time the switch is thrown. When the number reaches 9 the display must return to 0 after the next switch throw.

Solution The program is shown in Table 7-11. It starts by initializing the A port for outputs. It then monitors control/status register A. A switch throw causes a transition on CA1 and causes CRA7 to go HIGH. When this occurs, the program falls through to location 35 where it:

1 reads the A data register to reset CRA7;

2 increments X and resets it to 0 if X has gone beyond 9;

3 jumps to a table to get the proper codes to drive the seven-segment display.

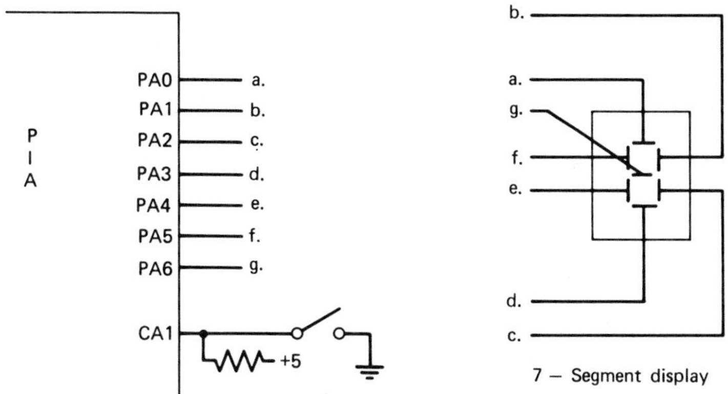

Figure 7-19 Control of a seven-segment display using the PIA. (From Greenfield and Wray, *Using Microprocessors and Microcomputers: The 6800 Family*, Wiley, 1981.)

Table 7-11 **Program and data table for Example 7-34**

a. Program

Address	*Code*		*Mnemonic*	*Comments*
20	CE 0000		LDX #0	Clear X
23	7F 8005		CLR $8005	CLR bit 2 to SELECT DIR REG
26	86 FF		LDA A #$FF	SET TO ALL 1s
28	B7 8004		STA A $8004	SET DIRECTION FOR OUTPUTS
2B	86 04		LDA A #$4	GET WORD FOR NEG GOING CA1 &
2D	B7 8005		STA A $8005	SET CRA2 TO SELECT DATA REG
30	B6 8005	LOOP	LDA A $8005	GET STATUS
33	2A FB		BPL LOOP	WAIT FOR CRA7 TO BECOME 1
35	B6 8004		LDA A $8004	CLEAR BIT 7
38	08		INX	INCREMENT X
39	8C 000A		CPX #$A	IS IT > 9 ?
3C	26 03		BNE *+5	NO- SKIP NEXT INSTRUCTION
3E	CE 0000		LDX #0	YES-CLEAR X
41	A6 A0		LDA A $A0,X	GET THE 7-SEGMENT CODE
43	B7 8004		STA A $8004	OUTPUT IT TO DISPLAY
46	20 E8		BRA LOOP	RTN TO 30 AGAIN

b. Data table

Location	*Contents*	*Decimal number to be displayed*
A0	3F	0
A1	06	1
A2	5B	2
A3	4F	3
A4	66	4
A5	6D	5
A6	7D	6
A7	07	7
A8	7F	8
A9	6F	9

In this program the table starts at location A0. To show a 0 on the display, the data must cause all segments except g to light. The code in A0 must therefore be 3F. If A1 is accessed, a 1 should appear by lighting segments B and C, so that A1 should contain 06. (Figure 7-19 shows the segments with their PIA interconnections.)

Many μP kits such as the **MEK-6800-D2** drive their displays directly by using similar tables. Note that this program provides a way for the μP to count and display external events as they occur.

7-15.2 Control Lines CA2 and CB2

Lines CA2 and CB2 can be used either as input or output control lines, and are controlled by bits 3, 4, and 5 of the control/status register. If bit 5 of the control/status register is a 0, the lines function as interrupt inputs as shown in Table 7-12. Table 7-12 reveals that these lines function exactly as CA1 and CB1 do except that transitions caused by the external devices set bit 6 instead of bit 7 of the control/status register.

EXAMPLE 7-35 Assume a tape drive is connected to a **6800** system and it must send the **6800** either data or status information on the same I/O lines. The data would be the words read from the tape, and the status information tells the system what the tape is doing (e.g., running forward, rewinding, at end-of-tape). How can the system distinguish between data and status information?

Solution One solution is to connect both CA1 and CA2 to the tape drive. If the tape drive is sending data, it raises CA1 every time it has a byte to send, while if it is sending status information, it raises CA2. The μP system can distinguish between status and data requests by examining bits 6 and 7 of the PIAs control/status register.

7-15.3 Use of CB2 as an Output in the Handshake Mode

The action of the CB2 line as an *output* is described in Table 7-13. Note that the CB2 line goes LOW after a WRITE to the data register. This simplifies the programming and therefore makes it preferable for the B section of the PIA to be used to send data to external devices (output).

The top line of Table 7-13 illustrates a mode of operation commonly called the handshaking mode. This case is illustrated in Figure 7-20 and the sequence of events is as follows:

1 The control word to the B side is written as shown. Note that CRB 5, 4, and 3 are 100, respectively.

2 When the system must send data out it writes the data to data register B. This causes CB2 to go LOW.

3 The peripheral device acknowledges receipt of the data by placing an acknowledge pulse on CB1. The negative transition of this pulse causes CB2 to return HIGH and raises the CRB7 flag.

Table 7-12 **Control of CA2 and CB2 as interrupt inputs. CRA5 (CRB5) is LOW**

CRA-5 (CRB-5)	*CRA-4 (CRB-4)*	*CRA-3 (CRB-3)*	*Interrupt input CA2 (CB2)*	*Interrupt flag CRA-6 (CRB-6)*	*MPU interrupt request $\overline{IRAQ}$ ($\overline{IRQB}$)*
0	0	0	↓ Active	Set HIGH on ↓ of CA2 (CB2)	Disabled—$\overline{\text{IRQ}}$ remains HIGH
0	0	1	↓ Active	Set HIGH on ↓ of CA2 (CB2)	Goes LOW when the interrupt flag bit CRA-6 (CRB-6) goes HIGH
0	1	0	↑ Active	Set HIGH on ↑ of CA2 (CB2)	Disabled—$\overline{\text{IRQ}}$ remains HIGH
0	1	1	↑ Active	Set HIGH on ↑ of CA2 (CB2)	Goes LOW when the interrupt flag bit CRA-6 (CRB-6) goes HIGH

Notes:
1 ↑ indicates positive transitive (LOW to HIGH).
2 ↓ indicates negative transition (HIGH to LOW).
3 The interrupt flag bit CRA-6 is cleared by an MPU read of the A data register and CRB-6 is cleared by an MPU read of the B data register.
4 If CRA-3 (CRB-3) is LOW when an interrupt occurs (interrupt disabled) and is later brought HIGH, $\overline{\text{IRQA}}$ ($\overline{\text{IRQB}}$) occurs after CRA-3 (CRB-3) is written to a 1.

Table 7-13 **Control of CB2 as an output. CRB5 is HIGH**

CRB-5	*CRB-4*	*CRB-3*	*CB2* Cleared	*CB2* Set
1	0	0	LOW on the positive transition of the first E pulse following an MPU WRITE B data register operation	HIGH when the interrupt flag bit CRB-7 is set by an active transition of the CB1 signal
1	0	1	LOW on the positive transition of the first E pulse after an MPU WRITE B data register operation	HIGH on the positive edge of the first E pulse following an E pulse which occurred while the part was deselected
1	1	0	LOW when CRB-3 goes LOW as a result of an MPU write in control register B	Always LOW as long as CRB-3 is LOW. Will go HIGH on an MPU WRITE in control register B that changes CRB-3 to 1.
1	1	1	Always HIGH as long as CRB-3 is HIGH. Will be cleared when an MPU write control register B results in clearing CRB-3 to 0.	HIGH when CRB-3 goes high as a result of an MPU WRITE into control register B

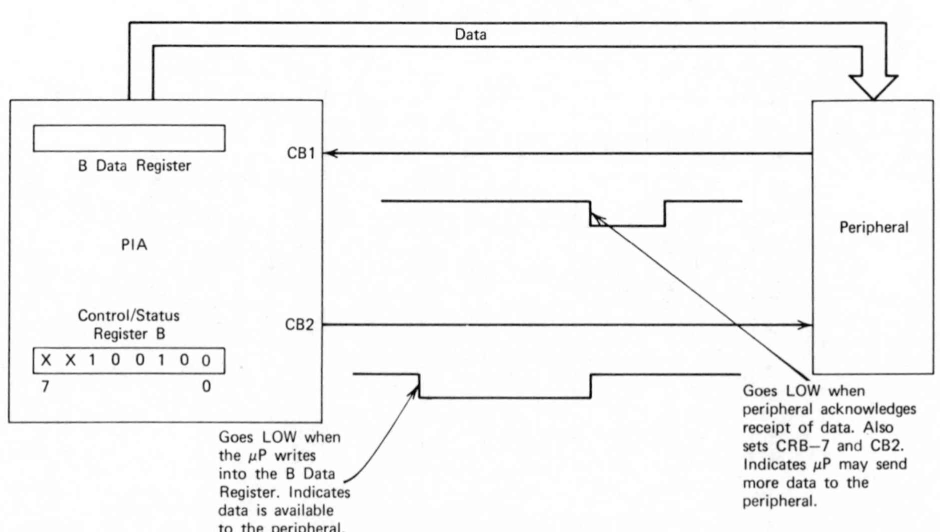

Figure 7-20 Handshaking with the B side of the PIA. (From Greenfield and Wray, *Using Microprocessors and Microcomputers: The 6800 Family*, Wiley, 1981.)

4 The **6800** system responds to a HIGH on CRB7 as an indication that the data has been accepted by the peripheral, and the next byte can be written to the PIA.

5 Before the next output byte can be written to the PIA, data register B must be read to reset CRB7.

EXAMPLE 7-36 The data between memory locations 1000 and 104F must be sent to a peripheral using the system of Figure 7-20. Draw a flowchart to show how this is accomplished.

Solution The solution is shown in Figure 7-21 and proceeds in the following way.

1 The control/status register is set to 00 (or the PIA is reset).

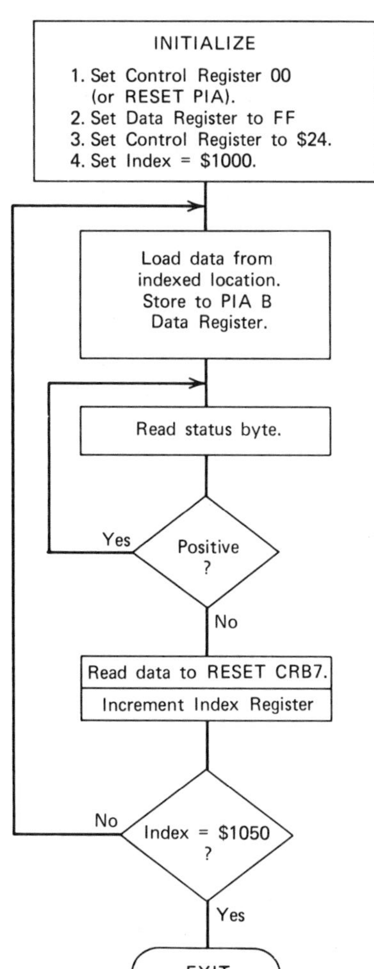

Figure 7-21 Flowchart for Example 7-36. (From Greenfield and Wray, *Using Microprocessors and Microcomputers: The 6800 Family*, Wiley, 1981.)

2 Direction register B is initialized to FF (all bits to be outputs) and then the control/status register is set to 24 (hex) to initialize the handshaking procedure described above.

3 The index register is set equal to 1000 and the first memory word to be transmitted is loaded from that location into the accumulator and stored in data register B. This causes CB2 to go LOW.

4 The program goes into a loop until the peripheral accepts the data and causes a negative transition (↓) on CB1. This SETS CRB7 and CB2. Before the transition, the result is positive (MSB = 0) and the program continues to loop. After the transition the result is negative and the program exits from the loop.

5 The program reads the B data register to reset CRB7. It then tests to determine if it has exhausted its data area by comparing the index register with 1050, each time after it has been incremented. If it has, it stops; if it has not, it loads the next data word causing CB2 to go LOW again and repeats the above steps.

7-15.4 Use of CB2 in the Pulse Mode

If a peripheral device is connected to a PIA as shown in Figure 7-22 and bits 5, 4, and 3 of the control/status register are 101 as also shown, the CB2 line will be pulsed LOW as data is written into the B data register. The pulse width is one clock cycle. This line can be used to inform the peripheral that new data is available on the PIA output lines. If the peripheral can accept the data without fail, in the few microseconds it takes before the program can output the next byte, there is no need for an acknowledgment. The pulse mode of the PIA is outstanding for its simplicity of programming. Every WRITE into the B data register causes CB2 to be pulsed. This mode is capable of very fast operation and is best used for high speed peripherals like a floppy disk system.

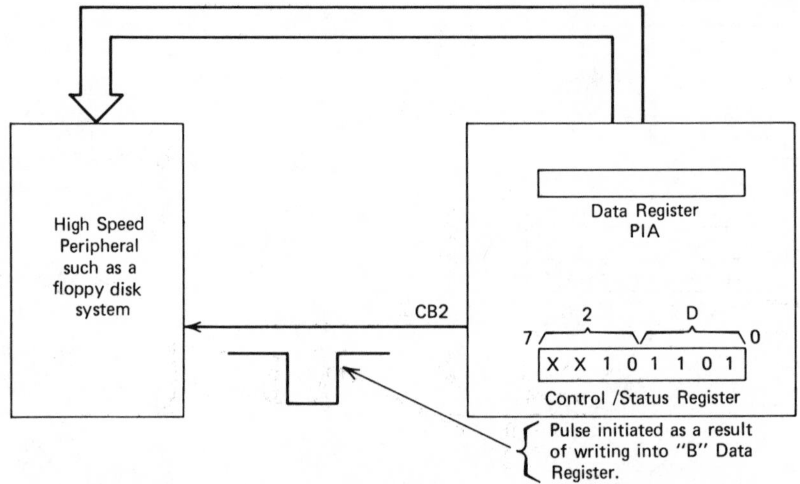

Figure 7-22 Pulse mode of the PIA used with B side. (From Greenfield and Wray, *Using Microprocessors and Microcomputers: The 6800 Family*, Wiley, 1981.)

EXAMPLE 7-37 Show how the pulse mode can be used on the B side to output data to a high speed device like a floppy disk system. Give an example of a program. Assume the base address of the PIA is 8004, and the PIA has been initialized with a control word of 2D.

Solution Refer once more to Figure 7-22 and to the program shown in Table 7-14. Again, this pulse mode assumes that data can be accepted as fast as it is put out by the program. The CB2 line can be used to strobe a data latch, or to increment an address counter so that the data can be stored in memory in the peripheral, for example. The program shown in Table 7-14 is written to reside at 1000 and assumes that the data to be transmitted is in memory at 2000 to 20FF (256 bytes).

Table 7-14 **Program for Example 7-37**

Address	*Data*	*Label*	*Mnemonics*	*Comments*
1000	CE 2000		LDX #$2000	Get pointer to data.
1003	A6 00	LOOP	LDA A 0,X	Get data.
1005	B7 8006		STA A $8006	Store to B data register.
1008	08		INX	Increment pointer.
1009	8C 2100		CPX #$2100	End of data?
100C	26 F5		BNE LOOP	No. Get next byte.
100E	.. ..		etc.	

The first instruction sets the index register to the starting address of the data. The instruction at 1003 loads the A accumulator from the location specified by the index register. This byte is then stored in the PIA data register (or output), which informs the peripheral by pulsing the CB2 line. The program then increments the index register to the address of the next byte. The compare index (immediate) instruction is used to determine if all of the data has been sent out. This is done by the instruction at location 1009 to see if the index register has gone past the end address of the data and, if not, looping back for the next byte.

7-15.5 ON-OFF Control of CB2

The last two lines of Table 7-13 specify a mode of operation in which the level of CB2 can be directly programmed. If CRB5 and CRB4 are both 1s, the CB2 line assumes the same level as CRB3. This allows the program to control the length of time CB2 is LOW or HIGH, or allows CB2 to function as an additional output.

7-15.6 Control of CA2 as an Output (Handshaking Mode)

CA2 can be used as an output line to regulate the flow of data from the peripheral to the PIA in the same way that CB2 does (see Example 7-36), except that the CA2 line is taken LOW on the negative transition of E instead of on the positive, and after a READ of the A data register, instead of a WRITE of B (See Table 7-15). Use of CA2 is therefore to be preferred when data input is involved.

Table 7-15 **Control of CA2 as an output. CRA-5 is HIGH.**

CRA-5	*CRA-4*	*CRA-3*	*CA2* Cleared	*CA2* Set
1	0	0	LOW on negative transition of E after an MPU READ A data operation	HIGH when the interrupt flag bit CRA-7 is set by an active transition of the CA1 signal
1	0	1	LOW on negative transition of E after an MPU READ A data operation	HIGH on the negative edge of the first E pulse which occurs during a deselect
1	1	0	LOW when CRA-3 goes LOW as a result of an MPU WRITE to control register A	Always LOW as long as CRA-3 is LOW. Will go HIGH on an MPU WRITE to control register A that changes CRA-3 to 1.
1	1	1	Always HIGH as long as CRA-3 is HIGH. Will be cleared on an MPU WRITE to control register A that clears CRA-3 to a 0.	HIGH when CRA-3 goes HIGH as a result of an MPU WRITE to control register A

EXAMPLE 7-38 A **6800** system must read several words from a disk. To do so, it must first send the disk controller several bytes of information that tell it, for example, the disk address and the number of words to be read. Describe how the transfer can be accomplished.

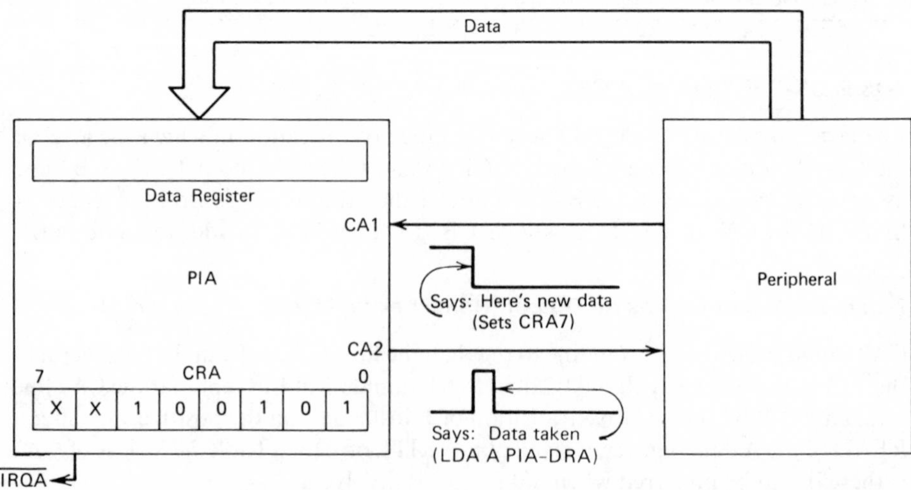

Figure 7-23 Handshaking with a peripheral on the A side. (From Greenfield and Wray, *Using Microprocessors and Microcomputers: The 6800 Family*, Wiley, 1981.)

Solution

1 The direction register (B side) is set up for output (FF), and the A side direction register is set for input (00).

2 The **6800** sends commands to the disk controller via the data lines PB0 through PB7, using the handshaking procedure discussed in section 7-15.3. CB2 controls the flow of commands as shown in Figure 7-20.

3 When the first word is ready, the controller causes a transition on CA1, which SETS CRA7 and CA2 (see Figure 7-23).

4 The **6800** system now reads the first word from the **PIA** and places it in memory. This resets CA2, which requests new data from the disk. The read also resets CRA-7.

5 This procedure continues until the required number of bytes have been transferred from the disk to the μC's memory.

7-15.7 Pulse Mode for CA2

If CRA5, 4, and 3 are 101, respectively, the A side of the PIA operates in a pulse mode identical to that described for the B side, but it is triggered by a READ instead of a WRITE data operation.

7-15.8 ON-OFF Mode for CA2

When CRA5 and CRA6 are both 1s, the state of CA2 will be the same as that of bit CRA3 and, therefore, CA2 can be set HIGH or LOW as desired. This gives the program total control of CA2.

7-16 REFERENCES

Ron Bishop, *Basic Microprocessors and the 6800*, Hayden, Rochelle Park, N.J., 1979.

Andrew C. Staugaard, Jr., *How to Program and Interface the 6800*, Howard W. Sams & Co., Indianapolis, Ind., 1980.

Lance A. Leventhal, *Microcomputer Experimentation with the Motorola MEK 6800D2*, Prentice-Hall, Englewood Cliffs, N.J., 1981.

Joseph D. Greenfield and William C. Wray, *Using Microprocessors and Microcomputers: The 6800 Family*, Wiley, New York, 1981.

Lance A. Leventhal, *6800 Assembly Language Programming*, Osborne & Associates, Inc., Berkeley, Calif., 1978.

CHAPTER 8

The MC6809

Tim Ahrens
Motorola
Austin, Texas

8-1 ARCHITECTURE OF THE MC6809

The **M6809** (both the **MC6809** or **MC6809E**) was designed by both software and hardware experts, with ease of programming and system design kept in mind. Although many features of the **M6800** were retained, many improvements were made to allow the **M6809** to be the most efficient 8-bit μP. The architecture remained basically identical to the **M6800**, although enhancements such as additional registers (a Y index register, a U stack pointer, and a direct page register) and new instructions (such as MUL) simplify software designs. The original addressing modes were kept, but several improved modes were also added.

The **M6800** was Motorola's initial entrance into the μP marketplace. Experience gained using the **M6800** showed that many features could be added to improve the μP. Inputs from both previous users and the new designers were taken into account in the design of the **M6809**. These inputs (PUSH X, PULL X, better access time, etc.) were incorporated, and the new **M6809** exhibits all of these features, and much more.

The register set of the **M6809**, quite expanded over that of the **M6800**, is shown in Figure 8-1.

8-1.1 Accumulators

As seen in Figure 8-1, the two accumulator registers (A and B) are general-purpose 8-bit registers that may be used for arithmetic calculations and data manipulations. To allow for certain 16-bit operations, the two registers are concatenated to form a single 16-bit-wide D register. The A accumulator forms the most significant byte.

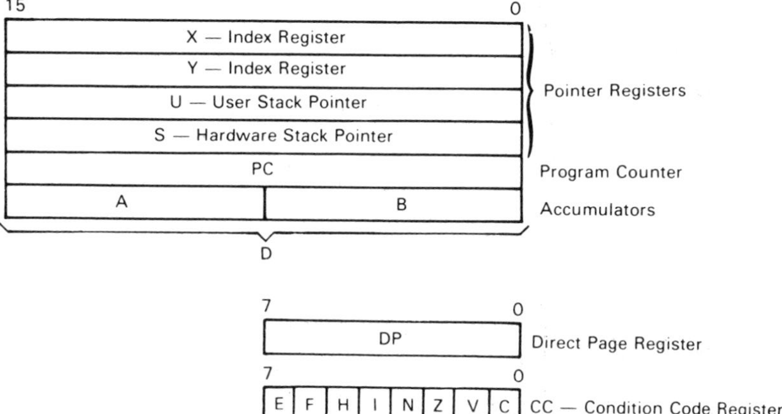

Figure 8-1 Programming model of the **MC6809** μP. (From the *MC6809-MC6809E Microprocessor Programming Manual*, Motorola, Inc., Austin, TX, 1981. Reprinted courtesy of Motorola, Inc.)

8-1.2 Index Registers

The **M6809** contains two index registers referred to as X and Y. These registers are used during the indexed addressing modes. The address information in an index register is used in the calculation of an effective address. This address may be used to point directly to data, or may be modified by an optional constant or register offset to produce the effective address. The second index register allows the programmer more flexibility than had been previously available.

8-1.3 Stack Pointers (S, U)

There are two stack pointers available to the programmer in the **M6809**. They are a hardware stack pointer (S), which is used automatically by the processor during subroutine calls and interrupts, and a user stack pointer (U) which is controlled totally by the programmer. It is used to temporarily store register contents and other data using PSHU and PULU instructions. Both stack pointers may be used by the programmer and always point to the top of the stack (the highest vacant location).

Both of these registers have the same indexed addressing mode capabilities as the index registers, and also support the PUSH and PULL instructions. All four indexable registers (X, Y, S, U) may be referred to as *pointer registers*.

8-1.4 Direct Page Register (DP)

The DP register contains the most significant byte of the address to be used in the *direct addressing mode*. The contents of this register are concatenated with the byte following the direct addressing mode Op code to form the 16-bit effective address.

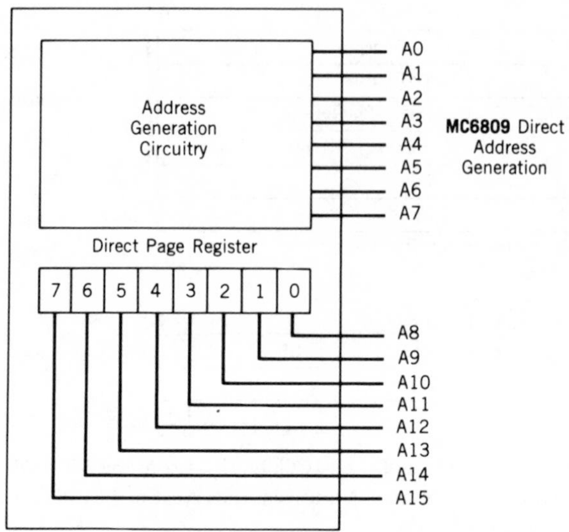

Figure 8-2 Direct page register. (From the *MC6809-MC6809E Microprocessor Programming Manual*, Motorola, Inc., Austin, TX, 1981. Reprinted courtesy of Motorola, Inc.)

Use of this register allows direct addressing on any "page" within the entire **M6809** memory map. The direct page register contents appear as bits A15 through A8 of the address, as shown in Figure 8-2.

During RESET, this register is automatically cleared to allow **M6800** compatibility.

EXAMPLE 8-1 If the DP register contains \$3C, where does the instruction LDA A \$21 get its data?

Solution The direct address is the concatenation of the DP register and the instruction address. This instruction causes the data to be fetched from location \$3C21.

8-1.5 Condition Code Register (CC)

The condition code register contains the condition codes and the interrupt masks as shown in Figure 8-3.

Condition Code Bits Five bits in the condition code register are used to indicate the results of instructions that manipulate data. They are: half-carry (H), negative (N), zero (Z), overflow (V), and carry (C).

Half-Carry (H), Bit 5. This bit is used to indicate that a carry was generated from bit 3 in the arithmetic-logic unit as a result of an 8-bit addition. This bit is undefined in all subtractlike instructions. The decimal addition adjust (DAA)

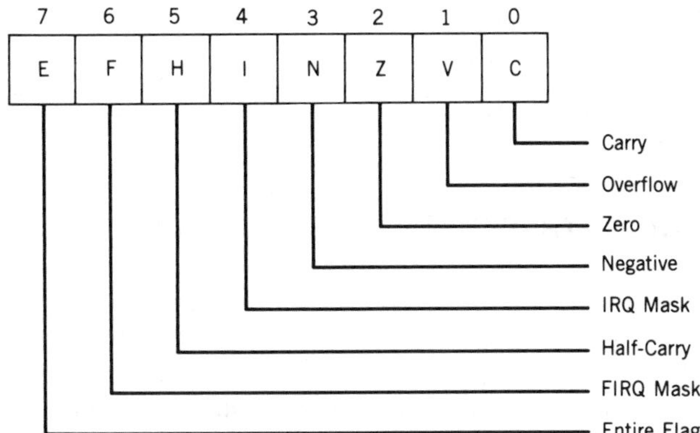

Figure 8-3 Condition code register. (From the *MC6809-MC6809E Microprocessor Programming Manual*, Motorola, Inc., Austin, TX, 1981. Reprinted courtesy of Motorola, Inc.)

instruction uses the state of this bit to perform the adjust operation for BCD arithmetic.

Negative (N), Bit 3. This bit contains the value of the most significant bit of the result of the previous data operation.

Zero (Z), Bit 2. This bit is used to indicate that the result of the previous operation was zero.

Overflow (V), Bit 1. This bit is used to indicate that the previous operation caused a signed arithmetic overflow.

Carry (C), Bit 0. This bit is used to indicate that a carry or a borrow was generated from bit 7 in the arithmetic-logic unit as a result of an 8-bit mathematical operation.

Interrupt Bits

Fast Interrupt Request (F), Bit 6. This bit is used to mask (disable) any interrupt on the FIRQ line. This bit is automatically set by a hardware RESET, or after recognition of another interrupt. Execution of certain instructions such as SWI will also inhibit recognition of a FIRQ input. A description of FIRQ is given in section 8-10.12.

Interrupt Request (I), Bit 4. This bit is used to mask (disable) any interrupt on the IRQ line. This bit is automatically set by a hardware reset, or after recognition of another interrupt. Execution of certain instructions such as SWI will also inhibit recognition of an IRQ input.

Entire Flag (E), Bit 7. This bit is used to indicate how many registers were stacked. When set, all of the registers were stacked during the last interrupt stacking operation. When clear, only the program counter and condition code registers were stacked during the last interrupt. The state of the E bit in the STACKED condition code register is used by the return from interrupt (RTI) instruction to determine how many registers need to be pulled from the stack.

8-1.6 Program Counter (PC)

The program counter is used by the processor to store the address of the next instruction to be executed. It may also be used as an index register in certain addressing modes.

8-2 MODES OF INSTRUCTION EXECUTION (ADDRESSING MODES)

One major attribute of a microprocessor is how efficiently code can be generated. The only way to do this is to have a set of addressing modes that lend themselves to easy code generation. The **M6809** has the most complete set of addressing modes available on any microprocessor today. For example, the **M6809** has 59 basic instructions; however, it recognizes 1464 different variations of instructions and addressing modes. These addressing modes were designed to support modern programming techniques such as position independence, modular programming, and reentrancy/recursion.

The addressing modes available on the **M6809** are listed below:

Inherent
Immediate
Extended
  Extended indirect
Direct
Register
Indexed
  Zero-offset
  Constant-offset
  Accumulator-offset
  Auto increment/decrement
  Indexed indirect
Relative
  Short/long relative branching
  Program counter/relative

Many instructions are followed by a *postbyte*, which is a byte immediately following the Op code byte and further defines the instruction. The instructions and modes that take a postbyte include:

Indexed instructions
Exchanges
Pushes
Pulls
Indirect instructions

The configuration of the postbyte will be defined when the instructions that use them are discussed.

Table 8-1 which begins on page 340, is a tabular presentation of the **MC6809** instructions.

The following paragraphs describe the instruction modes and give examples of their use.

8-2.1 Inherent

In this addressing mode, the Op code of the instruction contains all of the information necessary. Examples of inherent addressing are: ABX, DAA, SWI, ASRA, and CLRB. Inherent instructions do not require a second memory reference.

8-2.2 Immediate Addressing

In immediate addressing, the effective address of the data is the location immediately following the Op code (i.e., the data to be used in the instruction immediately follows the Op code of the instruction). The **M6809** uses both 8- and 16-bit immediate values, depending on the size of argument specified by the Op code. Examples of instructions with immediate addressing are:

```
LDA #$20      (1 byte)
LDX #$F000    (2 bytes)
LDY #CAT      (CAT is a 2-byte number)
```

Note: # signifies immediate addressing, $ signifies hexidecimal value.

8-2.3 Extended Addressing

In extended addressing, the contents of the two bytes immediately following the Op code fully specify the 16-bit effective address used by the instruction. Note that the address generated by an extended instruction defines an *absolute address* and is *not position independent*. Examples of extended addressing include:

```
LDA CAT
STX MOUSE
LDD $2000
```

EXAMPLE 8-2 What does LDD $2000 mean?

Solution LDD $2000 is an extended instruction that must load 16 bits into the double register. Therefore it LOADs the contents of $2000 into A and the contents of $2001 into B.

8-2.4 Extended Indirect

As a special case of indexed addressing (discussed below), one level of indirection may be added to extended addressing. In extended indirect, the two bytes following the postbyte of an indexed instruction contain the address of the data.

```
LDA [CAT]
LDX [$FFFE]
STU [DOG]
```

The postbyte for these instructions is discussed in section 8-3.

8-2.5 Direct Addressing

Direct addressing is similar to extended addressing except that only 1 byte of address follows the Op code. This byte specifies the lower 8 bits of the address to be used. The upper 8 bits of the address are supplied by the direct page register. Since only 1 byte of address is required in direct addressing, this mode requires less memory and executes faster than extended addressing. Of course, only 256 locations (one page) may be accessed without redefining the contents of the DP register. Indirection is not allowed in direct addressing. Some examples of direct addressing are:

```
LDA $30
SETDP $10   (assembler directive)
LDD <CAT
```

Note: < is an assembler directive that forces direct addressing.

EXAMPLE 8-3 A portion of a program is to run starting at location $1C00. How can it be made to execute faster?

Solution The program can be simplified and will execute faster if the direct page register is first loaded with $1C. Then many memory references in this area can be made using the direct addressing mode, rather than extended. Not only does this speed up the execution of the program, but it will also save many bytes of code.

8-2.6 Register Addressing

Register addressing instructions allow the transfer of data between registers or between a register and the stack. Some examples of register addressing are:

`TFR X,Y`	Transfers X into Y	
`EXG A,B`	Exchanges A with B	
`PSHS A,B,X,Y`	Push Y, X, B, and A onto S	(the program stack)
`PULU X,Y,D`	Pull D, X, and Y from U	(the user stack)

These instructions take a postbyte and are discussed in section 8-4.3.

8-3 INDEXED ADDRESSING

In all indexed addressing, one of the pointer registers (X, Y, U, S, and sometimes PC) is used in a calculation of the effective address of the operand to be used by the instruction. Five basic types of indexing are available and are discussed below. The postbyte of an indexed instruction specifies the basic type and variation of the addressing mode as well as the pointer register to be used. Figure 8-4 lists the legal formats for the postbyte. Table 8-2 gives the assembler form and the number of cycles and bytes added to the basic values for indexed addressing for each variation.

***Table 8-2* Indexed addressing mode**

Type	Forms	Nonindirect: Assembler form	Nonindirect: Postbyte Op code	$\overset{+}{\sim}$	$\overset{+}{\#}$	Indirect: Assembler form	Indirect: Postbyte Op code	$\overset{+}{\sim}$	$\overset{+}{\#}$
Constant offset from R	No offset	,R	1RR00100	0	0	[,R]	1RR10100	3	0
(2s complement offsets)	5-bit offset	n, R	0RRnnnnn	1	0	Defaults to 8-bit			
	8-bit offset	n, R	1RR01000	1	1	[n, R]	1RR11000	4	1
	16-bit offset	n, R	1RR01001	4	2	[n, R]	1RR11001	7	2
Accumulator offset from R	A register offset	A, R	1RR00110	1	0	[A, R]	1RR10110	4	0
(2s complement offsets)	B register offset	B, R	1RR00101	1	0	[B, R]	1RR10101	4	0
	D register offset	D, R	1RR01011	4	0	[D, R]	1RR11011	7	0
Auto increment/decrement R	Increment by 1	,R +	1RR00000	2	0	Not allowed			
	Increment by 2	,R + +	1RR00001	3	0	[,R + +]	1RR10001	6	0
	Decrement by 1	,− R	1RR00010	2	0	Not allowed			
	Decrement by 2	,− − R	1RR00011	3	0	[,− − R]	1RR10011	6	0
Constant offset from PC	8-bit offset	n, PCR	1xx01100	1	1	[n, PCR]	1xx11100	4	1
(2s complement offsets)	16-bit offset	n, PCR	1xx01101	5	2	[n, PCR]	1xx11101	8	2
Extended indirect	16-bit address	—	—	—	—	[n]	10011111	5	2

R = X, Y, U or S
x = Don't care

RR:
00 = X
01 = Y
10 = U
11 = S

$\overset{+}{\sim}$ and $\overset{+}{\#}$ indicate the number of additional cycles and bytes for the particular variation.

Post byte register bit								*Index addressing mode*
7	*6*	*5*	*4*	*3*	*2*	*1*	*0*	
0	R	R	d	d	d	d	d	EA = R + 5-bit offset
1	R	R	0	0	0	0	0	,R +
1	R	R	i	0	0	0	1	,R + +
1	R	R	0	0	0	1	0	,– R
1	R	R	i	0	0	1	1	,– – R
1	R	R	i	0	1	0	0	EA = ,R + 0 offset
1	R	R	i	0	1	0	1	EA = ,R + ACCB offset
1	R	R	i	0	1	1	0	EA = ,R + ACCA offset
1	R	R	i	1	0	0	0	EA = ,R + 8-bit offset
1	R	R	i	1	0	0	1	EA = ,R + 16-bit offset
1	R	R	i	1	0	1	1	EA = ,R + D offset
1	x	x	i	1	1	0	0	EA = ,PC + 8-bit offset
1	x	x	i	1	1	0	1	EA = ,PC + 16-bit offset
1	R	R	i	1	1	1	1	EA = [,Address]

Addressing mode field (bits 3–0)

Indirect field (bit 4)
(sign bit when $b_7 = 0$)

Register field: RR (bits 6–5)
00 = X
01 = Y
10 = U
11 = S

x = Don't care
d = Offset bit
i = 0 = Not indirect
1 = Indirect

Figure 8-4 Indexed addressing postbyte register bit assignments.

8-3.1 Zero-Offset Indexed

In this mode, the selected pointer register contains the effective address of the data to be used by the instruction. This is the fastest indexing mode. The postbyte for this mode is on line 6 of Figure 8-4. Examples are:

```
LDD 0,X
LDA S
```

8-3.2 Constant-Offset Indexed

In this mode, a 2s complement offset and the contents of one of the pointer registers are added to form the effective address of the operand. The pointer register's initial content is unchanged by the addition. Three sizes of offsets are available: 5-bit (−16 to +15), 8-bit (−128 to +127), and 16-bit (−32768 to +32767).

The 2s complement 5-bit offset is included in the postbyte and, therefore, is most efficient in use of bytes and cycles. The 2s complement 8-bit offset is contained in a single byte following the postbyte. The 2s complement 16-bit offset is in the 2 bytes following the postbyte. In most cases the programmer need not be concerned with the size of this offset since the assembler will select the optimal size automatically. Examples of constant-offset indexing and their required offsets are:

```
LDA 23,X        (8-bit offset)
LDX -2,S        (5-bit offset)
LDY 300,X X     (16-bit offset)
LDU CAT,Y Y     (Depends upon the value of CAT)
```

EXAMPLE 8-4 How does the constant-offset indexed instruction for a 16-bit offset appear in memory?

Solution In memory it takes 4 bytes as shown:

Op code
Postbyte
Upper byte of offset
Lower byte of offset

EXAMPLE 8-5 What does LDX −2,S do? What numbers are in the postbyte and the offset?

Solution The instruction subtracts 2 from the S register and loads the contents of that location into X (i.e., if S = 210, then the instruction would load the contents of 20E and 20F into the X register). Note that the postbyte would be 11101001. The second pair of ones denotes the register set used. In this case, 11 = S. This instruction could be coded three different ways:

1 AE   Op code
  7E   (Postbyte specifying a 5-bit offset of −2)

```
2 AE    Op code
  E8    (Postbyte specifying an 8-bit offset)
  FE    (Offset of -2)
3 AE    Op code
  E9    (Postbyte specifying a 16-bit offset)
  FF
  FE    (-2 as a 16-bit number)
```

The first way is obviously the most economical and would be selected by the assembler. Note also that in each case bits 5 and 6 of the postbyte are 11, because a 11 specifies the S register.

8-3.3 Accumulator-Offset Indexed

This mode is similar to constant-offset indexed except that the 2s complement value in one of the accumulators (A, B, or D) and the contents of one of the pointer registers are added to form the effective address of the operand. The contents of both the accumulator and the pointer register are unchanged by the addition. The postbyte specifies which accumulator to use as an offset and no additional bytes are required. The advantage of an accumulator offset is that the value of the offset can be calculated at run time. Some examples are:

```
LDA B,Y
LDX D,Y
LEAX B,X
```

Note: For a discussion of LEAX, see section 8-4.4.

8-3.4 Auto Increment/Decrement Indexed

In the auto increment addressing mode, the pointer register (X, Y, U, or S) contains the address of the operand. Then, *after* the pointer register is used it is incremented by one or two. This addressing mode is useful in stepping through tables, moving data, or for the creation of software stacks. In auto decrement, the pointer register is decremented *prior* to use as the address of the data. The use of auto decrement is similar to that of auto increment, but the tables, and so on, are scanned from the high to low addresses. The size of the increment/decrement can be either one or two to allow for tables of either 8- or 16-bit data to be accessed, and is selectable by the programmer. The predecrement, postincrement nature of these modes allows them to be used to create additional software stacks that behave identically to the U and S stacks. Some examples of the auto increment/decrement addressing modes are:

```
LDA ,X+
STD ,Y++
LDB ,-Y
LDX ,--S
```

Care should be taken in performing operations on 16-bit pointer registers (X, Y, U, S) where the same register is used to calculate the effective address. Consider the following instruction.

EXAMPLE 8-6 We want to store a 0 in locations \$0000 and \$0001, then increment X to point to \$0002. Will the following instructions do it?

Solution

`STX 0,X++` (X initialized to 0)

In reality, the following operations occur:

`0 --> temp`	Calculate the EA; temp is a holding register
`X+2 --> X`	Perform auto increment
`X --> temp`	Do store operation

At this time, locations 0000 and 0001 contain 0002, and the X register contains 0002.

8-3.5 Indexed Indirect

All of the indexing modes, with the exception of auto increment/decrement by one, or a +/− 4-bit offset, may have an additional level of indirection specified. In indirect addressing, the *effective address* is contained at the location specified by the contents of the index register plus any offset.

EXAMPLE 8-7 Show how the A accumulator is loaded indirectly using an effective address calculated from the index register and an offset.

Before Execution

```
A = XX (don't care)
X = $F000
```

Solution The following locations are assumed to contain the given data:

`$0100 LDA [$10,X]`		EA is now \$F010
`$F010 $F1`		\$F150 is now the
`$F011 $50`		new EA
`$F150 $AA`		

After Execution

```
A = $AA Actual data loaded
X = $F000
```

All modes of indexed indirect are included except those that are meaningless (e.g., auto increment/decrement by one indirect). Some examples of indexed indirect are:

```
LDA [,X]
LDD [10,S]
LDA [B,Y]
LDD [,X++]
```

8-3.6 Relative Addressing

The byte(s) following the branch Op code is (are) treated as a signed offset which may be added to the program counter. If the branch condition is true, then the calculated (PC + signed offset) is loaded into the program counter. Program execution continues at the new location as indicated by the PC; short (1 byte offset) and long (2 bytes offset) relative addressing modes are available. All of memory can be reached in long relative addressing as an effective address is interpreted modulo 2©16. Some examples of relative addressing are:

```
BEQ CAT               (Short)
BGT DOG               (Short)
CAT LBEQ RAT          (Long)
DOG LBGT RABBIT       (Long)
        :
RAT NOP
RABBIT NOP
```

8-3.7 Program Counter Relative

The PC can be used as the pointer register with 8- or 16-bit signed offsets. As in relative addressing, the offset is added to the current PC to create the effective address. The effective address is then used as the address of the operand or data. Program counter relative addressing is used for writing position independent programs. Tables related to a particular routine will maintain the same relationship after the routine is moved, if referenced relative to the program counter. Examples are:

```
LDA CAT,PCR
LEAX TABLE,PCR
```

Since program counter relative is a type of indexing, an additional level of indirection is available.

```
LDA [CAT,PCR]
LDU [DOG,PCR]
```

EXAMPLE 8-8 If CAT = $0100, what does the instruction 0010 LDA CAT, PCR do?

Solution The effective address for this instruction is $0110 (CAT + PC). Since the address has been calculated, the A register is loaded from location 0110.

8-4 M6809 INSTRUCTION SET

The instruction set of the **M6809** is similar to that of the **M6800** and is upward compatible at the source code level. The number of instructions has been reduced from 72 to 59, but because of the expanded architecture and additional addressing

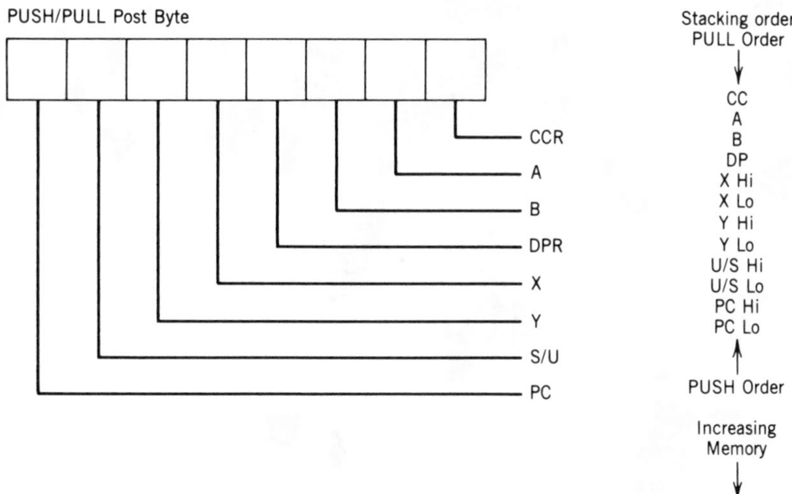

Figure 8-5 PUSH/PULL postbyte. (From the *MC6809-MC6809E Microprocessor Programming Manual*, Motorola, Inc., Austin, TX, 1981. Reprinted courtesy of Motorola, Inc.)

modes, the number of available Op codes (with different addressing modes) has risen from 197 to 1464.

The complete instruction set is given in Table 8-1, which begins on page 340. Some of the new instructions are described in detail below.

8-4.1 PSHU/PSHS

The push instructions have the capability of pushing onto either the hardware stack (S) or the user stack (U) any single register, or set of registers with a single instruction.

8-4.2 PULU/PULS

The pull instructions have the same capability of the push instruction, except in reverse order. The postbyte immediately following the PUSH or PULL Op code determines which register or set of registers are to be pushed or pulled. The actual PUSH/PULL sequence is fixed; each bit defines a unique register to push or pull, as shown in Figure 8-5.

EXAMPLE 8-9 If it is necessary to push A, B, X, and CC onto the user's stack, what does the instruction look like? What does the postbyte look like? In what order are they placed on the stack?

Solution The instruction to do this looks like PSHU A, B, X, CC. The postbyte (00010111) uses a "1" to represent registers which are to be pushed. The stacking order would be CC, A, B, and X.

8-4.3 TFR/EXG

Within the **M6809**, any register may be transferred to or exchanged with another of like size; that is 8-bit to 8-bit or 16-bit to 16-bit. Bits 4–7 of the postbyte define the source register, while bits 0–3 represent the destination register as shown in Figure 8-6.

Source	Destination

Register field

0000	D(AB)	1000	A
0001	X	1001	B
0010	Y	1010	CCR
0011	U	1011	DPR
0100	S		
0101	PC		

Note: All other combinations are undefined and invalid, although there is an obvious link between 8-bit and 16-bit registers through the 16-bit D accumulator.

Figure 8-6 TRANSFER/EXCHANGE postbyte.

EXAMPLE 8-10 How can a user load the direct page register with $1C?

Solution There is no instruction that loads the direct page register but the user may load A and then transfer it into the DPR. The program might be:

```
LDA#$1C
TFR DP,A
```

Figure 8-6 shows that the postbyte on the transfer instruction would be 8B.

8-4.4 LEAX/LEAY/LEAU/LEAS

The LEA (load effective address) works by calculating the effective address used in an indexed instruction and stores that address value, rather than the data at that address, in a pointer register. This makes all the features of the internal addressing hardware available to the programmer. Some of the implications of this instruction are illustrated in Table 8-3. The LEA instruction also makes use of a postbyte.

The LEA instruction also allows the user to access data and tables in a position independent manner. For example:

```
     LEAX MSG1,PCR
     LBSR PDATA   (Print message routine)
     :
MSG1 FCC 'MESSAGE'
```

This sample program prints: "MESSAGE". By writing MSG1, PCR, the assembler computes the distance between the present address and MSG1. This result is placed as a constant into the X register which will be indexed from the PC value at the time of execution. No matter where the code is located, when it is executed, the computed offset from the PC will put the absolute address of MSG1 into the X pointer register. This code is totally position independent.

The LEA instructions are very powerful and use an internal holding register (temp). Care must be exercised when using the LEA instructions with the auto increment and auto decrement addressing modes because of the sequence of internal operations. The LEA internal sequence is outlined as follows:

```
LEAa ,b+                (Any of the 16-bit pointer registers X, Y, U, or S may
                        be substituted for a and b.)
1 b --> temp            (Calculate the EA)
2 b + 1 --> b           (Modify b, postincrement)
3 temp --> a            (Load a)
LEAa ,-b
1 b --> temp            (Calculate EA with predecrement)
2 b - 1 --> b           (Modify b, predecrement)
3 temp --> a            (Load a)
```

Auto increment by two and auto decrement by two instructions work similarly. Note that LEAX ,X+ does not change X. LEAX, −X, however does decrement X. LEAX 1,X should be used to increment X by one.

Table 8-3 **LEA examples**

Instruction	*Operation*	*Comment*
LEAX 10,X	X + 10 → X	Adds 5-bit constant 10 to X.
LEAX 500,X	X + 500 → X	Adds 16-bit constant 500 to X.
LEAY A,Y	Y + A → Y	Adds 8-bit A accumulator to Y.
LEAY D,Y	Y + D → Y	Adds 16-bit D accumulator to Y.
LEAU -10,U	U - 10 → U	Subtracts 10 from U.
LEAS -10,S	S - 10 → S	Used to reserve area on stack.
LEAS 10,S	S + 10 → S	Used to unreserve stack.
LEAX 5,S	S + 5 → X	Transfers as well as adds.

EXAMPLE 8-11 What does LEAX ,S+ do?

Solution This is an example of the LEAa ,b+ instruction discussed above. This instruction loads the value in S into X, then increments S. Symbolically:

```
(X) <--- (S)
(S) <--- (S + 1)
```

8-4.5 MUL

MUL multiplies the unsigned binary numbers in the A and B accumulator and places the unsigned result into the 16-bit D accumulator. This unsigned multiply also allows multiple-precision multiplications.

8-5 LONG AND SHORT RELATIVE BRANCHES

The **M6809** has the capability of program counter relative branching throughout the entire memory map. In this mode, if the branch is to be taken, the 8- or 16-bit signed offset is added to the value of the program counter to be used as the effective address. This allows the program to branch anywhere in the 64K memory map. Position independent code may be easily generated through the use of relative branching. Both short (8-bit) and long (16-bit) branches are available. For short branches the byte following the Op code is the offset. For long branches, the offset is contained in the bytes following the Op code.

8-6 SYNC

After encountering a SYNC instruction, the MPU enters a sync state, stops processing instructions, and waits for an interrupt. If the pending interrupt is nonmaskable (NMI) or maskable (FIRQ, IRQ) with its mask bit clear, the processor will clear the SYNC state and perform the normal interrupt stacking and service routine. Since FIRQ and IRQ are not edge triggered, a low level with a minimum duration of three bus cycles is required to assure that the interrupt will be taken. If the pending interrupt is maskable with its mask bit set, the processor will clear the SYNC state and continue processing by executing the next in-line instruction.

Stacking of registers during an interrupt is accomplished in the following order:

```
PC, U, Y, X, DP, B, A, CC
```

Note that the condition code register is the last register pushed. This means that it is the first one pulled, and a determination is made to see how many registers are to be pulled (E bit).

8-7 SOFTWARE INTERRUPTS

A SOFTWARE INTERRUPT is an instruction that will cause an interrupt and its associated vector fetch. These SOFTWARE INTERRUPTs are useful in operating system calls, software debugging, trace operations, memory mapping, and software development systems. Three levels of SWI are available on the **M6809**, and are prioritized in the following order: SWI, SWI2, and SWI3. The SOFTWARE INTERRUPTs cause the processor to go through the normal interrupt request sequence of stacking the complete machine state even though the interrupting source is the processor itself. These interrupts are commonly used for program debugging and for calls to an operating system. Normal processing of the SWI input sets the I and F bits to prevent either of these interrupt requests from affecting the completion of a SOFTWARE INTERRUPT request. The remaining SOFTWARE INTERRUPT request inputs (SWI2 and SWI3) do not have the priority of the SWI input, and therefore do not mask off the two hardware request inputs (IRQ and FIRQ).

8-8 16-BIT OPERATION

The **M6809** has instructions that give the MPU the capability of processing 16-bit data. These instructions include LOADS, STOREs, COMPAREs, ADDs, SUBTRACTs, TRANSFERs, EXCHANGEs, PUSHes, and PULLs.

The instruction set may be functionally divided into five categories. They are:

8-bit accumulator and memory instructions
16-bit accumulator and memory instructions
Index register/stack pointer instructions
BRANCH instructions
Miscellaneous instructions

Tables 8-4 through 8-8 are listings of the **M6809** instructions and their variations grouped into the five categories listed.

8-9 PIN OUT AND SIGNAL DESCRIPTIONS

After producing the **MC6809** Motorola built a more specialized μP, the **MC6809E**. The **MC6809** was designed before the **MC6809E**, and was destined for applications that did not require an extensive clocking circuit, as would be required in multiprocessor systems. As described below, the **MC6809** has a relatively simple system of clocking, although some sophisticated DMA systems may still be implemented using the HALT or DMA/BREQ lines. The **MC6809E** was designed with the multiprocessing environment in mind. The pin diagrams are basically the same, with only necessary changes in pin functions. Radio Shack used the **MC6809E** in their color computer. Figure 8-7 gives the pin outs for both the **MC6809** and **MC6809E** microprocessors.

The following signal descriptions refer to the **MC6809**. Following these the **MC6809E** differences will be discussed. Any pin that has an asterisk beside it is not available on the **MC6809E**.

8-9.1 Power (Vss, Vcc)

Two pins are used to supply power to the part: Vss is ground, and Vcc is 5 V $\pm$ 5 per cent.

Table 8-4 **8-bit accumulator and memory instructions**

Mnemonic(s)	Operation
ADCA, ADCB	Add memory to accumulator with carry
ADDA, ADDB	Add memory to accumulator
ANDA, ANDB	And memory with accumulator
ASL, ASLA, ASLB	Arithmetic shift of accumulator or memory left
ASR, ASRA, ASRB	Arithmetic shift of accumulator or memory right
BITA, BITB	Bit test memory with accumulator
CLR, CLRA, CLRB	Clear accumulator or memory location
CMPA, CMPB	Compare memory from accumulator
COM, COMA, COMB	Complement accumulator or memory location
DAA	Decimal adjust A-accumulator
DEC, DECA, DECB	Decrement accumulator or memory location
EORA, EORB	Exclusive or memory with accumulator
EXG R1, R2	Exchange R1 with R2 (R1, R2 = A, B, CC, DP)
INC, INCA, INCB	Increment accumulator or memory location
LDA, LDB	Load accumulator from memory
LSL, LSLA, LSLB	Logical shift left accumulator or memory location
LSR, LSRA, LSRB	Logical shift right accumulator or memory location
MUL	Unsigned multiply (A x B → D)
NEG, NEGA, NEGB	Negate accumulator or memory
ORA, ORB	Or memory with accumulator
ROL, ROLA, ROLB	Rotate accumulator or memory left
ROR, RORA, RORB	Rotate accumulator or memory right
SBCA, SBCB	Subtract memory from accumulator with borrow
STA, STB	Store accumulator to memory
SUBA, SUBB	Subtract memory from accumulator
TST, TSTA, TSTB	Test accumulator or memory location
TFR, R1, R2	Transfer R1 to R2 (R1, R2 = A, B, CC, DP)

NOTE: A, B, CC, or DP may be pushed to (pulled from) either stack with PSHS, PSHU, (PULS, PULU) instructions.

Table 8-5 **16-bit accumulator and memory instructions**

Mnemonic(s)	Operation
ADDD	Add memory to D accumulator
CMPD	Compare memory from D accumulator
EXG D, R	Exchange D with X, Y, S, U or PC
LDD	Load D accumulator from memory
SEX	Sign Extend B accumulator into A accumulator
STD	Store D accumulator to memory
SUBD	Subtract memory from D accumulator
TFR D, R	Transfer D to X, Y, S, U or PC
TFR R, D	Transfer X, Y, S, U or PC to D

Table 8-6 **Index register/stack pointer instructions**

Mnemonic(s)	Operation
CMPS, CMPU	Compare memory from stack pointer
CMPX, CMPY	Compare memory from index register
EXG R1, R2	Exchange D, X, Y, S, U, or PC with D, X, Y, S, U or PC
LEAS, LEAU	Load effective address into stack pointer
LEAX, LEAY	Load effective address into index register
LDS, LDU	Load stack pointer from memory
LDX, LDY	Load index register from memory
PSHS	Push any register(s) onto hardware stack (except S)
PSHU	Push any register(s) onto user stack (except U)
PULS	Pull any register(s) from hardware stack (except S)
PULU	Pull any register(s) from hardware stack (except U)
STS, STU	Store stack pointer to memory
STX, STY	Store index register to memory
TFR R1, R2	Transfer D, X, Y, S, U or PC to D, X, Y, S, U or PC
ABX	Add B accumulator to X (unsigned)

Table 8-7 **BRANCH instructions**

Mnemonic(s)	Operation
BCC, LBCC	Branch if carry clear
BCS, LBCS	Branch if carry set
BEQ, LBEQ	Branch if equal
BGE, LBGE	Branch if greater than or equal (signed)
BGT, LBGT	Branch if greater (signed)
BHI, LBHI	Branch if higher (unsigned)
BHS, LBHS	Branch if higher or same (unsigned)
BLE, LBLE	Branch if less than or equal (signed)
BLO, LBLO	Branch if lower (unsigned)
BLS, LBLS	Branch if lower or same (unsigned)
BLT, LBLT	Branch if less than (signed)
BMI, LBMI	Branch if minus
BNE, LBNE	Branch if not equal
BPL, LBPL	Branch if plus
BRA, LBRA	Branch always
BRN, LBRN	Branch never
BSR, LBSR	Branch to subroutine
BVC, LBVC	Branch if overflow clear
BVS, LBVS	Branch if overflow set

Table 8-8 **Miscellaneous instructions**

Mnemonic(s)	Operation
ANDCC	AND condition code register
CWAI	AND condition code register, then wait for interrupt
NOP	No operation
ORCC	OR condition code register
JMP	Jump
JSR	Jump to subroutine
RTI	Return from interrupt
RTS	Return from subroutine
SWI, SWI2, SWI3	Software interrupt (absolute indirect)
SYNC	Synchronize with interrupt line

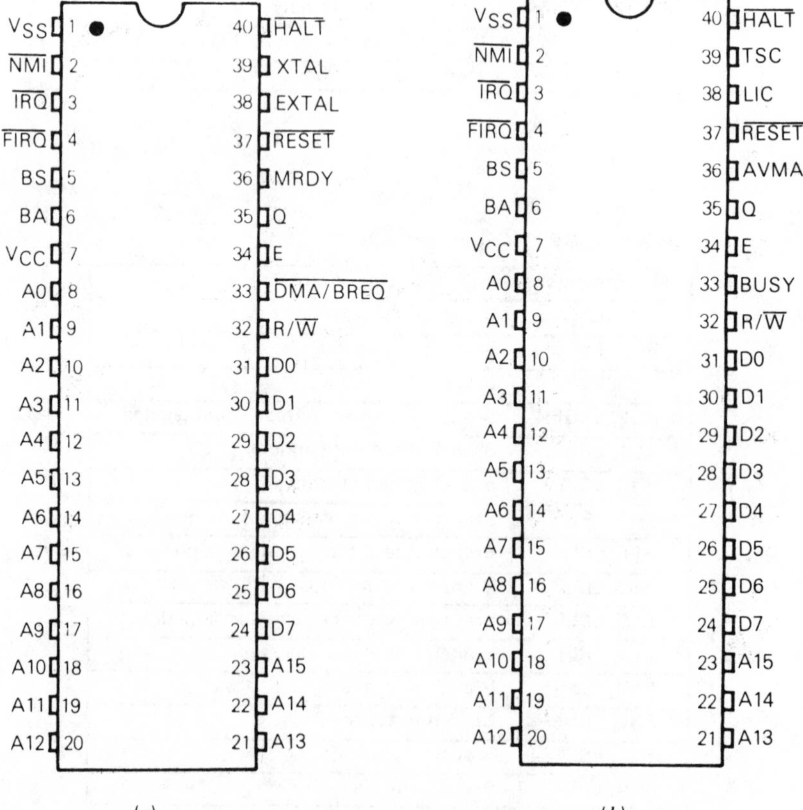

Figure 8-7 Pin outs for the **MC6809** and the **MC6809E**. (*a*) **MC6809** pin out. (*b*) **MC6809E** pin out. (From the *MC6809-MC6809E Microprocessor Programming Manual*, Motorola, Inc., Austin, TX, 1981. Reprinted courtesy of Motorola, Inc.)

8-9.2 XTAL, EXTAL*

These inputs are used to connect the on-chip oscillator to an external parallel-resonant crystal. Alternately, the pin EXTAL may be used as a TTL level input for external timing by grounding XTAL. The crystal or external frequency is four times the bus frequency.

8-9.3 E, Q*

E is similar to the **M6800** bus timing signal $\phi 2$; Q is a quadrature clock signal which leads E. Q has no parallel on the **M6800**. Addresses from the MPU will be valid with the leading edge of Q. Data is latched on the falling edge of E. Timing relationships between E and Q are shown in Figure 8-8.

8-9.4 Address Bus (A0–A15)

Sixteen pins are used to output address information from the MPU onto the address bus. When the processor does not require the bus for a data transfer, it will output address $FFFF, R/W = 1, and BS = 0. This *dummy access* cycle is provided so that the address bus and R/W line will be in a known condition during these nonused bus cycles. The **M6800** required a separate VMA line to determine if the addresses were valid on the bus. Addresses are valid on the rising edge of Q (see timing diagrams). All address bus drivers are made high impedance when output bus available (BA) is high. Each pin will drive one Schottky TTL load or four LS TTL loads, and 90 pF.

8-9.5 Data Bus (D0–D7)

These eight pins provide communication with the system bidirectional data bus. Each pin will drive one Schottky TTL load or four LS TTL loads, and 130 pF.

8-9.6 READ/WRITE (R/W)

This signal indicates the direction of data transfer on the data bus. A LOW indicates that the MPU is writing data onto the data bus. R/W is made high impedance when BA is HIGH. R/W, like the addresses, is valid on the rising edge of Q.

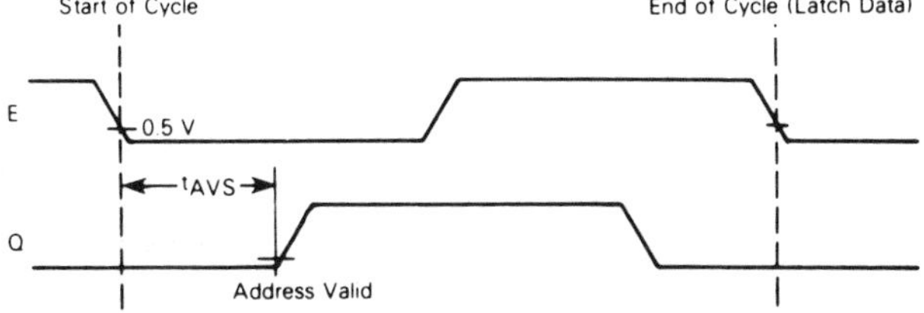

NOTE: Waveform measurements for all inputs and outputs are specified at logic high 2.0 V and logic low 0.8 V unless otherwise specified.

Figure 8-8 E/Q relationship. (From the *MC6809-MC6809E Microprocessor Programming Manual*, Motorola, Inc., Austin, TX, 1981. Reprinted courtesy of Motorola, Inc.)

8-9.7 RESET

A low level on this Schmitt-trigger input for greater than one bus cycle will reset the MPU. The RESET vectors are fetched from locations $FFFE and $FFFF when interrupt acknowledge is true. During initial power-on, the RESET line should be held low until the clock oscillator is fully operational.

Because the **M6809** RESET pin has a Schmitt-trigger input with a threshold voltage higher than that of standard peripherals, a simple RC network may be used to reset the entire system. This higher threshold voltage ensures that all peripherals are out of the RESET state before the MPU.

8-9.8 HALT

A low level on this input pin will cause the MPU to stop running at the end of the present instruction and remain halted indefinitely without loss of data. When halted, the BA output is driven HIGH, indicating the buses are high impedance. BS is also HIGH, which indicates the processor is in the HALT or BUS GRANT state. While halted, the MPU will not respond to external real-time requests (FIRQ, IRQ) although DMA/BREQ will always be accepted, and NMI or RESET will be latched for later response. During the HALT state, E and Q continue to run normally. If the MPU is not running (in RESET, or DMA/BREQ), a halted state may be achieved by pulling HALT LOW while RESET is still LOW. If DMA/BREQ and HALT are both pulled LOW, the processor will reach the last cycle of the instruction (by reverse cycle stealing). The machine will then enter the HALT state.

8-9.9 BUS AVAILABLE, BUS STATUS (BA, BS)

Two lines on the **MC6809** and **MC6809E** microprocessors are used to determine which of four possible states the **M6809** is operating in. These four states are shown in Figure 8-9.

The BUS AVAILABLE output is an indication of an internal control signal that makes the MOS buses of the MPU high impedance. This signal does not imply that the bus will be available for more than one cycle. When BA goes LOW, a dead cycle will elapse before the MPU acquires the bus.

MPU state		
BA	*BS*	*MPU state definition*
0	0	Normal (running)
0	1	INTERRUPT or RESET ACKNOWLEDGE
1	0	SYNC ACKNOWLEDGE
1	1	HALT or BUS GRANT ACKNOWLEDGE

Figure 8-9 State definitions for the **6809**. (From the *MC6809-MC6809E Microprocessor Programming Manual*, Motorola, Inc., Austin, TX, 1981. Reprinted courtesy of Motorola, Inc.)

The BUS STATUS (BS) output signal, when decoded with BA, represents the MPU state (valid with the leading edge of Q).

8-9.10 INTERRUPT ACKNOWLEDGE

INTERRUPT ACKNOWLEDGE is indicated during both cycles of a hardware vector fetch. This signal, plus decoding of the lower four address lines, can provide the user with an indication of which interrupt level is being serviced and allow vectoring by device. Once an actual interrupt occurs on the inputs, the **M6809** stacks the appropriate number of registers (IRQ, NMI, OR FIRQ) and then fetches the 2 bytes of address information from the vector locations. This procedure is similar to that for a SWI interrupt, except that no hardware signals are involved. Table 8-9 shows the vector locations.

SYNC ACKNOWLEDGE is asserted while the MPU is waiting for external synchronization on an interrupt line.

HALT/BUS GRANT is true when the **M6809** is in a HALT or BUS GRANT condition. In this condition other devices may make DMA requests to the **M6809**'s memory.

8-9.11 NONMASKABLE INTERRUPT (NMI)

A negative transition on this input requests that a NONMASKABLE INTERRUPT sequence be generated. A NONMASKABLE INTERRUPT cannot be inhibited by the program, and also has a higher priority than FIRQ, IRQ, or other software interrupts. During the recognition of an NMI, the entire machine state is saved on the hardware stack. After RESET, an NMI will not be recognized until the first program load of the hardware stack pointer (S). The pulse width of NMI low must be at least one E cycle. If the NMI input does not meet the minimum setup with respect to Q, the interrupt will not be recognized until the next cycle.

Table 8-9 **Memory map for interrupt vectors**

Memory map for vector locations		*Interrupt vector description*
MS	*LS*	
FFFE	FFFF	$\overline{\text{RESET}}$
FFFC	FFFD	$\overline{\text{NMI}}$
FFFA	FFFB	SWI
FFF8	FFF9	$\overline{\text{IRQ}}$
FFF6	FFF7	$\overline{\text{FIRQ}}$
FFF4	FFF5	SWI1
FFF2	FFF3	SWI3
FFF0	FFF1	Reserved

8-9.12 FAST INTERRUPT REQUEST (FIRQ)

A low level on this input pin will initiate a FAST INTERRUPT sequence, provided its mask bit (F) in the CC is clear. This sequence has priority over the standard INTERRUPT REQUEST (IRQ), and is fast in the sense that it stacks only the contents of the condition code register and the program counter. The INTERRUPT SERVICE routine should clear the source of the interrupt before doing an RTI.

When the μP encounters an RTI instruction (necessary to return from the interrupt service routine), the CC is recovered first. If the recovered E bit is clear, it indicates that a FAST INTERRUPT REQUEST occurred and only the program counter address is additionally pulled. If the bit is set, it indicates that a standard IRQ sequence occurred, and all registers must be pulled.

8-9.13 INTERRUPT REQUEST (IRQ)

A low-level input on this pin will initiate an INTERRUPT REQUEST sequence, provided the mask bit (I) in the CC is clear. Since IRQ stacks the entire machine state, it provides a slower response to interrupts than FIRQ. IRQ also has a lower priority than FIRQ. Again, the INTERRUPT SERVICE routine should clear the source of the interrupt before doing an RTI.

Note: NMI, FIRQ, and IRQ requests are sampled on the falling edge of Q. One cycle is required for synchronization before these interrupts are recognized. The pending interrupt(s) will not be serviced until the completion of the current instruction, unless a SYNC or CWAI condition is present. If IRQ and FIRQ do not remain low until completion of the current instruction, they may not be recognized. However, NMI is latched and need only remain low for one cycle. No interrupts are recognized or latched between the falling edge of RESET and the rising edge of BS indicating RESET acknowledge.

8-9.14 MRDY*

This input control signal allows stretching of E and Q to extend data access time. E and Q operate normally while MRDY is high. When MRDY is low, E and Q may be stretched in integral multiples of one-quarter bus cycles, thus allowing interface to slow memories. During nonvalid memory access (VMA cycles), MRDY has no effect on the stretching of E and Q; this inhibits slowing the processor during "don't care" bus accesses. MRDY may also be used to stretch clocks (for slow memory) when bus control has been transferred to an external device (through the use of HALT and DMA/BREQ).

Note: Some early **MC6809**s required synchronization of the MRDY input with the 4f clock. Refer to the data sheet for particular information.

8-9.15 DMA/BREQ*

The DMA/BREQ input provides a method of suspending execution and acquiring the MPU bus for another use, such as DMA and dynamic memory refresh.

Transitions of DMA/BREQ should occur during Q. A low level on this pin will stop instruction execution at the end of the current cycle unless preempted by self-refresh. The MPU will acknowledge DMA/BREQ by setting BA and BS to a 1. The requesting device will now have up to 15 bus cycles before the MPU retrieves the bus for self-refresh. Self-refresh requires one bus cycle with a leading and trailing dead cycle. The self-refresh counter is only cleared if DMA/BREQ is inactive for two or more MPU cycles.

The self-refresh condition happens whenever the DMA/BREQ line is held for enough time to put the MPU in a mode where it needs to refresh itself or lose data. The **MC6809**, like the **MC6800**, is a dynamic device. This means that if the clock stops, only a short time may pass before certain parts of the MPU will cease functioning properly. To guard against this condition from inadvertantly happening, the **MC6809** will automatically keep up with the number of clock cycles it needs. In the DMA/BREQ mode the MPU must be refreshed once every 15 cycles.

Typically, the DMA controller will request the bus by asserting DMA/BREQ pin LOW on the leading edge of E. When the MPU replies by setting BA and BS to a 1, that cycle will be a dead cycle which should be used to transfer bus mastership to the DMA controller.

False memory access may be prevented during any dead cycles by generating a system DMA/VMA signal which is LOW in any cycle when BA has changed.

When BA goes LOW (either as a result of DMA/BREQ = HIGH or MPU self-refresh), the DMA device should be taken off of the bus. Another dead cycle will elapse before the MPU accesses memory, to allow transfer of bus mastership without contention.

8-10 PINS IMPLEMENTED ONLY ON THE MC6809E

The following pin descriptions apply only to the **MC6809E**.

8-10.1 Clock Inputs E, Q

The clock signals required by the **MC6809E** are E and Q. Addresses will be valid from the MPU, tAD after the falling edge of E, and data will be latched from the bus by the falling edge of E. While the Q input is fully TTL compatible, the E input directly drives internal MOS circuitry, and thus requires a high level above normal TTL levels. This approach minimizes clock skew inherent with an internal buffer. Figure 8-10 shows a simple clock generator for the **MC6809E**.

8-10.2 BUSY

BUSY will be high for the READ and MODIFY cycles of a READ-MODIFY-WRITE instruction, and during the access of the first byte of a double-byte operation (e.g., LDX, STD, ADDD). BUSY is also high during the first byte of any indirect or vector fetch (e.g., jump extended, SWI indirect, etc.).

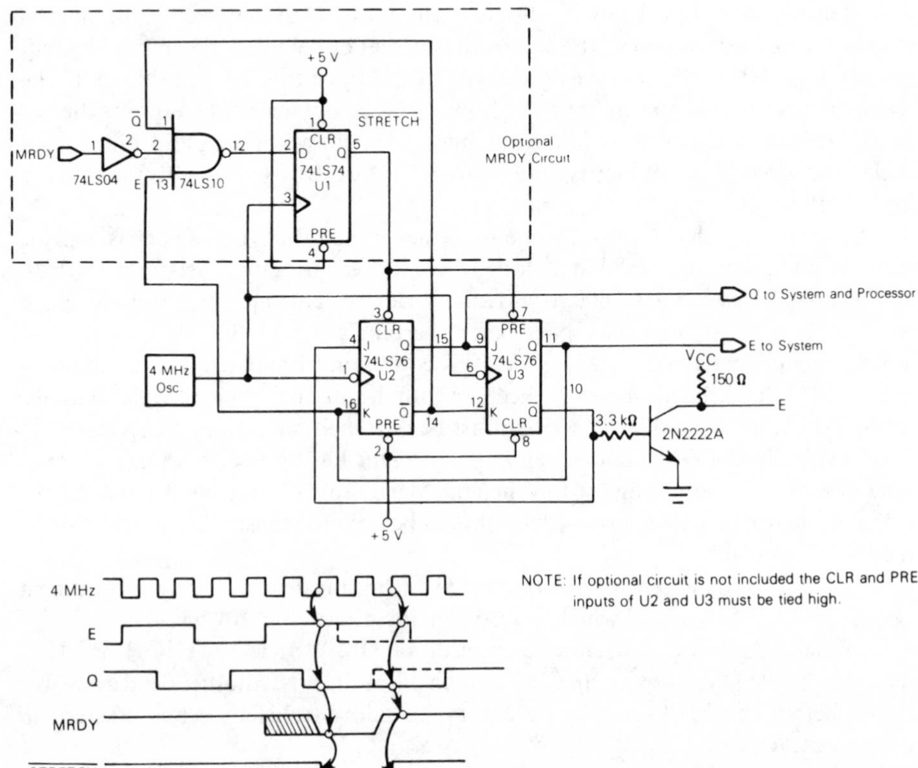

Figure 8-10 **MC6809E** clock generator. (From the *MC6809-MC6809E Microprocessor Programming Manual*, Motorola, Inc., Austin, TX, 1981. Reprinted courtesy of Motorola, Inc.)

In a multiprocessor system, BUSY indicates the need to defer the rearbitration of the next bus cycle to ensure the integrity of the above operations. This difference provides the indivisible memory access required for a "test-and set" primitive, using any one of several READ-MODIFY-WRITE instructions.

BUSY does not become active during PSH or PUL operations.

8-10.3 AVMA

AVMA is the *advanced* VMA signal and indicates that the MPU will use the bus in the following bus cycle. The predictive nature of the AVMA signal allows efficient shared-bus multiprocessor systems. AVMA is LOW when the MPU is in either a HALT or SYNC state.

8-10.4 LIC

LIC (last instruction cycle) is HIGH during the last cycle of every instruction, and its transition from HIGH to LOW indicates that the first byte of an Op code will be latched at the end of the present bus cycle. LIC will be high when the MPU is halted at the end of an instruction (i.e., not in CWAI or RESET), in SYNC state, or while stacking during interrupts.

8-10.5 TSC

TSC (tri-state control) will cause MOS address, data, and R/W buffers to assume a high-impedance state. The control signals (BA, BS, BUSY, AVMA, and LIC) will not go into the high-impedance state. TSC is intended to allow a single bus to be shared with other bus masters (processors or DMA controllers).

While E is low, TSC controls the address buffers and R/W directly. The data bus buffers during a WRITE operation are in a high-impedance state until Q rises, at which time, if TSC is true, they will remain in a high-impedance state. If TSC is held beyond the rising edge of E, then it will be internally latched, keeping the bus drivers in a high-impedance state for the remainder of the bus cycle.

8-11 MPU OPERATION

During normal operation, the MPU fetches an instruction from memory and then executes the requested function. This sequence begins after a RESET and is repeated indefinitely unless altered by a special instruction or hardware occurrence. Software instructions that alter normal MPU operations are SWI, SWI2, SWI3, CWAI, RTI, and SYNC. An interrupt or HALT input can also alter the normal execution of instructions. The flowcharts for the **MC6809** and **MC6809E** are shown in Figures 8-11 and 8-12.

8-12 THE MC6809 EVALUATION BOARD

All of the features of the **MC6809** make it a processor that is not only very efficient but also very easy to design systems around.

An evaluation board shown in Figure 8-13 was designed to allow the **MC6809** user to do an evaluation on the μP to determine if it would be acceptable in his system.

The board consists of the following hardware items:

MC6809 μP
MC6840 programmable timer
MC6850 Asynchronous Communication Interface Adapter (for **RS-232**)
4K RAM
6K EPROM
Exorciser bus interface

When used with the ASSIST09 program (see the *Motorola 6809 Microprocessor Programming Manual*), this board allows the user to debug small programs with the monitor program on board.

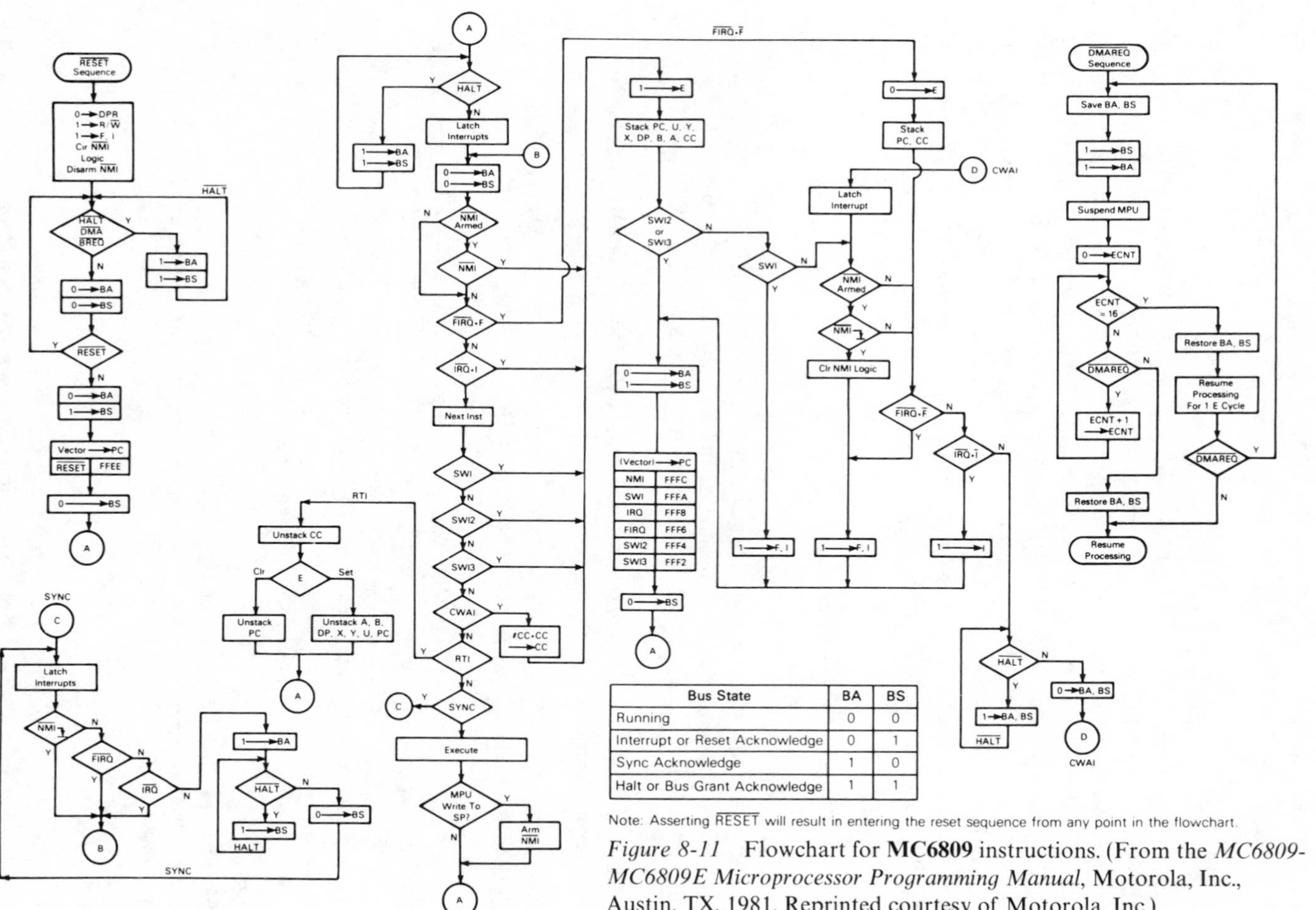

Bus State	BA	BS
Running	0	0
Interrupt or Reset Acknowledge	0	1
Sync Acknowledge	1	0
Halt or Bus Grant Acknowledge	1	1

Note: Asserting $\overline{\text{RESET}}$ will result in entering the reset sequence from any point in the flowchart.

Figure 8-11 Flowchart for **MC6809** instructions. (From the *MC6809-MC6809E Microprocessor Programming Manual*, Motorola, Inc., Austin, TX, 1981. Reprinted courtesy of Motorola, Inc.)

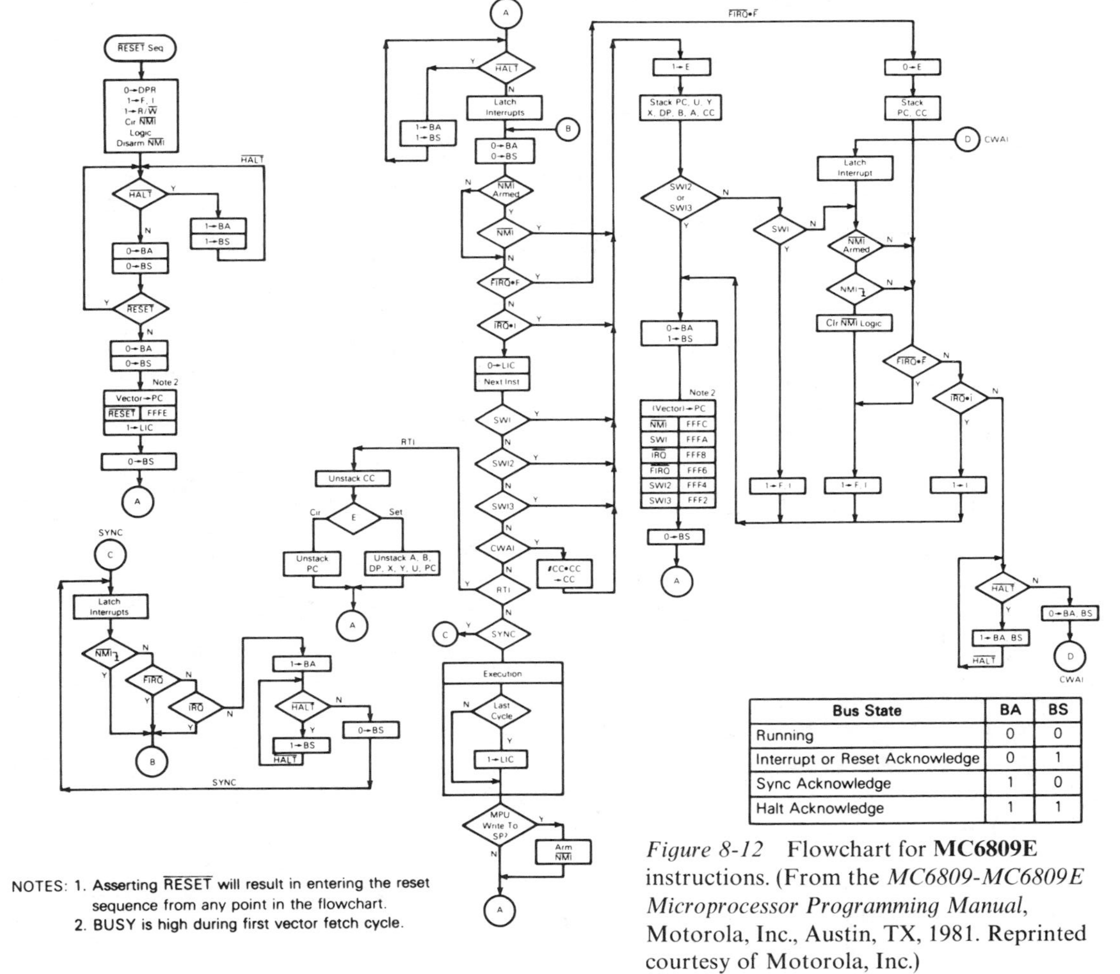

Bus State	BA	BS
Running	0	0
Interrupt or Reset Acknowledge	0	1
Sync Acknowledge	1	0
Halt Acknowledge	1	1

NOTES: 1. Asserting $\overline{\text{RESET}}$ will result in entering the reset sequence from any point in the flowchart.
2. BUSY is high during first vector fetch cycle.

Figure 8-12 Flowchart for **MC6809E** instructions. (From the *MC6809-MC6809E Microprocessor Programming Manual*, Motorola, Inc., Austin, TX, 1981. Reprinted courtesy of Motorola, Inc.)

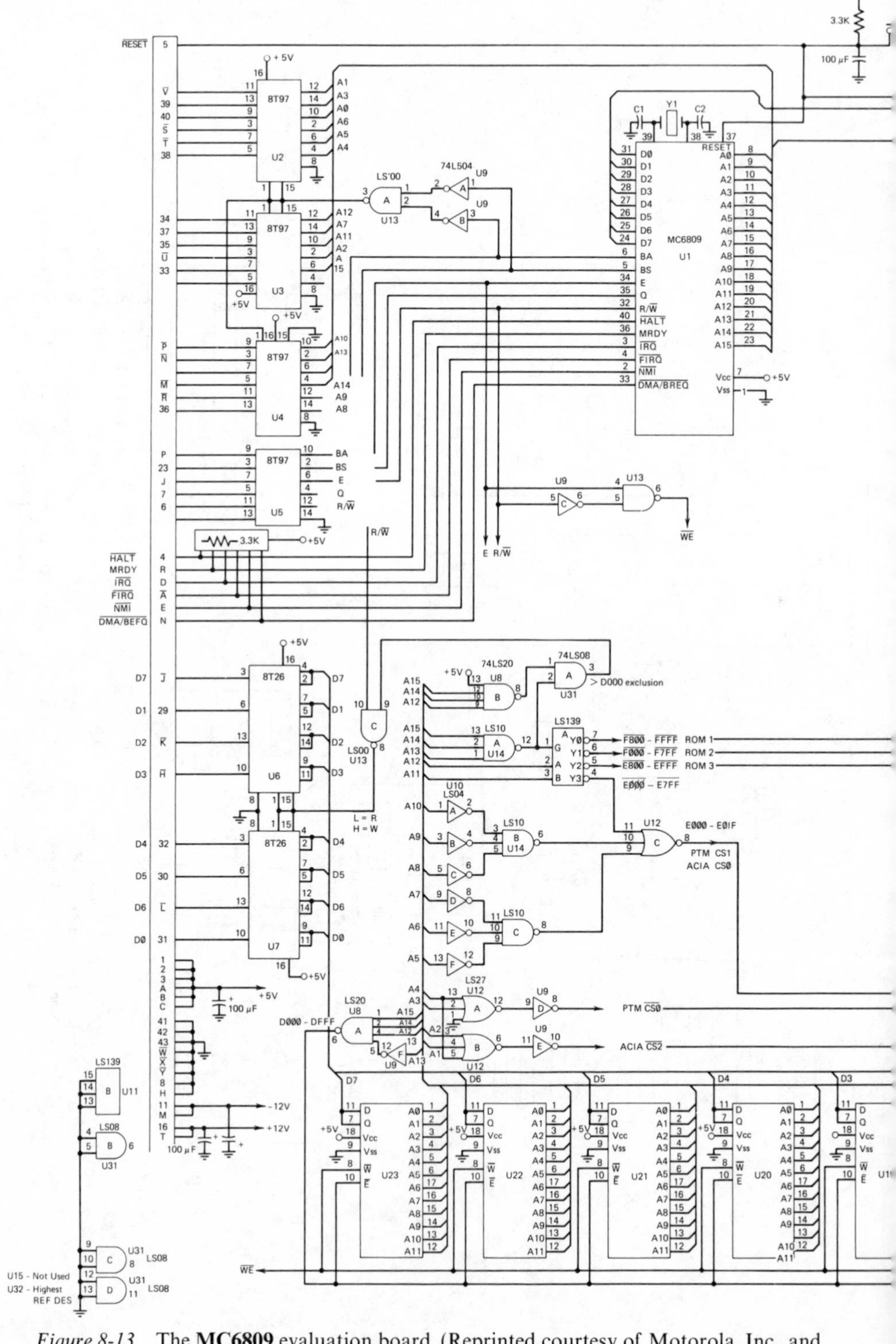

Figure 8-13 The **MC6809** evaluation board. (Reprinted courtesy of Motorola, Inc., and Tim Ahrens.)

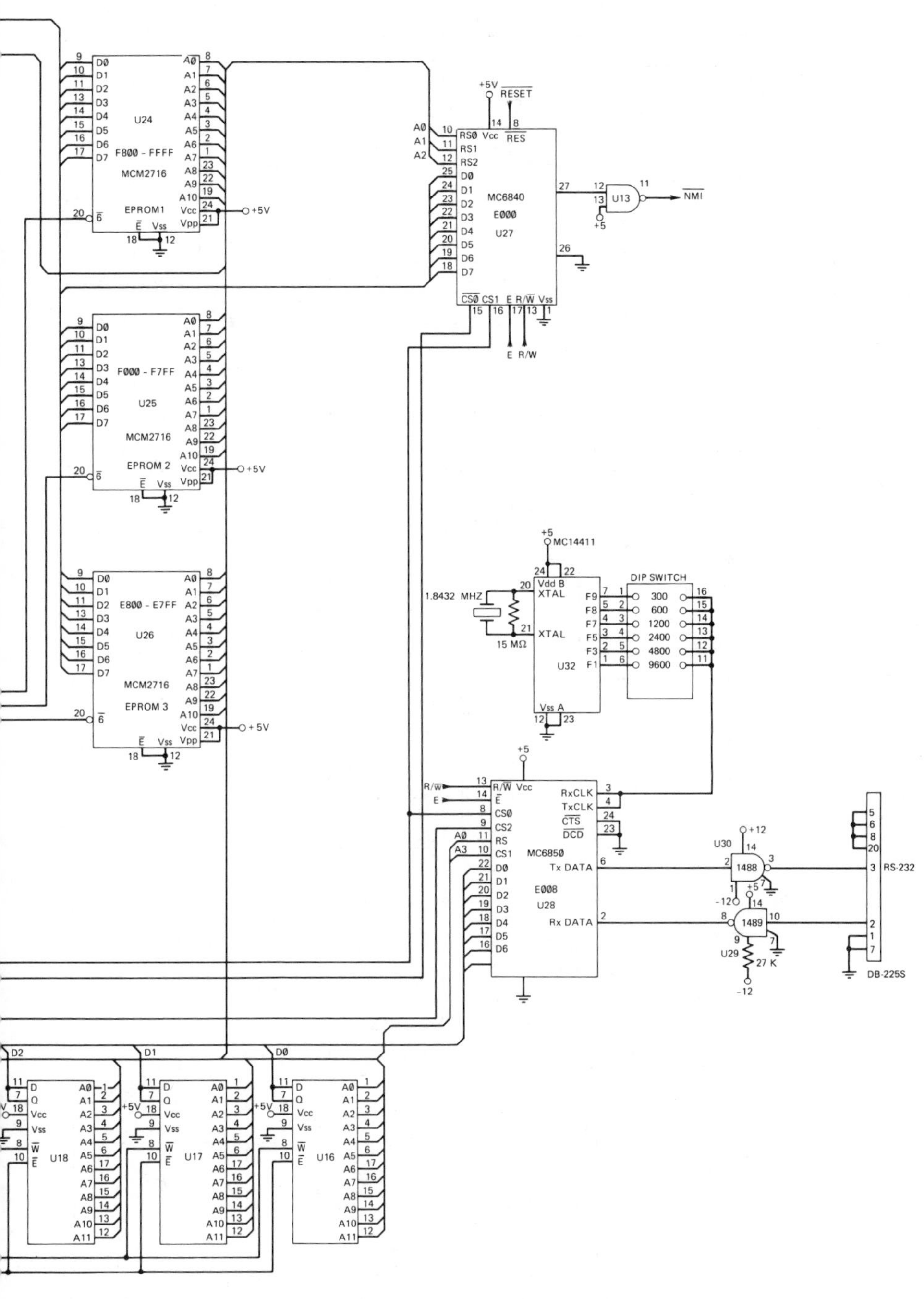

F800 - FFFF
U24
MCM2716
EPROM1
F000 - F7FF
U25
MCM2716
EPROM 2
E800 - E7FF
U26
MCM2716
EPROM 3
MC6840
E000
U27
RESET
NMI
U13
E R/W
MC14411
1.8432 MHZ
15 MΩ
U32
DIP SWITCH
300
600
1200
2400
4800
9600
MC6850
E008
U28
Tx DATA
Rx DATA
U30
1488
1489
U29
27 K
RS-232
DB-225S
U18
U17
U16

Table 8-1 The MC6809 instruction set

Branch instructions

Instruction	Forms	Addressing mode: Relative Op	~	#	Description	5 H	3 N	2 Z	1 V	0 C
BCC	BCC LBCC	24 10 24	3 5(6)	2 4	Branch C = 0 Long branch C = 0	• •	• •	• •	• •	• •
BCS	BCS LBCS	25 10 25	3 5(6)	2 4	Branch C = 1 Long branch C = 1	• •	• •	• •	• •	• •
BEQ	BEQ LBEQ	27 10 27	3 5(6)	2 4	Branch Z = 0 Long branch Z = 0	• •	• •	• •	• •	• •
BGE	BGE LBGE	2C 10 2C	3 5(6)	2 4	Branch ≥ zero Long branch ≥ zero	• •	• •	• •	• •	• •
BGT	BGT LBGT	2E 10 2E	3 5(6)	2 4	Branch > zero Long branch > zero	• •	• •	• •	• •	• •
BHI	BHI LBHI	22 10 22	3 5(6)	2 4	Branch higher Long branch higher	• •	• •	• •	• •	• •
BHS	BHS LBHS	24 10 24	3 5(6)	2 4	Branch higher or same Long branch higher or same	• •	• •	• •	• •	• •
BLE	BLE LBLE	2F 10 2F	3 5(6)	2 4	Branch ≤ zero Long branch ≤ zero	• •	• •	• •	• •	• •
BLO	BLO LBLO	25 10 25	3 5(6)	2 4	Branch lower Long branch lower	• •	• •	• •	• •	• •
BLS	BLS LBLS	23 10 23	3 5(6)	2 4	Branch lower or same Long branch lower or same	• •	• •	• •	• •	• •
BLT	BLT LBLT	2D 10 2D	3 5(6)	2 4	Branch < zero Long branch < zero	• •	• •	• •	• •	• •
BMI	BMI LBMI	2B 10 2B	3 5(6)	2 4	Branch minus Long branch minus	• •	• •	• •	• •	• •
BNE	BNE LBNE	26 10 26	3 5(6)	2 4	Branch Z ≠ 0 Long branch Z ≠ 0	• •	• •	• •	• •	• •
BPL	BPL LBPL	2A 10 2A	3 5(6)	2 4	Branch plus Long branch plus	• •	• •	• •	• •	• •
BRA	BRA LBRA	20 16	3 5	2 3	Branch always Long branch always	• •	• •	• •	• •	• •
BRN	BRN LBRN	21 10 21	3 5	2 4	Branch never Long branch never	• •	• •	• •	• •	• •
BSR	BSR LBSR	8D 17	7 9	2 3	Branch to subroutine Long branch to subroutine	• •	• •	• •	• •	• •
BVC	BVC LBVC	28 10 28	3 5(6)	2 4	Branch V = 0 Long branch V = 0	• •	• •	• •	• •	• •
BVS	BVS LBVS	29 10 29	3 5(6)	2 4	Branch V = 1 Long branch V = 1	• •	• •	• •	• •	• •

Table 8-1 (Continued)

Simple branches			
	Op	~	#
BRA	20	3	2
LBRA	16	5	3
BRN	21	3	2
LBRN	1021	5	4
BSR	8D	7	2
LBSR	17	9	3

Simple conditional branches (notes 1–4)				
Test	*True*	*Op*	*False*	*Op*
N = 1	BMI	2B	BPL	2A
Z = 1	BEQ	27	BNE	26
V = 1	BVS	29	BVC	28
C = 1	BCS	25	BCC	24

Signed conditional branches (notes 1–4)				
Test	*True*	*Op*	*False*	*Op*
r > m	BGT	2E	BLE	2F
r ≥ m	BGE	2C	BLT	2D
r = m	BEQ	27	BNE	26
r ≤ m	BLE	2F	BGT	2E
r < m	BLT	2D	BGE	2C

Unsigned conditional branches (notes 1–4)				
Test	*True*	*Op*	*False*	*Op*
r > m	BHI	22	BLS	23
r ≥ m	BHS	24	BLO	25
r = m	BEQ	27	BNE	26
r ≤ m	BLS	23	BHI	22
r < m	BLO	25	BHS	24

Notes:

1 All conditional branches have both short and long variations.
2 All short branches are 2 bytes and require 3 cycles.
3 All conditional long branches are formed by prefixing the short branch Op code with $10 and using a 16-bit destination offset.
4 All conditional long branches require 4 bytes and 6 cycles if the branch is taken or 5 cycles if the branch is not taken.

Table 8-1 (Continued)

Instruction	Forms	Immediate Op	Immediate ~	Immediate #	Direct Op	Direct ~	Direct #	Indexed Op	Indexed ~	Indexed #	Extended Op	Extended ~	Extended #	Inherent Op	Inherent ~	Inherent #	Description	5 H	3 N	2 Z	1 V	0 C
ABX														3A	3	1	B + X → X (unsigned)	•	•	•	•	•
ADC	ADCA	89	2	2	99	4	2	A9	4+	2+	B9	5	3				A + M + C → A	↕	↕	↕	↕	↕
	ADCB	C9	2	2	D9	4	2	E9	4+	2+	F9	5	3				B + M + C → B	↕	↕	↕	↕	↕
ADD	ADDA	8B	2	2	9B	4	2	AB	4+	2+	BB	5	3				A + M → A	↕	↕	↕	↕	↕
	ADDB	CB	2	2	DB	4	2	EB	4+	2+	FB	5	3				B + M → B	↕	↕	↕	↕	↕
	ADDD	C3	4	3	D3	6	2	E3	6+	2+	F3	7	3				D + M:M + 1 → D	•	↕	↕	↕	↕
AND	ANDA	84	2	2	94	4	2	A4	4+	2+	B4	5	3				A ∧ M → A	•	↕	↕	0	•
	ANDB	C4	2	2	D4	4	2	E4	4+	2+	F4	5	3				B ∧ M → B	•	↕	↕	0	•
	ANDCC	1C	3	2													CC ∧ IMM → CC					7
ASL	ASLA													48	2	1	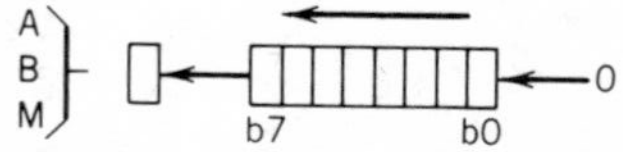 A	8	↕	↕	↕	↕
	ASLB													58	2	1	B ← b7 b0 ← 0	8	↕	↕	↕	↕
	ASL				08	6	2	68	6+	2+	78	7	3				M	8	↕	↕	↕	↕
ASR	ASRB													47	2	1	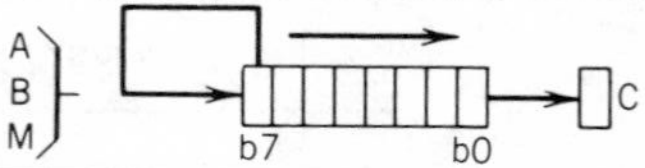 A	8	↕	↕	•	↕
	ASR													57	2	1	B → b7 b0 → C	8	↕	↕	•	↕
	ASR				07	6	2	67	6+	2+	77	7	3				M	8	↕	↕	•	↕
BIT	BITA	85	2	2	95	4	2	A5	4+	2+	B5	5	3				Bit Test A (M ∧ A)	•	↕	↕	0	•
	BITB	C5	2	2	D5	4	2	E5	4+	2+	F5	5	3				Bit Test B (M ∧ B)	•	↕	↕	0	•
CLR	CLRA													4F	2	1	0 → A	•	0	1	0	0
	CLRB													5F	2	1	0 → B	•	0	1	0	0
	CLR				0F	6	2	6F	6+	2+	7F	7	3				0 → M	•	0	1	0	0
CMP	CMPA	81	2	2	91	4	2	A1	4+	2+	B1	5	3				Compare M from A	B	↕	↕	↕	↕
	CMPB	C1	2	2	D1	4	2	E1	4+	2+	F1	5	3				Compare M from B	B	↕	↕	↕	↕
	CMPD	10 83	5	4	10 93	7	3	10 A3	7+	3+	10 B3	8	4				Compare M:M + 1 from D	•	↕	↕	↕	↕
	CMPS	11 8C	5	4	11 9C	7	3	11 AC	7+	3+	11 BC	8	4				Compare M:M + 1 from S	•	↕	↕	↕	↕
	CMPU	11 83	5	4	11 93	7	3	11 A3	7+	3+	11 B3	8	4				Compare M:M + 1 from U	•	↕	↕	↕	↕
	CMPX	BC	4	3	9C	6	2	AC	6+	2+	BC	7	3				Compare M:M + 1 from X	•	↕	↕	↕	↕
	CMPY	10 BC	5	4	10 9C	7	3	10 AC	7+	3+	10 BC	8	4				Compare M:M + 1 from Y	•	↕	↕	↕	↕

COM	COMA													43	2	1	$\bar{A} \rightarrow A$	•	$\updownarrow$	$\updownarrow$	0	1
	COMB													53	2	1	$\bar{B} \rightarrow B$	•	$\updownarrow$	$\updownarrow$	0	1
	COM				03	6	2	63	6+	2+	73	7	3				$\bar{M} \rightarrow M$	•	$\updownarrow$	$\updownarrow$	0	1
CWAI		3C	≥20	2													CC ∧ IMM → CC Wait for interrupt					7
DAA														19	2	1	Decimal adjust A	•	$\updownarrow$	$\updownarrow$	0	$\updownarrow$
DEC	DECA													4A	2	1	$A - A \rightarrow A$	•	$\updownarrow$	$\updownarrow$	$\updownarrow$	•
	DECB													5A	2	1	$B - 1 \rightarrow B$	•	$\updownarrow$	$\updownarrow$	$\updownarrow$	•
	DEC				0A	6	2	6A	6+	2+	7A	7	3				$M - 1 \rightarrow M$	•	$\updownarrow$	$\updownarrow$	$\updownarrow$	•
EOR	EORA	88	2	2	98	4	2	A8	4+	2+	B8	5	3				$A \veebar M \rightarrow A$	•	$\updownarrow$	$\updownarrow$	0	•
	EORB	C8	2	2	D8	4	2	E8	4+	2+	F8	5	3				$B \veebar M \rightarrow B$	•	$\updownarrow$	$\updownarrow$	0	•
EXG	R1,R2	1E	8	2													$R1 \leftrightarrow R2_2$	•	•	•	•	•
INC	INCA													4C	2	1	$A + 1 \rightarrow A$	•	$\updownarrow$	$\updownarrow$	$\updownarrow$	•
	INCB													5C	2	1	$B + 1 \rightarrow B$	•	$\updownarrow$	$\updownarrow$	$\updownarrow$	•
	INC				0C	6	2	6C	6+	2+	7C	7	3				$M + 1 \rightarrow M$	•	$\updownarrow$	$\updownarrow$	$\updownarrow$	•
JMP					0E	3	2	6E	3+	2+	7E	4	3				$EA^3 \rightarrow PC$	•	•	•	•	•
JSR					9D	7	2	AD	7+	2+	BD	8	3				Jump to subroutine	•	•	•	•	•
LD	LDA	86	2	2	96	4	2	A6	4+	2+	B6	5	3				$M \rightarrow A$	•	$\updownarrow$	$\updownarrow$	0	•
	LDB	C6	2	2	D6	4	2	E6	4+	2+	F6	5	3				$M \rightarrow B$	•	$\updownarrow$	$\updownarrow$	0	•
	LDD	CC	3	3	DC	5	2	EC	5+	2+	FC	6	3				$M:M + 1 \rightarrow D$	•	$\updownarrow$	$\updownarrow$	0	•
	LDS	10 CE	4	4	10 DE	6	3	10 EE	6+	3+	10 FE	7	4				$M:M + 1 \rightarrow S$	•	$\updownarrow$	$\updownarrow$	0	•
	LDU	CE	3	3	DE	5	2	EE	5+	2+	FE	6	3				$M:M + 1 \rightarrow U$	•	$\updownarrow$	$\updownarrow$	0	•
	LDX	8E	3	3	9E	5	2	AE	5+	2+	BE	6	3				$M:M + 1 \rightarrow X$	•	$\updownarrow$	$\updownarrow$	0	•
	LDY	10 BE	4	4	10 9E	6	3	10 AE	6+	3+	10 BE	7	4				$M:M + 1 \rightarrow Y$	•	$\updownarrow$	$\updownarrow$	0	•
LEA	LEAS							32	4+	2+							$EA^3 \rightarrow S$	•	•	•	•	•
	LEAU							33	4+	2+							$EA^3 \rightarrow U$	•	•	•	•	•
	LEAX							30	4+	2+							$EA^3 \rightarrow X$	•	•	$\updownarrow$	•	•
	LEAY							31	4+	2+							$EA^3 \rightarrow Y$	•	•	$\updownarrow$	•	•

Legend:

Op	Operation code (hexadecimal)	—	Transfer into	•	Not affected
~	Number of MPU cycles	H	Half-carry (from bit 3)	CC	Condition code register
#	Number of program bytes	N	Negative (sign bit)	:	Concatenation
+	Arithemetic plus	Z	Zero (reset)	∧	Logical or
−	Arithmetic minus	V	Overflow, 2s complement	∨	Logical and
•	Multiply	C	Carry from ALU	⊻	Logical exclusive or
$\bar{M}$	Complement of M	t	Test and set if true, cleared otherwise		

Table 8-1 (Continued)

Instruction	Forms	Immediate			Direct			Indexed			Extended			Inherent			Description	5	3	2	1	0
		Op	~	#	Op	~	#	Op	~	#	Op	~	#	Op	~	#		H	N	Z	V	C
ABX														3A	3	1	B + X → X (unsigned)	•	•	•	•	•
ADC	ADCA ADCB	89 C9	2 2	2 2	99 D9	4 4	2 2	A9 E9	4+ 4+	2+ 2+	B9 F9	5 5	3 3				A + M + C → A B + M + C → B	↕ ↕	↕ ↕	↕ ↕	↕ ↕	↕ ↕
LSL	LSLA LSLB LSL				 08	 6	 2	 68	 6+	 2+	 78	 7	 3	48 58	2 2	1 1	A B M C ← b7 … b0 ← 0	• • •	↕ ↕ ↕	↕ ↕ ↕	↕ ↕ ↕	↕ ↕ ↕
LSR	LSRA LSRB LSR				 04	 6	 2	 64	 6+	 2+	 74		 3	44 54	2 2	1 1	A B M 0 → b7 … b0 → C	• • •	0 0 0	↕ ↕ ↕	• • •	↕ ↕ ↕
MUL														3D	11	1	A × B → D (unsigned)	•	•	↕	•	9
NEG	NEGA NEGB NEG				 00	 6	 2	 60	 6+	 2+	 70	 7	 3	40 50	2 2	1 1	$\overline{A}$ + 1 → A $\overline{B}$ + 1 → B $\overline{M}$ + 1 → M	8 8 8	↕ ↕ ↕	↕ ↕ ↕	↕ ↕ ↕	↕ ↕ ↕
NOP														12	2	1	No operation	•	•	•	•	•
OR	ORA ORB ORCC	8A CA 1A	2 2 3	2 2 2	9A DA	4 4	2 2	AA EA	4+ +	2+ 2+	BA FA	5 5	3 3				A V M → A B V M → B CC V IMM → CC	• •	↕ ↕	↕ ↕	0 0 7	• •
PSH	PSHS PSHU	34 36	5 + 4 5 + 4	2 2													Push registers on S stack Push registers on U stack	• •	• •	• •	• •	• •
PUL	PULS PULU	35 37	5 + 4 5 + 4	2 2													Pull registers from S stack Pull registers from U stack	• •	• •	• •	• •	• •
ROL	ROLA ROLB ROL				 09	 6	 2	 69	 6+	 2+	 79	 7	 3	49 59	2 2	1 1	A B M C ← b7 … b0 (b0 ← C)	• • •	↕ ↕ ↕	↕ ↕ ↕	↕ ↕ ↕	↕ ↕ ↕

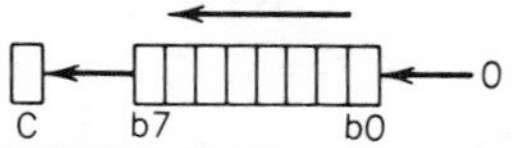

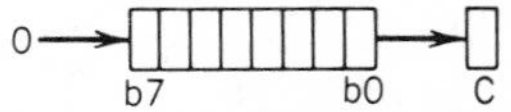

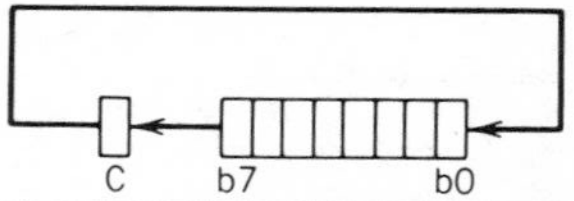

ROR	RORA RORB ROR				 06	 6	 2	 66	 6+	 2+	 76	 7	 3	46 56	2 2	1 1	A B M (b7 … b0)	• • •	↕ ↕ ↕	↕ ↕ ↕	• • •	↕ ↕ ↕
RTI														3B	6/15	1	Return from interrupt					7
RTS														39	5	1	Return from subroutine	•	•	•	•	•
SBC	SBCA SBCB	82 C2	2 2	2 2	92 D2	4 4	2 2	A2 E2	4+ 4+	2+ 2+	B2 F2	5 5	3 3				A − M − C → A B − M − C → B	8 8	↕ ↕	↕ ↕	↕ ↕	↕ ↕
SEX														1D	2	1	Sign extend B into A	•	↕	↕	0	•
ST	STA STB STD STS STU STX STY				97 D7 DD 10 DF DF 9F 10 9F	4 4 5 6 5 5 6	2 2 2 3 2 2 3	A7 E7 ED 10 EF EF AF 10 AF	4+ 4+ 5+ 6+ 5+ 5+ 6+	2+ 2+ 2+ 3+ 2+ 2+ 3+	B7 F7 FD 10 FF FF BF 10 BF	5 5 6 7 6 6 7	3 3 3 4 3 3 4				A → M B → M D → M:M + 1 S → M:M + 1 U → M:M + 1 X → M:M + 1 Y → M:M + 1	• • • • • • •	↕ ↕ ↕ ↕ ↕ ↕ ↕	↕ ↕ ↕ ↕ ↕ ↕ ↕	0 0 0 0 0 0 0	• • • • • • •
SUB	SUBA SUBB SUBD	80 C0 83	2 2 4	2 2 3	90 D0 93	4 4 6	2 2 2	A0 E0 A3	4+ 4+ 6+	2+ 2+ 2+	B0 F0 B3	5 5 7	3 3 3				A − M → A B − M → B D − M:M + 1 → D	8 8 •	↕ ↕ ↕	↕ ↕ ↕	↕ ↕ ↕	↕ ↕ ↕
SWI	SWI[6] SWI2[6] SWI3[6]													3F 10 3F 11 3F	19 20 20	1 2 1	Software interrupt 1 Software interrupt 2 Software interrupt 3	• • •	• • •	• • •	• • •	• • •
SYNC														13	≥4	1	Synchronize to interrupt	•	•	•	•	•
TFR	R1,R2	1F	6	2													R1 → R2[2]	•	•	•	•	•
TST	TSTA TSTB TST				 0D	 6	 2	 6D	 6+	 2+	 7D	 7	 3	4D 5D	2 2	1 1	Test A Test B Test M	• • •	↕ ↕ ↕	↕ ↕ ↕	0 0 0	• • •

Notes:

1 This column gives a base cycle and byte count.

2 R1 and R2 may be any pair of 8-bit or any pair of 16-bit registers.
The 8-bit registers are: A, B, CC, DP
The 16-bit registers are: X, Y, U, S, D, PC

3 EA is the effective address.

4 The PSH and PUL instructions require 5 cycles plus 1 cycle for each byte pushed or pulled.

5 5(6) means: 5 cycles if branch not taken, 6 cycles if taken (branch instructions).

6 SWI sets 1 and F bits. SW12 and SW13 do not affect 1 and F.

7 Conditions codes set as a direct result of the instruction.

8 Value of half-carry flag is undefined.

9 Special case—carry set if b7 is SET.

The circuit diagram is quite straightforward and consistent with **MC6809** design. The board has provisions for 4K worth of static RAM, and bus extenders for expanding the system. There are provisions for three EPROMs in the top of the memory map, one of which is the monitor ASSIST09, described in the *Motorola MC6809–MC6809E Microprocessor Programming Manual.* The board may run at 1, 1.5, or 2 MHz, depending on what is required. As can be seen, the connections and peripheral chips required to make a small system with the **MC6809** are minimal.

8-13 CONVERSION CONSIDERATIONS

Converting to the **MC6809** from existing **MC6800** systems is generally very easy. For most systems, the bus timing requirements are better than those provided by the **MC6800**, so they may be ignored. Of course, the clock generator may be replaced by a crystal and two capacitors, thus relieving the user from the more stringent requirements of the 01 and 02 clocks of the **MC6800**. The VMA signal used in most chip-decoding schemes may be deleted, as all addresses are valid, with the **MC6809** putting $FFFF on the address bus on unused cycles. As with all other parts, be sure to refer to the individual data sheet for particular timing diagrams and timing numbers.

8-14 SUMMARY

The **MC6809** family of processors may be used in systems ranging from simple to systems which are of the multiprocessor variety and very complex. The **MC6809** was designed to fill both of these types of systems with ease of programming and hardware design. Chapter 14 on the **MC6800–MC6809** peripherals give a total picture of what auxiliary devices may be placed directly on the bus to provide the user with the complexity of system required.

8-15 REFERENCES

Lance Leventhal, *Assembly Language Programming*, Osborne/McGraw-Hill, Berkeley, Calif., 1981.

Andrew C. Staugaard, Jr., *6809 Microcomputer Programming & Interfacing*, Howard W. Sams & Co, Indianapolis, Ind., 1981.

T. J. Wagner and G. J. Lipovski, *Fundamentals of Microcomputer Programming*, Macmillan, New York, 1984.

MC6809–MC6809E Microprocessor Programming Manual, Motorola, Inc., Austin, Tex., 1981.

CHAPTER 9

The 6500 Family of Microprocessors

Marvin L. De Jong
Department of Mathematics–Physics, The School of the Ozarks
Point Lookout, Missouri

9-1 INTRODUCTION

The **6500** family of μPs, of which the **6502** is the most well-known member, is one of the most popular μP families [1]. In addition to being used as a controller in scientific, industrial, and entertainment devices, the **6502** is used in many personal computers including the Apple, Commodore, and the Atari. Chronologically, the **6502** was designed after the Motorola **6800** μP as an enhancement of this device. The **6502** appeared on the market after the **8080A** and the **6800** but before the **6809** and the **8085**. The **6502** was originally manufactured by MOS Technology (subsequently purchased by Commodore Business Machines). Since then it has been second sourced by Rockwell International and Synertek.

The **6500** family of microprocessors consists of ten μPs and one single-chip μC, the **6500/1**. The family members use the same instruction set, and they are available in 1-, 2-, or 3-MHz versions, corresponding to the frequency of the two-phase clock. In the **6500** family, a memory reference cycle is one clock cycle. The principal differences between the members of the family are in the size of the address space, the number of interrupt pins, and in the system clock support circuitry. The discussion here focuses on the **6502**, but it applies with only minor differences to the other members of the **6500** family. More details, including specification sheets, can be obtained from:

Rockwell International Corp.
Microelectronic Devices
P.O. Box 3669
Anaheim, CA 92803

Synertek, Inc.
P.O. Box 552
Santa Clara, CA 95052

Both of these companies offer development systems with high-level language support for the **6500** family. The **6500** family also includes a number of peripheral integrated circuits used for input/output, timing, counting, and program storage. These chips include the **6520**, **6522**, **6530**, **6532**, **6545**, and the **6551**, a few of which will be discussed later in this chapter.

9-2 A PROGRAMMER'S MODEL OF THE 6500 ARCHITECTURE

The register structure of the **6502** is one of the simplest among the popular 8-bit μPs. This structure is illustrated in Figure 9-1. There is an accumulator (A) used for data transfers to and from memory, shifts, and all arithmetic and logical operations. There are two 8-bit index registers, X and Y. Their main purpose is to serve as an 8-bit index (or offset or subscript) to a base address when one of the six indexed addressing modes is used (see section 9-6). Because there are instructions that allow the index registers' contents to be incremented or decremented one unit at a time, they are also used as loop counters. The X and Y index registers may also be used for data transfers.

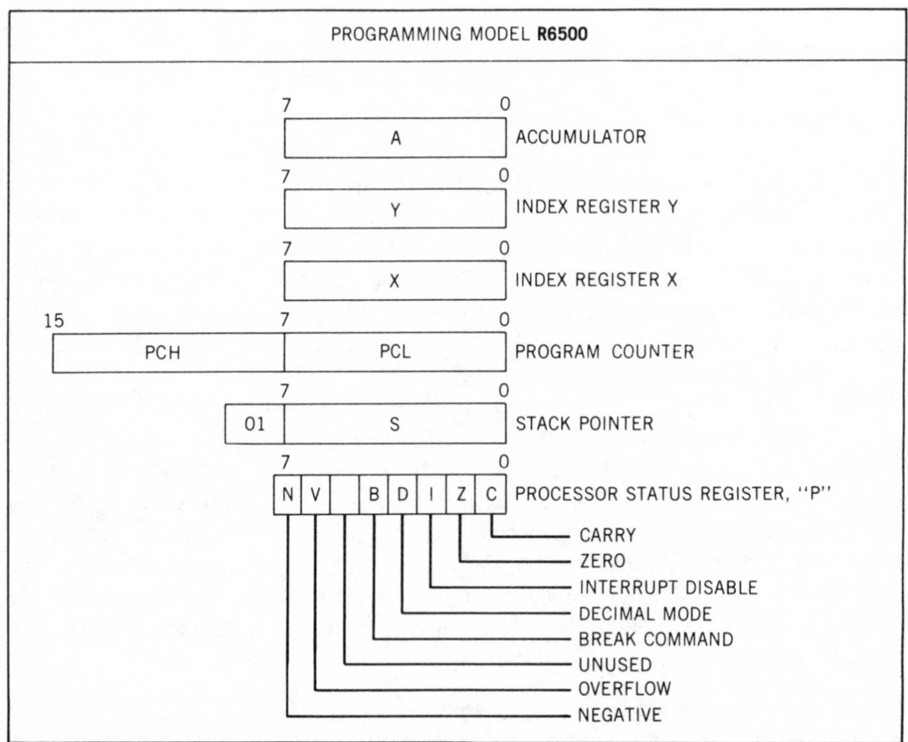

Figure 9-1 Register structure of the **6500** family of μPs. (Courtesy of Rockwell International.)

The processor status register (P) contains the flags and is detailed in Figure 9-2. The flags (or condition codes) in this register may change with the execution of each instruction. The flags that are affected by the execution of a particular instruction are given in the "Condition Codes" column of the instruction set summary in Table 9-1. A brief description of each flag follows:

1 The carry (C) flag is set when an addition, shift, or rotate instruction generates a *carry*, and it is set when a subtraction or a compare instruction does not produce a *borrow*. (See Example 9-2.) The carry flag can also be cleared with a CLI instruction or set with a SEI instruction.

2 The zero (Z) flag is set when the accumulator or index register contains *all zeros* in it as the result of an arithmetic, logical, shift, rotate, or load data instruction, and so on. (See Example 9-2.)

3 The negative (N) flag is set when the accumulator or index register has a 1 in bit 7 as the result of an arithmetic, logical, shift, rotate, or load data instruction, and so on. (See Example 9-2.)

4 The overflow (V) flag is set when an addition or subtraction operation involving *signed* numbers produces a result that cannot be correctly interpreted as a signed number; that is, if a single-precision addition produces a result in excess of \$7F (= 127) or less than \$80 (= − 128). More precisely, the V flag is the result of an EXCLUSIVE OR between the carry flag (C) and any carry from bit 6. That is, $V = C \oplus C_6$, where C is the content of the carry flag and C_6 is any carry from bit 6. The V flag can also be cleared with a CLV instruction.

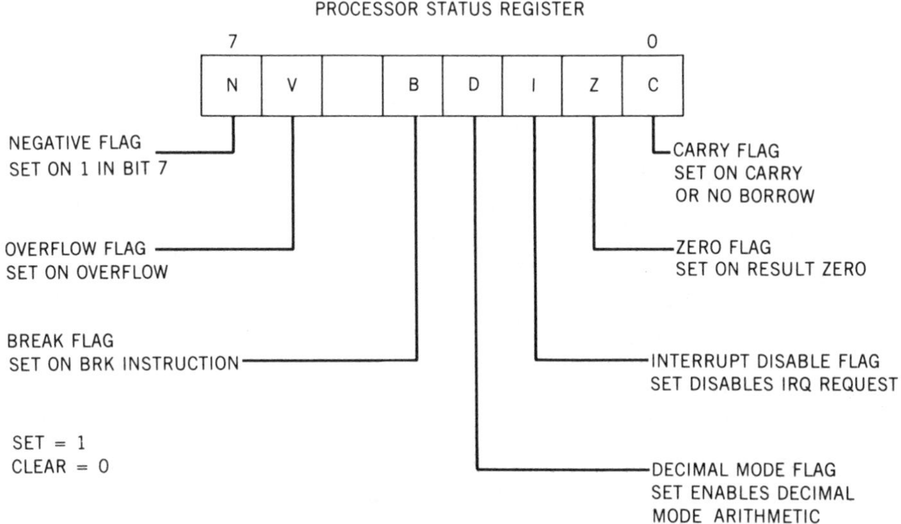

Figure 9-2 Detail of the processor status register.

Table 9-1 The 6500 Instruction Set Summary

Instructions		Immediate			Absolute			Zero page			Accum			Implied			(Ind. X)			(Ind). Y			Z page, X			Ass. X			Abs. Y			Relative			Indirect			Z page, Y			Processor status codes								
Mnemonic	Operation	Op	n	#	Op	n	#	Op	n	#	Op	n	#	Op	n	#	Op	n	#	Op	n	#	Op	n	#	Op	n	#	Op	n	#	Op	n	#	Op	n	#	Op	n	#	7 N	6 V	5 •	4 B	3 D	2 I	1 Z	0 C	Mnemonic
A D C	A + M + C → A (4) (1)	69	2	2	6D	4	3	65	3	2							61	6	2	71	5	2	75	4	2	7D	4	3	79	4	3										N	V	•	•	•	•	Z	C	A D C
A N D	A ∧ M → A (1)	29	2	2	2D	4	3	25	3	2							21	6	2	31	5	2	35	4	2	3D	4	3	39	4	3										N	•	•	•	•	•	Z	•	A N D
A S L	C ← [7 0] ← 0				0E	6	3	06	5	2	0A	2	1										16	6	2	1E	7	3													N	•	•	•	•	•	Z	C	A S L
B C C	BRANCH ON C = 0 (2)																															90	2	2							•	•	•	•	•	•	•	•	B C C
B C S	BRANCH ON C = 1 (2)																															B0	2	2							•	•	•	•	•	•	•	•	B C S
B E Q	BRANCH ON Z = 1 (2)																															F0	2	2							•	•	•	•	•	•	•	•	B E Q
B I T	A ∧ M				2C	4	3	24	3	2																															M_7	M_6	•	•	•	•	Z	•	B I T
B M I	BRANCH ON N = 1 (2)																															30	2	2							•	•	•	•	•	•	•	•	B M I
B N E	BRANCH ON Z = 0 (2)																															D0	2	2							•	•	•	•	•	•	•	•	B N E
B P L	BRANCH ON N = 0 (2)																															10	2	2							•	•	•	•	•	•	•	•	B P L
B R K	BREAK													00	7	1																									•	•	•	1	•	1	•	•	B R K
B V C	BRANCH ON V = 0 (2)																															50	2	2							•	•	•	•	•	•	•	•	B V C
B V S	BRANCH ON V = 1 (2)																															70	2	2							•	•	•	•	•	•	•	•	B V S
C L C	0 → C													18	2	1																									•	•	•	•	•	•	•	0	C L C
C L D	0 → D													D8	2	1																									•	•	•	•	0	•	•	•	C L D
C L I	0 → I													58	2	1																									•	•	•	•	•	0	•	•	C L I
C L V	0 → V													B8	2	1																									•	0	•	•	•	•	•	•	C L V
C M P	A − M	C9	2	2	CD	4	3	C5	3	2							C1	6	2	D1	5	2	D5	4	2	DD	4	3	D9	4	3										N	•	•	•	•	•	Z	C	C M P
C P X	X − M	E0	2	2	EC	4	3	E4	3	2																															N	•	•	•	•	•	Z	C	C P X
C P Y	Y − M	C0	2	2	CC	4	3	C4	3	2																															N	•	•	•	•	•	Z	C	C P Y
D E C	M − 1 → M				CE	6	3	C6	5	2													D6	6	2	DE	7	3													N	•	•	•	•	•	Z	•	D E C
D E X	X − 1 → X													CA	2	1																									N	•	•	•	•	•	Z	•	D E X
D E Y	Y − 1 → Y													88	2	1																									N	•	•	•	•	•	Z	•	D E Y
E O R	A ∨ M → A (1)	49	2	2	4D	4	3	45	3	2							41	6	2	51	5	2	55	4	2	5D	4	3	59	4	3										N	•	•	•	•	•	Z	•	E O R
I N C	M + 1 → M				EE	6	3	E6	5	2													F6	6	2	FE	7	3													N	•	•	•	•	•	Z	•	I N C
I N X	X + 1 → X													E8	2	1																									N	•	•	•	•	•	Z	•	I N X
I N Y	Y + 1 → Y													C8	2	1																									N	•	•	•	•	•	Z	•	I N Y
J M P	JUMP TO NEW LOC				4C	3	3																												6C	5	3				•	•	•	•	•	•	•	•	J M P
J S R	JUMP SUB				20	6	3																																		•	•	•	•	•	•	•	•	J S R
L D A	M → A (1)	A9	2	2	AD	4	3	A5	3	2							A1	6	2	B1	5	2	B5	4	2	BD	4	3	B9	4	3										N	•	•	•	•	•	Z	•	L D A

L D X	M → X (1)	A2	2	2	AE	4	3	A6	3	2																			BE	4	3							B6	4	2	N	•	•	•	•	•	Z	•	L D X
L D Y	M → Y (1)	A0	2	2	AC	4	3	A4	3	2													B4	4	2	BC	4	3													N	•	•	•	•	•	Z	•	L D Y
L S R	0 → [7 0] → C				4E	6	3	46	5	2	4A	2	1										56	6	2	5E	7	3													0	•	•	•	•	•	Z	C	L S R
N O P	NO OPERATION													EA	2	1																									•	•	•	•	•	•	•	•	N O P
O R A	A ∨ M → A	09	2	2	0D	4	3	05	3	2							01	6	2	11	5	2	15	4	2	1D	4	3	19	4	3										N	•	•	•	•	•	Z	•	O R A
P H A	A → Ms S − 1 → S													48	3	1																									•	•	•	•	•	•	•	•	P H A
P H P	P → Ms S − 1 → S													08	3	1																									•	•	•	•	•	•	•	•	P H P
P L A	S + 1 → S Ms → A													68	4	1																									N	•	•	•	•	•	Z	•	P L A
P L P	S + 1 → S Ms → P													28	4	1																									(RESTORED)								P L P
R O L	[7 0] ← [C] (rotate left)				2E	6	3	26	5	2	2A	2	1										36	6	2	3E	7	3													N	•	•	•	•	•	Z	C	R O L
R O R	[C] → [7 0] (rotate right)				6E	6	3	66	5	2	6A	2	1										76	6	2	7E	7	3													N	•	•	•	•	•	Z	C	R O R
R T I	RTRN INT													40	6	1																									(RESTORED)								R T I
R T S	RTRN SUB													60	6	1																									•	•	•	•	•	•	•	•	R T S
S B C	$A - M - \overline{C} \rightarrow A$ (1)	E9	2	2	ED	4	3	E5	3	2							E1	6	2	F1	5	2	F5	4	2	FD	4	3	F9	4	3										N	V	•	•	•	•	Z	(3)	S B C
S E C	1 → C													38	2	1																									•	•	•	•	•	•	•	1	S E C
S E D	1 → D													F8	2	1																									•	•	•	•	1	•	•	•	S E D
S E I	1 → I													78	2	1																									•	•	•	•	•	1	•	•	S E I
S T A	A → M				8D	4	3	85	3	2							81	6	2	91	6	2	95	4	2	9D	5	3	99	5	3										•	•	•	•	•	•	•	•	S T A
S T X	X → M				8E	4	3	86	3	2																												96	4	2	•	•	•	•	•	•	•	•	S T X
S T Y	Y → M				8C	4	3	84	3	2													94	4	2																•	•	•	•	•	•	•	•	S T Y
T A X	A → X													AA	2	1																									N	•	•	•	•	•	Z	•	T A X
T A Y	A → Y													A8	2	1																									N	•	•	•	•	•	Z	•	T A Y
T S X	S → X													BA	2	1																									N	•	•	•	•	•	Z	•	T S X
T X A	X → A													8A	2	1																									N	•	•	•	•	•	Z	•	T X A
T X S	X → S													9A	2	1																									•	•	•	•	•	•	•	•	T X S
T Y A	Y → A													98	2	1																									N	•	•	•	•	•	Z	•	T Y A

1. Add 1 to "N" if page boundary is crossed.
2. Add 1 to "N" if branch occurs to same page.
   Add 2 to "N" if branch occurs to different page.
3. Carry not = borrow.
4. If in decimal mode Z flag is invalid,
   Accumulator must be checked for zero result.

X Index X
Y Index Y
A Accumulator
M Memory per effective address
Ms Memory per stack pointer

\+ Add
− Subtract
∧ And
∨ Or
⊻ Exclusive or

M_7 Memory bit 7
M_6 Memory bit 6
n No cycles
\# No bytes.

5 The decimal mode (D) flag signals the processor that addition and subtraction are to be performed in the *decimal mode*. In this mode each byte is assumed to represent two BCD digits. This mode allows the user to do decimal arithmetic. In the decimal mode the carry flag is set when the result of adding 2 bytes exceeds 99. The D flag can only be set and cleared by the SED and the CLD instructions, respectively. (See Example 9-3.)

6 The interrrupt disable (I) flag is set whenever an interrupt occurs or when a BRK instruction is executed. (Interrupts are discussed in more detail in section 9-5.) The P register is restored to the value it had before the interrupt (or BRK) when a return from interrupt (RTI) instruction is executed, clearing the I flag. If the interrupt disable flag is set, any interrupt request made via the $\overline{\text{IRQ}}$ pin on the μP will not be recognized. The interrupt flag *does not* disable any interrupt request made via the $\overline{\text{NMI}}$ pin on the μP, *nor* does it disable execution of the BRK instruction, a software forced interrupt request. The I *flag* can also be set with a SEI instruction or cleared with a CLI instruction.

7 The break (B) flag is set whenever a BRK instruction is executed. The I flag will also be set in this case. Both flags will be cleared when the P register is restored upon returning from the interrupt. The B flag permits the programmer to distinguish between a software forced interrupt request, commonly used in debugging programs, and a hardware generated interrupt request on the $\overline{\text{IRQ}}$ pin.

The program counter (PC) is a 16-bit register that "points" to the address of a location in memory that contains the next byte of the program. When the μC system is reset the program counter is set internally to $FFFC. The number in location $FFFC is the *low-order byte* of the address of the first byte in the program. Next the program counter is incremented to $FFFD to fetch the *high-order byte* of the address of the first byte in the program. Locations $FFFC and $FFFD contain the address of the first byte in the program. Refer to Example 9-1.

EXAMPLE 9-1 A program starts at $FE00. What must be done to start program execution there?

Solution Location $FFFC must contain $00 and location $FFFD must contain $FE. When the $\overline{\text{RES}}$ pin on the μP is allowed to go to logic 1 from logic 0, the μP will fetch the starting address from these locations and the user's program will commence.

The stack pointer (S) is an 8-bit register that is used to point to a location in page 1 ($0100–$01FF) of memory. (The address space of a μP with 16 address lines may be conveniently divided into 256 *pages* each with 256 memory locations. The high-order 8 bits of the address identify the page number.) The stack pointer is used to implement a *first-in-last-out* stack that is confined to page 1 of memory. This confinement is unique to the **6500** family. When the stack is referenced by the μP, the high-order byte on the address bus is $01. This is why an "01" is shown preceding the stack pointer in Figure 9-1.

The stack is used to store return addresses, register contents, and the contents of the P register when interrupts and subroutine calls occur. When power is applied to the **6502**, a random number appears in the stack pointer. The user can initialize the stack pointer with the LDX and TXS instructions.

Since the μP uses page 1 of memory for the stack, it is good programming practice not to place programs in this page. Of course, READ/WRITE memory *must* be provided for the stack.

9-3 THE 6500 FAMILY INSTRUCTION SET

One of the most important tools in programming the **6502** is the instruction set summary in Table 9-1. With it the user can write and assemble short machine language programs, although an assembler is necessary for longer programs. Because of its usefulness, the instruction set summary will be described in some detail and referred to frequently. The first column lists the entire **6500** instruction set by *mnemonics* in alphabetical order. The next column gives a logical description of the instruction. The next 13 columns give three elements of information for each of the 13 addressing modes. These elements are (1) the operation code (or Op code) expressed in hexadecimal code; (2) the number of clock cycles required to execute the instruction; and (3) the number of bytes of memory required by each instruction. The Op code is *always the first byte* of an instruction. The meaning of the second and third bytes will be explained in section 9-6. If an entry is missing, that addressing mode is not available for the instruction. Refer to the example programs in this chapter for more details.

The second-to-the-last column indicates which flags in the processor status register are affected by the execution of that instruction. For example, Table 9-1 shows that the ADC instruction (add with carry) affects the carry flag, the zero flag, the overflow flag, and the negative flag. This information, combined with the detailed information about the P register in section 9-2, may be used to determine the condition of the P register after the execution of an instruction, provided that the values of the numbers that enter the operation are known. Example 9-2 illustrates this.

EXAMPLE 9-2 How will the flags in the P register be affected after a CMP instruction is executed if the accumulator contains \$3F and the memory location referenced contains \$B3?

Solution

a Table 9-1 indicates that the logical expression for CMP is A − M. No data is transferred by this instruction, hence A and M are not modified by its execution, and only the P register is changed.

b The CMP instruction affects the C, Z, and N flags. First observe that \$3F − \$B3 = \$8C, with a borrow.

c Since the result is not zero, the Z flag is cleared. The result has a 1 in bit 7, so the N flag is set. The operation produced a borrow, so the carry flag is cleared (no borrow = carry).

Note that the **6502** instruction set does not include an add *without* carry nor a subtract *without* borrow. A general rule is to clear the carry flag (CLC) before an addition instruction and set the carry flag (SEC) before a subtraction. The exception to the rule occurs when doing multibyte arithmetic, and the least significant bytes have already been combined. Example 9-3 illustrates a simple single-byte addition program using the decimal mode. Note especially that the carry flag is cleared before the addition operation. Example 9-3 also illustrates the general format of **6502** assembly language programs.

Example 9-3 also shows how the **6502** performs decimal arithmetic. Several other μPs accomplish the same thing with a decimal adjust (DAA) instruction. The ability to do decimal arithmetic greatly simplifies the processing of BCD data and BCD-to-binary conversions.

We conclude this section with a simple programming example that clarifies a few of the instructions and concepts introduced thus far. Example 9-3 also illustrates the format of **6502** assembly language programs that is commonly used.

EXAMPLE 9-3 Write a program segment that adds (in the decimal mode) the contents of location $0010 to the number 65 and stores the result in location $03FF. If 35 is the BCD number in location $0010, describe the status of the carry flag.

Solution

Location	Instruction B1	B2	B3	Label	Mnemonic	Operand field	Comments
$0200	F8			START	SED		Put the processor in the decimal mode.
$0201	18				CLC		Clear the carry flag.
$0202	A5	10			LDA	ADND	Get the first addend.
$0204	69	65			ADC	#65	Add it to the second addend.
$0206	8D	FF	03		STA	SUM	Store the result in $03FF.

Since the decimal sum of 35 and 65 is 100, location $03FF will contain 00 after the addition and the carry flag will be set.

To make the instructions more understandable, an English language explanation for each instruction is given in Table 9-2. Space does not permit an exposition of each instruction. Beginners may wish to consult De Jong's introductory text on the **6502** [2]. More advanced programmers will find a wealth of information in Leventhal's book [3] and in Scanlon's text [4]. In the next two sections we give additional attention to the instructions that have no simple logical expression, such as the JMP, JSR, and RTI instructions.

Table 9-2 **Description of the 6500 instruction set**

Mnemonic	*Logical expression*	*Data transfer instructions*
LDA	$M \rightarrow A$	Transfer the contents of a memory location M to the accumulator A.
LDX	$M \rightarrow X$	Transfer the contents of a memory location M to the X register.
LDY	$M \rightarrow Y$	Transfer the contents of a memory location M to the Y register.
STA	$A \rightarrow M$	Transfer the contents of the accumulator to a memory location.
STX	$X \rightarrow M$	Transfer the contents of the X register to a memory location.
STY	$Y \rightarrow M$	Transfer the contents of the Y register to a memory location.
TAX	$A \rightarrow X$	Transfer the contents of the accumulator to the X register.
TXA	$X \rightarrow A$	Transfer the contents of the X register to the accumulator.
TAY	$A \rightarrow Y$	Transfer the contents of the accumulator to the Y register.
TYA	$Y \rightarrow A$	Transfer the contents of the Y register to the accumulator.
		Arithmetic and logical operation instructions
ADC	$A + M + C \rightarrow A$	Add the contents of the accumulator, a memory location, and the carry flag; store the result in the accumulator.
SBC	$A - M - \overline{C} \rightarrow A$	Subtract the contents of a memory location from the contents of the accumulator. Also invert and subtract the carry flag; store the result in the accumulator.
AND	$A \wedge M \rightarrow A$	Form the logical AND of the contents of the accumulator and a memory location; store the result in the accumulator.
ORA	$A \vee M \rightarrow A$	Form the logical OR of the contents of the accumulator and a memory location; store the result in the accumulator.
EOR	$A \veebar M \rightarrow A$	Form the logical EXCLUSIVE OR of the contents of the accumulator and a memory location; store the result in the accumulator.
		Test instructions
CMP	$A - M$	Subtract the contents of a memory location from the accumulator; the result is used only to set flags in the P register.
CPX	$X - M$	Subtract the contents of a memory location from the X register; the result is used only to set flags in the P register.

Table 9-2 (Continued)

Mnemonic	Logical expression	
		Data transfer instructions
CPY	Y − M	Subtract the contents of a memory location from the Y register; the result is used only to set flags in the P register.
BIT	$A \wedge M$, $M_7 \rightarrow N$, $M_6 \rightarrow V$	Form the logical AND of the contents of the accumulator and a memory location; use the result to set the Z flag. Transfer bit 7 of the memory location to the N flag, and transfer bit 6 of the memory location to the V flag.
		Register shift and modify instructions
DEC	$M - 1 \rightarrow M$	Decrement the contents of a memory location by one unit.
INC	$M + 1 \rightarrow M$	Increment the contents of a memory location by one unit.
DEX	$X - 1 \rightarrow X$	Decrement the contents of the X register by one unit.
INX	$X + 1 \rightarrow X$	Increment the contents of the X register by one unit.
DEY	$Y - 1 \rightarrow Y$	Decrement the contents of the Y register by one unit.
INY	$Y + 1 \rightarrow Y$	Increment the contents of the Y register by one unit.
ASL	C ← [7 … 0] ← 0	Shift the contents of a location left, zero into bit 0, bit 7 into carry.
LSR	0 → [7 … 0] → C	Shift the contents of a location right; zero into bit 7, bit 0 into carry.
ROL	C ← [7 … 0] ← (C)	Rotate the contents of a location left; carry into bit 0, bit 7 into carry.
ROR	(C) → [7 … 0] → C	Rotate the contents of a location right; carry into bit 7, bit 0 into carry.
		Flag set and clear instructions
CLC	$0 \rightarrow C$	Clear the carry flag in the processor status register.
SEC	$1 \rightarrow C$	Set the carry flag.
CLD	$0 \rightarrow D$	Clear the decimal mode flag in the processor status register to do binary arithmetic.
SED	$1 \rightarrow D$	Set the decimal mode flag to do BCD arithmetic.
CLI	$0 \rightarrow I$	Clear the interrupt disable flag to allow $\overline{IRQ}$ interrupts.
SEI	$1 \rightarrow I$	Set the interrupt disable flag to prevent interrupts from the $\overline{IRQ}$ pin.
CLV	$1 \rightarrow V$	Clear the overflow flag.

		No operation instruction
NOP		No operation.
		Branch instructions
BCC	PC = PC + OFFSET[a]	If the carry flag is clear, obtain the next instruction at location PC + OFFSET.
BCS	PC = PC + OFFSET	If the carry flag is set, obtain the next instruction at location PC + OFFSET.
BEQ	PC = PC + OFFSET	If the Z flag is set, obtain the next instruction at location PC + OFFSET.
BNE	PC = PC + OFFSET	If the result was not zero, obtain the next instruction at location PC + OFFSET.
BMI	PC = PC + OFFSET	If the N flag is set, obtain the next instruction at location PC + OFFSET.
BPL	PC = PC + OFFSET	If the result is not minus, obtain the next instruction at location PC + OFFSET.
BVC	PC = PC + OFFSET	If the arithmetic operation cleared the V flag, obtain the next instruction at PC + OFFSET.
BVS	PC = PC + OFFSET	If the V flag is set, obtain the next instruction at PC + OFFSET.
		Stack operation instructions
PHA	$A \rightarrow M_S$, $S - 1 \rightarrow S$	Push the contents of the accumulator on the stack, and decrement the stack pointer.
PLA	$S + 1 \rightarrow S$, $M_S \rightarrow A$	Increment the stack pointer, and pull the accumulator contents from the stack.
PHP	$P \rightarrow M_S$, $S - 1 \rightarrow S$	Push the P register contents on the stack, and decrement the stack pointer.
PLP	$S + 1 \rightarrow S$, $M_S \rightarrow P$	Increment the stack pointer, and pull the P register contents from the stack.
TXS	$X \rightarrow S$	Transfer the contents of the X register to the stack pointer.
TSX	$S \rightarrow X$	Transfer the contents of the stack pointer to the X register.
		Jump, subroutine call, interrupt, and return instructions
JMP	No simple logic.	Jump to a new location to continue program execution. PC is modified.
JSR	No simple logic.	Jump to a subroutine to continue execution. PC is saved.
RTS	No simple logic.	Return to a calling program from a subroutine. PC is restored.
RTI	No simple logic.	Return to a program from an interrupt routine.
BRK	No simple logic.	Force a JUMP to an interrupt routine with software.

[a] OFFSET is the 2s complement code of the second byte of any of the branch instructions, and PC is identical to the address of the first operation code following the branch instruction.

9-4 BRANCHES, JUMPS, AND SUBROUTINE CALLS

Several instructions and processes require a more detailed explanation than Tables 9-1 and 9-2 afford. We begin with the BRANCH instructions, BNE, BEQ, and so on. The BRANCH instructions are 2-byte instructions, and the μP interprets the second byte as an 8-bit *offset* to be added to the program counter *if* the BRANCH condition is met. The offset is interpreted as a 2s complement number, allowing both forward and backward BRANCHes. The BRANCH instructions *test the flags in the P register.* If the condition is met the offset is added to the program counter, otherwise the program counter is not modified and execution continues with the instruction following the BRANCH instruction. Example 9-4 illustrates this concept.

It is *very important* to realize that (because the program counter is incremented after each program byte is fetched) the value of the program counter that is added to the offset is the address of the first Op code *following* the BRANCH instruction. The notation PC = PC + OFFSET in Table 9-2 refers only to the situation where the BRANCH condition is met. Example 9-4 and Example 9-5 illustrate these ideas.

EXAMPLE 9-4 Locations $B035 and $B036 of a program contain a BEQ $F2 instruction. Where will the program continue if **(a)** Z = 0, **(b)** Z = 1?

Solution

a If Z = 0 the program will not branch and the next instruction whose Op code is in location $B037 will be executed.

b If Z = 1 the branch condition is met and the branch will be taken. The destination of the branch is $B037 + $F2 = $B029. Note that the program branched back to $B029 because the offset was negative ($F2 = −$0E).

EXAMPLE 9-5 When a program reaches location $B035 it must go to location $B063 if the carry flag is set. What instruction should be in locations $B035 and $B036?

Solution A branch on carry set (BCS) instruction is required. The offset required is $B063 − $B037 = $2C. In machine language the instruction is $B0 $2C.

A jump (JMP) instruction is a 3-byte instruction; the second 2 bytes provide the processor with the destination address in the order low-order byte first, high-order byte second. In the case of the *indirect* JMP, the second and third bytes of the instruction give the address (low-order byte followed by high-order byte) of the location where the low-order byte of the destination of the JMP is found. The high-order byte of the destination address of the JMP is found in the next higher location in memory. See Example 9-6.

EXAMPLE 9-6 A JMP indirect instruction consists of the following 3 bytes: 6C FA 1F. Assume location $1FFA contains $50 and location $1FFB contains $03. Where will execution of the program continue after the JMP instruction?

Solution The program counter low (PCL) will be loaded with the number in \$1FFA and the program counter high (PCH) will be loaded with the number in \$1FFB. Program execution continues at \$0350, the number stored in these two locations.

It will be convenient in what follows to continue the practice introduced in Example 9-6 in which the low-order byte of the program counter is called PCL and the high-order byte is called PCH. Further, the low-order byte of an address will be called ADL, while the high-order byte will be called ADH.

A subroutine call (JSR) is a 3-byte instruction that provides the processor with the starting address of the subroutine. The second byte of the JSR instruction is the ADL of the first instruction of the subroutine, while the third byte of the JSR instruction is the ADH of the first instruction in the subroutine. A JSR instruction produces the following sequence of events:

1 The ADH of the third byte of the JSR instruction is stored on the stack and the stack pointer is decremented.

2 The ADL of the third byte of the JSR instruction is stored on the stack and the stack pointer is decremented.

3 The second and third bytes of the JSR instruction are placed in the PCL and the PCH, respectively.

4 Execution of the subroutine commences.

The last instruction in the subroutine is an RTS (return from subroutine) instruction. It produces the following sequence of events:

1 The stack pointer is incremented and the PCL is loaded from this location in the stack.

2 The stack pointer is incremented and the PCH is loaded from this location in the stack.

3 The program counter is incremented and execution continues. Example 9-7 clarifies these concepts.

EXAMPLE 9-7 Write a subroutine that reads an ASCII encoded keyboard and returns with a 7-bit ASCII character in the accumulator. The keyboard is accessed at location \$1700, an input port labeled Pad. A key depression results in a 10-μs logic zero strobe pulse on bit 7 of the input port. The subroutine should wait until a key is depressed. Describe the calling instruction and indicate what numbers are stored on the stack.

Solution

Location	*Instruction*	*Label*	*Mnemonic operand*	*Comments*
\$0800	AD 00 17	SUB	LDA PAD	Read the keyboard location.
\$0803	30 FB		BMI SUB	Wait for the strobe pulse.
\$0805	60		RTS	Return to the calling program.

The calling program instruction will look like this:

```
$032D    20 00 08  CALL   JSR SUB  Go to keyboard input subroutine.
```

When this calling instruction is executed, \$03 will be stored at the top of the stack and \$2F will be stored in the next location down. If the stack pointer was \$6A before the JSR instruction, then \$03 will be stored in location \$016A and \$2F will be stored in \$0169.

9-5 INTERRUPTS

The **6502** supports three kinds of interrupts, two of which occur when the external circuitry produces logic level changes on either the $\overline{IRQ}$ (interrupt request) pin or the $\overline{NMI}$ (nonmaskable interrupt) pin. The third interrupt is produced by a BRK instruction in a program. The $\overline{IRQ}$-type interrupt will be described in some detail and the other two interrupt types will be described by comparison.

An $\overline{IRQ}$-type interrupt occurs when an external circuit produces a logic-0 voltage on the $\overline{IRQ}$ pin on the **6502** for approximately eight clock cycles. If the I flag in the P register is set, the interrupt request will *not* be recognized and execution of the program will continue normally. If the I flag is cleared, the following sequence of events occurs:

1 The instruction currently being executed is completed.
2 PC is stored on the stack in the order PCH first, PCL second.
3 The P register is stored on the stack.
4 The I flag is set to disable interrupts.
5 The μP loads the contents of location \$FFFE into PCL.
6 The μP loads the contents of location \$FFFF into PCH.
7 Execution continues with the Op code located at PCH–PCL.

The set of instructions starting at the location whose address is in \$FFFE and \$FFFF is called the *interrupt routine.* It ends with an RTI (return from interrupt) instruction that produces the following sequence of events:

1 The stack pointer is incremented and P is pulled from the stack.
2 The stack pointer is incremented and PCL is pulled from the stack.
3 The stack pointer is incremented and PCH is pulled from the stack.
4 Execution continues at PCH–PCL, the location of the first instruction after the instruction that was interrupted.

The $\overline{NMI}$ interrupt differs from the $\overline{IRQ}$ interrupt in several important ways:

1 The $\overline{NMI}$ pin is edge sensitive (negative transition) rather than level sensitive.
2 An $\overline{NMI}$ interrupt is *not* disabled by the I flag or any other flag.
3 The new PCL and the new PCH are obtained from locations \$FFFA and \$FFFB, respectively.

Clearly, the $\overline{\text{NMI}}$ has a higher priority than the $\overline{\text{IRQ}}$ since it cannot be disabled. $\overline{\text{NMI}}$ interrupts are used to implement 24-hour clocks, handle panic situations, and implement single-step execution in some μC systems. The number stored in $FFFE and $FFFF is called the *$\overline{IRQ}$ vector*, and it points to the first instruction in the $\overline{\text{IRQ}}$ routine. The number stored in $FFFA and $FFFB is called the *$\overline{NMI}$ vector*, and it points to the first instruction in the $\overline{\text{NMI}}$ routine.

When a BRK instruction is executed in a program, program control switches to the $\overline{\text{IRQ}}$ routine in the same way that was described above for the $\overline{\text{IRQ}}$ request via the $\overline{\text{IRQ}}$ pin on the **6502**. However, the I flag in the P register *cannot* disable a BRK instruction. Also, the B flag is set when a BRK instruction is executed. After returning from the $\overline{\text{IRQ}}$ routine following a BRK instruction, the next Op code executed will be located at the address of the BRK instruction *plus two*. Usually a NOP instruction is inserted just after the BRK instruction to fill in the single meaningless program byte between the BRK Op code and the first Op code to be executed following a BRK.

EXAMPLE 9-8 How would the subroutine in Example 9-7 be modified to operate on an interrupt basis or from a BRK instruction?

Solution An interrupt vector ($0800) pointing to the start of the routine must be loaded into locations $FFFE and $FFFF. $00 should be in $FFFE and $08 should be in $FFFF. In most instances of interrupts the contents of the accumulator must be saved, so PHA (PUSH A) and PLA (PULL A) instructions are inserted. Assume that the ASCII code from the keyboard will be returned to the main program in the X register. Also assume that the negative strobe is connected to the $\overline{\text{IRQ}}$ pin. Bit 7 must be masked to return a 7-bit code. The $\overline{\text{IRQ}}$ or BRK routine follows:

Location	*Instruction*	*Label*	*Mnemonic operand*	*Comments*
$0800	48	IRQ	PHA	Save the accumulator on the stack.
$0801	AD 00 17		LDA PAD	Get the keyboard contents.
$0804	29 7F		AND #$7F	Mask bit 7.
$0806	AA		TAX	Transfer A to X.
$0807	68		PLA	Pull the accumulator from the stack.
$0808	40		RTI	Return.

To get to this routine from a BRK instruction, the main program should have this instruction:

$ABCD	00	BRK	Go to the interrupt routine.
$ABCE	EA	NOP	This instruction will be skipped.
$ABCF	.. .. ..	..	This instruction will be executed.

9-6 ADDRESSING MODES

We begin this discussion with an important definition. The *operand* of an instruction is the 8-bit number that is the *object* of the instruction. For example, in the case of a LDA instruction, the operand is the number that is transferred to the accumulator. In the case of an arithmetic or logical instruction, the operand is the number that becomes one of the two elements involved in the operation, the other element is already in the accumulator, and the result of the operation is stored in the accumulator. Thus, each instruction moves, modifies, or "uses" a number called the operand of the instruction. The addressing mode determines where that number is found; that is, where the operand is. In the Operation column of Table 9-1 and in the Logical Expression column of Table 9-2, the symbol M is frequently used to designate that the operand is in the *memory* space. The operand can also be in one of the internal registers of the **6502**. When the operand is in memory the symbol *ADL* stands for the low-order byte of the address of the operand and the symbol *ADH* stands for the high-order byte of the address of the operand.

In the *immediate addressing mode*, the operand is the second byte of the instruction. Note the use of the immediate mode in the fourth instruction (ADC) in Example 9-3.

In the *absolute addressing mode*, the ADL and the ADH of the operand are given by the second and third bytes of the instruction, respectively. Refer to the last instruction in Example 9-3 for an example of absolute addressing.

In the *zero-page addressing mode*, the second byte of the instruction is the ADL of the operand. The ADH of the operand is $00, thus the operand will always be in page zero of memory. See the third instruction (LDA) in Example 9-3 for an example of this mode.

In the *accumulator addressing mode*, the operand is in the accumulator. Only four instructions, the two ROTATE and the two SHIFT instructions, have access to the accumulator.

In the *implied addressing mode*, the location of the operand is implied by the instruction. For example, the INX instruction affects *only* the contents of the X register. All the information the processor needs to locate the operand is in the Op code, thus all implied instructions require only a *single byte*. The first two instructions in Example 9-3 use the implied mode.

Relative addressing has already been described in our explanation of branches. See section 9-4. The destination of the branch is relative to the location of the Op code following the branch instruction.

In the *zero page indexed by X addressing mode*, the ADL of the operand is the *sum* of the second byte of the instruction and the number in the X register. Any carry from this addition is ignored, so the ADH of the operand will *always* be $00. This addressing mode is illustrated in Example 9-9.

EXAMPLE 9-9 Write a program segment to compare the contents of a table located from $0020 to $002F with the contents of a table located from $036F to $037E. (The tables might contain ASCII strings.) If the contents differ, branch to OUT, otherwise continue execution.

Solution

Location	*Instruction*	*Label*	*Mnemonic operand*	*Comments*
$0200	A2 0F	START	LDX #$0F	LDX in the immediate mode.
$0202	B5 20	AGAIN	LDA TAB1,X	LDA in zero page indexed by X mode.
$0204	DD 6F 03		CMP TAB2,X	CMP in absolute indexed by X mode.
$0207	D0 20		BNE OUT	OUT is assumed to be at $0229.
$0209	CA		DEX	Implied mode to decrement X.
$020A	10 F6		BPL AGAIN	Relative mode to branch.

The *zero page indexed by Y addressing mode* is identical to the zero page indexed by X addressing mode except the number in the *Y register* is added to the second byte of the instruction to give the ADL of the operand.

In the *absolute indexed by X addressing mode*, the ADL of the operand is the sum of the number in the X register and the second byte of the instruction. The ADH of the operand is formed by adding any carry from the first sum to the third byte of the instruction. The third instruction in Example 9-9 illustrates this mode. In that example, when X = $0F, the operand of the CMP instruction is located at $036F + $0F = $037E.

Note that the *absolute indexed by Y addressing mode* is exactly like the absolute indexed by X mode except that the Y register is used as the index.

To explain the *indirect indexed addressing mode*, assume that the second byte of the instruction is symbolized by IAL (indirect address low). IAL is a *zero-page address.* The number in this zero-page location is added to the number in the Y register to give the ADL of the operand. The carry from this sum is added to the number in the zero-page location IAL + 1 to form the ADH of the operand. If the bracket notation [ ] is used to mean "the contents of," then we may symbolize this by saying:

```
    ADL = [IAL] + [Y],
    ADH = [IAL + 1],
OPERAND = [ADH,ADL],
```

if we remember that any carry from the first sum is added to [IAL + 1]. See Example 9-10 for an illustration.

EXAMPLE 9-10 What is the address of the operand of the LDA instruction in the following program segment? Assume location $0032 contains $2A and location $0033 contains $A0.

```
$0200 A0 55    LDY #$55        Initialize the Y register to $55.
$0202 B1 32    LDA (IAL),Y     LDA in indirect indexed mode.
```

Solution IAL points to the zero-page location \$0032. This location contains \$2A, so the ADL of the operand is \$2A + \$55 = \$7F. Since there is no carry from this sum, the ADH of the operand is the number in \$0032 + 1, and this number is \$A0. The operand is in location \$A07F, and it will be loaded into the accumulator by this instruction.

Critics of the **6502** who claim it has too few registers frequently overlook the fact that indirect indexed addressing makes page zero of memory a set of up to 128 register pairs, whose contents identify memory locations that may be accessed by eight different instructions in the **6502** instruction set.

Only the Y register may serve as an index in the indirect indexed addressing mode, and only the X register may serve as an index in the *indexed indirect addressing mode*. In this mode the number in the X register is added to the second byte of the instruction to give the address of a *zero-page* location. This zero-page location contains the ADL of the operand. The ADH of the operand is found in the next location (up) in memory. Call BAL the second byte of an instruction in the indexed indirect addressing mode. Then,

```
    ADL  = [BAL + [X]],
    ADH  = [BAL + [X] + 1],
OPERAND  = [ADH,ADL]
```

where all carrys are ignored. See Example 9-11.

EXAMPLE 9-11 Determine the location of the operand of the AND instruction in the following program segment. Assume location \$0032 contains \$2A and location \$0033 \$A0.

```
$0200 A2 32    LDX #$32        Initialize the X register to $32.
$0202 21 00    AND (BAL,X)     AND in indexed indirect mode.
```

Solution Note that for this example BAL, the byte in \$0203, is 00. BAL when added to X gives \$32. The ADL of the operand is found in this location, therefore it is \$2A. BAL + X + 1 is \$33 so the ADH is found at \$0033, and it is \$A0. The operand is in location \$A02A.

9-7 THE 6502 SIGNALS

The internal architecture of the **6500** family of μP forms the backdrop for the remainder of this chapter. A block diagram of the architecture of the **6500** family is shown in Figure 9-3. The pin assignments of the **6502** are shown in Figure 9-4. The pins can be divided into groups according to function: power, clock signals, address bus, bidirectional data bus, control bus, and interrupt pins. All output pins are rated at one standard TTL load; in many μC systems buffering will be required. All of the pin functions are summarized briefly in the next few paragraphs. A more detailed examination of the system timing requirements is given in section 9-8.

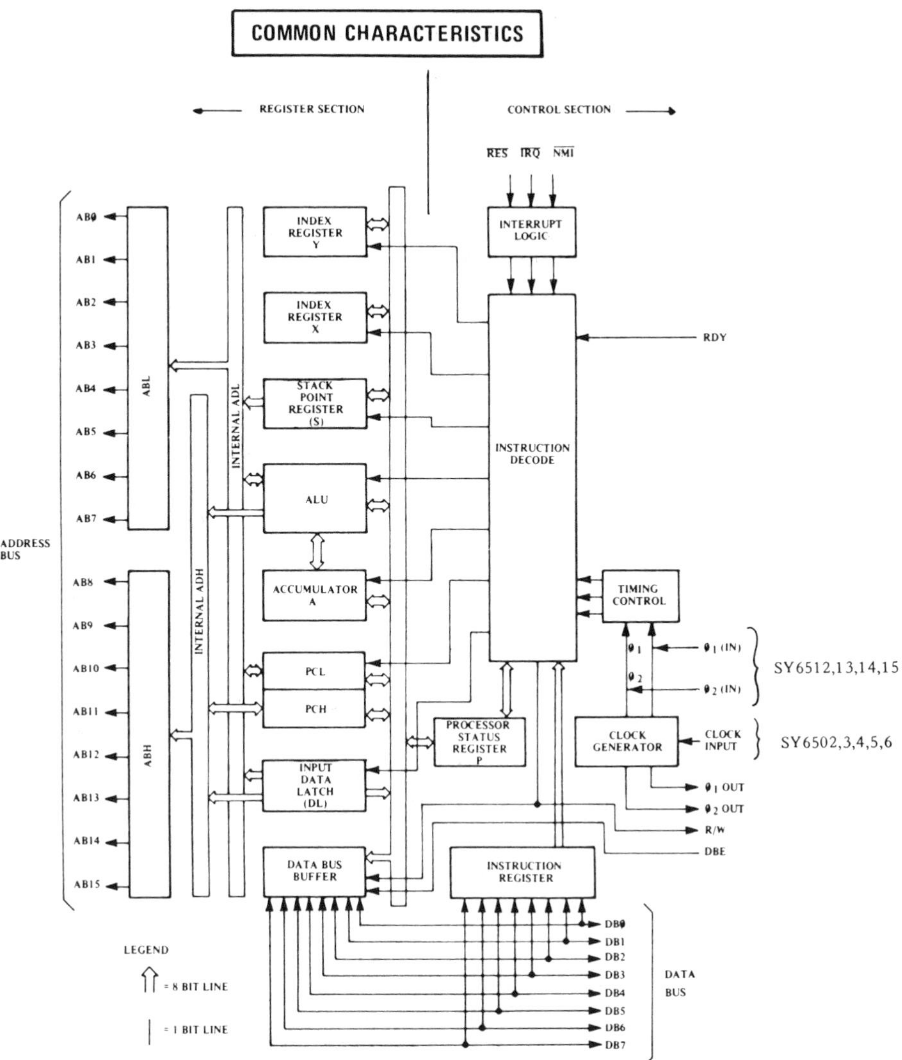

Figure 9-3 **SY6500** internal architecture. (Courtesy of Synertech, Inc.)

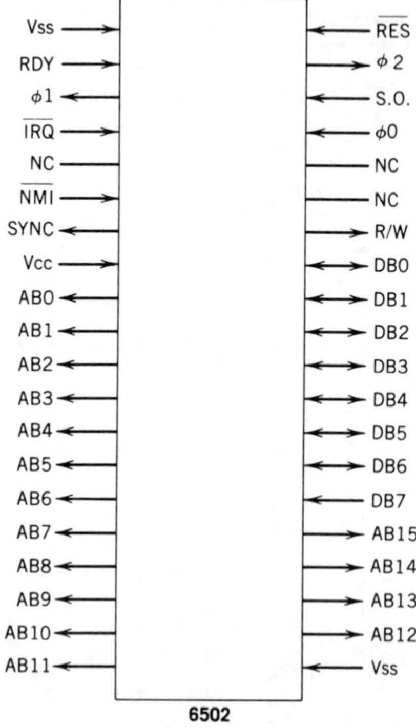

Figure 9-4 **6502** pin assignments.

Power. Vcc is connected to +5 V, Vss to ground.

Clock. The **6502** requires a single, TTL level clock input on the $\phi 0$ pin. The clock signal can be supplied by an external square wave generator or a crystal oscillator. Several clock circuits are shown in Figure 9-5. Clock circuitry internal to the **6502** generates the two-phase clock signals $\phi 1$ and $\phi 2$, both of which are output pins.

Address bus. The pins designated AB0–AB15 control the address bus. With 16 address lines the address space consists of 2^{16} memory locations. Note that the address bus drivers on the μP are output devices *rather than* tri-state devices. Direct memory access (DMA) operations will require special circuitry to isolate the address bus [5].

Bidirectional data bus. The pins designated DB0–DB7 are connected to the μC system's 8-bit data bus. These outputs are tri-state buffers rated at one standard TTL load.

Read/write. The R/W (sometimes called $R/\overline{W}$) pin is an output pin that controls the direction of a data transfer on the data bus. When the processor READs memory, R/W will be at logic 1: when the processor WRITEs to memory, then R/W is at logic 0. DMA operations must also make use of the R/W line.

Reset. The $\overline{RES}$ pin is an input to the **6502** that is used either to start the processor from a power-down condition or to reset it. This pin must be held at logic

SY6502

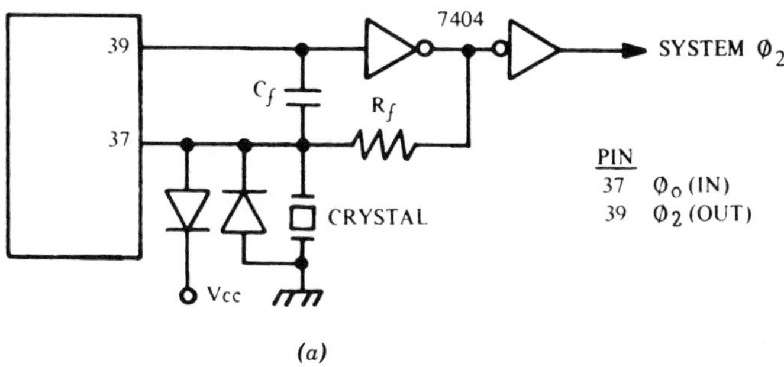

(*a*)

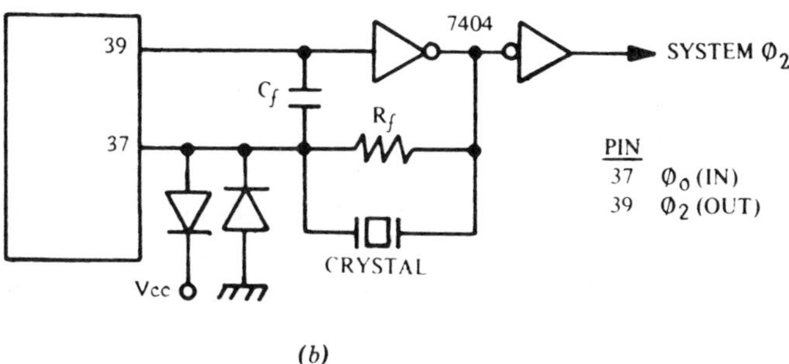

(*b*)

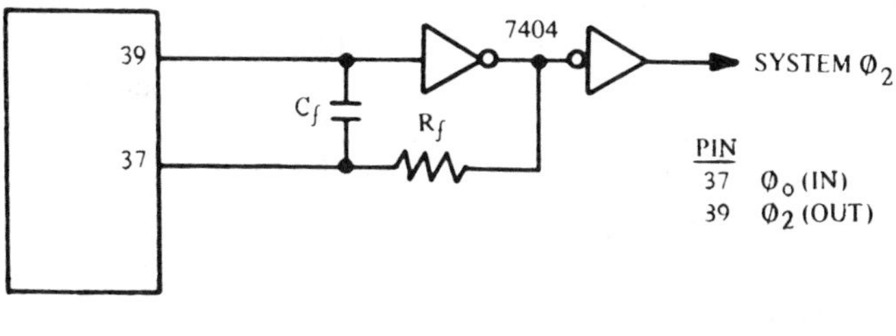

(*c*)

Figure 9-5 Clock circuits for the **6502**. Recommended values for R_f and C_f are 330 kΩ and 10 pF, respectively. (*a*) **SY6502** parallel mode crystal controlled oscillator. (*b*) **SY6502** series mode crystal controlled oscillator. (*c*) **SY6502** time base generator—RC network. (Courtesy of Synertech, Inc.)

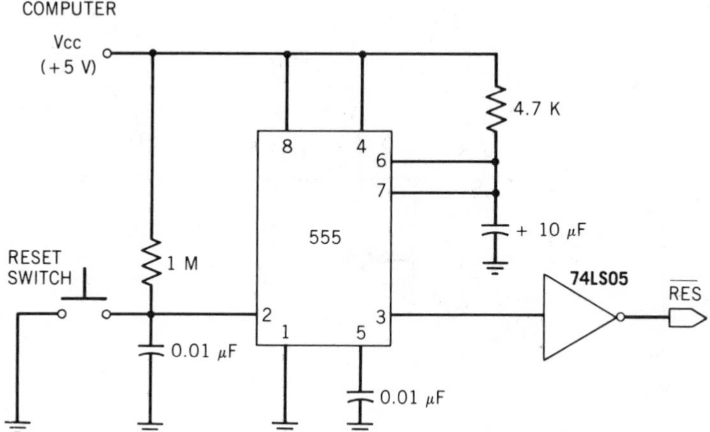

Figure 9-6 Circuit to reset the microcomputer system under power-up or pushbutton control.

0 for at least two clock cycles while Vcc is at 5 V. No data transfers take place when $\overline{\text{RES}}$ is at logic 0. Six cycles after it makes the transition to logic 1 it will load the PC from locations $FFFC and $FFFD as described in section 9-2. The numbers found in the various registers in the processor and in the peripheral interface adapters in the **6500** family will be random when power is applied. The system $\overline{\text{RES}}$ forces the important I/O registers to known values, preventing possible destruction of the devices being controlled by the system. A circuit to produce either a power-up reset signal or a pushbutton reset is shown in Figure 9-6. It holds the $\overline{\text{RES}}$ pin at logic 0 for about 500 ms before allowing it to go to logic 1; the system Vcc must reach 5 V within this time interval.

Ready. The *RDY* pin is an input that allows DMA operations and single-cycle instruction execution. It is also used to interface the processor with slow memory devices. A negative transition when $\phi 1$ is at logic 1, or when $\phi 1$ makes its negative transition during a READ cycle, halts the processor with the address lines static and the data bus in its high impedance state. A positive transition during a subsequent clock cycle causes the processor to resume operation. A circuit that ensures the correct timing for the $\overline{\text{RDY}}$ signal is shown in Figure 9-7. The $\overline{\text{WAIT}}$ line is pulled to logic 0 to halt the processor.

SYNC. The SYNC pin is an output that goes to logic 1 on a clock cycle during which the processor is fetching an Op code. It is used to implement single-instruction execution by pulling the $\overline{\text{RDY}}$ pin low during an Op code fetch, halting the μP just after the previous instruction was executed. Single-instruction execution may also be accomplished by NANDing SYNC with $\phi 2$ to make a $\overline{\text{NMI}}$ signal, interrupting the processor after each instruction is executed.

Set overflow. This is an input to the **6502**. A negative transition on the S.O. pin coincident with the negative transition of $\phi 1$ will set the overflow (V) flag in the

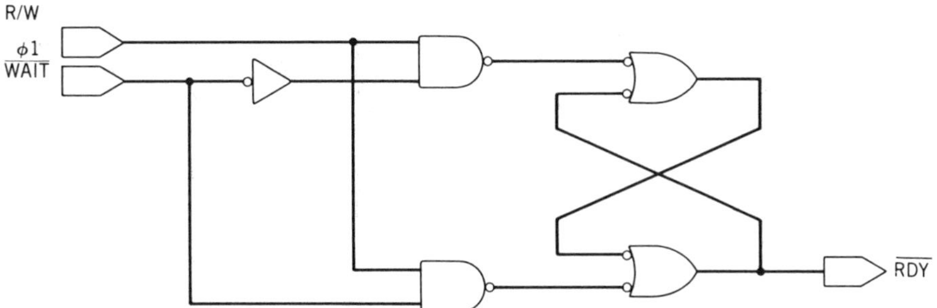

Figure 9-7 Circuit that produces a correctly timed $\overline{\text{RDY}}$ signal.

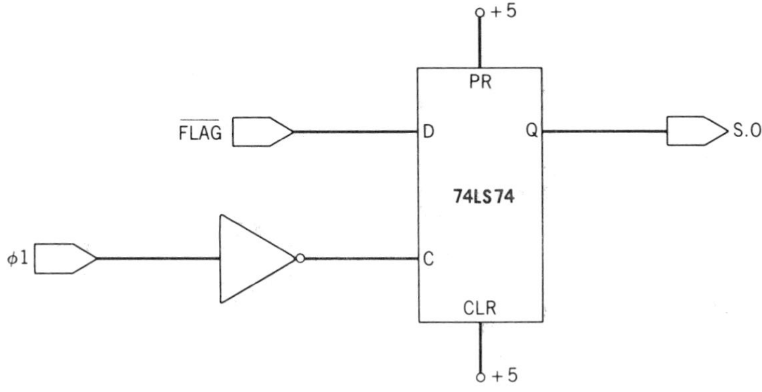

Figure 9-8 A logic 0 signal on $\overline{\text{FLAG}}$ produces a correctly timed transition on the S.O. pin.

P register. This gives the possibility of a hardware flag, but the user should be aware that ADC and SBC instructions also affect the same flag. A circuit to produce the correct timing for setting the V flag is shown in Figure 9-8. This signal is rarely used in applications.

Interrupts. The interrupt structure of the **6502** has been described in detail in section 9-5. The $\overline{\text{NMI}}$ pin and the $\overline{\text{IRQ}}$ pin require a 3.3 kΩ pull-up resistor, and these inputs may be wire-ORed to allow several interrupt sources to produce interrupts.

9-8 6502 SYSTEM TIMING

Each clock cycle in a **6502** system is either a READ cycle or a WRITE cycle. During some clock cycles there are internal operations taking place that are necessary in order to perform an instruction. However, even during these cycles the processor will either be reading or writing to memory, but the data will be discarded. Figures 9-9 and 9-10 show the signals and timing parameters during READ and WRITE cycles. The values for the important timing parameters are given in

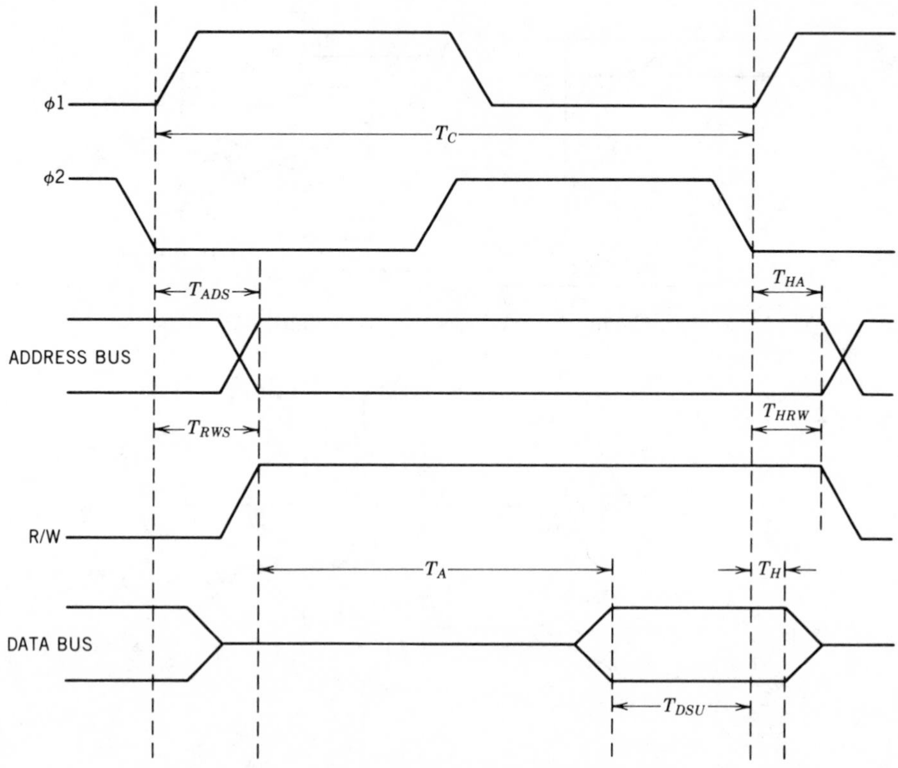

Figure 9-9 Timing diagram for a READ cycle.

Table 9-3. The value of these parameters for the 2- or 3-MHz versions of the processor may be estimated by scaling according to the clock period.

An important parameter in choosing memory devices is the access time T_A. Figure 9-9 shows that

$$T_A = T_C - T_{ADS} - T_{DSU}$$

Using the data given in Table 9-3 it is seen that the access time for a 1-MHz processor is 600 ns. The propagation delays through the decoders should be subtracted from the result given by the equation. Thus, any memory chip with such an access time, or less, will be suitable in the system.

The data on the bus is clocked into the **6502** by the trailing edge of $\phi 2$, and the data must be stable for a hold time, T_H, of at least 10 ns after $\phi 2$. The hold time is easily obtained from propagation delays either in the $\phi 2$ buffer/driver or in the data bus buffers. On the other hand, propagation delays in $\phi 2$ cannot be excessive because the **6502** only holds data on the bus for 30 ns after $\phi 2$ on a WRITE cycle, and again it is the trailing edge of $\phi 2$ that clocks the data into memory on a WRITE cycle. The designer should pay close attention to these timing restrictions.

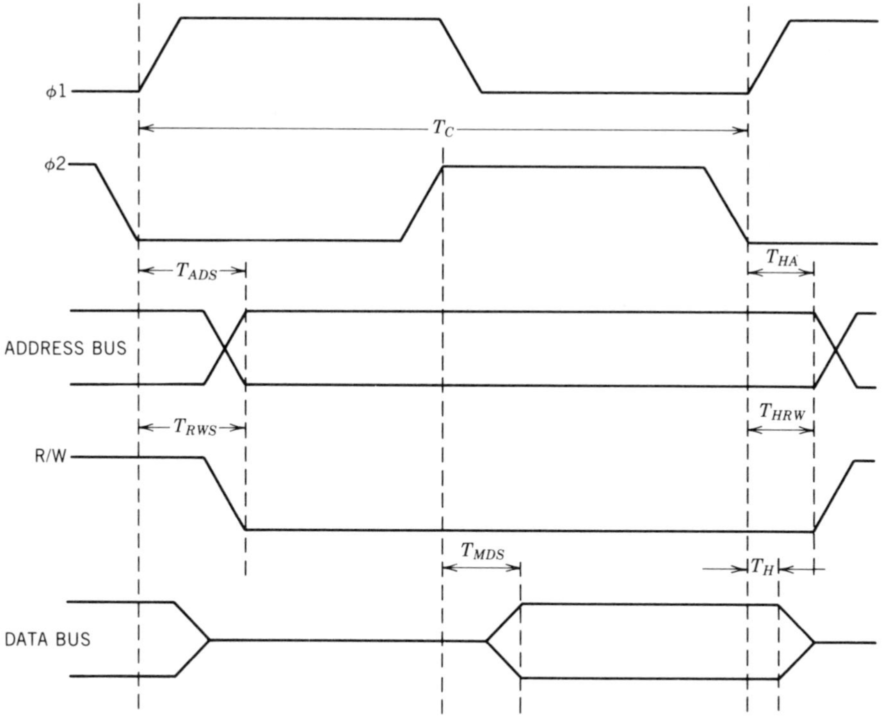

Figure 9-10 Timing diagram for a WRITE cycle.

Because the address lines and the R/W line are held stable for a time interval $T_{HA} = T_{HRW}$ after the conclusion of a READ cycle, it is possible that some data bus drive overlap may occur when two memory devices are accessed on successive clock cycles. This possibility can be removed by strobing the memory with $\phi 2$. One way in which this can be accomplished is by using $\phi 2$ to gate the address decoders that provide the chip select signals for the memory device. If the memory device has more

Table 9-3 **Timing parameters for the 6502 (1-MHz version)**

Symbol	*Characteristic*	*Value (ns)*
T_C	Cycle time	1000
T_{ADS}	Address setup time from **6502**	300 (max)
T_{RWS}	R/W setup time from **6502**	300 (max)
T_{DSU}	Data stability time period	100 (min)
T_H	Data hold time—READ	10 (min)
T_H	Data hold time—WRITE	30 (min)
T_{HA}	Address hold time	30 (min)
T_{HRW}	R/W hold time	30 (min)
T_{MDS}	Data setup time from **6502**	200 (max)

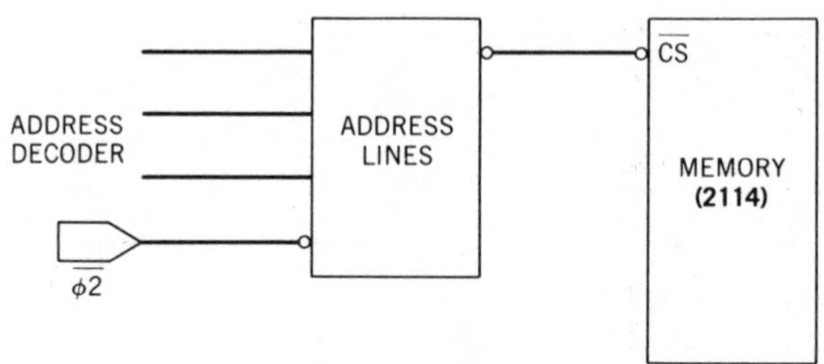

Figure 9-11 Use of the clock signals to strobe memory during phase 2 to prevent data bus drive overlap.

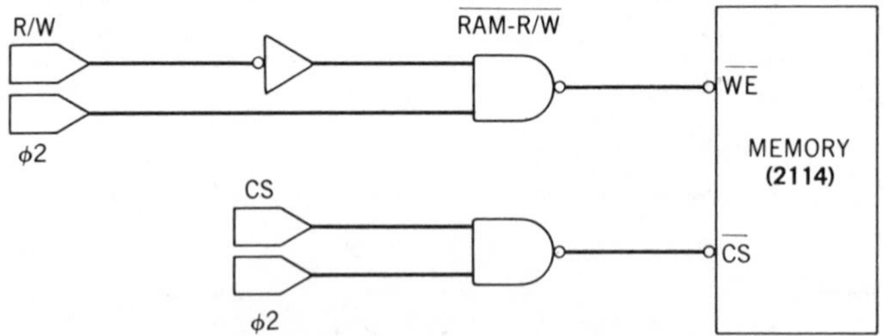

Figure 9-12 Circuit to form a $\overline{\text{RAM-R/W}}$ signal to write to static memory chips.

than one chip select, either $\phi 1$ or $\phi 2$ connected to the appropriate chip select will strobe the memory device during $\phi 2$. Figure 9-11 illustrates a possible solution.

The timing diagram for a WRITE cycle is shown in Figure 9-10. The R/W line is active over almost the entire clock cycle, but the data is stable only during $\phi 2$ and for at least 30 ns after $\phi 2$. Thus, the R/W line cannot be used as a WRITE ENABLE signal for static RAMs. The standard approach for **6502** designs is shown in Figure 9-12. R/W is gated with $\phi 2$ to form a signal that is frequently called $\overline{\text{RAM-R/W}}$. The appropriate logic for a **2114** memory chip is also shown in this figure.

Space does not permit a complete discussion of system timing for DMA operations or dynamic RAMs. An application note from Synertek [5] covers these topics in more detail. Also refer to the discussion in *Some Real Support Devices* [6]. Suffice it to say that some systems do not slow the processor because all DMA and refresh operations take place during $\phi 1$ of the cycle, while the processor uses $\phi 2$ for all its data transfers.

9-9 INPUT/OUTPUT

Input ports and output ports in **6502**-based μC systems are located in the address space of the processor. Reading an input port or writing to an output port is no different than reading or writing to a memory location. This implementation of input/output functions is called *memory-mapped I/O*. Like the **6800** but unlike the

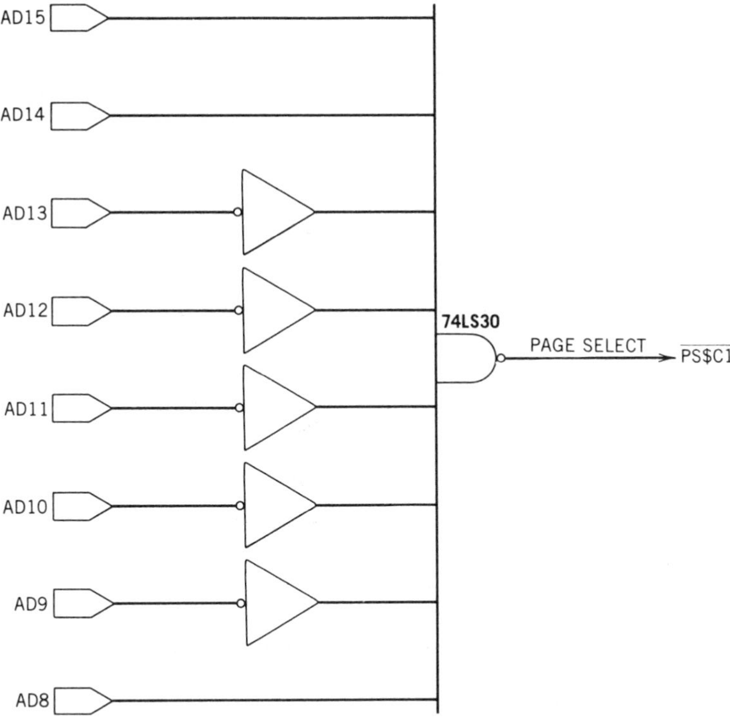

Figure 9-13 An address decoding circuit to select one page of the address space for I/O functions. As shown in this figure, page $C1 is selected. Adding to removing inverters will allow any other page to be selected.

8080 and **Z80** μCs, the **6502** has no IN or OUT instructions. Input and output ports are accessed in the same way as a memory location: the same instructions are used to access both.

Because of the special zero-page addressing modes and the use of zero-page locations in indirect indexed addressing, and because the stack is in page 1 of memory, **6502** system design philosophy usually places R/W memory at the bottom of the address space. It will extend upward into the address space as far as the memory requirements of the design dictate. On the other hand, because the reset and interrupt vectors are usually placed in ROM, the top of the address space is occupied by the read-only memory that contains the system program. This philosophy leaves the middle of the address space for I/O functions, interval timers, and counters.

Suppose, by way of example, that we allocate one page (256 locations) of the address space for input/output functions. A simple address decoding scheme that can be used to generate a page select pulse is shown in Figure 9-13. The page select pulse $\overline{\text{PS}}$ is used to enable the devices that decode the other eight address lines. One of many possible address decoding schemes to accomplish this is shown in

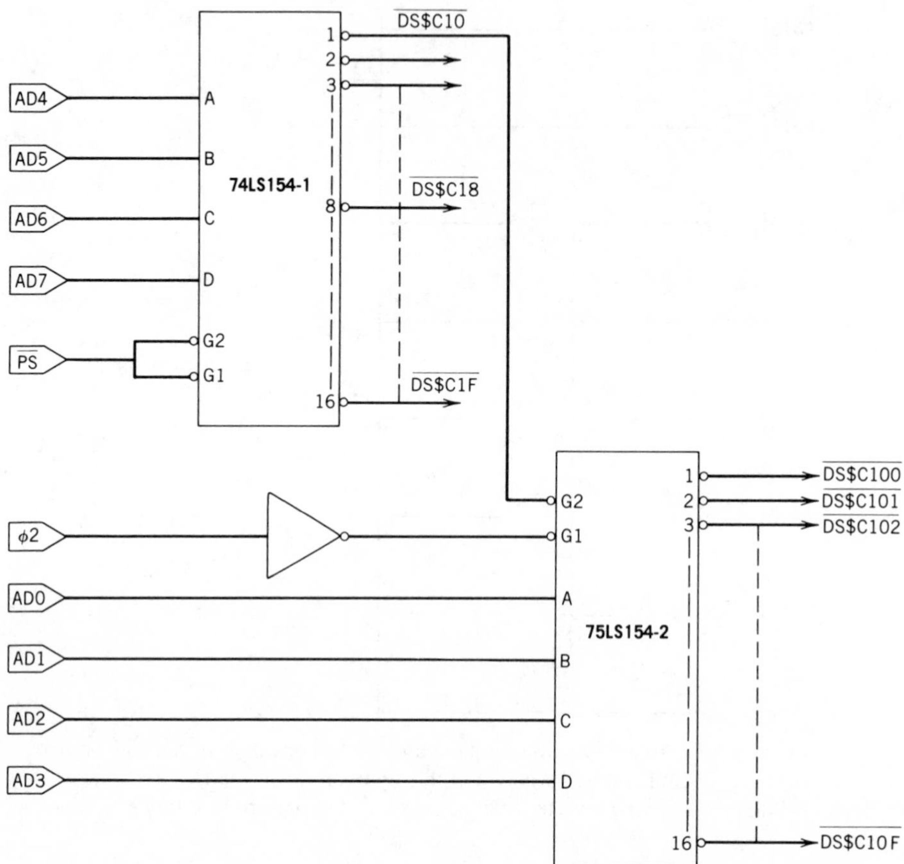

Figure 9-14 A circuit to select the addresses within a page of the address space. $\overline{PS}$ is a page-select pulse. Note that phase 2 is used to gate the second decoder.

Figure 9-14. The two **74LS154**s provide device selects for up to 16 I/O ports. More ports can be added by providing more decoders.

In Figure 9-14, the page select signal ($\overline{PS}$) from the eight-input NAND gate shown in Figure 9-13 is used to enable the first **74LS154**, labeled "**74LS154-1**" in Figure 9-14. This 4-to-16 line decoder is used to decode address lines AD4–AD7. Assuming that the page selected by $\overline{PS}$ is page $C1, the "1" output on the **74LS154-1** will be active for any address in the range $C100–$C10F, a total of 16 locations. The "2" output of the decoder will be active for any address in the range $C110–$C11F, and so on until the "16" pin which is active for addresses $C1F0–$C1FF.

A second 4-to-16 line decoder, labeled **74LS154-2** in Figure 9-14, is used to decode the lowest four address lines AD0–AD3. Thus, if the "1" pin from the **74LS154-1** decoder is used to enable the **74LS154-2** decoder then a device select for each of the 16 addresses in the range $C100–$C10F will be provided at the pins of the **74LS154-2** shown in Figure 9-14. Furthermore, using $\phi 2$ to gate the second

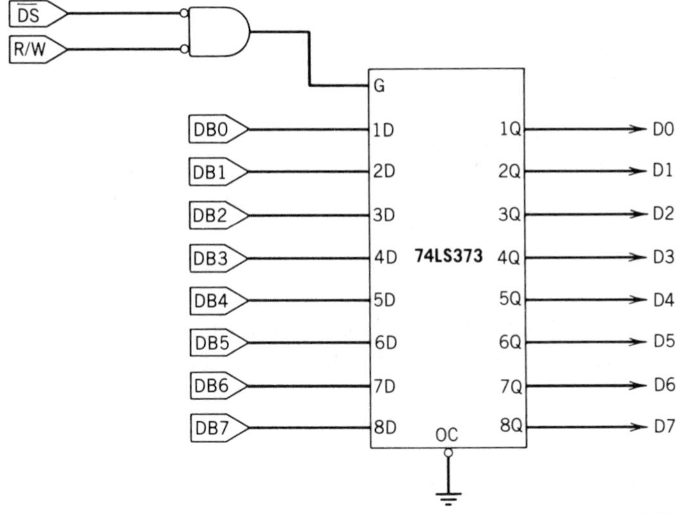

Figure 9-15 A memory-mapped output port using TTL chips. $\overline{DS}$ is generated by the circuit shown in Figure 9-14, and it is active only during phase 2. The outputs D0 to D7 are shown permanently enabled by tying 0C to a logic 0.

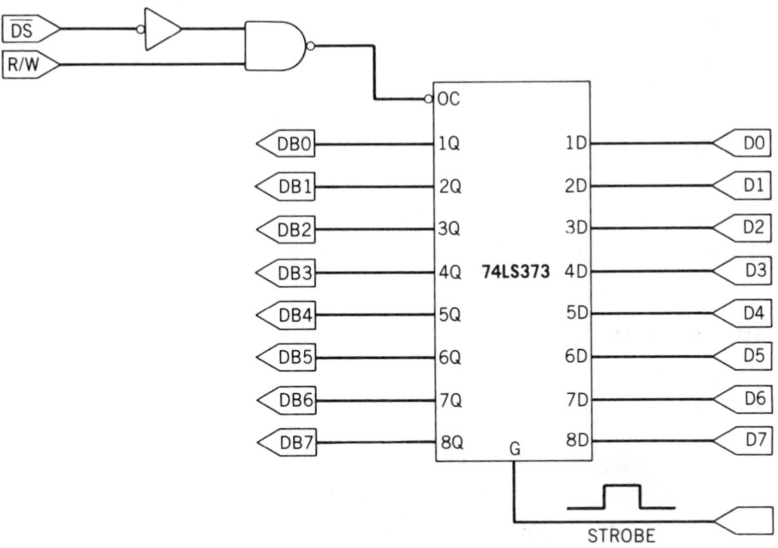

Figure 9-16 A memory-mapped input port. $\overline{DS}$ is generated by the circuit shown in Figure 9-14, and it is active only during phase 2. The input data may be latched by a positive strobe pulse on the G pin, or this pin may be tied to logic 1, making the latch permanently transparent.

decoder ensures that the trailing edge of each device select is properly timed to clock data into an output port or to gate data from an input port.

Memory-mapped input and output ports are shown in Figures 9-15 and 9-16. The circuits shown in Figures 9-13 to 9-16 can be used to implement input/output functions using inexpensive **74LS** series integrated circuits, avoiding the more expensive family-type chips. Note the following important points in connection with these circuits. First, the $\phi 2$ signal must be used to gate one of the **74LS154** decoders shown in Figure 9-14 to provide the proper timing and to clock the data into the output port. Second, READ-MODIFY-WRITE instructions (INC, DEC, ASL, ROR, etc.) cannot be used with the output port shown in Figure 9-15 because the processor cannot read the data at these kinds of ports. A STA instruction must be used. Third, output ports such as the one illustrated in Figure 9-15 can also be placed in the same address space as ROM, provided the ROM chips are enabled only during READ cycles. Finally, note that a variety of other circuits may be used to accomplish the same I/O functions; we have given only some examples.

A number of integrated circuits in the **6500** family are designed specifically for input/output functions as well as counting and timing functions. A particularly popular and useful chip is the **6522** Versatile Interface Adapter. It provides two 8-bit I/O ports for parallel I/O, two handshaking pins for each port, a serial port, and two interval timers, one of which may be used to count external pulses. Figure 9-17 illustrates how the **6522** can be interfaced to a **6500**-based μP. The **6522** may be located on the I/O card mentioned previously and can be selected by one of the device selects from the **74LS154-1** in Figure 9-14. In particular, for the applications described in the next section we will assume that device select $\overline{\text{DS\$C18}}$ is used to enable the **6522** by connecting it to the $\overline{\text{CS2}}$ pin. The **6522** has 16 internal registers, and it decodes address lines AD0–AD3 to access these registers. A specification sheet is absolutely essential when working with the **6522**.

Another family chip worth mentioning is the **6551** Asynchronous Communications Interface Adapter. The **6551** provides serial I/O at a variety of programmable baud rates, and is used frequently in **RS232-C** interfaces. It is closely related to the Motorola **6850**. The **6522** and the **6551** provide designers with virtually all of the I/O functions they will demand.

9-10 APPLICATIONS

The first application described is a parallel port line printer interfaced to a **6522** VIA in a **6502** μC system. The circuit is shown in Figure 9-17 and a driver program is given in Example 9-12. Assume that the simple handshaking protocol illustrated in Figure 9-18 is being used. The μC system produces a logic 0 DATA-ready pulse of 1 μs when the ASCII character is available at output register B (ORB) of the **6522**. The printer responds by bringing its BUSY line high until the printer has read the character. The trailing edge of the BUSY signal indicates that the printer is ready to accept another character. The ASCII character is transmitted over eight parallel data lines from output register B.

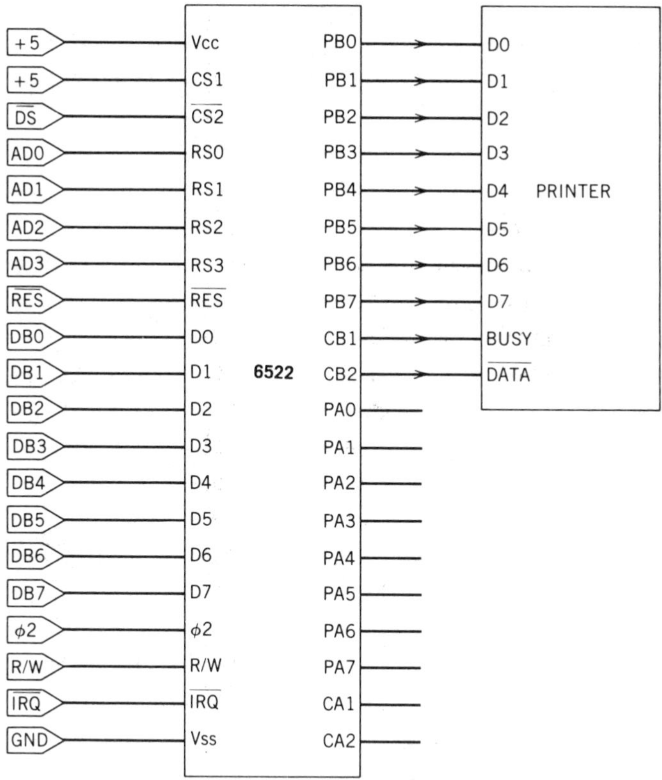

Figure 9-17 The **6522** interfaced to a **6500**-based system on the left and a line printer on the right. $\overline{\text{DS}}$ is from $\overline{\text{DS}}$\$C18 on the **74LS154-1** in Figure 9-14.

The **6522** handles this common handshaking sequence with ease. It is programmed to produce a 1-μs pulse on its CB2 pin following a write to ORB. Thus, the printer's $\overline{\text{DATA}}$ pin is connected to CB2. Pin CB1 of the **6522** is programmed to set a flag in the interrupt flag register of the **6522** when a negative transition on

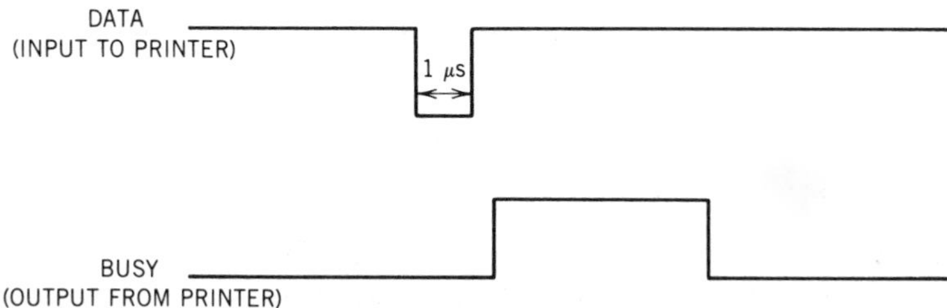

Figure 9-18 Handshaking protocol for the printer. BUSY stays at logic 1 until the character has been read by the printer and it is ready to read another character (buffer not full).

the BUSY line occurs, signaling that the printer is no longer busy. The **6522** initialization sequence is shown in the first nine lines of Example 9-12, a routine that would normally be part of the RESET routine. The actual output is shown in the next eight lines of Example 9-12.

EXAMPLE 9-12 Write a routine to initialize the **6522** for the printer interface shown in Figure 9-17. Also write a routine to handle the output of ASCII data to the printer.

Solution This is the initialization routine that would be part of the RESET procedure.

```
$7F09 A9 A0        INITIL   LDA #$A0    Set up the 6522 peripheral
                                          control.
$7F0B 8D 8C C1              STA PCR     Register to set a flag on a
$7F0E A9 10                 LDA #$10      negative transition on
                                          pin CB1.
$7F10 8D 8E C1              STA IFR     Clear any current interrupt
$7F13 8D 8D C1              STA IER       flags and interrupts.
$7F16 A9 FF                 LDA #$FF    Initialize port B to be an
$7F18 8D 82 C1              STA DDRB      output port by loading its
                                          DDR with 1s.
$7F1B A9 0C                 LDA #$0C    Write a form feed to the
                                          printer.
$7F1D 8D 80 C1              STA ORB
```

This is the output subroutine. Assume that the character is passed to the subroutine in the accumulator.

```
$7F21 48           OUTPUT   PHA         Save the character on the
                                          stack.
$7F22 A9 10                 LDA #$10    Set up the mask for the flag
                                          register.
$7F24 2C 8D C1     WAIT     BIT IFR     Has the BUSY line gone to
                                          logic 0?
$7F27 F0 FB                 BEQ WAIT    No. Then wait here.
$7F29 8D 8D C1              STA IFR     Yes. Then clear the flag.
$7F2C 68                    PLA         Get the character from the
                                          stack.
$7F2D 8D 80 C1              STA ORB     Output it to the printer.
$7F30 60                    RTS         Return to the calling program.
```

The next application is a simple but fast analog-to-digital interface and driver routine. An **AD570** or **AD571** A/D converter (manufactured by Analog Devices, Inc.) is interfaced to a **6522** VIA with the circuit shown in Figure 9-19. The **AD570/1** has a typical conversion time of 25 μs, and it has provision for both bipolar or unipolar inputs. In Figure 9-19 the $B/\overline{C}$ (blank and convert) pin of the **AD570** is

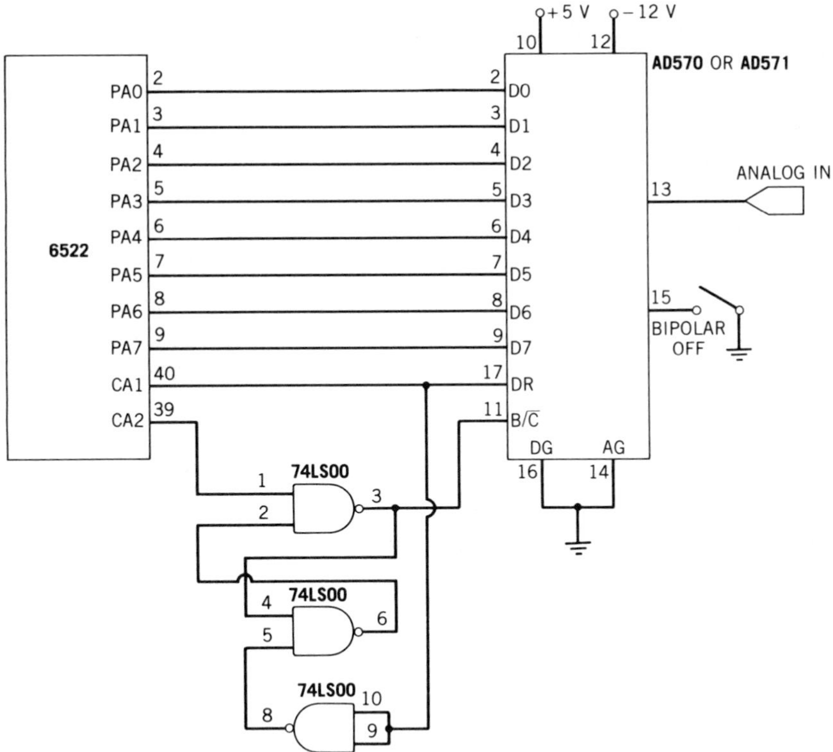

Figure 9-19 A **6522** to the **AD570** analog-to-digital converter interface.

connected to the CA2 handshaking pin on the **6522**. The CA2 pin is programmed to produce a negative pulse of one clock cycle in duration when port A (IRA) is read. In conjunction with the logic circuitry in Figure 9-19, this initiates a conversion. When the conversion ends approximately 25 μs later, the **AD570** brings its $\overline{DR}$ (data already) pin to logic 0. It is connected to pin CA1 on the **6522**, and a negative transition on this pin sets bit 2 in the interrupt flag register (IFR). Detection of this event causes the program to read the converter and store the data, as well as initiating another conversion.

Example 9-13 illustrates a routine to perform 256 conversions and store the results in page 2 of memory. These conversions will be performed as fast as the converter and the software allow. Delay loops can be inserted between successive conversions to slow the rate at which data is collected. It is not difficult to write software to make rather sophisticated data collection schemes once the basic operation of the **AD570** or **AD571** is understood. We have made a simple and inexpensive storate oscilloscope [7] with the **AD570** and a **NE5018** (Signetics) digital-to-analog converter. The **NE5018** or the Analog Devices **AD558** D/A converters can be attached to port B of the **6522**, giving A/D and D/A capability with one **6522**.

EXAMPLE 9-13 Write a routine to perform 256 analog-to-digital conversions and store the results in page 2 of memory.

Solution

```
0F00 A2 00      BEGIN  LDX #00      Clear index to point to first
0F02 A9 0A             LDA #$0A       location in the table.
0F04 8D 8C C1          STA PCR      Initialize PCR to pulse CA2
                                      and detech negative
                                      transition on CA1.
0F07 AD 81 C1          LDA IRA      Start a conversion.
                                      Disregard the data.
0F0A A9 02      BACK   LDA #02      Set up mask for IFR.
0F0C 2C 8D C1   WAIT   BIT IFR      Check the flag register.
                                      Conversion complete?
0F0F F0 FB             BEQ WAIT     No, then wait for it to finish.
0F11 AD 81 C1          LDA IRA      Yes, read the converter and
0F14 9D 00 02          STA TABLE,X    start a new conversion.
                                      Store the result.
0F17 E8                INX          Get 256 points.
0F18 D0 F0             BNE RACK     Finished?
0F1A 00                BRK          Yes, then quit.
```

The last application illustrated in this chapter is an interface to measure the time between two events. The events might be the heartbeat of a human, the arrival of cosmic rays, the start and end of a race, the start and end of a wheel rotation cycle, and many others. The interface circuit makes use of the fact that the T1 timer on the **6522** can be operated in a free-running mode. In that mode, the T1 timer produces a square wave output on pin PB7 of the **6522**. The period of the square wave is T_p, where

$$T_p = 2(N + 2)T_c$$

N is the 16-bit number loaded into the two T1 timer registers, and T_c is the system clock period.

The interface also makes use of the fact that the T2 timer on the **6522** can be used to count pulses from an external device. In this case, the pulses will be gated onto PB6, the pulse-counting pin of the **6522**, by a timing circuit shown in Figure 9-20. The signal to the CB1 pin on the **6522** signals the μC that the timing is completed when the positive transition to CB1 occurs.

Some useful values for the period of the square wave that appears at PB7 are given in Table 9-4. The numbers to be loaded into the two 8-bit T1 timer registers to produce these periods are also given in the table. The time T between the successive

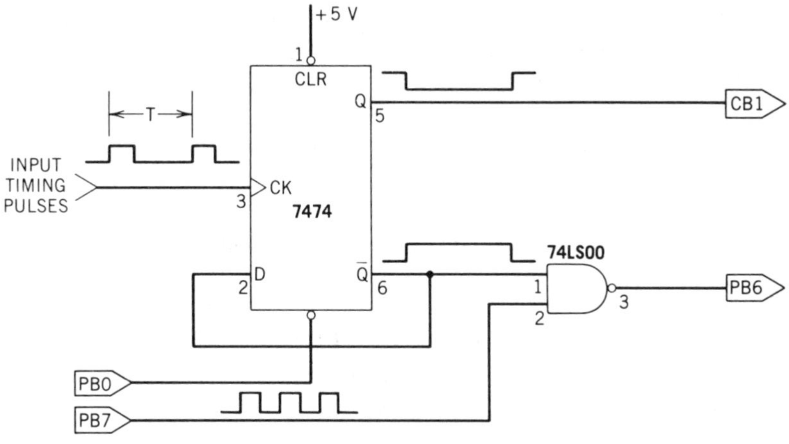

Figure 9-20 A **6522** timing circuit.

positive pulses that clock the flip-flop is given by

$$T = 2(N_1 + 2)(\$FFFF - N_2)T_c$$

where N_1 is the number in the T1 timer, N_2 is the number in the T2 timer at the end of the timing period, and T_c is the system clock period.

The maximum time interval that can be measured for a particular value of N_1, the number in the T1 timer, is

$$T_{max} = 65536(2)(N_1 + 2)T_c$$

Clearly, there is a trade-off between the largest time interval that can be measured and the resolution which is $\pm T_p$. The greatest resolution is 4 μs, while 0.1 s is near the smallest resolution. The user must decide which values he will choose, based on the requirements of the application.

A program to measure time intervals is given in Example 9-14. As shown it measures time in units of 0.01 s, but with the use of Table 9-4 it may be easily modified to give greater or less resolution. Note also that we have not provided the

Table 9-4 **Data for the timing program in Example 9-14**

	N + 2		*N*
Period T_p	*Decimal*	*Hex*	*Hex*
0.10 s	50000	\$C350	\$C34E
0.01 s	5000	\$1388	\$1386
1.00 ms	500	\$01F4	\$01F2
0.10 ms	50	\$0032	\$0030
0.01 ms	5	\$0005	\$0003
4.00 μs	2	\$0002	\$0000

subroutine OUTPUT to convert the hexadecimal number of T_p (0.01 s) intervals to a decimal result. The number of T_p intervals is found by subtracting the contents of timer T2 from $FFFF. After the OUTPUT subroutine has processed the data, the program should return to AGAIN to time another interval. We have used a variation of this program to implement a cardiotachometer [8].

EXAMPLE 9-14 Write a program to operate the timing circuit shown in Figure 9-20.

Solution

```
$0F00 A9 00       ORIGIN  LDA #00      Clear the two locations
$0F02 85 01               STA LEAST      that hold the number
$0F04 85 02               STA MOST       of 0.01-s intervals.
$0F06 A9 01               LDA #01      Set up port B so pin zero
$0F08 8D 80 C1            STA ORB        is an output pin at
$0F0B 8D 82 C1            STA DDRB       logic 1.
$0F0E CE 80 C1            DEC ORB      Flip-flop is preset.
$0F11 A9 10               LDA #$10     Initialize peripheral
$0F13 8D 8C C1            STA PCR        control register to set
                                         flag with positive
                                         transition on CB1.
$0F16 A9 E0               LDA #$E0     Set up auxiliary control
$0F18 8D 8B C1            STA ACR        register so T1 timer runs
                                         free and T2 timer counts.
$0F1B A9 86               LDA #$86     Put $1386 into T1 to give a
$0F1D 8D 86 C1            STA T1LL       period of Tp = 0.01 s,
                                         f = 100 Hz.
$0F20 A9 13               LDA #$13     $1386 + 2 = 5000.
$0F22 8D 85 C1            STA T1LH     T1 is now loaded.
$0F25 A9 FF       AGAIN   LDA #$FF     Start T2 counting down
                                         from $FFFF.
$0F27 8D 88 C1            STA T2LL
$0F2A 8D 89 C1            STA T1CH     T2 is now loaded.
$0F2D EE 80 C1            INC ORB      Allow flip-flop to clock
                                         by removing preset.
$0F30 A9 10               LDA #$10     Timing now begins.
                                         Set up mask.
$0F32 2C 8D C1    WAIT    BIT IFR      Has CB1 gone positive yet?
$0F35 F0 FB               BEQ WAIT     No. Wait here.
$0F37 CE 80 C1            DEC ORB      Preset flip-flop again.
$0F3A 20 ?? ??            JSR OUTPUT   Convert time to decimal
                                         and output it.
```

Recently, a new CMOS version of the **6502** called the **65C02** has been introduced. It contains all the **6502** instructions, plus some additional instructions, and is scheduled to be used in the Apple 2C and Apple 2E computers. For further details on the **65C02**, consult the manufacturers literature.

9-11 REFERENCES

1. S. Libes, "Byte News," *Byte*, **4,** February 1979, p. 64.
2. M. L. De Jong, *Programming and Interfacing the 6502, With Experiments*, Howard W. Sams & Co., Indianapolis, Ind., 1981.
3. L. A. Leventhal, *6502 Assembly Language Programming*, Osborne/McGraw-Hill, Berkeley, Calif., 1979.
4. L. Scanlon, *6502 Software Design*, Howard W. Sams & Co., Indianapolis, Ind., 1980.
5. *SY6500 Microprocessor Family Applications Information AN2*, Synertek, Inc., 1980.
6. J. Kane with A. Osborne, *Some Real Support Devices*, Osborne & Associates, Inc., Berkeley, Calif., 1978, pp. A7-1 to A7-29.
7. M. L. De Jong, "Some A/D and D/A Conversion Techniques," *COMPUTE II*, June/July 1980, p. 5.
8. M. L. De Jong, "A Digital Cardiotachometer Implemented with the AIM 65," *COMPUTE II*, August/September 1980, p. 32.

SECTION THREE

SIXTEEN-BIT MICROPROCESSORS

CHAPTER 10

Intel 8086 and 8088 Microprocessors

Windsor Thomas
Professor of Electrical Engineering Technology
State University of New York
Utica–Rome, New York

10-1 INTRODUCTION

The Intel **8086** is the latest in the line of μPs that started with the **8008** in 1972 and is part of Intel's compatible family of μPs. The **8086** is the first of Intel's 16-bit μPs. It has a 16-bit data bus, a 20-bit address bus, and uses 16-bit operands. The **8086** is upward compatible at the assembly language level with its predecessors, the **8080A** and the **8085** (with the exception of the RIM and SIM instructions which are peculiar to the **8085**). Thus any **8080A** instruction can be simulated by a combination of **8086** instructions. As will be seen in section 10-4, the **8080A** registers are a subset of the **8086** registers.

The **8086** architecture will be covered first, followed by the addressing modes and the instruction set.

10-2 8086 ARCHITECTURE

The **8086** and **8088** μPs are internally divided into two separate processing units. The *execution unit* (EU) executes instructions and the *bus interface unit* (BIU) fetches instructions, reads operands, and writes results. The two units operate almost independently and normally overlap the instruction fetch with the execution phases. This increases effective execution speed because instruction fetch time almost disappears. The **8088** is an 8-bit version of the **8086**. The **8088** is a μP with an 8-bit interface or I/O bus, but 16-bit internal registers, so it computes using 16-bit values as the **8086** does. The **8088** is discussed further in section 10-9.1.

The execution unit (EU) is the same on both the **8086** and the **8088**. The EU contains the 16-bit arithmetic-logic unit (ALU) that maintains the status and control flags and manipulates the general registers and instruction operands. The EU's only connection to the rest of the system is through the BIU.

The bus interface unit (BIU) performs all bus operations for the EU. Data is transferred between the μP and memory or I/O devices by request from the EU. In addition to the increased efficiency from the overlap of FETCH and execution phases, the efficiency is further increased by the BIU design that includes an instruction stream queue which the BIU can fill by prefetching instructions, that is, fetch the next consecutive instruction so it will be available as soon as the EU needs it. The instruction stream queue holds up to 6 bytes (4 bytes for the **8088**). If the EU executes an instruction that transfers control to another location, the BIU discards the instructions stored in the queue, fetches the instruction from the new address, passes it immediately to the EU, and then begins refilling the queue from the new locations. Whenever the EU requests a memory or I/O READ or WRITE, the BIU suspends instruction fetching until the EU's request has been satisfied.

10-3 8086 REGISTERS

The **8086** registers are discussed in the following groupings: general registers, segment registers, instruction pointer, and status register.

10-3.1 General Registers

The **8086** μP has eight 16-bit general registers, similar to the traditional accumulator. Figure 10-1 shows the general registers. The first four general registers (AX, BX, CS, DX) are the data registers (sometimes also referred to as the "H and L" group for high and low). Each of these data registers may be used interchangeably as

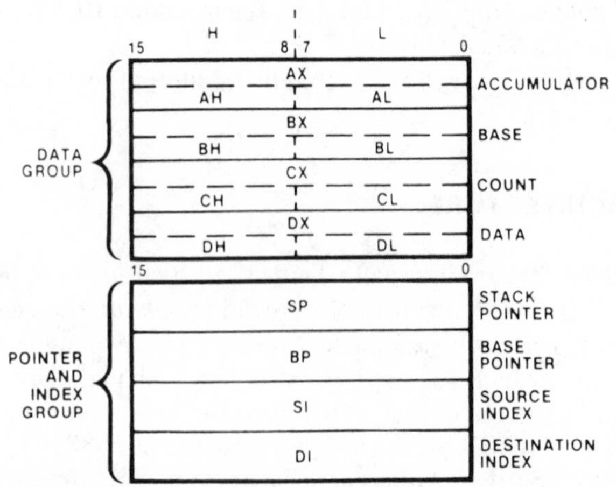

Figure 10-1 The **8086** general registers. (Courtesy of Intel Corporation.)

Table 10-1 **Use of the 8086 registers**

REGISTER	OPERATIONS
AX	Word Multiply, Word Divide, Word I/O
AL	Byte Multiply, Byte Divide, Byte I/O, Translate, Decimal Arithmetic
AH	Byte Multiply, Byte Divide
BX	Translate
CX	String Operations, Loops
CL	Variable Shift and Rotate
DX	Word Multiply, Word Divide, Indirect I/O
SP	Stack Operations
SI	String Operations
DI	String Operations

either a 16-bit register (AX, BX, CX, DX) or two 8-bit registers (AH and AL, BH and BL, CH and CL, DH and DL). For arithmetic and logical operations the data registers can be used without limitation; however some instructions do make implicit use of certain registers. Table 10-1 shows this use of general registers.

The other four 16-bit registers are pointer and index registers which can be used only as 16-bit registers. These 16-bit registers can also be used in most arithmetic and logical operations. These four registers include the traditional *stack pointer* in addition to three index or pointer registers, the *base pointer* (BP), the *source index* (SI), and the *destination index* (DI). The use of the BP, SI, and DI registers is discussed in section 10-7.

10-3.2 Segment Registers

In addition to the registers shown in Figure 10-1, the **8086** has a 16-bit *instruction pointer* register and four 16-bit *segment registers* that allow it to address different areas of memory. The **8086** is capable of addressing 1 megabyte of memory space, which requires 20 bits of address. The four segment registers are added, in a unique manner, to the 16-bit effective address formed by the various addressing modes to generate the 20-bit address. A segment is a logical unit of contiguous memory which may be up to 64K bytes long. Each segment is assigned a *base address* (under software control), which is its *starting location* in memory. All segments begin on 16-byte memory boundaries (i.e., the four least significant bits of the base address are zero). The segments are completely independent and therefore may overlap fully, partially, or not at all. Thus a given physical memory location may be in more than one logical segment (see Examples 10-1 and 10-2).

The segment registers are 16-bit registers and contain the most significant 16 bits of the 20-bit base address of the segment associated with that register (recall that the least significant 4 bits of the base address are zero). Programs may obtain access to data and instructions in different areas of memory by changing the segment

Table 10-2 **Default and alternative segment registers**

TYPE OF MEMORY REFERENCE	DEFAULT SEGMENT BASE	ALTERNATE SEGMENT BASE	OFFSET
Instruction Fetch	CS	NONE	IP
Stack Operation	SS	NONE	SP
Variable (except following)	DS	CS,ES,SS	Effective Address
String Source	DS	CS,ES,SS	SI
String Destination	ES	NONE	DI
BP Used As Base Register	SS	CS,DS,ES	Effective Address

registers to point to the desired areas of memory. Instructions and stack locations occupy words, whereas data locations are measured in bytes. The use of segmentation provides the user immediate access to 64K bytes of instruction code, 64K bytes of stack, and 128K bytes of data storage. By changing the associated segment register, the full 1 megabyte of memory can be utilized. Each of the addressing modes has a default segment register that it uses and some may optionally select an alternate segment register.

The 16-bit address that the μP forms is a 16-bit offset register referred to as the *logical address*. The 20-bit address is the *physical address*, which actually goes on the address lines. The physical address is generated in the μP by shifting the appropriate segment register left 4 bits and adding the 16-bit logical address to it. There are four segment registers, the *code segment* (CS), *data segment* (DS), *stack segment* (SS), and the *extra segment* (ES). Every operation that accesses memory uses at least one of these segment registers to generate a physical address. Each memory reference has a default segment register and an alternative set of segment registers which may be utilized. Table 10-2 shows the default and alternative segment registers for each addressing mode. Note that it is only the data operations that have an alternate segment register.

The offset in Table 10-2 is a register that contains the 16 LSBs of the address. The physical address is the sum of the shifted segment register and the offset register.

10-3.3 Instruction Pointer

The *instruction pointer* (IP) is an offset register analogous to the program counter (PC) in the 8-bit μPs. The instruction pointer normally contains the logical address (the offset from the beginning of the current code segment) of the next instruction to be fetched by the BIU. Whenever the IP is saved on the stack, as the result of a subroutine jump or interrupt, it is first adjusted to point to the next instruction to be executed. This register is not directly accessible to the programmer.

EXAMPLE 10-1 An instruction fetch memory reference is being performed with the instruction pointer (IP) set to 17E4. From Table 10-2, the appropriate segment register for an instruction fetch is the code segment register (CS) which contains 6A11. What is the physical address that appears on the address bus?

Solution The physical address (20 bits) is formed by using the contents of the segment register (CS) as the most significant 16 bits of the 20-bit address, with the 4 least significant bits equal to zero. To this base address (6A110) the 16-bit logical address of 17E4 is added.

6A110	Base address (from segment register)
017E4	Logical address (from IP)
6B8F4	Physical address

The 20-bit result 6B8F4 is the physical address that goes out on the address lines. Figure 10-2 shows this symbolically.

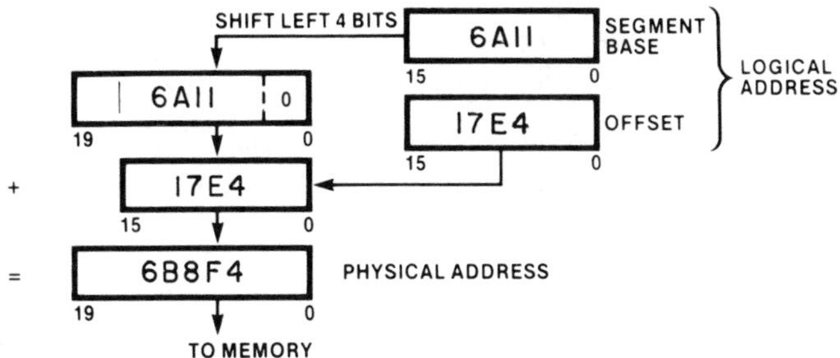

Figure 10-2 Physical address generation. (Courtesy of Intel Corporation.)

EXAMPLE 10-2 Assume the logical address of a data byte is C474 and the data segment register contains 5F48. Calculate the physical address.

Solution Again the logical address is added to the base address.

5F480	Base address (from segment register)
0C474	Logical address

6B8F4	Physical address

The example was chosen so that the same physical address would be generated as in the previous example to show the effect of overlapping segments. Note that the base addresses are also different, while the physical addresses are the same and therefore they access the same memory location.

10-3.4 Status Register

The **8086** has a status register that contains six status flags (AF, CF, OF, SF, PE, and ZF) and three control flags (DF, IF, TF) that the EU uses to indicate certain characteristics of the result of arithmetic and logic operations. Different instructions affect the status flags differently. These flags are shown in Figure 10-3 and are used as follows:

The *auxiliary carry flag* (AF) is set when there has been a carry out of the low nibble into the high nibble of an 8-bit number. The flag is used by decimal arithmetic instructions.

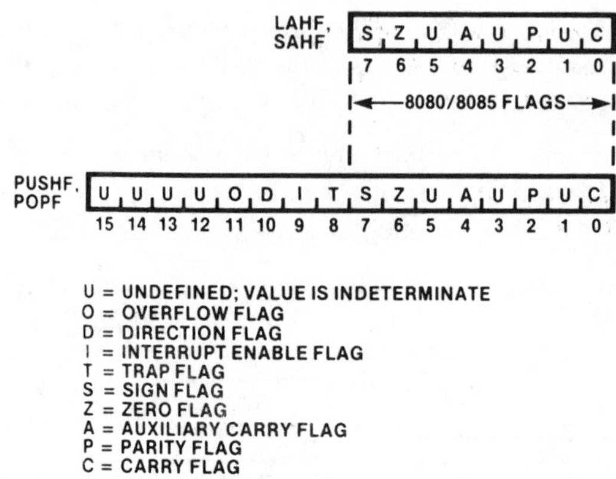

Figure 10-3 Flag storage formats. (Courtesy of Intel Corporation.)

The *carry flag* (CF) is set when there has been a carry out of, or a borrow into, the most significant bit of the result (8-bit or 16-bit).

The *overflow flag* (OF) is set when an *arithmetic overflow* has occurred. An INTERRUPT ON OVERFLOW instruction is available which will generate an interrupt in this situation.

The *sign flag* (SF), if set, indicates that the most significant bit of the result is a 1. In 2s complement notation the most significant bit indicates the sign (0 = positive and 1 = negative) of the number.

The *parity flag* (PF) is set if the result has even parity, an even number of 1 bits. The PF is cleared if the result has odd parity.

The *zero flag* (ZF) is set when the result is zero and cleared for nonzero result.

The *direction flag* (DF), if set, causes the string instructions to auto decrement. Clearing the DF causes the string instructions to auto increment.

The *interrupt enable flag* (IF), if set, allows the **8086** to recognize external (maskable) interrupt requests. Clearing the IF disables these maskable interrupts.

The *trap flag* (TF), if set, puts the processor into single-step mode for debugging. In this mode the **8086** automatically generates an internal interrupt after every instruction.

10-4 COMPARISON OF THE 8086 AND 8080/8085 ARCHITECTURE

The register and flags of the **8080/8085** all have counterparts in the **8086**. The A register of the **8080/8085** corresponds to the AL register of the **8086**. The **8080/8085** H, L, B, C, D, E correspond to the BH, BL, CH, CL, DH, DL, respectively, in the **8086**. The **8080/8085** stack pointer (SP) and program counter (PC) have their counterparts in the **8086** stack pointer (SP) and instruction pointer (IP). The **8086** flag register contains 5 flag bits that are the same as the **8080/8085** flag bits; these are the AF, CF, PF, SF, and ZF flag bits. The OF, DF, IF and TF flag bits are unique to the **8086**. This close correspondence of **8080/8085** flags, shown in Figure 10-3, allows most existing assembly language programs to be directly translated into **8086** code.

10-5 THE STACK

The **8086** stack structure is located in memory by the standard physical address generation techniques using the stack segment (SS) and the stack pointer register (SP). The number of stacks used by the system is only limited by the memory available on a system. Any one stack can only be 64K bytes long, and only one stack at a time is directly addressable (the current stack). The SS contains the base address of the current stack and SP points to the top of the stack. The stack advances toward the beginning of memory.

A PUSH instruction PUSHes a word onto the stack by first decrementing the SP by 2 (the memory addresses are actually byte addresses) and then writing the word to the location addressed by the SP. A POP instruction removes a word from the stack by copying it from the top of the stack and then incrementing the SP by 2. Therefore successive PUSHes cause the SP address to move *down* in memory toward the stack segments base address.

10-6 SYSTEM RESET

The **8086** RESET line is an active-high signal, which, when activated, initializes the μP. The activation of RESET performs the following initialization of the **8086**: the flag register is cleared and the queue set to empty. The instruction pointer register is cleared to zero as are all the segment registers, except the code segment register (CS), which is set to FFFF. The physical address from which the first instruction is fetched is found by adding the shifted CS register contents (FFFF0) to the instruction pointer contents (0000) to get FFFF0 as the first address. Therefore, there must be memory that responds to address FFFF0, since this is the starting location of the program after a RESET occurs. The maskable interrupts are disabled by the RESET operation. The reset does not modify any of the accumulators or index registers.

The **8086** instruction set and description are given in Tables 10-3 through 10-8. Space in this Handbook precludes a detailed description of the format of each instruction, but instructions can be from 1 to 6 bytes long and their mode is implied by the Op code. For a detailed description of each instruction, see the references at the end of the chapter.

10-7 ADDRESSING MODES

The **8086** μP provides many ways of accessing data. The data may be part of the instruction itself, in a register, in memory, or in an I/O port. The 16-bit Op code allows 256 times as many Op codes (combinations of instructions and addressing modes) as a single-byte Op code on an 8-bit μP. Thus the 16-bit μP allows for a much more complex instruction set and addressing modes. The **8086** takes full advantage of this to provide a very flexible instruction set. Along with this flexibility comes complexity. The **8086** addressing modes fall into two general categories, those that do not require an effective address calculation and those that do. The first group is the simplest and will be discussed first.

10-7.1 Register Addressing

The register addressing mode allows the source and/or destination data to be stored in a register within the μP. This mode provides the shortest instruction since it only requires 3 bits in the instruction to specify a register. This addressing mode also executes quickly since the **8086** does not have to perform a bus operation to get the data.

10-7.2 Immediate Addressing

The immediate addressing mode assumes the data immediately follows the instruction Op codes in memory. This mode of addressing is also relatively fast for two reasons: first, because the **8086** does not have to calculate an effective address since the data is in the next location; and secondly, since the data is located in memory immediately after the instruction Op code, the BIU of the **8086** has already performed a bus operation and prefetched the data into the queue on the **8086**.

10-7.3 Effective Address Calculation

The *effective address*, or EA, is calculated by the EU and is the offset relative to the beginning of the segment. The EA is used along with the appropriate segment register to produce the 20-bit physical address. The EU calculates the EA by summing a displacement, the contents of a base register, and the contents of an index register. The variety of addressing modes results because the EU may use any combination of these three components.

The displacement is an 8-bit or 16-bit number contained in the instruction. The base register may be either the BX or BP and the index register may be either the SI or the DI.

10-7.4 Direct Addressing

The direct addressing mode uses no registers. The EA is taken from the displacement field in the instruction.

10-7.5 Register Indirect Addressing

The register indirect addressing mode takes the EA from one of the base or index registers. For the CALL and JMP instructions, any 16-bit general register may be used.

10-7.6 Based Addressing

The based addressing mode adds a displacement to the contents of the BX or BP register. Using the BP as a base register causes the BIU to use the current stack segment as the default segment register. This makes this addressing mode with the BP register a very convenient method of passing data on the stack to a subroutine.

10-7.7 Indexed Addressing

The indexed addressing mode calculates the EA by adding the displacement to the contents of either the SI or the DI index register.

10-7.8 Based Indexed Addressing

The based indexed addressing mode forms the EA by the sum of a base register (BX or BP), an index register (SI or DI), and a displacement. This mode is also sometimes considered *doubly indexed* because it is indexed by an index register and a base register.

10-7.9 String Addressing

The string instructions (see section 10-8.3) do not use the normal memory addressing modes but implicitly use the two index registers SI and DI. This addressing mode assumes that SI points to the next character of the *source string* and DI points to the next character position in the *destination string*. As the string operations are repeated, the **8086** automatically adjusts both the SI and DI to point to the next character after every operation. This addressing mode uses the direction flag bit of the status register to decide whether the SI and DI should be incremented or decremented after each string instruction.

10-7.10 I/O Port Addressing

I/O ports on the **8086** systems may be *memory mapped* and therefore addressable by any of the memory addressing instructions. I/O ports may alternatively be configured so that they can only be addressed by special I/O *port addressing* instructions. In the direct port addressing mode, an 8-bit immediate operand is the port number. Direct port addressing allows the system to address 256 ports.

Indirect port addressing uses the DX register to contain a 16-bit port number, which allows the **8086** to address 65,536 ports.

10-8 8086 INSTRUCTION SET

The majority of the **8086** instruction set is made up of the standard data transfer, arithmetic, SHIFT, and ROTATE types of instructions. These instructions are shown in Tables 10-4 and 10-5 and will not be discussed in detail. There are several instructions in the **8086** which are major improvements over those available in 8-bit processors, and these will be covered in more detail.

Table 10-3 **The 8086 data transfer instructions**

GENERAL PURPOSE	
MOV	Move byte or word
PUSH	Push word onto stack
POP	Pop word off stack
XCHG	Exchange byte or word
XLAT	Translate byte
INPUT/OUTPUT	
IN	Input byte or word
OUT	Output byte or word
ADDRESS OBJECT	
LEA	Load effective address
LDS	Load pointer using DS
LES	Load pointer using ES
FLAG TRANSFER	
LAHF	Load AH register from flags
SAHF	Store AH register in flags
PUSHF	Push flags onto stack
POPF	Pop flags off stack

10-8.1 Data Transfer Instruction

In the data transfer instruction group, shown in Table 10-3, the XLAT is new and extremely powerful. It is a special translate table instruction. This instruction uses a 256-byte table to convert the contents of AL register into a different byte. The instruction uses BX to point to the memory location of the beginning of the table. The original value in AL is used as the offset from the beginning of the table. The XLAT instruction takes the byte pointed to in the table and loads it into the AL register. This instruction provides a very convenient method of converting from one character representation to another, such as from EBCDIC to ASCII or back. This would also simplify the connection of an unencoded keyboard to an **8086** system.

EXAMPLE 10-3 An **8086** system has BX containing 2000 and the short table shown below in memory. If AL contains a 0B what will AL contain after executing an XLAT instruction? What operation does this XLAT perform?

Address	*Contents*
2000	30
2001	31
2002	32

Address	*Contents*
2003	33
2004	34
2005	35
2006	36
2007	37
2008	38
2009	39
200A	41
200B	42
200C	43
200D	44
200E	45
200F	46

Solution The **8086** adds 0B from AL to 2000 from BX to get 200B and gets the data in this location (42) and loads it into the AL register. Thus the contents of AL is 42. The way the table is set up, it allows the **8086** to convert a hexidecimal digit (0B) in AL into the corresponding ASCII character (B = 42) in one instruction.

The power of the XLAT instruction is that by loading a different number into the BX register a conversion to a different character set can be performed because BX now points to a different table.

10-8.2 Arithmetic and Logical Instructions

The arithmetic instruction group shown in Table 10-4 has been greatly expanded over the **8080**. The MUL and IMUL instructions allow the **8086** to perform unsigned and signed integer multiplication on either bytes or words. The corresponding DIV and IDIV allow unsigned and signed integer division on either bytes or words. This group also includes two conversion instructions, CBW and CWD, which convert a byte operand into a word or a word operand into a double word.

The bit manipulation instruction group shown in Table 10-5 includes the standard AND, OR, XOR, and NOT in addition to SHIFTs and ROTATEs. The TEST instruction is very useful because it performs the logical AND of the destination and the source. The flags are set based on this result, which may be used by conditional jumps. Neither the source operand nor the destination operand are modified.

10-8.3 String Instructions

A *string* is a group of consecutive memory locations, where each location contains an ASCII character. The **8086** contains several special instructions designed to work directly with strings.

Table 10-4 **The 8086 arithmetic instructions**

ADDITION	
ADD	Add byte or word
ADC	Add byte or word with carry
INC	Increment byte or word by 1
AAA	ASCII adjust for addition
DAA	Decimal adjust for addition
SUBTRACTION	
SUB	Subtract byte or word
SBB	Subtract byte or word with borrow
DEC	Decrement byte or word by 1
NEG	Negate byte or word
CMP	Compare byte or word
AAS	ASCII adjust for subtraction
DAS	Decimal adjust for subtraction
MULTIPLICATION	
MUL	Multiply byte or word unsigned
IMUL	Integer multiply byte or word
AAM	ASCII adjust for multiply
DIVISION	
DIV	Divide byte or word unsigned
IDIV	Integer divide byte or word
AAD	ASCII adjust for division
CBW	Convert byte to word
CWD	Convert word to doubleword

Table 10-5 **The 8086 logical and shift instructions**

LOGICALS	
NOT	"Not" byte or word
AND	"And" byte or word
OR	"Inclusive or" byte or word
XOR	"Exclusive or" byte or word
TEST	"Test" byte or word
SHIFTS	
SHL/SAL	Shift logical/arithmetic left byte or word
SHR	Shift logical right byte or word
SAR	Shift arithmetic right byte or word
ROTATES	
ROL	Rotate left byte or word
ROR	Rotate right byte or word
RCL	Rotate through carry left byte or word
RCR	Rotate through carry right byte or word

The string instructions are shown in Table 10-6. While at first glance these instructions seems to be a duplication of the other instructions, they are actually a well-constructed set of primitive operations which can be used to construct very complicated assembly routines to handle strings. These instructions get their power

Table 10-6 **The 8086 block transfer and string instructions**

REP	Repeat
REPE/REPZ	Repeat while equal/zero
REPNE/REPNZ	Repeat while not equal/not zero
MOVS	Move byte or word string
MOVSB/MOVSW	Move byte or word string
CMPS	Compare byte or word string
SCAS	Scan byte or word string
LODS	Load byte or word string
STOS	Store byte or word string

SI	Index (offset) for source string
DI	Index (offset) for destination string
CX	Repetition counter
AL/AX	Scan value Destination for LODS Source for STOS
DF	0 = auto-increment SI, DI 1 = auto-decrement SI, DI
ZF	Scan/compare terminator

from the implicit use of index registers and segment registers. The **8086** assumes that the source string is in the current data segment and uses the SI index register and the DS segment to generate the physical address. A segment prefix byte can be added to change the default source segment. The destination string must be in the extra segment and the **8086** uses the DI index register and the ES segment register to generate the physical address. The **8086** will automatically increment SI and DI if the direction flag bit (DF) in the status register is 0 or decrement SI and DI if the direction flag bit is 1. The amount of the increment or decrement will be two for word operands or one for byte operands. Table 10-6 also shows default uses which the string instructions make. Note that the CX register is used as a repetition counter.

A string instruction can be preceded by a prefix instruction. There are three single-byte prefix instructions, REP, REPE, and REPNE, which enhance the power of string instructions. These prefixes control the repetition of a subsequent string instruction. The REP prefix is interpreted as "repeat while not end of string," that is, repeat until CS = 0. This prefix is used with the MOVS (move string) and STOS (store string) instructions to allow multibyte or multiword transfers.

The REPE (also called REPZ) is used with the CMPS (compare string) and SCAS (scan string) instructions and will repeat the string instruction if the zero flag, ZF, is set to 1 and it is not the end of the string (CX, not 0).

The REPNE (also called REPNZ) works the same as the REPE except that the zero flag ZF must be cleared to zero in order to repeat the string instruction.

The MOVS, move string instruction, transfers a byte or word from the source string to the destination string and increments or decrements both SI and DI. When REP is used with the MOVS instruction, it effectively performs a single-instruction block move.

The MOVSB and MOVSW are alternate mnemonics for the MOVS and allow the programmer to explicitly define whether a byte or a word is to be moved.

The CMPS, compare string instruction, subtracts the destination operand from the source operand (either byte or word operands). Neither the source operand nor the destination operand are modified but SI and DI are updated; the flags AF, CF, OF, PF, SF, and ZF are modified as appropriate to the result of the subtraction. By prefixing the CMPS with REPE the **8086** will compare the two strings and will continue comparing consecutive elements in the strings until either the end of the string is encountered (CX = 0) or the two elements being compared are unequal (ZF = 0).

The SCAS, scan string instruction, subtracts the element of the destination string from the contents of AL (for byte strings) or AX (for word strings) and updates the flags, but does not change the destination string element, AL or AX. The destination string index register DI is also updated. By adding the REPNE prefix, this can be used to search a string for the first occurrence of a byte or word string.

The LODS, load string instruction, transfers the byte or word string element, pointed to by the SI register, into the AL or AX register. The repeat prefixes are not appropriate for this instruction since AL or AX can only hold one element.

The STOS, store string instruction, moves a byte or word from the AL or AX register into the string element pointed to by DI. The STOS instruction could be used with the REP prefix if it were desired to fill the string with the same character. For example, this would be a simple way to set a string to all ASCII space characters.

10-8.4 Program Transfer Instruction

The program transfer instructions are shown in Table 10-7 and include CALL, RET, JMP, and conditional JUMP instructions, plus several new instructions.

Table 10-7 **The 8086 JUMP and INTERRUPT instructions**

UNCONDITIONAL TRANSFERS	
CALL	Call procedure
RET	Return from procedure
JMP	Jump
CONDITIONAL TRANSFERS	
JA/JNBE	Jump if above/not below nor equal
JAE/JNB	Jump if above or equal/not below
JB/JNAE	Jump if below/not above nor equal
JBE/JNA	Jump if below or equal/not above
JC	Jump if carry
JE/JZ	Jump if equal/zero
JG/JNLE	Jump if greater/not less nor equal
JGE/JNL	Jump if greater or equal/not less
JL/JNGE	Jump if less/not greater nor equal
JLE/JNG	Jump if less or equal/not greater
JNC	Jump if not carry
JNE/JNZ	Jump if not equal/not zero
JNO	Jump if not overflow
JNP/JPO	Jump if not parity/parity odd
JNS	Jump if not sign
JO	Jump if overflow
JP/JPE	Jump if parity/parity even
JS	Jump if sign
ITERATION CONTROLS	
LOOP	Loop
LOOPE/LOOPZ	Loop if equal/zero
LOOPNE/LOOPNZ	Loop if not equal/not zero
JCXZ	Jump if register CX = 0
INTERRUPTS	
INT	Interrupt
INTO	Interrupt if overflow
IRET	Interrupt return

There are three types of JMPs: short, near, and far. A short JUMP takes a 1-byte displacement and can only jump ± 127 words from the instruction pointer. A near JUMP takes a 2-byte displacement and can jump $\pm 32{,}767$ bytes. A far JUMP can jump all over memory, but it takes 4 bytes and loads both the CS and IP registers. There is also a series of conditional JUMPS on the **8086**, but these are all short JUMPS.

There are two types of CALLs, near and far, that direct the IP and CS (for a far CALL) to a subroutine. The subroutine must end with the proper RETURN (near or far).

The LOOP instruction will decrement CX by 1 and transfer control to the specified address if CX is not zero; otherwise the next instruction is executed. This is similar to the Z80 DECREMENT AND BRANCH IF NOT ZERO instruction. Note that CX is decremented before it is tested.

The LOOPE (also called LOOPZ) instruction is similar to LOOP but the transfer will occur only if CX is not zero and ZF = 1. The LOOPNE (also called LOOPNZ) instruction works like the LOOPE, except ZF = 0 instead of 1.

The JCXZ is like the LOOP but does not decrement CX. This allows the programmer to put a JCXZ at the beginning of a loop to detect that the user wants the loop to be executed zero times if CX contains zero.

10-8.5 Processor Control Instructions

The processor control instruction group is shown in Table 10-8 and includes the standard NOP, set or clear flag bit instructions, and halt instructions, plus several

Table 10-8 **The 8086 processor control instructions**

FLAG OPERATIONS	
STC	Set carry flag
CLC	Clear carry flag
CMC	Complement carry flag
STD	Set direction flag
CLD	Clear direction flag
STI	Set interrupt enable flag
CLI	Clear interrupt enable flag
EXTERNAL SYNCHRONIZATION	
HLT	Halt until interrupt or reset
WAIT	Wait for $\overline{\text{TEST}}$ pin active
ESC	Escape to external processor
LOCK	Lock bus during next instruction
NO OPERATION	
NOP	No operation

new instructions. The ESC is an escape instruction which provides a means for an external coprocessor to obtain an instruction and operand. If the operand is a memory variable, the **8086** will fetch the data from memory, so that the coprocessor can grab the data as it comes over the data bus.

The LOCK instruction is a simple-byte prefix which causes the **8086**, configured in the maximum mode, to retain control of the bus until the next instruction has been completely executed. The sole purpose of this prefix is for multi-CPU systems having shared resources such as printers, disk storage, or files. A typical multi-CPU system uses a memory location to indicate whether a device is being used by the CPU. When a CPU wants the device it has to read the status and if it is not being used, then the CPU writes the busy indication into the status location. The LOCK prevents another CPU from using the bus between the time that the first CPU reads the status and the time it writes the busy value into the status location.

10-9 8086/8088 PINS AND MODE SELECTION

The **8086/8088** pins are described in this section, followed by the special use of the MN/MX pin to select the minimum or maximum mode. Figures 10-4 and 10-5 show the pin outs of the **8086** and **8088**. The pins of the **8086** will be discussed first, followed by a discussion of the differences between the **8088** and the **8086**. The pins that are common between the minimum and maximum mode will be covered first, followed by the minimum mode signals, then the maximum mode signals.

10-9.1 8086/8088 Pin Out

The pins on the **8086** and their function are described in this section.

AD0–AD15 The address/data bus pins are used jointly as the full 16 bits of the bidirectional data bus and also as the lower 16 bits of the address bus. The ALE pin is used to enable an external 16-bit latch to store the address information while these pins are used to transfer data.

There are eight hardware status pins on the **8086** that can be used by other devices. The first three pins, $\overline{S0}$, $\overline{S1}$, $\overline{S2}$, are used by the **8288** bus controller to determine the type of bus cycle. S3 and S4 indicate which of the four segment registers was used to produce the physical address. S5 indicates the state of the interrupt enable flag. S6 is always 0 and S7 is a spare line which is undefined. The address appears on the shared lines during the first two clock cycles of a bus cycle and the status information on the third and fourth clock cycles of the bus cycle.

A16/S3 to A19/S6 These four output pins are used as the most significant 4 bits of the addresses' 20-bit address bus and are also time shared as 4 status bits S3 to S6.

$\overline{BHE}$/S7—Bus High Enable/Status Bit 7 This is an output that the **8086** uses to enable data transfer on the most significant 8 bits of the data bus or as bit 7 of the status information.

Common Signals		
Name	**Function**	**Type**
AD15-AD0	Address/Data Bus	Bidirectional, 3-State
A19/S6-A16/S3	Address/Status	Output, 3-State
$\overline{BHE}$/S7	Bus High Enable/Status	Output, 3-State
MN/$\overline{MX}$	Minimum/Maximum Mode Control	Input
$\overline{RD}$	Read Control	Output, 3-State
$\overline{TEST}$	Wait On Test Control	Input
READY	Wait State Control	Input
RESET	System Reset	Input
NMI	Non-Maskable Interrupt Request	Input
INTR	Interrupt Request	Input
CLK	System Clock	Input
V_{CC}	+5V	Input
GND	Ground	

Minimum Mode Signals (MN/MX = V_{CC})		
Name	**Function**	**Type**
HOLD	Hold Request	Input
HLDA	Hold Acknowledge	Output
$\overline{WR}$	Write Control	Output, 3-State
M/$\overline{IO}$	Memory/IO Control	Output, 3-State
DT/$\overline{R}$	Data Transmit/Receive	Output, 3-State
$\overline{DEN}$	Data Enable	Output, 3-State
ALE	Address Latch Enable	Output
$\overline{INTA}$	Interrupt Acknowledge	Output

Maximum Mode Signals (MN/MX = GND)		
Name	**Function**	**Type**
$\overline{RQ}/\overline{GT1}$, 0	Request/Grant Bus Access Control	Bidirectional
$\overline{LOCK}$	Bus Priority Lock Control	Output, 3-State
$\overline{S2}$-$\overline{S0}$	Bus Cycle Status	Output, 3-State
QS1, QS0	Instruction Queue Status	Output

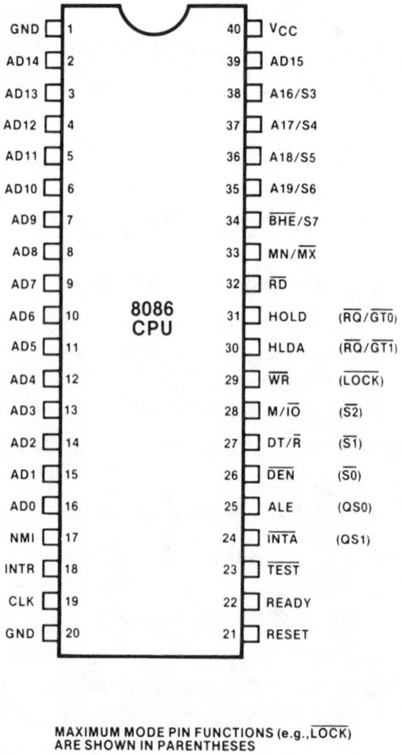

Pin	Signal	Pin	Signal	(Max mode)
1	GND	40	V_{CC}	
2	AD14	39	AD15	
3	AD13	38	A16/S3	
4	AD12	37	A17/S4	
5	AD11	36	A18/S5	
6	AD10	35	A19/S6	
7	AD9	34	$\overline{BHE}$/S7	
8	AD8	33	MN/$\overline{MX}$	
9	AD7	32	$\overline{RD}$	
10	AD6	31	HOLD	($\overline{RQ}/\overline{GT0}$)
11	AD5	30	HLDA	($\overline{RQ}/\overline{GT1}$)
12	AD4	29	$\overline{WR}$	($\overline{LOCK}$)
13	AD3	28	M/$\overline{IO}$	($\overline{S2}$)
14	AD2	27	DT/$\overline{R}$	($\overline{S1}$)
15	AD1	26	$\overline{DEN}$	($\overline{S0}$)
16	AD0	25	ALE	(QS0)
17	NMI	24	$\overline{INTA}$	(QS1)
18	INTR	23	$\overline{TEST}$	
19	CLK	22	READY	
20	GND	21	RESET	

8086 CPU

MAXIMUM MODE PIN FUNCTIONS (e.g., $\overline{LOCK}$) ARE SHOWN IN PARENTHESES

Figure 10-4 **8086** pin definitions. (Courtesy of Intel Corporation.)

Common Signals		
Name	**Function**	**Type**
AD7–AD0	Address/Data Bus	Bidirectional, 3-State
A15–A8	Address Bus	Output, 3-State
A19/S6–A16/S3	Address/Status	Output, 3-State
MN/$\overline{MX}$	Minimum/Maximum Mode Control	Input
$\overline{RD}$	Read Control	Output, 3-State
$\overline{TEST}$	Wait On Test Control	Input
READY	Wait State Control	Input
RESET	System Reset	Input
NMI	Non-Maskable Interrupt Request	Input
INTR	Interrupt Request	Input
CLK	System Clock	Input
V_{CC}	+5V	Input
GND	Ground	

Minimum Mode Signals (MN/$\overline{MX}$ = V_{CC})		
Name	**Function**	**Type**
HOLD	Hold Request	Input
HLDA	Hold Acknowledge	Output
$\overline{WR}$	Write Control	Output, 3-State
IO/$\overline{M}$	IO/Memory Control	Output, 3-State
DT/$\overline{R}$	Data Transmit/Receive	Output, 3-State
$\overline{DEN}$	Data Enable	Output, 3-State
ALE	Address Latch Enable	Output
$\overline{INTA}$	Interrupt Acknowledge	Output
$\overline{SS0}$	S0 Status	Output, 3-State

Maximum Mode Signals (MN/$\overline{MX}$ = GND)		
Name	**Function**	**Type**
$\overline{RQ}/\overline{GT1}$, 0	Request/Grant Bus Access Control	Bidirectional
$\overline{LOCK}$	Bus Priority Lock Control	Output, 3-State
$\overline{S2}$–$\overline{S0}$	Bus Cycle Status	Output, 3-State
QS1, QS0	Instruction Queue Status	Output

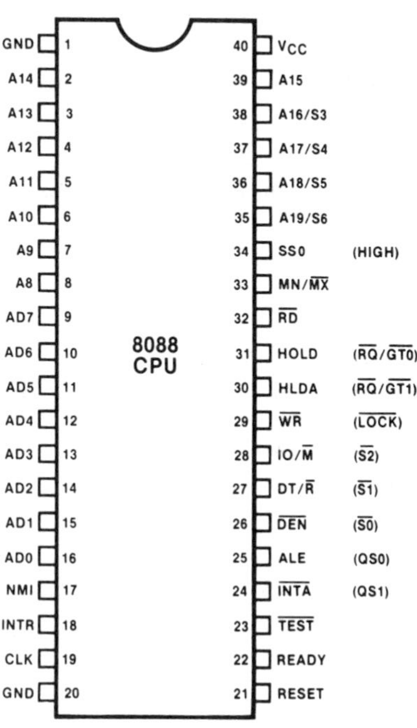

Figure 10-5 **8088** pin definitions. (Courtesy of Intel Corporation.)

MN/$\overline{MX}$ The minimum/maximum mode control pin places the μP in a single μP mode (minimum mode) or in a multiprocessor mode (maximum mode). The minimum/maximum mode is discussed in section 10-9.2.

$\overline{RD}$ The READ signal is low when the μP wants to read data and is high when not doing a READ or not using the data bus.

$\overline{TEST}$ The TEST input allows the μP to check the condition of an external signal and execute an INTERRUPT ON TEST instruction.

READY This is the READY input which is used by external devices to force the μP to add WAIT states. It allows the **8086** to be used with slower speed memory.

RESET The RESET is an active-high input used to force the μP into the RESET condition. The RESET is really a special type of interrupt and is discussed further in section 10-10.

NMI The NMI is the nonmaskable interrupt request input which is one of the interrupts which will be discussed in section 10-10. The nonmaskability means the CLI (clear interrupt instruction) does not prevent the NMI input from causing an interrupt.

INTR The INTR is the interrupt request input. Interrupts on this pin are maskable and can be disabled by the CLI instruction.

CLK The CLK input is the system clock pin. The square wave input on this pin determines the speed of instruction execution.

The following pin designations apply when the μP is in the *minimum mode*. In the minimum mode the **8086** generates its own control signals and does not require a bus controller chip (**8288**) to generate these signals. In the maximum mode, these signals are generated by a bus controller chip (**8288**). The status lines tell the bus controller when to generate these signals.

HOLD This input pin allows an external device to request the use of the system bus. The **8086** will put the data bus/address bus and control lines into a tri-state condition and then activate HLDA to tell the external device that it can have the bus. When the external device releases the HOLD pin, the **8086** will again take control of the bus and continue executing its program.

HLDA The hold acknowledge output pin is used to tell the device that activated the HOLD input that it may start using the bus.

$\overline{WR}$ The WRITE signal is the standard WRITE output line which is low when the μP wants to write data and is high when the μP is not writing data.

M/$\overline{IO}$ This output pin tells the memory or input/output devices whether the address on the address bus should be interpreted as a memory address or a port number.

DT/$\overline{R}$ This output is the data transmit/receive pin. This pin, plus the $\overline{DEN}$ pin, is used by the **8286** (noninverting) and **8287** (inverting) Octal Bus Transceivers. These two pins work with the clock pin to assure proper timing of the data bus and also help to keep the address and data on the shared bus separated.

$\overline{DEN}$ The data enable output works with the DT/$\overline{R}$ pin to control the shared data/address bus. The DEN is similar to the ALE output, except that the DEN enables a bidirectional bus driver which is connected to the shared address/data bus. This bus driver separates the address and data information and only passes data bus information. This separation is done by the DEN signal.

ALE The address latch enable output provides a control signal to external latches which can latch or hold the address while the shared data/address bus is used to transfer data.

$\overline{INTA}$ The interrupt acknowledge output is used to signal an interrupting device that it should proceed with the interrupt procedure as described in section 10-10.

The following pin designations apply when the μP is in the *maximum mode*. In this mode the **8086** requires a bus controller chip (**8288**) to generate all of the control signals it generated in the minimum mode. The **8086** then generates special signals which can be used for bus arbitration, that is, to control the shared use of the system with other μPs.

$\overline{RQ}/\overline{GTI}$ and $\overline{RQ}/\overline{GTO}$ These two request/grant bus access control lines serve the identical function of allowing an external device to request the use of the bus. The **8086** is unique in that these lines are bidirectional and only one of these lines will be used (either line may be chosen). The requesting coprocessor, μP, or other device only needs to send a pulse to the **8086** on one of these lines (BUS REQUEST action). The **8086** will respond by sending a pulse back to the device, on the same line, when it has released the bus (BUS GRANT action). When the device has finished with the bus it must send another pulse on the same line to the **8086**, which will inform the **8086** that it can again start using the bus (BUS RELEASE action). The reason for having two identical lines is probably that this allows two other processors or coprocessors to be used on the system without adding any additional hardware. The timing of the transfer of pulses on these lines is determined by the system clock, so all devices using these lines must use the same system clock.

$\overline{LOCK}$ The bus priority lock control output pin is used with the **8289** bus arbiter to ensure that the **8086** retains control of the bus until it finishes the entire instruction. This output is a result of executing a LOCK instruction.

S2, S1, S0 These three outputs indicate the bus cycle status. They are used in the maximum mode by the **8288** bus controller to generate all the control signals required for a bus cycle.

QS1 and QS0 These two outputs indicate the instruction queue status. These signals allow external monitoring of the **8086** instruction queue to allow extension of the instruction set by a coprocessor.

The differences between the **8086** and the **8088** are very minor. The major difference is that the **8086** can transfer a 16-bit word to memory in one step because it has a 16-bit data bus, while the **8088** must use two steps to transfer a 16-bit word to memory because it only has an 8-bit data bus.

The *instruction queue* in the execution unit of the **8086** is 6 bytes long and the **8086** will prefetch 16-bit words in its attempt to keep the queue full. The **8088** has a 4-byte queue and it will fetch single bytes to try to keep the queue full.

The final difference is in the pin definitions as shown in Figures 10-4 and 10-5. Since the **8088** only handles bytes and not 16-bit words, the BHE pin is not needed so it is used as S0 status line. The other major difference in the pin definitions is in pin 28, which is defined as $M/\overline{IO}$ on the **8086**, but has a complemented definition on the **8088** ($IO/\overline{M}$). This makes the **8088** more compatible with the **8085**.

10-9.2 Mode Selection

Both the **8086** and **8088** have two modes of operation, a maximum mode and a minimum mode. The selection of the mode changes the functional characteristics of several of the μP pins. The mode of the μP is selected by using the $MN/\overline{MX}$ pin (pin 33). When this pin is connected to +5 V the minimum mode is selected. In the minimum mode the μP is configured internally to provide the bus control signals needed by memory and peripherals. The minimum mode is ideal for small system configurations which seek to minimize cost and parts count.

When the $MN/\overline{MX}$ pin is LOW, the μP is configured in the maximum mode. In the maximum mode the **8086** encodes control signals on three lines (S2, 21, S0). An **8288** bus controller must be added to decode the signals from the **8086**. It is the **8288**'s job to provide an expanded set of control signals to the rest of the system. The **8086** uses the other status lines, in the maximum mode, to help coordinate the activities of other processors in the system. The maximum mode is utilized for large systems which may include multiprocessors and coprocessors.

10-10 INTERRUPT CAPABILITIES

The **8086** allows interrupts to come from hardware (both maskable and non-maskable interrupts) and from the software and **8086** error trapping.

There are three types of software and error trapping interrupts. The INTERRUPT ON OVERFLOW instruction, INTO, will force an interrupt if the overflow status bit is set when this instruction is executed. The second type is an interrupt instruction, INT, which allows a program to use an interrupt service routine. Both of these types are under direct program control. The third type is an error interrupt which occurs when the program attempts a divide by zero. This simplifies automatic recovery from the error.

There are two pins on the **8086** which allow an external device to request an interrupt. The first of these is the *nonmaskable interrupt*, NMI, which is an edge-triggered input activated on a low-to-high transition on the NMI input. The second is the INTR input, which is level sensitive and activated by a high level on this input.

The interrupt processing of the **8086** is similar to most of the other 16-bit μPs in that it uses a table to contain information determining how each of the different interrupts is to be processed. Figure 10-6 shows the physical arrangement of the table of vectors. Each vector is numbered 0 to 255 and consists of two words (4 bytes). The first word will be loaded into the code segment register after the previous value is pushed onto the stack. The second word will be loaded into the instruction pointer after the previous contents of the program counter is pushed onto the stack. The status register is also saved on the stack. Loading these two registers will transfer execution to the appropriate *interrupt service routine.* When the interrupt service routine is completed, it will execute an IRET instruction which will POP the

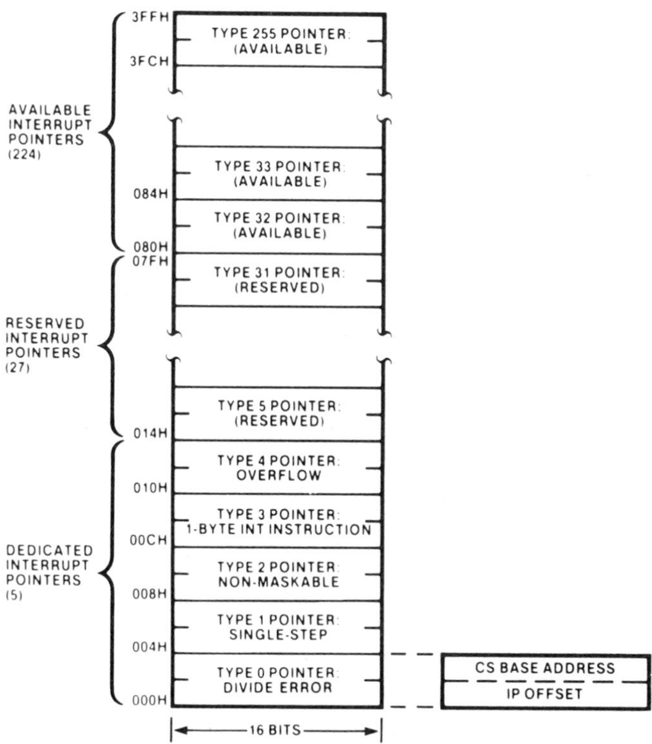

Figure 10-6 Interrupt pointer table. (Courtesy of Intel Corporation.)

status register, the previous program counter, and the previous code segment register off the stack and execution will continue where it was interrupted.

If the interrupt came in on the INTR pin, then the **8086** goes through an *interrupt acknowledge* procedure by sending out an acknowledge. The interrupting device then sends an 8-bit code to the **8086** on the least significant 8 bits of the data bus to indicate which one of the 256 vectors should be used for this particular interrupt. As Figure 10-6 shows, the first five vectors are used for special purposes. Vector 0 is used for the "divide by zero" error processing. Vector 1 is used when the single-step bit in the status register is set to allow the **8086** to single-step through user instructions and then transfer control to a monitor program that will perform whatever tasks the user requires, such as displaying the register contents. Vector 2 is used by the nonmaskable interrupt request. Note that the NMI only has one service routine while the INTR has many. This is consistent with the normal usage of the NMI for very high priority actions, such as loss of power. Vectors 3 and 4 are used by the INT and INTO instructions. The INT instruction has the capability of using the second byte of the instruction to select one of the 256 vectors to use. This provides a convenient method for having a user program request a service from the operating system.

Of the 256 vectors in the table, Intel has identified vectors 5 to 31 as reserved for use by Intel. There is no hardware to prevent the user from using these; this is only a warning that Intel plans to use these vectors on several of their peripheral boards and if the user intends to use their board level system, then he should not use these vectors.

10-11 COPROCESSORS

The Intel **8086** family of devices provides extremely sophisticated and powerful computing hardware. The real strength of the family is due not only to the power of the **8086** instruction set, but to the capability of the **8086** to have *coprocessors* incorporated into the system. The coprocessors effectively expand the instruction set by adding new instructions which add special capabilities. There are two coprocessors currently available, the **8089**, which is an input/output coprocessor, and the **8087**, which is an arithmetic coprocessor. The term *coprocessor* is a unique and innovative idea, but the novelty of the concept is that the coprocessor is connected to the data and address bus in parallel with the **8086.** This allows the assembly language programmer to write one program which will control the **8086** and the coprocessor. The advantage of the coprocessor is that the internal architecture, registers, and instruction set are optimized to perform the specialized operations and therefore are much more efficient at performing the task.

10-11.1 The 8089 Input/Output Processor

The **8089** Input/Output Processor (IOP) is a coprocessor to be used with the **8086** and **8088** systems when they are configured in the maximum mode. The pin diagram of the **8089** is shown in Figure 10-7. The IOP contains two independent

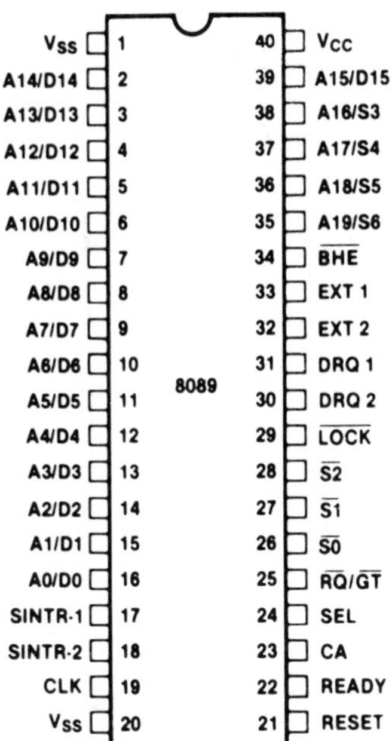

Figure 10-7 **8089** input/output processor pin diagram. (Courtesy of Intel Corporation.)

input/output channels. This smart peripheral chip combines the flexibility of direct CPU controlled input/output with the speed of DMA (direct memory access) on each channel. The instruction set of the IOP allows it to manipulate or search through the data as it is being transferred.

The advantage of the **8089** is that it relieves the CPU of the character-by-character transfer task because the **8089** performs this for the CPU. The CPU only has to build a set of commands that describe the task in memory. The IOP then reads and carries out the commands and notifies the CPU when the task is completed. Thus, the CPU can deal in a higher level of I/O; that is, it can deal in block or buffer transfer, instead of byte or character transfer. The unique feature of the **8089** is that it shares the data/address bus with the **8086/8088**.

10-11.2 Functional Description

Figure 10-8 shows the **8089** block diagram and the channel register set (one set of registers for each channel). As Figure 10-7 indicates, the **8089** is really a CPU, with its own arithmetic-logic unit (ALU), set of registers, control lines, and address and data lines. The **8089**, however, has an instruction set which tailors it to handling data input and output and the manipulation of the data as it is transferred.

Figure 10-8 shows that the **8089** consists of the following components.

Assembly/Disassembly Registers The assembly/disassembly registers are used internally by the **8089** to accommodate data transfers between different width data

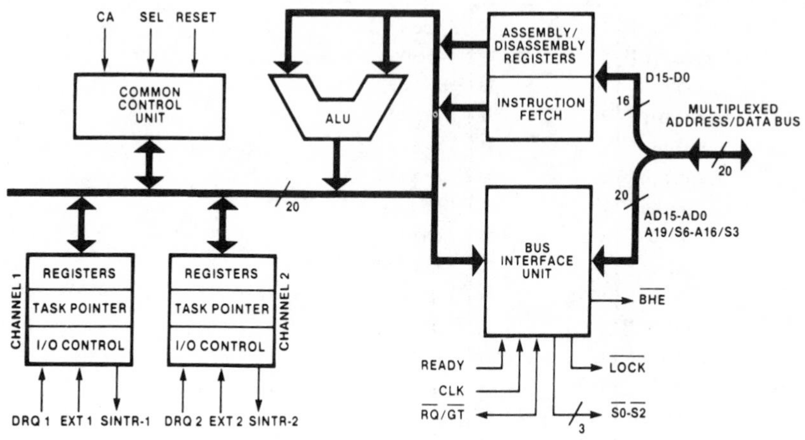

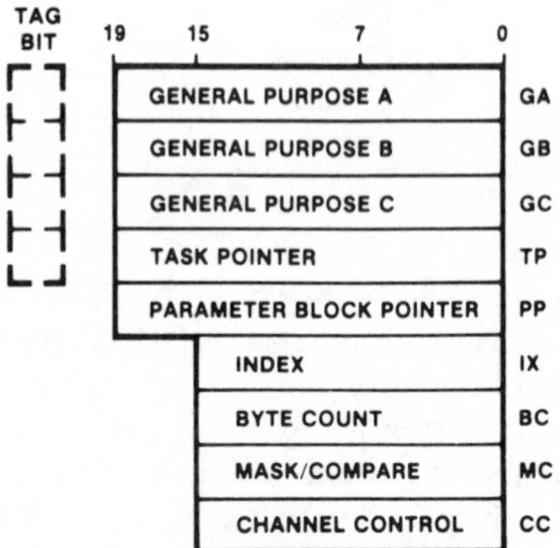

Figure 10-8 **8089** block diagram and channel register set. (Courtesy of Intel Corporation.)

buses, such as between the 16-bit data bus to the **8086** memory and an 8-bit I/O device. Thus, the IOP could read data from an 8-bit I/O device such as an **8251** or an **8255** and after reading 2 bytes into the assembly/disassembly registers, the **8089** would then transfer one 16-bit word to the appropriate memory location.

Instruction Fetch Unit The instruction fetch unit controls the fetching of instructions for whichever channel is executing. This unit also adjusts to using either an 8-bit or 16-bit bus to fetch instructions.

Bus Interface Unit The BIU of the **8089** handles all bus cycles to transfer data and instructions between the **8089** and memory and peripheral devices. The **8089** generates control and status signals, similar to the **8086**.

I/O Control Section The I/O control section of each channel handles the three control lines (DRQ, EXT, and SINTR) on each channel. If the data transferred is synchronized, the channel waits for a signal on its DRQ line before performing the next transfer. If the transfer is to be terminated by an external signal, the **8089** monitors its EXT line and stops the transfer when this line goes active. Each channel has a SINTR line that can be activated by software to send an interrupt request to the CPU.

Channel Registers The channel registers are shown in Figure 10-8. The first five registers (GA, GB, GC, TP, and PP) are 20-bit registers, which allows them to address any location in the one megabyte address space of the **8086**. The remaining four registers (IX, BC, MC, and CC) are 16-bit registers. The register use and capabilities are shown in Figure 10-9.

General-Purpose A and B The two general-purpose registers, GA and GB, may be used as source and destination registers. Their use may be interchanged.

General-Purpose C The GC register may be used to point to a translation table, if the data is to be translated during the transfer. This register is not altered by the transfer operation.

Task Pointer (TP) The channel control unit (CCU) loads the TP from the parameter block when it starts or restarts a channel program. The TP points to the next instruction to be executed by the channel. During **8089** execution, the TP is automatically updated as each instruction for that channel is executed.

Register	Size	Program Access	System or I/O Pointer	Use by Channel Programs	Use in DMA Transfers
GA	20	Update	Either	General, base	Source/destination pointer
GB	20	Update	Either	General, base	Source/destination pointer
GC	20	Update	Either	General, base	Translate table pointer
TP	20	Update	Either	Procedure return, instruction pointer	Adjusted to reflect cause of termination
PP	20	Reference	System	Base	N/A
IX	16	Update	N/A	General, auto-increment	N/A
BC	16	Update	N/A	General	Byte counter
MC	16	Update	N/A	General, masked compare	Masked compare
CC	16	Update	N/A	Restricted use recommended	Defines transfer options

Figure 10-9 Channel register summary. (Courtesy of Intel Corporation.)

Parameter Block Pointer (PP) The parameter block is a block of memory that defines the I/O operation. The CCU loads the PP with the address of the parameter block before it starts a channel program. The PP register cannot be altered by the channel program, which makes this an ideal register to use as a base register for addressing data in the parameter block. PP is not used in DMA transfers.

Index (IX) The IX register may be used as another general register or as an index register (with a base register). When IX is used as an index register it may be auto incremented to simplify accessing consecutive elements in an array, buffer, or string. IX is not used in DMA transfers.

Byte Count (BC) The BC register may also be used as a general register. During DMA transfer, BC will be decremented for each byte transferred, and may be used to terminate the DMA operation when the register reaches zero.

Mask/Compare (MC) The MC may be used as a general register. This register may also be used during either DMA or a channel program to check selected bits within a byte. In order to do this, the program must load a value to be used for the compare into the eight least significant bits of the MC register and a mask value into the upper 8 bits of the MC register. A "1" in a mask bit selects the bit in the corresponding position in the compare value; a 0 in a mask bit masks the corresponding bit in the compare value.

EXAMPLE 10-4 What value would be loaded into the mask/compare register (MC) to look for a byte of data with the least significant 4 bits being binary 1010?

Solution The most significant 8 bits of the MC register select which bits in the byte being transferred are to be checked. Since it is desired to check only the least significant 4 bits of the data, a value of 00001111 should be in the most significant 8 bits of the MC register. The least significant 8 bits contain the bit pattern that is being checked for. Since the data is to be checked for 1010, the value 00001010 can be loaded into the least significant 8 bits of the MC register. The four zeros are arbitrary in this example because the comparison is being based only on the lower 4 bits. Thus the value to be loaded into the MC register is binary 0000111100001010 or hexidecimal 0F0A.

Channel Control (CC) The contents of the channel control register control the execution of the I/O transfer. Figure 10-10 shows the function of the various bits in the channel control register.

Program Status Word (PSW) The program status word is not available to the programmer and is used internally by the **8089** to maintain the status of each channel. Each channel has its own status word. The channel program does not have access to the PSW. If the CPU suspends the I/O command, then the TP, PSW, and TP TAG bits are stored in the first 4 bytes of the parameter block for that channel.

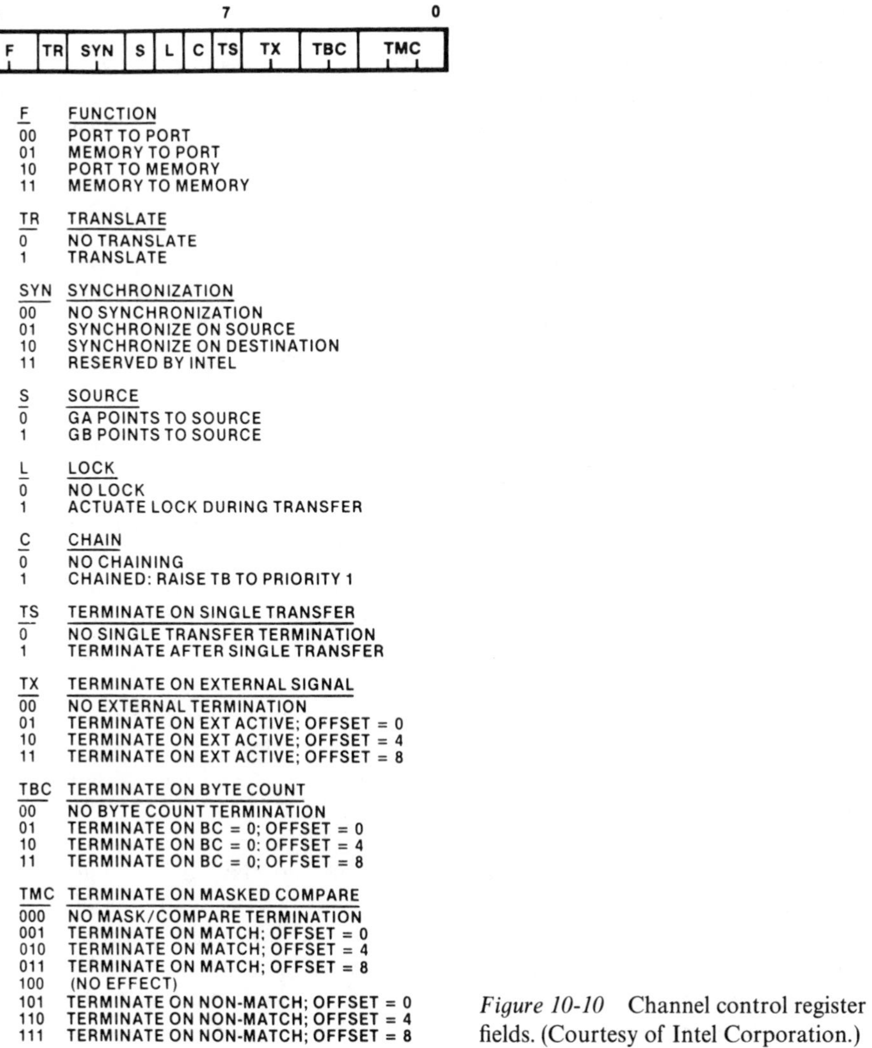

Figure 10-10 Channel control register fields. (Courtesy of Intel Corporation.)

This allows the channel to continue where it left off, if the CPU sends it a resume command.

TP Tag Bits The TP tag bits are each associated with one of the four channel registers (GA, GB, GC, TP). If the tag bit is a 0, then the register associated with that tag bit points to system memory space. If the tag bit is a 1, then the register associated with that tag bit points to I/O space. The CCU sets or clears the tag bits based on commands received from the CPU.

The LOAD POINTER instruction clears the tag bit and enables the addressing of system memory space. The MOVE instruction sets the tag bit to 1 and enables the addressing of I/O space.

10-11.3 I/O Coprocessor Operation

The **8089** I/O Coprocessor can operate in two modes. The first mode is programmed I/O which is similar to the manner in which the **8086** and **8088** operate with I/O devices. The second mode is the DMA (direct memory access) mode which is usually used for high-speed transfer of blocks of data.

Programmed I/O With programmed I/O, for each byte or word to be transferred, the **8089** executes one or more instructions to cause the transfer. This results in a maximum data transfer rate that is several times slower than the DMA transfer. This technique of I/O transfer is very useful with slow devices. It is also used to send commands to an I/O device to set up a DMA transfer or to read the status from the I/O device.

Direct Memory Access I/O The **8089**'s DMA mode allows the transfer of blocks of data. The transfer may be from one section of memory to another section of memory, or from one I/O device to another I/O device, or between memory and an I/O device. To perform a DMA transfer, the CPU (**8086** or **8088**) usually has the **8089** execute a channel program which writes commands to the device controller to enable the I/O device to perform the DMA. The channel program also initializes the channel registers in the **8089** which will be used in the transfer. The **8089** registers GA and GB must be initialized as the source and destination pointers. The tag bit associated with each register designates whether the register points to an I/O location or a memory location. If the tag bit indicates that GA or GB are pointers to memory, then the full 20 bits of the register will be used and the register will be incremented after each data transfer. If the tag bit for GA and GB indicates the register points to an I/O device, then only the lower 16 bits of the register will be used (corresponding to the 64K I/O addresses) and the register will not be incremented after each transfer.

The channel control register is 16 bits long, as shown in Figure 10-10, and contains ten fields that determine how the DMA transfer is implemented. This is the last of the three required registers. (The first two are GA and GB.) Bits 15 and 14 select the type of transfer (memory to memory, I/O port to memory, memory to I/O port, or I/O port to I/O port). Bit 13 is used to indicate whether the **8089** should *translate* the data. If bit 13 is set to 1, then the **8089** translates the data using a translation table in memory and pointed to by register GC. Data translation by the **8089** can only be performed on byte transfers and the destination bus must have a logical width of 8 bits.

Bits 12 and 11 specify if the transfer is synchronized by the source device, the destination device, or unsynchronized (free running).

Bit 10 selects the source register (GA or GB) to be used. If bit 10 is a 0, then GA is the source register and GB is the destination register. If bit 10 is a 1, then GB is the source register and GA is the destination register.

Bit 9 is the LOCK bit, which indicates to the channel that is should assert the processor's bus lock (LOCK) during the transfer. The LOCK will be asserted at the beginning of the transfer and will be released when the channel enters the termination sequence.

Bit 8 is the CHAIN bit, which will raise the channel program execution to priority level 1, when set.

Bit 7 is the TERMINATE ON SINGLE TRANSFER field. When this bit is a 1, the channel will perform one complete transfer and then resume the channel program. When this bit is a 1, the other termination conditions are ignored. This will frequently be used when the I/O device is relatively slow.

Bits 6 to 0 specify the termination condition to stop the transfer. There are three types of termination conditions which may be selected individually or in combination. The three conditions are: an external signal coming in on the channel EXT line, or on a byte count becoming zero, or on a masked compare (either match or nonmatch condition).

To put the **8089** channel into the DMA transfer mode, the **8089** must execute a XFER instruction. The **8089** will be in the DMA mode after it executes one instruction following the XFER instruction. This allows the **8089** channel program to send a final command to the I/O device to enable it to start the transfer.

10-11.4 Initialization

Before the **8089** can start handling I/O tasks, it must be initialized. The initialization process defines the physical bus width, request/grant mode, and the location of the channel control block. The **8089** initializes itself by reading information from three *initialization control blocks* located in memory, shown in Figure 10-11. These three blocks are the system configuration pointer (SCP), the system configuration block (SCB), and the channel control block (CB). The SCP will usually be in ROM, the SCB can be in either RAM or ROM, and the CB will usually be in RAM. It is the responsibility of the CPU to set up the SCB and the CB if they are in RAM.

The initialization sequence is started when the CPU issues a *channel attention* to channel 1 or channel 2. The channel attention is issued to the **8089** and uses the CA and SEL pins on the **8089**. The SEL pin selects either channel 1 or 2. The CA pin then causes the selected channel to be sent a channel attention signal. If channel 1 was selected, then the **8089** considers itself the master unit. If channel 2 was selected, then the **8089** considers itself as a slave unit. The **8089** then accesses the system bus to read the SYSBUS field from location FFFF6H in system memory (the **8089** assumes an 8-bit bus initially). The least significant bit of SYSBUS tells the **8089** whether the system data bus is 8 bits or 16 bits wide as shown in Figure 10-12. If the bit is a 0 then the bus is 8 bits. If the bit is a 1, the bus is 16 bits wide. Next the **8089** gets the address of the SCB from the SCP. Then the **8089** reads the system operation command (SOC) field from the SCB. The SOC bit encoding is shown in Figure 10-12 and tells the **8089** the request/grant mode and the width of the I/O bus. The **8089** then reads the pointer to the channel control block and stores the address in an internal register which is not available to the channel program. Next the **8089** clears the channel 1 BUSY flag in the CB. The clearing of the BUSY flag indicates that the **8089** is now ready to handle an I/O task. After the **8089** has been initialized, any channel attention is interpreted as a command to the channel.

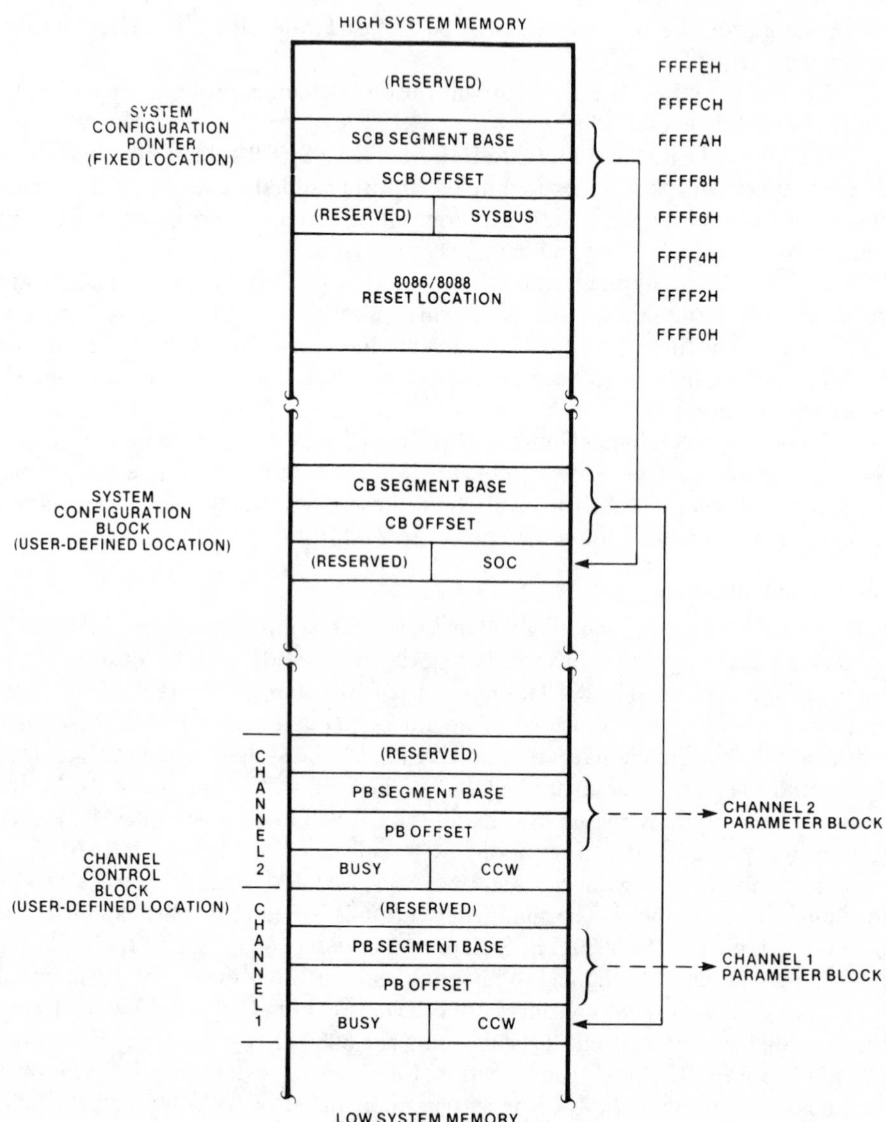

Figure 10-11 Initialization control blocks. (Courtesy of Intel Corporation.)

To initiate an I/O task, the CPU sends a channel attention to the channel and the channel sets its BUSY flag in the CB to FFH. This provides a busy status indication to the CPU. Next the channel reads the channel command word (CCW) from its CB and executes the command set up there by the CPU. The CCW bit encoding is shown in Figure 10-12. The command field of the CCW shows that there are four commands:

1 START CHANNEL PROGRAM

2 SUSPEND CHANNEL OPERATION

3 RESUME SUSPENDED CHANNEL PROGRAM

4 HALT CHANNEL OPERATION

The **8089** knows where the channel program is located by two 16-bit registers located in the channel control block. They are the parameter block segment base and offset. The **8089** uses these two 16-bit values to form a 20-bit physical address in exactly the same way that the **8086** does. The parameter block contains the starting address of the channel program. The channel program is composed of **8089** instructions that perform the desired I/O task. The **8089** instructions are shown in Table 10-9.

The **8089** I/O Coprocessor and the **8086** or **8088** make a very powerful combination because the **8089** can run its programs at the same time that the CPU is running its own program and yet have almost no effect on slowing the CPU. This is because the CPU has a prefetch queue to store the next instruction to be executed, thus the sharing of the system bus does not adversely affect the CPU speed.

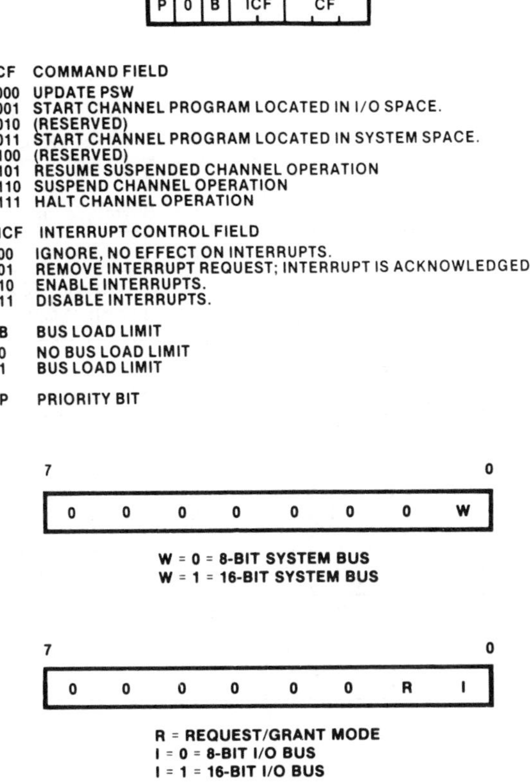

Figure 10-12 Encoding of CCW, SYSBUS, and SOC. (Courtesy of Intel Corporation.)

Table 10-9 **The 8089 instructions**

ADD destination, source		Add Word Variable	
Operands	**Clocks**	**Bytes**	**Coding Example**
register, mem16	11/15	2-3	ADD BC, [GA].LENGTH
mem16, register	16/26	2-3	ADD [GB], GC

ADDB destination, source		Add Byte Variable	
Operands	**Clocks**	**Bytes**	**Coding Example**
register, mem8	11	2-3	ADDB GC, [GA].N_CHARS
mem8, register	16	2-3	ADDB [PP].ERRORS, MC

ADDBI destination, source		Add Byte Immediate	
Operands	**Clocks**	**Bytes**	**Coding Example**
register, immed8	3	3	ADDBI MC,10
mem8, immed8	16	3-4	ADDBI [PP+IX+].RECORDS, 2CH

ADDI destination, source		Add Word Immediate	
Operands	**Clocks**	**Bytes**	**Coding Example**
register, immed16	3	4	ADDI GB, 0C25BH
mem16, immed16	16/26	4-5	ADDI [GB].POINTER, 5899

AND destination, source		Logical AND Word Variable	
Operands	**Clocks**	**Bytes**	**Coding Example**
register, mem16	11/15	2-3	AND MC, [GA].FLAG_WORD
mem16, register	16/26	2-3	AND [GC].STATUS, BC

ANDB destination, source		Logical AND Byte Variable	
Operands	**Clocks**	**Bytes**	**Coding Example**
register, mem8	11	2-3	AND BC, [GC]
mem8, register	16	2-3	AND [GA+IX].RESULT, GA

ANDBI destination, source		Logical AND Byte Immediate	
Operands	**Clocks**	**Bytes**	**Coding Example**
register, immed8	3	3	GA, 01100000B
mem8, immed8	16	3-4	[GC+IX], 2CH

Table 10-9 (Continued)

ANDI destination, source		Logical AND Word Immediate	
Operands	**Clocks**	**Bytes**	**Coding Example**
register, immed16 mem16, immed16	3 16/26	4 4-5	IX, 0H [GB+IX].TAB, 40H

CALL TPsave, target		Call	
Operands	**Clocks**	**Bytes**	**Coding Example**
mem24, !label	17/23	3-5	CALL [GC+IX].SAVE, GET_NEXT

CLR destination, bit select		Clear Bit To Zero	
Operands	**Clocks**	**Bytes**	**Coding Example**
mem8, 0-7	16	2-3	CLR [GA], 3

DEC destination		Decrement Word By 1	
Operands	**Clocks**	**Bytes**	**Coding Example**
register mem16	3 16/26	2 2-3	 DEC [PP].RETRY

DECB destination		Decrement Byte By 1	
Operands	**Clocks**	**Bytes**	**Coding Example**
mem8	16	2-3	DECB [GA+IX+].TAB

HLT (no operands)		Halt Channel Program	
Operands	**Clocks**	**Bytes**	**Coding Example**
(no operands)	11	2	HLT

INC destination		Increment Word by 1	
Operands	**Clocks**	**Bytes**	**Coding Example**
register mem16	3 16/26	2 2-3	INC GA INC [GA].COUNT

Table 10-9 (Continued)

INCB destination		Increment Byte by 1	
Operands	**Clocks**	**Bytes**	**Coding Example**
mem8	16	2-3	INCB [GB].POINTER

JBT source, bit-select, target		Jump if Bit True (1)	
Operands	**Clocks**	**Bytes**	**Coding Example**
mem8, 0-7, label	14	3-5	JBT [GA].RESULT_REG, 3, DATA_VALID

JMCE source, target		Jump if Masked Compare Equal	
Operands	**Clocks**	**Bytes**	**Coding Example**
mem8, label	14	3-5	JMCE [GB].FLAG, STOP_SEARCH

JMCNE source, target		Jump if Masked Compare Not Equal	
Operands	**Clocks**	**Bytes**	**Coding Example**
mem8, label	14	3-5	JMCNE [GB+IX], NEXT_ITEM

JMP target		Jump Unconditionally	
Operands	**Clocks**	**Bytes**	**Coding Example**
label	3	3-4	JMP READ_SECTOR

JNBT source, bit-select, target		Jump if Bit Not True (0)	
Operands	**Clocks**	**Bytes**	**Coding Example**
mem8, 0-7, label	14	3-5	JNBT [GC], 3, RE READ

JNZ source, target		Jump if Word Not Zero	
Operands	**Clocks**	**Bytes**	**Coding Example**
register, label	5	3-4	JNZ BC, WRITE LINE
mem16, label	12/16	3-5	JNZ [PP].NUM CHARS, PUT BYTE

JNZB source, target		Jump if Byte Not Zero	
Operands	**Clocks**	**Bytes**	**Coding Example**
mem8, label	12	3-5	JNZB [GA], MORE_DATA

Table 10-9 (Continued)

JZ source, target		Jump if Word is Zero	
Operands	**Clocks**	**Bytes**	**Coding Example**
register, label	5	3-4	JZ BC, NEXT_LINE
mem16, label	12/16	3-5	JZ [GC+IX].INDEX, BUF_EMPTY

JZB source, target		Jump if Byte Zero	
Operands	**Clocks**	**Bytes**	**Coding Example**
mem8, label	12	3-5	JZB [PP].LINES_LEFT, RETURN

LCALL TPsave, target		Long Call	
Operands	**Clocks**	**Bytes**	**Coding Example**
mem24, label	17/23	4-5	LCALL [GC].RETURN_SAVE, INIT_8279

LJBT source, bit-select, target		Long Jump if Bit True (1)	
Operands	**Clocks**	**Bytes**	**Coding Example**
mem8, 0-7, label	14	4-5	LJBT [GA].RESULT, 1, DATA_OK

LJMCE source, target		Long Jump if Masked Compare Equal	
Operands	**Clocks**	**Bytes**	**Coding Example**
mem8, label	14	4-5	LJMCE [GB], BYTE_FOUND

LJMCNE source, target		Long Jump if Masked Compare Not Equal	
Operands	**Clocks**	**Bytes**	**Coding Example**
mem8, label	14	4-5	LJMCNE [GC+IX+], SCAN_NEXT

LJMP target		Long Jump Unconditional	
Operands	**Clocks**	**Bytes**	**Coding Example**
label	3	4	LJMP GET_CURSOR

LJNBT source, bit-select, target		Long Jump if Bit Not True (0)	
Operands	**Clocks**	**Bytes**	**Coding Example**
mem8, 0-7, label	14	4-5	LJNBT [GC], 6, CRCC_ERROR

Table 10-9 (Continued)

LJNZ source, target		Long Jump if Word Not Zero	
Operands	**Clocks**	**Bytes**	**Coding Example**
register, label mem16, label	5 12/16	4 4-5	LJNZ BC, PARTIAL_XMIT LJNZ [GA+IX].N_LEFT, PUT_DATA

LJNZB source, target		Long Jump if Byte Not Zero	
Operands	**Clocks**	**Bytes**	**Coding Example**
mem8, label	12	4-5	LJNZB [GB+IX+].ITEM, BUMP_COUNT

LJZ source, target		Long Jump if Word Zero	
Operands	**Clocks**	**Bytes**	**Coding Example**
register, label mem16, label	5 12/16	4 4-5	LJZ IX, FIRST_ELEMENT LJZ [GB].XMIT_COUNT, NO_DATA

LJZB source, target		Long Jump if Byte Zero	
Operands	**Clocks**	**Bytes**	**Coding Example**
mem8, label	12	4-5	LJZB [GA], RETURN_LINE

LPD destination, source		Load Pointer With Doubleword Variable	
Operands	**Clocks**	**Bytes**	**Coding Example**
ptr-reg, mem32	20/28*	2-3	LPD GA, [PP].BUF_START

*20 clocks if operand is on even address; 28 if on odd address

LPDI destination, source		Load Pointer With Doubleword Immediate	
Operands	**Clocks**	**Bytes**	**Coding Example**
ptr-reg, immed32	12/16*	6	LPDI GB, DISK_ADDRESS

*12 clocks if instruction is on even address; 16 if on odd address

MOV destination, source		Move Word	
Operands	**Clocks**	**Bytes**	**Coding Example**

register, mem16
mem16, register
mem16, mem16
	8/12
	10/16
	18/28
		2-3
		2-3
		4-6
			MOV IX, [GC]
			MOV [GA].COUNT, BC
			MOV [GA].READING, [GB]

MOVB destination, source		Move Byte	
Operands	**Clocks**	**Bytes**	**Coding Example**

register, mem8
mem8, register
mem8, mem8
	8
	10
	18
		2-3
		2-3
		4-6
			MOVB BC, [PP].TRAN_COUNT
			MOVB [PP].RETURN_CODE, GC
			MOVB [GB+IX+], [GA+IX+]

Table 10-9 (Continued)

MOVBI destination, source		Move Byte Immediate	
Operands	**Clocks**	**Bytes**	**Coding Example**
register, immed8	3	3	MOVBI MC, 'A'
mem8, immed8	12	3-4	MOVBI [PP].RESULT, 0

MOVI destination, source		Move Word Immediate	
Operands	**Clocks**	**Bytes**	**Coding Example**
register, immed16	3	4	MOVI BC, 0
mem16, immed16	12/18	4-5	MOVI [GB], 0FFFFH

MOVP destination, source		Move Pointer	
Operands	**Clocks**	**Bytes**	**Coding Example**
ptr-reg, mem24	19/27*	2-3	MOVP TP, [GC+IX]
mem24, ptr-reg	16/22*	2-3	MOVP [GB].SAVE ADDR, GC

*First figure is for operand on even address; second is for odd-addressed operand.

NOP (no operands)		No Operation	
Operands	**Clocks**	**Bytes**	**Coding Example**
(no operands)	4	2	NOP

NOT destination/destination, source		Logical NOT Word	
Operands	**Clocks**	**Bytes**	**Coding Example**
register	3	2	NOT MC
mem16	16/26	2-3	NOT [GA].PARM
register, mem16	11/15	2-3	NOT BC, [GA+IX].LINES_LEFT

NOTB destination/destination, source		Logical NOT Byte	
Operands	**Clocks**	**Bytes**	**Coding Example**
mem8	16	2-3	NOTB [GA].PARM_REG
register, mem8	11	2-3	NOTB IX, [GB].STATUS

OR destination, source		Logical OR Word	
Operands	**Clocks**	**Bytes**	**Coding Example**
register, mem16	11/15	2-3	OR MC, [GC].MASK
mem16, register	16/26	2-3	OR [GC], BC

ORB destination, source		Logical OR Byte	
Operands	**Clocks**	**Bytes**	**Coding Example**
register, mem8	11	2-3	ORB IX, [PP].POINTER
mem8, register	16	2-3	ORB [GA+IX+], GB

Table 10-9 (Continued)

ORBI destination, source		Logical OR Byte Immediate	
Operands	**Clocks**	**Bytes**	**Coding Example**
register, immed8 mem8, immed8	3 16	3 3-4	ORBI IX, 00010001B ORBI [GB].COMMAND, 0CH

ORI destination, source		Logical OR Word Immediate	
Operands	**Clocks**	**Bytes**	**Coding Example**
register, immed16 mem16,immed16	3 16/26	4 4-5	ORI MC, 0FF0DH ORI [GA], 1000H

SETB destination, bit-select		Set Bit to 1	
Operands	**Clocks**	**Bytes**	**Coding Example**
mem8, 0-7	16	2-3	SETB [GA].PARM_REG, 2

SINTR (no operands)		Set Interrupt Service Bit	
Operands	**Clocks**	**Bytes**	**Coding Example**
(no operands)	4	2	SINTR

TSL destination, set-value, target		Test and Set While Locked	
Operands	**Clocks**	**Bytes**	**Coding Example**
mem8, immed8, short-label	14/16*	4-5	TSL [GA].FLAG, 0FFH, NOT_READY

*14 clocks if destination ≠ 0; 16 clocks if destination = 0

WID source-width, dest-width		Set Logical Bus Widths	
Operands	**Clocks**	**Bytes**	**Coding Example**
8/16, 8/16	4	2	WID 8, 8

XFER (no operands)		Enter DMA Transfer Mode After Next Instruction	
Operands	**Clocks**	**Bytes**	**Coding Example**
(no operands)	4	2	XFER

10-11.5 Numeric Data Processor

The **8087** Numeric Data Processor (NDP) is a coprocessor to be used with the **8086** and **8088** systems when they are configured in the maximum mode. The **8087** pin diagram and block diagram are shown in Figure 10-13. Because of the complexity of the **8087** only a brief description of its capabilities will be provided.

The most important thing to note is the eight 80-bit registers. This gives the **8087** the capabilities for very accurate mathematical computations. The **8087** meets the standards proposed by the IEEE in 1979 for binary floating point arithmetic. The

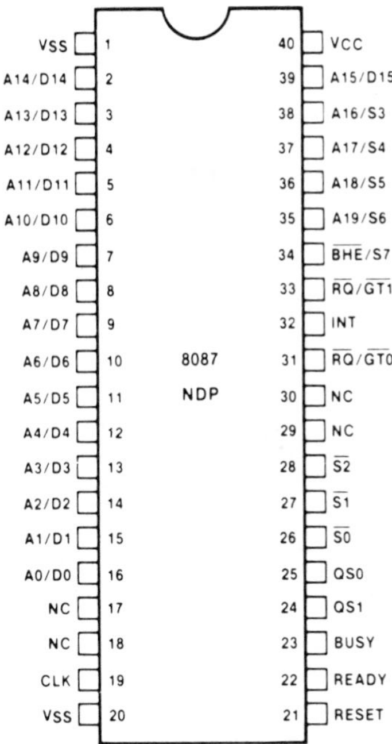

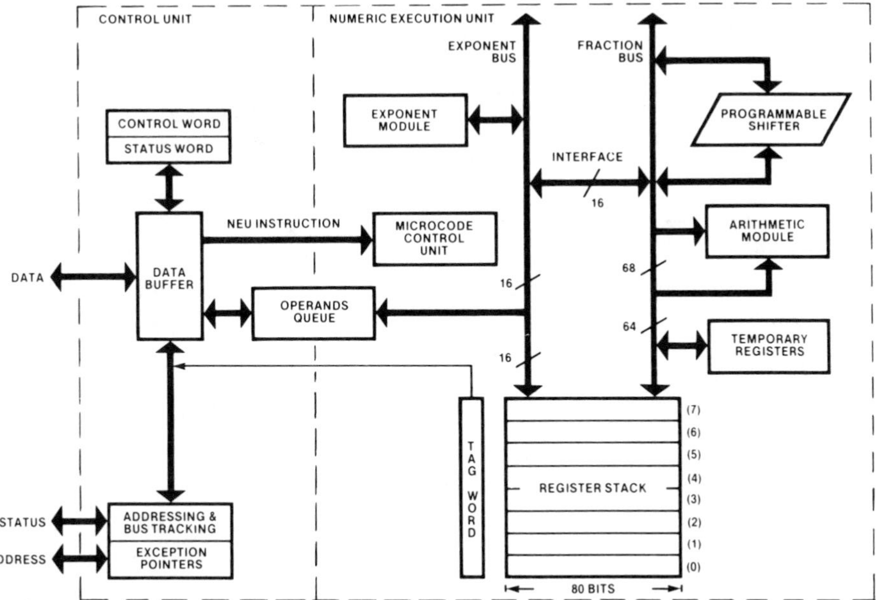

Figure 10-13 **8087** pin diagram and block diagram. (Courtesy of Intel Corporation.)

real advantage of the **8087** is in systems that have to do a large number of numerical calculations, such as 32-bit and 64-bit multiplies or divides or computations such as square roots, or trigonometric or transcendental function calculation. Table 10-10 shows a timing comparison for certain operations; single precision refers to 32-bit floating point numbers and double precision refers to 64-bit floating point numbers.

Table 10-11 shows the wide range of data types which are available with the **8087** and their data formats. The full instruction set of the NDP is shown in Table 10-12. The major difference in the operation of the **8087** is in the control unit (CU), which handles the bus interface. **8087** instructions are mixed in with the instructions for the **8086**. By monitoring the status signals from the **8086**, the NDP can determine when its instruction is being fetched and the CU of the **8087** just copies the data off the bus. The **8086** knows that this instruction was for the **8087**, so it ignores the instruction. The NDP has its own instruction queue to store instructions as they come in. The first 5 bits of all **8087** instructions Op codes are all the same; these bits designate the coprocessor escape (ESC) group of instructions. This is how the **8087** knows which instructions are meant for it, and how the **8086** knows that it should ignore this instruction. The CPU also cooperates in the operation of the **8087**; for example, if the **8087** instruction is an instruction that requires data to be fetched from memory, then the CPU calculates the operand address and performs a "dummy read" of the data from that location. In this case the CPU ignores the data that was read, but the NDP picks it off the bus and uses it.

The combination of an **8086**, **8089**, and **8087** makes a system with superior capabilities. The performance of this three-processor system will compare very favorably with many of the newer 32-bit processors.

Table 10-10 **A timing comparison between 8086 and 8087 operations**

Instruction	Approximate Execution Time (μs) (5 MHz Clock)	
	8087	8086 Emulation
Multiply (single precision)	19	1,600
Multiply (double precision)	27	2,100
Add	17	1,600
Divide (single precision)	39	3,200
Compare	9	1,300
Load (single precision)	9	1,700
Store (single precision)	18	1,200
Square root	36	19,600
Tangent	90	13,000
Exponentiation	100	17,100

Table 10-11 **8087 instruction formats**

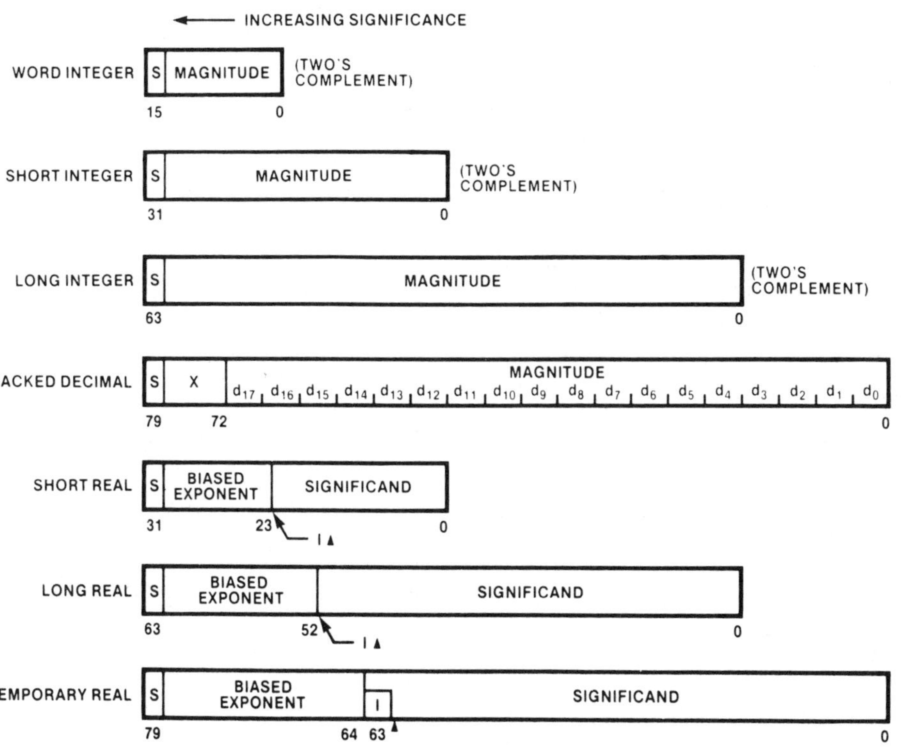

NOTES:
S = Sign bit (0 = positive, 1 = negative)
d_n = Decimal digit (two per byte)
X = Bits have no significance; 8087 ignores when loading, zeros when storing.
▲ = Position of implicit binary point
I = Integer bit of significand; stored in temporary real, implicit in short and long real
Exponent Bias (normalized values):
Short Real: 127 (7FH)
Long Real: 1023 (3FFH)
Temporary Real: 16383 (3FFFH)

Data Type	Bits	Significant Digits (Decimal)	Approximate Range (Decimal)
Word integer	16	4	$-32,768 \leq X \leq +32,767$
Short integer	32	9	$-2\text{x}10^9 \leq X \leq +2\text{x}10^9$
Long integer	64	18	$-9\text{x}10^{18} \leq X \leq +9\text{x}10^{18}$
Packed decimal	80	18	$-99...99 \leq X \leq +99...99$ (18 digits)
Short real*	32	6-7	$8.43\text{x}10^{-37} \leq \|X\| \leq 3.37\text{x}10^{38}$
Long real*	64	15-16	$4.19\text{x}10^{-307} \leq \|X\| \leq 1.67\text{x}10^{308}$
Temporary real	80	19	$3.4\text{x}10^{-4932} \leq \|X\| \leq 1.2\text{x}10^{4932}$

*The short and long real data types correspond to the single and double precision data types defined in other Intel numerics products.

Table 10-12 **NDC instruction set**

FABS

FABS (no operands)
Absolute value

Exceptions: I

Operands	Execution Clocks		Transfers		Bytes	Coding Example
	Typical	Range	8086	8088		
(no operands)	14	10-17	0	0	2	FABS

FADD

FADD //source/destination,source
Add real

Exceptions: I, D, O, U, P

Operands	Execution Clocks		Transfers		Bytes	Coding Example
	Typical	Range	8086	8088		
//ST,ST(i)/ST(i),ST	85	70-100	0	0	2	FADD ST,ST(4)
short-real	105+EA	90-120+EA	2/4	4	2-4	FADD AIR_TEMP [SI]
long-real	110+EA	95-125+EA	4/6	8	2-4	FADD [BX].MEAN

FADDP

FADDP destination,source
Add real and pop

Exceptions: I, D, O, U, P

Operands	Execution Clocks		Transfers		Bytes	Coding Example
	Typical	Range	8086	8088		
ST(i),ST	90	75-105	0	0	2	FADDP ST(2),ST

FBLD

FBLD source
Packed decimal (BCD) load

Exceptions: I

Operands	Execution Clocks		Transfers		Bytes	Coding Example
	Typical	Range	8086	8088		
packed-decimal	300+EA	290-310+EA	5/7	10	2-4	FBLD YTD_SALES

FBSTP

FBSTP destination
Packed decimal (BCD) store and pop

Exceptions: I

Operands	Execution Clocks		Transfers		Bytes	Coding Example
	Typical	Range	8086	8088		
packed-decimal	530+EA	520-540+EA	6/8	12	2-4	FBSTP [BX].FORECAST

FCHS

FCHS (no operands)
Change sign

Exceptions: I

Operands	Execution Clocks		Transfers		Bytes	Coding Example
	Typical	Range	8086	8088		
(no operands)	15	10-17	0	0	2	FCHS

Table 10-12 (Continued)

FCLEX/FNCLEX — **FCLEX** (no operands)
Clear exceptions — **Exceptions:** None

Operands	Execution Clocks		Transfers		Bytes	Coding Example
	Typical	Range	8086	8088		
(no operands)	5	2-8	0	0	2	FNCLEX

FCOM — **FCOM** //source
Compare real — **Exceptions:** I, D

Operands	Execution Clocks		Transfers		Bytes	Coding Example
	Typical	Range	8086	8088		
//ST(i)	45	40-50	0	0	2	FCOM ST(1)
short-real	65+EA	60-70+EA	2/4	4	2-4	FCOM [BP].UPPER_LIMIT
long-real	70+EA	65-75+EA	4/6	8	2-4	FCOM WAVELENGTH

FCOMP — **FCOMP** //source
Compare real and pop — **Exceptions:** I, D

Operands	Execution Clocks		Transfers		Bytes	Coding Example
	Typical	Range	8086	8088		
//ST(i)	47	42-52	0	0	2	FCOMP ST(2)
short-real	68+EA	63-73+EA	2/4	4	2-4	FCOMP [BP+2].N_READINGS
long-real	72+EA	67-77+EA	4/6	8	2-4	FCOMP DENSITY

FCOMPP — **FCOMPP** (no operands)
Compare real and pop twice — **Exceptions:** I, D

Operands	Execution Clocks		Transfers		Bytes	Coding Example
	Typical	Range	8086	8088		
(no operands)	50	45-55	0	0	2	FCOMPP

FDECSTP — **FDECSTP** (no operands)
Decrement stack pointer — **Exceptions:** None

Operands	Execution Clocks		Transfers		Bytes	Coding Example
	Typical	Range	8086	8088		
(no operands)	9	6-12	0	0	2	FDECSTP

FDISI/FNDISI — **FDISI** (no operands)
Disable interrupts — **Exceptions:** None

Operands	Execution Clocks		Transfers		Bytes	Coding Example
	Typical	Range	8086	8088		
(no operands)	5	2-8	0	0	2	FDISI

Table 10-12 (Continued)

FDIV

FDIV //source/destination,source
Divide real

Exceptions: I, D, Z, O, U, P

Operands	Execution Clocks		Transfers		Bytes	Coding Example
	Typical	Range	8086	8088		
//ST(i),ST	198	193-203	0	0	2	FDIV
short-real	220+EA	215-225+EA	2/4	4	2-4	FDIV DISTANCE
long-real	225+EA	220-230+EA	4/6	8	2-4	FDIV ARC [DI]

FDIVP

FDIVP destination,source
Divide real and pop

Exceptions: I, D, Z, O, U, P

Operands	Execution Clocks		Transfers		Bytes	Coding Example
	Typical	Range	8086	8088		
ST(i),ST	202	197-207	0	0	2	FDIVP ST(4),ST

FDIVR

FDIVR //source/destination,source
Divide real reversed

Exceptions: I, D, Z, O, U, P

Operands	Execution Clocks		Transfers		Bytes	Coding Example
	Typical	Range	8086	8088		
//ST,ST(i)/ST(i),ST	199	194-204	0	0	2	FDIVR ST(2),ST
short-real	221+EA	216-226+EA	2/4	6	2-4	FDIVR [BX].PULSE RATE
long-real	226+EA	221-231+EA	4/6	8	2-4	FDIVR RECORDER.FREQUENCY

FDIVRP

FDIVRP destination,source
Divide real reversed and pop

Exceptions: I, D, Z, O, U, P

Operands	Execution Clocks		Transfers		Bytes	Coding Example
	Typical	Range	8086	8088		
ST(i),ST	203	198-208	0	0	2	FDIVRP ST(1),ST

FENI/FNENI

FENI (no operands)
Enable interrupts

Exceptions: None

Operands	Execution Clocks		Transfers		Bytes	Coding Example
	Typical	Range	8086	8088		
(no operands)	5	2-8	0	0	2	FNENI

FFREE

FFREE destination
Free register

Exceptions: None

Operands	Execution Clocks		Transfers		Bytes	Coding Example
	Typical	Range	8086	8088		
ST(i)	11	9-16	0	0	2	FFREE ST(1)

Table 10-12 (Continued)

FIADD — FIADD source — Integer add — Exceptions: I, D, O, P

Operands	Execution Clocks		Transfers		Bytes	Coding Example
	Typical	Range	8086	8088		
word-integer	120+EA	102-137+EA	1/2	2	2-4	FIADD DISTANCE TRAVELLED
short-integer	125+EA	108-143+EA	2/4	4	2-4	FIADD PULSE COUNT [SI]

FICOM — FICOM source — Integer compare — Exceptions: I, D

Operands	Execution Clocks		Transfers		Bytes	Coding Example
	Typical	Range	8086	8088		
word-integer	80+EA	72-86+EA	1/2	2	2-4	FICOM TOOL.N_PASSES
short-integer	85+EA	78-91+EA	2/4	4	2-4	FICOM [BP+4].PARM_COUNT

FICOMP — FICOMP source — Integer compare and pop — Exceptions: I, D

Operands	Execution Clocks		Transfers		Bytes	Coding Example
	Typical	Range	8086	8088		
word-integer	82+EA	74-88+EA	1/2	2	2-4	FICOMP [BP].LIMIT [SI]
short-integer	87+EA	80-93+EA	2/4	4	2-4	FICOMP N_SAMPLES

FIDIV — FIDIV source — Integer divide — Exceptions: I, D, Z, O, U, P

Operands	Execution Clocks		Transfers		Bytes	Coding Example
	Typical	Range	8086	8088		
word-integer	230+EA	224-238+EA	1/2	2	2-4	FIDIV SURVEY.OBSERVATIONS
short-integer	236+EA	230-243+EA	2/4	4	2-4	FIDIV RELATIVE_ANGLE [DI]

FIDIVR — FIDIVR source — Integer divide reversed — Exceptions: I, D, Z, O, U, P

Operands	Execution Clocks		Transfers		Bytes	Coding Example
	Typical	Range	8086	8088		
word-integer	230+EA	225-239+EA	1/2	2	2-4	FIDIVR [BP].X_COORD
short-integer	237+EA	231-245+EA	2/4	4	2-4	FIDIVR FREQUENCY

FILD — FILD source — Integer load — Exception: I

Operands	Execution Clocks		Transfers		Bytes	Coding Example
	Typical	Range	8086	8088		
word-integer	50+EA	46-54+EA	1/2	2	2-4	FILD [BX].SEQUENCE
short-integer	56+EA	52-60+EA	2/4	4	2-4	FILD STANDOFF [DI]
long-integer	64+EA	60-68+EA	4/6	8	2-4	FILD RESPONSE.COUNT

Table 10-12 (Continued)

FIMUL

FIMUL source
Integer multiply

Exceptions: I, D, O, P

Operands	Execution Clocks		Transfers		Bytes	Coding Example
	Typical	Range	8086	8088		
word-integer	130+EA	124-138+EA	1/2	2	2-4	FIMUL BEARING
short-integer	136+EA	130-144+EA	2/4	4	2-4	FIMUL POSITION.Z AXIS

FINCSTP

FINCSTP (no operands)
Increment stack pointer

Exceptions: None

Operands	Execution Clocks		Transfers		Bytes	Coding Example
	Typical	Range	8086	8088		
(no operands)	9	6-12	0	0	2	FINCSTP

FINIT/FNINIT

FINIT (no operands)
Initialize processor

Exceptions: None

Operands	Execution Clocks		Transfers		Bytes	Coding Example
	Typical	Range	8086	8088		
(no operands)	5	2-8	0	0	2	FINIT

FIST

FIST destination
Integer store

Exceptions: I, P

Operands	Execution Clocks		Transfers		Bytes	Coding Example
	Typical	Range	8086	8088		
word-integer	86+EA	80-90+EA	2/4	4	2-4	FIST OBS.COUNT [SI]
short-integer	88+EA	82-92+EA	3/5	6	2-4	FIST [BP].FACTORED PULSES

FISTP

FISTP destination
Integer store and pop

Exceptions: I, P

Operands	Execution Clocks		Transfers		Bytes	Coding Example
	Typical	Range	8086	8088		
word-integer	88+EA	82-92+EA	2/4	4	2-4	FISTP [BX].ALPHA_COUNT [SI]
short-integer	90+EA	84-94+EA	3/5	6	2-4	FISTP CORRECTED TIME
long-integer	100+EA	94-105+EA	5/7	10	2-4	FISTP PANEL.N READINGS

FISUB

FISUB source
Integer subtract

Exceptions: I, D, O, P

Operands	Execution Clocks		Transfers		Bytes	Coding Example
	Typical	Range	8086	8088		
word-integer	120+EA	102-137+EA	1/2	2	2-4	FISUB BASE_FREQUENCY
short-integer	125+EA	108-143+EA	2/4	4	2-4	FISUB TRAIN_SIZE [DI]

Table 10-12 (Continued)

FISUBR — **FISUBR** source — Integer subtract reversed — **Exceptions:** I, D, O, P

Operands	Execution Clocks		Transfers		Bytes	Coding Example
	Typical	Range	8086	8088		
word-integer	120+EA	103-139+EA	1/2	2	2-4	FISUBR FLOOR [BX] [SI]
short-integer	125+EA	109-144+EA	2/4	4	2-4	FISUBR BALANCE

FLD — **FLD** source — Load real — **Exceptions:** I, D

Operands	Execution Clocks		Transfers		Bytes	Coding Example
	Typical	Range	8086	8088		
ST(i)	20	17-22	0	0	2	FLD ST(0)
short-real	43+EA	38-56+EA	2/4	4	2-4	FLD READING [SI].PRESSURE
long-real	46+EA	40-60+EA	4/6	8	2-4	FLD [BP].TEMPERATURE
temp-real	57+EA	53-65+EA	5/7	10	2-4	FLD SAVEREADING

FLDCW — **FLDCW** source — Load control word — **Exceptions:** None

Operands	Execution Clocks		Transfers		Bytes	Coding Example
	Typical	Range	8086	8088		
2-bytes	10+EA	7-14+EA	1/2	2	2-4	FLDCW CONTROL_WORD

FLDENV — **FLDENV** source — Load environment — **Exceptions:** None

Operands	Execution Clocks		Transfers		Bytes	Coding Example
	Typical	Range	8086	8088		
14-bytes	40+EA	35-45+EA	7/9	14	2-4	FLDENV [BP+6]

FLDLG2 — **FLDLG2** (no operands) — Load $\log_{10} 2$ — **Exceptions:** I

Operands	Execution Clocks		Transfers		Bytes	Coding Example
	Typical	Range	8086	8088		
(no operands)	21	18-24	0	0	2	FLDLG2

FLDLN2 — **FLDLN2** (no operands) — Load $\log_e 2$ — **Exceptions:** I

Operands	Execution Clocks		Transfers		Bytes	Coding Example
	Typical	Range	8086	8088		
(no operands)	20	17-23	0	0	2	FLDLN2

Table 10-12 ***(Continued)***

FLDL2E

FLDL2E (no operands)
Load $\log_2 e$

Exceptions: I

Operands	Execution Clocks		Transfers		Bytes	Coding Example
	Typical	Range	8086	8088		
(no operands)	18	15-21	0	0	2	FLDL2E

FLDL2T

FLDL2T (no operands)
Load $\log_2 10$

Exceptions: I

Operands	Execution Clocks		Transfers		Bytes	Coding Example
	Typical	Range	8086	8088		
(no operands)	19	16-22	0	0	2	FLDL2T

FLDPI

FLDPI (no operands)
Load π

Exceptions: I

Operands	Execution Clocks		Transfers		Bytes	Coding Example
	Typical	Range	8086	8088		
(no operands)	19	16-22	0	0	2	FLDPI

FLDZ

FLDZ (no operands)
Load +0.0

Exceptions: I

Operands	Execution Clocks		Transfers		Bytes	Coding Example
	Typical	Range	8086	8088		
(no operands)	14	11-17	0	0	2	FLDZ

FLD1

FLD1 (no operands)
Load +1.0

Exceptions: I

Operands	Execution Clocks		Transfers		Bytes	Coding Example
	Typical	Range	8086	8088		
(no operands)	18	15-21	0	0	2	FLD1

FMUL

FMUL //source/destination,source
Multiply real

Exceptions: I, D, O, U, P

Operands	Execution Clocks		Transfers		Bytes	Coding Example
	Typical	Range	8086	8088		
//ST(i),ST/ST,ST(i)[1]	97	90-105	0	0	2	FMUL ST,ST(3)
//ST(i),ST/ST,ST(i)	138	130-145	0	0	2	FMUL ST,ST(3)
short-real	118+EA	110-125+EA	2/4	4	2-4	FMUL SPEED_FACTOR
long-real[1]	120+EA	112-126+EA	4/6	8	2-4	FMUL [BP].HEIGHT
long-real	161+EA	154-168+EA	4/6	8	2-4	FMUL [BP].HEIGHT

[1] occurs when one or both operands is "short"—it has 40 trailing zeros in its fraction (e.g., it was loaded from a short-real memory operand).

Table 10-12 (Continued)

FMULP

FMULP destination,source
Multiply real and pop

Exceptions: I, D, O, U, P

Operands	Execution Clocks		Transfers		Bytes	Coding Example
	Typical	Range	8086	8088		
ST(i),ST[1]	100	94-108	0	0	2	FMULP ST(1),ST
ST(i),ST	142	134-148	0	0	2	FMULP ST(1),ST

[1] occurs when one or both operands is "short"—it has 40 trailing zeros in its fraction (e.g., it was loaded from a short-real memory operand).

FNOP

FNOP (no operands)
No operation

Exceptions: None

Operands	Execution Clocks		Transfers		Bytes	Coding Example
	Typical	Range	8086	8088		
(no operands)	13	10-16	0	0	2	FNOP

FPATAN

FPATAN (no operands)
Partial arctangent

Exceptions: U, P (operands not checked)

Operands	Execution Clocks		Transfers		Bytes	Coding Example
	Typical	Range	8086	8088		
(no operands)	650	250-800	0	0	2	FPATAN

FPREM

FPREM (no operands)
Partial remainder

Exceptions: I, D, U

Operands	Execution Clocks		Transfers		Bytes	Coding Example
	Typical	Range	8086	8088		
(no operands)	125	15-190	0	0	2	FPREM

FPTAN

FPTAN (no operands)
Partial tangent

Exceptions: I, P (operands not checked)

Operands	Execution Clocks		Transfers		Bytes	Coding Example
	Typical	Range	8086	8088		
(no operands)	450	30-540	0	0	2	FPTAN

FRNDINT

FRNDINT (no operands)
Round to integer

Exceptions: I, P

Operands	Execution Clocks		Transfers		Bytes	Coding Example
	Typical	Range	8086	8088		
(no operands)	45	16-50	0	0	2	FRNDINT

Table 10-12 **(*Continued*)**

FRSTOR

FRSTOR source
Restore saved state

Exceptions: None

Operands	Execution Clocks		Transfers		Bytes	Coding Example
	Typical	Range	8086	8088		
94-bytes	210+EA	205-215+EA	47/49	96	2-4	FRSTOR [BP]

FSAVE/FNSAVE

FSAVE destination
Save state

Exceptions: None

Operands	Execution Clocks		Transfers		Bytes	Coding Example
	Typical	Range	8086	8088		
94-bytes	210+EA	205-215+EA	48/50	94	2-4	FSAVE [BP]

FSCALE

FSCALE (no operands)
Scale

Exceptions: I, O, U

Operands	Execution Clocks		Transfers		Bytes	Coding Example
	Typical	Range	8086	8088		
(no operands)	35	32-38	0	0	2	FSCALE

FSQRT

FSQRT (no operands)
Square root

Exceptions: I, D, P

Operands	Execution Clocks		Transfers		Bytes	Coding Example
	Typical	Range	8086	8088		
(no operands)	183	180-186	0	0	2	FSQRT

FST

FST destination
Store real

Exceptions: I, O, U, P

Operands	Execution Clocks		Transfers		Bytes	Coding Example
	Typical	Range	8086	8088		
ST(i)	18	15-22	0	0	2	FST ST(3)
short-real	87+EA	84-90+EA	3/5	6	2-4	FST CORRELATION [DI]
long-real	100+EA	96-104+EA	5/7	10	2-4	FST MEAN_READING

FSTCW/FNSTCW

FSTCW destination
Store control word

Exceptions: None

Operands	Execution Clocks		Transfers		Bytes	Coding Example
	Typical	Range	8086	8088		
2-bytes	15+EA	12-18+EA	2/4	4	2-4	FSTCW SAVE_CONTROL

Table 10-12 (Continued)

FSTENV/FNSTENV — **FSTENV** destination. Store environment. **Exceptions:** None

Operands	Execution Clocks		Transfers		Bytes	Coding Example
	Typical	Range	8086	8088		
14-bytes	45+EA	40-50+EA	8/10	16	2-4	FSTENV [BP]

FSTP — **FSTP** destination. Store real and pop. **Exceptions:** I, O, U, P

Operands	Execution Clocks		Transfers		Bytes	Coding Example
	Typical	Range	8086	8088		
ST(i)	20	17-24	0	0	2	FSTP ST(2)
short-real	89+EA	86-92+EA	3/5	6	2-4	FSTP [BX].ADJUSTED_RPM
long-real	102+EA	98-106+EA	5/7	10	2-4	FSTP TOTAL_DOSAGE
temp-real	55+EA	52-58+EA	6/8	12	2-4	FSTP REG_SAVE[SI]

FSTSW/FNSTSW — **FSTSW** destination. Store status word. **Exceptions:** None

Operands	Execution Clocks		Transfers		Bytes	Coding Example
	Typical	Range	8086	8088		
2-bytes	15+EA	12-18+EA	2/4	4	2-4	FSTSW SAVE_STATUS

FSUB — **FSUB** //source/destination,source. Subtract real. **Exceptions:** I,D,O,U,P

Operands	Execution Clocks		Transfers		Bytes	Coding Example
	Typical	Range	8086	8088		
//ST,ST(i)/ST(i),ST	85	70-100	0	0	2	FSUB ST,ST(2)
short-real	105+EA	90-120+EA	2/4	4	2-4	FSUB BASE_VALUE
long-real	110+EA	95-125+EA	4/6	8	2-4	FSUB COORDINATE.X

FSUBP — **FSUBP** destination,source. Subtract real and pop. **Exceptions:** I,D,O,U,P

Operands	Execution Clocks		Transfers		Bytes	Coding Example
	Typical	Range	8086	8088		
ST(i),ST	90	75-105	0	0	2	FSUBP ST(2),ST

FSUBR — **FSUBR** //source/destination,source. Subtract real reversed. **Exceptions:** I,D,O,U,P

Operands	Execution Clocks		Transfers		Bytes	Coding Example
	Typical	Range	8086	8088		
//ST,ST(i)/ST(i),ST	87	70-100	0	0	2	FSUBR ST,ST(1)
short-real	105+EA	90-120+EA	2/4	4	2-4	FSUBR VECTOR[SI]
long-real	110+EA	95-125+EA	4/6	8	2-4	FSUBR [BX].INDEX

Table 10-12 (Continued)

FSUBRP — **FSUBRP** destination,source — Subtract real reversed and pop — **Exceptions:** I,D,O,U,P

Operands	Executon Clocks		Transfers		Bytes	Coding Example
	Typical	Range	8086	8088		
ST(i),ST	90	75-105	0	0	2	FSUBRP ST(1),ST

FTST — **FTST** (no operands) — Test stack top against +0.0 — **Exceptions:** I, D

Operands	Execution Clocks		Transfers		Bytes	Coding Example
	Typical	Range	8086	8088		
(no operands)	42	38-48	0	0	2	FTST

FWAIT — **FWAIT** (no operands) — (CPU) Wait while 8087 is busy — **Exceptions:** None (CPU instruction)

Operands	Execution Clocks		Transfers		Bytes	Coding Example
	Typical	Range	8086	8088		
(no operands)	3+5n*	3+5n*	0	0	1	FWAIT

*n = number of times CPU examines $\overline{\text{TEST}}$ line before 8087 lowers BUSY.

FXAM — **FXAM** (no operands) — Examine stack top — **Exceptions :** None

Operands	Execution Clocks		Transfers		Bytes	Coding Example
	Typical	Range	8086	8088		
(no operands)	17	12-23	0	0	2	FXAM

FXCH — **FXCH** //destination — Exchange registers — **Exceptions:** I

Operands	Execution Clocks		Transfers		Bytes	Coding Example
	Typical	Range	8086	8088		
//ST(i)	12	10-15	0	0	2	FXCH ST(2)

FXTRACT — **FXTRACT** (no operands) — Extract exponent and significand — **Exceptions:** I

Operands	Execution Clocks		Transfers		Bytes	Coding Example
	Typical	Range	8086	8088		
(no operands)	50	27-55	0	0	2	FXTRACT

Table 10-12 (Continued)

FYL2X	**FYL2X** (no operands) Y • Log_2 X					**Exceptions:** P (operands not checked)
Operands	**Execution Clocks**		**Transfers**		**Bytes**	**Coding Example**
	Typical	**Range**	**8086**	**8088**		
(no operands)	950	900-1100	0	0	2	FYL2X

FYL2XP1	**FYL2XP1** (no operands) Y • $log_2(X+1)$					**Exceptions:** P (operands not checked)
Operands	**Execution Clocks**		**Transfers**		**Bytes**	**Coding Example**
	Typical	**Range**	**8086**	**8088**		
(no operands)	850	700-1000	0	0	2	FYL2XP1

F2XM1	**F2XM1** (no operands) 2^{X}-1					**Exceptions:** U, P (operands not checked)
Operands	**Execution Clocks**		**Transfers**		**Bytes**	**Coding Example**
	Typical	**Range**	**8086**	**8088**		
(no operands)	500	310-630	0	0	2	F2XM1

10-12 REFERENCES

Intel, iAPX 86, *88 User's Manual*, July 1981, AFN-01300C-1.

Intel, *The 8086 Family User's Manual Numeric Supplement*, July, 1980, # 121586-001 REV A.

James W. Coffron, *Programming the 8086/8088*, Sybex, Berkeley, Calif., 1983.

CHAPTER 11

The Z8000 16-Bit Microprocessors

Steve Sharp
American Microsystems, Inc.
Santa Clara, California
(formerly of Zilog)

11-1 INTRODUCTION

The **Z8000**[1] is the generic name for a series of Zilog 16-bit μPs. The user can select from one of three central processing units (CPUs), the **Z8001**, the **Z8002**, or the **Z8003**. The **Z8002** is for systems that require less than 64K words of memory; it only provides a 16-bit address bus. The **Z8001** and **Z8003** have a 23-bit address bus and can be used in systems with up to 8M words of memory. Other differences between the CPUs are discussed in section 11-3.

The **Z8000** is a 16-bit μP family composed of central processing units (CPUs), CPU support devices, and peripherals. While the family started with the design of the **Z8001** and **Z8002** CPUs, much of the strength of the **Z8000** family is found in its CPU support devices and peripherals. In this chapter, we will examine the **Z8000** CPUs in detail, but some mention of the **Z8000** family in general is in order.

The **Z8000** family was conceived as an expandable architecture in which the different CPUs and peripherals could be used freely with one another, allowing the designer the freedom to select the CPU/peripheral combination that best suited the particular design task.

The central element of the entire family is the Z-Bus, a system of chip interconnections that every device is designed to interface to. This is a multiplexed bus in which address and data share a common set of lines. By allowing enough signals for address/data, this bus is readily expandable to 32 bits when the new 32-bit processors and peripherals become available.

[1] Zilog, **Z80**, **Z8000**, and so on, are trademarks of Zilog, Inc., with whom the publisher is not associated.

The major architectural features of the **Z8000** CPU that enhance throughput and processing power are a general-purpose register set, a powerful instruction set, multiple data types, numerous addressing modes, multiple addressing spaces, system and normal modes of operation, separate I/O address spaces, a sophisticated interrupt instruction, and provisions for multiprocessing. For the **Z8001** and **Z8003**, a large address space and segmented memory addressing are provided.

All of these features combine to produce a powerful, versatile μP. Some of the benefits that result from these features include improved code density and compiler efficiency, and support for typical operating system features.

The **Z8001** and **Z8003** CPUs have been designed to work with the **Z8010** Memory Management Unit (MMU) to improve the way main memory is utilized and provide memory protection capabilities. Although the MMU is not a necessary part of the system—the **Z8001** and **Z8003** are extremely powerful processors even without the MMU—the CPUs have features to allow easy integration with the MMU.

Finally, a general mechanism has been provided for extending the basic instruction set through the use of external devices called *extended processing units* (EPUs). In general, an EPU is an IC included in a system to perform complex and time-consuming tasks so as to unburden the CPU. Examples of these kinds of tasks include floating point arithmetic, data base search and maintenance operations, network interfaces, and many others. Multiple EPUs may exist in the same system, each performing certain operations. The EPU concept will be treated in section 11-4.10.

11-2 GENERAL ARCHITECTURE

The **Z8000** architecture is based on several basic concepts. The first of these deals with timing. The basic unit of time in a **Z8000** system is a *clock cycle*. This is one cycle of the CPU clock (the CLK signal). The second concept deals with execution. The fundamental element of all **Z8000** operations is the *machine cycle*, and it is composed of from three to ten clock cycles (assuming no WAIT states). A typical machine cycle is a memory READ or memory WRITE. The type of machine cycle in progress is always indicated by the four status lines (see section 11-2.5), and this fact forms the basis for most **Z8000** system architecture and design. The term instruction cycle applies to the sequence of single or multiple machine cycles that are necessary to complete any particular instruction. This is not an extremely useful concept, however, because there is no convenient way to detect when a particular instruction cycle begins and ends.

The architectural resources of the **Z8000** CPUs include sixteen 16-bit general-purpose registers, seven data types ranging from bits to byte strings and 32-bit long words, eight user-selectable addressing modes, and an instruction set more powerful than that of most minicomputers. There are 110 distinct instruction types, which combine with the various data types and addressing modes to form a set of 414 instructions. In addition, this set of instructions exhibits a high degree of regularity.

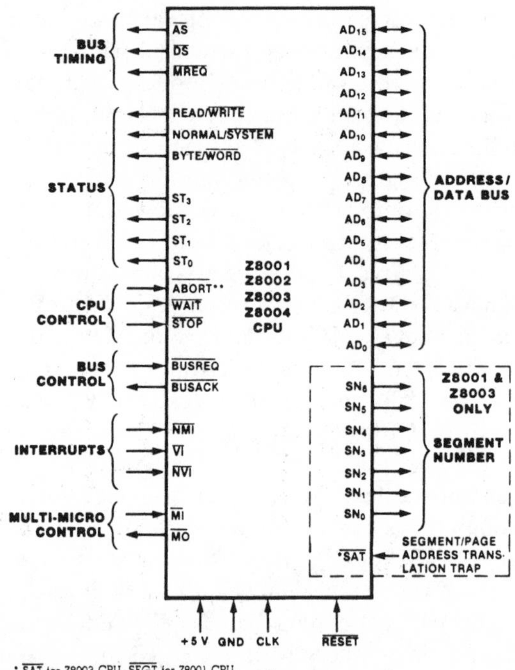

Figure 11-1 **Z8000** pin-out and fractional description. (Reproduced by permission © Zilog, Inc. This material shall not be reproduced without the written consent of Zilog, Inc.

More that 90 percent of the instructions can use any of the five main addressing modes with 8-bit byte, 16-bit word, or 32-bit-long word data types.

The CPU generates status signals to indicate the type of machine cycle in progress. This status information can be used to implement multiple address spaces as well as facilitate hardware interfacing. The CPU also has two operating modes, system and normal (see section 11-2.6), and an external signal to indicate the mode. This feature can be used to separate operating system functions from normal applications processes. I/O operations have been given their own status codes and address spaces, further enhancing the capability and integrity of **Z8000** systems, and the sophisticated interrupt structure allows for efficient operation of peripheral devices. The extended instruction capability of the **Z8000** allows very time-consuming tasks to be handled by specialized processing units. The pin out is shown in Figure 11-1.

11-2.1 General-Purpose Register Set

The architecture of the **Z8000** CPUs is based on a set of sixteen 16-bit general-purpose registers. The fact that the registers are general purpose is the major factor that contributes to the power and regularity of the **Z8000** instruction set. General-purpose registers can be used as accumulators, memory pointers, or index registers interchangeably. This ability to vary the usage of a register as the needs of a program change is very valuable. It avoids bottlenecks present in an implied or dedicated register architecture, which must save and restore the contents of dedicated registers when more registers of a particular type are needed than are available. With the **Z8000** register set, if more memory pointers are needed at a particular time, then the registers may be used as such. If some of those registers are later needed as arithmetic accumulators, then they may be used that way.

For example, the instruction

```
ADD   R1,R2
```

adds the contents of registers 1 and 2 and puts the result in register 1. If, however, R2 was instead a pointer to a value in memory, the instruction

```
ADD   R1,@R2
```

would add the contents of register 1 to the contents of the memory location addressed by R2. The "@" sign signifies *indirect addressing* in this case.

The **Z8000** register set may be accessed in several ways. It may be accessed as 16 single-byte (8-bit) registers (occupying one-half of the file), as 16-word (16-bit) registers, as eight long-word (32-bit) registers, or as four quadruple-word (64-bit) registers. Because of this flexibility, it is not necessary to use a 32-bit register to hold a single byte of data.

Figure 11-2 shows the register files for the **Z8001** and the **Z8002**. The register file for the **Z8003** is identical to that of the **Z8001**, so in further discussions we will concentrate on the differences between the **Z8001** and **Z8002**. The 16-word registers are designated as R0 through R15. The 16-byte registers are designated as RH0

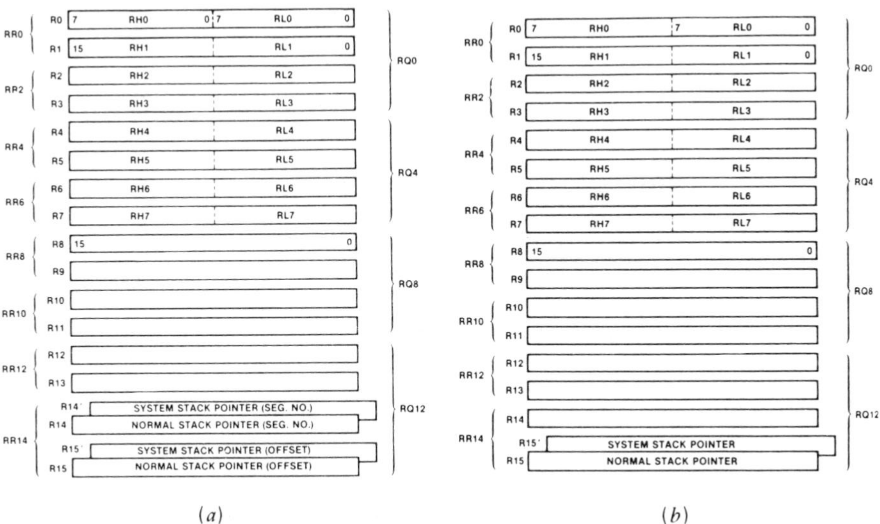

Figure 11-2 Registers' address space. (*a*) **Z8001** general-purpose registers. (*b*) **Z8002** general-purpose registers. (Reproduced by permission © Zilog, Inc. This material shall not be reproduced without the written consent of Zilog, Inc.)

through RL7, and they overlap the first eight-word registers. For example, RH0 and RL0 together make up R0. As implied by the letters, RH0 is the high-order half (most significant byte) of R0 and RL0 is the low-order half (least signifcant byte). The eight long-word registers are designated as RR0 through RR14, and the four quad-word registers are designated as RQ0 through RQ12. In each case, the number in the designation is that of the lowest order word register in that grouping, that is, RQ8 is composed of the word registers R8, R9, R10, and R11.

As Figure 11-2 illustrates, the CPUs have two hardware stack pointers, one dedicated to each of the two operating modes, system and normal. The **Z8001** and **Z8003** use a long-word stack pointer for each mode (RR14 or RR14′), whereas the nonsegmented **Z8002** uses only one word register for each mode (R15 or R15′). The *system stack pointer* is used for saving status information when an interrupt or trap occurs and for supporting subroutine calls in system mode. The *normal stack pointer* is used for subroutine calls and stack operations while in normal mode. When the CPU is in normal mode, only the normal mode stack pointer is accessible. While in system mode, both stack pointers are accessible—the system stack pointer as a register in the register file, and the normal stack pointer as a special control register.

In addition to the general-purpose registers, there are some special-purpose registers. These include the program status registers, the program status area pointer (PSAP), and the refresh counter. They are illustrated in Figure 11-3. Each register can be manipulated by software executing in system mode, and some are modified automatically by certain operations.

The program status registers include the flag and control word (FCW) and the program counter (PC). As the name implies, they are used to keep track of the state of an executing program.

In the **Z8002**, the FCW and PC are both one word. In the **Z8001/3**, there are four-word registers, one reserved word, one word for the FCW, and two words for the segmented PC.

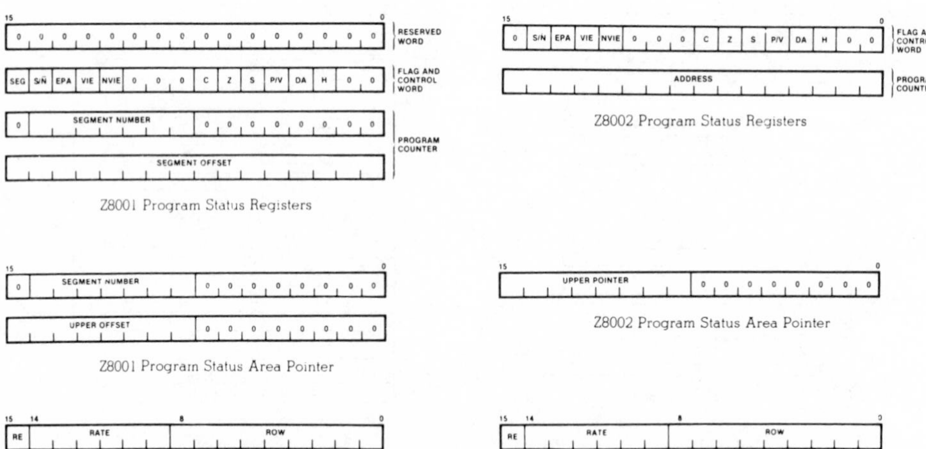

Figure 11-3 CPU special registers. (Reproduced by permission © Zilog, Inc. This material shall not be reproduced without the written consent of Zilog, Inc.)

The low-order byte of the FCW contains the six status flags, from which the condition codes used for program flow control are derived. The six flags are:

Carry (C), which generally indicates a carry out of the high-order bit position of a register being used as an accumulator.

Zero (Z), which is generally used to indicate that the result of an operation is zero.

Sign (S), which is generally used to indicate that the result of an operation is a negative number.

Parity/overflow (P/V), which is generally used to indicate either even parity (after logical operations on byte operands) or overflow (after arithmetic operations).

Decimal adjust (D), which is used in BCD arithmetic to indicate the type of instruction that executed (addition or subtraction).

Half-carry (H), which is used to convert the binary result of a previous decimal addition or subtraction into the correct decimal (BCD) result.

The control bits, which occupy the high-order half of the FCW, are used to enable various interrupts or to control CPU operating modes. The control bits are:

Nonvectored interrupt enable (NVIE), vectored interrupt enable (VIE). These bits determine whether or not the CPU will accept nonvectored or vectored interrupts, respectively. Note that vectored and nonvectored interrupts are received on different CPU pins.

System/normal mode (S/N). When this bit is set to 1, the CPU is operating in system mode. When it is cleared to 0, the CPU is in normal mode. The CPU output status line (N/S pin) is the complement of this bit. (See section 11-2.6.)

Extended processor architecture mode (EPA). This bit, when set to 1, indicates that the system contains one or more extended processing units (EPUs), and hence extended instructions encountered by the CPU are sent to the EPUs for execution. When this bit is cleared to 0, these extended instructions are trapped for a software emulator to handle.

The *program status area pointer* (PSAP) points to an array of program status values (FCWs and PCs) in main memory called the *program status area.* New program status register values are fetched from the program status area when an interrupt or trap occurs. As shown in Figure 11-3, the PSAP is either one word (**Z8002**) or two words (**Z8001/3**). For either configuration, the lower byte of the pointer must be 0.

The refresh counter is a programmable counter that can be used to refresh dynamic memory automatically. The refresh counter register consists of a 9-bit row counter, a 6-bit rate counter, and an enable bit (see Figure 11-3).

11-2.2 Instruction Set

The **Z8000** has a very powerful instruction set, as shown in the Instruction Set Summary table beginning on page 466. The instruction set is one measure of the flexibility and versatility of a processor. Having commonly used operations implemented in hardware can save memory and improve speed. In addition, the completeness of the operations available on a given data type is often more important than additional, esoteric instructions that are not likely to significantly affect performance. The **Z8000** CPU provides a full complement of arithmetic, logical, BRANCH, I/O, SHIFT, ROTATE, and STRING instructions. In addition, special instructions have been included to aid in multiprocessing and typical high-level language and operating system functions. The general philosophy of the **Z8000** instruction set is that most operations are two-operand, register-to-memory operations, with register-to-register operations as a special subset. To improve code density, however, some memory-to-memory operations are included for string manipulation. Having one operand in an easily accessible general-purpose register facilitates the use of an intermediate result in subsequent calculations.

The majority of instructions deal with byte, word, or long-word operands, providing a high degree of regularity within the instruction set. Also included in the instruction set are compact, one-word instructions for common operations such as branching short distances within a program or transferring data from one register to another.

Section 11-4 is devoted to summarizing the various groups of instructions.

11-2.3 Data Types

Multiple data types are supported by the **Z8000** architecture. A data type is supported when it has instructions that directly apply to it. Other data types can always be created by combining the basic data types, but hardware support provides faster execution and more convenient programming.

The basic data type is the byte, which is also the smallest addressable element. The architecture also supports the following data types: words (16 bits), long words (32 bits), byte strings, and word strings. In addition, bits are fully supported and addressed by a number within a word or byte. BCD digits are supported and represented as two 4-bit BCD digits in a byte. Arrays are supported by the indexed addressing mode. Stacks are supported by the instruction set and by an external device (the **Z8010** Memory Management Unit) available for use with the **Z8001** and **Z8003**.

11-2.4 Addressing Modes

The term *addressing mode* is used to describe the way in which an address is generated. The addressing mode for an operand is specified in each instruction. The **Z8000** CPUs support eight addressing modes. The combination of a large instruction set, multiple data types, and these eight addressing modes improves processing power and makes programming much easier. The addressing modes available are register, immediate, indirect register, direct address, indexed, relative address, base address, and base indexed addressing. Several other addressing modes are implied by certain instructions, such as auto increment and auto decrement.

In register addressing the operand is contained in a register. We have already seen an example of an ADD instruction using register addressing. (See section 11-2.1.) Immediate addressing is where the operand is contained within the instruction itself. Indirect addressing is where a register holds the address in memory where the operand is located. Direct addressing is similar to indirect addressing, except that the address itself is contained within the instruction. An indexed address

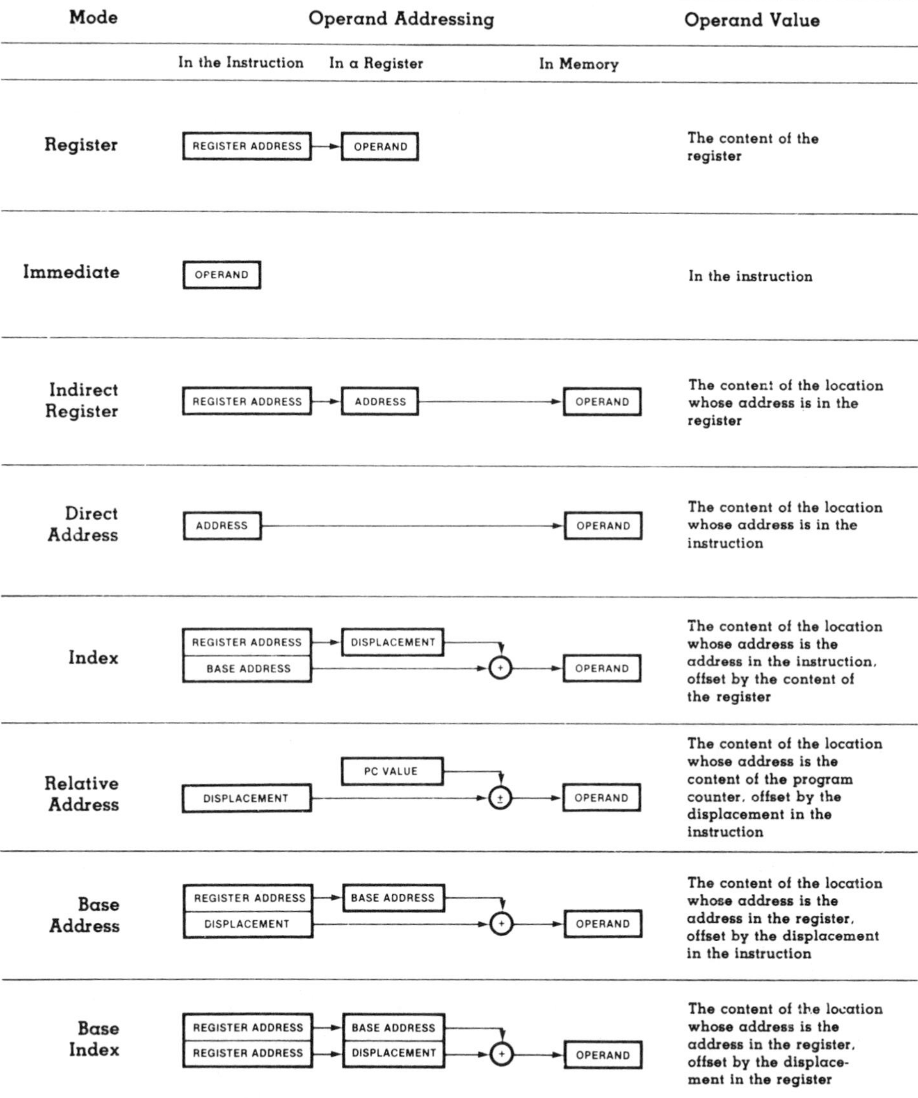

Figure 11-4 The **Z8000** basic addressing modes. (Reproduced by permission © Zilog, Inc. This material shall not be reproduced without the written consent of Zilog, Inc.)

has an address within the instruction and an offset in a register that is added to the address from the instruction to get the address of the operand. Base addressing is essentially the same as indexed addressing, except that the offset is contained in the instruction and the main address is held in a register. Base indexed addressing is a combination of the two, where both the main address and the offset are contained in registers. Relative addressing is indexed addressing from the program counter (PC). In relative addressing, an offset contained in the instruction is added to the PC to get the final address. Figure 11-4 is a tabular summary of addressing modes.

The first five modes listed in Figure 11-4 are considered the basic addressing modes that are used most frequently, and they apply to most instructions having more than one addressing mode. Section 11-4, which is devoted to discussing the instruction set in detail, goes into further detail concerning which addressing modes are available with which instructions and how they are most frequently used.

EXAMPLE 11-1 If the contents of R6 are 50 and the contents of R8 are 70, what will the following LOAD instructions load into R5?

```
a LD R5,R6          !register addressing       !
b LD R5,#2000       !immediate addressing      !
c LD R5,2000        !direct addressing         !
d LD R5,@R6         !indirect addressing       !
e LD R5,R6(#5)      !based addressing          !
f LD R5,2000(R6)    !indexed addressing        !
g LD R5,R6(R8)      !based indexed addressing!
```

Solution

a The contents of R6 (the value 50).

b The value 2000.

c The contents of memory location 2000.

d The contents of memory location 50.

e The contents of memory location 55.

f The contents of memory location 2050.

g The contents of memory location 2070.

11-2.5 Memory Address Spaces

The **Z8000** CPUs facilitate the use of multiple address spaces. When a **Z8000** CPU generates an address, it also outputs status signals corresponding to the type of activity which led to the particular memory request: instruction fetch, operand reference, or stack reference. This information can be used to increase memory space available to the CPU by allowing the program to be split, for example, by putting program code in one space and data in another. This would be accomplished by

Table 11-1 **Status codes**

Kind of transaction	ST_3-ST_0	*Additional information*
Internal operation	0000	
Refresh	0001	
I/O transaction	0010	Standard I/O
	0011	Special I/O
INTERRUPT ACKNOWLEDGE transaction	0100	Segment trap
	0101	Nonmaskable interrupt
	0110	Nonvectored interrupt
	0111	Vectored interrupt
Memory transaction	1000	Data address space
	1001	Stack address space,
	1010	Data address space, EPU transfer
	1011	Stack address space, EPU transfer
	1100	Program address space,
	1101	Program address space, first word of instruction
EPU transfer	1110	
reserved	1111	

designing the memory hardware such that a particular memory module responded to memory accesses only when the 4-bit status code generated by the CPU matched the code that it checks for. This status information also allows us to protect portions of the memory and allow only certain types of accesses (for example, by allowing only instruction fetches from an area of memory known to contain proprietary software). The **Z8010** Memory Management Unit has been designed to provide precisely these kinds of protection features by using this CPU-generated status information. The status codes output by the **Z8000** CPU are given in Table 11-1.

11-2.6 System/Normal Modes of Operation

The **Z8000** CPUs can run in either system mode or normal mode. In system mode, all of the instructions in the instruction set may be executed and all of the CPU registers may be used. This mode is intended to be used by programs needing access to all of these CPU resources. An example of this kind of program would be an operating system kernel. In normal mode, some instructions (called privileged instructions) may not be executed, and some of the control registers of the CPU are not accessible. An example of privileged instructions includes the entire group of I/O instructions. This separation of CPU resources preserves the integrity of the system, since programs running in normal mode are denied access to those aspects of the CPU dealing with time-dependent or system-interface operations. A classic example of this partitioning comes from current minicomputer and mainframe systems: the operating system runs in system mode and the individual applications programs run in normal mode.

To further support this partitioning, there are two copies of the stack pointer—one for system mode and another for normal mode. These two stacks facilitate the task switching that occurs when interrupts or traps occur. To ensure that the normal stack is free of system information, the information saved when an interrupt or trap occurs is always saved on the system stack using the system stack pointer. Because of the way interrupts are handled, this switch from normal mode to system mode for handling interrupts, and back to normal mode when the interrupt has been serviced, happens automatically.

11-2.7 Separate I/O Address Spaces

The architecture of the **Z8000** distinguishes between memory and I/O address spaces, and thus requires specific I/O instructions. This separation allows better protection and has more potential for expansion. We have already mentioned that the group of I/O instructions may not be executed when the CPU is in normal mode. This is possible only because I/O address space is separate from memory address space and is so indicated by the status lines. There are in fact two separate I/O address spaces: standard I/O and special I/O. The main reason for these two spaces is to support two types of peripheral support chips. Standard I/O peripherals are usually configured to respond to standard I/O commands by decoding the status code for normal I/O accesses. Special I/O peripherals such as the **Z8010** MMU are designed to respond to special I/O commands. This allows us to separate the address space for special I/O devices such as the MMU from the address space for normal I/O devices such as serial communications devices and parallel I/O devices.

11-2.8 Interrupt Structure

The sophisticated interrupt structure of the **Z8000** allows the CPU to continue performing useful work while waiting for peripheral events to occur, and to process efficiently those events when they do occur. The CPU supports three kinds of interrupts. A nonmaskable interrupt is available for handling catastrophic events which require immediate handling in order to preserve system integrity. In addition, two maskable interrupts are available: nonvectored and vectored. The vectored interrupt provides an automatic call to separate interrupt service routines based on the vector presented by the peripheral and information in the program status area, while the nonvectored interrupt allows for only one service routine, but does provide for a device "identifier" to be passed into the service routine from the external device.

The **Z8000** has implemented a priority system for handling interrupts. Vectored interrupts have priority over nonvectored interrupts, and nonmaskable interrupt has priority over both of the maskable interrupts.

When an interrupt is acknowledged, the program status of the currently executing program is saved on the system stack along with a code describing the reason for the switch (the vector in the case of a vectored interrupt and the "identifier" in the case of a nonvectored interrupt). The new program status for the interrupt service routine is then loaded from the program status area, and the program control is then passed to the interrupt service routine. The fact that the system stack is used for saving the program status allows recursive task switches to occur while leaving the normal stack undisturbed by system information.

The use of the system stack and a pointer to the program status area is a specific choice made to allow architectural compatibility if new interrupts or traps were to be added to the architecture at a later date.

11-2.9 Multiprocessing

With today's computer systems getting more complex, it is often desirable to have multiple processors, each doing a small set of tasks and communicating through common memory or high-speed buffers. The **Z8000** CPUs provide some support for such a mechanism by including a TEST AND SET instruction to allow testing of semaphores and by including a multi-micro input and output and instructions to handle these signals. These multi-micro instructions can sample the state of the multi-micro input, set and reset the multi-micro output, and also perform a conditional resource request using the multi-micro input and output lines and the processor flags.

11-2.10 Large Address Space for Z8001 and Z8003

For some applications, the 16-bit addresses generated by the **Z8002** will be more than sufficient. With status codes available to allow separation of code and data, this addressing range is often large enough to handle smaller applications. For other applications, especially those involving processing of large data bases and arrays, it is more convenient to have the entire program, code and data, in memory at one time. The **Z8001** and **Z8003** generate segmented 23-bit addresses and have a basic address space of 8 megabytes. When contrasted with the basic address space of the **Z8002** at 64 kilobytes, the **Z8001/3** provides the addressing necessary to handle larger arrays and programs. This larger address space reduces the need for minimizing program size and allows the use of higher-level languages.

11-2.11 Segmented Address for Z8001 and Z8003

The **Z8001** and **Z8003** both generate 23-bit segmented addresses. These addresses are divided into a 16-bit offset and a 7-bit segment number. The segment number serves as a *logical name* of a segment. It is not altered by address calculations (by indexing, for example). This concept is used to gain advantages in the areas of memory protection, relocation, and memory access time. Even without a memory management unit (MMU), however, the 23-bit segmented address is still useful.

A **Z8001/3** system without any MMUs can still address 8 megabytes in each status-selected address space. The only major difference between a **Z8001** without an MMU and a linear addressed processor is that the segment number in a segmented address does not automatically increment when the offset reaches its maximum value. This is viewed by many people as a major disadvantage, but it does not have to be so. There are only a few times when a linear address is genuinely needed, such as when addressing linear arrays larger than 64K bytes (the size of one segment), or when a single program must be larger than 64K bytes. In the case of the program spanning multiple segments, only a couple of instructions are necessary to span the segment boundary because the programmer knows ahead of time when it is necessary to cross the boundary, and these few instructions do not significantly affect the execution time of such a large program.

There are significant advantages to segmentation when memory management is used. Because the segment number is not part of address calculations, it is available from the processor in advance of the offset. This allows memory address decoding logic to be slower and permits the use of slower, less expensive, memories. Thus, segmentation allows the use of slower memories than linear addressing schemes allow. In addition, segments provide a convenient way of partitioning memory so that each partition is given particular access attributes (for example, read-only). When used with the **Z8010** MMU, attribute checking is done automatically, and a segment trap is issued if errors are found. The MMU also has a value for the length of each segment (up to 64K bytes), and a segment trap is also generated if an attempt is made to access memory beyond the designated end of a segment. Relocation is also easier with the MMU, because each segment has a base physical address stored in the MMU, so to relocate a particular section of code, only the base address in the MMU need be changed.

11-3 THE Z8000 FAMILY OF CPUs

The **Z8000** CPU currently comes in three versions: the nonsegmented **Z8002**, the segmented **Z8001**, and the segmented, virtual memory **Z8003**. There are a few distinguishing characteristics about each CPU which bear discussion.

11-3.1 Z8002 Nonsegmented CPU

The **Z8002** is a 40-pin device that is essentially a **Z8000** CPU that operates only in nonsegmented mode. It produces 16-bit addresses only, and as such does not have segment lines or a segment trap input. In all other respects it functions identically to the **Z8001**. As mentioned previously, there are a few internal differences because of the fact that there is no segmented operation. The two stack pointers, one for system and one for normal mode, are each one word long instead of two. This means that R14 is available for general use in the **Z8002**. The bit in the FCW to select segmented operation does not function in the **Z8002**, and the PC and PSAP in the **Z8002** are only one word long instead of two words long as in the **Z8001**. For applications where large amounts of memory are not needed, the **Z8002** is recommended because of its lower cost and simpler hardware interface. There is no measurable difference between a **Z8002** and **Z8001** operating at the same clock frequency.

11-3.2 Z8001 Segmented CPU

The **Z8001** is a 48-pin device that operates in either nonsegmented mode or in segmented mode. When a **Z8001** is operating in nonsegmented mode, it is fully compatible with code written for the **Z8002**. The most important difference is that the **Z8001** generates 23-bit segmented addresses, so for applications requiring large amounts of memory, or requiring the protection and relocation features of the **Z8010** MMU, the **Z8001** should be used.

11-3.3 Z8003 Virtual Memory CPU

The **Z8003** CPU is identical to the **Z8001** in every respect except for two additional features. The **Z8003** has an ABORT input for processing virtual memory faults, and it has a unique status code for the TEST AND SET instruction. The ABORT input is similar to the segment trap on the **Z8001**, except that the ABORT input aborts the current instruction instead of the next instruction the way a segment trap does. This means that when the processor is attempting to execute an instruction that does not exist in physical memory, the virtual memory handler can bring that section of the program in from mass storage and then reexecute the aborted instruction properly. The **Z8003** is completely hardware and software compatible with the **Z8001** with the single exception of the ABORT input, so that a **Z8001** system may be upgraded to a **Z8003** with no loss of hardware or software investment. Of course it is necessary to add some hardware and software to take advantage of the two additional features of the **Z8003**.

11-4 INSTRUCTION SET

This section presents a brief overview of the **Z8000** instructions. This is not intended to be a detailed explanation of individual instructions, but rather a general overview of the types of instructions available and the basic operations they can do. For this purpose, the instructions may be divided into ten functional groups:

LOAD and EXCHANGE
Arithmetic
Logical
Program control
Bit manipulation
ROTATE and SHIFT
Block transfer and string manipulation
Input/output
CPU control
Extended instructions

In this summary we will list the instructions (by mnemonics) in each group, and summarize the type of operations they perform. Table 11-2 is a quick reference guide to all of the instructions taken from the actual **Z8000** *CPU Technical Manual*. Readers desiring a more in-depth breakdown of the instructions may find it useful.

11-4.1 LOAD and EXCHANGE

The instructions in this group are clear, exchange, load, load address, load address relative, load constant, load multiple, load relative, pop, and push (CLR, CLRB, EX, EXB, LD, LDB, LDL, LDA, LDAR, LDK, LDM, LDR, LDRB, LDRL, POP, POPL, PUSH, and PUSHL).

The LOAD and EXCHANGE group includes a variety of instructions that provide for movement of data between registers, memory, and the program itself (i.e., immediate data). This group of instructions is supported by the widest range of addressing modes. The base (BA) and base index (BX) address modes are only available on instructions in this group. None of these instructions affect any CPU flags.

EXAMPLE 11-2 How can the contents of memory locations 2000–2005 be loaded into registers R4–R9?

Solution The single-load multiple instruction

```
LDM R4,2000,#6
```

will transfer the contents of the memory locations to the registers.

11-4.2 Arithmetic

The instructions in this group are add with carry, add, compare, decimal adjust, decrement, divide, extend sign, increment, multiply, negate, subtract with carry, and subtract (ADC, ADCB, ADD, ADDB, ADDL, CP, CPB, CPL, DAB, DEC, DECB, DIV, DIVL, EXTS, EXTSB, EXTSL, INC, INCB, MULT, MULTL, NEG, NEGB, SBC, SBCB, SUB, SUBB, and SUBL).

The arithmetic group consists of instructions for performing integer arithmetic. The basic instructions use standard 2s complement binary format. Support is also available for BCD arithmetic.

Most of the instructions in this group perform an operation between a register operand and a second operand designated by any of the five basic addressing modes (R, IM, IR, DA, and X), and load the result into the register.

The arithmetic instructions in general alter the C, Z, S, and P/V flags. These flags may then be tested by conditional JUMP instructions. In this case, the P/V flag indicates arithmetic overflow, and hence is referred to as the V (overflow) flag. The byte version of these instructions generally alters the D and H flags as well.

The basic integer operations are performed on byte, word, or long-word values, although not all operand sizes are supported by all instructions. Multiple precision operations can be implemented using the add with carry (ADC, ADCB), subtract with carry (SBC, SBCB), and extend sign (EXTS, EXTSB, EXTSL) instructions.

BCD operations are not supported directly, but they can be implemented using binary addition or subtraction (ADDB, ADCB, SUBB, SBCB) followed by a decimal adjust (DAB) instruction.

11-4.3 Logical

The instructions in this group are and, complement, or, test, and exclusive or (AND, ANDB, COM, COMB, OR, ORB, TEST, TESTB, TESTL, XOR, and XORB).

This group of instructions performs logical operations on each of the bits of the operands. The operands may be bytes or words. Logical operations on long words are not supported (except for TESTL), but are easily implemented with pairs of instructions.

11-4.4 Program Control

The instructions in this group are call procedure (subroutine), call procedure relative, decrement and jump if not zero, interrupt return, jump, jump relative, return from procedure, and system call (CALL, CALR, DJNZ, DBJNZ, IRET, JP, JR, RET, and SC).

This group of instructions all affect the program counter (PC), and thereby control program flow. General-purpose registers and memory are not altered except for the processor stack pointer and the system stack, which play a significant role in procedures and interrupts. (An exception is the DJNZ instruction, which uses a general-purpose register as a loop counter.) The flags are also preserved except for IRET which reloads the program status, including the flags, from the system stack.

EXAMPLE 11-3 The block of code starting at LOOP is to be executed 12 times. How should the code look?

Solution The following sequence would be used (R0 is used as the loop counter):

```
LOOP:   LD R0,#12
        !Loop code goes here!
        DJNZ R0,LOOP
NEXT:
```

11-4.5 Bit Manipulation

The instructions in this group are bit test, reset bit, set bit, test and set, and test condition code (BIT, BITB, RES, RESB, SET, SETB, TSET, TSETB, TCC, and TCCB).

The instructions in this group are useful for manipulating individual bits in registers or memory. This is easily done using this group of instructions, whereas in most computers this has to be done using logical instructions with suitable masks.

11-4.6 Rotate and Shift

The instructions in this group are rotate left, rotate left through carry, rotate left digit, rotate right, rotate right through carry, rotate right digit, shift dynamic arithmetic, shift dynamic logical, shift left arithmetic, shift left logical, shift right arithmetic, and shift right logical (RL, RLB, RLC, RLCB, RLDB, RR, RRB, RRC, RRCB, RRDB, SDA, SDAB, SDAL, SDL, SDLB, SDLL, SLA, SLAB, SLAL, SLL, SLLB, SLLL, SRA, SRAB, SRAL, SRL, SRLB, and SRLL).

The group contains a wide variety of instructions for shifting and rotating data registers.

Instructions for shifting arithmetically or logically in either direction are available. Three operand lengths are supported: 8, 16, and 32 bits. The amount of the shift, which may be any value up to the operand length, can be specified statically by a field in the instruction or dynamically by the contents of another register. The ability to determine the amount of a shift dynamically is a useful feature not available in most μPs.

EXAMPLE 11-4 How can the contents of R5 be shifted 3 bits to the right?

Solution The following **Z8000** instruction will do it:

```
RR R5,#3
```

11-4.7 Block Transfer and String Manipulation

The instructions in this group are compare (with decrement, increment, and repeat options), compare string (with increment, decrement, and repeat options), load with increment, decrement, and repeat options, translate (with increment, decrement, and repeat options), and translate and test (with increment, decrement, and repeat options). The Op codes for these instructions are CPD, CPDB, CPDRB, CPI, CPIB, CPIR, CPIRB, CPSD, CPSDB, CPSDR, CPSDRB, CPSI, CPSIB, CPSIR, CPSIRB, LDD, LDDB, LDDR, LDRB, LDI, LDIB, LDIR, LDIRB, TRDB, TRDRB, TRIB, TRIRB, TRTDB, TRTDRB, TRTIB, and TRTIRB.

This is an exceptionally powerful group of instructions that provides a full complement of string comparison, string translation, and block transfer operations. With these instructions, a byte or word block of any length up to 64K bytes can be moved in memory, a byte or word string can be searched for a given value, 2-byte or word strings can be compared, and a byte string can be translated using the value of each byte as the address of its own replacement in a translation table. The TRANSLATE and TEST instructions can skip over a class of bytes specified by a translation table, detecting bytes with values of special interest.

All of the operations in this group can proceed through the data in either direction. In addition, the operation may be repeated automatically while decrementing a length counter until it is zero, or they may operate on one storage unit per execution with the length counter decremented by 1 and the source and destination counters properly adjusted. The latter form is useful when it is necessary to implement more complex operations in software and other instructions will be used in a loop along with the block instructions.

The P/V flag is used by these instructions to indicate that the length counter has decremented to zero. The D and H flags are not affected by any of these instructions, while the C and S flags are used only by the COMPARE instructions.

These instructions use indirect register addressing, and follow all rules of segmented addressing (they do not modify the high-order half of the 16-bit register pair used as a pointer in the **Z8001** and **Z8003**).

The repetitive forms of these instructions are interruptible after each iteration. The address of the instruction itself, rather than the address of the next one, is saved on the stack, and the contents of the pointer registers and repetition counter are such that the instruction can be restarted after returning from the interrupt without any visible effect on its execution.

EXAMPLE 11-5 What instructions are needed to copy data from memory locations 2000–2800 to memory locations 8000–8800?

Solution The following **Z8000** instructions will execute this task:

```
LD    R1,#8000      !destination address!
LD    R2,#2000      !source address     !
LD    R3,#800       !word count         !
LDIR  @R1,@R2,R3    !perform block move !
```

11-4.8 Input/Output

The instructions in this group are input (with increment, decrement, and repeat options), output (with increment, decrement, and repeat options), special input (with increment, decrement, and repeat options), and special output (with increment, decrement, and repeat options). The mnemonics for these instructions are IN, INB, IND, INDB, INDR, INDRB, INI, INIB, INIR, INIRB, OUT, OUTB, OUTD, OUTDB, OTDR, OTDRB, OUTI, OUTIB, OTIR, OTIRB, SIN, SINB, SIND, SINDB, SINDR, SINDRB, SINI, SINIB, SINIR, SINIRB, SOUT, SOUTB, SOUTD SOUTDB, SOTDR, SOTDRB, SOUTI, SOUTIB, SOTIR, and SOTIRB.

This group of instructions transfers a byte, word, or block of data between peripheral devices and the CPU registers or memory. Two separate I/O address spaces are recognized, standard I/O and special I/O. The two sets of instructions are identical except that they generate different status codes, and for special I/O instructions the port address can only be specified statically, whereas for standard I/O instructions the port address may be specified statically or dynamically by the contents of a CPU register.

All I/O instructions are privileged, and as such can only be executed in system mode.

11-4.9 CPU Control

The instructions in this group are complement flag, disable interrupt, enable interrupt, halt, load control register, load program status, multi-micro bit test, multi-micro request, multi-micro reset, multi-micro set, no operation, reset flag, and set flag (COMFLG, DI, EI, HALT, LDCTL, LDCTLB, LDPS, MBIT, MREQ, MRES, MSET, NOP, RESFLG, and SETFLG).

The instructions in this group relate CPU control and status registers (FCW, PSAP, REFRESH, etc.). They also perform unusual operations that do not fit into any of the other categories, such as the instructions that support the multi-micro input and output pins. Most of these instructions are privileged with the exception of NOP and the flag operations (SETFLG, RESFLG, COMFLG, LDCTLB).

11-4.10 Extended Instructions

As we have mentioned earlier, the **Z8000** architecture supports external processing units. A group of six Op codes (0E, 0F, 4E, 4F, 8E, and 8F hexadecimal) is dedicated for the implementation of extended instructions using the extended processing architecture. The five basic addressing modes may be used with these reserved Op codes. The action taken by the CPU when it encounters one of these reserved Op codes depends on the state of the EPA bit in the FCW. If this bit is set, it is assumed that the system contains EPUs, therefore the instruction is allowed to execute. If this bit is clear, the CPU traps (extended instruction trap) so that a trap handler can process the instruction in software.

The instructions available on the **Z8000** are given in Table 11-2. It lists the mnemonics, the address modes, and clock cycles for each instruction. It also contains a brief symbolic description of the action of each instruction.

11-5 HARDWARE INTERFACE

11-5.1 Multiplexed Bus (Z-Bus)

The Z-Bus is shown in Figure 11-5. It is the central element of the **Z8000** family. It is a multiplexed address/data bus with control signals which was designed as a system of interconnection between chips. Although the Z-bus was not intended as a system backplane definition, backplane designs can easily be implemented using the Z-Bus as a foundation. The basic concept behind the Z-Bus is that transactions are identified by the status lines, and information is transferred by the address and data strobes with the actual addresses or data appearing on the bidirectional address/data lines. The use of status lines makes hardware interfacing easier, and also reduces the number of signals needed.

11-5.2 Address Strobe and Data Strobe

The address and data strobes indicate that either an address or data is stable on the address/data lines. Each machine cycle contains an address strobe followed by a data strobe. The address becomes stable during the time that address strobe is active, and is guaranteed to be stable a defined time before the rising edge of address strobe. This allows the use of either transparent latches or edge-triggered latches for addresses. The use of transparent latches will increase the time valid addresses are available, thereby increasing the available memory access time. This part of the machine cycle is then followed by a data strobe, which indicates either that valid output data is present on the address/data lines, or that the slave device should place input data on the address/data lines.

An important point to remember is that the status lines and the READ/WRITE, byte/word, and system/normal lines define the exact type of machine cycle in progress. In almost any hardware design using Z-Bus components, these lines are used to control the access to various memory or peripheral modules.

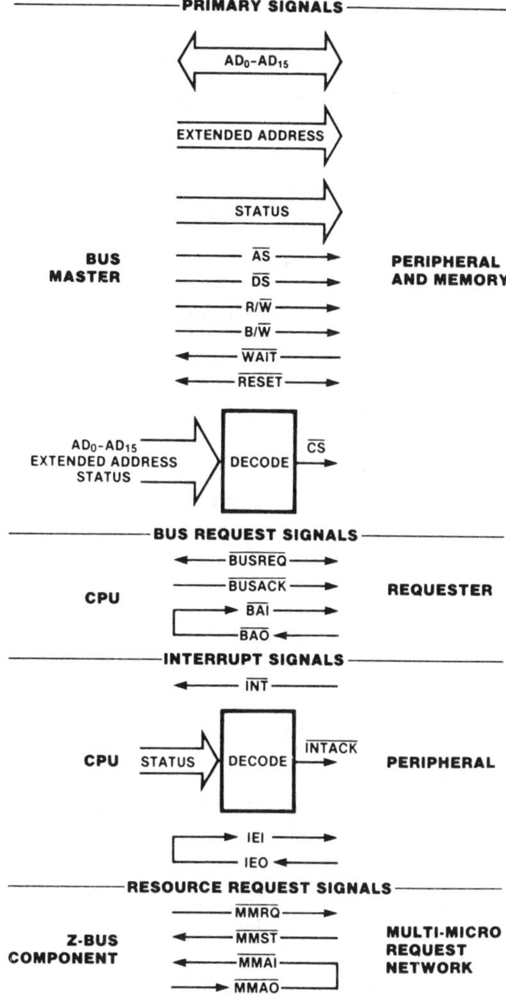

Figure 11-5 Z-Bus signals. (Reproduced by permission © Zilog, Inc. This material shall not be reproduced without the written consent of Zilog, Inc.)

11-5.3 Input/Output Operation

Because a memory access machine cycle looks the same as an input/output machine cycle except for the status code, interfacing to I/O devices is a simple matter of decoding any address bits necessary and including in the decoding the status code for I/O or special I/O. An extra clock cycle is included in I/O machine cycles, but the designer could just as easily attach memory to the processor so that it was accessed by I/O instructions. In practice, though, this extra clock cycle provides the time necessary for slower peripheral devices to respond, so the I/O status is used for I/O devices.

11-5.4 Interrupts and Traps

The hardware interface for interrupts and traps in the **Z8000** is structured and easy to use. Any device desiring service may pull one of the four interrupt and trap lines LOW. Because the interrupt lines are active LOW, several devices may drive a line LOW at the same time. The interrupt acknowledge (INTACK) procedure in the **Z8000** resolves these potential conflicts. When an interrupt is recognized, the CPU will go through an INTACK cycle, which provides a unique status code on the four status lines. There are, in fact, separate status codes for nonmaskable INTACK, vectored INTACK, nonvectored INTACK, and segment trap acknowledge. It is necessary for all devices sharing a common interrupt line to be able to resolve any contention so that only one device will respond to the INTACK cycle. The Z-Bus definition does this with an interrupt enable daisy chain. In this system, devices closest to the beginning of the daisy chain have the option of disabling lower devices and responding to the INTACK cycle. If they have no interrupts pending, they allow the enable signal to pass to the next-lower-priority device. When a device does respond to an INTACK cycle, it places its interrupt vector or "identifier" on the address/data lines during the time data strobe is active in the INTACK cycle. While this method of interrupt priority resolution allows for only one daisy chain per interrupt type, it is easy to implement a multiple daisy chain system where each interrupt can have several priority daisy chains, each of them having a relative priority.

11-5.5 Bus Request and Acknowledge

While the **Z8000** CPU is normally the bus master, there is a provision for allowing other devices to gain control of the bus temporarily. The bus request (BUSREQ) and bus acknowledge (BUSACK) signals allow an external device to request the bus by pulling BUSREQ LOW (active). When the BUSACK signal goes LOW (active), the requesting device knows that it has control of the bus. In order to maintain control of the bus, the external device must continue to hold BUSREQ LOW. When BUSREQ is allowed to go HIGH, the CPU will take BUSACK HIGH (inactive) and regain control of the bus. In order to preserve refresh of dynamic memories, the CPU will remember if the refresh counter expired during the time the CPU was disconnected from the bus, and the missed refresh cycle will be issued as soon as the CPU regains control of the bus. The CPU can remember up to two such "missed" refresh cycles. Knowing this fact, a designer would be wise not to allow an external device to hold control of the bus for more than two refresh periods if refresh is being used.

11-6 CPU SUPPORT DEVICES

There are currently three devices designed to support the **Z8000** CPUs. They are not properly called peripherals because they do tasks tied very closely with CPU operation, and as such have special operating characteristics that distinguish them from normal peripheral devices. We have already mentioned the **Z8010** MMU frequently in talking about memory addressing and protection. The **Z8016** DMA Transfer Controller (DTC) was designed to do DMA (direct memory access) transfers on the Z-Bus using the bus request/acknowledge protocol already described. The **Z8070** Arithmetic Processing Unit (APU) works within the EPU architecture already described and performs IEEE standard floating point operations. Some discussion of each device is in order so that we may show how these devices work with the CPU to expand its power and flexibility.

11-6.1 Z8010 MMU

The **Z8010** MMU (hereafter referred to as the MMU) is a device designed to work with the segmented addresses generated by the **Z8001** and **Z8003** CPUs to provide memory protection and relocation. Each MMU has provisions for handling 128 segments of memory, storing information on each segment relating to the location of that segment in physical memory and the allowable accesses to that segment. Because the **Z8001** and **Z8003** can address up to 256 segments, two MMUs are necessary if it is necessary to have memory management on all 256 segments at the same time. It is also possible to have a system with multiple MMUs in which some MMUs handle memory that responds only to program accesses and others handle memory that responds only to data accesses, and so forth.

11-6.2 Z8016 DTC

The **Z8016** DMA Transfer Controller (DTC) has two independent DMA channels that will transfer data between memory and a peripheral, two memory areas, or between two peripherals. The DTC is both a master and a slave device on the Z-Bus. When the CPU has control of the bus, the DTC can be programmed as a peripheral. This is how the CPU loads the DTC registers to program the type of transfers desired. The DTC can also request the bus via the BUSREQ line and become the bus master to perform the transfer. It has daisy chain inputs and outputs for implementing a bus request priority chain. In this way multiple DTCs can exist in the same system and be capable of resolving any conflicts when requesting the bus at the same time.

In a system containing MMUs, the DTC may be used in either of two ways. It may be connected between the CPU and any MMU so that the addresses generated by the DTC are translated by the MMU. A signal called DMASYNC enables the MMU to differentiate between CPU-generated addresses and DTC-generated addresses. It is also possible to connect the DTC directly to the physical memory address bus, and deal with physical addresses. This is somewhat easier to understand, but gives up the relocation and attribute checking the MMU can provide.

11-6.3 Z8070 APU

The **Z8070** Arithmetic Processing Unit (APU) is a new device designed to do very high-speed floating point arithmetic in Z-Bus systems. It works with any of the **Z8000** CPUs, and was also designed with the future 32-bit CPUs in mind. It performs IEEE standard floating point operations and will also operate on "double-extended" precision numbers (80 bits). This device works using the EPU architecture designed into the **Z8000** in which certain Op codes are designated as "extended instructions." A bit in the FCW, the EPA bit, tells the CPU that an EPU is present in the system. When the EPA bit is set, any extended instructions are not trapped, but are left for the EPU to process. The APU is one type of EPU designed to do floating point operations. In this architecture, the CPU fetches the Op codes and does any address calculations necessary, while the APU does the actual operation specified. In this system, the APU is neither a bus master nor a bus slave, it is an extended processing unit. EPUs have this unique characteristic of only doing a portion of the job of executing a particular extended instruction. The CPU is already capable of doing the address calculation and signal generation, so the job left to the EPU is that specialized part of the task that the CPU cannot do.

11-7 SOFTWARE INTERFACE

A great deal of the cost of designing a μP system today lies in the software design. It would not be fair to dwell on the hardware features of a processor without mentioning the features present to aid in software design.

We have already seen how the regularity of the instruction set in the **Z8000** CPU, combined with its multiple addressing modes and data types, makes assembly language programming easier.

There are other features of the **Z8000** that have been designed with the software designer in mind. They include context switching features, interrupt service routine initiation, the SYSTEM CALL instruction, and segment trap and abort handling.

11-7.1 Context Switching

A very useful feature in any complex system is the ability to switch the context of a program. A *context switch* is necessary whenever the program flow must be altered to service an interrupt, call another subroutine that will use working registers, or perform some operating system function. In these cases it will be necessary to save the current state of the CPU (the current context) and load the new state (the new context). The **Z8000** instruction set provides instructions to help accomplish this. The LDM (load multiple) instruction is commonly used to load a group of registers (possibly the entire register file) into memory, then to load the new data desired. In this manner, a subroutine can save the current contents of all registers, load any data necessary to its function, and then restore the original register contents upon exiting. The original calling program never sees any of its data modified unexpectedly.

11-7.2 Interrupts

Interrupts are a way of signaling the CPU that an external device requires service of one kind or another. The **Z8000** CPUs have four such external interrupts: the nonmaskable interrupt (NMI), the vectored interrupt (VI), nonvectored interrupt (NVI), and the segment trap (SEGT). The segment trap input will be discussed later in this chapter.

When an interrupt is recognized, the processor will actually fetch the next instruction, but this instruction is never executed (this is referred to as an aborted instruction fetch). The CPU then issues an *interrupt machine cycle* corresponding to the interrupt recognized. It then saves the current program status on the system stack and loads the new program status from the appropriate locations in the program status area. At this time the PC will be loaded with the value from the program status area, which was set up ahead of time to be the address of the interrupt service routine. At the end of the interrupt service routine, the interrupt return instruction (IRET) will reverse the process, putting the CPU back in the original program with the original program status that was in effect when the interrupt was first recognized.

Because much of the actual interrupt process is handled automatically, the bulk of the programming effort necessary to handle interrupts is in the setup of the program status area. Once the FCW and PC values for each interrupt used are entered, handling an interrupt requires only doing the task necessary in the interrupt service routine, and then executing an IRET instruction to return to the original program. Any switches from normal to system mode, or from nonsegmented to segmented mode, are handled automatically.

11-7.3 SYSTEM CALL Instruction

We did mention that the software must prevent unauthorized system calls that would allow normal users to obtain system status. After a casual look at the CPU architecture, a valid concern could be: I can access the FCW while in system mode and switch to normal mode, but how do I get back to system mode once I am in normal mode? The SYSTEM CALL instruction answers this question.

The SYSTEM CALL instruction provides a way to handle requests for system mode operations while operating in normal mode. A SYSTEM CALL can be thought of as a *software interrupt*. A SYSTEM CALL instruction causes the CPU to fetch a new FCW and PC from the program status area, just as with an external interrupt. The difference is that with a SYSTEM CALL, there is no need to abort the current instruction or to acknowledge the system call itself. The saving of current program status, loading of new program status, and return to the original program are handled just as for an interrupt.

11-7.4 Segment Trap and Abort

The SEGMENT TRAP input on the **Z8001** is another form of interrupt input. It has its own acknowledge status code just as the other interrupts do, and there is a place in the program status area for a FCW and PC that are loaded when a segment trap is recognized. It is nothing more than an interrupt that has been given a special name and suggested for use in processing segment traps from a MMU. The timing of the segment trap input has been given careful consideration to be certain it will be compatible with the SEGT output of the **Z8010** MMU, although there is nothing to prevent a user from using the SEGT input of a **Z8001** or **Z8003** CPU as another interrupt input, providing there was no need for memory management and its associated segment trap.

In contrast to the SEGMENT TRAP input, the abort input (ABORT) of the **Z8003** is a unique input. It is used for processing *virtual memory page faults*, and as such cannot tolerate the delay in recognition inherent in the segment trap input. Because the instruction being fetched may not exist in real memory, we must be able to abort the current instruction, not the next one. This is the principal difference between the abort and segment trap inputs. The abort input causes the current instruction to be aborted, so that when the appropriate processing has been done, that instruction may be restarted and executed now that it exists in real memory.

11-8 REFERENCES

The Zilog 1983/84 Data Book, Zilog, Campbell, Calif., 1983.

The Z8000 CPU Technical Manual, Zilog, Campbell, Calif., 1983.

Table 11-2 **Instruction set summary**

Load and Exchange

Mnemonics	Operands	Addr. Modes	Clock Cycles* Word, Byte NS	SS	SL	Long Word NS	SS	SL	Operation
CLR	dst	R	7	-	-				**Clear**
CLRB		IR	8	-	-				dst ← 0
		DA	11	12	14				
		X	12	12	15				
EX	R, src	R	6	-	-				**Exchange**
EXB		IR	12	-	-				R ↔ src
		DA	15	16	18				
		X	16	16	19				
LD	R, src	R	3	-	-	5	-	-	**Load into Register**
LDB		IM	7	-	-	11	-	-	R ← src
LDL		IM	5 (byte only)						
		IR	7	-	-	11	-	-	
		DA	9	10	12	12	13	15	
		X	10	10	13	13	13	16	
		BA	14	-	-	17	-	-	
		BX	14	-	-	17	-	-	
LD	dst, R	IR	8	-	-	11	-	-	**Load into Memory** (Store)
LDB		DA	11	12	14	14	15	17	dst ← R
LDL		X	12	12	15	15	15	18	
		BA	14	-	-	17	-	-	
		BX	14	-	-	17	-	-	
LD	dst, IM	IR	11	-	-				**Load Immediate into Memory**
LDB		DA	14	15	17				dst ← IM
		X	15	15	18				

*** NS = Non-Segmented SS = Segmented Short Offset SL = Segmented Long Offset**

Table 11-2 (continued)

Load and Exchange (Continued)	Mnemonics	Operands	Addr. Modes	Clock Cycles						Operation
				Word, Byte			Long Word			
				NS	SS	SL	NS	SS	SL	
	LDA	R, src	DA	12	13	15				**Load Address**
			X	13	13	16				R ← source address
			BA	15	-	-				
			BX	15	-	-				
	LDAR	R, src	RA	15	-	-				**Load Address Relative**
										R ← source address
	LDK	R, src	IM	5	-	-				**Load Constant**
										R ← n (n = 0 . . . 15)
	LDM	R, src, n	IR	11	-	-	+3 n			**Load Multiple**
			DA	14	15	17	+3 n			R ← src (n consecutive words)
			X	15	15	18	+3 n			(n = 1 . . . 16)
	LDM	dst, R, n	IR	11	-	-	+3 n			**Load Multiple** (Store Multiple)
			DA	14	15	17	+3 n			dst ← R (n consecutive words)
			X	15	15	18	+3 n			(n = 1 . . . 16)
	LDR	R, src	RA	14	-	-	17	-	-	**Load Relative**
	LDRB									R ← src
	LDRL									(range -32768 . . . +32767)
	LDR	dst, R	RA	14	-	-	17	-	-	**Load Relative** (Store Relative)
	LDRB									dst ← R
	LDRL									(range -32768 . . . +32767)
	POP	dst, IR	R	8	-	-	12	-	-	**Pop**
	POPL		IR	12	-	-	19	-	-	dst ← IR
			DA	16	16	18	23	23	25	Autoincrement contents of R
			X	16	16	19	23	23	26	
	PUSH	IR, src	R	9	-	-	12	-	-	**Push**
	PUSHL		IM	12	-	-	-	-	-	Autodecrement contents of R
			IR	13	-	-	20	-	-	IR ← src
			DA	14	14	16	21	21	23	
			X	14	14	17	21	21	24	
Arithmetic	**ADC**	R, src	R	5	-	-				**Add with Carry**
	ADCB									R ← R + src + carry
	ADD	R, src	R	4	-	-	8	-	-	**Add**
	ADDB		IM	7	-	-	14	-	-	R ← R + src
	ADDL		IR	7	-	-	14	-	-	
			DA	9	10	12	15	16	18	
			X	10	10	13	16	16	19	
	CP	R, src	R	4	-	-	8	-	-	**Compare with Register**
	CPB		IM	7	-	-	14	-	-	R - src
	CPL		IR	7	-	-	14	-	-	
			DA	9	10	12	15	16	18	
			X	10	10	13	16	16	19	
	CP	dst, IM	IR	11	-	-				**Compare with Immediate**
	CPB		DA	14	15	17				dst - IM
			X	15	15	18				
	DAB	dst	R	5	-	-				**Decimal Adjust**
	DEC	dst, n	R	4	-	-				**Decrement by n**
	DECB		IR	11	-	-				dst ← dst - n
			DA	13	14	16				(n = 1 . . . 16)
			X	14	14	17				

Table 11-2 (continued)

	Mnemonics	Operands	Addr. Modes	Clock Cycles: Word, Byte NS	SS	SL	Long Word NS	SS	SL	Operation
Arithmetic (Continued)	**DIV**	R, src	R	107	-	-	744	-	-	**Divide** (signed)
	DIVL		IM	107	-	-	744	-	-	Word: $R_{n+1} \leftarrow R_{n,n+1} + src$
			IR	107	107	107	744	744	744	$R_n \leftarrow$ remainder
			DA	108	109	111	745	746	748	Long Word: $R_{n+2,n+3} \leftarrow R_{n \ldots n+3} + src$
			X	109	109	112	746	746	749	$R_{n,n+1} \leftarrow$ remainder
	EXTS	dst	R	11	-	-	11	-	-	**Extend Sign**
	EXTSB									Extend sign of low order half of dst
	EXTSL									through high order half of dst
	INC	dst, n	R	4	-	-				**Increment by n**
	INCB		IR	11	-	-				dst ← dst + n
			DA	13	14	16				(n = 1 ... 16)
			X	14	14	17				
	MULT	R, src	R	70	-	-	282*	-	-	**Multiply** (signed)
	MULTL		IM	70	-	-	282*	-	-	Word: $R_{n,n+1} \leftarrow R_{n+1} \cdot src$
			IR	70	-	-	282*	-	-	Long Word: $R_{n \ldots n+3} \leftarrow R_{n+2,\, n+3}$
			DA	71	72	74	283*	284*	286*	* Plus seven cycles for each 1 in the
			X	72	72	75	284*	284*	287*	multiplicand
	NEG	dst	R	7	-	-				**Negate**
	NEGB		IR	12	-	-				dst ← 0 - dst
			DA	15	16	18				
			X	16	16	19				
	SBC	R, src	R	5	-	-				**Subtract with Carry**
	SBCB									R ← R - src - carry
	SUB	R, src	R	4	-	-	8	-	-	**Subtract**
	SUBB		IM	7	-	-	14	-	-	R ← R - src
	SUBL		IR	7	-	-	14	-	-	
			DA	9	10	12	15	16	18	
			X	10	10	13	16	16	19	
Logical	**AND**	R, src	R	4	-	-				**AND**
	ANDB		IM	7	-	-				R ← R AND src
			IR	7	-	-				
			DA	9	10	12				
			X	10	10	13				
	COM	dst	R	7	-	-				**Complement**
	COMB		IR	12	-	-				dst ← NOT dst
			DA	15	16	18				
			X	16	16	19				
	OR	R, src	R	4	-	-				**OR**
	ORB		IM	7	-	-				R ← R OR src
			IR	7	-	-				
			DA	9	10	12				
			X	10	10	13				
	TCC	cc, dst	R	5	-	-				**Test Condition Code**
	TCCB									Set LSB if cc is true
	TEST	dst	R	7	-	-	13	-	-	**Test**
	TESTB		IR	8	-	-	13	-	-	dst OR 0
	TESTL		DA	11	12	14	16	17	19	
			X	12	12	15	17	17	20	
	XOR	R, src	R	4	-	-				**Exclusive OR**
	XORB		IM	7	-	-				R ← R XOR src
			IR	7	-	-				
			DA	9	10	12				
			X	10	10	13				

Table 11-2 (continued)

	Mnemonics	Operands	Addr. Modes	Clock Cycles Word, Byte NS	SS	SL	Long Word NS	SS	SL	Operation
Program Control	**CALL**	dst	IR DA X	10 12 13	- 18 18	15 20 21				**Call Subroutine** Autodecrement SP @ SP ← PC PC ← dst
	CALR	dst	RA	10	-	15				**Call Relative** Autodecrement SP @ SP ← PC PC ← PC + dst (range -4094 to +4096)
	DJNZ **DBJNZ**	R, dst	RA	11	-	-				**Decrement and Jump if Non-Zero** R ← R - 1 If R ≠ 0: PC ← PC + dst (range -254 to 0)
	IRET*	-	-	13	-	16				**Interrupt Return** PS ← @ SP Autoincrement SP
	JP	cc, dst	IR IR DA X	10 7 7 8	- - 8 8	15 7 10 11		(taken) (not taken)		**Jump Conditional** If cc is true: PC ← dst
	JR	cc, dst	RA	6	-	-				**Jump Conditional Relative** If cc is true: PC ← PC + dst (range -256 to +254)
	RET	cc	-	10 7	- -	13 7		(taken) (not taken)		**Return Conditional** If cc is true: PC ← @ SP Autoincrement SP
	SC	src	IM	33	-	39				**System Call** Autodecrement SP @ SP ← old PS Push instruction PS ← System Call PS
Bit Manipulation	**BIT** **BITB**	dst, b	R IR DA X	4 8 10 11	- - 11 11	- - 13 14				**Test Bit Static** Z flag ← NOT dst bit specified by b
	BIT **BITB**	dst, R	R	10	-	-				**Test Bit Dynamic** Z flag ← NOT dst bit specified by contents of R
	RES **RESB**	dst, b	R IR DA X	4 11 13 14	- - 14 14	- - 16 17				**Reset Bit Static** Reset dst bit specified by b
	RES **RESB**	dst, R	R	10	-	-				**Reset Bit Dynamic** Reset dst bit specified by contents R
	SET **SETB**	dst, b	R IR DA X	4 11 13 14	- - 14 14	- - 16 17				**Set Bit Static** Set dst bit specified by b
	SET **SETB**	dst, R	R	10	-	-				**Set Bit Dynamic** Set dst bit specified by contents of R
	TSET **TSETB**	dst	R IR DA X	7 11 14 15	- - 15 15	- - 17 18				**Test and Set** S flag ← MSB of dst dst ← all 1s

Table 11-2 (continued)

	Mnemonics	Operands	Addr. Modes	Clock Cycles Word, Byte NS	SS	SL	Long Word NS	SS	SL	Operation
Rotate and Shift	**RL** **RLB**	dst, n	R R	6 for n = 1 7 for n = 2						**Rotate Left** by n bits (n = 1, 2)
	RLC **RLCB**	dst, n	R R	6 for n = 1 7 for n = 2						**Rotate Left through Carry** by n bits (n = 1, 2)
	RLDB	R, src	R	9	-	-				**Rotate Digit Left**
	RR **RRB**	dst, n	R R	6 for n = 1 7 for n = 2						**Rotate Right** by n bits (n = 1, 2)
	RRC **RRCB**	dst, n	R R	6 for n = 1 7 for n = 2						**Rotate Right through Carry** by n bits (n = 1, 2)
	RRDB	R, src	R	9	-	-				**Rotate Digit Right**
	SDA **SDAB** **SDAL**	dst, R	R	(15 + 3 n)			(15 + 3 n)			**Shift Dynamic Arithmetic** Shift dst left or right by contents of R
	SDL **SDLB** **SDLL**	dst, R	R	(15 + 3 n)			(15 + 3 n)			**Shift Dynamic Logical** Shift dst left or right by contents of R
	SLA **SLAB** **SLAL**	dst, n	R	(13 + 3 n)			(13 +3 n)			**Shift Left Arithmetic** by n bits
	SLL **SLLB** **SLLL**	dst, n	R	(13 + 3 n)			(13 + 3 n)			**Shift Left Logical** by n bits
	SRA **SRAB** **SRAL**	dst, n	R	(13 + 3 n)			(13 + 3 n)			**Shift Right Arithmetic** by n bits
	SRL **SRLB** **SRLL**	dst, n	R	(13 + 3 n)			(13 + 3 n)			**Shift Right Logical** by n bits
Block Transfer and String Manipulation	**CPD** **CPDB**	R_X, src, R_Y, cc	IR	20	-	-				**Compare and Decrement** R_X - src Autodecrement src address $R_Y \leftarrow R_Y - 1$
	CPDR **CPDRB**	R_X, src, R_Y, cc	IR	(11 + 9 n)						**Compare, Decrement and Repeat** R_X - src Autodecrement src address $R_Y \leftarrow R_Y - 1$ Repeat until cc is true or $R_Y = 0$
	CPI **CPIB**	R_X, src, R_Y, cc	IR	20	-	-				**Compare and Increment** R_X - src Autoincrement src address $R_Y \leftarrow R_Y - 1$
	CPIR **CPIRB**	R_X, src, R_Y cc	IR	(11 + 9 n)						**Compare, Increment and Repeat** R_X - src Autoincrement src address $R_Y \leftarrow R_Y - 1$ Repeat until cc is true or $R_Y = 0$
	CPSD **CPSDB**	dst, src, R, cc	IR	25	-	-				**Compare String and Decrement** dst - src Autodecrement dst and src addresses $R \leftarrow R - 1$

Table 11-2 (continued)

Block Transfer and String Manipulation (Continued)	Mnemonics	Operands	Addr. Modes	Clock Cycles Word, Byte NS	SS	SL	Long Word NS	SS	SL	Operation
	CPSDR **CPSDRB**	dst, src, R, cc	IR	(11 + 14 n)						**Compare String, Decr. and Repeat** dst - src Autodecrement dst and src addresses R ← R - 1 Repeat until cc is true or R = 0
	CPSI **CPSIB**	dst, src, R, cc	IR	25	-	-				**Compare String and Increment** dst - src Autoincrement dst and src addresses R ← R - 1
	CPSIR **CPSIRB**	dst, src, R, cc	IR	(11 + 14 n)						**Compare String, Incr. and Repeat** dst - src Autoincrement dst and src addresses R ← R - 1 Repeat until cc is true or R = 0
	LDD **LDDB**	dst, src, R	IR	20	-	-				**Load and Decrement** dst ← src Autodecrement dst and src addresses R ← R - 1
	LDDR **LDDRB**	dst, src, R	IR	(11 + 9 n)						**Load, Decrement and Repeat** dst ← src Autodecrement dst and src addresses R ← R - 1 Repeat until R = 0
	LDI **LDIB**	dst, src, R	IR	20	-	-				**Load and Increment** dst ← src Autoincrement dst and src addresses R ← R - 1
	LDIR **LDIRB**	dst, src, R	IR	(11 + 9 n)						**Load, Increment and Repeat** dst ← src Autoincrement dst and src addresses R ← R - 1 Repeat until R = 0
	TRDB	dst, src, R	IR	25	-	-				**Translate and Decrement** dst ← src (dst) Autodecrement dst address R ← R - 1
	TRDRB	dst, src, R	IR	(11 + 14 n)						**Translate, Decrement and Repeat** dst ← src (dst) Autodecrement dst address R ← R - 1 Repeat until R = 0
	TRIB	dst, src, R	IR	25	-	-				**Translate and Increment** dst ← src (dst) Autoincrement dst address R ← R - 1
	TRIRB	dst, src, R	IR	(11 + 14 n)						**Translate, Increment and Repeat** dst ← src (dst) Autoincrement dst address R ← R - 1 Repeat until R = 0
	TRTDB	src 1, src 2, R	IR	25	-	-				**Translate and Test, Decrement** RH1 ← src 2 (src 1) Autodecrement src 1 address R ← R - 1

Table 11-2 (continued)

Block Transfer and String Manipulation (Continued)	Mnemonics	Operands	Addr. Modes	Clock Cycles Word, Byte NS	SS	SL	Long Word NS	SS	SL	Operation
	TRTDRB	src1, src2, R	IR	(11 + 14 n)						**Translate and Test, Decr. and Repeat** RH1 ← src 2 (src 1) Autodecrement src 1 address R ← R - 1 Repeat until R = 0 or RH1 = 0
	TRTIB	src1, src2, R	IR	25						**Translate and Test, Increment** RH1 ← src 2 (src 1) Autoincrement src 1 address R ← R - 1
	TRTIRB	src1, src2, R	IR	(11 + 14 n)						**Translate and Test, Incr. and Repeat** RH1 ← src 2 (src 1) Autoincrement src 1 address R ← R - 1 Repeat until R = 0 or RH1 = 0
Input/ Output	**IN*** **INB***	R, src	IR DA	10 12	- -	- -				**Input** R ← src
	IND* **INDB***	dst, src, R	IR	21	-	-				**Input and Decrement** dst ← src Autodecrement dst address R ← R - 1
	INDR* **INDRB***	dst, src, R	IR	(11 + 10 n)						**Input, Decrement and Repeat** dst ← src Autodecrement dst address R ← R - 1 Repeat until R = 0
	INI* **INIB***	dst, src, R	IR	21	-	-				**Input and Increment** dst ← src Autoincrement dst address R ← R - 1
	INIR* **INIRB***	dst, src, R	IR	(11 + 10 n)						**Input, Increment and Repeat** dst ← src Autoincrement dst address R ← R - 1 Repeat until R = 0
	OUT* **OUTB***	dst, R	IR DA	10 12	- -	- -				**Output** dst ← R
	OUTD* **OUTDB***	dst, src, R	IR	21	-	-				**Output and Decrement** dst ← src Autodecrement src address R ← R - 1
	OTDR* **OTDRB***	dst, src, R	IR	(11 + 10 n)						**Output, Decrement and Repeat** dst ← src Autodecrement src address R ← R - 1 Repeat until R = 0
	OUTI* **OUTIB***	dst, src, R	IR	21	-	-				**Output and Increment** dst ← src Autoincrement src address R ← R - 1
	OTIR* **OTIRB***	dst, src, R	IR	(11 + 10 n)						**Output, Increment and Repeat** dst ← src Autoincrement src address R ← R - 1 Repeat until R = 0

Table 11-2 (continued)

	Mnemonics	Operands	Addr. Modes	Clock Cycles Word, Byte NS	SS	SL	Long Word NS	SS	SL	Operation
Input/Output (Continued)	**SIN*** **SINB***	R, src	DA	12	-	-				**Special Input** R ← src
	SIND* **SINDB***	dst, src, R	IR	21	-	-				**Special Input and Decrement** dst ← src Autodecrement dst address R ← R - 1
	SINDR* **SINDRB***	dst, src, R	IR	(11 + 10 n)						**Special Input, Decrement and Repeat** dst ← src Autodecrement dst address R ← R - 1 Repeat until R = 0
	SINI* **SINIB***	dst, src, R	IR	21	-	-				**Special Input and Increment** dst ← src Autoincrement dst address R ← R - 1
	SINIR* **SINIRB***	dst, src, R	IR	(11 + 10 n)						**Special Input, Increment and Repeat** dst ← src Autoincrement dst address R ← R - 1 Repeat until R = 0
	SOUT* **SOUTB***	dst, src	DA	12	-	-				**Special Output** dst ← src
	SOUTD* **SOUTDB***	dst, src, R	IR	21	-	-				**Special Output and Decrement** dst ← src Autodecrement src address R ← R - 1
	SOTDR* **SOTDRB***	dst, src, R	IR	(11 + 10 n)						**Special Output, Decr. and Repeat** dst ← src Autodecrement src address R ← R - 1 Repeat until R = 0
	SOUTI* **SOUTIB***	dst, src, R	IR	21	-	-				**Special Output and Increment** dst ← src Autoincrement src address R ← R - 1
	SOTIR* **SOTIRB***	dst, src, R	R	(11 + 10 n)						**Special Output, Incr. and Repeat** dst ← src Autoincrement src address R ← R - 1 Repeat until R = 0
CPU Control	**COMFLG**	flags	-	7	-	-				**Complement Flag** (Any combination of C, Z, S, P/V)
	DI*	int	-	7	-	-				**Disable Interrupt** (Any combination of NVI, VI)
	EI*	int	-	7	-	-				**Enable Interrupt** (Any combination of NVI, VI)
	HALT*	-	-	(8 + 3 n)						**HALT**
	LDCTL*	CTLR, src	R	7	-	-				**Load into Control Register** CTLR ← src
	LDCTL*	dst, CTLR	R	7	-	-				**Load from Control Register** dst ← CTLR

Table 11-2 (continued)

CPU Control (Continued)

Mnemonics	Operands	Addr. Modes	Clock Cycles Word, Byte NS	SS	SL	Long Word NS	SS	SL	Operation
LDCTLB	FLGR, src	R	7	-	-				**Load into Flag Byte Register** FLGR ← src
LDCTLB	dst, FLGR	R	7	-	-				**Load from Flag Byte Register** dst ← FLGR
LDPS*	src	IR DA X	12 16 17	- 20 20	16 22 23				**Load Program Status** PS ← src
MBIT*	-	-	7	-	-				**Test Multi-Micro Bit** Set S if $\overline{M_I}$ is Low; reset S if $\overline{M_I}$ is High
MREQ*	dst	R	(12 + 7 n)						**Multi-Micro Request**
MRES*	-	-	5	-	-				**Multi-Micro Reset**
MSET*	-	-	5	-	-				**Multi-Micro Set**
NOP	-	-	7	-	-				**No Operation**
RESFLG	flag		7	-	-				**Reset Flag** (Any combination of C, Z, S, P/V)
SETFLG	flag	-	7	-	-				**Set Flag** (Any combination of C, Z, S, P/V)

*Privileged instructions. Executed in system mode only.

Condition Codes

Code	Meaning	Flag Settings	CC Field
	Always false	-	0000
	Always true	-	1000
Z	Zero	Z = 1	0110
NZ	Not zero	Z = 0	1110
C	Carry	C = 1	0111
NC	No Carry	C = 0	1111
PL	Plus	S = 0	1101
MI	Minus	S = 1	0101
NE	Not equal	Z = 0	1110
EQ	Equal	Z = 1	0110
OV	Overflow	P/V = 1	0100
NOV	No overflow	P/V = 0	1100
PE	Parity is even	P/V = 1	0100
PO	Parity is odd	P/V = 0	1100
GE	Greater than or equal (signed)	(S XOR P/V) = 0	1001
LT	Less than (signed)	(S XOR P/V) = 1	0001
GT	Greater than (signed)	[Z OR (S XOR P/V)] = 0	1010
LE	Less than or equal (signed)	[Z OR (S XOR P/V)] = 1	0010
UGE	Unsigned greater than or equal	C = 0	1111
ULT	Unsigned less than	C = 1	0111
UGT	Unsigned greater than	[(C = 0) AND (Z = 0)] = 1	1011
ULE	Unsigned less than or equal	(C OR Z) = 1	0011

Note that some condition codes have identical flag settings and binary fields in the instruction:
Z = EQ, NZ = NE, C = ULT, NC = UGE, OV = PE, NOV = PO

Status Code Lines

ST_3-ST_0	Definition	ST_3-ST_0	Definition
0 0 0 0	Internal operation	1 0 0 0	Data memory request
0 0 0 1	Memory refresh	1 0 0 1	Stack memory request
0 0 1 0	I/O reference	1 0 1 0	Data memory request (EPU)
0 0 1 1	Special I/O reference (e.g., to an MMU)	1 0 1 1	Stack memory request (EPU)
0 1 0 0	Segment trap acknowledge	1 1 0 0	Program reference, nth word
0 1 0 1	Non-maskable interrupt acknowledge	1 1 0 1	Instruction fetch, first word
0 1 1 0	Non-vectored interrupt acknowledge	1 1 1 0	Extension processor transfer
0 1 1 1	Vectored interrupt acknowledge	1 1 1 1	Reserved

Source: Reproduced by permission © Zilog, Inc. This material shall not be reproduced without the written consent of Zilog, Inc.

CHAPTER 12

The Motorola 68000

Dennis Pfleger
Motorola Microsystem
Tempe, Arizona

The **MC68000**, Motorola's 16-bit microprocessor unit (MPU) takes maximum advantage of the improvements in design and manufacturing technology which took place during the late 1970s. The 16-bit **MC68000** packs ten times as much VLSI circuitry on a single chip as the previous generation of 8-bit MPUs. The primary goals in the design of this MPU are to create a very high-performance device that is also user friendly. The **68000** also meets the increasing need to easily support high-level languages and complex operating systems.

12-1 PRIMARY FEATURES

The primary features of the **MC68000** are:

1 16-megabyte linear address space;

2 16-bit data bus;

3 32-bit internal architecture with 17 registers available to the programmer;

4 a particularly rich instruction set with 56 instructions and 14 addressing modes;

5 hardware and software mechanisms which allow a highly secure operating system environment;

6 a high degree of fault tolerance.

The standard **MC68000** has a primary clock speed of 8 MHz. This allows an aggregate of 2 million instruction and data word transfers a second with readily available standard product memories. Versions of the **MC68000** are available now with clock speeds of 10 MHz, 12.5 MHz, and 16 MHz.

Figure 12-1 Silicon wheel containing **MC68000** die and various packaging options.

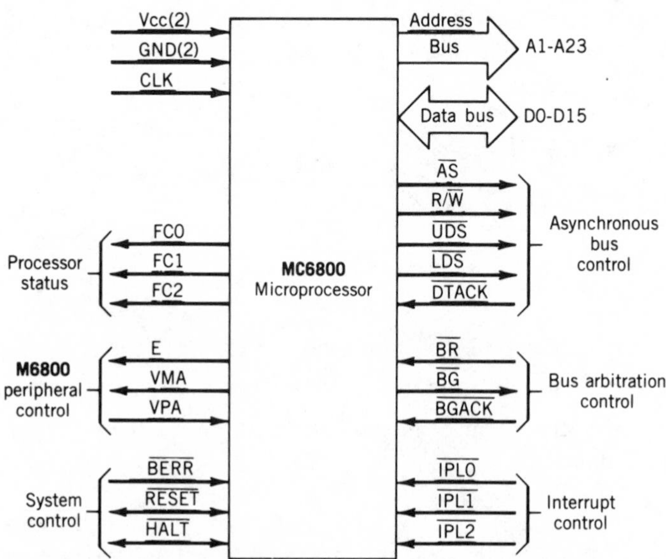

Figure 12-2 General pin assignments for the **MC68000**. (From the *M68000 16/32-Bit Microprocessor Programmer's Reference Manual*, 4th Edition, courtesy of Motorola, Inc.)

The **MC68000** is available in four packaging options, as shown in Figure 12-1. The most common package is the 64-pin dual-in-line (DIP) in either plastic or ceramic. This allows for separate, non-multiplexed address and data buses, as well as a large number of control interrupt signals. Other packaging options include a 68-lead JEDEC chip carrier and a 68-pin grid array (see Figure 12-1). In each packaging option there are 60 signal lines, including the clock, as well as two +5 V power and two ground pins. Figure 12-2 shows the general pin assignments for any **MC68000**. Figure 12-3 shows the exact pin-out for the **MC68000** and the dual-in-line package. The function of each of the pins is described in section 12-9.

The **MC68000** bus structure is designed for speed and flexibility. The address and data lines are not multiplexed but are in parallel, which provides an increase in

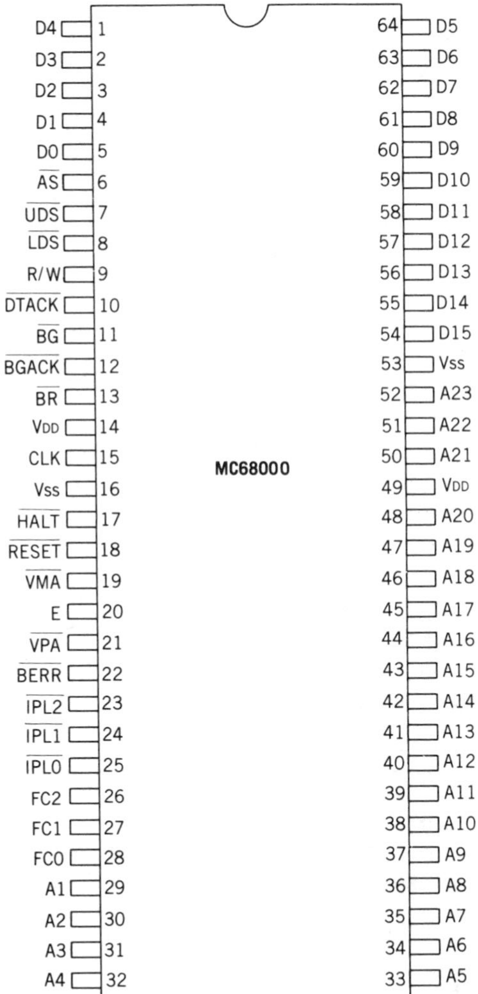

Figure 12-3 **MC68000** pin assignments. (From the *M68000 Programmer's Manual*, 4th Edition, courtesy of Motorola, Inc.)

performance over multiplexed buses. The data bus is asynchronous. This eliminates the need to provide synchronizing signals around the system. The use of handshaking signals, such as DTACK, allows the connection of devices and memories with large variations in response time to the processor bus. The processor can wait an arbitrary amount of time until the device or memory signals the transfer is complete. This MPU bus architecture is also convenient for connecting to system buses of varying lengths.

12-2 THE SOFTWARE DESIGNER'S VIEW OF THE MC68000

The internal register set of the **MC68000** is shown in Figure 12-4. It is designed to allow efficient program construction. A large set of data registers encourages the programmer to store intermediate results on the MPU chip itself. A large set of accumulators allows complex addressing variations without the need to access external information. Instructions which operate exclusively on internal registers are much faster than those which must access external data or addressing information.

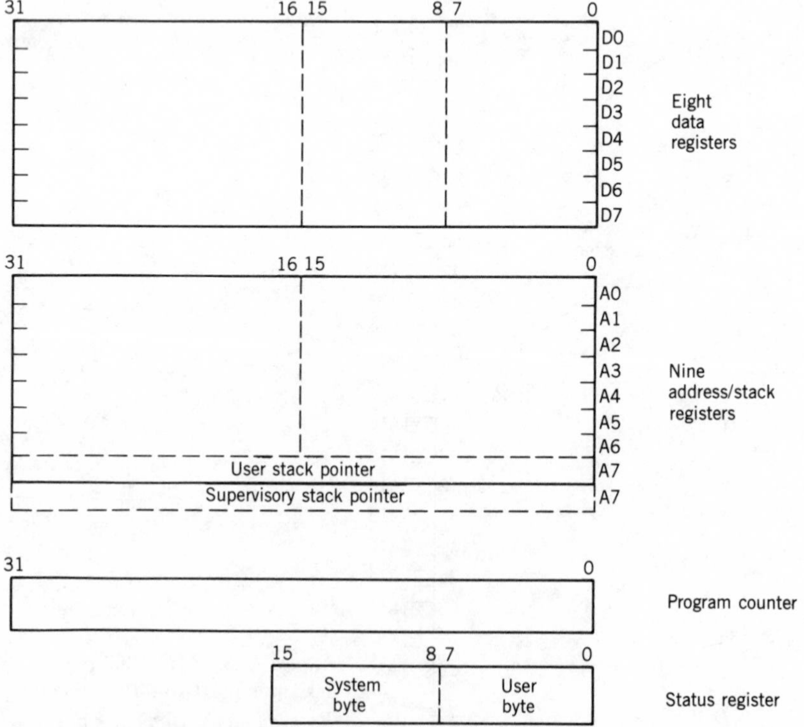

Figure 12-4 **MC68000** programming model. (From the *M68000 Programmer's Reference Manual*, 4th edition, courtesy of Motorola, Inc.)

There are eight data registers and eight address registers on the **MC68000** which are available to the programmer. Actually, there are nine address registers in the MPU; address register A7 is the *user stack pointer* and address register (A7)′ is the *supervisory stack pointer* that is available only to supervisory programs. The supervisory state programs are covered in section 12-6 of this chapter.

In addition to the eight data registers and eight address registers, there is a program counter and a status register. With the exception of the status register, each internal register is 32 bits wide. In the case of the program counter, bits 24–31 are unused when accessing instruction locations. The status register is 16 bits wide, with 6 unused bits.

12-2.1 Data Registers

The general form of a **68000** instruction is operation, source, destination. The data registers are generally used as operands in logical and arithmetic operations and as temporary storage for the results of those operations. Data registers provide the same function as accumulators in more primitive MPU architectures. For example,

```
ADD D1,D3
```

will add the contents of data register 1 and data register 3 and place the results in data register 3. The data register also may be used as an address modifier or index register in certain addressing modes. For example,

```
MOVE (A3),(D3,A4)
```

means move the data contained in the location pointed to by register A3 to the location pointed to by register A4 plus the contents of register D3. Here data register D3 functions as an index register.

12-2.2 Address Registers

The address registers are general-purpose registers which can be used to generate addresses in several different ways. Address registers can be thought of as pointers to memory locations and, depending on the addressing mode, can be modified during execution of an instruction. For example, the **MC68000** allows predecrement and postincrement of address registers.

12-2.3 Status Registers

The status register, shown in Figure 12-5, is divided into two bytes. The upper byte is called the *system byte*. It contains bits which control the operation of the processor. When the *trace mode bit* is set, the processor will trap at the completion of every instruction to the trace trap vector location (see section 12-6). Once there it will execute a routine provided by the user. Trace mode is often used in single-step operation and a typical routine will print out the register contents.

The *supervisor status bit* indicates whether a program is running in the supervisor or the user state. The differences between the user and supervisory states

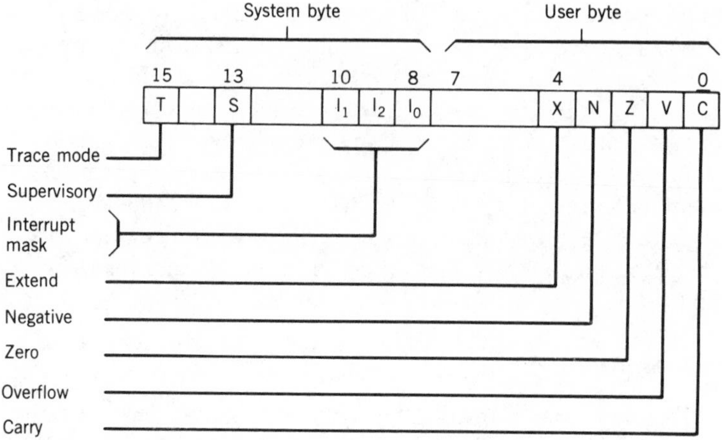

Figure 12-5 Status register. (From the *M68000 Programmer's Reference Manual*, 4th Edition, courtesy of Motorola, Inc.)

is discussed in section 12-6. The three *interrupt mask bits* are decoded as a binary value which will mask all interrupts up to and including the level indicated by that value. For example, 011 will mask all interrupt levels from 0 through 3.

The low-order byte of the status register is called the *user byte* or *condition code register*. It contains the *flags* which indicate the results of an instruction. For example, an instruction which creates a zero result will cause the Z bit to be set. The instruction set summary indicates how the condition code register is set for each instruction.

12-3 ADDRESSING TYPES

Memory is logically addressed in 8-bit bytes, 16-bit words, or 32-bit-long words. The **MC68000** requires that word and long-word data be aligned on even byte boundaries. There are six basic addressing types that include 14 modes. These six types are:

1 **Register direct.** The register itself (one of the data or address registers) is the address. The instruction ADD D1, D3 is an example of the register direct mode; only registers, not memory operands, are involved in the instruction.

2 **Register indirect.** The address of a memory operand is contained in one of the address registers. This is similar to the operation of the H and L registers in the Intel **8080/85**.

3 **Absolute.** The byte(s) following the instruction contains the address of the data.

4 **Immediate.** The byte(s) following the instruction contains the data or operand to be used in the instruction. Note that both absolute and immediate instructions require additional bytes within the program to specify the address or data.

5 **Program counter relative.** The address is specified by an offset that is added to the program counter. This mode is typically used with JUMP and BRANCH instructions.

6 **Implied.** Implied instructions need only one address, not both a source and destination. SHIFT or NEGATE instructions are implied instructions. The address can be a register or in memory.

Included in the register indirect mode is the capability to do postincrementing, predecrementing, offsetting, and indexing. Program counter relative mode can also be modified by indexing and offsetting.

Table 12-1 summarizes the addressing modes and the assembler syntax. Not all addressing modes apply to all instructions. To determine what addressing modes may be applied to a specific instruction, it is necessary to know which of the following general addressing categories are allowed:

Data. If an effective address mode may be used to refer to *data operands* (the contents of a data register), it is considered a data addressing effective address mode.

Memory. If an effective address mode may be used to refer to *memory operands*, it is considered a memory addressing effective address mode.

Alterable. If an address mode may be used to refer to alterable (writeable) operands, it is considered to be an alterable addressing effective address mode. All addressing modes that do not involve the PC are alterable.

Control. If an effective address mode may be used to refer to memory operands without an associated size, it is considered a control addressing effective address mode. For example, the JMP instruction uses the control addressing modes, meaning those modes where the effective address is a memory location. The JMP instruction does not perform postincrement or predecrement. The allowed addressing modes are consistent with the nature of the instruction. The program should be allowed to jump to a location, but not to a register.

In Table 12-1, the addressing modes which fall into each of these categories are defined with an "X" in the appropriate column. To determine the allowed addressing mode for a specific instruction, determine the addressing category from the instruction set summary (Tables 12-2 through 12-9). Then look up the allowed addressing modes in Table 12-1.

EXAMPLE 12-1 What address modes can be used with the instruction:

NEGX (Create the 2s complement negative of a value with the signbit extended)

Solution This instruction appears in Table 12-4 and the allowable addressing modes are "data alterable." This means that those addressing modes in Table 12-1 which have an "X" in both the *data* and the *alterable* columns are allowed.

Looking at Table 12-1 we can see that the NEG X instruction can take all addressing modes except ADDRESS REGISTER DIRECT, IMMEDIATE, and program counter. This allows the user to negate data registers and memory operands.

Note: Text continues on page 492.

Table 12-1 **Addressing modes**

Addressing mode	*Mode*	*Register*	*Addressing categories*				*Assembler syntax*
			Data	*Memory*	*Control*	*Alterable*	
Data register direct	000	reg. no.	X	—	—	X	Dn
Address register direct	001	reg. no.	—	—	—	X	An
Address register indirect	010	reg. no.	X	X	X	X	(An)
Address register indirect with postincrement	011	reg. no.	X	X	—	X	(An)+
Address register indirect with predecrement	100	reg. no.	X	X	—	X	−(An)
Address register indirect with displacement	101	reg. no.	X	X	X	X	d(An)
Address register indirect with index	110	reg. no.	X	X	X	X	d(An, ix)
Absolute short	111	000	X	X	X	X	xxx.W
Absolute long	111	001	X	X	X	X	xxx.L
Program counter with displacement	111	010	X	X	X	—	d(PC)
Program counter with index	111	011	X	X	X	—	d(PC, ix)
Immediate	111	100	X	X	—	—	xxx

Table 12-2 **Data movement instructions**

Instruction	*Operand size*	*Operation*	*Notation*	*Allowable effective address modes*
MOVE	8,16,32	(SOURCE) → DESTINATION	MOVE ⟨ea⟩, ⟨ea⟩	SOURCE ALL DEST DATA ALTERABLE
MOVE from SR	16	SR → DESTINATION	MOVE SR, ⟨ea⟩	DATA ALTERABLE
MOVE to CC	16	(SOURCE) → CCR	MOVE ⟨ea⟩, CCR	DATA
MOVE to SR	16	(SOURCE) → SR	MOVE ⟨ea⟩, SR	DATA
MOVE USP	32	USP → An or An → USP	MOVE USP, An MOVE An, USP	—
MOVEA	16,32	(SOURCE) → REGISTERS	MOVEA ⟨ea⟩, An	ALL
MOVEM	16,32	REGISTERS → DESTINATION (SOURCE) → REGISTERS	MOVEM REGISTER LIST ⟨ea⟩	ALTERABLE CONTROL AND PREDECREMENT
			MOVEM ⟨ea⟩ REGISTER LIST	CONTROL AND POST INCREMENT
MOVEP	16,32	(SOURCE) → DESTINATION	MOVEP Dx, d(Ay) MOVEP d(Ay), Dx	—
MOVEQ	32	IMMEDIATE DATA → DESTINATION	MOVEQ # data, Dn	—
EXG	32	Rx ↔ Ry	EXG Rx,Ry	—
SWAP	16	Dnhw ↔ Dnhw	SWAP Dn	—

Table 12.3 **Logic instructions**

Instruction	*Operand size*	*Operation*	*Notation*	*Allowable effective address modes*
AND	8,16,32	(SOURCE) ∧ (DESTINATION) → DESTINATION	AND ⟨ea⟩, Dn	DATA
			AND Dn, ⟨ea⟩	ALTERABLE MEMORY
ANDI	8,16,32	IMMEDIATE DATA ∧ (DESTINATION) → DESTINATION	ANDI # ⟨data⟩, ⟨ea⟩	DATA ALTERABLE OR [a]STATUS REGISTER
EOR	8,16,32	(SOURCE) ⊕ (DESTINATION) → DESTINATION	EOR Dn, ⟨ea⟩	DATA ALTERABLE
EORI	8,16,32	IMMEDIATE DATA ⊕ (DESTINATION) → DESTINATION	EOR1 # ⟨data⟩, ⟨ea⟩	DATA ALTERABLE OR [a]STATUS REGISTER
NOT	8,16,32	$\overline{\text{(DESTINATION)}}$ → DESTINATION	NOT ⟨ea⟩	DATA ALTERABLE
OR	8,16,32	(SOURCE) ∨ (DESTINATION) → DESTINATION	OR DN, ⟨ea⟩	ALTERABLE MEMORY
			OR ⟨ea⟩, Dn	DATA
ORI	8,16,32	IMMEDIATE DATA ∨ (DESTINATION) → DESTINATION	ORI # ⟨data⟩, ⟨ea⟩	DATA ALTERABLE OR [a]STATUS REGISTER

[a] *Source: M68000 Programmer's Reference Manual*, 4th Edition, courtesy of Motorola, Inc.

Table 12-4 **Integer arithmetic instructions**

Instruction	*Operand size*	*Operation*	*Notation*	*Allowable effective address modes*
ADD	8,16,32	(DESTINATION) + (SOURCE) → DESTINATION	ADD Dn, ⟨ea⟩	ALTERABLE MEMORY
			ADD ⟨ea⟩, Dn	ALL
ADDA	16,32	(DESTINATION) + (SOURCE) → DESTINATION	ADD ⟨ea⟩, An	ALL
ADDI	8,16,32	(DESTINATION) + IMMEDIATE DATA → DESTINATION	ADDI # ⟨data⟩, ⟨ea⟩	DATA ALTERABLE
ADDQ	8,16,32	(DESTINATION) + IMMEDIATE DATA → DESTINATION	ADDQ # ⟨data⟩, ⟨ea⟩	ALTERABLE
ADDX	8,16,32	(DESTINATION) + (SOURCE) + X → DESTINATION	ADDX Dy, Dx ADDX −(Ay), −(Ax)	— —
SUB	8,16,32	(DESTINATION) − (SOURCE) → DESTINATION	SUB Dn, ⟨ea⟩	ALTERABLE MEMORY
			SUB ⟨ea⟩, Dn	ALL
SUBA	16,32	(DESTINATION) − (SOURCE) → DESTINATION	SUBA ⟨ea⟩, An	ALL
SUBI	8,16,32	(DESTINATION) − IMMEDIATE DATA → DESTINATION	SUBI # ⟨data⟩, ⟨ea⟩	DATA ALTERABLE
SUBQ	8,16,32	(DESTINATION) − IMMEDIATE DATA → DESTINATION	SUBQ # ⟨data⟩, ⟨ea⟩	ALTERABLE
SUBX	8,16,32	(DESTINATION) − (SOURCE) − X → DESTINATION	SUBX Dy, Dx SUBX −(Ay), −(Ax)	—

Table 12-4 (Continued)

Instruction	*Operand size*	*Operation*	*Notation*	*Allowable effective address modes*
CMP	8,16,32	(OPERAND2) – (OPERAND1)	CMP ⟨ea⟩, Dn	ALL
CMPA	16,32	(OPERAND2) – (OPERAND1)	CMPA ⟨ea⟩, An	ALL
CMPI	8,16,32	(OPERAND) – IMMEDIATE DATA	CMPI # ⟨data⟩,⟨ea⟩	DATA ALTERABLE
CMPM	8,16,32	(OPERAND2) – (OPERAND1)	CMPM (Ay) +,(Ax) +	
TST	8,16,32	(DESTINATION) – 0 (DESTINATION) TESTED → CC	TST ⟨ea⟩	DATA ALTERABLE
EXT	16,32	(DESTINATION) Sign-EXTENDED → DESTINATION	EXT Dn	
MULS	16	(SOURCE) × (DESTINATION) → DESTINATION	MULS ⟨ea⟩, Dn	DATA
MULU	16	(SOURCE) × (DESTINATION) → DESTINATION	MULU ⟨ea⟩, Dn	DATA
NEG	8,16,32	0 – (DESTINATION) → DESTINATION	NEG ⟨ea⟩	DATA ALTERABLE
NEGX	8,16,32	0 – (DESTINATION) – X → DESTINATION	NEGX ⟨ea⟩	DATA ALTERABLE
CLR	8,16,32	0 → DESTINATION	CLR ⟨ea⟩	DATA ALTERABLE
DIVS	16	(DESTINATION) + (SOURCE) → DESTINATION	DIVS ⟨ea⟩, Dn	DATA
DIVU	16	(DESTINATION) + (SOURCE) → DESTINATION	DIVU ⟨ea⟩, Dn	DATA

Table 12-5 BCD operations

Instruction	*Operand size*	*Operation*	*Notation*	*Allowable effective address modes*
ABCD	8	$(\text{SOURCE})_{10} + (\text{DESTINATION})_{10} + X \rightarrow$ DESTINATION	ABCD Dy, Dx ABCD −(Ay), −(Ax)	—
NBCD	8	$0 - (\text{DESTINATION})_{10} - X \rightarrow$ DESTINATION	NBCD ⟨ea⟩	DATA ALTERABLE
SBCD	8	$(\text{DESTINATION})_{10} - (\text{SOURCE})_{10} - X \rightarrow$ DESTINATION	SBCD Dy, Dx SBCD −(Ay), −(Ax)	—

Table 12-6 Bit manipulation instructions

Instruction	*Operand size*[a]	*Operation*	*Notation*	*Allowable effective address modes*
BCHG	8,32	~(⟨bit number⟩ OF Destination) → Z ~(⟨bit number⟩ OF Destination) → ⟨bit number⟩ OF Destination	BCHG Dn, ⟨ea⟩ BCHG # ⟨data⟩, ⟨ea⟩	DATA ALTERABLE
BCLR	8,32	~(⟨bit number⟩ OF Destination) → Z 0 → ⟨bit number⟩ OF Destination	BCLR Dn, ⟨ea⟩ BCLR # ⟨data⟩, ⟨ea⟩	DATA ALTERABLE
BSET	8,32	~(⟨bit number⟩ OF Destination) → Z; 1 → ⟨bit number⟩ OF Destination	BSET Dn, ⟨ea⟩ BSET # ⟨data⟩ ⟨ea⟩	DATA ALTERABLE
BTST	8,32	~(⟨bit number⟩ OF Destination) → Z	BTST ⟨Dn⟩, ⟨ea⟩ BTST # ⟨data⟩, ⟨ea⟩	DATA

[a] For memory operation, the data size is byte. For data reg. operation, the data size is long word.

Table 12-7 Shift and Rotate instructions

Instruction	Operand size	Operation	Notation	Allowable effective address modes
ASL ASR	8,16,32	ASL: C, X, OPERATION, 0	ASd Dx, Dy	—
			ASd # ⟨data⟩, Dy	—
	16	ASR: OPERAND, C, X	ASd ⟨ea⟩	MEMORY ALTERABLE
LSL LSR	8,16,32	LSL: C, X, OPERAND, 0	LSd Dx, Dy	—
			LSd # ⟨data⟩, Dy	—
	16	LSR: 0, OPERAND, C, X	LSd ⟨ea⟩	MEMORY ALTERABLE
ROL ROR	8,16,32	ROL: C, OPERAND	ROd Dx, Dy	—
			ROd # ⟨data⟩, Dy	—
	16	ROR: OPERAND, C	ROd ⟨ea⟩	MEMORY ALTERABLE
ROXL ROXR	8,16,32	ROXL: C, X, OPERAND	ROXd Dx, Dy	—
			ROXd # ⟨data⟩, Dy	—
	16	ROXR: OPERAND, C, X	ROXd ⟨ea⟩	MEMORY ALTERABLE

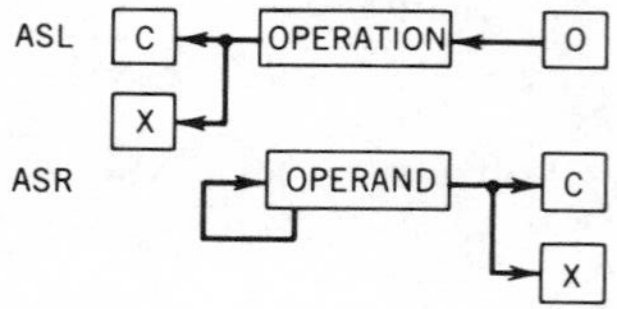

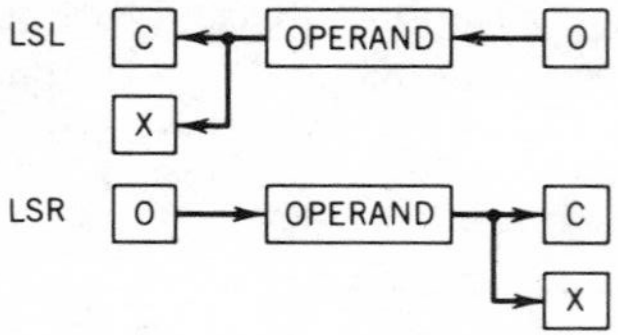

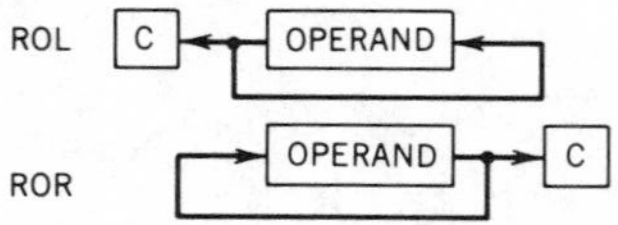

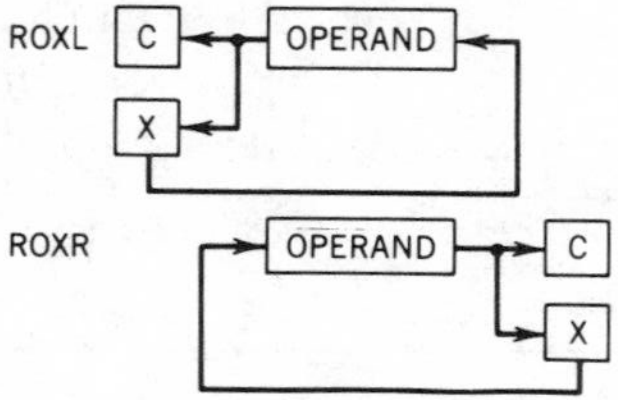

Table 12-8 **Program control instructions**

Instruction	*Operand size*	*Operation*	*Notation*	*Allowable effective address modes*
Bcc	8,16	If cc then PC + d → PC	Bcc ⟨label⟩	—
BRA	8,16	PC + d → PC	BRA ⟨label⟩	—
BSR	8,16	PC → −(SP); PC + d → PC	BSR ⟨label⟩	—
JMP	—	DESTINATION → PC	JMP ⟨ea⟩	CONTROL
JSR	—	PC → −(SP); DESTINATION → PC	JSR ⟨ea⟩	CONTROL
NOP	—	PC + 2 → PC	NOP	—
RESET	—	RESET EXTERNAL DEVICES	RESET	—
RTE	—	(SP)+ → SR; (SP)+ → PC	RTE	—
RTR	—	(SP)+ → CC; (SP)+ → PC	RTR	—
RTS	—	(SP)+ → PC	RTS	—
STOP	—	STOP PROGRAM EXECUTION	STOP # ⟨data⟩	—
TRAP	—	PC → −(SSP); SR → −(SSP): (VECTOR) → PC	TRAP ⟨VECTOR⟩	—
TRAPV	—	If V then TRAP	TRAPV	—

Table 12-9 **Special instructions**

Instruction	*Operand size*	*Operation*	*Notation*	*Allowable address category*
Scc	8	IF cc THEN 1's → DEST. ELSE 0's → DESTINATION	Scc ⟨ea⟩	DATA ALTERABLE
DBcc[a]	16	IF cc THEN Dn − 1 → Dn; IF Dn ≠ −1 THEN PC + d → PC	DBcc Dn, LABEL	—
CHK	16	IF Dn IS LESS THAN 0 OR GREATER THAN ⟨ea⟩ THEN EXCEPTION	CHK ⟨ea⟩, Dn	DATA
LINK	—	An → −(SP); SP → An; SP + d → SP	LINK An, # (disp.)	—
UNLK	—	An → SP; (SP) + →An	UNLK An	—
TAS	8	(DESTINATION) TESTED → CC 1 → DESTINATION AT BIT 7	TAS ⟨ea⟩	DATA ALTERABLE

Special instructions description

S_{CC} Set according to condition is used to save the result of a logical condition by setting a byte to true (all 1s). For example:

```
SMI  LOC1
```

means SET ON MINUS and would set all bits in LOC1 to 1 if the N bit in the condition code register is 1.

D_{BCC} Decrement and branch is a looping instruction that causes a branch to occur until the logical condition occurs. For example:

```
DBMI D1, LOC1
```

will branch *until* a minus condition occurs.

CHK	The compare against bounds instruction creates an exception if a value in a data register is zero or greater than a specified value.

```
CHK $22555,D0
```

would generate an exception if the value in D0 exceeds $22555. This might be used in Fortran array processing to guarantee that operating system intervention occurs if the program attempts to access an area outside of the array boundary.

LINK	The LINK instruction pushes the contents of an address register onto the stack and the new stack pointer value is placed in the register. The stack pointer is adjusted by a specified new displacement. This effectively allocates a temporary block of memory on the stack.
UNLK	Reverses the processes of the LINK instruction, effectively bringing the stack back to the status prior to the previous link instruction.
TAS	The test and set instruction sets the N and Z bit of the condition code register based on the current value of the operand. The high-order bit of the operand is set, regardless of the result of the instruction. This instruction is indivisible, meaning that no other external device on the MPU bus (such as a DMA controller) can change the operand once this instruction starts. TAS is used frequently to send synchronization signals between processors sharing the same bus.

Tables 12-2 through 12-9 list the **MC68000** instruction set. In general, the addressing mode is independent of the data type and, in cases where it makes sense (integers, logicals, and addresses), the size of the operand may be specified independent of the operation. Sources for operands may be either registers or memory locations, and the destinations may be registers or memory locations. Operations can be specified as register to register, register to memory, memory to register, or memory to memory.

Since not every 16-bit code is recognized as a valid instruction in the **MC68000**, an invalid instruction trap is implemented. Whenever an undefined Op code is encountered in the instruction stream, a trap will occur to a routine provided by the user. This routine allows a method of recovering from improperly coded programs.

A more detailed discussion of the instruction set is given in the *16-Bit Microprocessor Programmer's Reference Manual* published by Motorola (see References). Figure 12-7 is a page of this manual that defines the ADD instruction. It consists of four major parts:

1 a description of the instruction;

2 the effect of the instruction on the condition codes or flags;

3 the format of the instruction word;

4 definitions of the fields in the instruction format.

EXAMPLE 12-2 What does the instruction D019 do?

Solution The instruction is disassembled as shown in Figure 12-6. Bits 12–15 are a hexadecimal D, which indicates an ADD instruction. Bits 9–11 determine that data register 0 is the data register involved in this instruction. The Op mode is also 0. This indicates:

1 A byte transfer is the data length.

2 Register 0 is one of the operands and the destination, or where the results will reside.

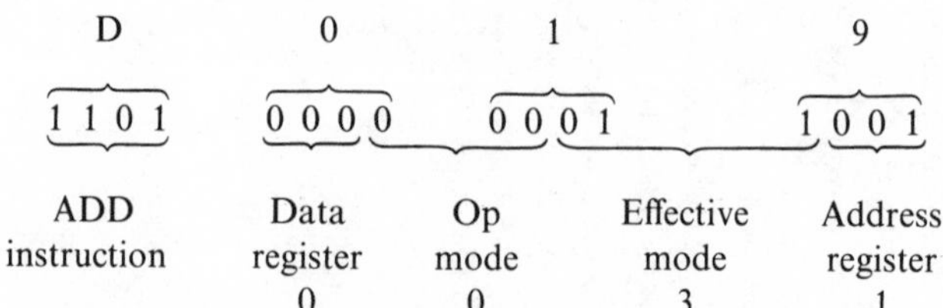

Figure 12-6 Disassembling the instruction D019. (From the *M68000 Programmer's Reference Manual*, 4th Edition, courtesy of Motorola Inc.)

Bits 0–5 determine the address of the other operand. The operand mode is 011 or $(An)^+$ and the address register involved is address register 1.

The effect of this instruction is to ADD the number in data register 0 to the number in the memory location pointed to by address register 1. The results go to data register 0. Also, the mode is auto incrementing so that address register 1 is incremented at the end of the instruction.

Operation: (Source) + (destination) → destination

Assembler Syntax: ADD ⟨ea⟩, Dn
ADD, Dn, ⟨ea⟩

Attributes: Size = (byte, word, long)

Description: Add the source operand to the destination operand, and store the result in the destination location. The size of the operation may be specified to be byte, word, or long. The mode of the instruction indicates which operand is the source and which is the destination as well as the operand size.

Condition Codes:

X	N	Z	V	C
*	*	*	*	*

N Set if the result is negative. Cleared otherwise.
Z Set if the result is zero. Cleared otherwise.
V Set if an overflow is generated. Cleared otherwise.
C Set if a carry is generated. Cleared otherwise.
X Set the same as the carry bit.

Instruction Format:

15	14	13	12	11 10 9	8 7 6	5 4 3	2 1 0
1	1	0	1	Register	Op-mode	Effective mode	Address register

Instruction Fields:

Register field—Specifies any of the eight data registers.
Op-mode field—

Byte	**Word**	**Long**	**Operation**
000	001	010	(⟨Dn⟩) + (⟨ea⟩) → ⟨Dn⟩
100	101	110	(⟨ea⟩) + (⟨Dn⟩) → ⟨ea⟩

Effective Address field—Determines addressing mode:

If the location specified is a source operand, then all addressing modes are allowed as shown:

Addressing mode	*Mode*	*Register*	*Addressing mode*	*Mode*	*Register*
Dn	000	Register number	d(An, Xi)	110	Register number
An[a]	001	Register number	Abs.W	111	000
(An)	010	Register number	Abs.L	111	001
(An)+	011	Register number	d(PC)	111	010
−(An)	100	Register number	d(PC, Xi)	111	011
d(An)	101	Register number	Imm	111	100

[a] Word and long only.

Figure 12-7 The ADD instruction. (From the *M68000 Programmer's Reference Manual*, 4th Edition, courtesy of Motorola, Inc.)

Operation: (Source) → destination

Assembler
Syntax: Move <ea>, <ea>

Attributes: Size = (byte, word, long)

Description: Move the content of the source to the destination location. The data is examined as it is moved, and the condition codes set accordingly. The size of the operation may be specified to be byte, word, or long.

Condition Codes:

X	N	Z	V	C
—	*	*	0	0

N Set if the result is negative. Cleared otherwise.
Z Set if the result is zero. Cleared otherwise.
V Always cleared.
C Always cleared.
X Not affected.

Instruction Format:

15	14	13 12	11 10 9	8 7 6	5 4 3	2 1 0
			Destination		Source	
0	0	Size	Register	Mode	Mode	Register

Instruction Fields:

Size field—specifies the size of the operand to be moved:
01—byte operation.
11—word operation.
10—long operation.

Destination effective address field—specifies the destination location. Only data alterable addressing modes are allowed as shown:

Addressing mode	*Mode*	*Register*	*Addressing mode*	*Mode*	*Register*
Dn	000	Register number	d(An, Xi)	110	Register number
An	—	—	Abs.W	111	000
(An)	010	Register number	Abs.L	111	001
(An)+	011	Register number	d(PC)	—	—
−(An)	100	Register number	d(PC, Xi)	—	—
d(An)	101	Register number	Imm	—	—

Source effective address field—specifies the source operand. All addressing modes are allowed as shown:

Addressing mode	*Mode*	*Register*
Dn	000	Register number
An[a]	001	Register number
(An)	010	Register number
(An)+	011	Register number
−(An)	100	Register number
d(An)	101	Register number
d(An, Xi)	110	Register number
Abs.W	111	000
Abs.L	111	001
d(PC)	111	010
d(PC, Xi)	111	011
Imm	111	100

[a] For byte size operation, address register direct is not allowed.

Notes: 1 MOVEA is used when the destination is an address register. Most assemblers automatically make this distinction.
2 MOVEQ can also be used for certain operations on data registers.

Figure 12-8 The MOVE instruction. (From the *M68000 Programmer's Reference Manual*, 4th Edition, courtesy of Motorola, Inc.)

Another common instruction format is shown in the MOVE instruction of Figure 12-8. The instruction contains an Op code field that declares it to be a MOVE instruction and specifies the size of the operand. It then has a 6-bit field to define the destination and another 6-bit field to define the source.

12-3.1 Assemblers

Much of the labor in Example 12-2 is eliminated by using an assembler. **MC68000** assemblers are available from Motorola and many other software vendors. In addition to making programming easier, they will detect and flag invalid instructions and addressing modes. It is recommended that the programmer use one of these assemblers to ensure the correctness of the code before attempting execution in the processor itself.

12-4 SPECIAL INSTRUCTIONS

The special instructions are given in Table 12-9. They are used to support modern programming techniques. The following are descriptions of **MC68000** instructions that support these techniques.

Array Processing The CHECK instruction can compare a previously calculated array index contained in a data register against zero and a limit addressed by the instruction. A trap will occur if the index being tested is out of bounds of the array.

Limited Precision Arithmetic The TRAP ON OVERFLOW instruction will cause a trap if the preceding operations resulted in the overflow condition code being SET. This allows for efficient testing of arithmetic results.

Looping The TEST CONDITION, DECREMENT BRANCH instruction is a restricted form of the FOR-LOOP construct, and is implemented in a single instruction that tests for the termination condition of the loop which, if not found, decrements the counter. When the counter reaches zero, this terminates the looping process.

Boolean-Expression Evaluation The SET ACCORDING TO CONDITION instruction assigns a true or false value to a Boolean variable on the same condition used by the CONDITIONAL BRANCH instruction. This instruction helps implement Boolean-expression evaluations by avoiding extra conditional branches.

EXAMPLE 12-3 The following "if-then-else" statement might be found in a Pascal program:

```
If AVAL < BVAL and BVAL ≥ CVAL
then PROC1
else PROC2;
```

How could it be coded in machine language?

Solution Assuming AVAL, BVAL and CVAL are 2s complement integers, the Boolean expression AVAL < BVAL and BVAL ⩾ CVAL might be compiled in machine language.

```
CMP AVAL,BVAL          Compare.
SLT BOOL1              Set BOOL1 if AVAL < BVAL.
COMP BVAL,CVAL
SGE BOOL2              Set BOOL2 if BVAL ⩾ CVAL.
AND B BOOL1,BOOL2
BNE PROC1              Branch if result nonzero.
BRA PROC2              Otherwise go to PROC2.
```

12-5 STACKS AND PROCEDURE CALLS

The **MC68000** uses a stack to build the nested environment of *called procedures.* Called procedures, unlike subroutines, create their own isolated operating environment. In Pascal, all variable data is contained on the stack (with one small exception called the "heap," which is not relevant to this example). The variable data on the stack is allocated when the procedure begins execution and is released when the procedure completes execution. This feature allows a procedure to call itself and is called *recursion.* When a procedure calls itself, it simply creates a new set of variables on the stack. When it completes, it returns to the old set of variables with their old values. The frame pointer points to the area on the stack that is active during the current execution of a procedure.

A procedure can then "call" itself and a whole new operating environment is created by simply moving the frame pointer a predefined number of locations. The procedure call in the **68000** uses only the stack and is completely reentrant. The instructions supporting procedure calls are as follows.

The MOVE and the PUSH EFFECTIVE ADDRESS (PEA) instructions can be used to push parameter values or addresses on the stack.

The JUMP TO SUBROUTINE instruction pushes the return address on the stack and jumps the processor to the procedure entry point.

The LINK instruction saves the old contents of the frame pointer (an address register) on the stack, points the frame pointer to the new top of stack, and subtracts the number of bytes of local storage required by the procedure from the stack pointer. This instruction establishes the local storage for the called procedure and a frame pointer for indexing of local variables and parameters. Figure 12-9 shows the action of the LINK and UNLINK instructions.

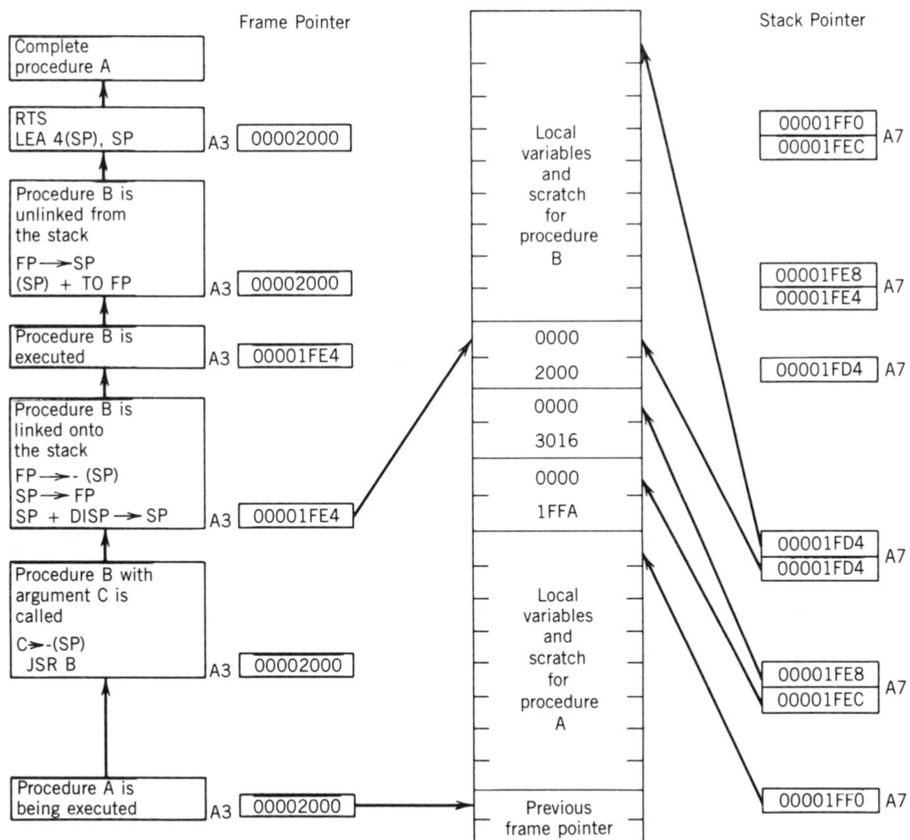

Figure 12-9 **MC68000** link and unlink. (From the MC68000 Training Note, courtesy of Motorola, Inc.)

The MOVE MULTIPLE REGISTERS instruction, MOVEM (see Table 12-2), saves a specified number of registers on the stack (or anywhere in memory). This is a single instruction, and the registers to be saved are indicated by setting their corresponding bit in the 16-bit data field of the instruction.

To restore the processor to the state prior to the procedure call, a reverse sequence of instructions is used. MOVE MULTIPLE REGISTERS instruction is again used, but this time with the processor as the destination. This is followed by the UNLINK instruction, which reverses the LINK instruction. The RETURN instruction is used to bring the return address from the stack and return to the calling procedure. Finally, the ADD IMMEDIATE instruction, used on the stack pointer, can bring any number of values off the stack.

In the following example, a high-level language procedure "B" (PROCB) is called within procedure "A" (PROCA). The LINK instruction is used to create a block of temporary memory during the execution of "B" and then release the memory via the UNLK instruction.

```
Motorola M68000 ASM Version  1.80 FIX :    0.          .CHAPTER .SA 10/02/84 08:51:07

         00030000                   ORG       $30000
                           *
                           *
                           *
00030000 47F900025000               L:A       $25000,A3
00030006 4FF900024FF0               LEA       $24FF0,SP
                           *
                           *
                           *
0003000C 4E71              PROCA    NOP
0003000E 4E71                       NOP                             THE ACTUAL PROCEDURE CODE
00030010 4E71                       NOP                             WOULD GO HERE
                           *
                           *  WHAT IS A TYPICAL CALLING SEQUENCE FOR
                           *  A PROCEDURE WHICH USES THE STACK FOR TEMPORARY
                           *  VARIABLE MEMORY AND RELEASES THE MEMORY
                           *  WHEN THE PROCEDURE ENDS EXECUTION.
                           *
00030012 486BFFFA                   PEA       -6(A3)                PICK UP THE ADDRESS OF A PARAMETER AND PUT
                           *                                IT ON THE STACK.
                           *
00030016 4EBA0010                   JSR       PROCB(PC)             CALL PROCEDURE PROCB
                           *
0003001A 4FEF0004                   LEA       4(SP),SP              REMOVE THE PARAMETER ADDRESS FROM THE STACK.
0003001E 4E71                       NOP
00030020 4E71                       NOP                             USER CODE WOULD NORMALLY REPLACE THE NOP
00030022 4E71                       NOP
00030024 4E5B                       UNLK      A3                    THIS PROCEDURE WAS CALLED FROM SOMEWHERE
                           *                                ELSE SO THIS WILL RELEASE THE TEMPORARY MEMORY
                           *
00030026 4E75                       RTS                             RETURN TO THE CALLING LOCATION FROM PROCA
                           *
                           *    END OF PROCA
                           *
                           *    BEGINNING OF PROCB
                           *
00030028 4E53FFF0          PROCB    LINK      A3,#-$10              SET ASIDE 10(HEX) WORDS ON THE STACK AND
                           *                                USE A3 TO SAVE THE PREVIOUS STACK CONTENTS
                           *                                FOR RESTORATION WHEN PROCB FINISHES.
0003002C 4E71                       NOP
0003002E 4E71                       NOP                             PROCB CODE GOES HERE
00030030 4E71                       NOP
                           *
                           *
00030032 3F420003                   MOVE      D2,3(SP)              THIS IS ONE WAY TO USE THE TEMPORARY
                           *                                STORAGE ON THE STACK.  SAVE THE CONTENTS OF
                           *                                D2 IN TEMPORARY LOCATION +3
                           *
```

```
    00030036 4E5B                UNLK    A3                  RESTORE THE STACK AND RELEASE THE TEMPORARY
                         *                               MEMORY LOCATIONS
                         *
    00030038 4E75                RTS                         END OF PROCB
                         *
                                 END

****** TOTAL ERRORS      0--
****** TOTAL WARNINGS    0--

Motorola M68000 ASM Version  1.80 FIX :    0.          .CHAPTER .SA 10/02/84 08:51:07


SYMBOL TABLE LISTING

SYMBOL NAME      SECT    VALUE         SYMBOL NAME      SECT    VALUE

PROCA                   0003000C       PROCB                   00030028
```

The area where the actual procedure code would go is indicated by NOP instructions.

12-6 TRAPS AND ERROR RECOVERY

Another major architectural feature of the **MC68000** is the extensive trap and error recovery capability. Table 12-10 provides a listing of all the traps and their vector addresses in memory. Each individual trap may have its own error recovery routine. This extensive repertoire of traps makes the **MC68000** one of the most powerful 16-bit processors in terms of flexibility and system integrity in both hardware and software.

EXAMPLE 12-4 What happens in a **68000** if an attempt is made to divide by zero?

Solution Table 12-10 shows that a zero divide causes a TRAP or JUMP to location 14. The user can write a routine for handling this situation. Location 14 should contain the starting address of this routine.

12-6.1 User and Supervisory States

The **MC68000** operates in one of two states—*user* or *supervisor*. In the supervisor state, the complete resources of the processor are available. In the user state, certain instructions such as STOP and RESET, as well as those that attempt to modify the supervisor portions of the control word, are not allowed. An attempt to execute these instructions while in the user state will cause a trap to the supervisor state. When this occurs, the routine address vector will indicate that a privilege violation has taken place. All exceptions to processing (illegal instructions, interrupts, illegal addressing, software traps, etc.) will cause the processor to trap and enter the supervisor state of operations. Information about the state of operation of the processor is available external to the processor on the processor status pins.

Table 12-10 **Exception vector assignments**

Vector number(s)	Address Dec	Address hex	Space	Assignment
0	0	000	SP	Reset: Initial SSP[b]
1	4	004	SP	Reset: Initial PC[b]
2	8	008	SD	Bus error
3	12	00C	SD	Address error
4	16	010	SD	Illegal instruction
5	20	014	SD	Zero divide
6	24	018	SD	CHK instruction
7	28	01C	SD	TRAPV instruction
8	32	020	SD	Privilege violation
9	36	024	SD	Trace
10	40	028	SD	Line 1010 emulator
11	44	02C	SD	Line 1111 emulator
12[a]	48	030	SD	(Unassigned, reserved)
13[a]	52	034	SD	(Unassigned, reserved)
14	56	038	SD	Format error[c]
15	60	03C	SD	Uninitialized interrupt vector
16–23[a]	64 95	040 05F	SD	(Unassigned, reserved) —
24	96	060	SD	Spurious interrupt[d]
25	100	064	SD	Level 1 interrupt autovector
26	104	068	SD	Level 2 interrupt autovector
27	108	06C	SD	Level 3 interrupt autovector
28	112	070	SD	Level 4 interrupt autovector
29	116	074	SD	Level 5 interrupt autovector
30	120	078	SD	Level 6 interrupt autovector
31	124	07C	SD	Level 7 interrupt autovector
32–47	128 191	080 08F	SD	TRAP instruction vectors[e]
48–63[a]	192 255	0C0 0FF	SD	(Unassigned, reserved) —
64–255	256 1023	100 3FF	SD	User interrupt vectors —

[a] Vector numbers 12, 13, 16 through 23, and 48 through 63 are reserved for future enhancements by Motorola. No user peripheral devices should be assigned these numbers.
[b] Reset vector (0) requires four words, unlike the other vectors which only require two words, and is located in the supervisor program space.
[c] **MC68010** only. See Return from Exception Section in the MC68010 data sheets. This vector is unassigned, reserved on the **MC68000** and **MC68008**.
[d] The spurious interrupt vector is taken when there is a bus error indication during interrupt processing.
[e] TRAP uses vector numbers 32 + n.

12-7 INTERRUPTS AND I/O

The **MC68000** has a very flexible interrupt structure. There are provisions for seven levels of interrupt priorities. Each level may have any number of interrupt-generating devices connected to it in a daisy-chained manner. Interrupt priority levels are numbered from 1 to 7. Level 7 is the highest priority and nonmaskable. Interrupts are vectored so that software has full control over the placement and execution of interrupt-handling routines. The status register (see Figure 12-5) contains a 3-bit mask which indicates the current processor priority, and interrupts are inhibited for all priority levels less than or equal to the current processor priority. All interrupts are acknowledged at the end of current instruction execution even though they are recognized earlier in the instruction cycle and made *pending*.

12-7.1 Memory-Mapped I/O

The **MC68000** was designed without specific input/output instructions. As with all Motorola μPs, all I/O device registers are addressed as memory locations. This *memory-mapped* I/O gives the programmer both the flexibility and the power of the entire instruction set for manipulating control and data registers in the I/O device. With no special instructions for I/O, the processor is simpler, and the instruction set is less complicated.

12-7.2 Interlocks

Two types of interlocks are provided with the **MC68000** to enable multiprocessor (or a more appropriate term, multiple bus master) operations. The first is a software interlock mechanism which is known as the TEST AND SET instruction. This is a READ-MODIFY-WRITE operation that cannot be interrupted or split by other requests for the processor bus. It can be used to provide communications between processors in a multiple processor environment or to reserve shared resource. It operates on a first come, first served basis.

The other mechanism for resolving bus mastership is the three-wire bus arbitration process supported by the **MC68000** (see section 12-9.3). In this manner all devices can contend for the system data and address buses in a prioritized fashion. The three-wire arbitration technique requires that the master-type devices (processors, direct memory access controllers, etc.) request, grant, and finally acknowledge control of the bus.

12-8 DATA ORGANIZATION

Figure 12-10 is a diagram of an **MC68000** basic system. The system is configured with random access memory (RAM), read-only memory (ROM), **MC68000** Peripheral Controllers, and **MC6800** Peripheral Controllers. To address and move data between these devices and the processor, it is important to understand how the **MC68000** organizes data and addresses memory. Because the **MC68000** utilizes the

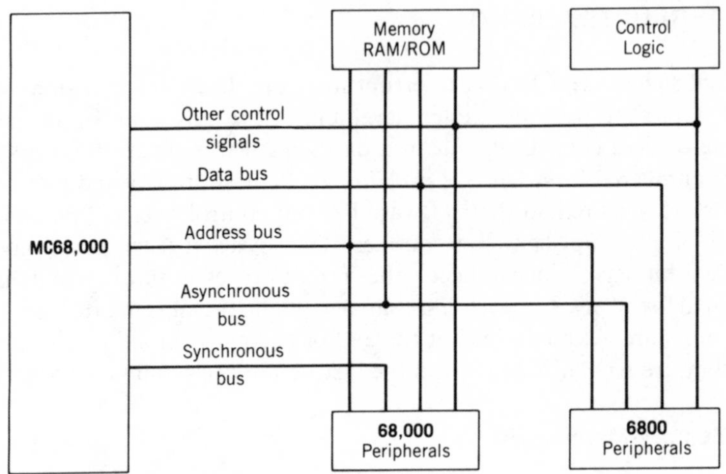

Figure 12-10 **MC68000** basic system. (From the MC68000 Training Notes courtesy of Motorola, Inc.)

technique of memory-mapped I/O, peripheral data and control registers are treated in the same manner as a memory location in addressing.

In bytes, words, or long words, bits are numbered with bit 0 being the least significant bit (LSB). Bytes can be addressed on byte boundaries, but words and long words can be addressed only on even byte boundaries. Several **MC68000** instructions permit the addressing of bit-data within words and long words. Figure 12-11 is a representation of a data word as seen by the processor—bit 0 being the LSB and bit 15 being the most significant bit (MSB) of the data word. The least significant word address is represented by N, N + 1, N + 2, N + 3,.... Bits in long words, module 32, are also addressable and follow the rules for addressing long words.

Binary coded decimal (BCD) digits are encoded two to a byte. Figure 12-12 is the representation of BCD character data as seen by the processor. The BCD instructions operate on data two BCD digits (a byte) at a time. BCD0 represents the most significant digit (MSD), followed by BCD1, which is the least significant digit (LSD) in the byte. N + 1 represents the address of the second byte of BCD data. followed by N + 2, N + 3, and so on, which follow the normal **MC68000** byte addressing rules.

Bytes are positioned in memory as in Figure 12-13. Byte 0, the position of the least significant byte, occupies bit positions 8 through 15 of the least significant word

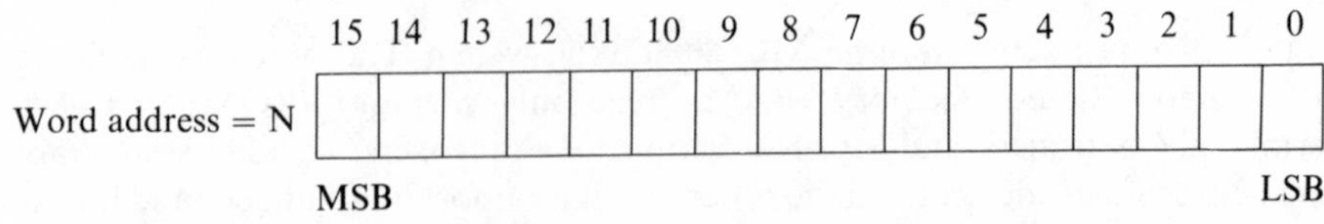

Figure 12-11 **MC68000** bit-numbering convention within a word.

Decimal Data
2 Binary Coded Decimal Digits = 1 Byte

15 14 13 12	11 10 9 8	7 6 5 4	3 2 1 0
MSD BCD 0	BCD 1 LSD	BCD 2	BCD 3
BCD 4	BCD 5	BCD 6	BCD 7

MSD = most significant digit
LSD = least significant digit

Figure 12-12 BCD data organization. (From the *M68000 Programmer's Reference Manual*, 4th Edition, courtesy of Motorola, Inc.)

1 byte = 8 bits

Address	15 … 8	7 … 0	
Address = N[a]	Byte 0	Byte 1	N + 1
N + 2	Byte 2	Byte 3	N + 3

1 word = 16 bits

Address	15 … 0	
Address = N	Word 0	N + 1
N + 2	Word 1	N + 3
N + 4	Word 2	N + 5

1 long word = 32 bits

Address	15 … 0	
Address = N	Long word 0 (H)	N + 1
N + 2	Long word 0 (L)	N + 3
N + 4	Long word 1 (H)	N + 5
N + 6	Long word 1 (L)	N + 7
N + 8	Long word 2 (H)	N + 9
N + 10	Long word 2 (L)	N + 11

[a] N is an even number.

Figure 12-13 Data organization in memory. (From the Motorola MC6840 Data Sheets, reprinted courtesy of Motorola, Inc.)

in a string of bytes. Byte 1, the next most significant byte address, occupies bit position 0 through 7 of the word. It is important to note that the **MC68000** has the capability to access directly bytes in both the read and write modes of operation, properly positioning these bytes in a processor register or memory and peripheral device address locations according to the byte address (even or odd), without going through any intermediate transfer process.

Words are addressed on even byte boundaries. Word 0 would be the lowest-order word, followed by word 1, word 2,... located in memory locations of ascending power, N, N + 2, N + 4,.... Again, bit position 0 is the LSB and bit position 15 is the MSB of the data word.

Long-word data and its organization is also shown in Figure 12-13. Addresses are also treated the same as long word data. Again, long words are positioned on even byte boundaries and occupy two words of memory. If the memory locations for a long word are specified by N and N + 2, the LSB would be bit 0 of N + 2, and the MSB would be bit 15 of N. The long word would be made up essentially of two half-words stored in memory, with the most significant half occupying the next-highest-order word (N + 2).

EXAMPLE 12-5 A long word consists of the hexadecimal digits AABBCCDD. AA is the most significant byte. It is to be placed in locations 100 and 102. How does it appear in memory?

Solution Here N is location 100, so the word would appear as shown in Figure 12-14.

Address	Data
100	A A B B
102	C C D D

Figure 12-14 Positioning a long word in memory.

The rules can be summarized as follows: words and long words must be accessed from an even address (otherwise a trap will occur), and bytes may be accessed from either an odd or even address.

In the **MC68000**'s hardware design, the allowance was made for the direct reading and writing of bytes from and to external devices, including memory. The 16-bit-wide data bus can be thought of as two 8-bit-wide data buses operating in parallel with independent control. Table 12-11 contains the rules of control of the data bus. UDS and LDS are mnemonics for upper and lower data strobes, while D_0–D_{15} represent the data lines for the bus, with D_0 being the least significant bit and D_{15} being the most significant. This is another feature of the flexibility of the **MC68000** and memory-mapped I/O. Independent byte control is also the implementation of error detection and correction circuitry to data movement on the bus.

The **MC68000**'s approach to the memory address space of the processor was to treat the total space as linear without internal segmentation. For users desiring segmentation, this can be provided externally. In this fashion, with a 2^{24} byte

Table 12-11 **MC68000: Memory bus control**

Memory control bus			Memory data bus	
UDS	*LDS*	*R/$\overline{W}$*	*D8–D15*	*D0–D7*
0	0	0	Valid Write data	Valid Write data
0	0	1	Valid Read data	Valid Read data
0	1	0	Valid Write data	*Same as D8–D15
0	1	1	Valid Read data	Don't care
1	0	0	*Same as D0–D7	Valid Write data
1	0	1	Don't care	Valid Read data
1	1	0	Don't care	Don't care
1	1	1	Don't care	Don't care

address space available, a user need not concern himself with trying to fit programs and data into pieces of memory constrained by arbitrary segmentation.

12-9 THE HARDWARE DESIGNER'S VIEW OF THE MC68000

The pin-out for the **68000** is given in Figure 12-3. The function of each pin is described in this section.

The **MC68000** input and output lines can be grouped into eight types in addition to the clock, power supply, and ground. Although only a single +5 V power supply is required, there are two power inputs and two ground pins to ensure a stable power supply and ground plane across the entire die. The eight types of I/O lines are:

Address bus
Data bus
Asynchronous bus control
Bus arbitration control
Interrupt control
System control
MC68000 Peripheral Control
Processor status

12-9.1 The Address Bus

This is a 23-bit bus capable of addressing eight megawords of data. It provides addresses for all bus operation cycles. During interrupt processing, lines A1, A2, and A3 display the current *level* of interrupt being processed. This can be used to select the proper vector when automatic vectoring is not used. In this case, an external circuit would use the data on A1, A2, A3 to select the proper value to present to the processor.

12-9.2 The Data Bus

This is a 16-bit bus which can transfer and accept data in either word or byte length. It is controlled by the signals listed below:

Address strobe ($\overline{\text{AS}}$). Signals that the address bus contains a valid signal.

Read/write (R/W). Determines if data is going out of the **MC68000** (write) or coming into the **MC68000** from some memory-mapped device (read).

Upper and lower data strobe ($\overline{\text{UDS}}$ and $\overline{\text{LDS}}$). Two lines which take the place of the least significant bit on the address bus. This allows individual byte addressing.

Data transfer acknowledge ($\overline{\text{DTACK}}$). An input from external devices which indicates that a data transfer has taken place. The processor is designed as an asynchronous bus device. This means, in general, that every time a bus transfer takes place, the processor will send out an address strobe. When transfer to or from the data bus occurs, the external device or external bus architecture must provide a proceed signal in the form of data transfer acknowledge.

12-9.3 System Control

The following signals control the action of the **68000** in a system:

Bus Arbitration Control This consists of three signals: bus request ($\overline{\text{BR}}$), bus grant ($\overline{\text{BG}}$), and bus grant acknowledge ($\overline{\text{BGACK}}$). These are used to determine which device will be a bus master. This is most frequently used for direct memory access data transfers such as disk input and output. However, it can be used for any peripheral which must periodically gain bus control, including other processors.

Interrupt Control This consists of three input lines (IPL0, IPL1, IPL2) that determine the priority of an interrupt. The interrupt lines can be thought of as a "one-of-eight" decoding scheme. An input of binary 000 means no interrupt present. An input of binary 111 is the highest priority. The **74148** is a TTL part that accepts eight inputs and creates the proper 3-bit binary input for the **MC68000** interrupt control. Note that the inputs are active LOW. Therefore, an electrical input of 111 is actually an input of 000.

When an interrupt occurs, it is made *pending* until the current instruction is finished. It is then necessary to indicate to the processor where the interrupt service routine resides. This is done in one of two ways. *Autovectoring* is the simplest method. Memory locations hex 64 through hex 7C are predefined *autovector locations*. When autovectoring is requested by the external device placing a LOW signal on (asserting) $\overline{\text{VPA}}$ during interrupt processing, the processor goes to the appropriate location in this area of memory and fetches the location of the interrupt service routine, which is prestored as data in these locations. The second method is a *forced vector* generated by the interrupting device. At the appropriate time in the interrupting process, the interrupting device provides a vector number on data lines D0 through D7. The processor translates this number into a memory address in the

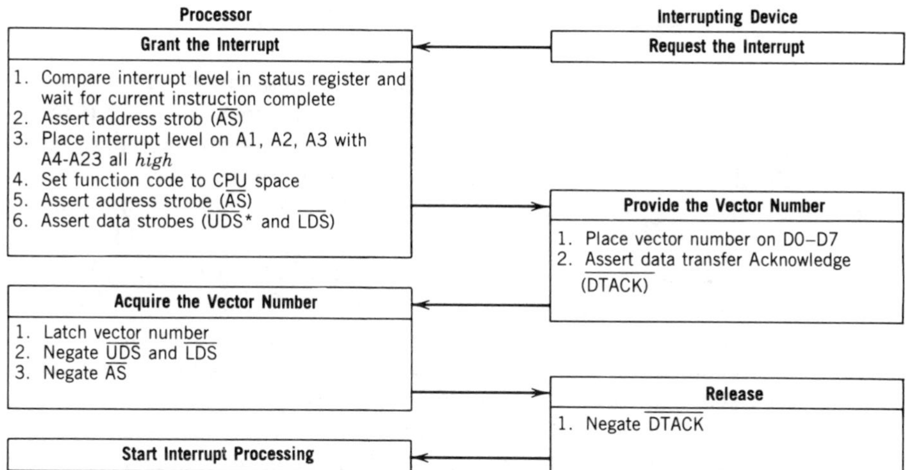

*Although a vector number is 1 byte, both data strobes are asserted due to the microcode used for exception processing. The processor does not recognize anything on data lines D8 through D15 at this time.

Figure 12-15 Vector acquisition flowchart. (From the *M68000 Programmer's Reference Manual*, 4th Edition, courtesy of Motorola, Inc.)

range of hex 100 to hex 3FF, where the predefined addresses of the interrupt service routines are stored.

Figure 12-15 is a flowchart showing the exchange of information between an interrupting peripheral device and the **MC68000**.

12-9.4 Systems Control

These signals are used to reset or halt the processor or to indicate that a bus error has occurred. BUS ERROR and HALT are both bidirectional signals. The BUS ERROR signal is provided so that the processor can respond to conditions where the proper handshake signals do not occur. The processor has two options when a BUS ERROR occurs; it either initiates a BUS ERROR exception or retries the bus operation. The exact response is determined by external circuitry and is a system designer's option.

Synchronous Peripheral Control These three signals (VPA, VMA, and E) provide proper timing for devices that perform bus transfers on specific edges of the primary clock. The 8-bit **MC6800** peripheral devices are typical of the devices that can interface to the **MC68000** using these signals.

Processor Status These three function code signals (F0, F1, F2) indicate the processor state and current cycle type whenever address strobe is active. These signals are used to select memory segments when operating with a memory management unit.

12-10 THE DATA SHEET AND USER'S GUIDE

When designing a system using the **MC68000**, there are a few documents which should be considered indispensable. The first of these documents is the **MC68000** data sheet, which is constantly being revised as manufacturing and design enhancements are made. The data sheet at the time this chapter was written contains specifications on a range of processors from the **MC68000L4** (4 MHz) through the **MC68000L10** (10 MHz). The second document necessary for the **MC68000** designer is the 16-bit microprocessor *Manual*. This is a book of approximately 230 pages which contains detailed information on the **MC68000** instruction set and addressing modes. One page of this manual has been used in Example 12-2. It also explains the functional characteristics of the processor in normal operating conditions. Finally, there are several compact pocket guides which can be used as a quick reference when programming an **MC68000** system. All three of these documents are available through the Motorola Semiconductor Sales offices in most major cities of the United States, Canada, Europe, and Japan, and in many other major cities of the world. The *Manual* is appearing in many retail book stores.

This section will examine the data sheet and *Manual* in more detail. The data sheet is primarily a hardware specification with the first two-thirds devoted to the signal characteristics of the 64 signal lines or pin outs on the **MC68000**.

12-10.1 Timing

The processor is a *dynamic* device. This means that it is constantly changing states. In theory, there are in excess of 2^{60} possible machine states. This is an impossibly large number of states to specify individually. Therefore, the machine is described in terms of normal predefined instruction operations and in terms of controlled exception response conditions and direct memory access conditions. All processor timing is keyed to the primary clock. This is the 50% duty cycle signal applied to pin 15 (CLK) of the processor. In the case of the **MC68000L8**, this signal is 8 MHz. A hardware designer would use this information to determine how external devices must respond to the **MC68000** and what the timing, current, and voltage constraints are. Two of the most important specifications to the hardware designer are the read cycle timing and the write cycle timing. Figures 12-16 through 12-19 show the flow of events and the timing of the processor for READ and WRITE instructions. Figure 12-16 shows the flow of events when a byte or word *WRITE cycle* takes place, and Figure 12-17 shows the actual signals on the external pins of the **MC68000** during a WRITE cycle. Figure 12-18 shows the flow of events when a byte or word *READ cycle* takes place. "Bus master" refers to the μP, and "slave" refers to the device transferring data, such as a RAM or ROM. Figure 12-19 shows the actual signals on the external pins of the **MC68000** during a READ cycle.

There is no explicit "read" or "write" instruction. This action is implicit in the addressing mode. For example,

```
Move (A3), LOC1        is a WRITE instruction
Move D6, (A4)          is a READ instruction
```

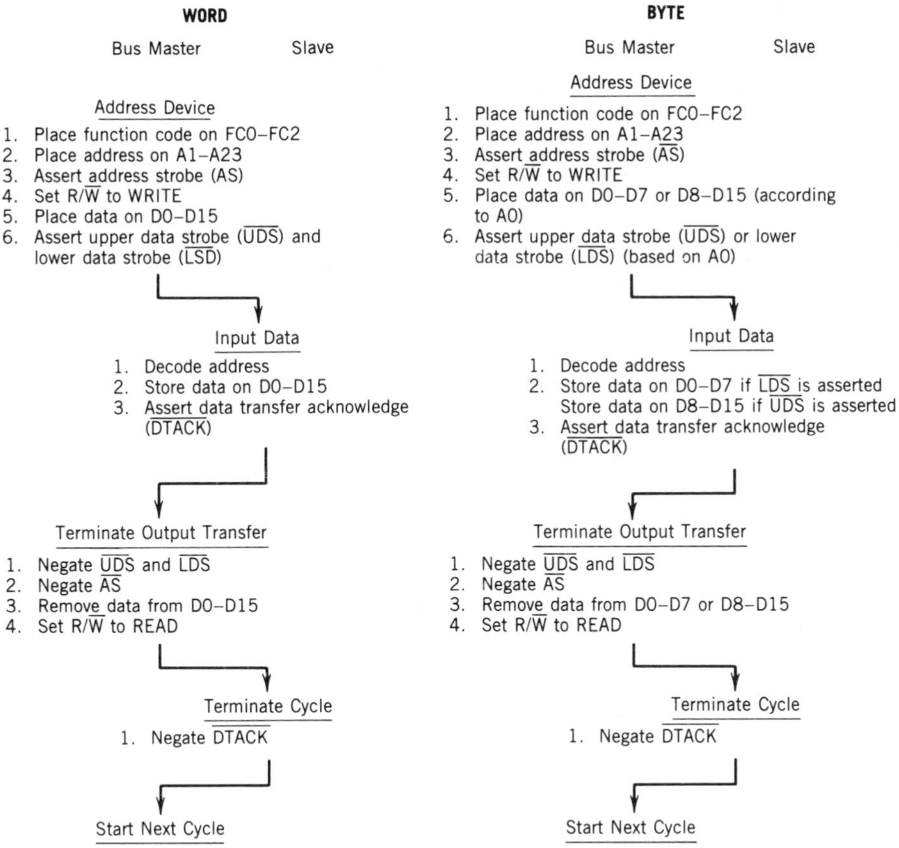

WORD

Bus Master	Slave

Address Device

1. Place function code on FC0–FC2
2. Place address on A1–A23
3. Assert address strobe (AS)
4. Set R/$\overline{\text{W}}$ to WRITE
5. Place data on D0–D15
6. Assert upper data strobe ($\overline{\text{UDS}}$) and lower data strobe ($\overline{\text{LSD}}$)

Input Data

1. Decode address
2. Store data on D0–D15
3. Assert data transfer acknowledge ($\overline{\text{DTACK}}$)

Terminate Output Transfer

1. Negate $\overline{\text{UDS}}$ and $\overline{\text{LDS}}$
2. Negate $\overline{\text{AS}}$
3. Remove data from D0–D15
4. Set R/$\overline{\text{W}}$ to READ

Terminate Cycle

1. Negate $\overline{\text{DTACK}}$

Start Next Cycle

BYTE

Bus Master	Slave

Address Device

1. Place function code on FC0–FC2
2. Place address on A1–A23
3. Assert address strobe ($\overline{\text{AS}}$)
4. Set R/$\overline{\text{W}}$ to WRITE
5. Place data on D0–D7 or D8–D15 (according to A0)
6. Assert upper data strobe ($\overline{\text{UDS}}$) or lower data strobe ($\overline{\text{LDS}}$) (based on A0)

Input Data

1. Decode address
2. Store data on D0–D7 if $\overline{\text{LDS}}$ is asserted Store data on D8–D15 if $\overline{\text{UDS}}$ is asserted
3. Assert data transfer acknowledge ($\overline{\text{DTACK}}$)

Terminate Output Transfer

1. Negate $\overline{\text{UDS}}$ and $\overline{\text{LDS}}$
2. Negate $\overline{\text{AS}}$
3. Remove data from D0–D7 or D8–D15
4. Set R/$\overline{\text{W}}$ to READ

Terminate Cycle

1. Negate $\overline{\text{DTACK}}$

Start Next Cycle

Figure 12-16 WRITE cycle flowchart. (From the *M68000 Programmer's Reference Manual*, 4th Edition, courtesy of Motorola, Inc.)

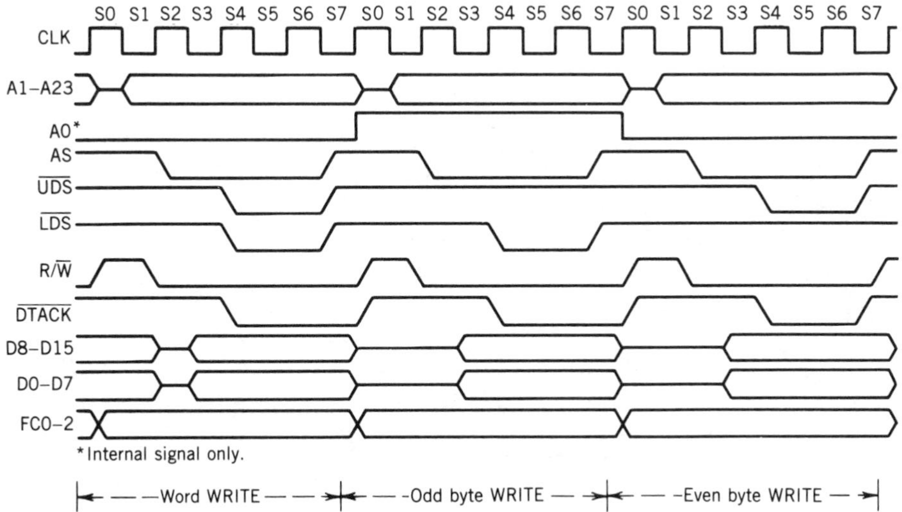

Figure 12-17 Word and byte WRITE cycle timing diagram. (From the *M68000 Programmer's Reference Manual*, 4th Edition, courtesy of Motorola, Inc.)

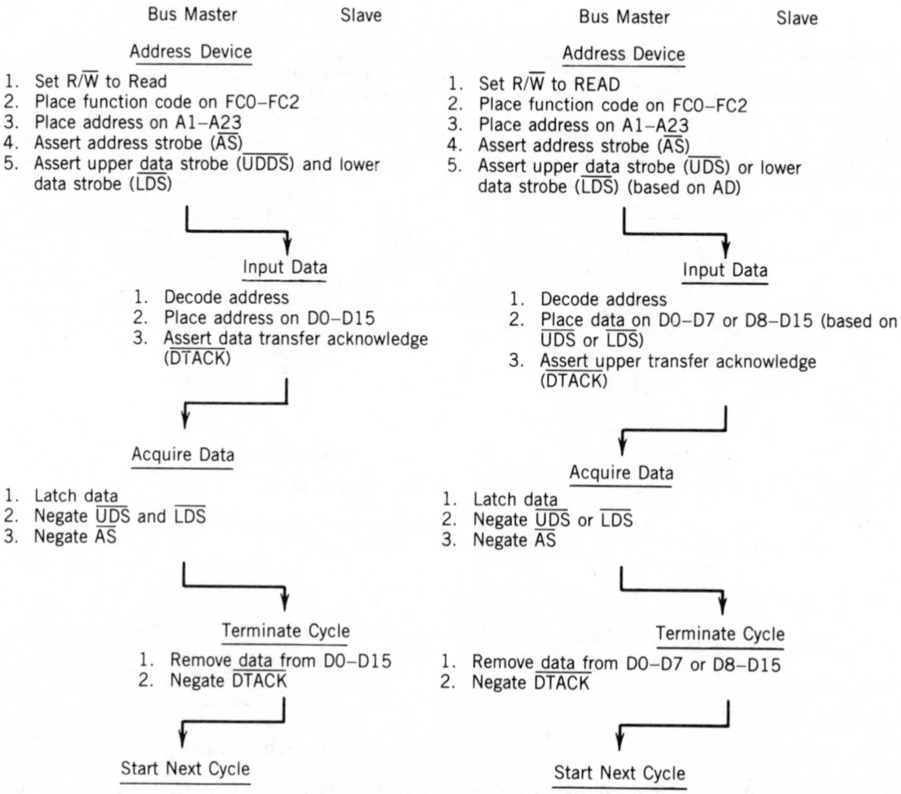

Bus Master
Slave
Address Device
1. Set R/$\overline{W}$ to Read
2. Place function code on FC0–FC2
3. Place address on A1–A23
4. Assert address strobe ($\overline{AS}$)
5. Assert upper data strobe ($\overline{UDDS}$) and lower data strobe ($\overline{LDS}$)
Input Data
1. Decode address
2. Place address on D0–D15
3. Assert data transfer acknowledge ($\overline{DTACK}$)
Acquire Data
1. Latch data
2. Negate $\overline{UDS}$ and $\overline{LDS}$
3. Negate $\overline{AS}$
Terminate Cycle
1. Remove data from D0–D15
2. Negate $\overline{DTACK}$
Start Next Cycle
Bus Master
Slave
Address Device
1. Set R/$\overline{W}$ to READ
2. Place function code on FC0–FC2
3. Place address on A1–A23
4. Assert address strobe ($\overline{AS}$)
5. Assert upper data strobe ($\overline{UDS}$) or lower data strobe ($\overline{LDS}$) (based on AD)
Input Data
1. Decode address
2. Place data on D0–D7 or D8–D15 (based on $\overline{UDS}$ or $\overline{LDS}$)
3. Assert upper transfer acknowledge ($\overline{DTACK}$)
Acquire Data
1. Latch data
2. Negate $\overline{UDS}$ or $\overline{LDS}$
3. Negate $\overline{AS}$
Terminate Cycle
1. Remove data from D0–D7 or D8–D15
2. Negate $\overline{DTACK}$
Start Next Cycle

Figure 12-18 READ cycle flowchart. (From the *M68000 Programmer's Reference Manual*, 4th Edition, courtesy of Motorola, Inc.)

S0 S1 S2 S3 S4 S5 S6 S7 S0 S1 S2 S3 S4 S5 S6 S7 S0 S1 S2 S3 S4 w w w w S5 S6 S7
CLK
A1–A23
$\overline{AS}$
$\overline{UDS}$
$\overline{LDS}$
R/W
$\overline{DTACK}$
D6–D15
D0–D7
FC0–2
READ
WRITE
Slow READ

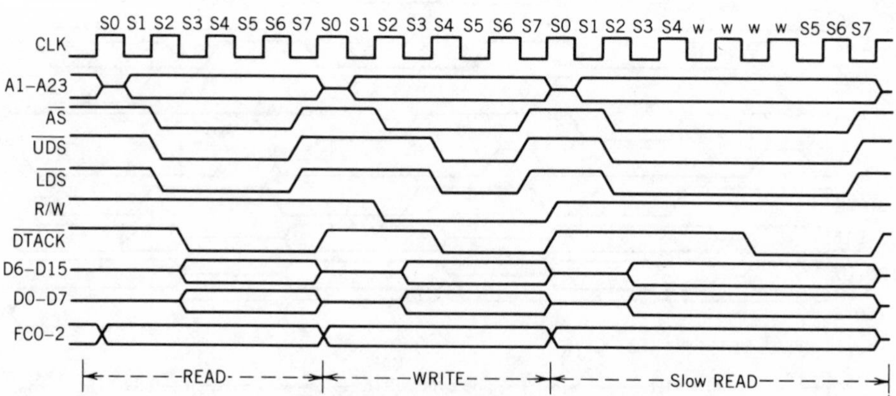

Figure 12-19 READ and WRITE cycle timing diagram. (From the *M68000 Programmer's Reference Manual*, 4th Edition, courtesy of Motorola, Inc.)

These are illustrated here to demonstrate the complexity of designing with a 16-bit MPU. In the case of a READ operation, there are approximately 34 critical timing events which occur (sometimes concurrently) in 1μs. In section 12-9, the signal lines of the **MC68000** are examined by their generic function. To understand the exact function of each individual line, it is necessary to consult the data sheet.

One word of advice—the most recent data sheet is usually the best one to use because as the product matures, many specifications are relaxed. This tends to make the hardware designer's job easier. In addition to the timing and signal information contained in the data sheet, there are explanations of several special conditions which occur during processing. These include a detailed description of *exception processing*. Exception processing is a general set of actions which the processor takes when an event occurs that is not included in the normal instruction stream. (This is not an entirely true statement because the TRAP and RESET instructions may be considered exceptions.)

The data sheet also explains the use of synchronous peripherals with the **MC68000**. The last one-third of the data sheet presents the addressing modes and instruction set in compact form, including the necessary tables to compute timing.

12-10.2 The *Programmer's Reference Manual*

The *Manual* elaborates on the **MC68000** from the programmer's point of view. The heaviest emphasis is on the addressing modes and instruction set. The *Manual* is organized into six chapters and six appendixes. The chapters of the **MC68000** *Manual* are:

General Description. An overview of the **MC68000** architecture.

Data Organization and Addressing Capabilities. The most comprehensive description of the addressing modes and the rules and regulations, and how data is manipulated in the registers and how it must be organized in memory.

Signal and Bus Operation and Description. A description of the 64 signal lines in less detail than the data sheet.

Exception Processing. Approximately the same description as contained in the data sheet.

Interface with the MC68000. Again approximately the same as the data sheet.

Instruction Set Summary. Explains the common features of the eight basic instruction types.

Appendix A—Condition Codes Computation. How condition codes are set by various instructions.

Appendix B—Instruction Set Details. The ultimate source of information on how each instruction operates.

Appendix C—Instruction Format Summary. Shows how the bit patterns are organized to form an instruction. Using this information and given a bit pattern, one can work backward to find the instruction it represents.

Appendix D—Instruction Execution Times. This requires a more detailed explanation. Each instruction can be thought of as having three components—an addressing mode, an instruction execution component, and a READ component if the instruction performs READ (because READ instructions take longer than WRITE instructions).

MOVE instructions have their own tables. One is for byte and word operations and one is for long-word instructions. To determine the time, look in the table in the row for the source addressing mode and the column for the destination operand. For example,

```
Move D2,A3+   8 cycles
Move.L 535A3, A4+   24 cycles
```

Non-MOVE instructions are a little more difficult. Find the instruction in Tables D4 through D12 of the *Manual.* Determine the column in the table which describes the addressing mode. Determine the number of cycles for the instruction. Add the number of cycles for the addressing mode. For example, the instruction

```
CMP (D3)A1, D4
```

is in Table D4 in the generic form

```
Op <ea> ,DN
```

The entry in the table is 4(1/0)+, which indicates that the instruction takes four cycles. The "(1/0)" means one READ cycle and zero WRITE cycles. The "+" indicates that the time for "⟨ea⟩" addressing mode must be added. In the case of CMP (D3) A1, D4, the effective address of the source is represented in Table D1 as An@(d, ix), where d = 0. The indicated time for this mode is 10 cycles. The net time is 4 + 10 or 14 cycles or 1.75 μs at 8 MHz.

Appendix E—Prefetch. An example of the instruction prefetch mechanism in the **MC68000**. This is a feature that enhances performance of the **MC68000** by bringing an instruction into the processor while a previous instruction is executing.

Appendix F—The 68451 Memory Management Unit. A description of the **MC68451** Memory Management Unit.

12-11 THE MC68451 MEMORY MANAGEMENT UNIT

In many applications, the **MC68000** is programmed using *multitasking* techniques. This implies a supervisory program—sometimes called an *operating system executive or kernel*—to control and allocate computer resources to several tasks. Each task may reside in different areas of memory and require data storage in other areas of memory. These tasks may require protection from one another so that one task will not alter conditions in another task and cause a software failure. A technique called *memory segmentation* is often used, particularly when memory management hardware is available. A task may operate in a logical memory space. This means that the program may be written using any address conventions that the programmer requires without regard to any other task in the system.

The Memory Management Unit (MMU) translates the logical addresses of any task into real physical addresses of the system. To access memory, the MMU *intercepts* the output of the address bus on the MPU and translates to *new physical addresses*. A task may be written to access memory locations $500 to $10000. If these locations are occupied by some other task, the supervisor can use some other locations—for instance, $C5500 to $D0000—and program the MMU to make the translation automatically.

The **MC68451** provides for 32 segments and uses the function code outputs to determine which segment is being accessed. It also provides physical protection for each segment so that no task may access or alter data in another segment controlled by another task unless specific rules are obeyed.

12-12 REFERENCES

M68000 16/32-Bit Microprocessor Programmer's Reference Manual, 4th Edition, © Motorola, Inc., Prentice-Hall, Englewood Cliffs, N.J., 1984.

Motorola MC68000 Course Notes, Motorola Technical Training, © Motorola, Inc., Phoenix, Ariz. 1984.

Motorola MC68000 16-Bit Microprocessor Data Sheet, © Motorola Semiconductor Products, Inc., Austin, Tex.

James W. Coffron, *Using and Troubleshooting the MC68000*, Reston Publishing Co, Reston, Va., 1983.

SECTION FOUR

PERIPHERAL ICs

CHAPTER 13

Intel Peripheral Circuits

Windsor Thomas
Professor of Electrical Engineering Technology
State University of New York
Utica/Rome, New York

13-1 INTRODUCTION

This chapter covers some of the most important Intel peripheral ICs. The **8255** Programmable Peripheral Interface has already been covered in Chapter 5. This chapter will cover the **8251A**, a serial interface chip, the **8253**, a triple 16-bit timer chip, the **8275**, a CRT controller chip, and the **8279** programmable keyboard/display interface.

13-2 8251A USART

The **8251A** Programmable Communications Interface is a USART (universal synchronous-asynchronous receiver/transmitter) that is designed to interface directly to an 8-bit μP data bus. It converts parallel data from the μP (bytes) into a series of bits for serial transmission, either to a serial input device such as a TTY, or for long-distance transmission via MODEMs and telephone lines.

The **8251A** peripheral chip may be programmed to operate in either synchronous mode at rates of DC to 64 kilobaud, or asynchronous mode at rates from DC to 19.2 kilobaud.[1] Each mode will be considered separately after a general discussion of the **8251A**.

13-2.1 Functional Description

The USART is used to convert 8-bit parallel formatted system data into serial format for transmission and to convert incoming serial data into parallel data for the

[1] For a discussion of asynchronous and synchronous transmission, see Greenfield, *Practical Digital Design Using ICs*, 2nd Edition, Sections 18-4 and 18-5.

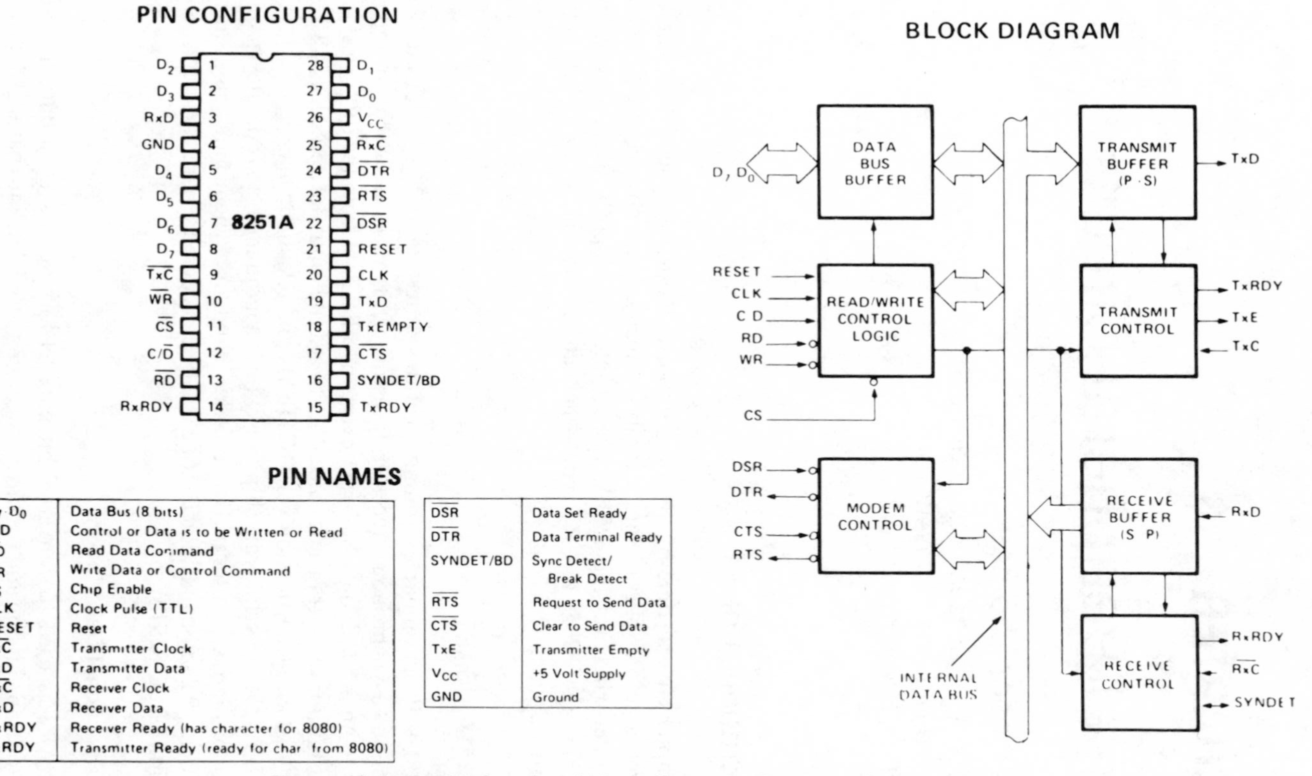

PIN NAMES

D_7-D_0	Data Bus (8 bits)
C/$\overline{D}$	Control or Data is to be Written or Read
$\overline{RD}$	Read Data Command
$\overline{WR}$	Write Data or Control Command
$\overline{CS}$	Chip Enable
CLK	Clock Pulse (TTL)
RESET	Reset
$\overline{TxC}$	Transmitter Clock
TxD	Transmitter Data
$\overline{RxC}$	Receiver Clock
RxD	Receiver Data
RxRDY	Receiver Ready (has character for 8080)
TxRDY	Transmitter Ready (ready for char from 8080)

$\overline{DSR}$	Data Set Ready
$\overline{DTR}$	Data Terminal Ready
SYNDET/BD	Sync Detect/ Break Detect
$\overline{RTS}$	Request to Send Data
$\overline{CTS}$	Clear to Send Data
TxE	Transmitter Empty
V_{CC}	+5 Volt Supply
GND	Ground

Figure 13-1 **8251A** functional block diagram. (Courtesy of Intel Corp.)

μP system. The **8251A** is functionally configured by system software and this is usually done during *system initialization* that immediately follows power-on or reset of the μP, or whenever it is necessary to alter the **8251A**'s functional operation (for example, to change the number of stop bits). Figure 13-1 shows the **8251A**'s functional block diagram with the functional pins and blocks discussed in section 13-2.2.

13-2.2 Major Functional Blocks and Pins

The major functional blocks and pins for the **8251A** are discussed in this section.

Data Bus Buffer These eight pins, and the buffer that they are connected to, allow the μP to exchange data, status information, and commands with the **8251A** over the μP system data bus.

Transmit Buffer The transmit buffer accepts parallel data from the μP via the data bus buffer, converts it to a serial stream of bits, inserting the appropriate SYNC characters (in synchronous mode) or START and STOP bits (in asynchronous mode), and outputs the combined serial stream on the TxD pin. The transmit buffer is *double buffered,* which means that it contains a *parallel buffer* for holding data from the μP and a *serial buffer*, which is essentially a *parallel-to-serial shift register* that sends out the data. Figure 13-2 is a block diagram of the transmit side of the **8251A**. It shows that data from the computer enters the parallel buffer, is transferred to the serial buffer, and is shifted out as the serial bit stream.

As the **8251A** is converting one parallel word to serial, the μP can send another word that will be stored in the parallel buffer. When the **8251A** finishes transmitting the first byte, the second byte is transferred to the serial buffer and the **8251A** immediately starts transmitting the second byte. The parallel buffer is now empty and the μP can send another byte to it at any time. In order to maintain a maximum data transfer rate, the μP can send another byte of data any time after the **8251A** starts transmitting the first bit of a byte. This allows the μP relative freedom in responding to the **8251A**'s need for the next byte of data.

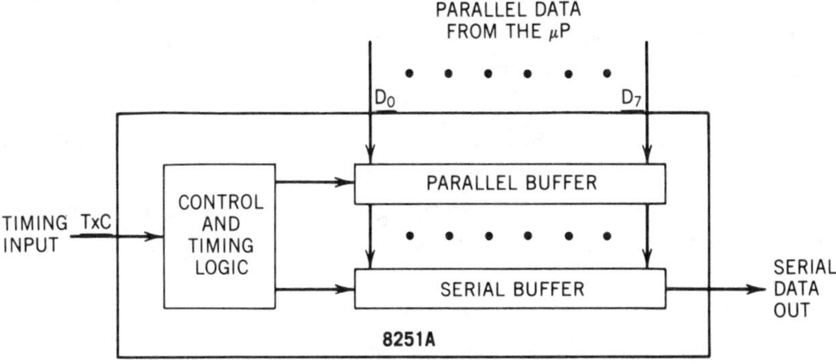

Figure 13-2 The transmit side of an **8251A**.

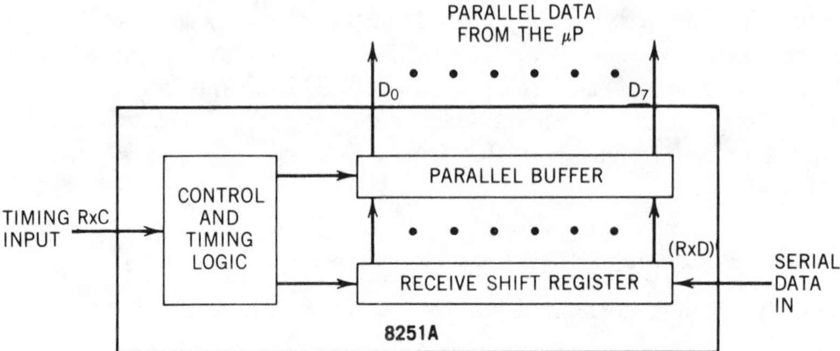

Figure 13-3 The receive side of an **8251A**.

Receive Buffer The receive buffer converts the serial data coming in on the RxD pin to parallel data to be sent to the μP and checks the format and framing bits or characters. A block diagram of the receive side of the **8251A** is shown in Figure 13-3. The receive buffer is double buffered in a manner similar to the transmit buffer. This allows the receive buffer to start converting the next serial input character to parallel form before the μP has read the previous character.

Receiver Control This section handles the initialization of the RxD line when the chip is reset, detects false start bits (it checks both the low-going edge and the center of the start bit to assure a valid start bit, thus increasing the noise immunity), calculates the character parity and indicates parity error, and detects framing errors (insufficient number of stop bits). The receiver control also handles the control of the RxRDY, RxC, and SYNDET/BRKDET pins.

13-2.3 Device Pins

The pin out for the **8251A** is given in Figure 13-1. The functions of these pins are described below.

RESET This active-high input is usually connected to the μP RESET pin so that a reset of the system also resets the **8251A** into an idle mode. This pin must be a logic 0 when the **8251A** is actually transmitting or receiving data.

CLK This is the clock input which is used for the internal clocking of the **8251A** and is completely independent of any input or output. The only requirement is that its frequency be greater than 30 times both the transmit and receive bit rates. The usual procedure is to connect one of the μP system clock phases to this input.

$\overline{WR}$ and $\overline{RD}$ These are the standard **8085A** types of write and read control lines which tell the peripheral device when the μP wants to write data or commands to the peripheral device or read data or status information from the **8251A**.

C/$\overline{D}$ and $\overline{CS}$ These two inputs are used as the decoding logic. The **8251A** looks like *two I/O ports* (or like two memory locations in a memory-mapped system), one for data and one for commands and status. When the C/$\overline{D}$ is 1, the command/status port is selected, and when the C/$\overline{D}$ pin is 0 the data port is selected. The CS should be used to enable the **8251A** when the proper port address or memory address is on the address bus and then C/$\overline{D}$ is used to select the desired port. C/$\overline{D}$ is usually connected to the A0 line of the address bus.

The next four pins are general-purpose control pins which are frequently used to simplify the connection of the **8251A** serial lines to a modem.

$\overline{DSR}$ (DATA SET READY) The logic level on this input pin is inverted and stored in the most significant bit of the status register. This pin is usually used to test the DATA SET READY output of a modem.

$\overline{DTR}$ (DATA TERMINAL READY) This output is the inverted logic state of whatever logic level is stored in bit 1 of the command instruction word. It is usually connected to the DATA TERMINAL READY input of a modem.

$\overline{RTS}$ (REQUEST TO SEND) This output, similar to the $\overline{DTR}$ output, is the inverted logic state of bit 5 of the command instruction word and is usually connected to the REQUEST TO SEND input of a MODEM.

$\overline{CTS}$ (CLEAR TO SEND) The fourth control line used to communicate with a modem is the $\overline{CTS}$ pin which is used to allow an external device such as a modem to enable the serial transmission. When the $\overline{CTS}$ input is low, the **8251A** can transmit serial data if the Tx enable bit in the command word is set to logic 1. If either the $\overline{CTS}$ input is set HIGH or the Tx enable bit in the command word is set LOW, the **8251A** will not transmit any serial data.

The next three pins control the interface between the μP and the **8251A** for data transmission.

TxRDY Transmitter ready output pin is used to indicate that the USART transmitter is ready to accept another byte of data. That is, the parallel transmitter buffer is empty. In interrupt-driven systems this pin is used to cause an interrupt. For polled I/O systems, the status register, which will be discussed in section 13-2.4, provides the same information.

TxE (TRANSMITTER EMPTY) This output pin is used to indicate that both transmitter buffers (or double buffers) are empty. In well-designed systems, the only time that both buffers would be empty would be at the end of a message; therefore this pin can be used as a hardware indication to the μP that the message transmission is complete.

$\overline{TxC}$ The transmitter clock is the third transmitter control pin. The $\overline{TxC}$ is used to control the baud rate (the number of bits per second, including all protocol bits) of the transmission. This clock frequency may be interpreted in one of three ways by the **8251A**. The software that initializes the **8251A** selects the proper interpretation. The three interpretations are that the clock signal on $\overline{\text{TxC}}$ input is at the same frequency as the desired bit rate (baud rate) on the serial transmit line, or the $\overline{\text{TxC}}$ is at a rate of 16 times the desired baud transmit baud rate, or that $\overline{\text{TxC}}$ is at a rate of 64 times the desired transmit baud rate.

EXAMPLE 13-1 The frequency of the signal on $\overline{\text{TxC}}$ input of the **8251A** is 9600 Hz. What is the actual transmit baud rates for each of the three interpretations of the $\overline{\text{TxC}}$ signal?

Solution For the times 1 case the transmit baud rate would be the same as the clock or 9600 bits/s. For the times 16 clock rate the transmit baud rate would be clock rate/16 or $9600/16 = 600$ bits/s. For the times 64 clock rate, the transmit baud rate would be $9600/64 = 150$ bits/s.

EXAMPLE 13-2 The **8251A** is to be interfaced to a serial line and should transmit at 2400 bits/s. What is the required clock rate on $\overline{\text{TxC}}$ for both the times 16 and the times 64 clock?

Solution The times 16 clock will have a frequency of $2400 \times 16 = 38400$ Hz. The times 64 clock will have a frequency of $2400 \times 64 = 153{,}600$ Hz, or 153.6 kHz.

The receive side of the **8251A** is controlled by the following signals.

RxRDY (RECEIVER READY) This indicates that the **8251A** has received a character and is ready for the μP to read the character from the receive buffer. This signal may be used to cause an interrupt in an interrupt-driven system. In a polled I/O system the μP can check the RxRDY bit (bit 1) of the status register. Whichever I/O technique is used, the μP must read the character from the receive buffer before the next character has been completely converted to parallel form, because when the next character is converted, it will be written into this buffer and erase the previous contents of the buffer. If the next character is received and transferred into this buffer before the μP has a chance to read the previous character, the previous character will be lost; this is called an OVERRUN error and will be detected by the **8251A** and indicated by setting bit 4 of the status register HIGH.

$\overline{\text{RxC}}$ (RECEIVE CLOCK) This input is used to clock the receive data and has the same capabilities at $\overline{\text{TxC}}$. The $\overline{\text{TxC}}$ and $\overline{\text{RxC}}$ may be tied together and run at the same frequency (this is the normal case), or they may be connected to two different frequency sources. For the asynchronous mode, both $\overline{\text{RxC}}$ and $\overline{\text{TxC}}$ must use the same multiplication ratio, that is, both must use a clock that is either the same as the desired baud rate, 16 times the desired baud rate, or 64 times the desired baud rate.

SYNDET/BRKDET (SYNC detect/BREAK detect) This pin may be programmed as either an input or an output pin. On RESET, this pin is an output pin at logic 0 (false); it will go HIGH when the **8251A** is in the synchronous mode and detects SYNC characters in the receiver, and will be reset LOW by a status register read operation. In the asynchronous mode this pin will be set HIGH when the receiver has detected a BREAK (RxD is LOW for all bits of two character times including stop bits). This will also be indicated by bit 6 of the status register being set to 1 and bit 6 is reset only on a master reset of the chip or the RxD returning to a 1 level.

When this pin is programmed as an input pin, the **8251A** assumes there is external hardware performing the SYNC detection operation and the **8251A** will start converting the character from serial to parallel on the rising edge of the next $\overline{RxC}$ after this input goes high. This mode disables the internal SYNC detection in the **8251A**.

13-2.4 General Operation

The **8251A** is a programmable I/O chip and *its operational modes and parameters must be initialized before the chip is functional.* This *initialization* is performed by the μP writing data (coded parameters) into the control register. These parameters define the mode of operation (asynchronous or synchronous), baud rate, character length and parity, and the number of stop bits. There are two types of instructions used to initialize and control the **8251A**, the MODE instruction and the COMMAND instructions. The MODE instruction is the *first instruction* written to the command register after a master reset of the **8251A**, and defines the overall operational mode. All instructions written to the command register after the MODE instruction bytes (synchronous) or byte (asynchronous) are *COMMAND instructions.*

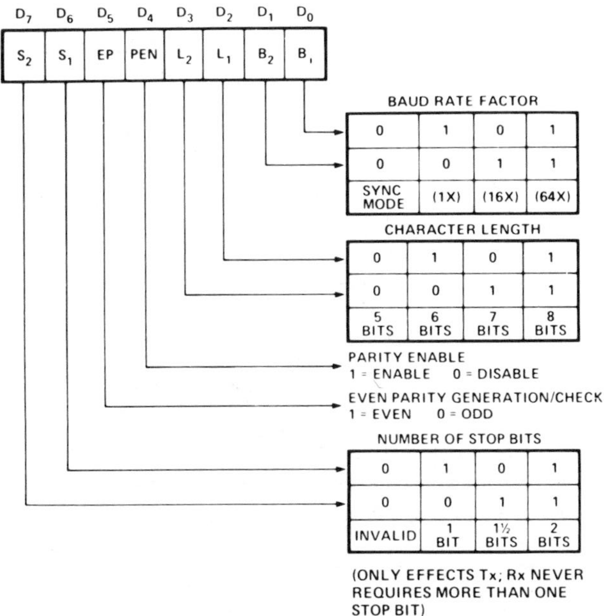

Figure 13-4 Asynchronous mode instruction. (Reprinted by permission of Intel Corp.)

The two least significant bits of the MODE instruction define the type of operation. If both of these bits are 0, then the synchronous mode is selected; otherwise the asynchronous mode instruction mode is selected. Figure 13-4 shows the asynchronous mode instruction format and the definition of bits. Example 13-3 shows how to assign the mode bits for a practical example.

EXAMPLE 13-3 An **8251A** is to be initialized to operate in the asynchronous mode at a rate of 300 bauds (bits per second) on a 4800-Hz clock, with 7 data bits (which is standard for ASCII encoded characters), one STOP bit, and even parity. What is the byte that the μP should send to the command register as a MODE instruction byte?

Solution 300 bits/s times 16 equals 4800 Hz. Therefore the baud rate ratio should be 16 ×, and bit 0 must be set to 0 and bit 1 set to 1. To specify 7 data bits, bit 2 must be set to 0 and bit 3 set to 1. The even parity is selected by setting bit 5 to 1 and the parity is enabled by setting bit 4 to 1. The 1 STOP bit is chosen by setting bit 6 to 1 and bit 7 to 0. Thus the byte is 01111010 in binary or 7A in hexadecimal.

Figure 13-5 shows the format of the MODE instruction for the asynchronous mode. The clearest way to explain this figure is by the use of the following example.

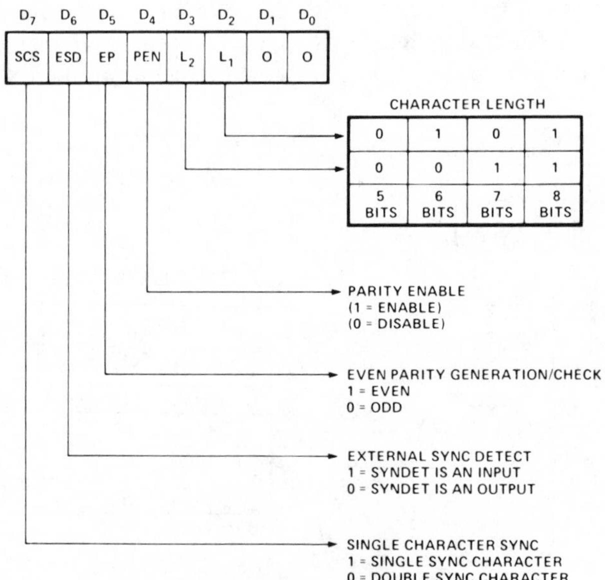

Figure 13-5 Synchronous mode instruction. (Reprinted by permission of Intel Corp.)

EXAMPLE 13-4 An **8251A** is to be initialized for synchronous communication with 8 data bits, odd parity, internal synchronization, and one SYNC character. What is the byte that should be written to the **8251A** as a MODE instruction?

Solution To choose the synchronous mode, bits 0 and 1 must be set to 0. To select the eight data bits, bits 2 and 3 must be set to 1. Parity is enabled by setting bit 4 to 1, and odd parity is selected by setting bit 5 to 0. The selection of internal SYNC detection is indicated by setting bit 6 to 0. A single SYNC character mode is chosen by setting bit 7 to 1. This yields a byte of 10011100 in binary or 9C in hexadecimal. Table 13-1 shows an **8080A** assembly language program that will perform this initialization.

Table 13-1 **8080/8085 code for initializing an 8251**

```
LXI    H,9001H    ;HL points to the command register
MVI    A,9CH      ;
MOV    M,A        ;Load 9C into the command register
```

13-2.5 Asynchronous Mode

In the asynchronous mode, whenever the μP writes a character to the **8251A**, the **8251A** automatically sends the START bit (low-level bit), followed by the data bits (least significant bit first), then calculates and adds the parity bit (if selected) and finally the STOP bit or bits. This data is sent out the TxD pin. The TxD output will remain at a HIGH level when it is not transmitting a character. The **8251A** can be commanded to transmit a BREAK code, which is a *continuous low level*. The BREAK code is used by many time-sharing systems as an interrupt from the terminal.

On receive, the **8251A** samples the RxC input on the high-to-low transition of the receive clock. When a low level is detected (the START bit), the chip waits until the middle of the START bit (about the eighth sample on the 16 × or thirty-second sample on the 64 × baud rate ratio) and rechecks the START bit. This helps to prevent the **8251A** from starting its conversion on a noise spike and also starts the conversion at the middle of the bit time which minimizes errors caused by mismatched transmit and receive clock rates. The receive section also compares the parity of the incoming character with the expected parity. The parity error bit in the status register is set if the incorrect parity is received; this allows detection of a single-bit error in a character. The STOP bit is also checked; if a LOW level (a valid STOP bit is a HIGH level) is detected, the framing error bit in the status register is set. The RxRDY pin is set to a 1 to indicate to the μP that there is a character to be read from the **8251A**. If the previous character has not been read by the μP, then the overrun error bit in the status register is set HIGH.

These errors can be reset by an ERROR RESET instruction. The occurrence of any of these errors does not disturb the normal operation of the **8251A** and errors do not cause interrupts. The user must read the contents of the status register to check for errors in receiving the data. Since the error status bits are reset by a RESET instruction, instead of being reset for each new character, the user's program only needs to check the error status at the end of the smallest retransmittable unit, such as a message or a block of data, instead of after each character. If an error is detected at the end of a block, the block is discarded and the sender is instructed to retransmit it.

13-2.6 Synchronous Mode

To transmit in synchronous mode, the TxD output will remain HIGH until the μP sends the **8251A** its first character, which is usually a SYNC character. The first character will then be transmitted out as soon as the modem drives the $\overline{\text{CTS}}$ signal LOW. All bits of the characters are shifted out on the high-to-low transition of the $\overline{\text{TxC}}$ clock. The data will be sent out at a rate of one bit per clock cycle and there will be no START or STOP bits used. Once the **8251A** receives the first character from the μP, the **8251A** will send out a continuous stream of bits on the TxD output. If the **8251A** has finished transmitting its character and the transmit buffers are empty, the **8251A** will transmit the SYNC character (or SYNC characters if a pair of characters were specified) and continue transmitting the SYNC character until another character is received from the μP. When the **8251A** receives a character from the μP, it finishes transmitting the current character or SYNC character(s) and then starts transmitting the new character. The TxEMPTY pin is set to 1 to indicate that the transmit buffers are empty and a SYNC character is being transmitted, and will stay at a HIGH level until the μP sends the **8251A** a data character.

In the synchronous mode there are no START and STOP bits on each character, as in the asynchronous mode. It is therefore necessary for the receiver to first find the *start of the bits for the first character.*

The purpose of the SYNC character is to aid in this process of synchronization of the receiver with the transmitter. To perform synchronization, both the transmitter and the receiver must be using the same SYNC character (or pair of characters). The **8251A** is directed to synchronize itself with the incoming signal by the ENTER HUNT command, which should be the first command after the mode selection. When the SYNC characters have been detected, the **8251A** exits the hunt mode and is synchronized. It indicates this by setting the SYNDET pin HIGH and setting the SYNDET bit in the status register HIGH. If external synchronization is selected in the mode instruction, then external hardware must be provided to do the synchronization and this hardware will send a sync detect signal to the **8251A** SYNDET pin which is now acting as an input pin.

13-2.7 Command Instructions

Once the MODE instruction (and the SYNC characters in the synchronous mode) has been written to the command register, the COMMAND instruction can then be written into the command register. The COMMAND instruction controls the actual operation of the **8251A** by performing the following functions: enable transmit/receive, error reset, modem control, internal reset, synchronization, and transmission of the break character. Figure 13-6 shows the format of the COMMAND instruction. In order to send a command to the **8251A**, the μP must write a byte to the command register and this may change all 8 bits. Thus multiple commands may be issued in one WRITE operation, but the programmer must be aware that all the bits will be programmed not just the desired bit. The following example will show how to initially program the **8251A** after the mode has been selected. Note that the command register is a *write-only* register, so once a command is written to the command register, the contents of the command register *cannot be read.*

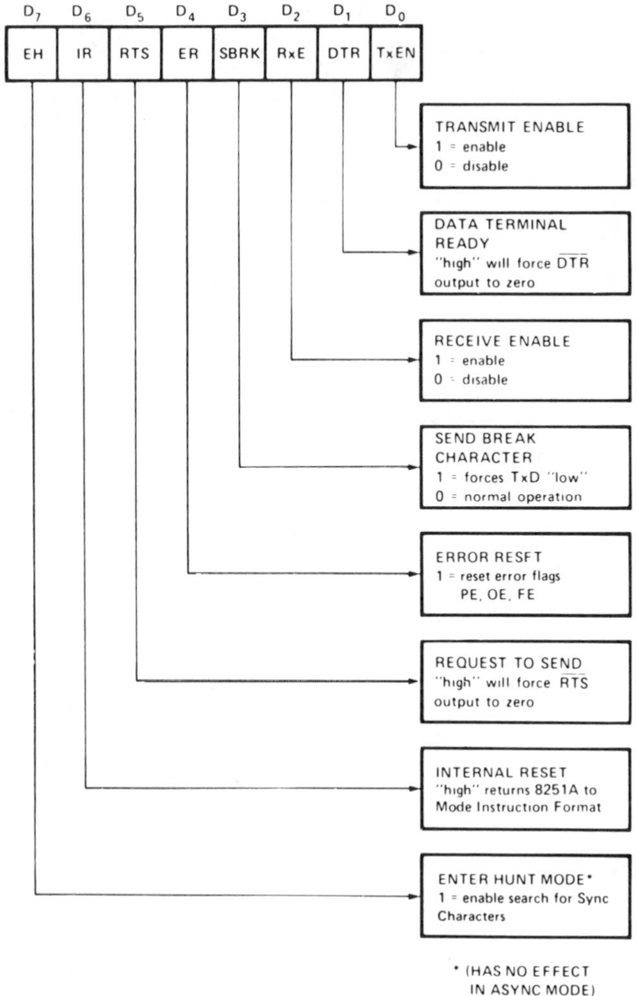

Figure 13-6 Format of COMMAND instruction. (Reprinted by permission of Intel Corp.)

EXAMPLE 13-5 What byte would have to be written to the command register to enable the transmitter, enable the receiver, set $\overline{DTR}$ output to zero, and set the $\overline{RTS}$ output LOW?

Solution From Figure 13-6 we can see that bit 0 should be set to 1 to enable the transmitter. Bit 1 should be set to 1 to set DTR to a LOW state. Bit 2 should be set to 1 to enable the receiver. Bit 3 should be set to 0 so that normal operation takes place instead of the transmission of a BREAK character. Bit 4 should be set to 0 so that the error reset operation is not performed. Bit 5 should be set to 1 to cause the RTS line to go to zero. Bit 6 should be set to 0 so that the **8251A** will not be internally reset. Bit 7 should be set to 0 so that the **8251A** is not put into the ENTER HUNT mode. Thus a value of 00100111 in binary or 27 in hexadecimal should be written.

13-2.8 Status Register

The status register contains 8 bits that reflect the current operational status of the **8251A**. Figure 13-7 shows the format of the status register. The bits labeled

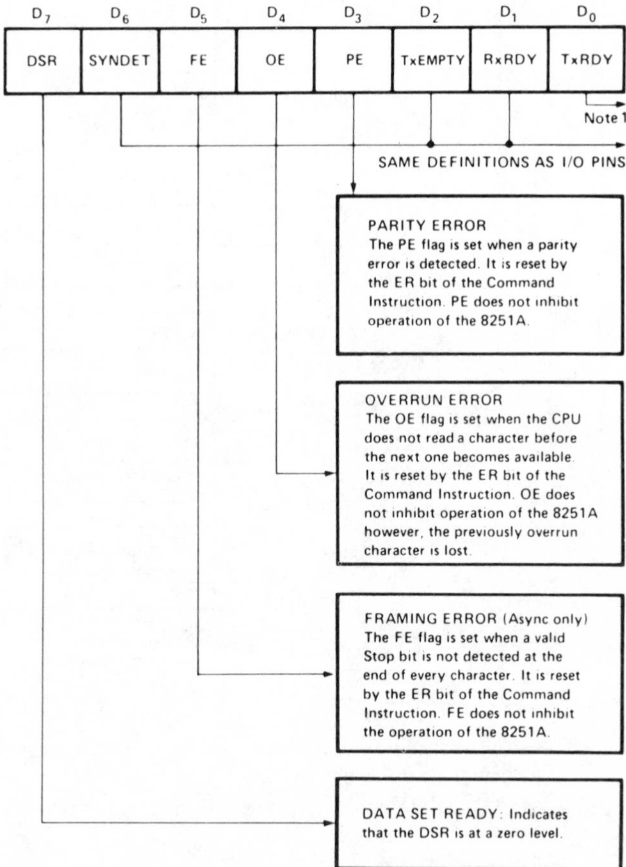

Note 1: TxRDY status bit has different meanings from the TxRDY output pin. The former is not conditioned by $\overline{CTS}$ and TxEN; the latter is conditioned by both $\overline{CTS}$ and TxEN.

i.e. TxRDY status bit = DB Buffer Empty

TxRDY pin out = DB Buffer Empty ·(CTS=0)·(TxEN

Figure 13-7 Status READ format. (Reprinted by permission of Intel Corp.)

SYNDET, TxEMPTY, and RxRDY have the same definition as the corresponding device pins. The $\overline{\text{DSR}}$ bit has a value that is the complement of the state of the pin. The FE (framing error), OE (overrun error), and the PE (parity error) bits are set to 1 whenever the corresponding error occurs. All three error flags will be cleared to 0 by either an error reset instruction or an internal reset instruction. The least significant bit of the status register is the TxRDY bit, which is similar in implementation to the corresponding pin, but there are differences. The TxRDY status bit indicates that the transmitter buffer is empty and is ready to receive a character from the μP. The TxRDY pin, however, also indicates that the transmitter is ready to receive a character from the μP but will do so only when the transmitter is enabled and $\overline{\text{CTS}}$ (clear to send) input signal is LOW.

13-2.9 Design Considerations

As shown in Figure 13-1, there is an I/O buffer labeled XMIT DATA/CMD BUFFER. Because of the shared nature of this buffer the programmer has to be extremely careful about when a command is written to the **8251A**. If a command is written when there is a data character in the buffer, both *the command and the data character will be modified in an undefined manner.* To avoid this problem when writing a command, the program should monitor TxRDY and should write the command to the **8251A** as soon as TxRDY is asserted. This is especially critical in the synchronous mode because the SYNC character uses this buffer also and the **8251A** will be continuously transmitting a character. Thus for the synchronous mode the program should continually monitor the TxRDY line and should write a command as soon as the TxRDY signal goes to 1.

The RxE bit acts as a mask to the RxRDY signal, but does not control the receiver. It is therefore possible that when the RxE is enabled, the receiver may already contain one or two characters in the buffers. When the RxRDY is first set it is advisable to read and *discard* two characters from the receiver. The extra characters can also cause problems in the synchronous mode. The following operations are recommended by the manufacturer for the synchronous mode.

1 Disable interrupts.

2 Send ENTER HUNT, clear errors, and enable the receiver.

3 Read and discard data.

4 Enable interrupts.

The next time RxRDY goes HIGH indicates that the **8251A** has found the SYNC character and has converted the first data character from serial to parallel format and is ready for the μP to read the newly received character.

The two lines CTS and TxE should remain true until all of the bits have been transmitted out of the **8251A** and any modem connected to it. If this is not observed, the last few bits may be lost.

The **8251A** sometimes sends out extraneous transitions on the TxEmpty status bit when data is transferred to the parallel-to-serial converter. It is therefore essential that several consecutive status reads are performed to assure that the transmitter is truly in an empty state.

The reception of a break character will result in several characters being received which have framing errors. The programmer must be aware of this when checking the status register.

13-3 8253 PROGRAMMABLE TIMER/COUNTER

The **8253** Programmable Interval Timer is a very flexible IC consisting of three identical 16-bit timer/counters. Each timer may be programmed to operate in one of six modes, independent of the mode of operation of the other two timers. Each timer may be used as a standard interval timer by providing it with an accurate frequency source from DC to 2 MHz. The timers are also flexible enough that they can count asynchronous events occurring at rates up to 2 MHz (or one event every 500 ns). The overall architecture of the chip will be discussed first. This will be followed by discussion of the device pins and then the operation and use of the six modes of operation.

13-3.1 Functional Description

Figure 13-8 shows the functional block diagram of the **8253**. The *data bus buffer* is bidirectional and is connected to the μP data bus. The operation of this buffer is controlled by the *chip select* line ($\overline{CS}$), which tells the **8253** that the μP is trying to transfer information to or from it. The $\overline{CS}$ is part of the READ/WRITE logic block, which controls the μP interface and the internal register/timer addressing. The last four functional blocks in the block diagram each correspond to one of the four addresses (either memory addresses or I/O port addresses) of the **8253**. The first of these blocks is the *control word register*, which is used to select the mode of operation of each counter and the various parameters required for operation. The next three blocks are the three 16-bit timers/counters. They are connected to an internal bus that provides them data from the data bus buffer and control information from the control word register. Each timer is a *presettable down counter* which can operate in either binary or BCD.

13-3.2 Device Pins

The pin out of the **8253** is also shown in Figure 13-8. Since the three timers are identical, the description of the pins associated directly with each timer will be discussed for only one timer.

D7 to D0 The eight data bus buffer pins D0 to D7 are bidirectional pins which allow the **8253** to receive data from and send data to the μP. These pins will be in a high-impedance (or tri-state) condition until the **8253** is selected by a LOW on the $\overline{CS}$ pin and either the read operation requested by a LOW on the $\overline{RD}$ input or a WRITE operation requested by the $\overline{WR}$ input going LOW.

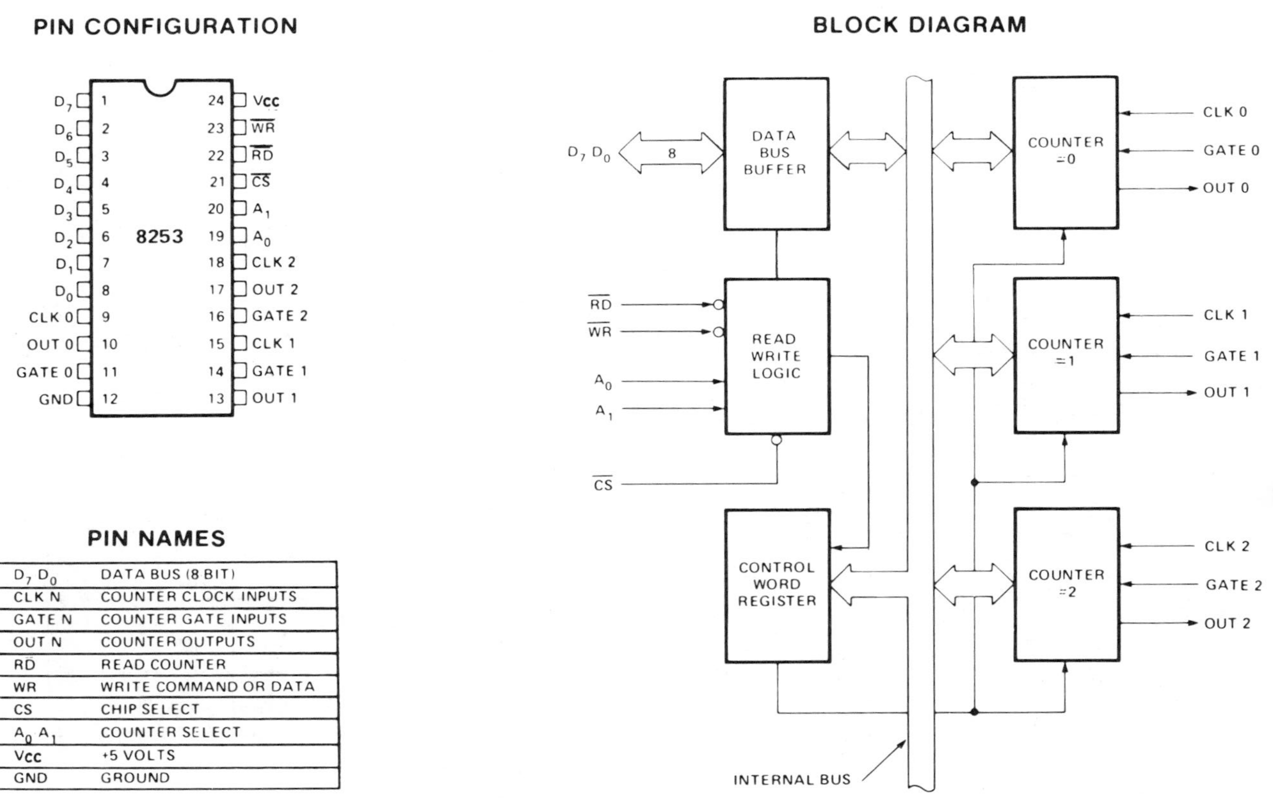

Figure 13-8 **8253** functional block diagram. (Reprinted by permission of Intel Corp.)

$\overline{CS}$ The chip select input is used to enable the communication between the **8253** and the μP by means of the data bus. A 0 on $\overline{\text{CS}}$ enables the data bus buffers, while a 1 disables the buffer. The $\overline{\text{CS}}$ input does not have any affect on the operation of the three timers once they have been initialized. The normal configuration of a system employs some *decode* logic which activates the $\overline{\text{CS}}$ line whenever a specific set of addresses that correspond to the **8253** appear on the address bus.

$\overline{RD}$ and $\overline{WR}$ The read ($\overline{\text{RD}}$) and write ($\overline{\text{WR}}$) pins control the direction of data transfer on the 8-bit data bus. When the $\overline{\text{RD}}$ input pin is LOW the **8253** is sending data to the μP. When $\overline{\text{WR}}$ is LOW the μP is sending data to the **8253**. The $\overline{\text{RD}}$ and $\overline{\text{WR}}$ pins should not both be LOW simultaneously. When both $\overline{\text{RD}}$ and $\overline{\text{WR}}$ pins are HIGH, the data bus buffer is disabled.

A0 and A1 These two input pins allow the μP to specify which one of the four registers in the **8253** is going to be used for the data transfer. Figure 13-9 shows how these two lines are used to select either the control word register or one of the 16-bit counters. For example, if there is a 1 on both A0 and A1 and a 0 on $\overline{\text{WR}}$, then the μP is writing a control byte to the control word register. These two input pins are usually connected to the address bus lines of the same name (i.e., A0 of the **8253** is connected to the A0 of the address bus and similarly for the A1 pin).

Each of the timers has three pins associated with it. These are the clock (CLK), the gate (GATE), and the output pin (OUT).

CLK This clock input pin provides the 16-bit timer with the signal that causes the timer to decrement. If the signal on this pin is generated by a fixed frequency oscillator then the user has implemented a standard timer. If the input signal is a

$\overline{\text{CS}}$	$\overline{\text{RD}}$	$\overline{\text{WR}}$	A_1	A_0	
0	1	0	0	0	Load Counter No. 0
0	1	0	0	1	Load Counter No. 1
0	1	0	1	0	Load Counter No. 2
0	1	0	1	1	Write Mode Word
0	0	1	0	0	Read Counter No. 0
0	0	1	0	1	Read Counter No. 1
0	0	1	1	0	Read Counter No. 2
0	0	1	1	1	No-Operation 3-State
1	X	X	X	X	Disable 3-State
0	1	1	X	X	No-Operation 3-State

Figure 13-9 Register selection. (Reprinted by permission of Intel Corp.)

string of randomly occurring pulses, then it is more appropriate to call this implementation a counter.

GATE The gate input pin is used to initiate or enable counting. The exact effect of the gate signal depends on which of the six modes of operation is chosen. More specific details will be covered in sections 13-3.5 on the **8253** operation.

OUTPUT The output pin provides an output from the timer. Its actual use depends on the mode of operation of the timer.

13-3.3 Principles of Operation

Each timer must be initialized into its mode of operation (one of the six modes) and selection of either binary or binary coded decimal (BCD) method of counting. The method of initializing the counters will be discussed in section 13-3.4 followed by the description of the six modes of operation in section 13-3.5

13-3.4 Counter Initialization

To initialize one of the **8253** counters the μP writes a *command* to the control word register to select the operational parameters for the counter, that is, to specify which of the six modes is to be used and to select either binary or BCD decrementing and a code to specify what operation that counter should perform (load the count or read the current counter value).

Figure 13-10 shows the format of the command that is written to the control word register. After the control word register has been programmed, the **8253** expects the count to be loaded into the counter as specified in the RL bits of the control word. If more than one counter is to be programmed at one time the software may be written to write a control word to each counter and then load the count into each counter, or each counter may be programmed completely with a control word and the count value before initializing the other counter.

EXAMPLE 13-6 An **8253** is part of an **8080** system and is addressed by the range of hexidecimal addresses 8000H to 8003H. What is the control byte that must be written to the **8253** to select timer two, in the binary mode for operation in mode 4 and the READ/LOAD operation of loading both 8-bit values into the timer? Write an **8080** assembly language program to perform this initialization and load the counter with a value of 07FCH.

Solution Timer number two is desired so bit 7 of the control word must be 1 and bit 6 must be 0. It is desired to load the 16-bit timer by loading in two 8-bit bytes, least significant byte first. This is indicated by setting bits 5 and 4 to 1. Mode 4 is selected by setting bit 3 to 1 and bits 2 and 1 to 0. The binary counting mode is selected by setting bit 0 to 0. Thus the value that should be written into the control word register is binary 10111000 or hexidecimal B8. The following program will perform this task.

Control Word Format

D_7	D_6	D_5	D_4	D_3	D_2	D_1	D_0
SC1	SC0	RL1	RL0	M2	M1	M0	BCD

Definition of Control

SC — Select Counter:

SC1	SC0	
0	0	Select Counter 0
0	1	Select Counter 1
1	0	Select Counter 2
1	1	Illegal

RL — Read/Load:

RL1	RL0	
0	0	Counter Latching operation (see READ/WRITE Procedure Section)
1	0	Read/Load most significant byte only
0	1	Read/Load least significant byte only
1	1	Read/Load least significant byte first, then most significant byte

M — MODE:

M2	M1	M0	
0	0	0	Mode 0
0	0	1	Mode 1
X	1	0	Mode 2
X	1	1	Mode 3
1	0	0	Mode 4
1	0	1	Mode 5

BCD:

0	Binary Counter 16 bits
1	Binary Coded Decimal (BCD) Counter (4 Decades)

Figure 13-10 Format of commands. (Reprinted by permission of Intel Corp.)

```
LXI   H,8003H   ;set HL to point to Cont. Word Reg
MVI   A,0B8H    ;
MOV   M,A       ;Load B8 into Cont. Word Reg.
DCX   H         ;HL points to counter #2.
MVI   A,0FCH    ;
MOV   M,A       ;Load low order byte to counter
MVI   A,07H     ;
MOV   M,A       ;Load high order byte to counter.
```

13-3.5 Modes of Operation

The mode of operation is chosen to produce the desired output signal. This will narrow the selection down to one or two modes. Next the user must supply a clock input signal to meet his needs and finally some external hardware is required to provide the proper input signal to the **8253** gate input. The gate input could be connected to an output port pin to allow computer control of the operation, or it could be connected to a switch or sensor provided by the user.

Figure 13-11 shows the different functions of the gate input in each mode of operation. The operation of the gate input will frequently determine the mode of

Modes \ Signal Status	Low Or Going Low	Rising	High
0	Disables counting	— —	Enables counting
1	— —	1) Initiates counting 2) Resets output after next clock	— —
2	1) Disables counting 2) Sets output immediately high	Initiates counting	Enables counting
3	1) Disables counting 2) Sets output immediately high	Initiates counting	Enables counting
4	Disables counting	— —	Enables counting
5	— —	Initiates counting	— —

Figure 13-11 Different functions of the gate input. (Reprinted by permission of Intel Corp.)

operation. The output pin from the counter can be used in the interrupt-related modes as the interrupt request signal; therefore this pin should be connected to the interrupt request input of the μP or to a priority interrupt controller (such as the **8259**) input pin. The **8253** has no built-in interrupt generating capability, other than the output pin of each timer. The **8253** is a general-purpose timer that can be used with any system. The six modes of operation are:

Mode Number	Mode Name
0	Interrupt on terminal count
1	Programmable one-shot
2	Rate generator
3	Square Wave rate generator
4	Software-triggered strobe
5	Hardware-triggered strobe

The operation of each of the modes is shown in Figure 13-12.

Mode 0: Interrupt on Terminal Count This mode of operation is a simple *down counter* with the output pin providing an indication of the counter reaching zero value. The output pin will go LOW when this mode is selected and will remain LOW until the counter reaches a count of zero, at which time the output pin will go HIGH and remain there until the counter has been reinitialized. The counter will start counting as soon as both bytes of the count value have been loaded and the gate is HIGH. After the counter has reached zero it will continue to count down, but will not change the output signal.

Mode 1: Programmable One-Shot This mode of operation provides a simple *retriggerable one-shot*. The output pin will go LOW on the clock pulse following the rising edge of the gate input. The rising edge of the gate also initiates the counting. The output pin will remain LOW until the counter has counted down to zero, at which time it will go HIGH. If a new value is loaded into the counter while the counter is counting, the counter will start using the new value and the output pin will remain low during the RELOAD operation.

This mode is very useful in that it provides a simple means of implementing a *watchdog timer* application. This can be done by connecting the output pin of the timer to the interrupt input of the μP. The software would then be required to reload the timer before it counted to zero. If the timer was not reloaded in the alloted time an interrupt would be generated, which would indicate to the operating system that the system was hung up in a loop and the operating system could then take appropriate action. If a 1-kHz clock signal was used, this would provide times up to 65 s with a resolution of 1 ms.

Mode 2: Rate Generator This mode of operation provides a divide by N counter or rate generator. The assumption is that a fixed frequency clock input is provided and it is desired that an output be generated for every N pulse supplied to the clock.

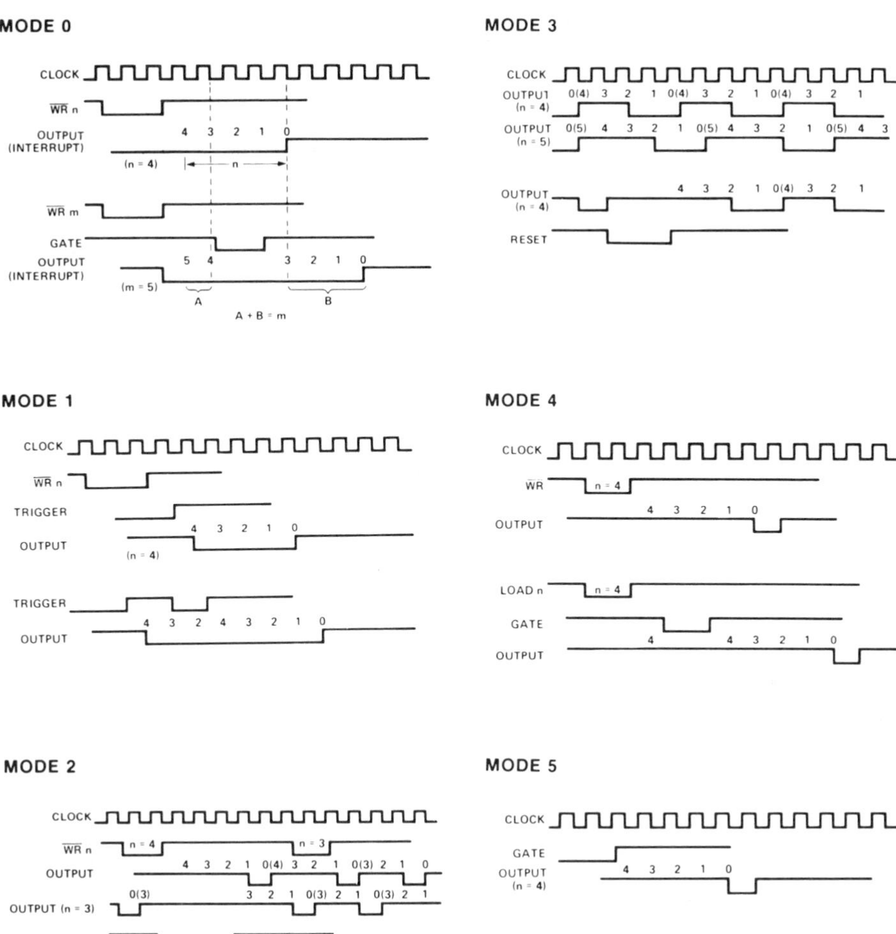

Figure 13-12 Timing diagrams for the six modes of operation. (Reprinted by permission of Intel Corp.)

The count only has to be loaded into the timer once and the timer will automatically reload itself when it has counted to zero. The output pin will remain HIGH until the counter reaches zero, at which time it will go LOW for one cycle of the input clock and then return HIGH until the counter has again counted to a zero value. If the counter is reloaded during counting, then the new count value will not be used until the counter finishes counting to zero using the previous value.

The gate input can be used to control the counter. If the gate is LOW, the output will be HIGH and no counting will be performed. When the gate input goes HIGH, then the counter will start counting from the initial value; thus this gate signal can be used by external hardware to synchronize the counting.

Mode 3: Square Wave Rate Generator This mode is similar to mode 2 except that the output signal will be a square wave with a symmetric wave shape (HIGH and LOW for equal times). This is accomplished internally by decrementing the counter by two on the falling edge of each clock pulse and then complementing the output signal. If the count value loaded was an odd value, then the output signal will be HIGH for (N + 1)/2 counts and LOW for (N − 1)/2 counts. Thus an odd value will introduce a small amount of asymmetry into the waveform. The rising edge of the gate signal will initiate the counting and the counting and output will continue as long as the gate is HIGH.

Mode 4: Software-Triggered Strobe In this mode of operation the output will go HIGH as soon as this mode is selected and the counter will begin counting as soon as the count has been loaded into the counter. When the counter reaches zero, the output will go LOW for one input clock period, then will go HIGH again.

If the counter was reloaded during the counting, the counter will immediately start counting using the new value. The counting will be enabled when the gate is HIGH and disabled when the gate is LOW.

Mode 5: Hardware-Triggered Strobe This mode provides the start of counting on the rising edge of the gate signal. The output pin will go LOW when the counter reaches zero, and remains LOW for one input clock period. The counter is retriggerable by activating the trigger line before the terminal count has been reached. The rising edge of the gate will cause the counter to be reloaded with the count value and counting to start again.

Figure 13-12 shows the timing diagrams for the six modes of operation. This diagram also clearly shows the effects of the gate signal on the operation of the counter and on the output signal.

13-3.6 Reading the Counter

When the timer is active, it is often desirable to read the current value of the timer. This is complicated on the **8253** because a 16-bit number must be read using an 8-bit data bus. This means the μP must read the 16-bits in two separate bytes. Trying to read the timer as it is in the process of counting down can often yield erroneous results. For example, if the timer had a value of 2000 when the first byte of 00 was read (the least significant byte is read first), then the timer decremented to 1FFF, and if the second byte was then read, it would have a value of 1F (the most significant byte of the current counter contents). This would make the user think that the timer contained a value of 1F00 instead of 2000 or 1FFF, which is a considerable error.

The **8253** provides a special READ operation that transfers the contents of the counter into a temporary register and lets the μP read the data from the register. The mode word format for latching the count is shown in Figure 13-10 and uses only the four most significant bits of the mode control word with bits 7 and 6 selecting the desired counter and bits 5 and 4 set to 0 to indicate a *latching count instruction.* After the count has been latched, either or both of the bytes can be read using the other three READ/LOAD operation shown in Figure 13-10.

A word of warning is necessary here. If the **8253** is in mode 3, it counts down by two; in all other modes the count decrements. Reading the count in mode 3 can give an ambiguous reading. Thus mode 3 should be used for generating square waves only, and not for counting.

EXAMPLE 13-7 An **8253** is part of an **8080A** system and is addressed by the range of addresses FF00 to FF03. It is desired that counter #0 be used in the "rate generator" mode with binary counting and a count value of 2C80H. Write an **8080A** program to perform this.

Solution First the number to be written to the mode word register must be determined. Bits 6 and 7 will be 0 to select timer #0. Bits 4 and 5 will both be 1 to indicate that we want to load the least significant byte followed by the most significant byte. The "rate generator" is mode 2, so bit 2 must be a 1 and bit 1 must be a 0 and bit 3 can be either a 1 or a 0. The binary mode is selected by setting bit 0 to 0. Since bit 3 can be either a 1 or a 0, a value of 0 will be used for simplicity. Thus, a value of binary 00110100 or hexidecimal 34H should be written to the mode word register. Based on Figure 13-7, the four addresses corresponding to the **8253** have the following functions:

Address	Register/Counter Number
FF00	Counter #0
FF01	Counter #1
FF02	Counter #2
FF03	Control word register

The following program will perform the initialization of the timer.

```
LXI   H,FF03   ;Set HL to point to Mode Word Reg.
MVI   A,34H    ;
MOV   M,A      ;Send 34H to Mode Word Reg.
LXI   H,FF00   ;Set HL to point to counter #0
MVI   A,80H    ;
MOV   M,A      ;Send LS byte to counter #0
MVI   A,2CH    ;
MOV   M,A      ;Send MS byte to counter #0
```

EXAMPLE 13-8 The **8253** described in Example 13-7 is assumed to be programmed and running and we now need to read the current value in the counter using the latched count technique and the value in the counter should be stored in the B and C registers (LS in B, and MS in C). Write a program to perform this operation.

Solution First the contents of the counter #0 must be latched into the temporary register on the **8253**. This is done by writing a byte to the control word register which has bits 4 and 5 set to 0 to indicate a latch instruction and with bits 6 and 7 set to 0 to select timer #0. The other four bits are not used and usually assumed to be 0. Thus a byte of binary 00000000 or hexidecimal 00 will perform this. Next a byte of 00110100 should be written to the control word register to indicate that 2 bytes will be read from counter #0. Then the 2 bytes should be read from counter 0.

```
LXI   H,FF03H   ;Set to point to mode word reg.
MVI   A,00H     ;
MOV   M,A       ;Latch counter #0
MVI   A,34H     ;
MOV   M,A       ;Set up 2 byte read of counter #0
INX   H         ;Set HL to point to counter #0
MOV   B,M       ;Load B with LS byte of counter #0
MOV   C,M       ;Load C with MS byte of counter #0
```

13-4 8275 PROGRAMMABLE CRT CONTROLLER

The **8275** programmable CRT controller is an LSI chip designed to perform many of the control functions required when a CRT (cathode ray tube, i.e., a video display) is interfaced to a μP system. This chip does not actually generate the video signal and therefore requires several auxiliary high-speed TTL gates and shift registers to produce the actual video output. The **8275** provides cursor control, light pen detection status and light pen data register, programmable screen and character format, and limited built-in graphics capability. The chip also has dual row buffers built into the chip so that the **8275** uses a minimum amount of CPU time performing its DMA (direct memory access) transfer from the CPU memory to the display. The **8275** requires an external character generator ROM, which allows an almost unlimited choice of character sets.

The **8275** normally uses an **8257** DMA controller to transfer data between the **8275** and the memory. Because of the complexity of the CRT controllers and the **8275**, this section will focus mainly on the **8275** itself and how it is programmed and used. There will be no detailed review of the operation of a video display system or complete design example.

13-4.1 Functional Description

Figure 13-13 shows the functional block diagram of the **8275** and Figure 13-15 is a typical system block diagram showing the **8275** and other required hardware. The data bus buffers provide the standard 8-bit bidirectional interface between the peripheral chip and the μP. This buffer allows the μP to write commands to the **8275** and to read status information from the **8275**. This buffer is also used during DMA operations to transfer characters from the μP system's memory directly to the **8275** without the direct intervention of the μP. This does, however, require the use of a special DMA controller such as the **8257**.

The control logic block of the **8275** is similar to the same block on the **8251** and **8253**, but this block has additional logic to handle the interface of a DMA controller with the **8275**. The rest of the functional blocks are associated directly with the CRT control operation. The character counter keeps track of which character within the row is currently having data displayed.

The two row buffers, shown in Figure 13-13, each 80 characters by 8 bits per character, are used for storing the characters for the row being displayed and the

PIN CONFIGURATION

Pin	Name	Pin	Name
1	LC_3	40	V_{CC}
2	LC_2	39	LA_0
3	LC_1	38	LA_1
4	LC_0	37	LTEN
5	DRQ	36	RVV
6	$\overline{DACK}$	35	VSP
7	HRTC	34	GPA_1
8	VRTC	33	GPA_0
9	$\overline{RD}$	32	HLGT
10	$\overline{WR}$	31	IRQ
11	LPEN	30	CCLK
12	DB_0	29	CC_6
13	DB_1	28	CC_5
14	DB_2	27	CC_4
15	DB_3	26	CC_3
16	DB_4	25	CC_2
17	DB_5	24	CC_1
18	DB_6	23	CC_0
19	DB_7	22	$\overline{CS}$
20	GND	21	A_0

8275

BLOCK DIAGRAM

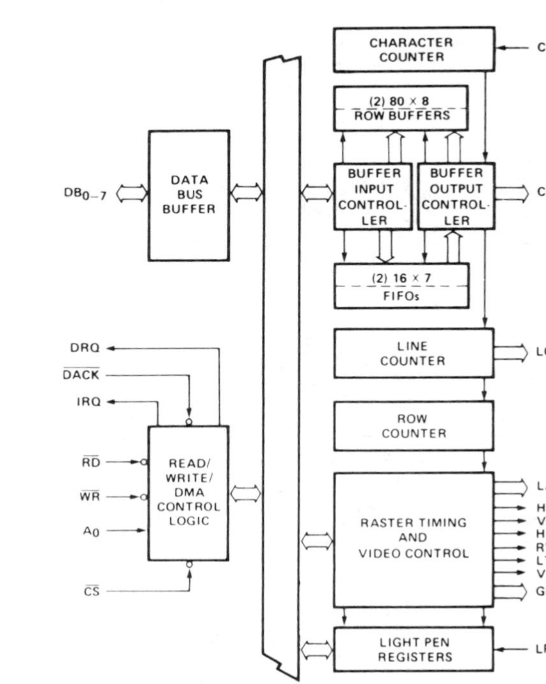

PIN NAMES

DB_{0-1}	BI-DIRECTIONAL DATA BUS	LC_{0-3}	LINE COUNTER OUTPUTS
DRQ	DMA REQUEST OUTPUT	LA_{0-1}	LINE ATTRIBUTE OUTPUTS
$\overline{DACK}$	DMA ACKNOWLEDGE INPUT	HRTC	HORIZONTAL RETRACE OUTPUT
IRQ	INTERRUPT REQUEST OUTPUT	VRTC	VERTICAL RETRACE OUTPUT
$\overline{RD}$	READ STROBE INPUT	HLGT	HIGHLIGHT OUTPUT
$\overline{WR}$	WRITE STROBE INPUT	RVV	REVERSE VIDEO OUTPUT
A_0	REGISTER ADDRESS INPUT	LTEN	LIGHT ENABLE OUTPUT
CS	CHIP SELECT INPUT	VSP	VIDEO SUPPRESS OUTPUT
CCLK	CHARACTER CLOCK INPUT	GPA_{0-1}	GENERAL PURPOSE ATTRIBUTE OUTPUTS
CC_{0-6}	CHARACTER CODE OUTPUTS	LPEN	LIGHT PEN INPUT

Figure 13-13 Functional block diagram and pin out of the **8275**. (Reprinted by permission of Intel Corp.)

next row to be displayed. One row buffer is being loaded from memory by way of the buffer input controller block while the other row buffer is sending characters out to the video generation circuit under the control of the buffer output controller. Both of these controllers use a dual 16-character by 7-bit FIFO buffer (first in, first out buffer) to simplify the handling of special control codes.

The line counter keeps track of which line of dots within the character is to be displayed. The row counter keeps track of which row of characters is currently being displayed.

The raster timing and video control generates all of the special control signals which are required to control the high-speed generation of the video signal by separate hardware. This requires a minimum amount of additional hardware.

The light pen registers allow the **8275** to store the row number and the character position within the row at which the light pen was pointed when activated. The light pen register contents can then be read by the μP.

13-4.2 Device Pins

The pins of the **8275** are shown in Figure 13-13 and will be described in two groups. The first group handles the interface to the μP system. The second group handles the interface to the CRT screen and high-speed video generation circuits.

The following set of device pins allow the **8275** to communicate with the μP system.

DB0 to DB7 These are the eight bidirectional pins that are connected to the data bus of the μP.

$\overline{RD}$ and $\overline{WR}$ The READ and WRITE input pins tell the **8275** the direction of the data transfer. If $\overline{\text{RD}}$ is LOW, then the μP expects data to come from the **8275** to the μP. When $\overline{\text{WR}}$ is LOW, the transfer is from the μP to the **8275**. Both $\overline{\text{RD}}$ and $\overline{\text{WR}}$ may not be 0 at the same time.

$\overline{CS}$ The chip select is used to inform the **8275** that the μP wants to communicate with it. The chip select signal is usually generated by some decode logic that will put out a 0 whenever the specific range of addresses corresponding to the **8275** appear on the address bus of the μP system.

DRQ This output pin is the DMA REQUEST pin used by the **8275** to request a DMA transfer of data by a DMA controller. A logic 1 requests a data transfer.

$\overline{DACK}$ This input pin is the DMA ACKNOWLEDGE input pin. A LOW on this input tells the **8275** that a DMA transfer is in progress.

IRQ This output pin is the INTERRUPT REQUEST output. The **8275** drives this pin HIGH to request an interrupt from the processor, indicating the **8275** requires interrupt servicing.

A0 The A0 input pin is used to select which register within the **8275** the μP is addressing. Figure 13-14 shows how the logic level of A0, $\overline{RD}$, $\overline{WR}$, and $\overline{CS}$ are used to select the proper register.

The following set of device pins allow the **8275** to interface to and to control the high-speed character generation by TTL (transistor-transistor logic) devices.

CCLK The character clock is an input pin on the **8275** which enables the external high-speed dot generation circuit to synchronize the output of 7-bit characters on the CC0 to CC6 pins by the **8275**, from the 80-character row buffer within the **8275**. The character clock is obtained by dividing the basic system dot clock by the width of the character in dots.

CC0 to CC6 These seven output pins transfer the character code (such as ASCII) for the next character to be displayed, from one of the row buffers in the **8275** to the external character generator ROM.

LC0 to LC3 These four output pins are the line count which go to the character generator ROM to indicate which row of dots of the character should be output.

LA0 to LA1 These two outputs indicate *attribute codes* which have to be decoded externally by the dot timing logic to generate limited graphics. (See section 13-4.4.)

HRTC The horizontal retrace output signal is active during the programmed horizontal retrace interval. This signal is used to control the external hardware, which generates the horizontal synchronization.

VRTC The vertical retrace output signal is active during the programmed vertical retrace interval and is used to control the vertical synchronization.

HLGT The highlight signal can be used to direct external hardware to increase the intensity of the video signal to make the character stand out.

RVV The reverse video output signal can be used by external hardware to cause the signal to be inverted in intensity. The reverse video may be used at the cursor

A_0	$\overline{RD}$	$\overline{WR}$	$\overline{CS}$	
0	0	1	0	Write 8275 Parameter
0	1	0	0	Read 8275 Parameter
1	0	1	0	Write 8275 Command
1	1	0	0	Read 8275 Status
X	1	1	0	Three-State
X	X	X	1	Three-state

Figure 13-14 **8275** register select logic. (Reprinted by permission of Intel Corp.)

position and or at positions specified by special characters in the data called field attribute codes.

LTEN The light enable output is used to enable the video signal to the CRT. This is active at the underline cursor position and at the locations specified by the field attribute codes.

VSP The video suppression output signal is used to blank or disable the video signal to the CRT. This signal is active during the horizontal and vertical retrace intervals, at the top and bottom line of each row, when a special end of row or end of screen field attribute code is detected, when a DMA underrun occurs, and when a blinking cursor has been programmed, or blinking characters have been selected by the field attribute code.

GPA0 and GPA1 These two general-purpose attribute outputs are enabled by the general-purpose field attribute codes. These two outputs can be used to activate special-purpose external hardware under the control of the **8275**.

LPEN The light pen input signal is driven by a photocell-triggered light pen which will output a pulse as the CRT raster scans past the point on the screen at which the light pen is pointing. This input allows the **8275** to internally store the row number and character position within the row of the character at which the light pen was pointing when activated.

13-4.3 General Operation

The **8275** CRT controller and the other necessary hardware to drive a video display is shown in Figure 13-15. The **8275** provides the control circuitry and interface between the μP system and the video generation hardware. The characters that are to be displayed on the CRT are stored in memory in a coded form such as ASCII. The memory is usually part of the memory space of the μP and the **8275** gets the character from memory with the help of a DMA controller, such as the **8257**. The DMA transfer provides the fastest possible method of transferring data from memory to the CRT controller while consuming a minimum amount of CPU time. When the **8275** receives the characters, they are stored in one of two 80-character (8 bits per character) row buffers. When a complete row of characters has been received, the **8275** will start filling the second row buffer with the next row of characters to be displayed. When the **8275** starts displaying a row of characters at the top of the screen, it will send the characters out to the character generator ROM at a rate of one character for each clock pulse input on the character clock input. The **8275** must send out the entire row of characters for each line of dots which will be displayed for the character. For example, if a character is nine dots high by seven dots wide, the string of characters must be sent out nine times before the **8275** can start displaying the second row of characters that are in the other 80-character row buffer. While the **8275** is displaying the second row of characters, it is also filling the first row buffer with the characters for the third row to be displayed. This operation

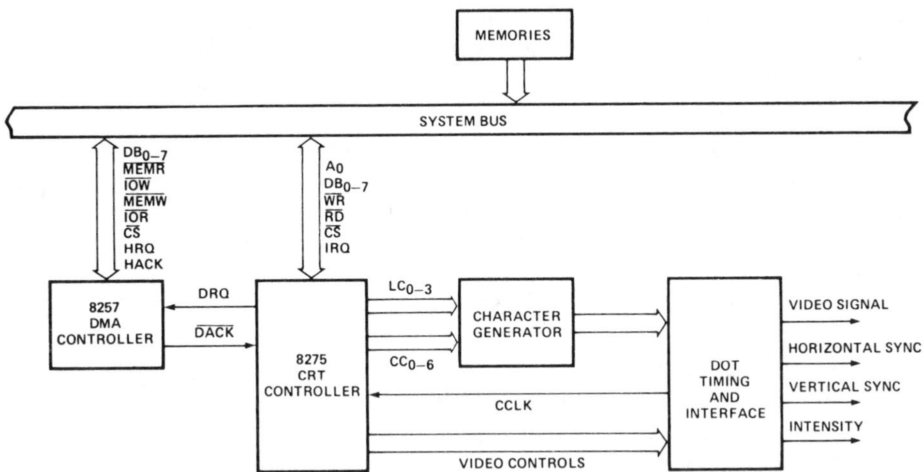

Figure 13-15 **8275** systems block diagram showing systems operation. (Reprinted by permission of Intel Corp.)

is repeated until the whole screen has been displayed once, which typically takes $\frac{1}{60}$ of a second, and then the whole operation repeats starting at the top of the screen again. Thus if we have a 20-row format with 80 characters per row, this yields 1600 characters which must be transferred 60 times a second, or 96,000 characters/s. Actually this is a worse-case number because the **8275** has *special character codes* which can be put at the end of a line or at the end of the row which is the last row to be displayed on the screen. These special characters allow the **8275** to stop the DMA operation and improve efficiency by not fetching a string of blank characters. The **8275** also improves operation by having two row buffers which allow the **8275** to transfer a row of characters from memory once, but send them out to the character generator ROM nine times without refetching them from memory.

The **8275** is programmable with a wide range of options for screen formats and DMA transfer rates. The next sections will consider the format options available and the initialization of the **8275**. Multiple displays or pages of displays may be maintained in memory and the display can be quickly changed simply by changing the starting address that the DMA controller is using to fetch data from memory. Scrolling can be implemented by the same method, that is, by changing the starting address for the DMA operation to the second row, instead of the first.

13-4.4 Display Format

The **8275** can be programmed to provide a display with from 1 to 80 characters per row and from 1 to 64 rows. The format may use single- or double-spaced format (with alternate rows blank). Each row of characters may consist of from one to 16 lines of dots (or horizontal sweeps). The placement of the underline character is programmable from line 0 to line 15. If the number of the underline is greater then 7, then the top and the bottom lines of the character field will be blanked to provide visible spacing between the rows. The blanking will be provided by the VSP signal and the underline is accomplished by the LTEN (light enable) signal. The dot width is a function of the dot timing circuitry. The width of each character (in dots) is a function of the character generator ROM.

The **8275** character counter is driven by the character clock (CCLK) and counts out the character being displayed. When the counter has reached the programmed row length, it increments the line counter and then counts out the programmed horizontal retrace interval, which can be set between 2 and 32 character clock counts.

The line counter outputs its contents on LC0 to LC3 to the character generator ROM to indicate which line of dots of the character should be output. The number of lines per character row is programmable from 1 to 16. When the line counter has counted the programmed number of lines, it resets itself, increments the row counter, and starts over.

The row counter keeps track of the current row number and controls the switching between the two row buffers. After the row counter has counted to the programmed number of rows, it then starts counting the vertical retrace interval which is selectable from 1- to 4-row intervals.

The **8275** can be programmed to request transfers of data in *bursts* of one to eight characters. The interval between the bursts can be programmed from 0 to 55 character clocks. The interval value of 0 implies that the data will be fetched continuously for the row of characters. The **8275** will make the first DMA request one row time before the end of the vertical retrace interval. The DMA requests will continue as programmed until the row buffer is filled. If the row is filled in the middle of a burst, the **8275** terminates the burst and resets the burst counter. The DMA actions will resume when the **8275** is ready to fill the second row buffer.

The **8275** can be programmed to generate an *interrupt* at the end of each frame. This interrupt may be used to reinitialize the DMA controller, at which time scrolling or a new display page could be substituted. The interrupt is cleared by reading the status register.

There are three types of special characters which are used by the **8275**. They are the character attribute codes, the special codes, and the field attributes.

A *character attribute code* is a nondisplayable code read from memory along with the data. The data is assumed to be 7-bit characters such as ASCII, where bit 7 is 0. A character attribute code causes the following displayable characters to have something special done to them, such as being underlined or highlighted. The 8-bit character attribute code is stored by the μP along with the regular characters. The character attribute codes have the following format:

```
bit    7 6 5 4 3 2 1 0
       1 1 C C C C B H
```

The two 1s in the most significant bits are used to distinguish it from the regular characters. The four bits with C in them are used by the external hardware to generate 16 special graphics characters. The B in bit position 1 signifies blinking. The H in bit position 0 indicates that the following characters should be highlighted.

There are also four *special control characters* to help reduce DMA overhead. The format for special codes is:

```
bit    7 6 5 4 3 2 1 0
       1 1 1 1 0 0 S S

SS     FUNCTION
00     End of Row
01     End of Row - Stop DMA
10     End of Screen
11     End of Screen - Stop DMA
```

The *field attributes* are control codes which affect the visual characteristics of a field of characters, starting at the character following the code, up to and including the character which precedes the next field attribute code, or up to the end of the frame. The format is as follows:

```
bit    7 6 5 4 3 2 1 0
       1 0 U R G G B H
```

where U = 1 for underline, R = 1 for reverse video, B = 1 for blinking characters, and H = 1 for highlighting. The 2-bit GG lines are output on the pins GPA1 and GPA0 and must be decoded by external hardware. The field attribute can specify any combination of the above display options.

The **8275** can handle the field attribute codes in two different ways, either as *visible* or *invisible* characters. In the invisible mode, the characters on each side of the field attribute code are displayed on the screen as adjacent characters, thus field attribute codes do not take up a character position on the screen and hence the description "invisible." In the *visible* character mode, the field attribute code is displayed as a *blank*. The visible mode may be useful for program debugging and checkout.

The cursor position on the screen is stored in two registers on the **8275**, the cursor row register and character position register. Both of these registers are loaded by the μP controller. The cursor may be programmed to one of the following four possibilities:

1 a blinking underline;

2 a blinking reverse video block;

3 a nonblinking underline;

4 a nonblinking reverse video block.

13-4.5 Device Initialization

The **8275** appears on the address bus as two memory locations or I/O ports, with A0 being used to distinguish between them. Figure 13-14 shows the selection of the registers based on A0 and whether the operation is a READ or a WRITE. The **8275** has three registers; the function and configuration of each register is shown in Figure 13-16. The parameter register (PREG) is used to accept the 0 to 4 bytes of

1. Reset Command:

	OPERATION	A_0	DESCRIPTION	DATA BUS MSB LSB
Command	Write	1	Reset Command	0 0 0 0 0 0 0 0
Parameters	Write	0	Screen Comp Byte 1	S H H H H H H H
	Write	0	Screen Comp Byte 2	V V R R R R R R
	Write	0	Screen Comp Byte 3	U U U U L L L L
	Write	0	Screen Comp Byte 4	M F C C Z Z Z Z

Action – After the reset command is written, DMA requests stop, 8275 interrupts are disabled, and the VSP output is used to blank the screen. HRTC and VRTC continue to run. HRTC and VRTC timing are random on power-up.

As parameters are written, the screen composition is defined.

Parameter – S Spaced Rows

S	FUNCTIONS
0	Normal Rows
1	Spaced Rows

Parameter – HHHHHHH Horizontal Characters/Row

H H H H H H H	NO. OF CHARACTERS PER ROW
0 0 0 0 0 0 0	1
0 0 0 0 0 0 1	2
0 0 0 0 0 1 0	3
.	.
.	.
.	.
1 0 0 1 1 1 1	80
1 0 1 0 0 0 0	Undefined
.	.
.	.
.	.
1 1 1 1 1 1 1	Undefined

Parameter – VV Vertical Retrace Row Count

V V	NO. OF ROW COUNTS PER VRTC
0 0	1
0 1	2
1 0	3
1 1	4

Parameter – RRRRRR Vertical Rows/Frame

R R R R R R	NO. OF ROWS/FRAME
0 0 0 0 0 0	1
0 0 0 0 0 1	2
0 0 0 0 1 0	3
.	.
.	.
.	.
1 1 1 1 1 1	64

Parameter – UUUU Underline Placement

U U U U	LINE NUMBER OF UNDERLINE
0 0 0 0	1
0 0 0 1	2
0 0 1 0	3
.	.
.	.
.	.
1 1 1 1	16

Parameter – LLLL Number of Lines per Character Row

L L L L	NO. OF LINES/ROW
0 0 0 0	1
0 0 0 1	2
0 0 1 0	3
.	.
.	.
.	.
1 1 1 1	16

Parameter – M Line Counter Mode

M	LINE COUNTER MODE
0	Mode 0 (Non-Offset)
1	Mode 1 (Offset by 1 Count)

Parameter – F Field Attribute Mode

F	FIELD ATTRIBUTE MODE
0	Transparent
1	Non-Transparent

Parameter – CC Cursor Format

C C	CURSOR FORMAT
0 0	Blinking reverse video block
0 1	Blinking underline
1 0	Nonblinking reverse video block
1 1	Nonblinking underline

Parameter – ZZZZ Horizontal Retrace Count

Z Z Z Z	NO. OF CHARACTER COUNTS PER HRTC
0 0 0 0	2
0 0 0 1	4
0 0 1 0	6
.	.
.	.
.	.
1 1 1 1	32

Note: uuuu MSB determines blanking of top and bottom lines (1 = blanked, 0 = not blanked).

Figure 13-16 The **8275** instruction set. (Reprinted by permission of Intel Corp.)

2. Start Display Command:

	OPERATION	A_0	DESCRIPTION	DATA BUS MSB ... LSB
Command	Write	1	Start Display	0 0 1 S S S B B
No parameters				

S S S	BURST SPACE CODE: NO. OF CHARACTER CLOCKS BETWEEN DMA REQUESTS
0 0 0	0
0 0 1	7
0 1 0	15
0 1 1	23
1 0 0	31
1 0 1	39
1 1 0	47
1 1 1	55

B B	BURST COUNT CODE: NO. OF DMA CYCLES PER BURST
0 0	1
0 1	2
1 0	4
1 1	8

Action – 8275 interrupts are enabled, DMA requests begin, video is enabled, Interrupt Enable and Video Enable status flags are set.

3. Stop Display Command:

	OPERATION	A_0	DESCRIPTION	DATA BUS MSB ... LSB
Command	Write	1	Stop Display	0 1 0 0 0 0 0 0
No parameters				

Action – Disables video, interrupts remain enabled, HRTC and VRTC continue to run, Video Enable status flag is reset, and the "Start Display" command must be given to re-enable the display.

4. Read Light Pen Command

	OPERATION	A_0	DESCRIPTION	DATA BUS MSB ... LSB
Command	Write	1	Read Light Pen	0 1 1 0 0 0 0 0
Parameters	Read	0	Char. Number	(Char. Position in Row)
	Read	0	Row Number	(Row Number)

Action – The 8275 is conditioned to supply the contents of the light pen position registers in the next two read cycles of the parameter register. Status flags are not affected.

Note: Software correction of light pen position is required.

5. Load Cursor Position:

	OPERATION	A_0	DESCRIPTION	DATA BUS MSB ... LSB
Command	Write	1	Load Cursor	1 0 0 0 0 0 0 0
Parameters	Write	0	Char. Number	(Char. Position in Row)
	Write	0	Row Number	(Row Number)

Action – The 8275 is conditioned to place the next two parameter bytes into the cursor position registers. Status flags not affected.

6. Enable Interrupt Command:

	OPERATION	A_0	DESCRIPTION	DATA BUS MSB ... LSB
Command	Write	1	Enable Interrupt	1 0 1 0 0 0 0 0
No parameters				

Action – The interrupt enable status flag is set and interrupts are enabled.

7. Disable Interrupt Command:

	OPERATION	A_0	DESCRIPTION	DATA BUS MSB ... LSB
Command	Write	1	Disable Interrupt	1 1 0 0 0 0 0 0
No parameters				

Action – Interrupts are disabled and the interrupt enable status flag is reset.

8. Preset Counters Command:

	OPERATION	A_0	DESCRIPTION	DATA BUS MSB ... LSB
Command	Write	1	Preset Counters	1 1 1 0 0 0 0 0
No parameters				

Action – The internal timing counters are preset, corresponding to a screen display position at the top left corner. Two character clocks are required for this operation. The counters will remain in this state until any other command is given.

This command is useful for system debug and synchronization of clustered CRT displays on a single CPU.

Status Flags

	OPERATION	A_0	DESCRIPTION	DATA BUS MSB ... LSB
Command	Read	1	Status Word	0 IE IR LP IC VE DU FO

IE – (Interrupt Enable) Set or reset by command. It enables vertical retrace interrupt. It is automatically set by a "Start Display" command and reset with the "Reset" command.

IR – (Interrupt Request) This flag is set at the beginning of display of the last row of the frame if the interrupt enable flag is set. It is reset after a status read operation.

LP – This flag is set when the light pen input (LPEN) is activated and the light pen registers have been loaded. This flag is automatically reset after a status read.

IC – (Improper Command) This flag is set when a command parameter string is too long or too short. The flag is automatically reset after a status read.

VE – (Video Enable) This flag indicates that video operation of the CRT is enabled. This flag is set on a "Start Display" command, and reset on a "Stop Display" or "Reset" command.

DU – (DMA Underrun) This flag is set whenever a data underrun occurs during DMA transfers. Upon detection of DU, the DMA operation is stopped and the screen is blanked until after the vertical retrace interval. This flag is reset after a status read.

FO – (FIFO Overrun) This flag is set whenever the FIFO is overrun. It is reset on a status read.

parameters associated with each command and is selected when A0 is 0. The command register (CREG) is selected when A0 is 1 and a WRITE operation is being performed. The status register is selected when A0 is 1 and a READ operation is performed. The **8275** is programmed by sending a single-byte command to the command register followed by 0 to 4 bytes of parameters, which are sent to the parameter register.

The following example demonstrates the initialization procedure for the **8275** and clearly demonstrates the interrelationship of the CRT parameters with the CRT controller hardware and the **8275** initialization.

EXAMPLE 13-9 Write the software required to initialize an **8275** that is to drive a CRT monitor approximately at the commercial US TV standard [horizontal sweep rate of 15,750 Hz (63.5 μs) and vertical sweep rate of 60 Hz (16.67 ms)] using a character generator ROM which displays the characters as 5×7 dots. The horizontal retrace time of the monitor is 28 character times and the vertical retrace time is two row times. The display format will be 80 characters per row with 25 rows on the screen.

Solution The first step of the initialization is to execute a RESET command and include the parameters to specify the screen format. After the screen format is defined the start display command should be executed.

The RESET command is executed by writing a 00 byte into the **8275** command register followed by 4 bytes of parameters written to the parameter register. The first parameter byte (see Figure 13-16) defines the number of characters per row and whether normal or spaced rows are required. Normal rows require bit 7 to be 0. The 7 least significant bits are a hexidecimal number which is one less than the number of characters per row. An 80-character-per-row format was selected, which means that these 7 bits must be 1001111 and the first parameter byte is 01001111 (or hexidecimal 4F).

The second parameter byte defines the number of rows per frame and the amount of time required for the vertical retrace time (in units of row counts). The most significant 2 bits specify the vertical retrace time which, for this example, is two row counts, so these bits should be 01. The least significant six bits specify the number of rows per frame, which is a hexidecimal number one less than the desired number of rows. Hence these 6 bits should be 011000, which yield the second byte value of 01011000 (or hexidecimal 58).

The third parameter byte specifies the number of lines of dots per character row and the line of dots on which the underline will be placed. Both of these are 4-bit numbers that specify a number between 1 and 16. Thus the 4-bit number is actually a value one less than the desired parameter value. For our characters we are using seven lines of dots to display the characters and three lines of blanks to separate the rows for a total of ten lines per character row, which means that the least significant 4 bits of the parameter should be 1001. Putting the underline on the middle of the three spacing lines would put the underline on line number nine, which means that the most significant 4 bits of the parameter would be 1000. Underline is a field attribute. The characters to be underlined must be preceded by an attribute character. This yields the third parameter byte of 10001001 (or hexidecimal 89).

The fourth parameter byte specifies the remaining four parameters. Selecting the normal line counter mode (nonoffset) means bit 7 is a 0. Bit 6 should also be 0 to select the transparent field attribute mode. Bits 4 and 5 select the desired cursor format, which can be selected based on the desire of the user. For this example a blinking reverse video cursor is used, so these 2 bits are both zero. We want a horizontal retrace time of 28 character counts to match the video monitor so we must set the 4 least significant bits to 1101. Thus the final parameter byte is 00001101 (or 0D hexidecimal).

Next we have to define the parameters required for the start display command. This command does not require additional parameter bytes, but includes two parameters in the command word. To do this we have to set up the DMA cycle by specifying the number of characters to be transferred on each DMA burst and the time between each burst. This has to be set up such that the entire row of 80 characters will have been loaded into the buffer in the time that it takes the **8275** to display all ten lines of dots plus the horizontal retrace on each line. That is, each line of dots requires 80 character times to display plus 28 character times for horizontal retrace, or a total of 108 character times per line. Therefore it will take 10×108 or 1080 character times to display the entire row. If we assume that the DMA transfer time per character is less than or equal to the character time, we can approximate how long it will take to transfer the characters. Assume that we want to transfer eight characters per DMA burst. Then we would require ten bursts to transfer all 80 characters. If we take a burst spacing of 55 character times this will transfer the entire line in $10 \times (8 + 55)$ or 630 character times, which is less than the 1080 character times, so this pair of numbers is satisfactory.

If we had picked two characters per burst this would require 40 bursts to transfer 80 characters. If we tried to again use the 55-character time spacing we would find that this required $40 \times (2 + 55)$ or 2280 character times, which is much greater than the maximum of 1080 character times, so this pair of numbers would not work.

To specify our start display command with 8 characters per burst and 55 character times between burst yields a value of 00111111 (or hexidecimal 3F) for our start command. The following program will perform this initialization.

```
LXI    H,CRTADDRESS    ;HL points to 8275 (A0 = 1)
MVI    M,00H           ;send reset command
DCX    H               ;HL points to PREG (A0 = 0)
MVI    M,4FH
MVI    M,58H
MVI    M,89H
MVI    M,0DH
INX    H               ;HL points to CREG (A0 = 1)
MVI    M,3FH           ;send start display command
```

13-5 THE 8279 PROGRAMMABLE KEYBOARD/DISPLAY INTERFACE

The **8279** is an I/O IC. It provides a μP interface to a keyboard and a multiplexed display output for driving LED or LCD seven-segment displays. It greatly simplifies the design of equipment such as a μP-controlled point of sales terminal (POS). This chip replaces many small-scale integrated circuits and reduces the part count and the power supply requirements.

13-5.1 Functional Description

The pin configuration of the **8279** is shown in Figure 13-17 and the functional block diagram of the **8279** is shown in Figure 13-18. The **8279** drives external displays

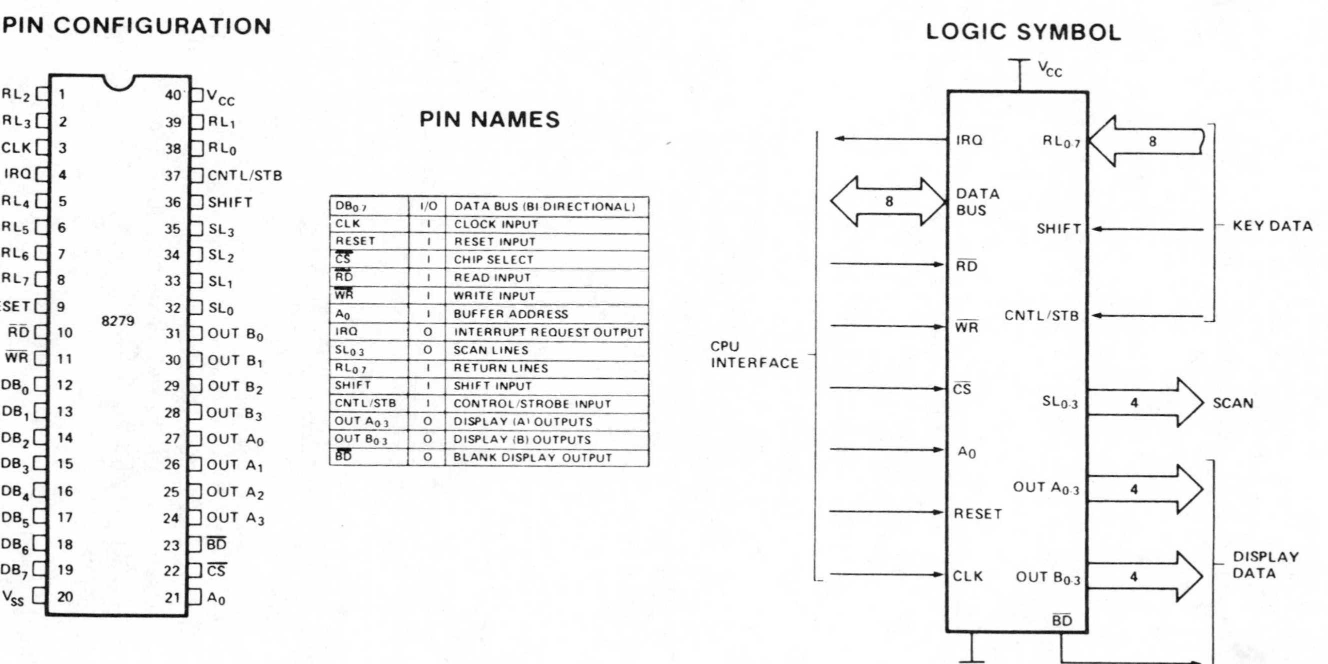

PIN NAMES

DB_{0-7}	I/O	DATA BUS (BI DIRECTIONAL)
CLK	I	CLOCK INPUT
RESET	I	RESET INPUT
$\overline{CS}$	I	CHIP SELECT
$\overline{RD}$	I	READ INPUT
$\overline{WR}$	I	WRITE INPUT
A_0	I	BUFFER ADDRESS
IRQ	O	INTERRUPT REQUEST OUTPUT
SL_{0-3}	O	SCAN LINES
RL_{0-7}	I	RETURN LINES
SHIFT	I	SHIFT INPUT
CNTL/STB	I	CONTROL/STROBE INPUT
OUT A_{0-3}	O	DISPLAY (A) OUTPUTS
OUT B_{0-3}	O	DISPLAY (B) OUTPUTS
$\overline{BD}$	O	BLANK DISPLAY OUTPUT

Figure 13-17 The pin configuration of the **8279**. (Reprinted by permission of Intel Corp.)

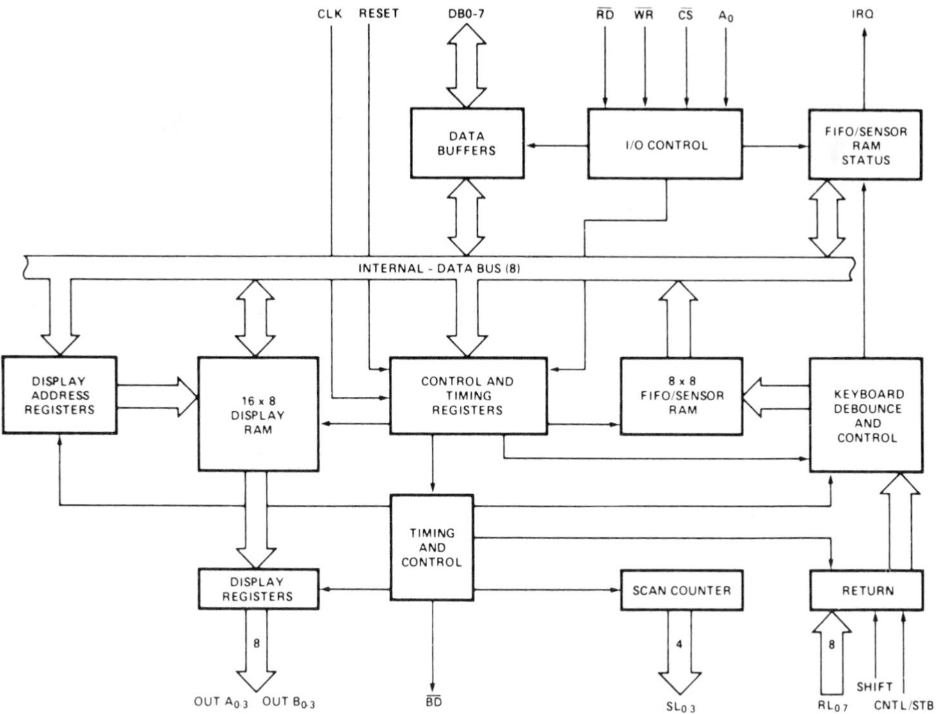

Figure 13-18 The functional block diagram of the **8279**. (Reprinted by permission of Intel Corp.)

using its eight OUT lines (A0 to A3 and B0 to B3). It receives information from a keyboard via the eight RL (RL0 to RL7) lines. It also has shift and CNTL/STB (control/strobe) inputs to accommodate an encoded keyboard.

The four *scan counter* outputs (SL0 to SL3) are used to control the keyboard line being scanned and also to determine which display is being selected. These signals relieve the user of having to multiplex signals for a keyboard scan or multiplexed display.

The data buffers, I/O control, and interrupt control allow the μP to communicate with the **8279**. The remainder of the **8279** can be partitioned into three main sections, the internal timing and control, the display addressing and storage, and the keyboard scanning and buffering.

The timing and control section is composed of two blocks, the timing and control logic and the timing and control registers. Together, these two blocks allow the **8279** to scan the keyboard to check for an entry and to drive the multiplexed displays independent of the μP. The control registers store the keyboard and display modes and other operating parameters. The timing control logic contains a timing chain, consisting of two counters. The first counter is a divide-by-N prescaler that can be programmed to generate an internal frequency. Programming this prescaler to generate a frequency of approximately 100 kHz yields a keyboard scan time of 5 ms and a keyboard debounce time of 10 ms. Another counter in the timing chain further divides the clock to provide the timing for keyboard scan, row scan, and display scanning. This effectively reduces the amount of control that the μP has to supply. The μP only has to communicate with the **8279** when a key has been pressed or when the μP wants to change the data being displayed.

The display address registers hold the address of the word currently being read or written by the μP or the 8 bits being sent to the display. The addresses are loaded by the μP and may also be set to auto increment after each READ or WRITE. The data that is stored in the display RAM may be stored in each location as a single byte or as two 4-bit nibbles.

EXAMPLE 13-10 How can BCD data be displayed using the **8279**?

Solution Each BCD digit can be entered into the display RAM as one nibble. When accessed it can go to a BCD to seven-segment decoder, like a 7447, and then to a seven-segment display.

The data may be entered into the display RAM from either the left side with successively entered characters being displayed in the next position to the right, or the data can be entered starting at the right most display position where each successive character entered goes into the rightmost position and all previously entered characters move to the left. Either method can be selected by the program when the **8279** is initialized.

The scan counter has two modes of operation. In the *encoded* mode, the scan counter puts out a 4-bit number that must be decoded by an external 1 of 16 decoder. This mode provides for the display of up to 16 decimal digits. In the other mode, the *decoded* mode, the same four output lines are each used to select one digit. This mode only allows the display of four digits. The scan counter is also used for selecting the row of the keyboard to be checked for a key pressed.

The keyboard section consists of the return buffers, keyboard debounce and control circuitry, and the FIFO/sensor RAM and status. The eight return lines are buffered and latched by the return buffers. The return buffers have three modes of operation, the keyboard mode, the scanned sensor mode, and the strobed input mode.

In the keyboard mode the **8279** scans the rows looking for a switch closure in each row. If a switch closure is detected, the debounce circuitry will wait the debounce time (typical debounce time for mechanical switches is 5 to 10 ms). If the switch is still closed then the address of the switch in the matrix (3-bit row address and 3-bit column address) and the status of the shift and control keys are transferred to the first-in-first-out (FIFO) buffer.

In the scanned sensor matrix mode, the contents of the return lines are directly transferred to the corresponding row of the FIFO each scan time. This method allows the μP to read the status of any sensor in the matrix simply by reading a location in the sensor RAM.

In the strobed input mode, the contents of the return lines are transferred to the FIFO on the rising edge of the CNTL/STB line pulse. This mode is ideally suited for systems using a keyboard that has built-in encoding.

The FIFO/sensor RAM is an 8-word by 8-bit RAM. In the keyboard or strobed input modes, the RAM acts as a FIFO buffer. The FIFO keeps track of where the next incoming entry will be placed in the RAM and which entry will be the next to be sent out, and also whether the FIFO is empty or full. The status logic will generate an interrupt when the FIFO is not empty.

In the scanned sensor matrix mode, the RAM is a sensor RAM. Each row of the sensor RAM (each 8-bit word) is loaded with the ON/OFF status of the eight sensors in the corresponding row of the sensor matrix. In this mode, an interrupt will be generated if a *change* in the status of any sensor is detected.

13-5.2 Device Pins

The device pins on the **8279** are shown in Figure 13-17 and are very closely related to the functional parts, which are described in section 13-5.1. The interface to the μP consists of the usual pins, which have been discussed in previous sections of this chapter, the eight data bus buffer pins, a read ($\overline{\text{RD}}$) and write ($\overline{\text{WR}}$), a chip select ($\overline{\text{CS}}$), a reset (RESET), an interrupt (IRQ), and a clock (CLK) which will not be covered in detail.

A0 The A0 input pin is usually connected to the least significant bit of the address bus and is used to select the appropriate internal register when the chip is selected. A HIGH on this line indicates that the μP is sending a command to the **8279** or reading the status. A LOW indicates that the μP is reading or writing data.

SL0 to SL3 These scan lines are used to scan the keyboard and the display.

RL0 to RL7 These return lines are inputs which are used to bring keyboard or sensor data into the **8279**.

SHIFT This input brings in the status of the shift key.

CNTL/STB This dual function input brings in the status of the control key in the keyboard and is used as the strobe input for the strobed input mode.

OUTA0 to OUTA3 and OUTB0 to OUTB3 These eight output lines output data to the display. The digit selected is determined by the output of the scan lines. These pins can alternately be considered as two 4-bit ports.

$\overline{\text{BD}}$ This output can be used to temporarily blank the display while new data and/or display digit is selected.

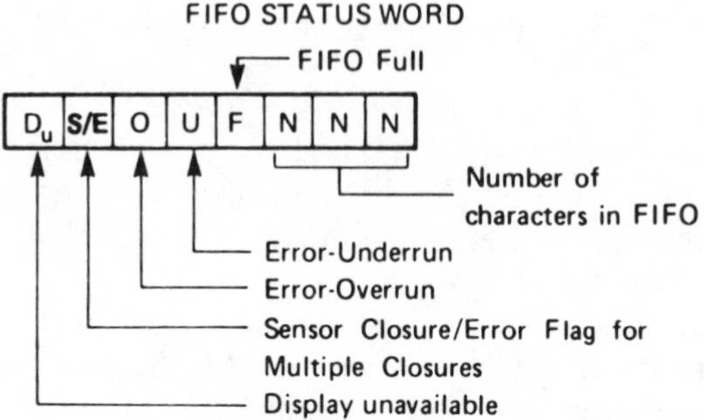

Figure 13-19 The **8279** commands and status format. (Reprinted by permission of Intel Corp.)

13-5.3 Device Operation

The command format and the definition of the status register are shown in Figure 13-19. Once the **8279** is initialized the μP only has to read data from the FIFO or write new data into the display RAM. The most complicated part of the software is the initialization of the **8279** when the system is first powered up. The clearest way to describe the initialization is with an example.

EXAMPLE 13-11 An **8279**-based system is shown in Figure 13-20. The system keyboard is a 64-key keyboard which requires that the scan counter work in the encoded mode and use the external 3-8 decoder shown in Figure 13-18. Assume that the keyboard will be scanned by the **8279** and the system is to have two-key lockout. The display is to be an eight-digit display with right entry. Assume that the clock input of the **8279** is the same as that of the μP in the system and that the clock rate is 2 MHz and the system should work with a keyboard that requires approximately 10 ms of debounce time.

Command description	**Code (8-bit word)**							
Keyboard/display mode set	0	0	0	D	D	K	K	E
Program clock	0	0	1	P	P	P	P	P
Read FIFO/sensor RAM	0	1	0	Ai	X	A	A	A
Read display RAM	0	1	1	Ai	A	A	A	A
Write display RAM	1	0	0	Ai	A	A	A	A
Display write inhibit/blanking	1	0	1	X	Wa	Wb	Ba	Bb
Clear	1	1	0	Cd	Cd	Cd	Cf	Ca
End interrupt/error mode set	1	1	1	E	X	X	X	X

Where:

D	*D*	*Display function*
0	0	Eight-character display —Left entry
0	1	Sixteen-character display—Left entry
1	0	Eight-character display —Right entry
1	1	Sixteen-character display—Right entry

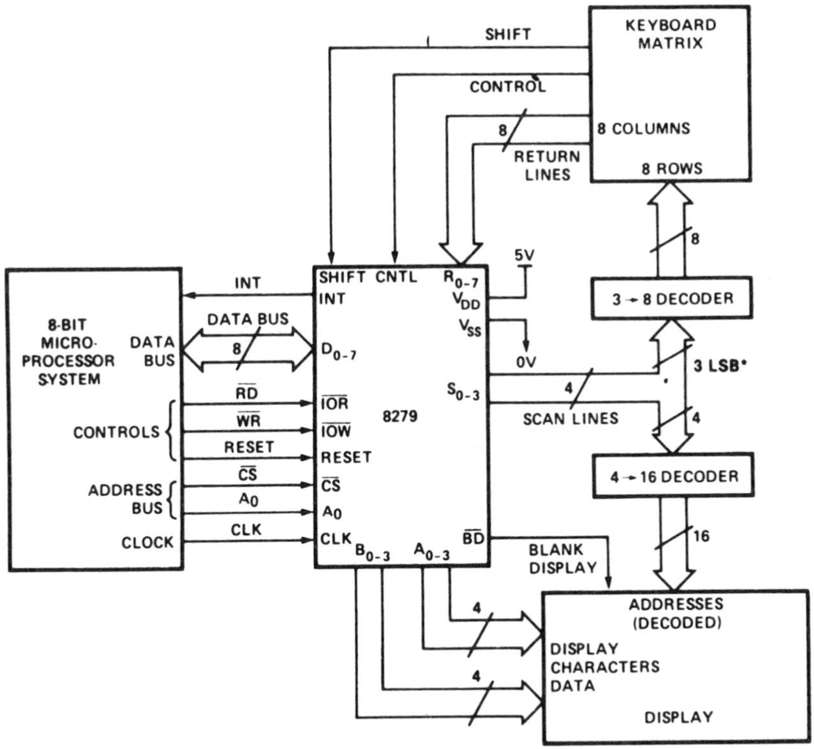

Figure 13-20 A typical application of **8279**. (Reprinted by permission of Intel Corp.)

K	*K*	*Keyboard type*
0	0	Scanned with two-key lockout
0	1	Scanned with N-key rollover
1	0	Scan sensor matrix
1	1	Strobed input

E	*Operation of scan counter*
0	Encoded
1	Decoded

PPPPP selects the N to be used by the prescaler counter to generate the internal timing values (valid range is from 2 to 31).

X Don't care value—This bit is not used by the system.

Ai The auto increment flag, a "1" indicates that the 8279 should increment the address on subsequent READS or WRITES.

AAA or AAAA This is the 3- or 4-bit address of either the display or the FIFO.

Wa or Wb When 4-bit ports are used, the Wa or Wb bit will mask either port A or port B to allow the **8279** to change one 4-bit port without changing the other.

Ba or Bb These bits blank the 4-bit ports (A and B) associated with each 8-bit display port.

Cd	*Cd*	*Cd*	*Clear display mode*
1	0	X	Clear to all 0s
1	1	0	Clear to hex 20 (ASCII blank)
1	1	1	Clear to all 1s

Cf—A "1" clears the FIFO status and resets the interrupt output line.

Solution The solution will be to first send out the keyboard/display MODE SET instruction, then the PROGRAM CLOCK instruction to set the internal timing, and finally the CLEAR instruction to clear the display and to reset the FIFO pointer.

The parameters in the MODE SET instruction must be determined first. The DD parameters must be set to 10 to indicate an eight-character display with right entry. The KK parameter must be set to 00 to indicate a scanned keyboard with two-key lockout. The E parameter must be 0 to set the scan counter to the encoded mode. This defines the MODE SET command.

Second, the PPPPP parameter in the PROGRAM CLOCK command must be determined. To get a 10-ms debounce time means that the 2-MHz clock must be divided down to a rate of 100 kHz by the internal prescaler. A value of N = 20 (2 MHz/100 kHz = 2,000,000/100,000 = 20) will do this. The hexidecimal number 14 is equal to decimal 20, so PPPPP = 10100 in binary.

Third, for the CLEAR command we want to clear the display and reset FIFO status. If we assume that the display is an ASCII character display then we must clear the display register to hex 20 (the ASCII blank character), and thus Cd = 110. To reset the FIFO, Cf = 1.

If the address of the command register of the **8279** in this system is at 8000, then the following assembly language program will initialize the **8279**.

```
LXI    H,8000H    ;set HL to point to
                  ;Command register
MVI    A,10H      ;
MOV    M,A        ;set mode
MVI    A,34H      ;
MOV    M,A        ;program clock
MVI    A,0DAH     ;
MOV    M,A        ;clear display
```

13-6 REFERENCES

The Intel 8080/8085 Microprocessor Book, Wiley-Interscience, New York, 1980.

Mohamed Rafiquzzaman, *Microcomputer Theory and Application*, Wiley, New York, 1982.

CHAPTER 14

Motorola Peripherals

Joseph D. Greenfield
Professor of Electrical Engineering
Rochester Institute of Technology

and Tom Hardy
Motorola
Austin, Texas

This chapter presents four of Motorola's most popular peripheral ICs. It includes the **6840** Programmable Timer Module (PTM); two communications control ICs, the **MC6850** ACIA for asynchronous communications, and the **MC6854** Advanced Data Link Controller (ADLC) for synchronous data communications; and the **6845** Cathode Ray Tube Controller. All Motorola peripheral ICs are memory mapped; they occupy several contiguous addresses. The ICs contain command registers, status registers, and data registers, and in most cases, separate addresses exist for each of the registers.

14-1 THE 6840 PROGRAMMABLE TIMER MODULE

The **MC6840** Programmable Timer Module (PTM) is a 28-pin IC counter/timer consisting of three independent 16-bit registers that can be used to count events. If the inputs to these registers are connected to a fixed-frequency source, they can also be used to generate timing waveforms.

Figure 14-1 is a drawing of one of the three counters in the **6840**. Each is a *presettable down-counter* that is controlled by an 8-bit control register that controls the action or mode of operation of the counter, and a 16-bit counter/latch register that holds the preset count. The control register and the 16-bit counter/latch register are accessed by the μP in control of the system. Each counter has two input lines and

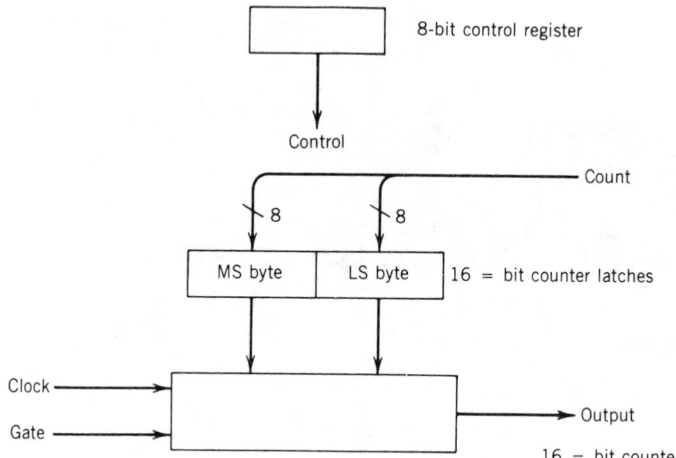

Figure 14-1 The registers associated with one of the three counters on the **6840**.

one output line associated with it. The input lines are the CLOCK and the GATE. The counter decrements on each positive edge of the CLOCK. The GATE input prevents or allows counting. A HIGH level on the GATE prevents counting, but a LOW level on the GATE allows the counter to decrement once for each clock pulse. The output line indicates the state of the counter. If a timing chain longer than 16 bits is required, the counters can be cascaded by tying the output of one counter to the clock of the succeeding counter.

There are nine registers within the **6840**, three for each counter. Each counter is associated with its own control register, the high byte of its counter/latches and the low byte of its counter/latches. The nine registers are accessed by eight addresses (see section 14-1.3).

14-1.1 The Hardware Interface to the 6840

Figure 14-2 shows a **6800** connected to a PTM and the pin out of the **6840**. Its interface consists of:

1 An 8-bit bidirectional data bus, D0–D7.

2 Three register select inputs (RS0, RS1, RS2). These select the register being accessed. Generally they are connected to A0, A1, and A2, the three LSBs of the address lines.

3 A READ/WRITE (R/$\overline{\text{W}}$) line.

4 Two chip select lines ($\overline{\text{CS0}}$ and CS1). The **6840** is selected only when $\overline{\text{CS0}} = 0$ and CS1 = 1. Two CS lines simplify chip selection.

5 The enable clock. This is usually the system's $\phi 2$ clock. The enable pin must be pulsed HIGH during a READ or WRITE to the **6840**.

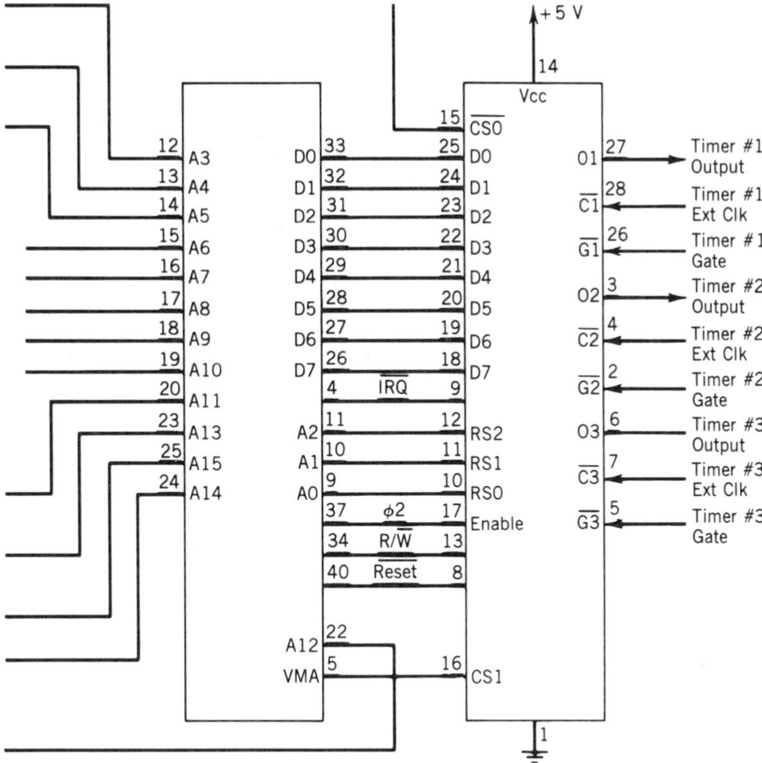

Figure 14-2 A **6840** PTM connected to an **MC6800** μP, and its pin out. (From the *Motorola Engineering Bulletin EB-69*, Motorola, Inc., Phoenix, AZ, 1978.)

6 A RESET input. A LOW signal on this pin resets the system.

7 An $\overline{\text{IRQ}}$. This is an output from the **6840** that can be used to interrupt the μP controlling it.

The pins listed above communicate with the μP. In addition, there are the CLOCKS, GATES, and OUTPUTS for each timer (C1, C2, C3, G1, G2, G3, and O1, O2, O3).

14-1.2 General System Operation

Table 14-1 relates the nine system registers to the eight combinations of register select inputs. The **6840** generally operates as follows:

1 The control registers are set up for the required function (see section 14-1.3).

2 The most significant byte of the count is entered into the MSB buffer register.

3 The least significant byte of the count is entered into the timer latches. This action enters the entire 16-bit count into the counter/timer of Figure 14-1.

Table 14-1 **Register selection**

Register select inputs			*Operations*		
RS2	*RS1*	*RS0*	*R/$\overline{W}$ = 0*		*R/$\overline{W}$ = 1*
0	0	0	CR20 = 0	WRITE control register #3	No operation
			CR20 = 1	WRITE control register #1	
0	0	1	WRITE control register #2		READ status register
0	1	0	WRITE MSB buffer register		READ timer #1 counter
0	1	1	WRITE timer #1 latches		READ LSB buffer register
1	0	0	WRITE MSB buffer register		READ timer #2 counter
1	0	1	WRITE timer #2 latches		READ LSB buffer register
1	1	0	WRITE MSB buffer register		READ timer #3 counter
1	1	1	WRITE timer #3 latches		READ LSB buffer register

4 When the **6840** starts operation, each counter counts down from the number in its latches to 0. When 0 is reached, the number in the latches is reloaded into the counter and the down-counting continues.

EXAMPLE 14-1 A μP system has no devices in addresses 4000–7FFF.[1] How can a **6840** be added to this system?

Solution Since these addresses all have A15 = 0 and A14 = 1, A15 can be connected to $\overline{\text{CS0}}$ and A14 can be connected to CS1. The **6840** will then respond to any address in the range. Most commonly the addresses 4000–4007 will be used to select the registers, although any set of eight contiguous addresses will suffice.

EXAMPLE 14-2 The 16-bit number 2ABC is to be loaded into the counter latches for timer 2. How can this be done? Assume the **6840** is at addresses 4000–4007.

Solution An examination of Table 14-1 shows that the MSB for register 2 is at $4004 and the timer #2 latches are at $4005. The writing can be accomplished by the following:

```
Program 1    LDA #2A
             STA $4004
             LDA #BC
             STA $4005
```

This program is used to show that the MSB buffer must be written first, followed by the timer #2 latches, or nothing will get in.

A simpler program is:

```
LDX #$2ABC
STX $4004
```

---

[1] This is true of the Motorola MEK-D2 system.

14-1.3 Programming the Control Registers

Each of the three counter/timers has an 8-bit control register associated with it. The function of the control register is to control the action of the counter/timer. Table 14-2 shows the function of each bit. Bit 0 of each control register has a slightly different function.

In control register 1, bit 0 determines whether the counters are held preset (see section 14-1.4) or allowed to operate.

Bit 0 of control register 2 is a *steering* bit. Table 14-1 shows that control register 2 has a unique address (RS0 = 1, RS1 = RS2 = 0), but control registers 1 and 3 have the same address (RS0 = RS1 = RS2 = 0). This allows the **6840** to place nine registers within eight addresses. A WRITE, when RS0 = RS1 = RS2 = 0, will access control register 1 if bit 0 of control register 2 is a 1, but will address control register 3 if bit 0 of control register 2 is a 0.

Bit 0 of control register 3 determines whether the input to control register 3 is *prescaled* by a divide-by-8 counter. If bit 0 of control register 3 is 1, it takes eight clock pulses to produce one output on register 3.

All the other bits of the control registers have identical functions, as shown in Table 14-2. They are:

Bit 1—internal/external clock. This bit determines whether the internal clock (coming in on the E pin) or an external clock, tied to the clock input of the counter, will act as the clock for that counter.

Bit 2. This bit determines whether the counter operates in 16-bit or dual 8-bit mode (see section 14-1.6).

Bits 3 and 4. If bit 3 is a 0, bit 4 determines whether a WRITE into the timer latches will initialize them. If bit 4 is a 0, the timers will initialize on a WRITE to the counter latches, but if bit 4 is a 1, a write will not initialize. If bit 3 is a 1, the timer

Table 14-2 **The function of each bit in the 8840s control registers**

CR10 Internal Reset Bit	CR20 Control Register Address Bit	CR30 Timer #3 Clock Control
0 All timers allowed to operate	0 CR#3 may be written	0 T3 $\overline{\text{Clock}}$ is not prescaled
1 All timers held in preset state	1 CR#1 may be written	1 T3 $\overline{\text{Clock}}$ is prescaled by ÷8

Bit	Function
CRX1*	Timer #X $\overline{\text{Clock}}$ Source
0	TX uses external clock source on $\overline{\text{CX}}$ input
1	TX uses Enable clock
CRX2	Timer #X Counting Mode Control
0	TX configured for normal (16-bit) counting mode
1	TX configured for dual 8-bit counting mode
CRX3 CRX4 CRX5	Timer #X Counter Mode and Interrupt Control (See Table 3)
CRX6	Timer #X Interrupt Enable
0	Interrupt Flag masked on $\overline{\text{IRQ}}$
1	Interrupt Flag enabled to $\overline{\text{IRQ}}$
CRX7	Timer #X Counter Output Enable
0	TX Output masked on output OX
1	TX Output enabled on output OX

*Control Register for Timer 1, 2, or 3, Bit 1.

operates in either frequency comparison or pulse width comparison modes, depending on bit 4. These modes are seldom used and will not be discussed further.

Bit 5—single-shot/continuous mode. This bit determines whether the counter will count down to 0 and then stop (single-shot mode), or reinitialize itself immediately and resume counting (continuous mode).

Bit 6. This bit determines whether interrupts are enabled. If enabled, the **6840** will interrupt when the count reaches 0.

Bit 7. This bit determines whether the outputs are masked or enabled.

14-1.4 RESETS

There are two types of RESETS on the **6840**, a hardware RESET and a software RESET.

A *hardware RESET* occurs when the RESET pin on the **6840** is brought to ground. A hardware RESET causes the following events:

1 All bits of all control registers will be 0, except for bit 0 or control register 1, which will be 1 (counters held preset).

2 All counters and latches will be loaded with the maximum count (FF).

The **6840** will be completely frozen in this position until the hardware RESET is removed.

A *software RESET* is caused by setting bit 0 of control register 1 to a 1. The counters and latches can be written to and read during a software RESET, but they will not count. The RESET condition can be removed by changing bit 0 of control register 1 to a 0.

14-1.5 Counter Initialization

A counter is initialized by transferring data from the latches into the counter. This can happen in one of four ways:

1 The counter is released and allowed to count by changing bit 0 of control register 0 from 1 to 0, with the gate LOW.

2 The gate associated with the counter is opened by placing a HIGH-to-LOW (↓) transition on it (bit 0 of CR0 = 0).

3 A write to the latches will initialize if bits 3 and 4 of the control register are 0.

4 The counter is counted down to 0 in continuous mode. It then reinitializes itself.

14-1.6 16-Bit and Dual 8-Bit Modes

Each counter of the **6840** can operate in either 16-bit mode or dual 8-bit mode, depending on bit 2 of its control register. The top part of Figure 14-3 (CRX2 = 0) shows the operation in 16-bit mode, where N is the 16-bit number entered into the counter/latches. If the counter/latches are divided into a most significant byte M and a least significant byte L, then

$$N = 256 \times M + L$$

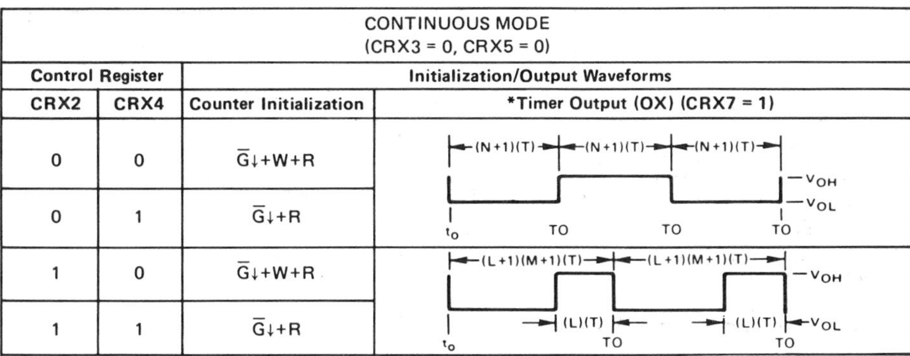

CONTINUOUS MODE (CRX3 = 0, CRX5 = 0)			
Control Register		**Initialization/Output Waveforms**	
CRX2	**CRX4**	**Counter Initialization**	***Timer Output (OX) (CRX7 = 1)**
0	0	$\overline{G}\downarrow$+W+R	(N+1)(T), (N+1)(T), (N+1)(T); V_{OH}, V_{OL}; t_o, TO, TO, TO
0	1	$\overline{G}\downarrow$+R	
1	0	$\overline{G}\downarrow$+W+R	(L+1)(M+1)(T), (L+1)(M+1)(T); (L)(T), (L)(T); V_{OH}, V_{OL}; t_o, TO, TO
1	1	$\overline{G}\downarrow$+R	

$\overline{G}\downarrow$ = Negative transition of $\overline{\text{Gate}}$ input.
W = Write Timer Latches Command.
R = Timer Reset (CR10 = 1 or External $\overline{\text{Reset}}$ = 0)
N = 16-Bit Number in Counter Latch.
L = 8-Bit Number in LSB Counter Latch.
M = 8-Bit Number in MSB Counter Latch.
T = Clock Input Negative Transitions to Counter.
t_o = Counter Initialization Cycle.
TO = Counter Time Out (All Zero Condition).

*All time intervals shown above assume the the $\overline{\text{Gate}}$ ($\overline{G}$) and $\overline{\text{Clock}}$ ($\overline{C}$) signals are synchronized to Enable (System $\phi 2$) with the specified setup and hold time requirements.

Figure 14-3 Continuous operating modes. (From the Motorola **MC6840** Data Sheets, reprinted courtesy of Motorola, Inc.)

EXAMPLE 14-3 A counter has the number 0403 set into its latches. How does it count down in 16-bit mode?

Solution The counter counts down as follows:

```
0403
0402
0401
0400
03FF
03FE
 :
0001
0000
0403
 :
```

Note that when the counter gets to 0 it will then be reloaded with the number in the counter/latches, 0403.

In dual 8-bit mode, the L counter resets to L instead of to FF. The output waveform for dual 8-bit mode is shown in the lower part of Figure 14-3 (CRX2 = 1).

EXAMPLE 14-4 Repeat Example 14-3 if the counter is in dual 8-bit mode.

Solution The counter now counts:

```
0403
0402
0401
0400
0303
0302
  :
0001
0000
0403
```

EXAMPLE 14-5 If counter 3 has 0403 loaded into its latches and it is driven by a 1-MHz clock on its E line, sketch the output if the control word for register 3 is:

a 83

b 86

Solution

a A control register containing 83 means that:

1 The outputs are enabled.

2 The divide-by-8 prescaler is operating.

3 The internal clock (1 MHz) is selected.

4 The counter is in 16-bit mode.

In 16-bit mode $N = 256 \times M + L = 256 \times 4 + 3 = 1027$.

Figure 14-3 shows that the output is down for $N + 1$ counts and up for $N + 1$ counts. Because of the prescaler it takes eight inputs to produce one count, so each count takes 8 μs. Thus the counter is up and down for $(N + 1)T = 1028 \times 8\ \mu s = 8.224$ ms. This output is shown in Figure 14-4a.

b If the control word contains 86, it means:

1 The prescaler is not invoked.

2 The internal clock is again selected.

3 The counter operates in dual 8-bit mode.

4 The outputs are enabled.

From Figure 14-3 we see that the total output time is $(M + 1)(L + 1)T = 5 \times 4 \times 1\ \mu s = 20\ \mu s$ and the output is HIGH for $L \times T$ or 3 μs. The output waveform is shown in Figure 14-4*b*.

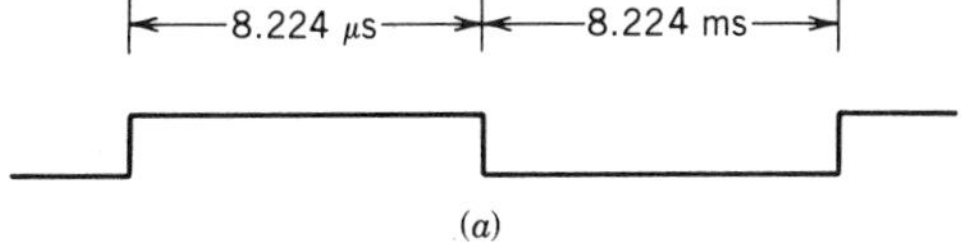

(a)

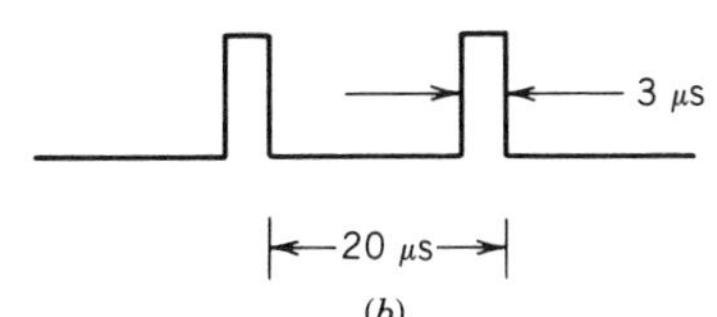

(b)

Figure 14-4 Waveforms for Example 14-5. (*a*) 16-bit continuous mode. (*b*) Dual 8-bit mode.

14-1.7 Single-Shot Mode

In single-shot mode (control register bit 3 = 0, control register bit 5 = 1), the **6840** acts like a monostable multivibrator on one shot; in response to a trigger or initialization pulse, it produces a single output pulse for a predetermined time period.

The single-shot waveforms are shown in Figure 14-5. In 16-bit mode the output is LOW for one clock pulse following initialization, and HIGH for N clock cycles thereafter. It then stays LOW until another trigger or initialization event occurs. In dual 8-bit mode, Figure 14-5 shows that the output is LOW for (L + 1)(M + 1) − L pulses and HIGH for L pulses. The output will then stay LOW until initialization occurs.

Single-shot mode
(CRX3 = 0, CRX7 = 1, CRX5 = 1)

Control register		*Initialization/output waveforms*	
CRX2	*CRX4*	*Counter initialization*	*Timer output (OX)*
0	0	$\overline{G}\downarrow + W + R$	(L + 1)(M + 1)(T); (L + 1)(M + 1)(T); (L)(T); t_0; TO; TO
0	1	$\overline{G}\downarrow + R$	
1	0	$\overline{G}\downarrow + W + R$	(N + 1)(T); (N + 1)(T); (N)(T); t_0; TO; TO
1	1	$\overline{G}\downarrow + R$	

Figure 14-5 Single-shot operating modes. (From the Motorola **MC6840** Data Sheets, reprinted courtesy of Motorola, Inc.)

Initialization or triggering occurs when:

1 The RESET is released.

2 The gate goes LOW.

3 Bit 4 of the control register is 0 and there is a WRITE into the counter latches. The initialization conditions are also shown in Figure 14-5.

A ↓ on the gate initializes the **6840**, but the gate need not remain LOW in single-shot mode. It can go HIGH without affecting the output.

EXAMPLE 14-6 A **6840** is located at addresses 4000–4007. How should it be initialized to provide a 520-μs pulse in response to a trigger on gate 1? Assume the internal clock is being used and is 1 μs.

Solution Since 520 pulses are required and $(520)_{10} = (0208)_{16}$, the counter can be initialized by the following program:

```
LDA A # 01      Set up register 2 to point to register 1.
STA A $4001
LDA A # A2      Send the control word (output enabled, single-shot 16-bit mode
STA A $4000     internal clock) to control register 1.
LDX # 0208      Store the count in counter 1s latches.
STX $4002
```

The counter will now produce a 520-μs pulse in response to a negative edge on the gate.

14-2 SERIAL DATA TRANSMISSION

When digital data is being transmitted or transferred between components in a μC system, it is moved a byte at a time by means of the 8-bit or 16-bit data bus. This is *parallel transmission*, and is synchronized by the system clock. When signals are sent to equipment not located in the same cabinet, the separate ground points create problems of noise or interfering signals. Extraneous current pulses and alternating currents (AC) are carried by the same ground wires and can induce unwanted pulses or glitches into the digital signals. To alleviate these problems, parallel digital signals are often converted to *serial* form on a single line, and transmitted *a bit at a time.*

When the distance is more than 50 or 100 ft, as in a system involving a main computer and several satellite terminals, this serial digital signal is frequently changed to audio tones by means of a modem (modulator-demodulator) and transmitted over telephone circuits. Most modems provide for duplex operation (one serial path in each direction) over one telephone circuit. Obviously, serial transmission with only one pair of wires is simpler and cheaper to implement than parallel transmission with eight or more lines, particularly since the grounding problems are eliminated. The operation of a full duplex data transmission system that transmits serial data in both directions simultaneously is shown in Figure 14-6.

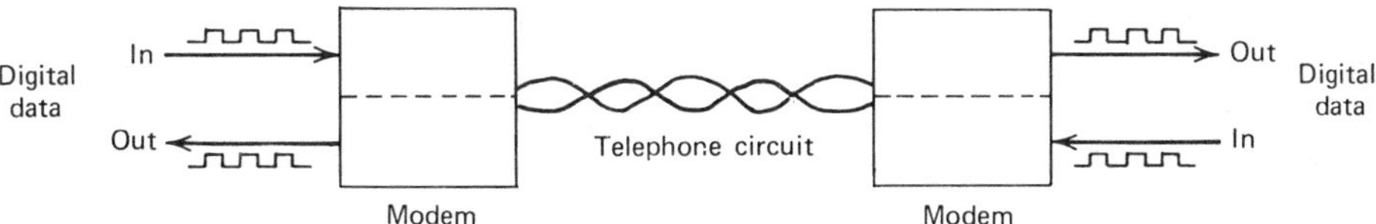

Figure 14-6 A full-duplex data transmission system. (From Greenfield and Wray, *Using Microprocessors and Microcomputers: The 6800 Family*, Wiley, 1981.)

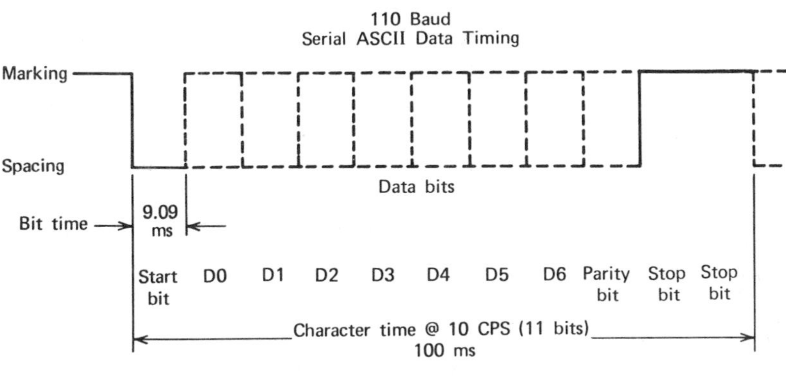

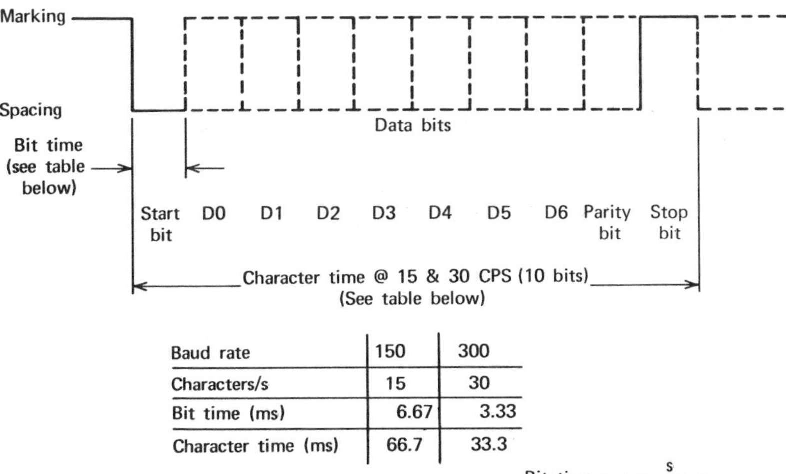

Baud rate	150	300
Characters/s	15	30
Bit time (ms)	6.67	3.33
Character time (ms)	66.7	33.3

$$\text{Bit time} = \frac{\text{s}}{\text{Baud rate}}$$

150 & 300 Baud Serial ASCII Data Timing

Figure 14-7 ASCII character bit timing. (From Greenfield and Wray, *Using Microprocessors and Microcomputers: The 6800 Family*, Wiley, 1981.)

In the transmit part of the modem, the digital information modulates an audio tone that is then transmitted to the distant device, usually over telephone circuits. The receive part of the remote modem demodulates the audio signals and sends them to the local equipment as digital data.

14-2.1 Asynchronous Transmission

Most serial systems use asynchronous (unclocked) data transmission. The characters are sent in a standard format or code so that equipment made by different manufacturers can be used together in a system. The most common code for asynchronous data transmission is the ASCII (American Standard Code for Information Interchange). As used in the Model 33 and 35 Teletypewriters (TTYs), it is an 11-bit START-STOP code. The basic pattern for this code is shown in Figure 14-7. When the line is quiescent (transmitting no data), it is constantly in the MARK or 1 state. The start of a character is signaled by the START bit that drives the line to the 0 or SPACE state for 1-bit time. The 8 bits immediately following the START bit are the data bits of the character. The bits are sent with the least significant bit (LSB) first. In most systems the ASCII code is used. The ASCII code (see Table 14-3) uses 7 bits to generate 128 unique codes. These include upper- and lower-case letters A to Z, the numbers 0 to 9, plus many punctuation and mathematical symbols. Many nonprintable control characters are also provided. The character consists of 7 data bits and a parity bit.

Table 14-3 **The ASCII code**

Bits 0 to 3 Second hex digit (LSB)	*Bits 4 to 6 First hex digit (MSB)*							
	0	*1*	*2*	*3*	*4*	*5*	*6*	*7*
0	NUL	DLE	SP	0	@	P		p
1	SOH	DC1	!	1	A	Q	a	q
2	STX	DC2	"	2	B	R	b	r
3	ETX	DC3	#	3	C	S	c	s
4	EOT	DC4	$	4	D	T	d	t
5	ENQ	NAK	%	5	E	U	e	u
6	ACK	SYN	&	6	F	V	f	v
7	BEL	ETB	'	7	G	W	g	w
8	BS	CAN	(	8	H	X	h	x
9	HT	EM	)	9	I	Y	i	y
A	LF	SUB	*	:	J	Z	j	z
B	VT	ESC	+	;	K	[	k	{
C	FF	FS	,	<	L	/	l	/
D	CR	GS	-	=	M	]	m	}
E	SO	RS	.	>	N	∧	n	≈
F	SI	US	/	?	O	-	o	DEL

Normally, *even* parity is used in the incoming direction because most TTY keyboards are connected to generate *even* parity characters (the number of 1s in each character are *even*). The TTY does not check parity on data to be printed, but many high-speed data terminals do.

After the last data bit, the transmission line must go HIGH for either 1- or 2-bit times. These are the STOP bits. TTYs use 2 STOP bits, but terminals operating at the higher baud rates use only 1. If no further data is to be transmitted, the line simply stays HIGH (marking) until the next START bit occurs. This data pattern thus uses 10 or 11 bits as follows:

a One START bit (always a space or 0).

b Eight data bits (including parity).

c One or two STOP bits (always a mark or 1).

EXAMPLE 14-7

a What is the bit pattern of the character shown in Figure 14-8?

b Is the parity odd or even?

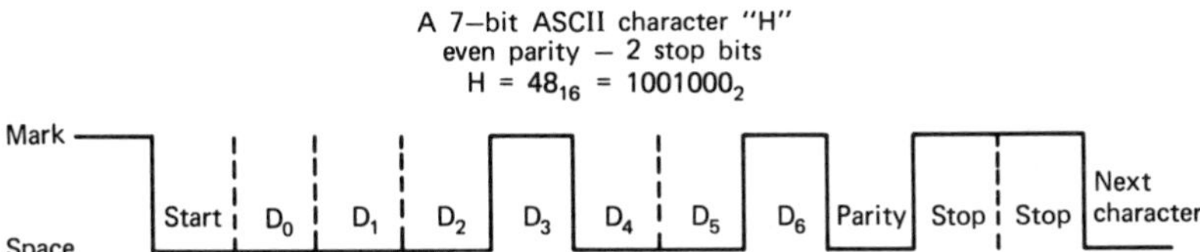

Figure 14-8 Character pattern for Example 14-7. (From Greenfield and Wray, *Using Microprocessors and Microcomputers: The 6800 Family*, Wiley, 1981.)

Solution

a As shown in Figure 14-8, the waveform bits are 00001001011. The first 0 is the START bit and the next eight are the character. Since the LSBs are transmitted first, they must be reversed to correspond to the convention used in most μP literature and in this book. Therefore the character is 01001000 (48 hex, or ASCII "H"). The two 1s following the last data bit are STOP bits. Any additional 1s following the STOP bit merely indicate that the line is idle.

b Since the character contains an even number of 1s, this is an even parity character.

14-2.2 Synchronous Communications

Asynchronous communications are used primarily with slow-speed terminals where information is generated on a keyboard (manually) and where the communication is not necessarily continuous. Synchronous communications are usually encountered where high-speed continuous transmission is required. This information is frequently read to modems, disk, or tape systems at 1200 bits/s or faster. Synchronous systems transmit a steady stream of bits even when no characters are

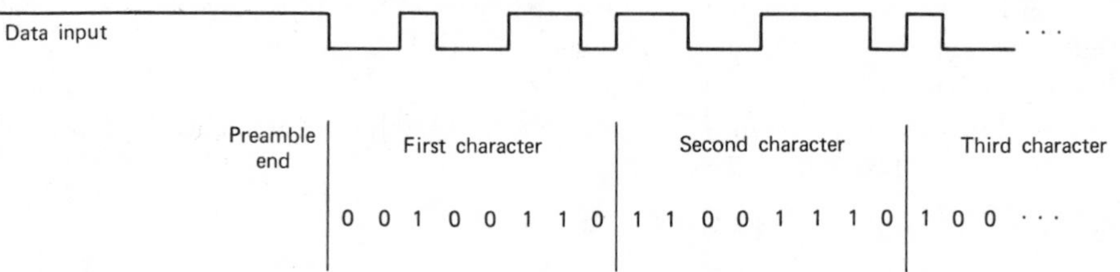

Figure 14-9 Synchronous transmission. (From Greenfield and Wray, *Using Microprocessors and Microcomputers: The 6800 Family*, Wiley, 1981.)

available (a *sync* character is substituted). Because there are no start and stop bits to separate the characters, care must be taken to synchronize the receiving device with the transmitted signal so that the receiver end of the circuit can determine which bit is bit 1 of the character.

Synchronous systems usually use a preamble (all 1s, for example) to establish synchronization between the receiver and transmitter and will then maintain sync by transmitting a sync pattern until interrupted. Because start and stop bits are not needed, the efficiency of transmission is 20 percent better for 8-bit words (8 instead of 10 bits/character).

Synchronous transmission is illustrated in Figure 14-9. The top line is the clock that is used in most systems to control the data. In this figure, all data changes occur on the positive edge of the clock. For maximum reliability, data should be sampled in the middle of the bit. Note that after the preamble, the data flows continuously.

14-3 THE ACIA

In Motorola systems, asynchronous serial data transmission is implemented by the **6850** asynchronous communications interface adapter (ACIA). The ACIA is designed to accept parallel data from the μC system data bus, a byte at a time, and to send the bits serially to an asynchronous serial data device such as a TTY, CRT terminal, line printer, or modem. At the same time, other circuits in the ACIA can accept serial data characters from a keyboard, a MODEM, or a tape reader, and place them on the μC bus as parallel bytes. Figure 14-10 shows the block diagram of the ACIA.

The left side of the diagram shows the lines that connect to the data, address, and control bus lines of the μP. The right side shows the lines used for the serial interface with external hardware.

The ACIA appends start, stop, and parity bits to the 7 or 8 data bits used for each character. The data could be a standard 7-bit ASCII character or any other

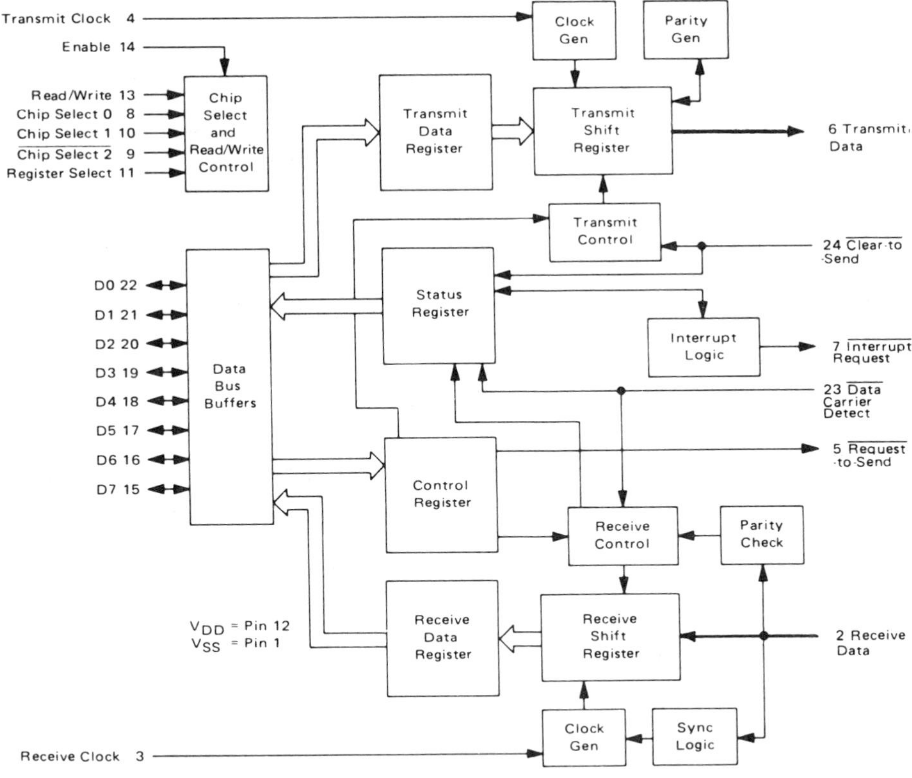

Figure 14-10 ACIA block diagram. (From Greenfield and Wray, *Using Microprocessors and Microcomputers: The 6800 Family*, Wiley, 1981.)

7- or 8-bit code such as EBCDIC, or even binary. The resulting character is either 10 or 11 bits long, depending on whether the character has 1 or 2 stop bits. Since the characters can be sent asynchronously, the time between each character can be from zero up. The ACIA is programmed during initialization via the μP data bus for the desired data configuration. It thus provides the following functions:

1 parallel-to-serial and serial-to-parallel conversion of data (simultaneously);

2 asynchronous transmission by means of start and stop bits;

3 error control by means of parity, framing, or overrun error detection.

14-3.1 Parallel-to-Serial and Serial-to-Parallel Conversion

The ACIA block diagram shown in Figure 14-10 includes TRANSMIT and RECEIVE shift registers. The transmit shift register is loaded in parallel from the data bus and then shifted right to send the bits out serially on one line. The receive shift register accepts serial data as input and sends it to the data bus in 8-bit bytes. The wide arrows in Figure 14-10 indicate the parallel side of the device (eight lines).

The receive and transmit bit rate clocks are used to shift these registers at the appropriate standard serial data rate (e.g., 110, 300, 2400, etc., bits/s). Note that these serial clock inputs are completely independent and can be used simultaneously at different rates if desired.

14-3.2 ACIA Registers

Figure 14-11 is a programmer's model of the ACIA. It shows the μP bus connections and the internal registers. Here is a list of the registers.

1 **Transmit data register.** The byte to be transmitted is written to the transmit data register by the μP. It is transferred to the transmit shift register, if it is empty. The byte is then shifted out serially. While 1 byte is being shifted out, a second byte can be loaded into the transmit data register. It is automatically loaded into the transmit shift register when transmission of the first byte is completed.

2 **Receive data register.** Information from external devices enters the ACIA serially via the receive shift register, which strips off the START and STOP bits and sends the byte in a parallel transfer to the receive data register. The μP must read the receive data register while the second byte is being received. If it is not read in time,

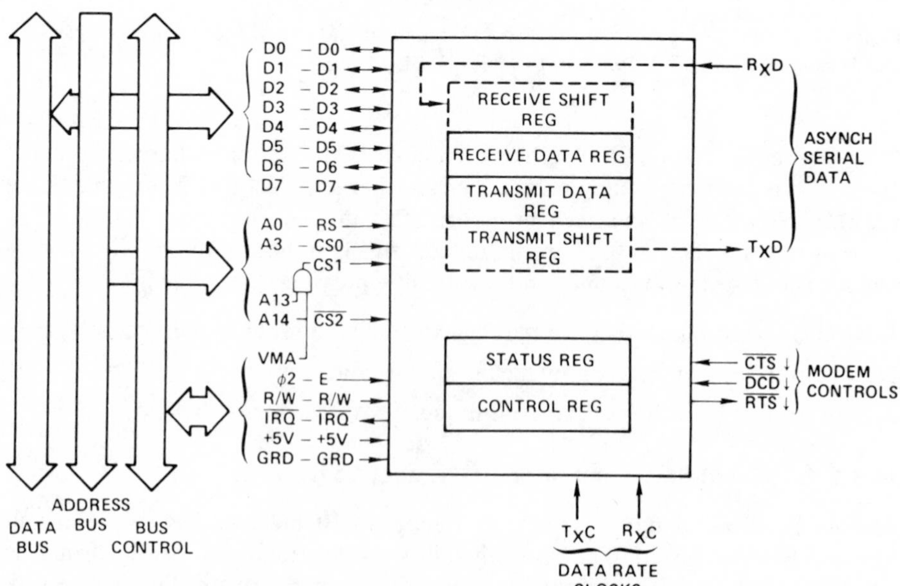

Figure 14-11 ACIA bus interface and register configuration. (From Greenfield and Wray, *Using Microprocessors and Microcomputers: The 6800 Family*, Wiley, 1981.)

the ACIA loses data, and causes the RECEIVE OVERRUN bit in the status register to be set (section 14-3.6).

3 **The control register.** This register controls the format of both the transmitted and received data. It is discussed in detail in section 14-3.4.

4 **The status register.** The status register monitors the progress of data transmission and reception and sends it to the μP. It is discussed in detail in section 14.3.6.

EXAMPLE 14-8 A standard 110 bits/s TTY is sending 11-bit characters continuously to the ACIA. How much time does the μP have to read each character?

Solution Since each character consists of 11 bits, the data rate is 10 characters per second. This allows the μP 0.1 s to read each character before the next character is assembled in the receive data register.

14-3.3 ACIA Signal Lines

The lines connected to the ACIA are shown in Figure 4-10. The IC pin number for each line is also shown. The lines and their functions are as follows.

1 **Eight bidirectional data lines.** These are connected to the **6800** data bus.

2 **Three chip select lines.** Like the PIA, the ACIA occupies specific locations in the address map. The chip select lines and register select line are connected to the address bus to select the ACIA.

3 **READ/WRITE and register select.** The combination of these two inputs selects one of the four major registers. The transmit data register and control register are *write only*; the μP cannot read them. If R/W is HIGH (for read), the receive data or status register is read (depending on whether the REGISTER SELECT pin is HIGH or LOW, respectively). If R/W is LOW, a word is written to either the transmit data register or to the control register (depending on whether REGISTER SELECT is HIGH or LOW, respectively).

14-3.4 The ACIA Control Register

Table 14-4 shows the contents of the ACIA registers. The Boolean statements at the top of the table are the signals required to address each register. The control register, for example, has the equation $\overline{RS} \cdot \overline{R/W}$. This means the control register is addressed only if both the RS and R/W inputs to the ACIA are 0.

The transmit and receive data registers hold the data to be transmitted or received. A word to be transmitted is written to the transmit data register, where it remains until the transmit shift register is empty. Received words remain in the receive data register until displaced by the next data word that is received. They must be read while they are available (see Example 14-8) or they will be lost.

The transmit control register is more complex and is explained below in greater detail.

Table 14-4 **Definition of ACIA register contents**

Data bus line number	Buffer address: $RS \cdot \overline{R/W}$ Transmit data register (WRITE only)	$RS \cdot R/W$ Receive data register (READ only)	$\overline{RS} \cdot \overline{R/W}$ Control register (WRITE only)	$\overline{RS} \cdot R/W$ Status register (READ only)
0	Data bit 0[a]	Data bit 0	Counter divide select 1 (CR0)	Receive data register full (RDRF)
1	Data bit 1	Data bit 1	Counter divide select 2 (CR1)	Transmit data register empty (TDRE)
2	Data bit 2	Data bit 2	Word select 1 (CR2)	Data carrier detect ($\overline{DCD}$)
3	Data bit 3	Data bit 3	Word select 2 (CR3)	Clear-to-send ($\overline{CTS}$)
4	Data bit 4	Data bit 4	Word select 3 (CR4)	Framing error (FE)
5	Data bit 5	Data bit 5	Transmit control (CR5)	Receiver overrun (OVRN)
6	Data bit 6	Data bit 6	Transmit control 2 (CR6)	Parity error (PE)
7	Data bit 7[b]	Data bit 7[c]	Receive interrupt enable (CR7)	Interrupt request (IRQ)

[a] Leading bit = LSB = Bit 0.
[b] Data bit is "don't care" in 7-bit plus parity modes.
[c] Data bit will be zero in 7-bit plus parity modes.

The function of the counter divide bits (CR0 and CR1) is shown in Table 14-5 and allows three choices.

It divides the incoming clock by either 1, 16, or 64, depending on CR1 and CR0.

The ÷ 1 mode can only be used if the receive clock is synchronized with the data being received and a bit is available at every positive transition of the receive clock. Most systems using an ACIA are asynchronous, however, and the arrival of a

Table 14-5 Counter divide select bits

CR1	*CR0*	*Function*
0	0	÷ 1
0	1	÷ 16
1	0	÷ 64
1	1	Master reset

byte is signaled by a START bit that can occur at any time. For these cases, the ÷ 16 or ÷ 64 options must be used.

EXAMPLE 14-9 An ACIA operates using the ÷ 16 mode.

a If the bit frequency is 100 bits/s, what receive clock frequency is required?

b At what point after the START bit begins should the data be sampled?

Solution

a Since the clock is divided by 16, the receive clock frequency must be 1600 bits/s to accept data at a 100 bits/s rate.

b The START bit can be thought of as occupying counts 1 to 16, the first data bit counts 17 to 32, and so on. For maximum accuracy, each bit should be sampled, or clocked into the receive shift register in the middle of its time slot or at counts 8, 24, 40, and so on. This is automatically accomplished by the internal logic of the ACIA. (See Figure 14-12.)

Bit synchronization in the ÷ 16 and ÷ 64 modes is initiated by the leading mark-to-space transition of the START bit. The START bit on the receiver data input sampled during the positive transitions of the external clock is shown in Figure 14-12*b*. If the input remains at a LOW level for a total of eight separate samplings in the ÷ 16 mode or 32 samplings in the ÷ 64 mode, which is equivalent to 50 percent of a bit time, the bit is assumed to be a valid START bit. This START bit is shifted into the ACIA circuitry on the negative edge of the internal clock. Once a valid START bit has been detected, the remaining bits are shifted into the shift register at their approximate midpoints.

If the receiver input returns to a mark state during the START bit sampling period, this false START bit is ignored and the receiver resumes looking for the mark-to-space transition or a valid START bit; this technique is called *false bit detection.*

Divide-by-1 mode selection will not provide internal bit synchronization within the receiver. Therefore, the external receive clock must be synchronized to the data under the following considerations. The sampling of the START bit occurs on the positive edge of the external clock, and the START bit is shifted into the shift register on the negative edge of the external clock, as shown in Figure 14-12*a*. For higher reliability of sampling the positive transition of the external clock (sampling point) should occur at the approximate midpoint of the bit interval. There is no requirement on the duty cycle of the external receive clock except that the clock must meet the minimum pulse width requirement, as noted on the ACIA data sheet.

Bits CR2, CR3, and CR4 of the control word are written to the ACIA during initialization and determine the configuration of the words being transmitted and received. The user can choose the number of data bits transmitted in each character (7 or 8), the parity (odd, even, or no parity), and the number of STOP bits (1 or 2). The options are given in Table 14-6. Note that when transmitting with parity, the

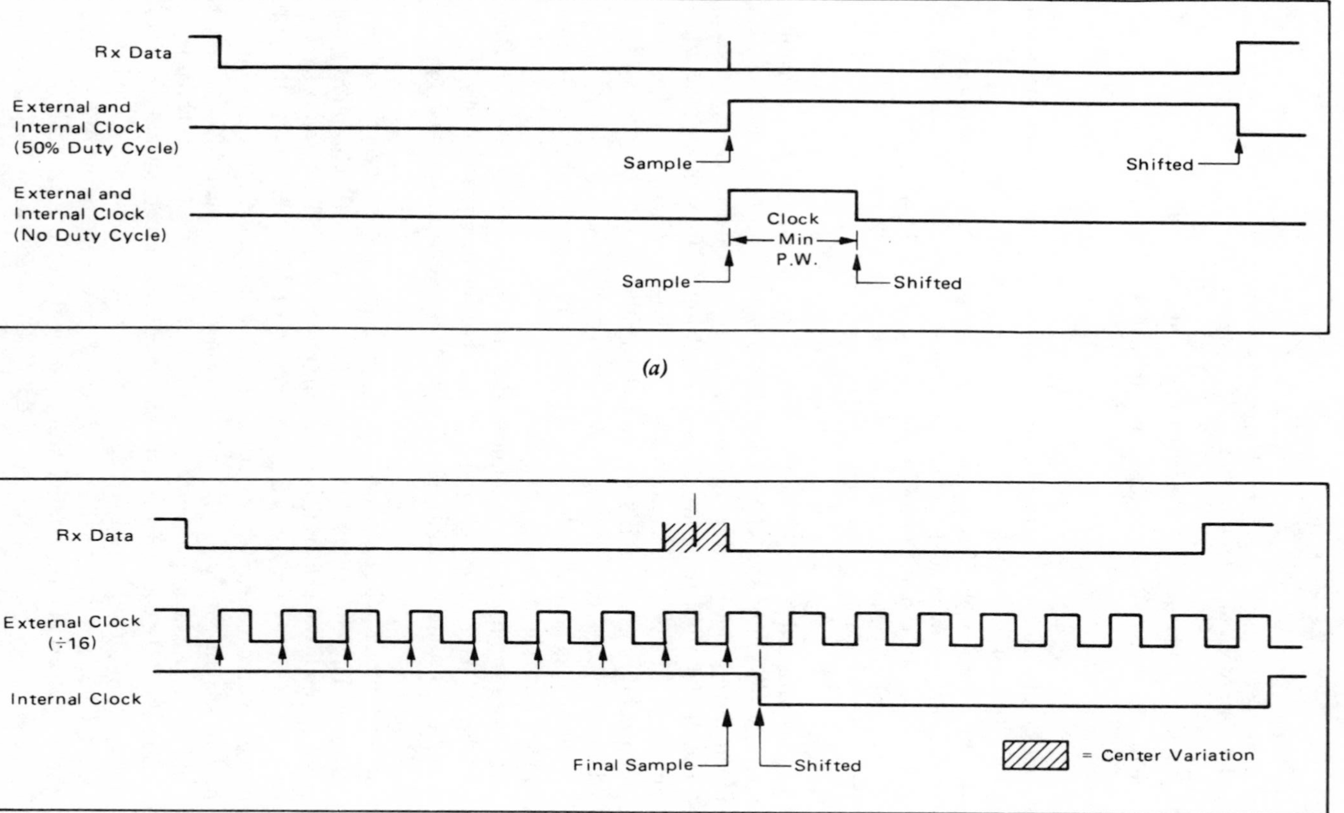

Figure 14-12 Relation of the data and sampling clock in an ACIA. (*a*) Divide by 1. (*b*) Divide by 16. (From Greenfield and Wray, *Using Microprocessors and Microcomputers: The 6800 Family*, Wiley, 1981.)

Table 14-6 **Word select bits**

CR4	*CR3*	*CR2*	*Function*
0	0	0	7 bits + even parity + 2 STOP bits
0	0	1	7 bits + odd parity + 2 STOP bits
0	1	0	7 bits + even parity + 1 STOP bit
0	1	1	7 bits + odd parity + 1 STOP bit
1	0	0	8 bits + 2 STOP bits
1	0	1	8 bits + 1 STOP bit
1	1	0	8 bits + even parity + 1 STOP bit
1	1	1	8 bits + odd parity + 1 STOP bit

Table 14-7 **Transmitter control bits**

CR6	*CR5*	*Function*
0	0	$\overline{\text{RTS}}$ = LOW, transmitting interrupt disabled.
0	1	$\overline{\text{RTS}}$ = LOW, transmitting interrupt enabled.
1	0	$\overline{\text{RTS}}$ = HIGH, transmitting interrupt disabled.
1	1	$\overline{\text{RTS}}$ = LOW, transmits a break level on the transmit data output. Transmitting interrupt disabled.

user need not concern himself with the parity of the data he sends to the ACIA. It calculates the correct parity and inserts the proper bit.

Bits CR5 and CR6 provide transmit interrupt control, as well as control of RTS, as shown in Table 14-7. (RTS is the request-to-send signal used with modems.) If CR6 and CR5 are 0 and 1, respectively, the ACIA interrupts the μP if IRQ is connected to the μP whenever the transmit data buffer is empty. This maximizes the data transmission rate since it causes the system to send the ACIA an output character as soon as it can accept one. If CR5 and CR6 are both 1s, the ACIA transmits a constant 0 level, called a *break*. A break is used as a control signal in some communications systems.

Bit CR7 is the receive side interrupt enable. If CR7 is a 1, the ACIA interrupts whenever the receive data register is full, or the overrun or data carrier detect conditions occur.

EXAMPLE 14-10 What are the characteristics of a transmission system if the control register contains C2?

Solution CR7 is a 1, so receive interrupts are enabled, but transmit interrupts are disabled because CR6 and CR5 are 1 and 0, respectively. Bits CR4, 3, and 2 are all 0s so the data word consists of 7 bits + even parity + 2 stop bits. Finally, because CR1 is a 1 and CR0 is a 0, the frequency of the input clock must be 64 times the bit rate of the data.

14-3.5 ACIA POWER-ON RESET

The ACIA contains an internal POWER-ON RESET circuit to detect the 5-V turn-on transition and to hold the ACIA in a RESET state until initialization by the μP is complete. This prevents any erroneous output transitions. In addition to initializing the transmitter and receiver sections, the POWER-ON RESET circuit holds the CR5 and CR6 bits of the control register at a logic 0 and logic 1, respectively, so that the request to send (RTS) output is held HIGH and any interrupt from the transmitter is disabled. The POWER-ON RESET logic is sensitive to the shape of the VDD power supply turn-on transition. To ensure correct operation of the reset function, the power turn-on transition must have a positive slope throughout its transition. The conditions of the status register and other outputs during POWER-ON RESET or software MASTER RESET are shown in Table 14-8.

The internal ACIA POWER-ON RESET logic must be released prior to the transmission of data by performing a software MASTER RESET, followed by a second control word. During MASTER RESET, control register bits CR0 and CR1 are set to 1s, which releases the latched condition of bits CR5 and CR6, allowing them to be programmed in the following control word. In recent production the processes have produced faster parts and this release may occur during master reset. To guard against the possibility of RTS going LOW, it is advisable to use a MASTER RESET word of 43. This retains the preset conditions of bits CR5 and CR6. The final condition can then be determined in the second control word without any false or momentary shifts in the RTS level. This also applies to receiver interrupt enable (RIE) which is controlled by bit CR7. The 43 will assure that the interrupt is inhibited until its state is specified in the second control word.

After MASTER RESET of the ACIA, the programmable control register must be set to select the desired options such as the clock divider ratios, word length, 1 or 2 stop bits, and parity (even, odd, or none). Bits CR5 and CR6 of the control register are no longer inhibited and can now be programmed for the options defined in Table 14-7.

14-3.6 The ACIA Status Register

The status of the ACIA, and what has happened to the data being handled, is determined by examining the status register at the proper time in the program. The function of each bit is given in Table 14-4.

Bit 0—Receive Data Register Full (RDRF) This bit is set when a character has been received by the ACIA and should be read by the CPU.

Bit 1—Transmit Data Register Empty (TDRE) This bit indicates that a character to be transmitted can be sent to the ACIA.

Bits 2 and 3—Data Carrier Detected (DCD) and Clear to Send (CTS) These bits will only be HIGH if an RS232C modem is connected to the ACIA and not ready for transmission or operating improperly. They must be tied LOW if a terminal rather than a modem is being used.

Table 14-8 **ACIA initialization sequence**

	POWER-ON RESET	*MASTER RESET (Release POWER-ON RESET)*	*MASTER RESET (General)*
	b7 b6 b5 b4 b3 b2 b1 b0	*b7 b6 b5 b4 b3 b2 b1 b0*	*b7 b6 b5 b4 b3 b2 b1 b0*
Status register	*0 0 0 0 X X 0 0*	*0 0 0 0 X X 0 0*	*0 0 0 0 X X 0 0*
$\overline{IRQ}$ output	1	1	1
$\overline{RTS}$ output	1	1	X
Transmit break capability	Inhibit	Inhibit	Optional
Internal: RIE	0	X	X
TIE	0	0	X

Note: X = independent of reset function. Held by POWER-ON RESET (applies to the $\overline{RTS}$ output, Transmit break capability, RIE and TIE entries under MASTER RESET (Release POWER-ON RESET)). Defined by control register (applies to the Transmit break capability, RIE and TIE entries under MASTER RESET (General)).

Bit 4—Framing Error (FE) A framing error indicates the loss of character synchronization, faulty transmission, or a break (all spaces) condition. If one of the above conditions is present, the internal receiver transfer signal will cause the FE bit to go HIGH. The next internal transfer signal will cause the FE status bit to be updated for the error status of the next character. A HIGH on the $\overline{\text{DCD}}$ input or a MASTER RESET will disable and reset the FE status bit.

Bit 5—Overrun Error (OVRN) A HIGH state on the OVRN status bit indicates that a character was received but not read from the receiver data register, resulting in the loss of one or more characters. The OVRN status bit is set when the last character prior to the overrun condition has been read. The READ DATA command forces the RDRF and OVRN status bits to go HIGH if an overrun condition exists. The next READ DATA command causes the RDRF and OVRN status bits to return to a LOW level. During an overrun condition, the last character in the receive data register that was not read subsequent to the overrun condition is retained since the internal transfer signal is disabled. A HIGH state on the $\overline{\text{DCD}}$ input or a MASTER RESET disables and resets the OVRN status bit.

Bit 6—Parity Error (PE) If the parity check function is enabled, the internal transfer signal causes the PE status bit to go HIGH if a parity error condition exists. The parity error status bit is updated by the next internal transfer signal. A HIGH state on the $\overline{\text{DCD}}$ input or a MASTER RESET disables and resets the PE status bit.

Bit 7—Interrupt Request (IRQ) A HIGH level on the IRQ status bit may be generated from three sources:

a Transmitter. If the Transmitter data register is empty (TDRE = 1), and TIE is SET.

b Receiver. If the receive data register is full (RDRF = 1), and RIE is SET.

c Data carrier loss. A loss of carrier (a HIGH level) on the $\overline{\text{DCD}}$ input, generates an interrupt, as indicated by the IRQ bit, if the RIE bit is SET.

EXAMPLE 14-11 The status register of an ACIA reads A3. What is the status of the ACIA?

Solution The data indicates that bits 0, 1, 5, and 7 are SET. Table 14-4 shows that:

1 The receive data register is full.

2 The transmit data register is empty.

3 A receive overrun error has occurred.

4 An interrupt request is pending.

The receive data register has overrun, indicating the μP did not fetch the last character during the time available. In addition, there is another character in the receive data register waiting to be read, and the ACIA is trying to interrupt. The transmit data register is available to accept any data for transmission. Essentially these conditions mean that the μP is not paying attention to the ACIA. They probably indicate that a timing problem (either hardware or software) has caused the system to malfunction.

14-3.7 Uses of the ACIA

The ACIA is typically used to communicate with asynchronous peripheral devices such as teletypes, printers, and low-speed modems. A teletype requires a 20-mA current loop. The ACIA outputs a TTL level so level converters must be used. Converters between TTL and 20-mA current loops often use optical couplers for noise isolation.

EXAMPLE 14-12 An ACIA is to transmit and receive data from a TTY simultaneously. The data to be transmitted is in memory starting at location 1000, and the received data is to be stored in consecutive locations starting at 2000. Explain how to set up the ACIA and what the program must do.

Solution First the timing must be set up, then the program must be written. A 1760-Hz clock would typically be used in the ÷16 mode to produce a 110 bit/s signal compatible with a TTY.

If polling is to be used, the control register must be initialized to 01. This does the following:

a Bits CR1 and CR0 are 01, selecting the ÷16 mode.

b Bits CR2, CR3, and CR4 are each 0, selecting a word format of 7 bits + even parity + 2 stop bits. This is the format used by standard TTYs.

c Bits CR5 and CR6 are each 0, disabling transmit interrupts.

d Bit CR7 is 0, disabling receive interrupts.

Before the program can start, four memory locations must be reserved for the two pointers: two locations for the transmit data area starting at 1000; two locations for the receive data area starting at 2000.

The program can then proceed as follows:

1 Read the ACIA status register.

2 Test bit 0. If it is 0, skip step 3.

3 If bit 0 equals 1, the receive data register is full. Place the receive pointer in X, read the receive data register, store the contents (indexed) into the receive data area, increment X (incrementing the receive pointer), and store X back into the receive pointer location.

4 Test bit 1. If it is 0, skip step 5.

Today most ACIAs communicate with printers and modems using RS232C signals.

All RS232C signals must be between +3 and +15 V for a 0 or *space*, or between −3 and −15 V for a 1 or *mark*. Consequently, level translators are required between the TTL levels or the ACIA and the modems. Two popular level translators are the **MC1488** and the **MC1489**, both manufactured by Motorola, Inc. The **MC1488** is a quad TTL-to-RS232C level translator for data going *to* the modem and the **MC1489** is a quad RS232C-to-TTL level translator for data coming *from* the modem to the digital ICs. Unfortunately, level translators require additional power supplies (typically, −12 V and +12 V) to generate the required signal voltages.

14-4 HIGH-SPEED SERIAL COMMUNICATION WITH THE MC6854 ADVANCED DATA LINK CONTROLLER

Synchronous data transmission is the transmission of data along with a clock, as shown in Figure 14-9. The data is synchronized with the clock and the middle of each data bit is at the LOW-to-HIGH transition of the clock. Synchronous data is also transmitted in accordance with a *protocol* that determines the format of the data. This protocol specifies the synchronizing characters, address and data portions of the message, and other characteristics of the message. Motorola has produced the **MC6854** IC to control synchronous data transmission.

The **MC6854** Advanced Data Link Controller (ADLC) provides the MPU/data communication interface for primary and secondary stations in a synchronous protocol communication system, as shown in Figure 14-13. In this type of network, there is one primary station and several secondary stations. All communication is between the primary station and one or more of the secondary stations. The computers controlling the ADLCs determine which is the primary station and which ADLCs in the communications network are secondary stations.

The primary station is the controller of the data link and issues commands serially over the communication channel to any number of secondary stations. These secondary stations then transfer data in response to a command issued by the primary station. The transfer data rate can reach 1.5 megabits/s, and the protocol used to transfer the serial information can be one of three defined standards listed below. The *bit-oriented protocol* (BOP) has essentially replaced the character-oriented serial protocol known as *bisync*. BOPs offer distinct advantages such as uniform frame formats and full-duplex operation. See References 6 through 10 concerning the origination of these 3-bit-oriented protocols and Reference 12 for data sheet information on the ADLC.

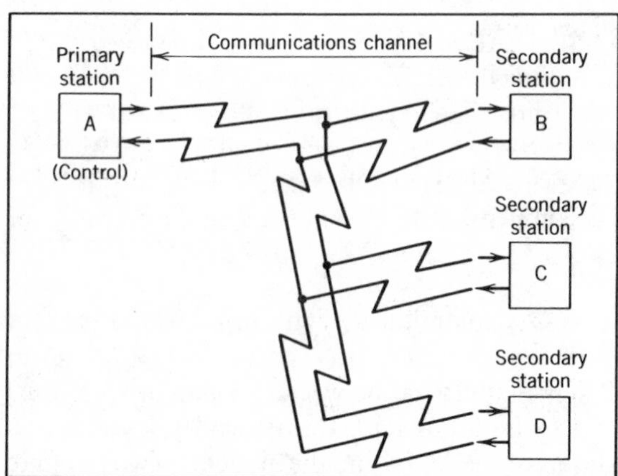

Figure 14-13 A synchronous data communications network. (From *Motorola Peripherals Document M6854 UM* (AD-1). "An Introduction to Data Communications," reprinted courtesy of Motorola, Inc.)

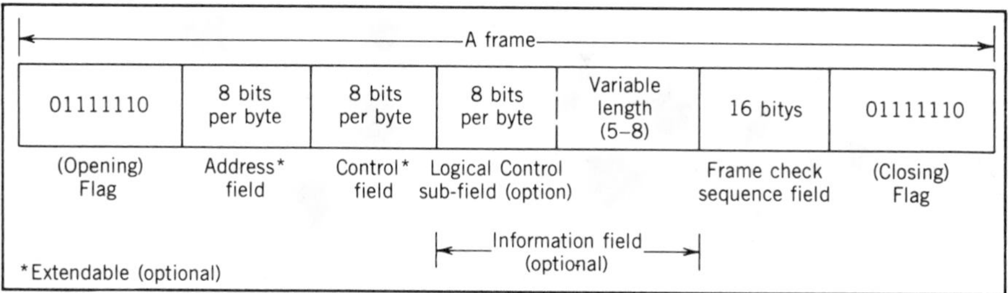

Figure 14-14 ADLC frame format. (From *Motorola Peripherals Document M6854 UM* (AD-1), "An Introduction to Data Communications," reprinted courtesy of Motorola, Inc.)

The protocols are:

1 advanced data communication control procedures (ADCCP);

2 high-level data link control (HDLC);

3 synchronous data link control (SDLC).

All three of these protocols are similar and have the same basic structure. However, differences occur in the extensions of the frame format. The SDLC protocol is fast becoming the industry standard and requires only 8 bits in the address and the control fields, while the other two protocols may add an additional eight bits of extension. This allows the HDLC and ADCCP protocols to have more addresses and more command words, but this is only required for very large systems. In this discussion, the SDLC protocol is assumed.

All data transfers over the communication channel are governed by a format referred to as a *frame*. Figure 14-14 illustrates the different fields which compose a frame implemented by the **MC6854** ADLC. The understanding of the ADLC device and its link to these defined protocols is made simple through an explanation of the frame format. The frame is composed of several different *fields* including flag, address, control, information, and the frame check sequence.

14-4.1 The Fields Within a Frame

A message consists of several frames of information. The frames are separated by *flags*, special bytes that form the boundaries between frames or between frames and sync characters. The basic fields in each frame are:

The Information Field This is the only field which is optional, although the closing flag of one frame may be used as the opening flag for the following frame which eliminates an additional field in back-to-back transfers. The flag (opening or closing) consists of a unique binary pattern (01111110) that provides the *frame boundary* and a reference for the position of each field in the frame. The transmitter on the **MC6854** (ADLC) transmits these flags with every frame and the receiver searches for this flag on a bit-by-bit basis to establish synchronization. Since the **MC6854** is a synchronous device, a clock must be provided which is *presynchronized* with the data to be transferred. The address field usually contains the addresses of the secondary station. If the frame contains a command (primary originated), the address identifies the secondary being commanded, assuming multiple secondary stations in the communication link. If a response is contained in the frame (secondary answering), the address identifies to the primary which secondary is responding. Some system planning provides for special addresses, like a *global* address (all 1s) which can be used to address all secondary stations. Simple systems which do not implement one of the three stated protocols, and involve information transfer between only two stations, may use the address field to transfer actual information, instead of an address. Even though the address field does not contain an address, it must still be present.

The data field contains the information being transmitted. It can be any number of data characters within a frame and each character can be between 5 and 8 bits long.

The Control Field This field defines the type of frame, keeps track of how many frames have been sent and received, and issues commands and control information. There are three different types of frames, which are defined by the bit-oriented protocol: information, supervisory, and nonsequenced. An *information frame* contains the *data to be transferred* along with a software counter indicating the number of frames transmitted or received. The *supervisory frames* are used by the primary station to acknowledge the reception of error-free frames. This is accomplished through the use of the same software counter present in the information frames. The function of the counter is to keep track of how many frames are successfully transferred. The transmitter increments the count each time it sends a frame and the receiver does the same when it receives a valid frame. If the receiver obtains an erroneous information frame, the software counter is not updated. When the message is complete, the receiver uses a supervisory frame to send its frame count back to the original transmitter. If an erroneous frame has been received, the transmitting station finds a mismatch of counters on the next supervisory frame. It is then the responsibility of the transmitting station to retransmit the appropriate frames that were received erroneously by the secondary. The supervisory frame can invoke commands that request these retransmissions of information frames or inhibit the sending of information frames.

The *nonsequenced frames* are used for data link management, such as the initialization of secondary stations. The information field contains the data to be transferred on the data link. Supervisory frames do not contain information fields, while selected nonsequenced frames may. The distinction between these frames is accomplished in software since the ADLC device makes no distinction in hardware.

The Frame Check Sequence Field These are the 16 bits preceding the closing flag. These 16 bits are obtained by performing a cyclic redundancy check (CRC) on the address, control, and information fields of the frame. The cyclic redundancy check is a complex calculation based on the polynomial superscripts

$X^{16} + X^{12} + X^5 + 1$, and is too involved to warrant comments in this text. See Reference 9 to obtain more information on the actual generation and check of this polynomial. The transmitter performs this calculation and sends the result out. The receiving station performs this same calculation on the data it receives and checks it against the frame check sequence field it was sent. Status registers implemented on the **MC6854** then reflect correct or erroneous data transfers between stations due to the result obtained from the calculations. This special feature replaces costly ICs which perform cyclic redundancy checks, and demonstrates the complex functions currently being implemented on peripherals.

14-4.2 Abort Conditions

The sending station can *abort* or abruptly end the transmission of a message. The abort condition is normally used by a sending station to end transmission in the middle of a frame and ensure that the receiving station ignores the frame. When an abort condition occurs, the frame check sequence field is not sent to the receiving station.

Since the ADLC provides flag (01111110) and abort (11111111) recognition, there must be some means to distinguish between the actual flag or abort and a normal character comprised of the same bits which make up these fields and conditions. This means of distinction is referred to as *zero insertion and deletion.* When the transmitter sends information which is not located in one of the flag fields, a 0 is inserted into the character stream after five consecutive 1s are detected. Similarly, when the receiver obtains five consecutive 1s which are not located in a flag field, it deletes the sixth character, which was a 0 placed in the data stream by the transmitter.

14-4.3 FIFOs

Figure 14-15 shows an internal block diagram of the ADLC. It shows both the transmit and receive sections, all the registers connected to them, and the interface lines that enable the ADLC to communicate with both the μP and the modem or other external device. The internal registers are discussed further in section 14-4.7.

The transmitter on the ADLC contains a 3-byte FIFO (first-in-first-out memory) that holds the characters to be sent out. This means that the transmitter is actually quadruply buffered since the transmit shift register also contains an 8-bit character and the software necessary to service this portion of the device will be invoked less frequently. The ADLC can be programmed to generate an interrupt when either 1 or 2 bytes inside the FIFO are empty. If the 2-byte mode is selected by programming the appropriate control register, a μP such as the **MC6809** can update 2 bytes of the FIFO in response to one interrupt and not be interrupted again by the transmitter until it has emptied 2 more bytes of the buffer. If, under any circumstances, the transmit FIFO becomes empty during frame transmission, an UNDERRUN will occur and be reflected in the appropriate status register of the ADLC and an ABORT will be generated (at least eight consecutive 1s).

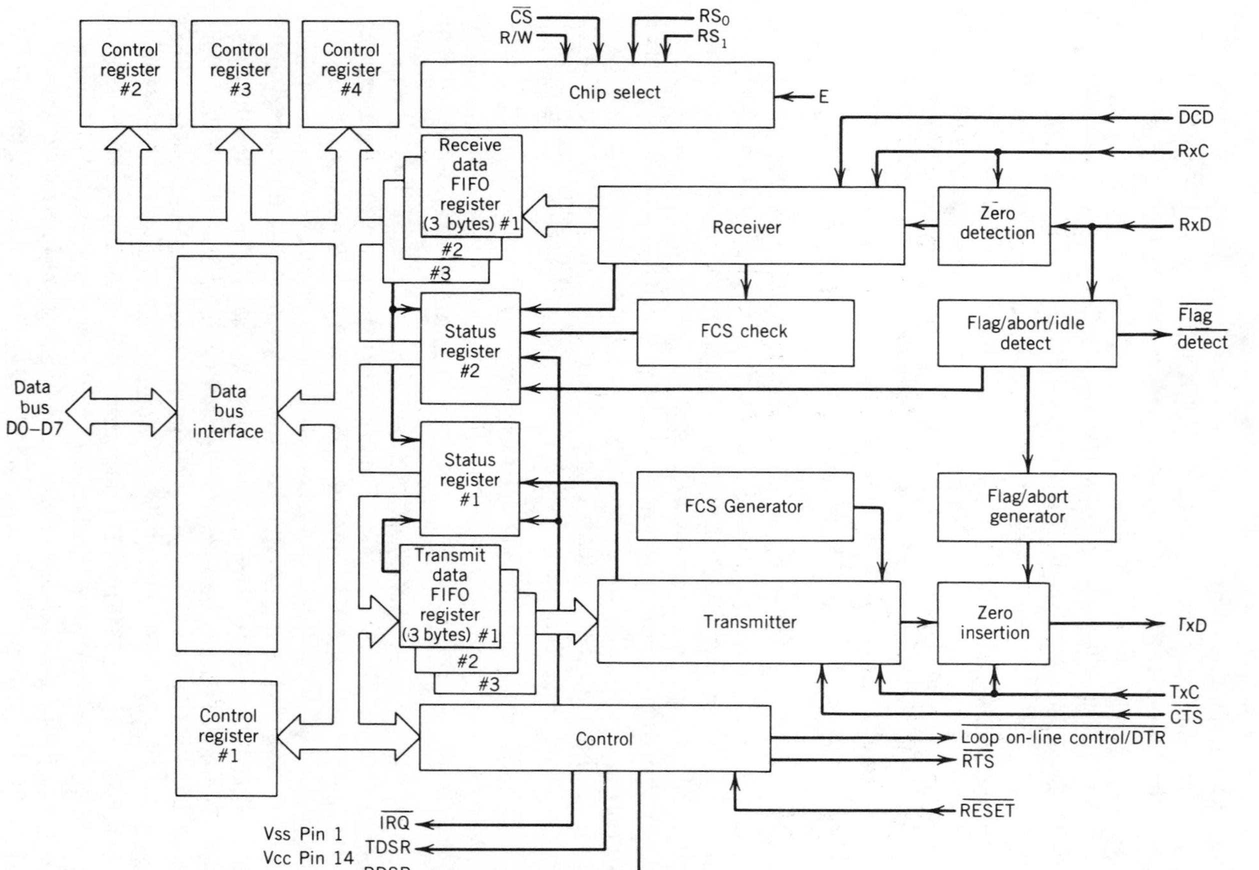

Figure 14-15 ADLC general block diagram. (From *Motorola Peripherals Document M6854 UM* (AD-1), "An Introduction to Data Communications," reprinted courtesy of Motorola, Inc.)

The receiver on the ADLC also contains a 3-byte FIFO and can be programmed to generate an interrupt when either 1 or 2 bytes of the FIFO is full. The receiver accepts a stream of binary bits, along with a presynchronized clock, and performs a continuous search on a bit-by-bit basis for flags and aborts. When a flag is detected, the receiver establishes a frame synchronization to the flag timing. If a series of flags is received, the receiver resynchronizes to each flag.

EXAMPLE 14-13 How does the receiver know when to resynchronize?

Solution Any sequence of six or more 1s is a flag. The receiver resynchronizes when it receives such a sequence.

The received serial data enters a 32-bit shift register clocked by the receiver clock before it is transferred to the FIFO. When the shift register is full, it is transferred byte-by-byte to the FIFO. The data is shifted through the FIFO on the positive and negative edges of the enable (E) clock generated by an MPU such as the **MC6809**. The sequence of each field in the received frame is automatically handled and when a closing flag is detected, the frame is terminated. The receiver also provides the ability to ignore any frame through special programming of a selected control register, and can discard current frame data without dropping synchronization. This feature can be used to ignore a frame which is addressed to another station.

14-4.4 Loop Transmission

In addition to the normal mode of operation, the ADLC provides an additional *loop mode* of operation. In this mode, a primary station communicates with any number of secondary stations in a loop configuration, as shown in Figure 14-16. The TxD output of the primary is wired to the RxD input of the first down-loop secondary station (clockwise data transfer in this figure). In sequence, each secondary station's TxD output is connected to the next down-loop station's RxD input until the primary is reached at the end of the loop. The last station's TxD output will be connected to the primary station's RxD input, thus terminating the loop. The primary transfers information to the first down-loop secondary station, which adds one bit of delay to the data transfer and passes it on to other stations down-loop until the same information transmitted arrives back at the primary. The loop mode of operation allows each secondary to transmit information to the primary and a set of protocols governing loop mode operation are defined below.

The four phases of loop mode operation are:

1 go on loop;

2 go active after poll;

3 go inactive when on loop;

4 go off loop.

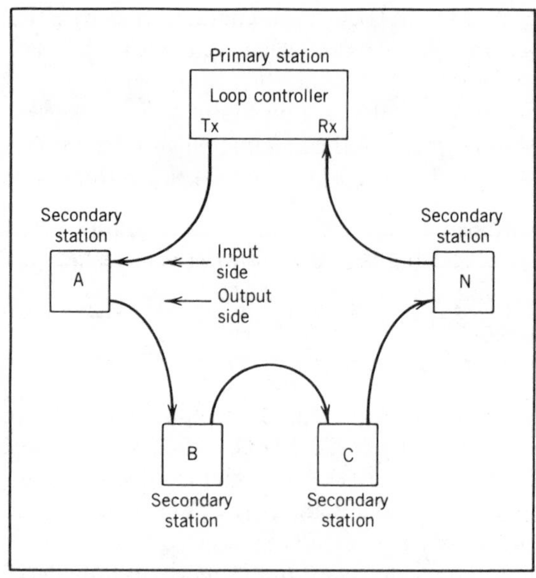

Figure 14-16 Loop configuration. (From *Motorola Peripherals Document M6854 UM* (AD-1), "An Introduction to Data Communications," reprinted courtesy of Motorola, Inc.)

Figure 14-17 shows an example of external loop logic used to implement an ADLC loop configuration. An ADLC goes on and off loop through the use of its $\overline{\text{LOC}}$ (loop on control) hardware output pin. POWER-ON RESET removes this signal (HIGH) and down-loop stations receive data from up-loop stations that have gone on loop, that is, stations that have connected their transmitters to the loop via the external loop logic. A device is placed on loop when it receives seven consecutive

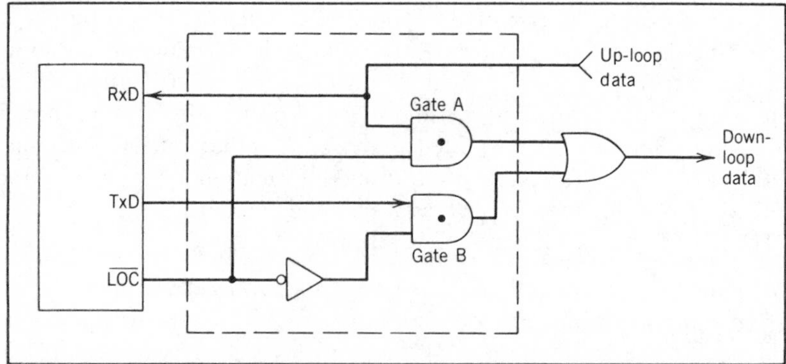

Figure 14-17 Typical loop configuration. (From *Motorola Peripherals Document M6854 UM* (AD-1), "An Introduction to Data Communications," reprinted courtesy of Motorola, Inc.)

1s sent by the primary. At this time $\overline{LOC}$ is asserted (LOW) and the device connects its transmit section to down-loop stations. After the device has gone on loop, it may then go active, that is, begin transmitting its own data. A device goes active on the loop when it receives a polling frame from the primary. After the primary sends the polling frame, it will follow with a transmission of mark idles (all 1s). The polling frame consists of a polling command for one or all devices and a sequence of seven 1s preceded by a 0. When the first up-loop station receives this sequence it should have its transmit FIFO preloaded to begin transmission immediately. This station will change the seventh 1 to a 0 and send this as its opening flag. This data is transmitted around the loop and back to the primary. When that station has finished transmitting, a closing flag is sent terminating the frame. The last 0 of the secondary's closing flag, followed by the mark idle that the primary is transmitting, becomes the sequence to activate transmission on the next down-loop station (0 followed by seven 1s). This continues until the primary receives the mark idle which it is transmitting. A device is considered inactive while on loop when it is not transmitting its own data stored in its FIFO, that is, when not transmitting data sent to it by up-loop stations. Any device may go off loop by special programming of a control register followed by reception of seven consecutive 1s sent to it by the primary. The loop mode of operation finds applications in multiterminal systems (e.g., department store terminals, airline terminals, local insurance company facilities, etc.).

14-4.5 MC6854 ADLC Hardware

The **MC6854** is packaged in a 28-pin DIP and a pin out is shown in Figure 14-18. The ADLC comes complete with a **6800** family interface which includes a data bus (D0–D7), R/W, and the enable clock (E). Two register select lines mean that the device must be memory mapped into four locations to access the internal registers. This device has several buried registers which can only be accessed after writing to a

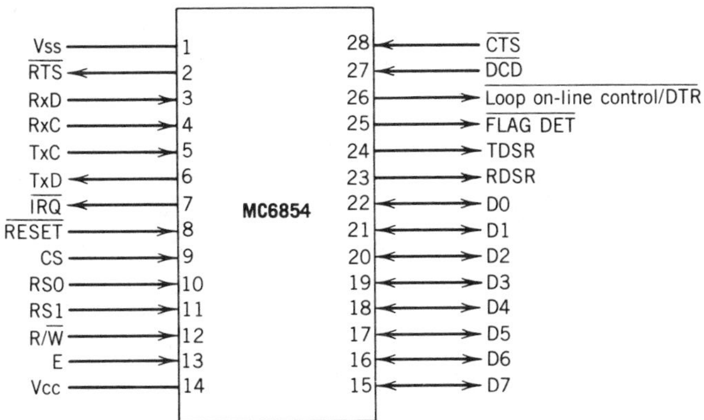

Figure 14-18 The pin out of the **MC6854**. (From *Motorola Peripherals Document M6854 UM* (AD-1), "An Introduction to Data Communications," reprinted courtesy of Motorola, Inc.)

special control register. This allows access to a total of nine separate registers although the ADLC occupies only four memory locations. Four pins on the device define the actual serial interface; they are RxD, RxC, TxD, and TxC. The transmitter clocks out data on the TxD pin when a *negative going* transition on the TxC input occurs; likewise the receiver clocks in data on the RxD input which is externally synchronized with the *positive going edge* of the RxC input. The transmitter and receiver may be programmed to operate in interrupt driven systems and the $\overline{\text{IRQ}}$ pin provides the hardware interface to make this task simple. A special test mode (loop back self-test) is also provided which internally connects the TxD and RxD pins so that test diagnostics may be written with minimal hardware configuration. The ADLC provides control signals such as $\overline{\text{CTS}}$ (clear to send), $\overline{\text{DCD}}$ (data carrier detect), $\overline{\text{RTS}}$ (request to send), and $\overline{\text{DTR}}$ (data terminal ready) which allow easy interface to modems. Two special control signals are provided in hardware to reflect the detection of an opening or closing flag and to indicate when a device is on loop while operating in the loop mode. These signals are $\overline{\text{FLAG DET}}$ (flag detect) and $\overline{\text{LOC}}$ (loop on control). The $\overline{\text{LOC}}$ and $\overline{\text{DTR}}$ pins have been multiplexed to conserve package costs, yet no performance is lost since the ADLC can operate in only one mode at a time and the pin provides different characteristics in loop and nonloop modes of operation. To increase the performance of ADLC-based communication systems the **MC6854** comes complete with a DMA (direct memory access) interface which is compatible with the **MC6844** DMA controller. See Reference 10 for data sheet information on the **MC6844**. Direct memory access is a process which uses a special controller (**MC6844**) to time share the system bus with μP such as the **MC6809** in order to provide high-speed data transfer between memory and peripheral (**MC6854**).

14-4.6 MC6854 Used with DMA

Two control signals on the ADLC, TDSR, and RDSR provide for DMA-type transfers to and from the on chip transmitter and receiver FIFOs. TDSR (transmit data service request) and RDSR (receive data service request) may be wired to the transfer request inputs of the **MC6844** DMA controller to provide increased system throughput. This type of system will be explained through an example showing the implementation of an intelligent terminal with data link capability. This example is further discussed in Application Note #830 available through Motorola. Figure 14-19 shows a block diagram of a system using the **MC6854**, **MC6844**, and several other **MC6800** family peripherals. Using the **MC6809**, **MC6854**, and **MC6844**, a small but powerful terminal complete with a high-speed data link can be constructed. Operating systems can be developed to make this terminal act as a word processor, point-of-sale terminal, data input source, and so on. The data link capability allows the operator to call in the resources of remote computers at synchronous serial data rates up to 1.5 MHz. To operate this fast, direct memory access must be used via the RDSR and TDSR outputs available on the ADLC. A data transfer can be processed every four bus cycles when a **MC6854** ADLC and **MC6844** DMA controller are used together.

The DMA signals available on the ADLC are extremely important in high-speed data transfer. If the **MC6854** were used at its highest communications speed

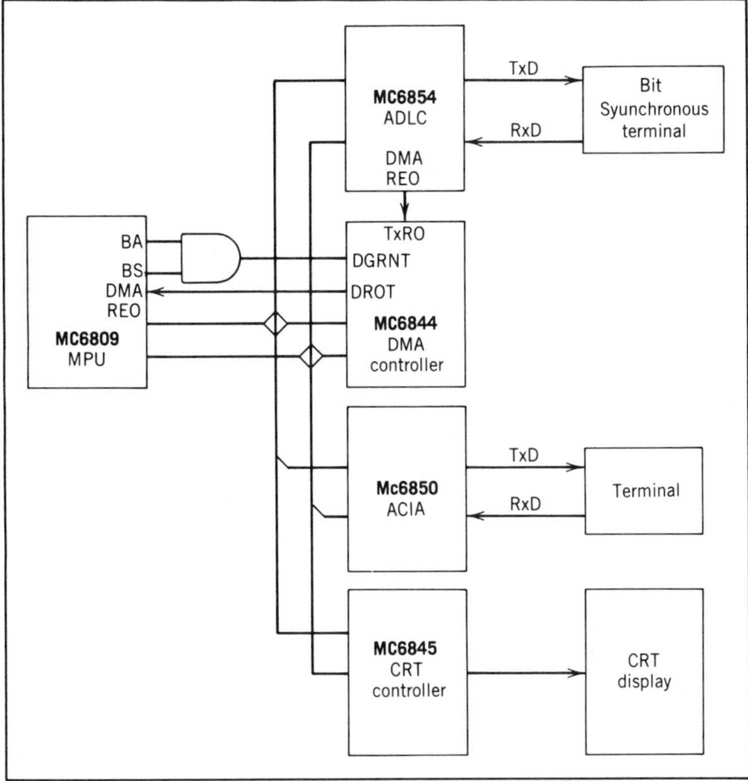

Figure 14-19 Intelligent terminal—block diagram. (From Motorola Applications Note #830. Reprinted courtesy of Motorola, Inc.)

(1.5 MHz) in full duplex operation, a polling routine would not be able to handle the transmitted and received data; therefore direct memory access capability is needed. At 1-megabit serial data transfer rates, a byte must be transferred to or from a FIFO every 4 μs if full duplex operation is used. The **MC6844** DMAC can transfer data to and from the **MC6854** FIFOs at that rate. The two control signals RDSR and TDSR are used to request information transfer on two channels of the **MC6844**. Access to these channels is provided through the use of two control signals, TxRQ0 and TxRQ1, located on the DMAC. When the transfer request line (TxRQ) goes HIGH in response to a service request from the ADLC, the DMAC requests the data bus from the MPU. When the data and address buses are available, the μP will assert bus available (BA) and bus status (BS). The logical AND of these two signals becomes the DMA grant signal (DGRANT) to the DMAC. This DMA grant is a signal to the DMAC that the address and data buses are free for it to control. When the DMA grant is received, the DMAC automatically takes control of the system bus in one cycle and performs the data transfer during the next cycle. The **MC6809** will not attempt to regain control of the bus until one full cycle after the DMAC has transferred the data to or from the ADLC device. When the DMAC completes its data transfer, control is passed back to the **MC6809** to continue its processing. The $\overline{CS}$ signal on the **MC6854** must be asserted when the DMAC requests data by issuing a transmit strobe (TxSTB), or when the **MC6809** addresses the internal registers of the device directly.

14-4.7 Internal Registers in the MC6854

The ADLC has eight internal registers that may be accessed via the data bus. Table 14-9 shows the actual register addressing inside the ADLC device and Reference (11) provides additional information to ease the burden of programming. The READ receiver FIFO register is used by an MPU or DMAC to acquire information which was received by the ADLC. The receiver data FIFO register consists of three 8-bit registers used for the buffer storage of received data. Likewise, the WRITE transmit FIFO register is used to store data that will be transmitted by the ADLC. The transmit FIFO also consists of three 8-bit registers which are used for buffer storage of data to be transmitted. A separate register is provided in the transmitter for storage of the last byte to be transferred. A WRITE to this register causes a frame check sequence field and closing flag to be sent, thus terminating the current frame.

Control register #1 on the ADLC provides the ability to reset the transmitter and the receiver, enable the transmitter and receiver interrupts, enable the DMA mode of operation, and access other buried registers implemented on the device. Control register #2 allows the user to control a modem via RTS output, clear the

Table 14-9 **Register addressing**

Register selected	$R/\overline{W}$	*RS1*	*RS0*	*Address control bit* $(C_1 b_0)$
WRITE control register #1	0	0	0	X
WRITE control register #2	0	0	1	0
WRITE control register #3	0	0	1	1
WRITE transmit FIFO (frame continue)	0	1	0	X
WRITE transmit FIFO (frame terminate)	0	1	1	0
WRITE control register #4	0	1	1	1
READ status register #1	1	0	0	X
READ status register #2	1	0	1	X
READ receiver FIFO	1	1	X	X

transmitter and receiver status conditions, terminate frames by different methods, and select various ways of interrupt by the transmitter and the receiver. The final control register is used to select various modes of operation including loop and nonloop modes, while also providing field extension capability as required by HDLC and ADCCP protocols.

Two status registers provide all information necessary to keep track and manage data transfers performed by the **MC6854** ADLC. An *interrupt request status bit* reflects the level asserted on the hardware IRQ pin, and 2 other bits determine when the receiver and transmitter FIFOs need servicing. There is an error bit which determines if the transmitter has experienced an underrun condition, that is, transmit FIFO was not loaded prior to the last data byte being transmitted out of the transmit shift register, along with another status bit which tells when the ADLC goes on and off loop (when operating in the loop mode). An additional bit in status register #1 indicates status information pending in status register #2. Status register #2 shows status information which deals primarily with the receiver section of the ADLC. Here receiver OVERRUN and modem error conditions such as LOSS OF CARRIER ($\overline{\text{DCD}}$) are acknowledged. Other status conditions indicated by this register include detection of an abort, inactive idle received (all 1s), invalid frames, and an error in the frame check sequence field.

14-4.8 The MC6852 Synchronous Serial Data Adapter (SSDA)

The **MC6854** ADLC is the most sophisticated synchronous communication device offered by Motorola; however the **MC6852** Synchronous Serial Data Adapter (SSDA) also provides data communication at the same rate (1.5 megabits/s) as the ADLC, but with less features. See Reference 12 for information on a data sheet for this device, and Figure 14-20 for an internal block diagram. The SSDA has a 3-byte FIFO in both the transmitter and receiver section similar to the ADLC and also provides the same modem control signals. Unlike the ADLC, the SSDA has no defined frame format, thus instead of beginning each frame with a flag, a sync byte defined by the primary is sent or received preceding the frame. Data synchronization may also be established externally by use of the $\overline{\text{DCD}}$ (data carrier detect input) on the device. Software programming will allow one or two sync characters, which improves system integrity by increasing noise immunity. The **MC6852** does not provide for error checking like that on the ADLC, and that places it second in comparison. The **MC6852** SSDA has typically been used in floppy disk controller subsystems as that found on the Motorola EXOR-cisor. Figure 14-21 is a block diagram of this controller. Take note of the external CRCC which is used to detect errors. If the **MC6854** ADLC had been used to implement this control system the CRCC hardware could have been eliminated.

14-5 THE MC6845 CRTC

The function of a *display generator* is to allow a computer or μP to control interaction on a CRT screen. Combinations of display generators, CRT screens, and

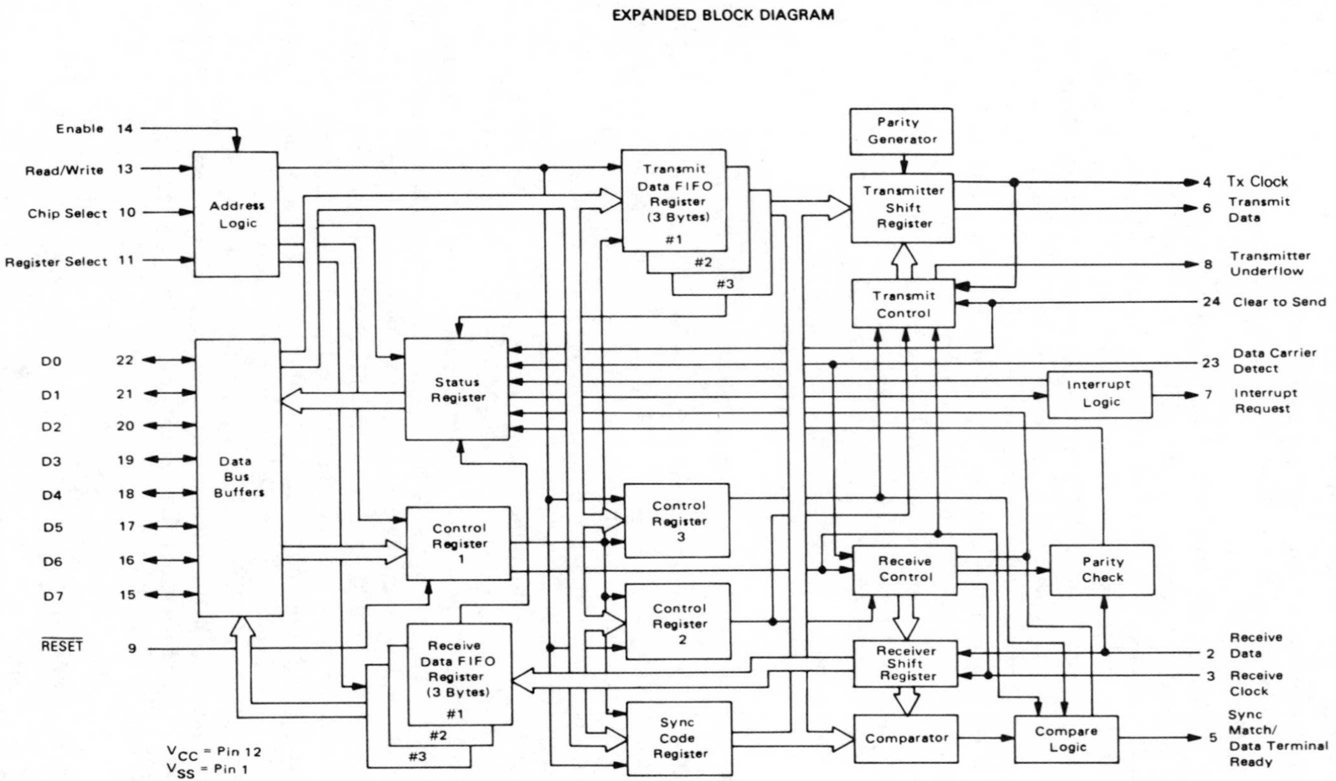

Figure 14-20 Expanded block diagram of the **6852** SSDA. (From the MC6852 Data Sheets. Reprinted courtesy of Motorola, Inc.)

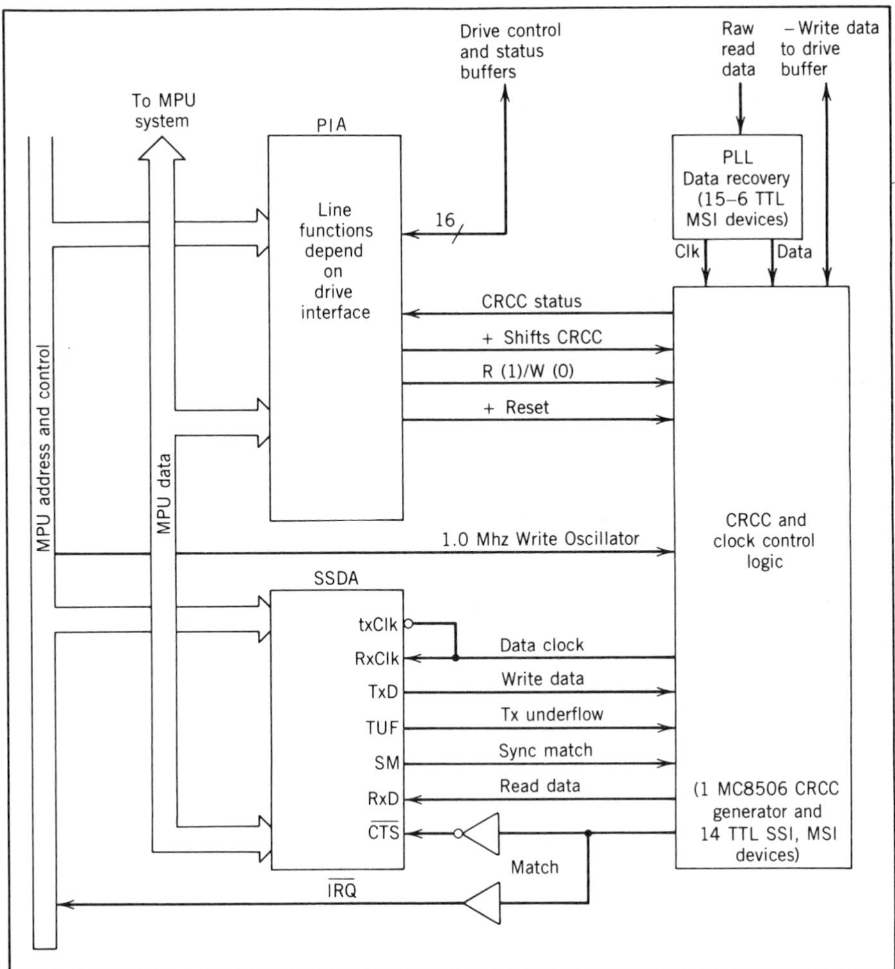

Figure 14-21 A **MC6852** used in a communications system. (From Motorola Applications Note # 764. Reprinted courtesy of Motorola, Inc.)

keyboards are usually called *terminals*, and allow a user to communicate with a computer.

Figure 14-22 is a block diagram of a display generator using an **MC6845** CRTC. The processor writes ASCII information into the refresh RAM[2] (random access memory), and it is the function of the rest of the circuit to translate the information in the refresh RAM into visible characters on a CRT screen.

[2] Microprocessor systems such as Apple, TRS-80, and so on, set aside a portion of their memories for the Refresh RAM. This part of memory is called the *screen image*, and characters can be written to the screen by writing (or poking in Basic) to the screen image area.

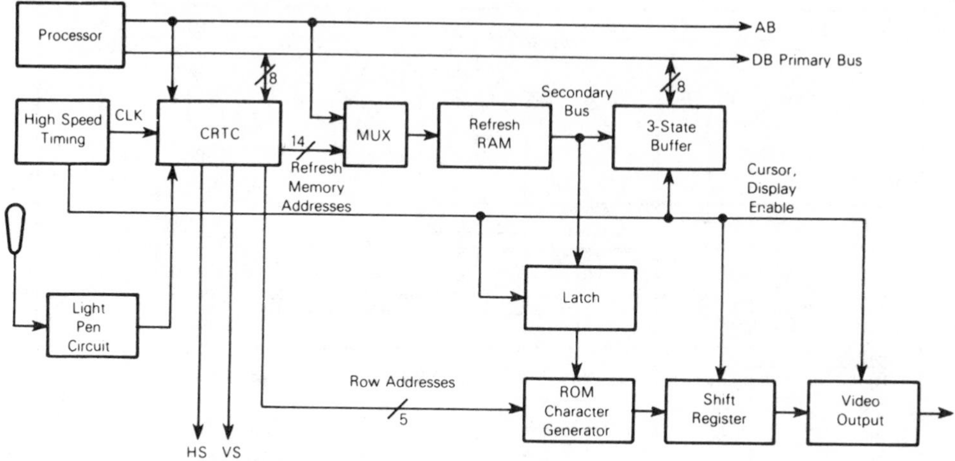

Figure 14-22 Typical CRT controller application. (From the **MC6845** Specification Sheets. Reprinted courtesy of Motorola, Inc.)

The processor only accesses the refresh RAM when it wants to change the display, which it does by writing new information into the RAM, or when it wants to read what is currently being displayed. The display generator must constantly read the RAM to get the characters to be displayed.

In order to understand the **MC6845** CRTC (cathode ray tube controller), the reader must understand the general operation of a display generator. This is beyond the scope of this chapter, but the reader who is unfamiliar with it can consult the references.[3]

The **6845** CRTC is a VLSI component that replaces several counters in a more primitive display generator. The **MC6845** does the following:

1 It generates horizontal and vertical sync pulses for the video output.

2 It generates the row addresses needed by the character generator.

3 It generates the proper addresses for the refresh RAM.

4 It generates a display enable signal when the display is active.

5 It generates a cursor signal when the cursor should be displayed.

6 It has an input for a light pen strobe and will store the position of a light pen in a set of registers.

14-5.1 The MC6845 Signals

Figure 14-23 shows the pin assignment for the **MC6845**. The processor interface consists of:

1 The μP data bus signals D0–D7.

[3] The fundamentals of display generators are discussed in Chapter 20 of Greenfield, *Practical Digital Design Using ICs* (see Reference 2) and in other texts.

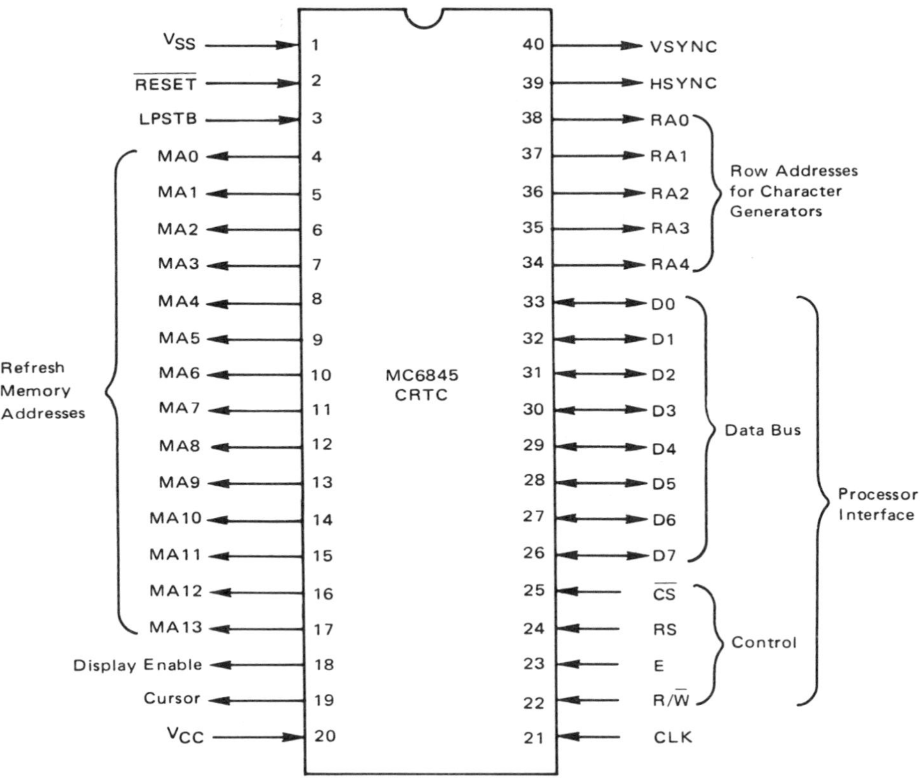

Figure 14-23 **MC6845** pin assignment. (From the **MC6845** Specification Sheets. Reprinted courtesy of Motorola, Inc.)

2 **Chip select $\overline{\text{CS}}$.** This signal must be active (LOW) when the μP is communicating with the **MC6845**. When $\overline{\text{CS}}$ is HIGH, however, the **MC6845** will continue to generate row addresses and refresh RAM addresses, so the display can be updated without any action by the μP.

3 **Register select ($\overline{\text{RS}}$).** When $\overline{\text{RS}}$ is LOW, a WRITE to the **MC6845** writes the address register (see section 14-5.2). When $\overline{\text{RS}}$ is HIGH, a READ or WRITE to the **MC6845** reads or writes data.

4 **Enable (E).** This signal is meant to be tied to the μP's clock signal to synchronize data transfers between the μP and the **MC6845**.

5 **Read/Write (R/$\overline{\text{W}}$).** As in all **6800** ICs, a LOW on this line indicates that the μP is *writing* data into the **MC6845**.

The other signals on the **MC6845** are: vertical and horizontal sync, the row addresses for the character generator, the refresh RAM addresses, light pen strobe, reset, display enable, cursor, and CLOCK (CLK). The clock signal is at the character rate (not the dot rate) of the display.

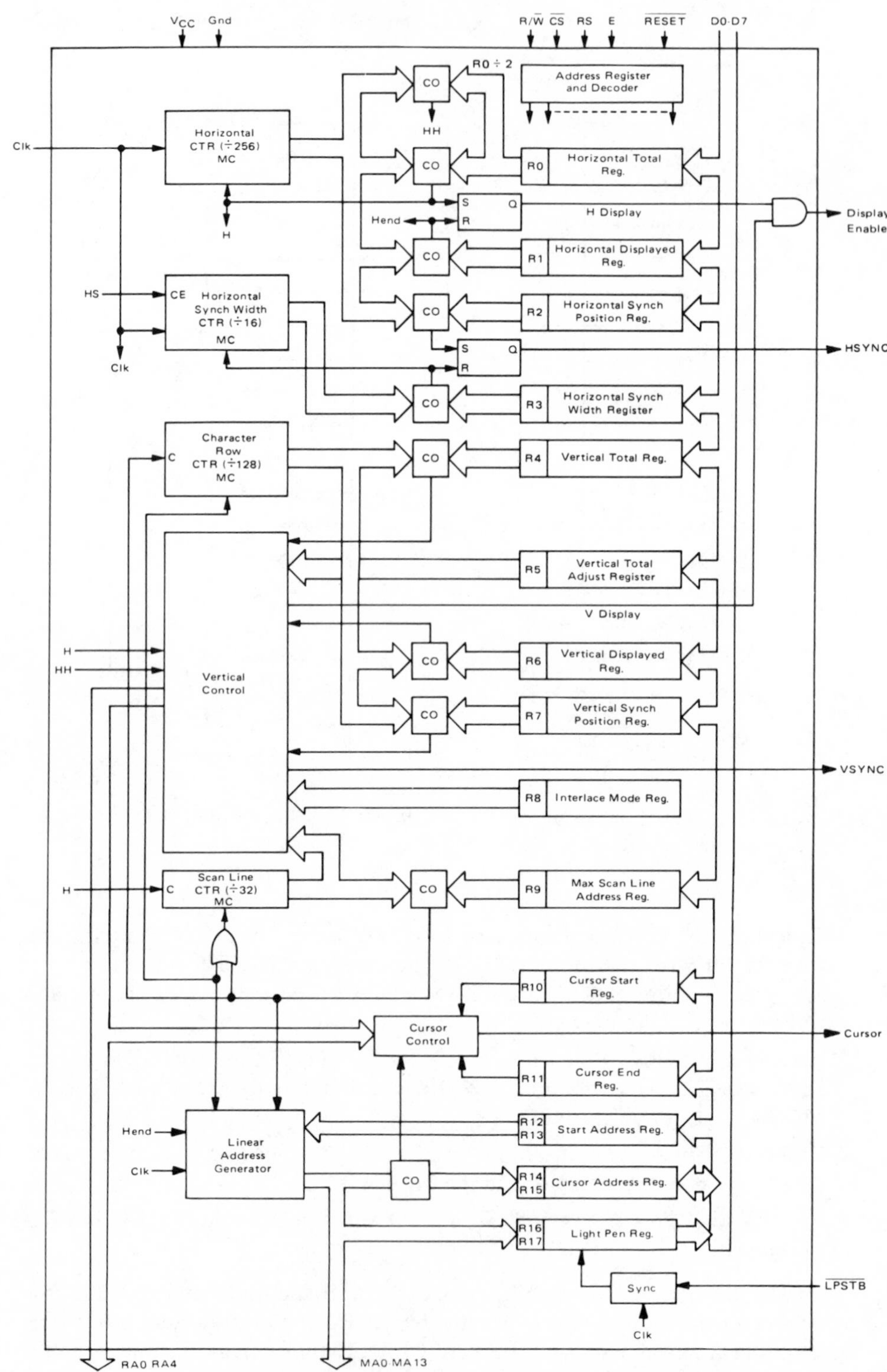

Figure 14-24 CRTC functional block diagram. (From the **MC6845** Specification Sheets. Reprinted courtesy of Motorola, Inc.)

EXAMPLE 14-14 A CRT screen displays 40 characters on a line in 40 μs (this is similar to the display on an Apple computer).

a What frequency must be applied to the CLK input of the **MC6845**?

b If there are 7 dots per character, what is the dot frequency of the display generator?

Solution

a With 40 characters in 40 μs, each character takes 1 μs. Therefore the **MC6845** must have a 1-MHz signal applied to its CLK input.

b With 7 dots per character, the dot rate is 7 MHz.

14-5.2 The MC6845 Registers

There are 18 control/status registers and one address register in the **MC6845** that are used to control the display and perform other peripheral functions, such as indicating the cursor position. A block diagram of the **MC6845** is shown in Figure 14-24, and an illustration of the CRT screen format that is controlled by the CRTC is shown in Figure 14-25.

Table 14-10 lists the 18 internal registers in the CRTC, and gives their functions. The READ and WRITE columns of Table 14-10 show that registers R0–R13 are write only (they cannot be read). The number of bits to be written into each register is also given in the table.

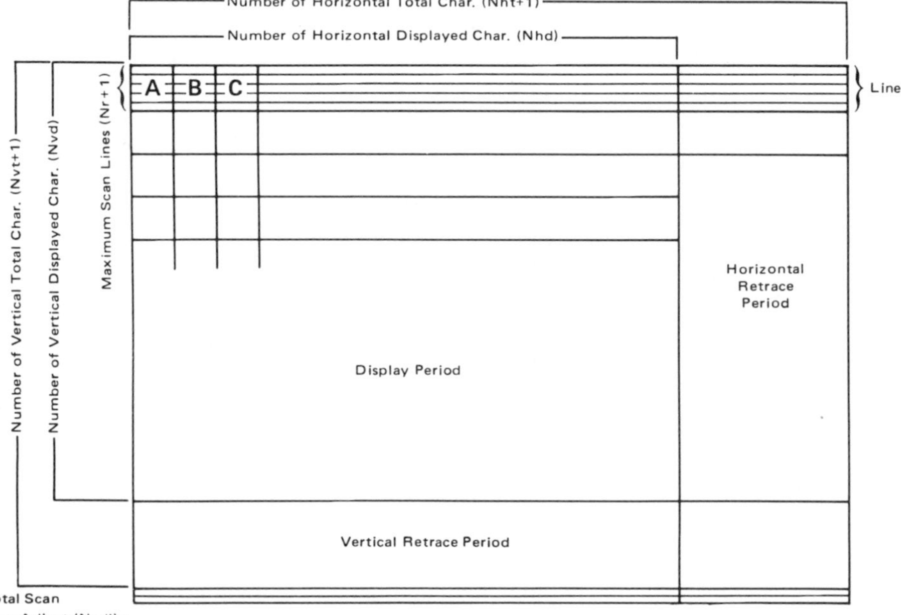

Figure 14-25 Illustration of the CRT screen format. (From the **MC6845** Specification Sheets. Reprinted courtesy of Motorola, Inc.)

Table 14-10 **CRTC internal register assignment**

		Address register					Register		Program			Number of bits							
$\overline{CS}$	RS	4	3	2	1	0	#	Register file	unit	READ	WRITE	7	6	5	4	3	2	1	0
1	X	X	X	X	X	X	X	—	—	—	—								
0	0	X	X	X	X	X	X	Address register	—	No	Yes								
0	1	0	0	0	0	0	R0	Horizontal total	Char.	No	Yes								
0	1	0	0	0	0	1	R1	Horizontal displayed	Char.	No	Yes								
0	1	0	0	0	1	0	R2	H. sync position	Char.	No	Yes								
0	1	0	0	0	1	1	R3	H. sync width	Char.	No	Yes								
0	1	0	0	1	0	0	R4	Vertical total	Char. row	No	Yes								
0	1	0	0	1	0	1	R5	V. total adjust	Scan line	No	Yes								
0	1	0	0	1	1	0	R6	Vertical displayed	Char. row	No	Yes								
0	1	0	0	1	1	1	R7	V. sync position	Char. row	No	Yes								
0	1	0	1	0	0	0	R8	Interlace mode	—	No	Yes								
0	1	0	1	0	0	1	R9	Max scan line address	Scan line	No	Yes								
0	1	0	1	0	1	0	R10	Cursor start	Scan line	No	Yes		B	P			(Note 1)		
0	1	0	1	0	1	1	R11	Cursor end	Scan line	No	Yes								
0	1	0	1	1	0	0	R12	Start address (H)	—	No	Yes								
0	1	0	1	1	0	1	R13	Start address (L)	—	No	Yes								
0	1	0	1	1	1	0	R14	Cursor (H)	—	Yes	Yes								
0	1	0	1	1	1	1	R15	Cursor (L)	—	Yes	Yes								
0	1	1	0	0	0	0	R16	Light pen (H)	—	Yes	No								
0	1	1	0	0	0	1	R17	Light pen (L)	—	Yes	No								

Note 1: Bit 5 of the Cursor Start Raster Register is used for blink period control, and Bit 6 is used to select blink or non-blink.

EXAMPLE 14-15 How many bits are written into the address register?

Solution Table 14-10 shows that the bits 7, 6, and 5 are crossed out, so that 5 bits are written to the address register. The address register must address one of 18 registers, so only 5 bits are required. The address of each register is given in the address register column of Table 14-9.

The function of each register in the **MC6845** is described in the rest of this section.

The address register holds the address of the control register to be written into. Addresses are written into the address register when $\overline{CS} = R/\overline{W} = RS = 0$. Control registers are written when $\overline{CS} = R/\overline{W} = 0$, and RS = 1. A typical way to write the control registers is to:

1 Write 0 into the address register;

2 change RS to 1 and write the data into R0;

3 change RS to 0 and write 1 into the address register;

4 change RS to 1 and write the data into control register 1.

⋮

Continue this procedure until all the control registers have been written into.

Control register 0 (R0) is the **horizontal total register**. It contains the total number of horizontal characters on each line (displayed and nondisplayed), minus 1.

Control register 1 (R1) is the **horizontal displayed register**. It contains the number of displayed characters on a line.

Control register 2 (R2) is the **horizontal sync position register**. It controls the position of the displayed characters relative to the horizontal sync pulse.

Control register 3 (R3) is the **horizontal sync width register**. It determines the width of the horizontal sync pulse.

Control registers R4 and R5 are the **vertical total** (R4) and **vertical total adjust registers**. This is the total number of rows (R4) and fractional rows (R5) in the field of the display.

Control register 6 (R6) is the **vertical displayed register**. It determines the number of character rows displayed on the CRT screen.

Control register 7 (R7) is the **vertical sync position register**. It determines the position of the displayed rows with respect to the vertical sync pulse.

Control register 8 (R8) is the **interlace mode register**. This 2-bit register determines whether the screen display is interlaced.

Control register 9 (R9) is the **maximum scan line address register**. It determines the number of scan lines per character row.

Registers R10 and R11 are the **cursor start** and **cursor end** registers. The cursor start register determines whether the cursor blinks, its blink rate, and its starting row. R11 determines the cursor end row. The action of these registers is shown in Figure 14-26.

Example of cursor display mode

Cursor Start Register
B *P*

Bit 6	Bit 5	Cursor display mode
0	0	Non-blink
0	1	Cursor non-display
1	0	Blink, 1/16 field rate
1	1	Blink, 1/32 field rate

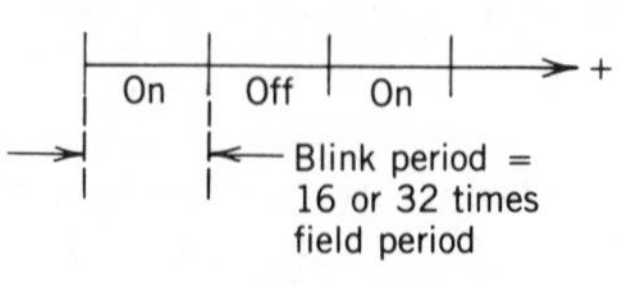

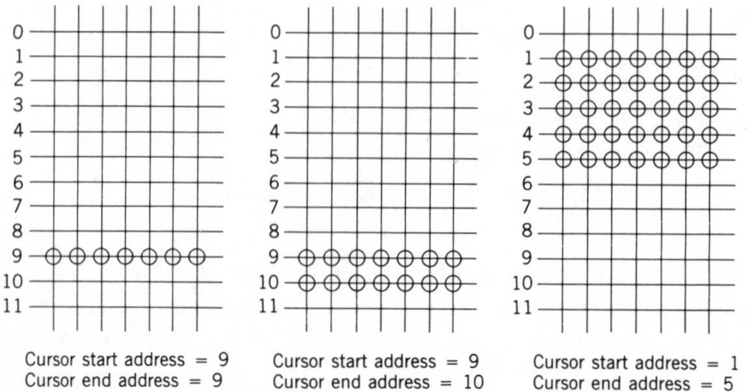

Figure 14-26 Cursor control. (From the MC6845 Specification Sheets. Reprinted courtesy of Motorola, Inc.)

Registers R12 and R13 are the **start address registers**. This consists of a 14-bit refresh RAM starting address. The six higher-order bits are in R12, and the 8 lower-order bits are in R13.

Registers R14 and R15 are the **cursor position registers**. They constitute a 14-bit register that determines the cursor location. These are the only registers in the **MC6845** that can both be read and written into.

Registers R16 and R17 are the *light pen registers.* When a light pen strobe occurs, the beam address is stored in these registers. They constitute a 14-bit read-only address register and give the μP the address of a light pen.

14-5.3 Setting Up a CRTC System

To set up a CRTC system, the following are required:

1 The hardware components, shown in Figure 14-22, must be in place.

2 The μP must write the data to be displayed into the refresh RAM. The multiplexer in Figure 14-22 determines whether the μP or the CRTC controls the addresses of the refresh RAM. Normally, the CRTC controls, but when the μP needs to read or

Table 14-11 CRTC format worksheet

Display Format Worksheet

	Item		Value	Unit
1.	Displayed Characters per Row		______	Char.
2.	Displayed Character Rows per Screen		______	Rows
3.	Character Matrix	a. Columns	______	Columns
		b. Rows	______	Rows
4.	Character Block	a. Columns	______	Columns
		b. Rows	______	Rows
5.	Frame Refresh Rate		______	Hz
6.	Horizontal Oscillator Frequency		______	Hz
7.	Active Scan Lines (Line 2 × Line 4b)		______	Lines
8.	Total Scan Lines (Line 6 ÷ Line 5)		______	Lines
9.	Total Rows Per Screen (Line 8 ÷ Line 4b)		______ Rows	and ______ Lines
10.	Vertical Sync Delay (Char. Rows)		______	Rows
11.	Vertical Sync Width (Scan Lines (16))		16	Lines
12.	Horizontal Sync Delay (Character Times)		______	Char. Times
13.	Horizontal Sync Width (Character Times)		______	Char. Times
14.	Horizontal Scan Delay (Character Times)		______	Char. Times
15.	Total Character Times (Line 1 + 12 + 13 + 14)		______	Char. Times
16.	Character Rate (Line 6 × 15)		______	Hz
17.	Dot Clock Rate (Line 4a × 16)		______	Hz

CRTC Registers

Register		Decimal	Hex
R0	Horizontal Total (Line 15 − 1)	______	______
R1	Horizontal Displayed (Line 1)	______	______
R2	Horizontal Sync Position (Line 1 + Line 12)	______	______
R3	Horizontal Sync Width (Line 13)	______	______
R4	Vertical Total (Line 9 − 1)	______	______
R5	Vertical Adjust (Line 9 Lines)	______	______
R6	Vertical Displayed (Line 2)	______	______
R7	Vertical Sync Position (Line 2 + Line 10)	______	______
R8	Interlace (00 Normal, 01 Interlace, 03 Interlace, and Video)		______
R9	Max Scan Line Add (Line 4b − 1)	______	______
R10	Cursor Start	______	______
R11	Cursor End	______	______
R12, R13	Start Address (H and L)	______	______
R14, R15	Cursor (H and L)		______

Table 14-11 (*Continued*)

Bits 0 to 3 Second Hex Digit (LSB)	**Bits 4 to 6 First Hex Digit (MSB)**							
	0	**1**	**2**	**3**	**4**	**5**	**6**	**7**
0	NUL	DLE	SP	0	@	P		p
1	SOH	DC1	!	1	A	Q	a	q
2	STX	DC2	"	2	B	R	b	r
3	ETX	DC3	#	3	C	S	c	s
4	EOT	DC4	$	4	D	T	d	t
5	ENQ	NAK	%	5	E	U	e	u
6	ACK	SYN	&	6	F	V	f	v
7	BEL	ETB	'	7	G	W	g	w
8	BS	CAN	(	8	H	X	h	x
9	HT	EM	)	9	I	Y	i	y
A	LF	SUB	*	:	J	Z	j	z
B	VT	ESC	+	;	K	[	k	{
C	FF	FS	,	<	L	/	l	/
D	CR	GS	-	=	M	]	m	}
E	SO	RS	.	>	N	∧	n	≈
F	SI	US	/	?	O	—	o	DEL

write the RAM, it must control the addresses. In some sophisticated systems, the μP has access when a clock is HIGH and the CRTC has access when the same clock is LOW.

3 The CRTC registers must be initialized to properly control the displays. This requires both a program and a hardware interface to the μP. A CRTC worksheet, shown in Table 14-11, greatly aids the designer.

This procedure is best illustrated by the example given in the next section.

14-5.4 An Example of a CRTC Design

This section presents a very simple example of a video display using the CRTC. We chose to have 16 displayed lines of 32 characters each.[4] The characters were chosen to be a 5×8 matrix embedded in a seven-column by ten-row block. This is compatible with a **2513** character generator.

The display was designed to operate at standard CRT specifications, which are 60 frames/s and a horizontal oscillator frequency of 15,750 Hz. These specifications determine the first nine entries in the display format worksheet (Table 14-10).

To complete the display format worksheet, the vertical sync delay was chosen as 0 rows, and the horizontal sync delay, horizontal sync width, and horizontal scan delay were all chosen as ten character times. This gave a total of 62 characters per line at a 15,750-Hz horizontal frequency, or a 976.5-Hz character rate.

Figure 14-27 shows the display format worksheet for this example, and the contents of the CRTC register as derived from the specifications.

[4] This example was tried in the laboratory at Rochester Institute of Technology.

Display Format Worksheet

			Value	Units
1	Displayed characters per row		32	Char.
2	Displayed character rows per screen		16	Rows
3	Character matrix	**a** Columns	5	Columns
		b Rows	8	Rows
4	Character block	**a** Columns	7	Columns
		b Rows	10	Rows
5	Frame refresh rate		60	Hz
6	Horizontal oscillator frequency		15,750	Hz
7	Active scan lines (line 2 × line 4b)		160	Lines
8	Total scan lines (line 6 + line 5)		262	Lines
9	Total rows per screen (line 8 + line 4b)		26 Rows	and 2 lines
10	Vertical sync delay (char. rows)		0	Rows
11	Vertical sync width (scan lines (16))		16	Lines
12	Horizontal sync delay (character times)		10	Char. times
13	Horizontal sync width (character times)		10	Char. times
14	Horizontal scan delay (character times)		10	Char. times
15	Total character times (Line 1 + 12 + 13 + 14)		62	Char. times
16	Character rate (line 6 × 15)		976.5	KHz
17	Dot clock rate (line 4a × 16)		6.836	MHz

	CRTC Registers	**Decimal**	**Hex**
R0	Horizontal total (Line 15–1)	61	3D
R1	Horizontal displayed (Line 1)	32	20
R2	Horizontal sync position (Line 1 + Line 12)	42	2A
R3	Horizontal sync width (Line 13)	10	A
R4	Vertical total (Line 9–1)	25	19
R5	Vertical adjust (Line 9 Lines)	2	2
R6	Vertical displayed (Line 2)	16	10
R7	Vertical sync position (line 2 + line 10)	16	10
R8	Interlace (00 normal, 01 interlace, 03 interlace, and video)		0
R9	Max scan line add (line 4b − 1)	9	9
R10	Cursor start	0	0
R11	Cursor end	9	9
R12, R13	Start address (H and L)	—	—
R14, R15	Cursor (H and L)		—

Figure 14-27 CRTC format worksheet. (From the MC6845 Specification Sheets. Reprinted courtesy of Motorola, Inc.)

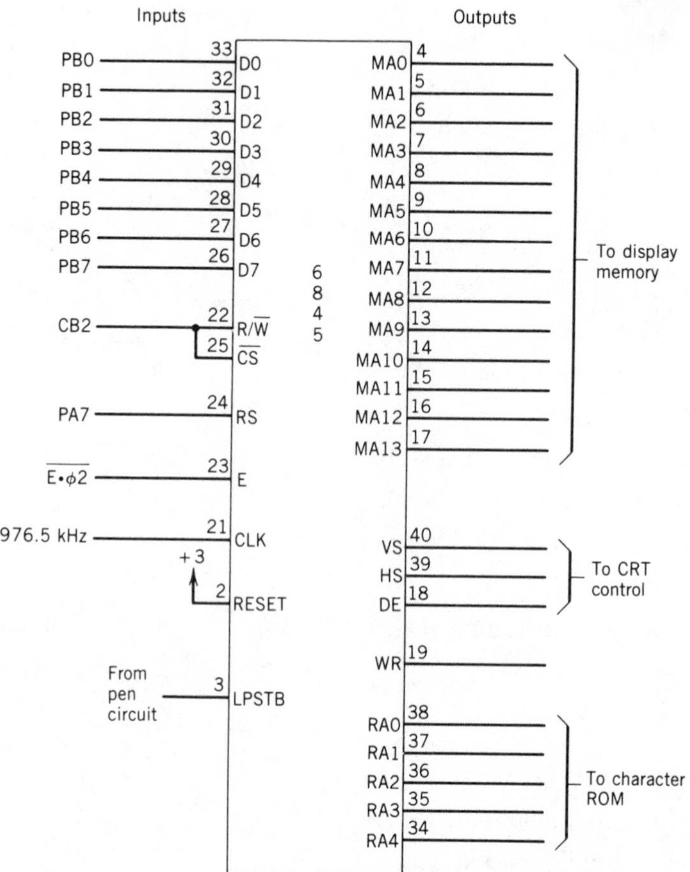

Figure 14-28 Schematic diagram showing the connections to the **MC6845**.

The **MC6845** was connected to a 6809-μP[5] (see Chapter 8) via a PIA (see section 7-14), as shown in Figure 14-28. The data bus on the **MC6845** was connected to the PB lines and the PIA was placed in pulse mode so that each time data was written to data register B, CB2 went LOW, causing a LOW on R/W and $\overline{\text{CS}}$. The RS input to the **6845** was connected to PA7.

Figure 14-29 shows the program. After initialization, the program addresses register 0, then writes register 0, repeats with register 1, and so on. The data is in REGTAB at $240 and is shown in Figure 14-30.

Many more sophisticated CRTC display drivers and terminals are described in Motorola's literature. Space limitations preclude discussing them, but the simple CRTC circuit presented here should give the reader a firm grasp of the fundamentals required to successfully use a **6845** CRTC in a display generator.

[5] The **6809** was part of the **6809-D4** kit manufactured by Motorola.

```
CRTINT   9-OCT-84 12:11:45  MC6809 V1.3   COPYRIGHT MOTOROLA 1980   PAGE   1

                 OPT   S,O,L
          E0FD  CRA     EQU   $E0FD      INIT NAMES FOR THE PIA
          E0FC  DRA     EQU   $E0FC
          E0FF  CRB     EQU   $E0FF
          E0FE  DRB     EQU   $E0FE
          000F  REGNUM  EQU   $0F
          0240  REGTAB  EQU   $240
0200                    ORG   $200       START AT $200
0200 7F   E0FD  START   CLR   CRA
0203 7F   E0FF          CLR   CRB
0206 96   FF            LDA   $FF        INIT PIA
0208 B7   E0FC          STA   DRA
020B B7   E0FE          STA   DRB
020E 86   3C            LDA   #$3C
0210 B7   E0FD          STA   CRA
0213 86   2C            LDA   #$2C
0215 B7   E0FE          STA   DRB
0218 5F                 CLRB
0219 8E   0240          LDX   #REGTAB    GET START OF TABLE

021C 4F         REGINT  CLRA
021D B7   E0FC          STA   DRA       SET RS LINE LOW
0220 F7   E0FE          STB   DRB       WRITE REG NUM INTO ADDRESS
0223 86   80            LDA   #$80
0225 B7   E0FC          STA   DRA       SET RS HIGH
0228 A6   80            LDA   0,X+      LOAD REG CONTENTS
022A B7   E0FE          STA   DRB       STORE IN REG
022D 5C                 INCB            NEXT REG
022E C1   10            CMPB  #REGNUM+1 DONE?
0230 26   EA            BNE   REGINT     DO IT AGAIN
0232 3F                 SWI
                        END

TOTAL ERRORS:   0     TOTAL WARNINGS:   0


SYMBOL TABLE

 CRA    E0FD  CRB    E0FF  DRA    E0FC  DRB    E0FE  REGINT 021C
 REGNUM 000F  REGTAB 0240  START  0200
```

Figure 14-29 A **6809** program to initialize the **MC6845**.

Location	*Register*	*Contents*	
240	R0	30	
241	R1	20	
242	R2	2A	
243	R3	0A	
244	R4	19	
245	R5	02	
246	R6	10	
247	R7	10	
248	R8	00	
249	R9	09	
24A	R10	00	
24B	R11	09	
24C	R12	-	USER DEFINED
24D	R13	-	
24E	R14	-	
24F	R15	-	

Figure 14-30 Register location contents.

14-6 REFERENCES

1. Joseph Greenfield and William Wray, *Using Microprocessors and Microcomputers: The 6800 Family*, Wiley, New York, 1981.
2. Joseph Greenfield, *Practical Digital Design Using ICs*, 2nd Edition, Wiley, New York, 1983.
3. *MC6840 Programmable Timer Fundamentals and Applications No. MC6840 UM (AD-I)*, Motorola Microsystems, Austin, Tex.
4. Motorola Engineering Bulletin No. EB-69.
5. *The Motorola MC6850 Specifications Sheets*, Motorola Semiconductor Division, Pheonix, Ariz.
6. *Advanced Data Communications Control Procedures (ADCCP)*, a BOP document of the American National Standards Institute (ANSI).
7. *High Level Data Link Control (HDLC)*, a BOP document of the Consultative Committee for International Telephony and Telegraphy (C-CITT).
8. *Synchronous Data Link Control (SDLC)*, a BOP document introduced by IBM.
9. *An Introduction to Data Communication*, Motorola Peripherals Document **MC6854** UM (AD-1), Motorola, Inc.
10. *Motorola MC6844 Direct Memory Access Controller Data Sheet #DS9520R2*, Motorola, Inc.
11. *Motorola MC6854 Advanced Data Link Controller Programming Reference Manual*, Issue A, Motorola, Inc.
12. *Motorola MC6852 Data Sheet #DS9495-R2*, Motorola, Inc.
13. *Motorola MC6845 Specification Sheets #ADI-465*, Motorola Semiconductor Division, Austin, Tex.

CHAPTER 15

Zilog Peripherals

Steve Sharp

American Microsystems, Inc.
Santa Clara, California
(formerly of Zilog)

15-1 OVERVIEW

This chapter discusses the **Z8000**[1] and **Z80** peripheral support chips, with the **Z8000** chips considered first. In chapter 11 the **Z8000** CPU and CPU support devices in the **Z8000** family were discussed. These are only a few of the members of this family of devices all designed to work with a common chip interconnect, the Z-Bus. Also in the **Z8000** family are several peripheral controllers and a Z-Bus memory device.

The **Z8000** peripherals are powerful, multifunction devices that can be custom tailored to a user's application by programming various internal registers. They use a common interrupt structure designed to interface easily to the **Z8000** CPUs, and they can also be used in a polled environment. The **Z8000** peripherals include:

1 the **Z8036** Counter/Timer Parallel I/O Unit (Z-CIO);

2 the **Z8030** Serial Communications Controller (Z-SCC);

3 the **Z8038** FIFO Input/Output Unit (Z-FIO);

4 the **Z8065** Burst Error Processor (Z-BEP);

5 the **Z8068** Data Ciphering Processor (Z-DCP).

The Z-CIO contains three parallel ports and three 16-bit counter/timers. It can also be used as a priority interrupt controller. The Z-SCC is a dual-channel serial I/O controller that supports all popular synchronous and asynchronous communications protocols. The Z-FIO is a byte-wide first in first out (FIFO) intelligent buffer for interfacing between CPUs or between a CPU and a peripheral. The Z-BEP

[1] Zilog, **Z80**, **Z8000**, and so on, are trademarks of Zilog, Inc., with whom the publisher is not associated.

provides error detection and correction during high-speed data transfers. The Z-DCP encrypts or decrypts data using the National Bureau of Standards encryption algorithms.

These peripherals come in two versions, a **Z8000** compatible version (the **8000** series) which works with the multiplexed Z-Bus, and a general nonmultiplexed bus version (the **8500** series). For example, the CIO is called the **Z8036** if it is the **Z8000** compatible part, and the **Z8536** if it is the nonmultiplexed bus part. The function of the two series of parts is the same, and all comments relating to function apply to both series of parts. The only difference is in the CPU interface, and in the fact that because the **8500** series parts do not use a multiplexed address/data bus, their internal registers are not all directly addressable, but must be accessed by way of a pointer register (similar to the way some of the older **Z80** peripherals were addressed).

15-2 HARDWARE INTERFACE

15-2.1 The Z-Bus Series of Peripherals

The **8000** series peripherals, also called the Z-Bus peripherals, interface very easily to the **Z8000** CPUs, requiring only a *chip select* signal in addition to the regular Z-Bus signals of address strobe, data strobe, READ/WRITE, and address/data lines. All of the Z-Bus peripherals are byte-wide devices, and are typically attached to the low-order half of the address/data bus. This is necessary because interrupt vectors must be placed on the lower half of the bus when using vectored interrupts. The timing of data transfers is controlled by address strobe ($\overline{\text{AS}}$) and data strobe ($\overline{\text{DS}}$), while the direction of the transfer is controlled by the read/write ($\overline{\text{R/}\overline{\text{W}}}$) signal. A CHIP SELECT ($\overline{\text{CS}}$) signal is also necessary to access a Z-Bus peripheral. CHIP SELECT is latched by the peripheral on the rising edge of address strobe, and should be generated by decoding the higher-order address bits during an I/O access. In order to ensure that the address being decoded is actually an I/O port address, the status for I/O reference is typically included in the decoding operation. The chip resets itself when both address strobe and data strobe are LOW (active) at the same time. (In normal operation, address strobe and data strobe are never active at the same time.)

Other signals, such as $\overline{\text{WAIT}}$ or REQ, may also be used as a part of the peripheral-to-CPU interface, depending on the application. Most of the Z-Bus peripherals also have a clock input (which is not always required for the part to function), but this clock does not have to be synchronized with the CPU clock in any way. In addition, the bus control signals do not have to be synchronized to any clocks.

The $\overline{\text{INT}}$, $\overline{\text{INTACK}}$, IEI, and IEO signals are used to interface the peripherals to the interrupt structure.

15-2.2 Signal Lines

The Z-Bus consists of a set of common signal lines that interconnect bus components. The signals on these lines can be grouped into four categories, depending on how they are used in transactions and requests. There are three groups of signals: primary, bus request, and interrupt.

Primary Signals These signals provide timing, control, and data transfer for Z-Bus transactions. The primary signals are:

AD_0–AD_{15}. *Address/data (active HIGH)*. These multiplexed data and address lines carry I/O addresses, memory addresses, and data during Z-Bus transactions. A Z-Bus may have 8 or 16 bits of data depending on the type of CPU. In the case of an 8-bit Z-Bus, data is transferred on AD_0–AD_7.

Extended address (active HIGH). These lines extend AD_0–AD_{15} to support memory addresses greater than 16 bits. The number of lines and the type of address information carried is dependent on the CPU.

Status (active HIGH). These lines designate the kind of transaction occurring on the bus and certain additional information about the transaction (such as program or data memory access or system versus normal mode).

$\overline{AS}$. *Address strobe (active LOW)*. The rising edge of $\overline{AS}$ indicates the beginning of a transaction and that the Address, Status, R/$\overline{W}$, and B/$\overline{W}$ signals are valid.

$\overline{DS}$. *Data strobe (active LOW)*. $\overline{DS}$ provides timing for data movement to or from the bus master.

R/$\overline{W}$. *Read/Write (LOW = WRITE)*. This signal determines the direction of data transfer for memory or I/O transactions.

B/$\overline{W}$. *Byte/word (LOW = word)*. This signal indicates whether a byte or word of data is to be transmitted on a 16-bit bus. The signal is not present on an 8-bit bus.

$\overline{WAIT}$ *(active LOW)*. A LOW on this line indicates that the responding device needs more time to complete a transaction.

$\overline{RESET}$ *(active LOW)*. A LOW on this line resets the CPU and bus users. Peripherals may be reset by $\overline{RESET}$ or by holding $\overline{AS}$ and $\overline{DS}$ LOW simultaneously.

$\overline{CS}$. *Chip select (active LOW)*. Each peripheral or memory component has a $\overline{CS}$ line that is decoded from the address and status lines. A LOW on this line indicates that the peripheral or memory component is being addressed by a transaction. The chip select information is latched on the rising edge of $\overline{AS}$.

CLOCK. This signal provides basic timing for bus transactions. Bus masters must provide all signals synchronously to the clock. Peripherals and memories do not need to be synchronized to the clock.

Bus Request Signals These signals make bus requests and establish which component should obtain control of the bus. The bus request signals are:

$\overline{BUSREQ}$. *Bus request (active LOW)*. This line is driven by all bus requesters. A LOW indicates that a bus requester has or is trying to obtain control of the bus.

$\overline{BUSACK}$. *Bus acknowledge (active LOW)*. A LOW on this line indicates that the Z-Bus CPU has relinquished control of the bus in response to a bus request.

$\overline{BAI}$, $\overline{BAO}$. *Bus acknowledge in, bus acknowledge out (active LOW)*. These signals form the bus-request daisy chain.

Interrupt Signals These signals are used for interrupt requests and for determining which interrupting component is to respond to an acknowledge. To support more than one type of interrupt, the lines carrying these signals can be replicated. (The **Z8000** CPU supports three types of interrupts; nonmaskable, vectored, and nonvectored.) The interrupt signals are:

$\overline{INT}$. *Interrupt* (*active LOW*). This signal can be driven by any peripheral capable of generating an interrupt. A LOW on $\overline{\text{INT}}$ indicates that an interrupt request is being made.

$\overline{INTACK}$. *Interrupt acknowledge* (*active LOW*). This signal is decoded from the status lines. A LOW indicates an interrupt acknowledge transaction is in progress. This signal is latched by the peripheral on the rising edge of $\overline{\text{AS}}$.

IEI, *IEO*. *Interrupt enable in*, *interrupt enable out* (*active HIGH*). These signals form the interrupt daisy chain.

Resource Request Signals These signals are used for resource requests. To manage more than one resource, the lines carrying these signals can be replicated. (The **Z8000** supports one set of resource request lines.) These are:

$\overline{MMRQ}$. *Multi-micro request* (*active LOW*). This line is driven by any device that can use the shared resource. A LOW indicates that a request for the resource has been made or granted.

$\overline{MMST}$. *Multi-micro status* (*active LOW*). This pin allows a device to observe the value of the $\overline{\text{MMRQ}}$ line. An input pin other than $\overline{\text{MMRQ}}$ facilitates the use of line drivers for $\overline{\text{MMRQ}}$.

$\overline{MMAI}$, $\overline{MMAO}$. *Multi-micro acknowledge in*, *multi-micro acknowledge out* (*active LOW*). These lines form the resource-request daisy chain.

15-2.3 Nonmultiplexed Bus Peripherals

The **8500** series of nonmultiplexed bus peripherals use a bus interface that is very similar to the bus used by the **Z80** and other common μPs. It uses read ($\overline{\text{RD}}$), write ($\overline{\text{WR}}$), chip enable ($\overline{\text{CE}}$), and one or two address lines. The address lines are typically used to select whether the access in progress is to a data buffer or a control register. Registers other than the data buffers must be accessed by writing a register address into a control register and then writing the data destined for that register. In these peripherals, the CHIP ENABLE signal is not latched as it was in the Z-Bus peripherals. The interrupt structure is essentially the same as in the Z-Bus peripherals, and a reset is indicated by $\overline{\text{RD}}$ and $\overline{\text{WR}}$ active (LOW) at the same time.

15-3 INTERRUPT STRUCTURE

The interrupt structure for both series of peripherals is the same, using an interrupt priority daisy chain to resolve contention, and an explicit interrupt acknowledge output. Returns from interrupt service routines are handled in software, so no special hardware is necessary.

A complete interrupt sequence consists of an interrupt request by a peripheral followed by an interrupt acknowledge cycle by the CPU, an interrupt service routine, and an exit from the interrupt service routine (return from interrupt), putting the peripheral back into the state it was in before the interrupt first occurred.

A peripheral can have more than one source of interrupts internally. The priority of these internal sources is usually fixed, and they can be thought of as individual interrupt sources just as different peripheral devices are individual interrupt sources.

The interrupt scheme showing several peripherals or sources of interrupts is shown in Figure 15-1.

Each interrupt source has 3 bits that control its operation. They are the interrupt pending (IP) bit, the interrupt enable (IE) bit, and the interrupt under service (IUS) bit. The state of these three bits at any point in time will determine how that interrupt source will react.

A single peripheral may have one or more interrupt vectors for identifying the source of an interrupt from that device. Each interrupt source will be associated with a particular vector, but there is nothing to prevent multiple interrupt sources from being associated with the same vector. Each vector will also have a vector includes status (VIS) bit to indicate whether or not that vector will include status information as to the source of the interrupt.

Finally, each peripheral has three bits in its control register for controlling the interrupt behavior of the entire device. They are the master interrupt enable (MIE) bit, the disable lower chain (DLC) bit, and the no vector (NV) bit.

The various peripherals within a system are connected together in a daisy chain using their IEI (interrupt enable in) and IEO (interrupt enable out) pins. The interrupt sources within a single device are also connected in a fixed daisy chain connecting all interrupt sources in a system. The *daisy chain* has two functions: during an INTERRUPT ACKNOWLEDGE cycle, it determines which interrupt source is being acknowledged, and at all other times it determines which interrupt sources can initiate and interrupt.

An interrupt source with an interrupt pending (IP = 1) makes an interrupt request (by pulling $\overline{\text{INT}}$ low) if and only if it is enabled (IE = 1 and MIE = 1), it does not have an interrupt under service (IUS = 0), no higher-priority interrupt is being serviced (IEI = 1), and no INTERRUPT ACKNOWLEDGE transaction is in progress (as indicated by $\overline{\text{INTACK}}$ at the last rising edge of address strobe). IEO is not pulled LOW at this time, but continues to follow IEI until an INTERRUPT ACKNOWLEDGE cycle occurs.

Some time after $\overline{\text{INT}}$ is pulled LOW, the CPU will recognize the interrupt and initiate an INTERRUPT ACKNOWLEDGE cycle (driving $\overline{\text{INTACK}}$ low). Between the rising edge of address strobe and the falling edge of data strobe of the INTERRUPT ACKNOWLEDGE cycle, the IEI/IEO daisy chain settles. Any interrupt source with an interrupt pending (IP = 1, IE = 1, MIE = 1) or under service (IUS = 1) holds its IEO line LOW. All other interrupt sources make IEO follow IEI. When data strobe falls, only the highest priority interrupt source (the first device in the daisy chain) with IP = 1 has its IEI input HIGH, its IE bit set to 1, and

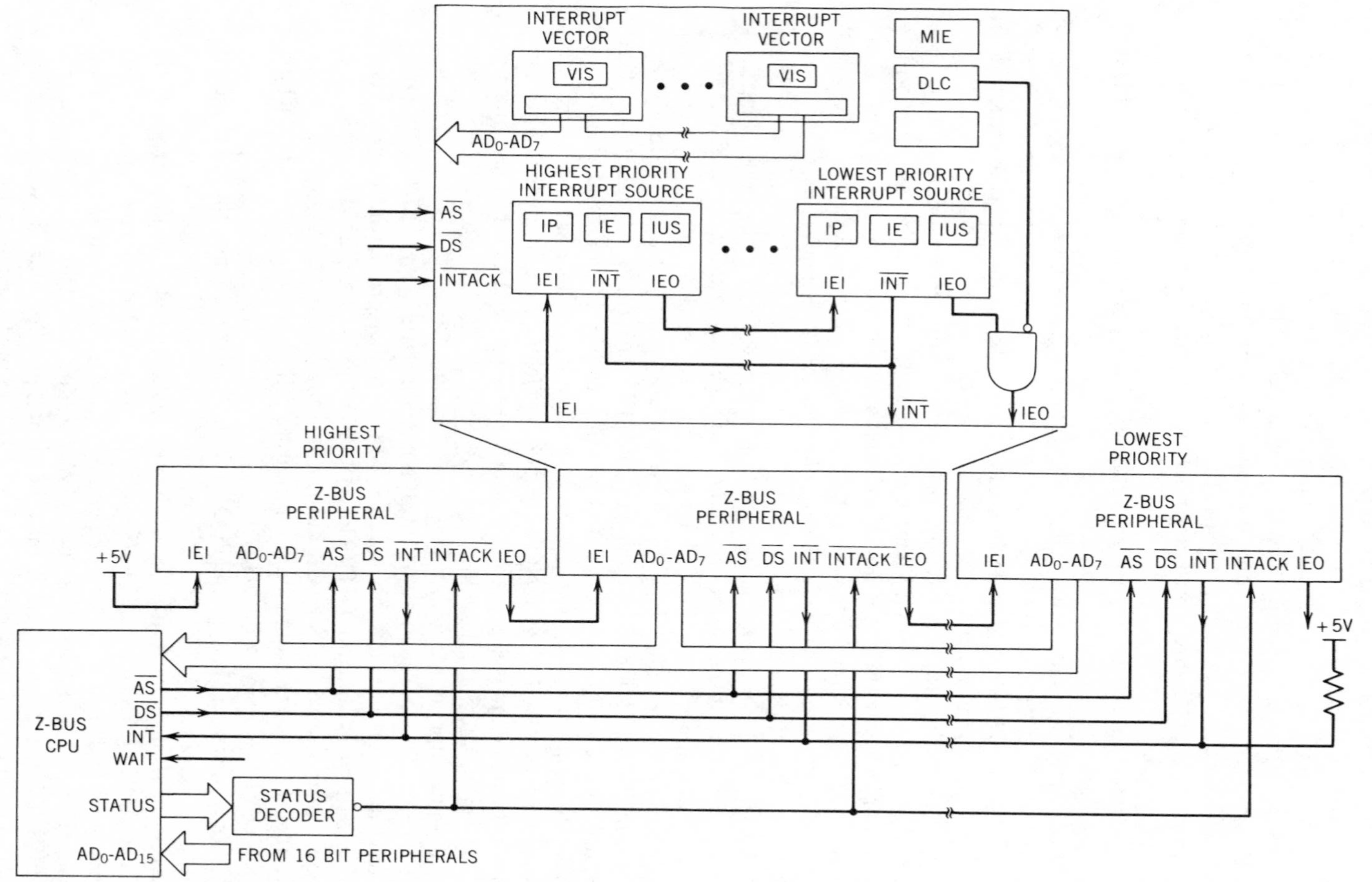

Figure 15-1 Z-Bus interrupt connections. (Reproduced by permission © Zilog, Inc. This material shall not be reproduced without the written consent of Zilog, Inc.)

its IUS bit set to 0. This is the interrupt source being acknowledged, and at this time it sets its IUS bit to 1, and if NV = 0, places its interrupt vector on the low-order 8 bits of the address/data bus. If NV = 1, the address/data lines remain tri-stated, allowing an external device to supply the vector.

If the VIS bit is set, the vector will include further status information to further identify the source of the interrupt. If VIS = 0, the vector supplied to the CPU will be the vector stored in the peripheral with no modification.

While an interrupt source has an interrupt under service (IUS = 1), it prevents any lower-priority device from requesting an interrupt by pulling IEO LOW. When the interrupt service routine is complete, the CPU must reset the IUS and, in most cases, the IP bit by means of an I/O operation. This restores the interrupt source to its quiescent state.

The master interrupt enable bit in a peripheral can affect all interrupt sources in that peripheral. If MIE = 0, it is as if all IE bits in that peripheral were set to 0; thus all interrupts from that peripheral are disabled. You will remember that in order for an interrupt to be generated, we must have a condition in which IP = 1, IE = 1, MIE = 1, IUS = 0, IEI = 1, and $\overline{\text{INTACK}}$ was not active on the last rising edge of $\overline{\text{AS}}$.

The disable lower chain bit (DLC) is used to control the daisy chain. If DLC = 1, that peripheral's IEO is forced LOW, thus disabling all lower-priority devices from generating an interrupt request until DLC is reset to 0.

In a **Z8000** system, the $\overline{\text{INTACK}}$ signal can be most easily generated by decoding the status lines. In systems using other CPUs, some other means must be found to generate a compatible $\overline{\text{INTACK}}$. When using the **8500** series of peripherals with a **Z80** CPU, for example, several logic chips are needed to recognize the **Z80** INTERRUPT ACKNOWLEDGE sequence and generate the $\overline{\text{INTACK}}$ signal.

15-4 Z8036 Z-CIO

The **Z8036** Counter/Timer Parallel I/O Unit (Z-CIO) contains three parallel I/O ports and three programmable counter/timers which allow it to perform most commonly needed parallel I/O and counter/timer functions in **Z8000** systems. A block diagram of the **Z8036** is shown in Figure 15-2.

The Z-CIO's parallel I/O capabilities consist of two 8-bit I/O ports and a special-purpose 4-bit port. The two 8-bit ports, port A and port B, can be linked together to form a 16-bit port. Either port can be configured as a byte port, input or output, or as a bit port in which the direction of each bit is individually programmable. Each timer requires four lines to access it. Port B provides access to counter/timers 1 and 2. With this one exception, port A and port B are identical. Port C is either a bit port or is used to provide handshake signals for ports A and B when they are used as byte ports. Port C also provides access to counter/timer 3.

When configured as byte ports, ports A and B can be input, output, or bidirectional ports. Both port A and port B are interrupt sources and each has its own unique interrupt vector. Byte ports can be single or double buffered, and the

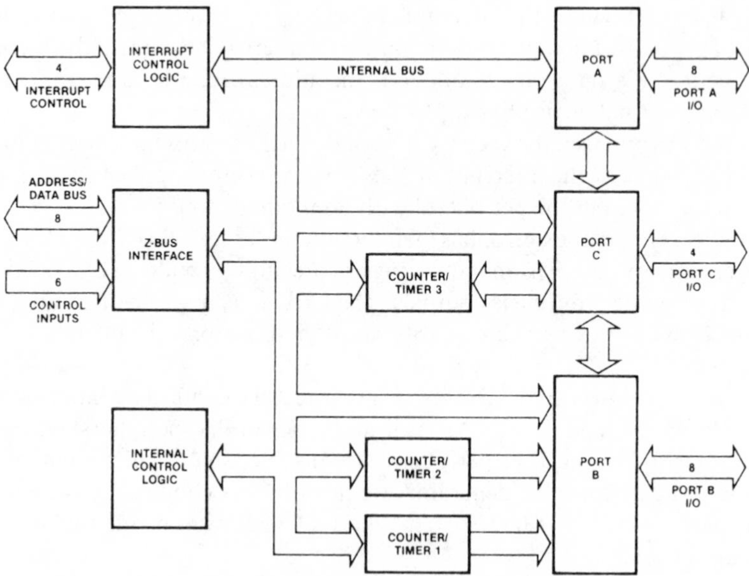

Figure 15-2 Z-CIO block diagram. (Reproduced by permission © Zilog, Inc. This material shall not be reproduced without the written consent of Zilog, Inc.)

interrupt logic can be programmed to interrupt on every byte transferred or on every second byte transferred, respectively. Optionally, port C can be used to provide handshake lines to control transfers on ports A and B. Four kinds of handshakes are available: interlocked, strobe, pulsed, and three-wire. The modes are illustrated in Figure 15-3. The interlocked, strobed, and pulsed handshakes are implemented with two signals: acknowledge in ($\overline{\text{ACKIN}}$) and ready for data (RFD) for input mode, and acknowledge in and data available ($\overline{\text{DAV}}$) for output mode. The three-wire handshake uses data available, ready for data, and data accepted (DAC), and is compatible with the handshake in the IEEE-488 bus specification. For output ports, a programmable 4-bit deskew timer can be used to generate a delay between output data valid and the falling edge of the $\overline{\text{DAV}}$ line. Port output lines can be configured as open-drain or active outputs. Data polarity is programmable on a bit-by-bit basis.

When they are used as bit ports, ports A and B may have their data direction and data polarity programmed on a bit-by-bit basis. In addition, *1s catchers* may be inserted into the data path of any or all bits. Ones catchers go to 1 when a transition on the input line occurs. The outputs of these 1s catchers remain at a logical 1 level until read (the bits are cleared when the port is read). Because of the randomness of bit port operation, no handshaking is available for bit ports. This fact is offset, though, by the increased flexibility of this mode.

Pattern match logic is available for use on both port A and port B, regardless of the mode that port is in. This allows interrupts to be generated when a specific data pattern is detected at the port. For each bit, the data may be specified to be a 1, 0, rising edge, falling edge, or both edges. Bits may also be masked off so as not to be

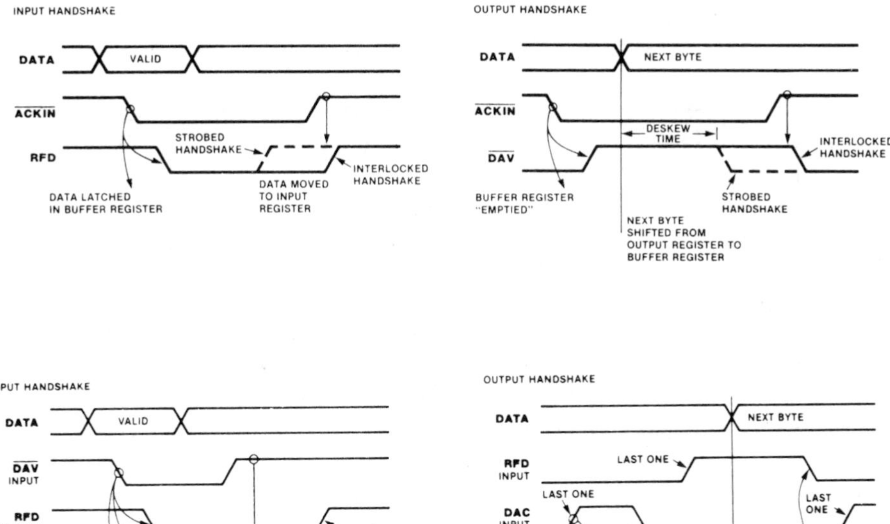

Figure 15-3 Three-wire handshake modes. (Reproduced by permission © Zilog, Inc. This material shall not be reproduced without the written consent of Zilog, Inc.)

considered in the match at all. Three pattern match modes are available: AND, OR, and OR-priority encoded vector (OR-PEV) modes. In the AND mode, a pattern match is not generated until all unmasked bits match their specification. In OR and OR-PEV modes, a pattern match will be generated when any one of the unmasked bits matches its specifications.

The OR-PEV mode also allows the Z-CIO to be used as a priority interrupt controller. In this mode, it is not necessary for the port to go from a match condition to a no-match condition and back to a match condition for another interrupt to be generated, as is the case for the OR and AND modes. In OR-PEV mode, if another bit is a match when the first interrupt is just finished being serviced, another interrupt will be generated immediately. If the vector-includes-status option has been selected, the vector returned to the CPU during the interrupt acknowledge cycle identifies the highest-priority bit matching its pattern match specification at the time of the interrupt acknowledge. This may or may not be the same bit that originally caused the interrupt. Using this mode, the Z-CIO can be set up to accept interrupts from other sources and generate interrupts to the CPU. This is useful in interfacing non Z-Bus devices to a **Z8000** system.

The function of the 4-bit, special-purpose port C depends on the modes ports A and B are being used in. Port C provides the handshake lines for ports A and B when they are being used as byte ports with handshaking. Port C also provides a $\overline{\text{WAIT}}$ or REQUEST signal to allow block transfers to and from the CPU. Port C also provides access to counter/timer 3. Because port C is only 4 bits wide, it is not possible to do handshaking on both ports A and B and also provide external access to counter/timer 3. Any bits in port C not being used for other functions may be used as bit I/O.

The three counter/timers are all 16-bit down counters. There are four control/status signals for each counter/timer: count input, gate input, trigger input, and counter/timer output. Each of these signals has a corresponding bit in the control/status register that can be accessed by software. Port B provides the signal lines for counter/timers 1 and 2, and port C provides access to counter/timer 3. It is possible to use a counter/timer under software control and generate interrupt without using any external port lines because the functions are available in the internal registers of the Z-CIO. It is also possible to connect the counter/timer 1 output to the trigger, gate, or count input of counter/timer 2. The count input of any counter/timer can come from an external pin or from the Z-CIO clock input (PCLK/2). If the counter/timer output is routed to an external pin, three output waveforms are available: pulse, one-shot, and square wave. Then end-of-count condition can be used to generate an interrupt. The counter/timers can be run in continuous- or single-cycle mode. If a trigger input is employed, it may be run in retriggerable or nonretriggerable mode. The current count can be *captured* and *read at any time*. Using these options, the counter/timers can be configured to perform a variety of functions, such as real-time clocks, event counter, pulse train generators, watch-dog timers, and baud rate generators.

With this wide array of features, the Z-CIO can be configured to do many different tasks, but the user decide how to best use all of these options.

15-5 Z8030 Z-SCC

The **Z8030** Serial Communications Controller (SCC) is a dual-channel programmable data communications controller that can support a wide variety of communications protocols. Refer to section 14-4 for further information on some of these protocols. The two channels of the SCC are independent, operate in full duplex mode, and can transfer data at rates up to 1 megabit/s. Each channel has its own crystal oscillator, baud rate generator, and digital-phase locked loop for clock recovery. Asynchronous, byte-synchronous, and bit-synchronous protocols are supported. The SCC also provides for data integrity checking (CRC) and modem control. This wide range of features allows the SCC to be used for virtually any serial data communications application. A block diagram of the SCC is shown in Figure 15-4.

In the asynchronous communications mode, the SCC can be programmed to send and receive 5, 6, 7, or 8 bits per character (plus an optional parity bit, if desired). The transmitter can supply 1, $1\frac{1}{2}$, or 2 stop bits per character, and can send a break sequence at any time. Parity checking and generation for odd or even parity are also provided. Framing and overrun errors are automatically detected, and an interrupt can be generated if desired. The transmit and receive clocks need not be symmetric, and data rates of 1, $\frac{1}{16}$, $\frac{1}{32}$, or $\frac{1}{64}$ of the base clock rate are supported.

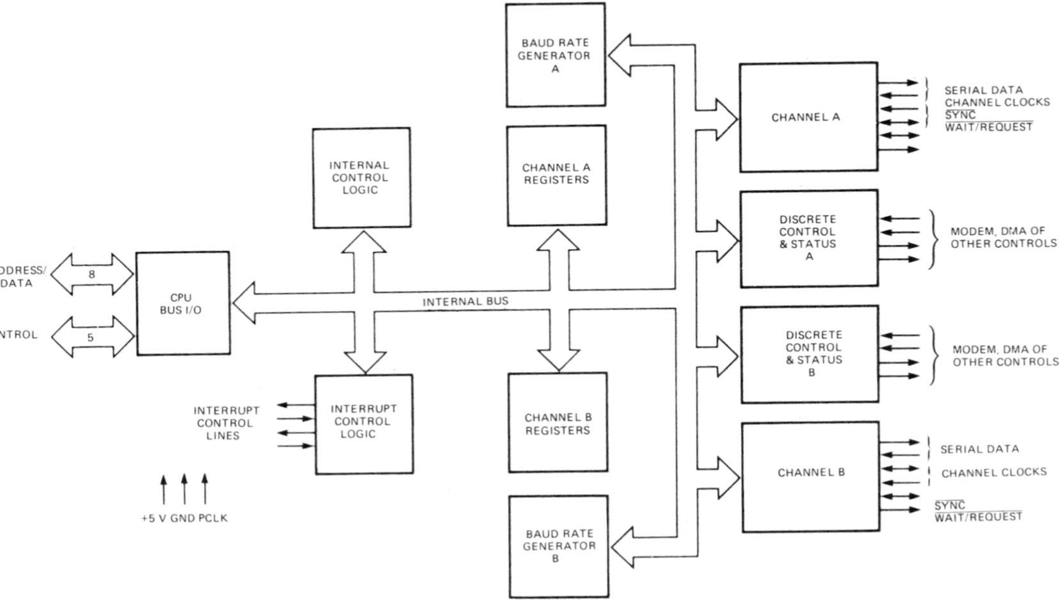

Figure 15-4 Block diagram of Z-SCC architecture. (Reproduced by permission © Zilog, Inc. This material shall not be reproduced without the written consent of Zilog, Inc.)

In the synchronous modes, both byte-oriented and bit-oriented protocols are supported. There are two cyclic redundancy codes (CRC) available for error detection. The CRC generator and CRC checker may be preset to all 1s or all 0s.

In the byte-oriented protocols, such as monosync and bisync, characters may be synchronized with a 6-bit, 8-bit, 12-bit, or 16-bit sync character, or they may be synchronized with an external signal. Leading sync characters are automatically deleted from the data stream by the receiver, without interrupting the CPU. The data protocols are shown in Figure 15-5.

The bit-oriented protocols, such as SDLC and HDLC, are supported by such features as automatic flag sending, address field recognition, automatic zero insertion and deletion, and abort sequence checking and generation. At the end of a message, the SCC automatically transmits the CRC code and trailing flags when the transmitter underruns. When doing address field recognition, the SCC can be programmed to respond to frames addressed by a byte, 4 bits within a byte, a user selected address, or a global broadcast address. The number of address bytes can be extended under software control. The SCC also supports SDLC loop mode operations, and can function as the controller or a secondary station on the loop.

The SCC has two special modes useful for debugging: *auto echo* and *local loopback*. Auto echo mode causes received data to be automatically routed to the transmit data line, continuously transmitting whatever is received. In local loopback, transmit data is automatically routed to the receive data line, allowing the SCC to receive the data it is transmitting.

In addition to the basic receiver and transmitter, there are other pieces of support circuitry within the SCC that provide support functions. They include the data encoder/decoder, baud rate generator, and digital-phase locked loop.

When used as a data encoder the data may be encoded in any of four ways in the SCC: FM0 (biphase space), FM1 (biphase mark), NRZ, or NRZI encoding, as

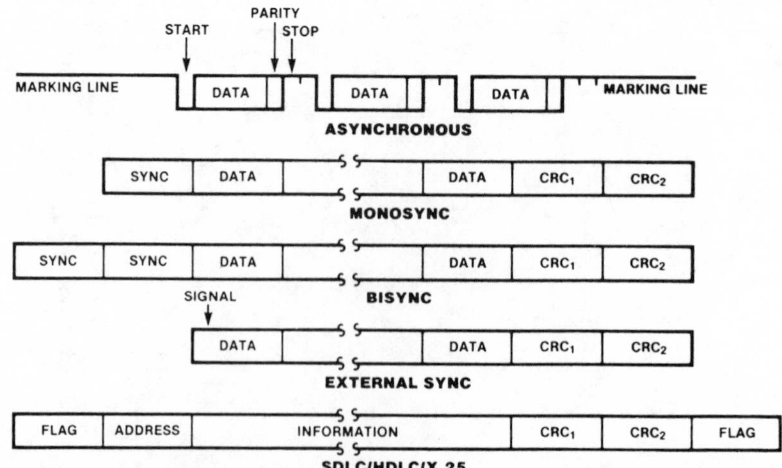

Figure 15-5 Some Z-SCC protocols. (Reproduced by permission © Zilog, Inc. This material shall not be reproduced without the written consent of Zilog, Inc.)

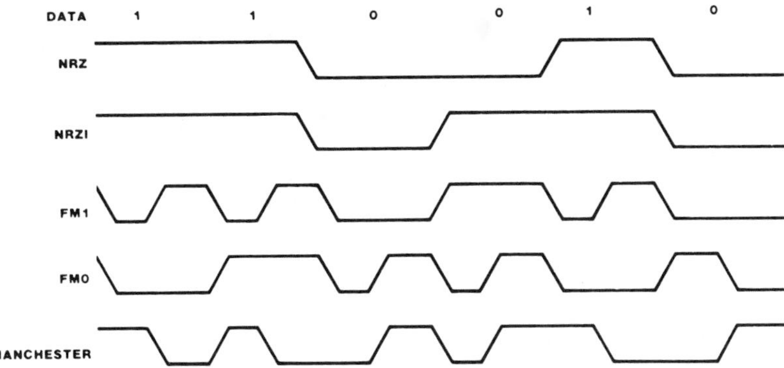

Figure 15-6 Data encoding methods. (Reproduced by permission © Zilog, Inc. This material shall not be reproduced without the written consent of Zilog, Inc.)

shown in Figure 15-6. In FM0 and FM1 encoding, a transition occurs at the beginning of every bit cell. In FM0 encoding, a 0 is represented by another transition at the center of the cell and a 1 is represented by no further transitions in the cell. FM1 is the inverse of FM0. In FM1, a 1 is represented by another transition at the center of the cell and a 0 is represented by no further transitions in the cell. For NRZ encoding, a 1 is represented by a high level and a 0 by a low level (this is essentially no encoding). In NRZI encoding, a 1 is represented by no change in level since the previous bit cell, and a 0 is represented by a change in level since the previous bit cell. In addition to decoding these four codes, the SCC can decode Manchester (biphase level) encoded data. Manchester data encoding always produces a transition in the center of the bit cell. If the transition is from 0 to 1, the bit is a 0. If the transition is from 1 to 0, the bit is a 1. The SCC can also encode Manchester with the addition of some simple external circuitry.

Each channel of the SCC has three possible sources of interrupts: receiver, transmitter, or external status/special condition. One interrupt vector is provided, and that vector can be encoded with status to indicate the source of the interrupt with respect to which channel and which interrupt source within that channel. A receive interrupt can be one of three cases: interrupt on first received character or special receive condition, interrupt on all received characters or special receive condition, or interrupt only on special receive conditions. The special receive conditions include overrun, parity error, framing error, and end-of-frame condition (SDLC mode). The transmit interrupt is activated when the transmit buffer becomes empty. External status interrupts are caused by active levels on the $\overline{\text{CTS}}$, $\overline{\text{DCD}}$, or $\overline{\text{SYNC}}$ pins, a transmit underrun, a break condition (asynchronous modes), an abort sequence (SDLC mode), an end-of-poll sequence (SDLC loop mode), or a zero count in the baud rate generator. Support is also provided for DMA- or CPU-controlled (using the $\overline{\text{WAIT}}$ line) high-speed data transfers.

In order to allow the CPU additional time to respond to a receive interrupt, receive data is routed through a 3-byte FIFO buffer. For each character in the FIFO, status information indicating if an error was detected is also sent through the FIFO so that error flags may be set properly. The register functions for the SCC are as follows:

READ Register Functions

RR0	Transmit/receive buffer status and external status
RR1	Special receive condition status
RR2	Modified interrupt vector (channel B only) Unmodified interrupt vector (channel A only)
RR3	Interrupt pending bits (channel A only)
RR8	Receive buffer
RR10	Miscellaneous status
RR12	Lower byte of baud rate generator time constant
RR13	Upper byte of baud rate generator time constant
RR15	External/Status interrupt information

WRITE Register Functions

WR0	CRC initialize, initialization commands for the various modes, SHIFT RIGHT/SHIFT LEFT command
WR1	Transmit/receive interrupt and data transfer mode definition
WR2	Interrupt vector (accessed through either channel)
WR3	Receive parameters and control
WR4	Transmit/receive miscellaneous parameters and modes
WR5	Transmit parameters and controls
WR6	Sync characters or SDLC address field
WR7	Sync character or SDLC flag
WR8	Transmit buffer
WR9	Master interrupt control and reset (accessed through either channel)
WR10	Miscellaneous transmitter/receiver control bits
WR11	Clock mode control
WR12	Lower byte of baud rate generator time constant
WR13	Upper byte of baud rate generator time constant
WR14	Miscellaneous control bits
WR15	External status interrupt control

15-6 Z8038 Z-FIO

The **Z8038** FIFO Input/Output Interface Unit (FIO) contains a 128-byte FIFO buffer that provides an asynchronous CPU-to-CPU or CPU-to-peripheral interface. A block diagram of **Z8038** is shown in Figure 15-7. Data written into the port 1 side of the FIO is read by the device connected to port 2 and vice versa. One side of the FIO, the port 1 side, can be configured as a Z-Bus or general-purpose, nonmultiplexed bus interface to a CPU. The other side, the port 2 side, can be

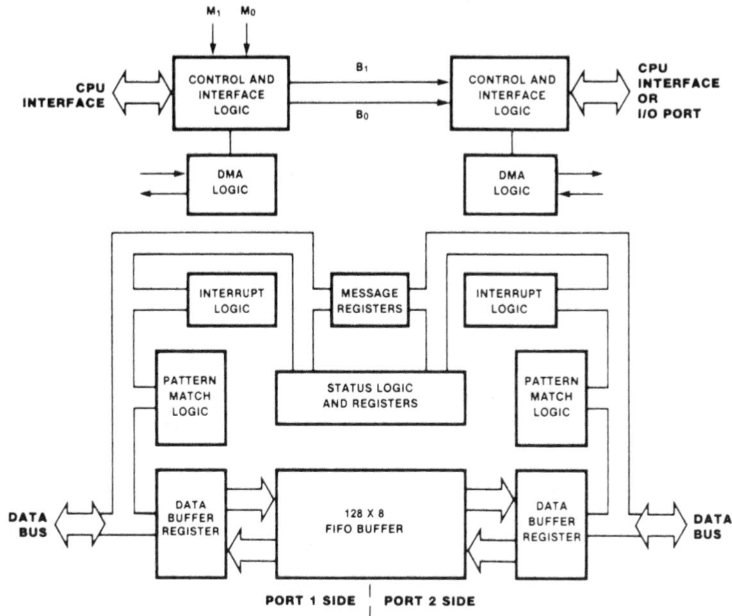

Figure 15-7 FIO block diagram. (Reproduced by permission © Zilog, Inc. This material shall not be reproduced without the written consent of Zilog, Inc.)

configured as a Z-Bus CPU interface, a nonmultiplexed CPU interface, a two-wire handshake I/O interface, or a three-wire handshake I/O interface. This flexibility in configuration allows the FIO to link CPUs or CPUs and peripherals operating at similar or different speeds, thus allowing asynchronous data transfers and reducing I/O overhead.

As mentioned previously, the port 1 side of the FIO is always a CPU interface. It can be a Z-Bus interface (either high or low byte), or a nonmultiplexed bus interface. The Z-Bus interface uses the same control signals present in the other Z-Bus peripherals ($\overline{\text{AS}}$, $\overline{\text{DS}}$, $\text{R}/\overline{\text{W}}$, and $\overline{\text{CS}}$). The nonmultiplexed bus interface is a general-purpose μP interface with eight data lines, chip enable ($\overline{\text{CE}}$), read ($\overline{\text{RD}}$), write ($\overline{\text{WR}}$), and control/data ($\text{C}/\overline{\text{D}}$) signals. The $\text{C}/\overline{\text{D}}$ signal determines if the current bus transfer involves a control register in the FIO or the FIFO data buffer itself. This interface is easily interfaced to μPs with separate, nonmultiplexed address and data buses such as the **Z80**, **8080**, **6800**, and **68000**.

The configuration of the port 1 side is determined by the condition of two pins, M0 and M1. The configuration of the port 2 side is controlled by programming 2 bits, B0 and B1, in an internal register of the port 1 side. The port 2 side can be a Z-Bus, nonmultiplexed bus, two-wire handshake, or three-wire handshake interface.

Pattern recognition logic is available on both sides of the FIO and can generate an interrupt when a specific pattern is written into or read from the FIFO buffer. The pattern can be specified to be any combination of 1s and 0s, and individual bits can be masked off if desired.

Special message passing registers, called *mailbox registers*, are available to allow messages to be passed from one CPU to another if the FIO is being used for CPU-to-CPU interfacing. These mailbox registers allow information to be passed between the two CPUs without using or affecting the contents of the FIFO buffer. An interrupt can be generated when a byte has been loaded into one of the mailbox registers, allowing one CPU to interrupt the other by writing a byte to the other CPU's mailbox register.

The FIO has been designed to work with DMA controllers to provide high-speed data transfer to and from the FIFO buffer. A byte count comparison register is available, and can be used to request a DMA transfer when a given number of bytes is in the buffer. For the input side of the FIFO buffer, the request (REQ) signal to the DMA controller becomes active when the number of bytes in the FIFO buffer equals the value in the byte count comparison register, and stays active until the buffer is full. For the output side, the REQ pin is inactive until the number of bytes in the buffer equals the value in the byte count comparison register. REQ then goes active and stays active until the buffer is empty. A $\overline{\text{WAIT}}$ L signal is also available and can be programmed to act in a similar manner to synchronize CPU-controlled block transfers.

Special control signals exist that can be used to clear the FIFO buffer or change the direction of data flow through the buffer. The clear and data direction functions are normally controlled by the port 1 side, but control of these functions can be passed to the port 2 side if desired.

Each side of the FIO has seven possible sources of interrupts. They are, in priority order, the mailbox register, a change in data direction, a pattern match, a status match (number of bytes in buffer equals the value in the byte count comparison register), overflow/underflow error, buffer full, and buffer empty. Each interrupt source has its own IE, IP, and IUS bits for controlling that interrupt. There is one interrupt vector for each side of the FIO, and that vector may be modified to include status information identifying the source of the interrupt.

15-7 FIFO BUFFER EXPANSION

Both the depth and width of the FIFO buffer may be expanded easily with additional **Z8038** FIOs and with another part, the **Z8060** FIFO. The **Z8060** is a 128 × 8 FIFO buffer with a 2-wire interlocked handshake interface on both sides of the buffer.

The buffer depth may be expanded to 256 bytes by putting two **Z8038**s in cascade with a 2-wire interface between them. In this configuration, the mailbox registers are no longer available, but all other functions of the FIO function normally. If more depth is desired, **Z8060** FIFOs may be inserted in between the two FIOs. For each FIFO added, the depth is expanded by 128 bytes. The FIFO is essentially an FIO without the intelligent features that are fixed in the 2-wire interface mode on both sides.

The buffer width may be expanded using multiple FIOs in parallel. Because of the way the internal registers are addressed in a Z-Bus system, two modes of FIO operation are provided: Z-Bus high byte and Z-Bus low byte. If a CPU-to-peripheral 16-bit word buffer is desired, some external logic will be necessary to synchronize the handshake signals from the two **Z8038**s.

15-8 Z8065 Z-BEP

The **Z8065** Burst Error Processor (BEP) is a device designed to provide high-speed serial or parallel data error detection and correction. It was designed for applications involving high-speed data transfers, such as high-performance disk systems. The BEP can operate at up to 20 megabytes/s and can detect errors in data streams up to 585K bits in length. A block diagram of the **Z8065** is shown in Figure 15-8.

The BEP uses one of four different polynomials, called *fire codes*, to detect and locate errors. Three different operations can be performed: writing data, reading data, and correcting data. When writing data, the BEP computes a check word by dividing the data stream by the desired polynomial. The remainder is a *check code* that is appended to the data stream. When reading data, the stream of data and check codes is divided by the polynomial to get a *syndrome*. If this syndrome is not zero, an error has been detected.

Two different read modes are available: normal and high speed. The normal method divides the data stream by the expanded form of the polynomial while the high-speed method performs parallel divisions using the factors of the polynomial. Both modes take the same amount of time during the read mode; however the high-speed mode can result in correction times shorter by orders of magnitude. The

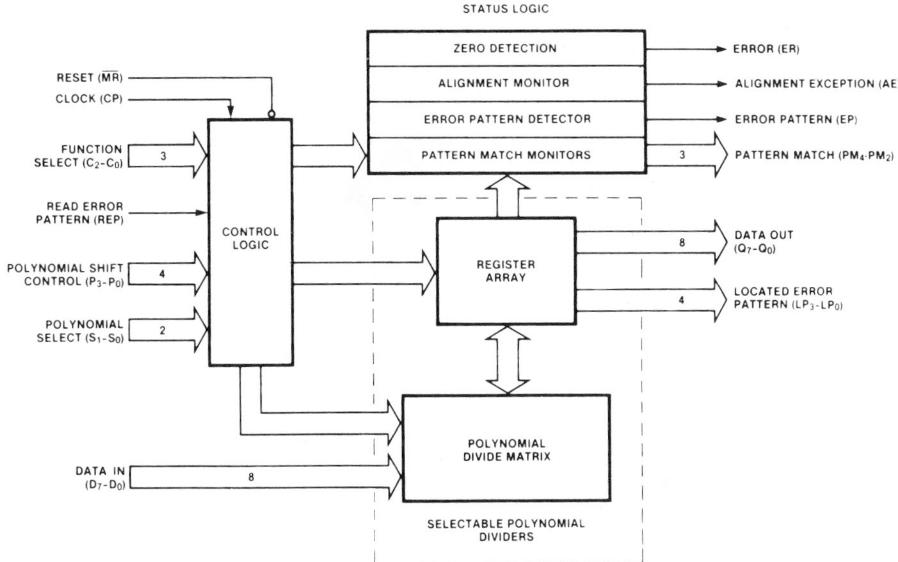

Figure 15-8 Block diagram of the **Z8065** burst error processor. (Reproduced by permission © Zilog, Inc. This material shall not be reproduced without the written consent of Zilog, Inc.)

syndrome is then used to correct the error using one of three correction methods, depending on the type of polynomial selected. For all but the 48-bit polynomial, the error can be located using one of two methods: the "full-period clock around" method (normal reads) or the "Chinese remainder theorem" (high-speed reads). For 48-bit polynomials, the "reciprocal polynomial" error-correction method is used. All of these correction algorithms extract the error pattern from the data stream for external correction.

15-9 Z8068 Z-DCP

The **Z8068** Data Ciphering Processor (DCP) is a data encryption/decryption device that conforms to the National Bureau of Standards Data Encryption Standard (Federal Information Processing Standards Publication 46). It can operate at a data rate of up to 1 megabyte/s. A block diagram of the **Z8068** is shown in Figure 15-9.

The DCP provides three ciphering options: Electronic code book, chain block cipher, and cipher feedback. Electronic code book is a relatively simple ciphering method used for disk systems and other similar applications. Chain block cipher encryption involves a feedback path whereby the ciphering of one data block is dependent on the previous data block. This method is commonly used in high-speed telecommunications applications. Cipher feedback encryption also involves a

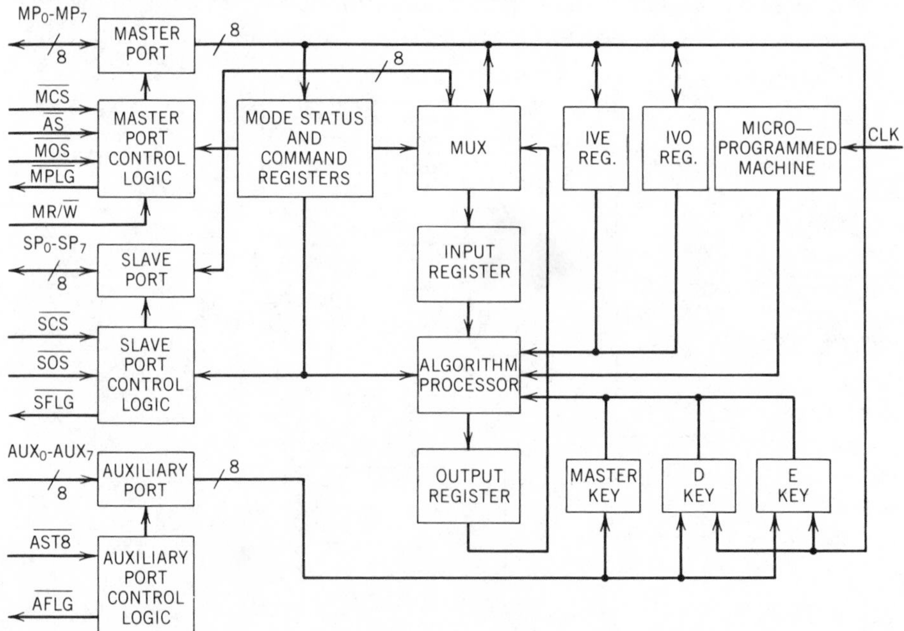

Figure 15-9 Block diagram of the **Z8068** data ciphering processor. (Reproduced by permission © Zilog, Inc. This material shall not be reproduced without the written consent of Zilog, Inc.)

feedback path, but adds a pseudorandom binary stream that is exclusive-ORed to the text to be encrypted. This method is slower and is commonly used in a low-speed, byte-oriented applications.

Three separate 8-bit ports are available for the cipher key, clear data, and encrypted data. The DCP can be used in a single-port configuration where the master port is used for both clear and encrypted data, or in a dual-port configuration where the master port is used for clear data and the slave port for encrypted data, or vice versa. Input, output, and ciphering of data are performed concurrently, which maximizes data throughput.

15-10 Z80 FAMILY PERIPHERALS

In addition to the newer **Z8000** family peripherals, Zilog has three peripheral devices that were designed to work with the **Z80** CPU. They are less complex devices than the newer generation peripherals, but can often be a very cost-effective solution for a **Z80** designer. They include the **Z80** Parallel Input/Output Controller (PIO), the **Z80** Counter/Timer Circuit (CTC), and the **Z80** Serial Input/Output Controller (SIO).

15-10.1 Interface

These devices interface to the CPU with **Z80**-compatible control signals. Eight data lines (D0–D7) are used to transfer data, status, and control information. One or two address inputs are used to select a data or control register in one of the channels of the device. (The PIO has only one control/data line, the SIO has two pins used to select control/data and channel A/channel B, and the CTC has two address bits to select one of four possible channels within the device.) A chip enable ($\overline{\text{CE}}$) signal is used to select the device, and an I/O request signal ($\overline{\text{IORQ}}$) is used to synchronize the transfers. A read signal ($\overline{\text{RD}}$) is used to indicate that the transfer in progress is a READ. No explicit WRITE signal is used; the peripheral generates its own WRITE signal when it sees $\overline{\text{CE}}$ active (LOW), $\overline{\text{IORQ}}$ active, and $\overline{\text{RD}}$ inactive. While the **Z8000** series of peripherals has an explicit interrupt acknowledge signal, the **Z80** series of peripherals recognizes the fact that the **Z80** CPU drives $\overline{\text{IORQ}}$ and $\overline{\text{M1}}$ active at the same time to indicate an INTERRUPT ACKNOWLEDGE cycle. In order to recognize this, the peripherals also have an $\overline{\text{M1}}$ input. The same interrupt priority daisy chain used in the **Z8000** peripherals is used in these peripherals, with an IEI input and an IEO output for each device.

The return from interrupt process is also handled differently in these peripherals. The CTC and PIO decode the **Z80** RETI instruction ("ED" followed by "4D"), and reset their IUS latch if they are the highest-priority devices currently under service. The SIO has the same feature, but also has a provision for resetting the highest-priority IUS bit under software control. The necessity of having this sequence appear on the bus in order to return from an interrupt does present a challenge when interfacing these peripherals to a processor other than the **Z80**.

15-11 Z80 PIO

The **Z80** Parallel Input/Output Controller (PIO) is a dual-port device designed to provide a TTL-compatible parallel interface between a **Z80** CPU and outside devices. The PIO is commonly used to interface between a **Z80** CPU and such devices as keyboards, PROM programmers, and printers.

The two ports of the PIO can be programmed by the CPU to act as input ports, output ports, bidirectional ports, or bit ports (in which the direction of each bit is individually programmable). The PIO also has interrupt capability and can interrupt the CPU when a data transfer is to be performed (input, output, or bidirectional ports), or when a specific pattern is detected (bit ports). Each port of the PIO has two dedicated handshake lines associated with it. These two lines are used to implement a two-wire handshake if the port is being used in the input, output, or bidirectional modes.

15-12 Z80 CTC

The **Z80** Counter/Timer Circuit (CTC) is a four-channel counter/timer device that can be programmed to suit a wide range of counting and timing applications. Examples of such tasks include event counting, interrupt and interval timing, and baud rate clock generation.

The **Z80** CTC has four independent counter/timer channels. Each channel is programmed with a channel control byte, a time constant byte, and an optional interrupt vector byte. Only one channel, channel 0, actually has an interrupt vector associated with it. The CTC automatically inserts 2 bits of information into the interrupt vector to identify the channel causing the interrupt. When used in a timer mode, a bit in the channel control word selects a prescale factor of either 16 or 256. The time constant is a value between 1 and 256.

In counter mode, the counter decrements on each CLK/TRG input pulse until a zero count is reached. Each decrement is synchronized by the system clock. For counts greater than 256, counters can be cascaded. At zero count, the downcounter is automatically reloaded with the time constant value. If interrupts are enabled, an interrupt will also be generated.

In timer mode, the prescaler factor selected is used to divide the system clock and the resulting signal feeds the down counter. Thus, the time interval is determined by the product of the system clock period, the prescaler value, and the time constant value. The timer may be automatically retriggered whenever the time constant is reloaded (zero count), or it may be triggered by an external CLK/TRG signal. Channels 0–2 have a zero count output that provides a pulse output whenever the timer reaches a zero count condition.

15-13 Z80 SIO

The **Z80** Serial Input/Output Controller (SIO) is a dual-channel serial data communications device. It has a wide range of capabilities, handling asynchronous and synchronous protocols, byte or bit oriented, and has many functions designed to lessen the work load of the CPU. It was a predecessor of the **Z8030** SCC (see section 15-5), and as such does not have some of the extra features of the SCC. It does, however, have all of the basic functions necessary to implement common asynchronous protocols as well as such synchronous protocols as monosync, bisync, SDLC, and HDLC. Full interfacing is provided for CPU-controlled (interrupt) or DMA data transfers.

In asynchronous mode, transmission and receptions can occur simultaneously on both channels with 5 to 8 bits per character, plus an optional parity bit. The transmitter can supply 1, $1\frac{1}{2}$, or 2 stop bits per character, and can provide a break output at any time. The receiver break-detection logic can interrupt the CPU both at the start and at the end of a break condition. Framing and overrun errors are detected and buffered along with the partial character on which they occurred. In asynchronous mode, the $\overline{\text{SYNC}}$ pin may be programmed as an input which can be used for such functions as monitoring a ring indicator.

The SIO does not require a symmetric clock. This feature allows the SIO to be used with a **Z80** CTC or many other clock sources. The transmitter and receiver can handle data at rates of 1, $\frac{1}{16}$, $\frac{1}{32}$, or $\frac{1}{64}$ of the transmit and receive clock inputs.

In synchronous mode, the SIO supports both byte-oriented and bit-oriented protocols.

Synchronous byte-oriented protocols can be handled in several modes that allow character synchronization with an 8-bit sync pattern (monosync), a 16-bit sync pattern (bisync), or an external sync signal. Leading sync characters can be removed automatically without interrupting the CPU. In the byte-oriented modes, CRC checking is delayed by one character time so that the CPU may disable CRC checking on specific characters.

Both CRC-16 and CCITT error checking polynomials are supported. In all non-SDLC modes, the CRC generator is preset to all 0s. In SDLC modes, it is preset to all 1s. The SIO can be programmed to transmit CRC data when no other data is available for transmission, allowing DMA transfers with no need for CPU intervention at the end of a message.

The SIO supports bit-oriented protocols such as SDLC and HDLC with such features as automatic flag sending, zero insertion, and automatic CRC generation. A special command is available to abort a frame currently being transmitted. The SIO will automatically transmit the CRC and trailing flag when the transmit buffer becomes empty. The transmitter can send 1 to 8 bits per character. The receiver will automatically synchronize on the leading flag of a frame and provide an external signal on the $\overline{\text{SYNC}}$ pin as well as provide an interrupt (if enabled). The receiver can be programmed to do address searching on 1 byte for either a user-selected address or a global broadcast address. Longer addresses and partial addresses must be handled in software.

Like the SCC, the SIO can generate a variety of interrupts. Each channel can generate receive, transmit, or external status interrupts. The transmitter interrupts when its buffer becomes empty (assuming there was a character there to start with). The receiver can interrupt on first received character or on all received characters. In the SIO, a special receive condition can cause an interrupt only if one of the two receive interrupt modes has been enabled. The external status interrupts possible include transitions on the clear to send, data carrier detect, and sync pins, a transmit underrun condition, or the beginning and end of a break condition.

15-14 REFERENCES

The Zilog 1983/84 Data Book, Zilog, Campbell, Calif., 1983.

The Z8000 CPU Technical Manual, Zilog, Campbell, Calif., 1983.

INDEX

Abort, 466, 587
Accumulator, 253, 368, 369
Addresses:
  bus, 505
  register, 479
  segmented, 453, 454
ALE (Address Latch Enable), 143, 148, 403, 407
AND, *see* Logic instructions
Arithmetic instructions, 93–97, 212–216, 397, 456
Arithmetic-Logic Unit (ALU), 12
Assembler, assembly language, 18, 58–62, 495
Asynchronous data transmission, 570–571

BCD (Binary Coded Decimal), 263–264
Binary Number System, 31–40
Bit instructions, 203, 220–221, 457
Block search, 210–212, 458
Block transfers, 208–212, 458
BRANCH instructions, 21–26, 50–52, 269–274, 324, 358
Break (B) flag, 352, 361, 579

CALL instructions, 108, 153–155, 224, 401, 402, 457
  system, 465
  see also JUMP TO SUBROUTINE
Carry (C) flag, 189, 261, 311, 349, 392, 447
Clock, 115, 143, 233, 283–285, 329, 333, 334, 366–372, 406, 443, 475, 508, 520, 613
Command register, 27, 526–528
Compare instructions, 106, 260, 267, 458
Condition codes, 13, 188, 189, 260–263, 310, 311, 349, 352, 353, 391, 393, 447, 460. *See also* Glags
Context switching, 464
Control registers, 561–567, 575–579, 584, 585, 601–609
Coprocessor, *see* Extended processor units
Cyclic Redundancy Check (CRC), 586, 587, 595

Decimal Adjust Accumulator (DAA), 103, 104, 189, 264, 265, 310, 311, 447
Decimal (D) flag, 352
DECREMENT AND JUMP (DJNZ) instruction, 223
Direct instructions, 63, 85, 257, 258, 314, 393, 449
Direct Memory Request (DMA), 76, 77, 230, 257, 283, 332, 333, 416, 417, 544–546, 592–595
Disable interrupts (DI), 111, 213, 352, 459

Enable interrupts (EI), 112, 213, 392, 459
EXCHANGE instructions, 185, 207, 455–456
EXCLUSIVE OR, *see* Logic instructions
Extended addressing (absolute addressing), 199, 201, 258, 259, 313, 314, 362
Extended processor units, 410–441, 447, 463, 464

FIFO (First-In-First-Out) memory, 587, 589, 594, 595, 626
Flags, 83, 84, 353, 396, 393. *See also* Condition codes
Flow charts, 18–20

H (Half carry bit), 189, 263, 264, 310, 391, 447
HALT, 112, 282, 330, 459, 507
Hexadecimal number system, 46–50
HOLD, 123, 406

Immediate instructions, 63, 85, 189, 199, 257, 313, 344, 362, 480
Implied addressing, 63, 85, 200, 259, 260, 313, 362
Indexed instructions, 63, 203, 259, 314–319, 363, 364, 395, 449, 450
Index registers, 188, 203–205, 259, 309, 389, 395, 449
Indirect addressing, 65, 66, 86, 201, 394, 449, 480
IN instruction, 111, 122, 147–149, 225–227
Input/Output (I/O), 5, 26, 27, 111, 146–149, 224–227, 290, 372–376, 395, 452, 459, 461, 462, 501

Interrupt acknowledge, 33, 121, 124, 150, 153, 331, 407, 410, 462, 614–617
Interrupts, 28–30, 70–74, 150, 229–233, 285–290, 311, 331–333, 369, 406, 408–410, 452, 462, 464, 465, 506, 507, 614–617
software, 324, 325
Interrupt vector register, 188, 205, 206, 286, 287, 462, 501, 506, 507
$IO/\overline{M}$, 144, 146, 148, 407

JUMP instructions, 107, 221–224, 268, 269, 358, 359, 401, 402, 457
JUMP TO SUBROUTINE, 359, 360, 497. *See also* CALLs

LEA (Load Effective Address) instructions, 322, 323
LIC (Last Instruction Cycle), 334, 335
LINK instruction, 497, 498
Logical instructions, 44, 104–106, 265, 397, 456, 457

Machine language, 56, 57
Memory, 4–12
Modem, 568–569, 592

NEGATE instruction, 268
Negative (N) flag, 261, 311, 349
Non-maskable interrupt (NMI), 72, 73, 230, 231, 289, 290, 331, 360, 361, 406, 409, 452, 465
NOP (No Operation) instruction, 112, 459

OR, *see* Logic instructions
OUT instruction, 111, 147–149, 227
Overflow (V) flag, 189, 261, 262, 311, 349, 392

Parity flag, 392
PCHL instruction, 107
Peripheral Interface Adapter (PIA), 290–307
POP (PULL), 70, 110, 275, 309, 321, 393, 455
Port (I/O), 146, 147, 230, 237, 372, 373
Postbyte, 312–319, 321–323
Program Counter (PC), 312, 352, 446
PROM, 141, 236
PUSH instruction, 69, 70, 110, 275, 321, 369, 393, 455

RAM, 141, 236
Ready, 116, 144, 283, 368, 406
Refresh register, 188, 447, 462
Relative addressing, 66, 202, 222–224, 320, 362, 450, 481
Reset, 125, 126, 146, 152, 236, 283, 287, 294, 330, 366, 368, 393, 406, 520, 564, 580, 581, 612, 613
Restart, 266, 287, 294
RESTART instruction, 109, 150–153, 224, 266
RETURN instruction, 108, 109, 224, 277, 278, 289
RIM (Read Input Mask) instruction, 158, 159
ROTATE instructions, 52–55, 97–100, 200, 216–217, 219, 267, 268, 457, 458

Segment registers, 389–391
SHIFT instructions, 52–55, 200, 217–218, 267, 268, 457, 458
SID (Serial Input Data) instruction, 150, 158
Sign flag, 188, 392, 447. *See also* Z flag.
SIM (Set Interrupt Mask) instruction, 156, 157
SOD (Serial Output Data), 150, 157
Stack, 68–70, 84, 201, 206, 274–279, 286, 353, 393, 496–499
Stack Pointer (SP), 274–279, 309, 352, 393, 446
Status lines, 121, 144, 163, 403, 451, 507, 613
Status register, 27, 177–178, 391, 392, 528, 529, 580–582
String, 395, 397–400
Subroutine, 67, 68, 275–279
Subtract flag, 189
SWI (Software Interrupt), 290, 324, 325, 465
SYNC, 324, 368
Synchronous communications, 571, 572

Trap, 152, 153, 392, 465, 466, 499
TSC (Tri-State Control), 335
Twos (2s) complement number system, 40–44

Valid Memory Address (VMA), 280, 334

WAI (Wait for Interrupt), 290
WAIT, 116, 123, 124, 126, 144, 164, 165, 230, 613

Z-bus, 460–464, 612–617
Zero (Z) flag, 189, 260, 311, 349, 447